COLLINS JUNIOR DICTIONARY

Compiled by
GINNY LAPAGE

with
Stewart Collins
Judith Fisher
Marguerite de la Haye

Consultant
Dr Paul Fletcher
Reader in Linguistic Science
University of Reading

Collins Educational

Acknowledgements

The authors and publishers wish to thank the following for their help in the preparation of the dictionary:

Hatch Ride Primary School, Crowthorne, Berkshire
Newtown Primary School, Reading, Berkshire
St Bartholomew's School, Newbury, Berkshire
Berkshire Centre for Computers in Education
LINCS (Language In-Service and Curriculum
     Support), Reading, Berkshire
Dr Richard Dorrance, Berkshire Science Advisor
Commission for Racial Equality
Equal Opportunities Commission

Thanks are due to the children, who made a major contribution, especially Tanaza Bibi, Robert Duff, Helen Eden, Craig Farr, Laura Harrall, Olu Ropo Olaofe, Norinder Jit Singh, Mai Yee Wan.

Illustrations by
Graham Allen (Linden Artists), Ted Bernstein, Jerry Collins, Angelika Elsebach, Peter Harper, Illustrated Arts Ltd, Mick Loates (Linden Artists), Alan Male (Linden Artists), John Rignall (Linden Artists), David Webb (Linden Artists), Martin Woodward

This dictionary was compiled using the Cobuild English Language Dictionary © Collins ELT 1987

Picture acknowledgements

The photographs have been reproduced by kind permission of the following:

Ace Photo Agency pp 5 (t.c. & c.r.), 13, 38, 56 (t.r.), 66 (b), 69, 156 (b), 158, 193, 197; Allsport pp 68 (1), 130, 154, 205, 208; Ancient Art & Architecture Collection pp 157 (b), 181, 185, 204, 261 (t), 282; Ardea Photographic Ltd pp 7 (1), 35 (b.1), 64; Barnaby's Picture Library pp 39 (1), 53 (b), 83, 119, 326; Beken of Cowes Ltd p 6; Bridgeman Art Library/British Library p 159; Caravan Magazine p 39 (t); Celtic Picture Agency p 50; J Allan Cash Ltd pp 9, 42 (b); John Cleare/Mountain Camera pp 33 ( ); 43 (1), 66 (t.1); Bruce Coleman Ltd pp 57 ( ), 97, 123, 148, 156 (t), 304, 309, 323, 325, 334 (1); Mary Evans Picture Library pp 73 (1), 88, 90 (b.1); S & R Greenhill pp 251, 256; Robert Harding Picture Library pp 5 (c.1 & b.c.), 33 ( ), 37, 38 (1), 56 (1), 81 (t), 124, 132, 184, 230, 249, 293, 300; Michael Holford pp 41, 120; London Features International Ltd p 53; NHPA pp 10 (r), 27, 38 (b.1), 43 (1), 62, 65 (1), 67, 70, 94, 111, 115, 117, 122, 125, 143, 159 (1), 168, 172, 173, 197 (r), 199, 230, 316; North of Scotland Hydro-Electric Board p 142; The Martin Library p 259; Medical Slide Bank p 338; Planet Earth Pictures pp 42 (t.r.), 161, 259, 261 (b), 334 (r); Ann Ronan Picture Library p 33 (t.1); Science Photo Library pp 96 (1), 190, 233, 235 (x 2), 287, 313; Brian Shuel p 33 ( ); Skyscan Balloon Photography p 179; Telegraph Colour Library pp 39 (b), 77; Wang p 336; Derek G Widdicombe p 7 (r); Woodmansterne Publications p 68 (r); all other photos by Nance Fyson.

HarperCollins Children's Books
A Division of HarperCollins*Publishers* Ltd
77-85 Fulham Palace Road, London W6 8JB

First published in 1990 in the United Kingdom
by Collins Educational as
Collins First Reference Dictionary
Second edition published in 1992 in the United
Kingdom by HarperCollins Children's Books as
Collins Illustrated Children's Dictionary
This edition published in 1995 in the
United Kingdom
This edition reprinted in 1997

Copyright © Ginny Lapage, Stewart Collins,
Judith Fisher, Marguerite de la Haye 1990

ISBN: 0 00 196477 1

A CIP record for this book is available from
the British Library

Printed and bound by Scotprint Ltd, Musselburg

4 6 8 10 9 7 5

Introduction

COLLINS JUNIOR DICTIONARY has been compiled by
practising teachers and tested with children. It contains a
range of words selected to meet the needs of children of nine
and upwards who are able to read and write independently
and who need to use a dictionary as a reference book for
meaning and for checking spelling.

The vocabulary includes words common in everyday use,
as well as those which reflect recent advances in technology
and changing social roles.

The derivatives of all headwords are given in full as an aid
to correct spelling. This includes forms of verbs, plurals,
comparatives and superlatives of adjectives. All words are
explained in full sentences showing the use of the word in
context, as well as making clear its meaning. Example
sentences are included where a word is particularly difficult
to explain. A guide to words which are pronounced in
different ways is also included.

Clearly labelled diagrams and photographs further extend
vocabulary and make the explanations accessible to children.

Entries give information about a wide variety of topics,
ranging from food and famous people to geographical,
religious and political subjects.

About this Dictionary

1 The words are listed in alphabetical order.

2 Each entry has one or more words at the beginning in bold type. The first is the **headword** and the following words are the different forms it has. For example,

> **calculate** **calculates calculating calculated** or **calm calmer calmest**
> A form ending in 's' can be either part of a verb or the plural form of a noun, for example, **click** **clicks clicking clicked**

3 The meaning of a word is explained in a complete sentence.

> **baker** **bakers** (n) A baker makes, cooks and sells cakes, pastries and bread.

4 If a word has two or more different meanings, each meaning is numbered. The word's part of speech (see pages iv–v) follows the number.

> **damage** **damages damaging damaged**
> **1** (n) Damage is harm done to someone or something.
> **2** (vb) If you damage something or somebody, you cause them physical harm.
> **3** (n) Damages refers to the amount of money awarded by a court as compensation for some harm done to a person.

5 Some entries have no part of speech given because the word is used in a special phrase.

> **resort** **resorts resorting resorted**
> **3** If you do something as a last resort, you do it after all other options have been tried.

6 If the meaning of the word is difficult to explain, or can be understood in several ways, an example sentence follows the explanation.

> **official** **officials**
> **1** (adj) If something is official, it is approved by those in authority. *The official explanation was published today.*
> **2** (n) An official is someone in authority in an organisation.

7 Words belonging to the same family as the headword and whose meaning can be easily worked out are shown at the end of the entry with their part of speech.

> **metal** **metals** (n) A metal is a hard substance such as iron, steel, silver, etc. **metallic** (adj)

8 Some words can be spelt in different ways. The most common spelling, sometimes with the alternative, is given.

> **caffeine** or **caffein** (n) is a chemical substance found in coffee, tea and cocoa which makes your brain and body more active.

Verbs with more than one syllable and which end in *-ise* (such as **authorise**) can also be spelt correctly as *-ize* but only the *-ise* ending has been used in this dictionary.

9 Some words are spelt the same way but are pronounced differently and have different meanings. The headwords have this symbol ⟷ by them.

> **abuse** **abuses abusing abused** ⟷
> **1** (vb) If you abuse someone you treat them badly either by saying unkind things to them or by being cruel.
> **2** (n) Abuse is cruel or violent treatment or unpleasant language, **abusive** (adj)

10 This symbol 👁, with a cross-reference, shows that there is an illustration which expands the information about that word.

> 👁
> tree
> p313
>
> **leaf leaves**
> **1** (n) A leaf is one of the green, flat growths on trees or plants. **leafy** (adj)

11 The diagrams, illustrations and photographs are included to give you more information about words in the dictionary and to show you specialised words about a subject.

12 At the end of this dictionary you will find some helpful lists of words for spelling; a list of abbreviations; and a topic section of information about endangered plant and animal species of Britain.

13 If you cannot find a word that you want in this dictionary or if an explanation does not give you all the information that you need, you should look in a larger, more advanced dictionary.

Parts of speech

The parts of speech used in this dictionary are as follows:

(n) noun

There are usually two forms of a noun. The singular shows there is only one, and the plural describes more than one of something. Many plurals are made by adding an 's' eg house, houses. Other plurals do not follow this rule, eg *mouse, mice; child, children*. Some nouns are the same in the singular as they are in the plural, eg *sheep*, or they do not have any singular form, eg *scissors*.

The abbreviations (fem. n) and (masc. n) appear after some words. These are nouns which have different forms when they are used to refer to the male or female person or animal. For example, *heiress* (fem. n) is the feminine form of *heir*.

(vb) verb

There are usually four forms of verbs, eg *hatch, hatches, hatching, hatched*. Some verbs do not follow this rule and have five, eg *break, breaks, breaking, broke, broken*.

(adj) adjective

Some adjectives can have three forms, eg *happy, happier, happiest*. For many adjectives, though, adding -er, -est to the end doesn't sound right, and in those cases we use **more** or **most** in front of the adjective, eg *more enthusiastic, most enthusiastic*.

Sometimes the -ed form of a verb can be used as an adjective, when it describes something permanent or fairly long lasting: *He had a **hooked** nose; the house was **isolated** and she felt very frightened.*

(adv) adverb

Often, but not always, adverbs end with -ly, eg *happily, quickly, eagerly*. There are some forms that do not follow this rule: *She did her work **well**.*

(pro) pronoun

Pronouns are general words used in place of specific nouns, eg *The boy played happily. **He** was absorbed in the game ... The girl listened. Something had startled **her** ... **Who** did that?*

(conj) conjunction

A conjunction is a word that links parts of a sentence, eg *The teacher shouted **because** the boy was asleep.*

(prep) preposition

Prepositions are used to show where things are, eg *The cat is **in** the box ... The slippers are **under** the sofa*; when things happen, eg *John left home **in** the morning ... Dinner will be ready **at** six o'clock*; or how something is done, eg *He opened the box **with** a chisel ... He threw the chair **in** a rage.*

Useful words spelling list

Months of the year

January
February
March
April
May
June
July
August
September
October
November
December

Days of the week

Monday
Tuesday
Wednesday
Thursday
Friday
Saturday
Sunday

Numbers

1 one	16 sixteen
2 two	17 seventeen
3 three	18 eighteen
4 four	19 nineteen
5 five	20 twenty
6 six	30 thirty
7 seven	40 forty
8 eight	50 fifty
9 nine	60 sixty
10 ten	70 seventy
11 eleven	80 eighty
12 twelve	90 ninety
13 thirteen	100 hundred
14 fourteen	1000 thousand
15 fifteen	1,000,000 million

Question words

how?	who?
what?	whose?
when?	which?
where?	why?

Verbs which do not follow rules

to be: am are is; being been; was were.
to come: comes, coming, came.
to do: does, doing, did, done.
to go: goes, going, went, gone.
to have: has, having, had.

Short forms:

The apostrophe shows that
a part of a word
has been left out.

I'm	I am
you're	you are
he's	he is
she's	she is
it's	it is
we're	we are
they're	they are
who's	who is
I've	I have
you've	you have
we've	we have
they've	they have
don't	do not
haven't	have not
doesn't	does not
aren't	are not
won't	will not
can't	can not
would've	would have
could've	could have
should've	should have

Aa

abandon abandons abandoning abandoned
1 (vb) If you abandon someone, you leave them behind, and do not return to them.
2 (vb) If you abandon a plan, you decide not to go ahead with it.

abbey abbeys (n) An abbey is a church with buildings attached to it where monks or nuns live.

abbreviation abbreviations (n) An abbreviation is the shortened form of a word. *Dr. is the abbreviation for Doctor.*
abbreviate (vb)

abdomen
abdomens (n) The abdomen is part of the body between chest and hips.

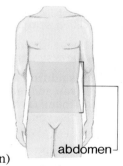
abdomen

able abler ablest
1 (adj) An able person or animal is good at doing things.
2 (adv) If you are able to do something, you can do it. **ability** (n)

abnormal (adj) things are not ordinary or usual. **abnormality** (n)

about
1 (prep) If you talk about a particular thing, your talk is in connection with it.
2 (prep) If you do something about a problem, you take action to solve it.
3 (adv) About is used with numbers or amounts to show that they are approximate.

above
1 (prep) If one thing is above another, it is higher up. *The plane flew above the clouds.*
2 (prep) A person who is above someone else in rank has higher status. *In the police force a sergeant is above a constable.*

abroad (adv) If you go abroad, you go to a foreign country.

absent (adj) If you are absent from a place, you are not there. *He was absent from school because he had a cold.*
absence (n)

absorb absorbs absorbing absorbed
1 (vb) If a towel, for example, absorbs liquid, it blots it up. **absorbent** (adj)
2 (vb) If you absorb knowledge, you learn it.
3 (vb) If you are absorbed in something, you are fascinated by it. *She was absorbed in her book and didn't hear me calling.*

abuse abuses abusing abused
1 (vb) If you abuse someone, you treat them badly either by saying unkind things to them or by being cruel.
2 (n) Abuse is cruel or violent treatment or unpleasant language. **abusive** (adj)

accelerate accelerates accelerating accelerated (vb) If a vehicle accelerates, it picks up speed and goes faster.

accelerator accelerators (n) The accelerator is the pedal in vehicles that is used to feed fuel to the engine to increase speed.

acceleration (n) is the rate at which the speed of something increases. *Paul admired the acceleration of his father's new car.*

accent accents (n) Someone who speaks with a particular accent says their words in a way which shows which area or country they come from. *She came from Glasgow and spoke with a Scottish accent.*

accept accepts accepting accepted (vb) If you accept something, you take what is being offered to you. **acceptable** (adj)

access accesses accessing accessed
1 (n) If you gain access to a place or a building, you succeed in getting into it; if you have access to a person (usually someone in authority) then you have the right to see that person. **accessible** (adj)
2 (vb) If you access information on a computer, you get it from the machine where it is stored.

accident accidents (n) An accident is something that happens by chance and without warning. *She found the book by accident . . . The accident left the motorway filled with wreckage.* **accidental** (adj)
accidentally (adv)

accomplice

accomplice accomplices (n) An accomplice helps in a crime.

account accounts accounting accounted
1 (vb) If you account for something, you explain how and why it happened.
2 (n) An account is a record of money which you have received or spent.
3 (n) An account is a spoken or written explanation of something that has happened. *The witness gave a clear account of the accident.*

accuse accuses accusing accused (vb) If you accuse someone of doing something, you blame them for it. **accusation** (n)

ace aces
1 (n) An ace is a playing card which has a single symbol on it. It can have the low value of only one or it can be a high card.
2 (n) An ace is a champion in sport.
3 (adj) If you describe something as ace, you mean it is very good indeed.

ache aches aching ached
1 (vb) If part of your body aches, you can feel a dull pain there.
2 (n) An ache is a constant dull pain.

achieve achieves achieving achieved (vb) If you achieve something, you do it usually after much effort. **achievement** (n)

acid acids
1 (n) An acid is a liquid which can burn the skin and eat through metals.
2 (adj) If you say a taste is acid, it is sour or bitter.
3 (adj) An acid remark is one that is meant to hurt or to be unkind.

acorn acorns (n) An acorn is the fruit of the oak tree.

acquaintance acquaintances (n) An acquaintance is someone you have met but do not know very well yet.

acrobat acrobats (n) An acrobat is a person who does difficult gymnastic acts, sometimes on a tightrope or a high wire.

across
1 (prep) If you go across a river or a field, you go from one side to the other.
2 (prep) If you say that you live across the road, it means that you live on the other side.

act acts acting acted
1 (vb) If you act, you do something. *She acted quickly to put the fire out.* **action** (n)
2 (vb) If you act in a play, you perform in it.
3 (n) An act is a thing done by someone. *His act of bravery saved the boy.*
4 (n) An act is a law passed by parliament.
5 (n) A play is in sections called acts.
6 (n) Short stage performances are called acts. *I saw a brilliant comedy act.*

active (adj) An active person or animal has a lot of energy and is always busy. **actively** (adv)

activity activities
1 (n) An activity is something which you do regularly for pleasure. *My favourite activity is walking.*
2 (n) If there is activity, there is a lot going on. *There was a lot of activity in the classroom when the maths project began.*

actor actors (n) An actor is a man or woman who takes part in a stage play, film or television drama.

actual (adj) Actual means real or true. *This is the actual spot where he fell.*

add adds adding added
1 (vb) If you add one thing to another, you combine them. *He added sugar to his tea.*
2 (vb) When you add numbers together, you combine them to give a total. **addition** (n)

adder adders (n) An adder, or viper, is a small, poisonous snake found in Britain.

addict addicts (n) An addict is someone who likes or needs something so much that they can't do without it. *She was addicted to nicotine and smoked thirty cigarettes a day.* **addiction** (n)

address addresses addressing addressed
1 (n) Your address is where you live. It gives details of your house number, street or road, town and post code.

2 (vb) If you address an envelope, you write someone's name and address on it.
3 (vb) If you address someone, you speak to them formally. *The Headteacher addressed the parents on Open Evening.*

adenoids (n) are lumps of flesh at the back of the throat. If they become infected and swell up they have to be removed.

adequate (adj) is just enough for what is needed. *The food was adequate and it kept them alive.* **adequately** (adv)

adjective adjectives (n) An adjective is a word that describes something or somebody. It tells you more about them. *The girl was quiet, but she had a noisy friend. Quiet* and *noisy* are adjectives.

adjust adjusts adjusting adjusted
1 (vb) If you adjust your seat-belt, you move it until it is safe and comfortable.
2 (vb) If you adjust a piece of machinery, you move the parts until it works smoothly.
3 (vb) If a person or animal adjusts to something, they get used to it. *The puppy adjusted to its new home after a few days.* **adjustment** (n)

admire admires admiring admired (vb) If you admire something or someone you like and respect them. **admiration** (n)

admit admits admitting admitted
1 (vb) If you admit someone to a place, you let them in.
2 (vb) If you are admitted to hospital, you are taken there for treatment.
3 (vb) If you admit to something, you agree that you did something that you shouldn't have done.
4 If you admit defeat, you stop doing something that has become very difficult. **admission** (n)

adolescence (n) is the time when you are changing from a child to an adult. **adolescent** (n)

adopt adopts adopting adopted
1 (vb) When a couple adopts someone else's child, they bring it up as part of their own family. **adoption** (n)
2 (vb) If you adopt an idea or practice, you take it up as your own.

adore adores adoring adored (vb) If you adore someone, you love them very much.

adult adults (n) An adult is a fully grown man, woman or animal.

advance advances advancing advanced
1 (vb) If you advance, you move forward.
2 (vb) When people advance their knowledge, they make progress in finding out about new things.
3 (n) If you have an advance of money, you get part or all of it before the full amount is due.

advantage advantages
1 (n) An advantage is something that puts you in a better position than other people. **advantageous** (adj)
2 If you take advantage of the situation, you make the most of it.
3 If you take advantage of a person, you use them unfairly for your own good.

adventure adventures (n) If you have an adventure, something strange and exciting and maybe dangerous happens to you. **adventurous** (adj)

adverb adverbs (n) Adverbs are words that usually give more information about verbs. They tell you how, when or where things are done. *He ran quickly . . . He saw her yesterday . . . Put it there. Quickly, yesterday* and *there* are adverbs.

advertise advertises advertising advertised (vb) When you advertise, you give people information through television, radio, papers etc., about something you want to sell, a job you want to fill or an event you want to publicise. **advertisement** (n)

advice (n) If you ask for advice about a problem, you ask for help in solving it. If you give advice you tell others how to sort out their problems.

advise advises advising advised (vb) If you advise someone, you give them helpful suggestions. **adviser (or advisor)** (n)

aerial aerials
1 (n) An aerial is made of metal rods or wires that send out or receive radio or television signals.
2 (adj) Aerial means in the air. An aerial photograph is taken from an aircraft.

aerobatics (n) are difficult and dangerous tricks done by a pilot flying an aircraft.

a

aerobics

aerobics (n) are exercises often done to music that help your muscles, heart and lungs to keep healthy.

aeroplane aeroplanes (n) An aeroplane is a flying machine with one or more engines and wings.

aerosol aerosols (n) An aerosol is a can filled with liquid under pressure. When a button is pushed the liquid comes out in a fine spray.

Aesop (?620-564BC) was the author of fables or moral tales where animals behave like human beings. "The Fox and The Grapes" and "The Tortoise and The Hare" are two of his best-known tales.

affair affairs
1 (n) An affair is something special that happens. *The party was a very grand affair.*
2 (n) A person's business affairs are the things connected with their work.
3 (n) If something is your own affair, then it is your concern only.

affect affects affecting affected (vb) If something affects you, it changes you in some way. *The weather affected his moods; if it was raining he was cross but if it was sunny he was happy.*

affection (n) is a fondness for someone. **affectionate** (adj) **affectionately** (adv)

affluent (adj) people or societies are rich. **affluence** (n)

afford affords affording afforded
1 (vb) If you can afford something, you have enough money to pay for it.
2 (vb) If you can afford to relax, you feel you have done enough work for the moment and have time to take things easy.

afraid
1 (adj) If you are afraid of something, it frightens you.
2 (adj) When you say, "I'm afraid I can't come," you are sorry you can't come.

after
1 (adv) The day after or the year after means the one following.
2 (prep) Close the door after you means you should close the door when you leave the room.
3 (prep) If you say that someone is after something, it means that they are trying to get it. *She's after a new job.*

afternoon afternoons (n) Afternoon is the time of day after 12.00 midday and before evening which starts at about 6.00pm.

afterwards (adv) means later.

again (adv) If you do something again, you do it one more time. If you do it again and again you keep on doing it.

against
1 (prep) If you put a chair against a wall, you put it so close that it touches it.
2 (prep) If you are against something, you don't agree with it. *He was against allowing girls to play football.*

age
1 (n) The age of something or someone is the length of time he, she or it has existed. *She was ten years of age.*
2 (n) An age is a certain number of years in history. *The Stone Age . . . The Victorian Age.*

agenda (n) An agenda is a list of things to be discussed at a meeting.

agent agents (n) An agent is someone who is paid to organise things for other people. *Showbusiness people pay agents to find work for them; estate agents find houses for people; travel agents arrange holidays; and secret agents spy for their governments.*

aggressive (adj) people or animals are bad-tempered and ready to attack others. **aggression** (n) **aggressively** (adv) **aggressor** (n)

agile (adj) people or animals can move quickly and easily. **agility** (n)

agitate agitates agitating agitated
1 (adj) A person who is agitated is very worried or nervous.
2 (vb) If you agitate a liquid, you stir it or move it around.
3 (vb) If you agitate for or against something, you campaign in public. **agitation** (n) **agitator** (n)

agnostic (n) An agnostic is a person who holds the view that you cannot prove God exists. **agnosticism** (n)

ago (adj) Ago means some time in the past. *It happened two years ago.*

agony agonies (n) Agony is great pain, which can be either physical or mental.

agree agrees agreeing agreed
1 (vb) If you agree with someone, you share the same idea. **agreement** (n)
2 (vb) If something agrees with someone, it does them good. *The sea air must have agreed with him, he looks so well.*

agreeable (adj) Someone or something that is agreeable is pleasant.

agriculture (n) Agriculture is everything to do with farming.

ahead
1 (adv) If you are ahead of someone, you are in front of them. *I walked ahead . . . Sally was ahead of her group. . . .*
2 (adv) If you look ahead, you look in front of you. *He looked ahead.*
3 (adv) If you think ahead, you plan for the future.
4 If someone says, "Go ahead" they mean carry on.

aid aids aiding aided
1 (vb) If you aid someone, you help them.

2 (n) An aid is a device which helps you to do or understand something.

AIDS (n) is an illness that destroys the body's ability to protect itself against disease. The letters stand for Acquired Immune Deficiency Syndrome.

aim aims aiming aimed
1 (vb) If you aim something such as a gun, ball or dart, you point it at what you want to hit.
2 (n) An aim is a target you set for yourself or for others. *My aim is to get into the first team this year.*

air airs airing aired
1 (n) Air is the mixture of gases all around us which we need to breathe.
2 (vb) If you air clothing or a house, you let air move around it to dry out dampness.

air-conditioning (n) is a way of keeping the air in buildings at a constant temperature. **air-conditioned** (adj)

aircraft (n) are aeroplanes, gliders and helicopters.

aircraft

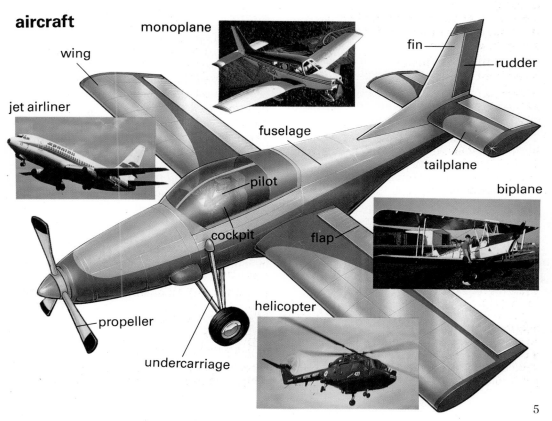

monoplane
wing
fin
rudder
jet airliner
fuselage
tailplane
biplane
pilot
cockpit
flap
helicopter
propeller
undercarriage

aircraft-carrier aircraft-carriers (n) An aircraft-carrier is a warship designed with a runway for aeroplanes to use.

airforce (n) The airforce is part of the fighting force of a country that defends or attacks from the air.

air-hostess air-hostesses (n) An air-hostess is a woman who works on an aeroplane and looks after passengers.

airline airlines (n) An airline is a company which owns aeroplanes and carries passengers and goods.

airgun airguns (n) An airgun is a gun that fires small pellets by air pressure.

airmail (n) is the way of sending letters and parcels between countries by aeroplane.

airport airports (n) An airport is an area with passenger facilities as well as runways where aeroplanes land and take off.

airtight (adj) containers stop air getting in or out of them. Some foods keep longer than usual in airtight containers.

aisle aisles (n) An aisle is the gap between blocks of seats in a theatre, cinema or church, or between shelving in a supermarket.

ajar (adj) If a door is ajar, it is partly open.

alarm alarms alarming alarmed
1 (vb) If you alarm someone, you frighten them in some way.
2 (n) An alarm is a warning given when there is danger.
3 (adj) If you are alarmed, you are afraid something unpleasant is about to happen.

album albums
1 (n) An album is a long-playing record with a collection of music on it.
2 (n) An album is a book where things such as photographs are collected.

alcohol
1 (n) Alcohol is the name for drinks such as beer, wine and spirits.
2 (n) Alcohol is also a name for a chemical found in beer, wine and spirits.

alert alerts alerting alerted
1 (vb) If you alert someone, you warn them of danger about to happen.
2 (adj) If a person or animal is alert, they pay attention to what is going on around them. **alertly** (adv)

algebra (n) is a type of mathematics where letters and symbols are used to represent numbers, for example, $x - y = 4$.

alibi alibis (n) You have an alibi if you can prove you were somewhere else when a crime was committed.

alien aliens
1 (n) An alien is someone who is not legally a citizen of a country where he lives.
2 (n) An alien is an imaginary creature from another planet.
3 (adj) If something is alien, it is strange, threatening or unusual.

alight alights alighting alighted
1 (adj) If something is alight, it is bright with light or on fire.
2 (vb) If you alight from a vehicle, such as a bus, you get off.
3 (adj) If someone's face is alight with joy or happiness, they show their emotion in their expression.

alike
1 (adj) People or objects that are similar in some way are alike.
2 (adv) Alike means in a similar way. *The teacher treated all the children alike.*

alive (adj) If something is alive, it is not dead. Stones can't be alive; plants and animals can.

alkali (n) An alkali is the chemical opposite of acids and will neutralise them in solution. Potash, ammonia and soda are alkalis.

Allah (n) is the name for God in Islam.

all right (or alright)
1 (adj) If you say that something is all right, you are satisfied with it.
2 (adj) If you ask someone if they are all right after a slight accident, you want to know if they have hurt themselves.

3 If you are asked to do something and you say, "All right", you agree to do it. If you have explained something to someone and you say, "All right?" you are asking if they understand.

allergic (adj) If a person or animal is allergic to something, their body reacts to it and may develop a rash or become ill in some way.

allergy allergies (n) If you are allergic to something, you have an allergy.

alligator alligators (n) An alligator is a large reptile like a crocodile. It has strong jaws and sharp teeth and lives mainly in America on the banks of rivers. It eats fish and other small animals.

allotment allotments (n) An allotment is a piece of ground, usually in a town, that a person can rent for growing vegetables or flowers.

allow allows allowing allowed (vb) If you allow someone to do something, you let them do it. **allowance** (n)

almost (adv) means nearly but not quite.

alone (adj) A person or thing that is alone is on its own.

along (prep) Anything that moves along a road or track travels forward on it.

aloud (adv) If you say something aloud, people can hear you.

alphabet alphabets (n) The twenty-six letters we use to make our words is called the alphabet. Many other languages have their own alphabets.

alphabetical (adj) Words in dictionaries and names on registers are arranged in alphabetical order, which means that they are listed in the order in which their first letters appear in the alphabet.

already (adv) If something has already happened, it has taken place beforehand.

altar altars (n) An altar is a place in a church, usually a block of stone or a table, which is the centre of worship.

alter alters altering altered
1 (vb) If you alter something, you change it in some way.
2 (vb) If your mood alters, it changes. *My happy mood altered when I saw the mess on the floor.* **alteration** (n)

alternative alternatives (n) An alternative is something you can choose instead of something else.

although (conj) is a word that joins two parts of a sentence. The part that it introduces has a comment in it that makes the other part seem to contradict it. *I really like watching television, although some of the programmes are not very good.*

altitude altitudes (n) The altitude of a place is its height above sea-level.

altogether (adv) means completely.

always (adv) If something happens in the same way every time, you say it always happens.

amateur amateurs (n) An amateur is someone who takes part in an activity or sport for the love of it rather than for payment.

amaze amazes amazing amazed (vb) If you are amazed, you are surprised and astonished. **amazement** (n)

ambassador ambassadors (n) An ambassador is an important official who lives in a foreign country and represents his or her own government there.

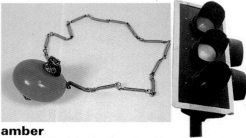

amber
1 (n) Amber is the hard yellowish-brown substance made from fossilized tree sap used for making jewellery.
2 (adj) The amber traffic light is the one in the middle of the set of traffic lights.

ambidextrous (adj) You are ambidextrous if you can use both hands equally well.

ambiguous (adj) If something ambiguous is said or written, it could have more than one meaning. **ambiguity** (n)

ambition ambitions (n) An ambition is a strong desire you have to do something well in the future. *Her ambition was to be an astronaut.* **ambitious** (adj)

ambulance ambulances (n) An ambulance is a vehicle used to carry patients to and from hospital.

ammonia (n) is a strong smelling gas or liquid sometimes used in cleaning fluids.

ammunition (n) is the rockets, bullets, shells and arrows which are fired from weapons.

amoeba (n) An amoeba is a tiny living creature which has only one cell.

among or **amongst**
1 (prep) If you are among a group of people you are in the middle of them.
2 (prep) If something is divided among several people it is shared between them.

amount amounts (n) An amount of something is the total that can be counted or measured. *An amount of money ... an amount of time ... an amount of interest.*

amphibious (adj) animals or machines are equally at home on land or in water.

amphibian amphibians (n) An amphibian is a creature that lives on land but breeds in water; frogs and toads are amphibians.

amplify amplifies amplifying amplified
1 (vb) If you amplify a sound you make it louder. **amplifier** (n)
2 (vb) If you amplify an idea, you explain it in further detail.

amputate amputates amputating amputated (vb) If you amputate a part of the body, you cut it off completely. *The surgeon amputated the man's leg because it could not be cured.* **amputation** (n)

amuse amuses amusing amused (vb) If you amuse somebody, you entertain them by making them laugh or smile. **amusement** (n)

anaemia (n) is a medical condition that makes you feel tired and look pale. It is caused by having too few red cells in your blood. **anaemic** (adj)

anaesthetic anaesthetics (n) This is a pain-killing injection or gas that doctors or dentists give their patients before an operation.

anagram anagrams (n) An anagram is a type of puzzle where the letters of a word or phrase are mixed up to make a new one. *Mate is an anagram of team.*

analyse analyses analysing analysed (vb) If someone analyses something they study it in great detail, often dividing it into parts. *The scientists analysed the temperature charts.* **analysis** (n) **analyst** (n)

anarchy (n) If there is anarchy in a place there are no rules or laws. **anarchist** (n)

anatomy (n) is the study of the structure of bodies, both animal and human, to find out how they work. **anatomical** (adj)

ancestor ancestors (n) Your ancestors are members of your family from past generations. *Queen Victoria is an ancestor of Prince Charles.* **ancestry** (n)

amphibian

This newt is a typical amphibian.

Newt eggs are produced singly and are attached to water weeds. The newt tadpoles live under water and breathe through gills until the newt is fully grown. The adult newts use lungs to breathe and live mainly on land.

An amphibious vehicle.

anchor anchors
1 (n) An anchor is the heavy metal hook which is used on ships and boats to stop them floating away.
2 (vb) If you anchor something, you hold it down firmly.

ancient (adj) If a thing is ancient, it is very old indeed, and belongs to the distant past.

Andrew, Saint is the patron saint of Scotland. He was one of the followers of Jesus who preached the gospels and he was eventually crucified by the Romans. His Feast day is November 30th.

anecdote anecdotes (n) An anecdote is a short, often humorous story.

anemometer anemometers (n) An anemometer is an instrument used to measure the strength of the wind.

angel angels
1 (n) An angel, some people believe, is a spiritual being and the messenger of God.

2 (n) The word angel is used to describe a person who acts in a particularly kind and thoughtful way. *What an angel you are to help me.* **angelic** (adj)

anger angers angering angered
1 (vb) If someone or something angers you, you feel cross and upset.
2 (n) Anger is a strong feeling which occurs when you think that you are being treated unfairly. **angrily** (adv)

angle angles angling angled
1 (n) An angle is the area created when two lines or plane surfaces meet.
2 (vb) Angle means to fish with a hook and line.

angry angrier angriest (adj) If you feel angry, you feel and show a strong reaction to someone or something that you feel is unfair or wrong.

animal

animal animals (n) The word animal describes all forms of life other than plants.

ankle ankles (n) Your ankle is the place where your leg joins your foot.

anniversary anniversaries (n) An anniversary is a date which is remembered because something special happened on that date in a previous year. *The couple celebrated their wedding anniversary in March.*

announce announces announcing announced (vb) If you announce that something has happened, you make it known publicly. *Tony and Susan announced their engagement through the newspaper.* **announcer** (n)

annoy annoys annoying annoyed (vb) If you annoy someone, you make them irritable or angry.

annual annuals
1 (adj) Annual events happen once a year. **annually** (adv)
2 (n) An annual is a book that is published once a year for children, usually at Christmas.
3 (n) An annual season ticket lasts a year.

anonymous (adj) If a person is anonymous their identity is unknown, either because it has been lost or because they want to keep it secret. **anonymously** (adv)

anorak anoraks (n) An anorak is a hooded jacket that is usually windproof and waterproof.

another If you want another item, you want one more than you already have.

answer answers answering answered (vb) If you answer a question, you reply.

answering machine (n) An answering machine can be connected up to your telephone to record messages for you if you are out when it rings.

ant ants (n) An ant is a small insect that lives in large groups underground.

antagonise antagonises antagonising antagonised (vb) If you antagonise another person, you upset them and make them angry.

Antarctic (n) The Antarctic is the area around the South Pole.

antelope antelopes (n) An antelope is an animal like a deer which can run very fast.

antenna antennae
1 (n) Antennae are long and thin feelers on the head of an insect.
2 (n) A radio antenna is its aerial.

anthem anthems (n) An anthem is a song, usually one of celebration and sometimes of a religious kind.

anthology anthologies (n) An anthology is a collection of poems, songs, stories etc. by different people put together in one book.

antibiotic antibiotics (n) An antibiotic is a drug used by doctors to help cure patients of infections.

anticlimax anticlimaxes (n) An anticlimax occurs when you are looking forward to an event very much and then are disappointed or let down by what takes place.

anticlockwise (adj) If anything moves in an anticlockwise direction, it goes in the opposite way to the hands on a clock face.

anticyclone anticyclones (n) An anticyclone refers to a mass of high pressure in the atmosphere which gives good weather.

anticipate anticipates anticipating anticipated (vb) If you anticipate something, you realise what may happen before it does. **anticipation** (n)

antidote antidotes (n) An antidote is a chemical substance used to overcome the effects of a poison.

antiseptic (n) is a liquid or a cream which kills germs and infections.

antique antiques (n) An antique is an old object, such as furniture or jewellery, that is valued highly because it is rare or beautiful.

antler antlers (n) Antlers are like branched horns and are found on the top of a male deer's head.

anus anuses (n) The anus is the hole between the buttocks of a person or an animal where waste matter leaves the body.

anvil anvils (n) An anvil is an iron block on which hot metal is beaten into shape.

anxious (adj) If you are anxious about an event or a person, you are worried and unsure about what will happen in the future. **anxiously** (adv) **anxiety** (n)

anybody see anyone.

anyhow
1 (adv) Anyhow means in any case. *Anyhow it is no use worrying about the test.*

anyone
1 (pron) You use the word anyone to refer to an unknown person or thing. *He did not see anyone in the park.*
2 (pron) The word anyone is also used to mean a person or people in general. *Anyone can make a mistake . . . It could happen to anyone.*

anything
1 (pron) You use the word anything to mean no particular thing. *He didn't give her anything.*
2 (pron) The word anything can be used when you are being vague about an event or an idea. *Anything could happen.*

anywhere (adv) Anywhere is in any place. *The boy would sleep anywhere he could find shelter.*

apart
1 (adv) If you live apart from your family, you do not live with them.
2 (adj) If you ask two people or more to move apart, you want them to make spaces between themselves. *The teacher made the two boys stand apart.*

apartheid (n) is a political system where black people and white people are required by law to live separately.

apartment apartments (n) An apartment is usually a flat where a family or group of friends can live.

ape apes (n) Apes are large animals similar to monkeys but without tails.

ape

gorilla

gibbon

orang-utan

chimpanzee

apex apexes (n) The apex is the highest point or the pointed end of anything. *The apex of the pyramid was 50 metres from the ground.*

apiary apiaries (n) An apiary is where bees are kept.

apology apologies (n) An apology is a written or spoken message to say that you are sorry for the trouble or hurt that you have caused. **apologetic** (adj) **apologetically** (adv)

apostrophe apostrophes
1 (n) An apostrophe is the sign used in writing to show where a letter or letters are left out. *"Don't do that" is the short form of "Do not do that".*
2 (n) An apostrophe is also used to show ownership. *The old woman's skirt blew in the wind.*

apparatus apparatuses
1 (n) Apparatus is the group of tools and instruments used for a particular job or piece of work.
2 (n) Apparatus is a specific piece of equipment constructed or used for a particular purpose.

apparent (adj) If something is apparent to you, you think that a situation exists even though you cannot be certain about it. **apparently** (adv)

appeal appeals appealing appealed
1 (vb) If you appeal for help, you ask with particular urgency. *The woman appealed for help when she was mugged.*
2 (n) An appeal is made when people are in particular need, or when attention must be drawn to an event. *The charity for sick children launched an appeal on Saturday.*

appear appears appearing appeared
1 (vb) If something or someone appears, they move from a place where they cannot be seen to a place where they can be seen. *The dog appeared from behind the bushes.*
2 (vb) If an actor appears in a play they have a part in it.
3 (vb) If someone appears in court, they come to answer charges brought against them.
4 (vb) The way you appear is how you look. **appearance** (n)

appendicitis (n) is a painful illness where a person has an infected appendix.

appendix appendices
1 (n) The appendix is a small part of the body's digestive system.
2 (n) An appendix is part of a book, usually at the end, which gives extra information.

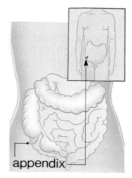

appendix

appetite appetites (n) Your appetite is your desire to eat. **appetising** (adj)

apple apples (n) An apple is a round red, yellow or green fruit with firm juicy flesh, and pips.

appliance appliances (n) An appliance is an instrument, tool or machine that is used for a particular job. *Washing machines, mixers and drills are electrical appliances.*

apply applies applying applied
1 (vb) If you apply for a job, you fill in a form, or contact the workplace to be considered for the job. **applicant** (n)
2 (vb) If you apply yourself to your work, you concentrate very hard on doing it.
3 (vb) If you apply something to a surface, you put it on it. *She applied the cream to her face.* **application** (n)

appoint appoints appointing appointed
(vb) If you appoint a person to a job, you choose them to do it.

appointment appointments (n) If you make an appointment, you arrange to visit a person at a particular time.

appreciate appreciates appreciating appreciated
1 (vb) When you appreciate people or books, you understand their best qualities.
2 (vb) When someone appreciates your efforts, they thank you to show that they have noticed what you have done. **appreciation** (n) **appreciative** (adj)

apprehensive (adj) If you feel apprehensive, you feel worried or unsure about what will happen. **apprehension** (n)

apprentice apprentices (n) An apprentice is someone who works with another person for a length of time to learn that person's job or trade. **apprenticeship** (n)

approach approaches approaching approached
1 (vb) If someone or something approaches another person or object, they come closer.
2 (n) The approach to a place is the road or path usually taken to it.

appropriate (adj) If you feel that a particular way of doing something is appropriate, you think that it is suitable for that occasion. **appropriately** (adv)

approve approves approving approved
(vb) If you approve of something, you like it or you agree with it.

approximate (adj) If you give an approximate answer, you make a guess that will be close but not exactly right. **approximately** (adv)

apricot apricots (n) An apricot is a small, soft orange-coloured fruit with a stone in the middle.

apron aprons (n) You wear an apron to protect the front of your clothes while you cook or paint.

aquarium aquariums or aquaria
1 (n) An aquarium is a large fish tank.
2 (n) An aquarium is a building, open to the public, where many kinds of fish and other water creatures are kept.

aquatic (adj) If something is aquatic, it lives or grows in water or it is an activity that takes place in or on water. *A duck is an aquatic bird; marsh marigolds are aquatic plants; skin diving and water skiing are aquatic sports.*

aqueduct aqueducts (n) An aqueduct is a high, long, arched structure that looks like a bridge, but which carries water across a valley.

arable (adj) land is used for growing crops.

arbitrary (adj) If someone makes an arbitrary decision, they do it without really thinking it through and without thinking about the people it might affect.

arc arcs
1 (n) An arc is a curved movement. *The stone rose through the air in an arc and smashed through the window.*
2 (n) An arc is a mathematical word for part of a circle.

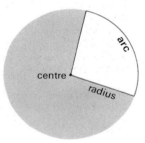

arcade arcades
1 (n) A shopping arcade is a covered area with lots of shops and stalls.
2 (n) An amusement arcade has fruit machines and games to play for money.

arch arches arching arched
1 (vb) If a cat arches its back, it curves its back upwards.

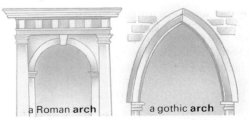

a Roman **arch**   a gothic **arch**

2 (n) An arch is a part of a building or bridge with pillars on either side of a space. It has a curving roof.

archaeology

archaeology (n) is the study of ancient times by excavating such things as very old buildings, burial grounds, weapons and tools. **archaeologist** (n)

archbishop archbishops (n) An archbishop is a very high-ranking bishop who is in charge of the churches and priests in a certain area.

archer archers (n) An archer shoots with a bow and arrow. **archery** (n)

architecture
1 (n) Architecture is the style in which buildings are designed.
2 (n) Architecture is the work of an architect. It includes planning and designing buildings. **architect** (n)

arctic
1 (n) The Arctic is the area around the North Pole.
2 (adj) If you say the weather is arctic, you mean that it is very cold.

area areas
1 (n) An area is a particular part of the world or a country, city or town.
2 (n) The area of something is the measurement of its flat surface. *The area of the playground is 1500 square metres.*

arena arenas (n) An arena is a large space where sports and entertainments are held.

argue argues arguing argued
1 (vb) If two people quarrel about something and go on doing so angrily, they argue. **argument** (n)
2 (vb) If you argue something, you say what you think is true and why. *The headteacher argued the case for building a new swimming pool so well that the governors agreed.*
3 (vb) When two or more people argue about a plan, they discuss the good and the bad points before making a decision.

arid (adj) regions are very dry and not able to support much life.

aristocrat aristocrats (n) An aristocrat is a member of a family of high social rank. **aristocratic** (adj) **aristocracy** (n)

arithmetic (n) is the part of mathematics that deals with adding, subtracting, dividing and multiplying numbers. **arithmetically** (adv)

ark (n) The Ark was the ship, in the Bible story, that Noah built to save his family and the animals from the Great Flood.

arm arms arming armed
1 (n) Your arm is the part of your body between your shoulder and your hand.
2 (vb) If a country arms itself, it prepares for war.
3 (n) Arms are weapons of war.
4 If you keep someone at arm's length, it means that you're not very friendly towards them.

armada armadas (n) An armada is a fleet of ships. The Spanish Armada was the fleet sent to destroy the English in 1588.

armchair armchairs (n) An armchair is a comfortable chair with supports for resting your arms.

armour (n) is metal clothing worn by soldiers hundreds of years ago to protect them from injury in battle. **armoured** (adj)

army armies (n) An army is a large group of people who are trained to fight on land in wartime.

aroma aromas (n) An aroma is a pleasant smell, usually of food.

around (prep or adv) If you say that something is around, it is on all sides. *There was fog around the house.*

arrange arranges arranging arranged
1 (vb) If you arrange something, you make plans and organise it.
2 (vb) When you arrange flowers or objects, you put them together in a tidy or interesting way. **arrangement** (n)

arrest arrests arresting arrested (vb) When the police arrest someone, they take them to the police station to be questioned about or charged with a crime.

arrive arrives arriving arrived
1 (vb) When you arrive somewhere after a journey, you reach your destination.
2 (vb) If you arrive at a decision, you make up your mind.
3 (vb) If something arrives, it has come. *Spring arrived early this year; the blossoms were out in April.*

armour from the Tudor period (1485-1603)

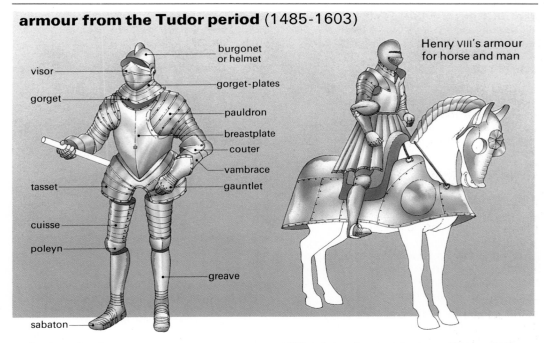

visor
gorget
tasset
cuisse
poleyn
sabaton

burgonet or helmet
gorget-plates
pauldron
breastplate
couter
vambrace
gauntlet
greave

Henry VIII's armour for horse and man

arrival arrivals
1 (n) The arrival is the moment when something or someone reaches a place or time. *The arrival of the flight from Paris has just been announced.*
2 (n) The beginning of something can be called an arrival. *The sudden arrival of winter made us get out our warm clothes.*
3 (n) A new arrival is a new-born baby.

arrogant (adj) people think that they are superior or cleverer than anyone else. They like to tell other people what to do and how to do it. **arrogance** (n)

arrow arrows
1 (n) An arrow is a long, thin weapon fired from a bow. It has a sharp point at one end and usually feathers at the other.
2 (n) An arrow is a sign pointing the way.

arsenal arsenals (n) An arsenal is a place where weapons and ammunition are stored.

arsenic (n) is a strong, dangerous poison.

arson (n) is the crime of setting fire to something on purpose.

art arts
1 (n) Art is the making of drawings, paintings, sculptures and carvings.

2 The Arts of a country are all its paintings, sculptures, poetry, plays, literature and music.
3 (n) The art of something is the skill of doing it. *The art of origami is fun to learn.*

artery

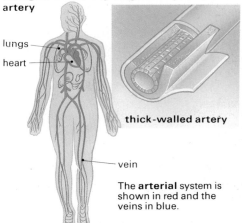

lungs
heart

thick-walled artery

vein

The **arterial** system is shown in red and the veins in blue.

artery arteries (n) An artery is one of the larger tubes that carries oxygenated blood from your heart around the body.

arthritis (n) is a disease that makes joints swollen and very painful.

Arthur, King

Arthur, King was the legendary king of the Britons, supposed to have lived at Camelot and who with his Knights of the Round Table, led a resistance against the Saxon invaders.

article articles
1 (n) An article is a piece of writing for a newspaper or magazine.
2 (n) An article is a particular thing. *He picked up an article of clothing from the floor.*

articulated lorry (n) An articulated lorry is a very long vehicle made in two parts with a steel bar joining them.

artificial
1 (adj) Artificial things are man-made and do not exist naturally. **artificially** (adv)
2 (adj) If someone is artificial, they put on an act and say and do things that they don't really mean.

artillery
1 (n) The artillery is the army's large guns.
2 (n) The Artillery is the army regiment which operates the large guns.

artist artists (n) An artist is a person who draws, paints or sculpts. **artistic** (adj) **artistically** (adv)

asbestos (n) is a material used for fire-proofing.

ascend ascends ascending ascended
1 (vb) If you ascend, you go up. *They ascended the mountain in the summer.*
2 (vb) When someone ascends a throne, they become king or queen. **ascent** (n)

ash ashes
1 (n) Ash is the grey powdery stuff that is left when something has been burned.
2 (n) An ash is a tree with smooth grey bark, small greenish flowers and wing-shaped seeds.
3 (n) The Ashes is the trophy for the winners of the England versus Australia cricket matches.

ashamed (adj) If you are ashamed, you feel very bad and guilty about something you have done which you think is wrong.

aside
1 (adv) If you push something aside, you push it out of the way.
2 (n) An aside is something that you say quietly that is not part of the general conversation.
3 (adv) If you take someone aside, you take them where you cannot be overheard and can talk privately.

ask asks asking asked
1 (vb) If you ask someone something, you put a question to them.
2 (vb) If you ask someone to do something, you hope they will do as you wish.
3 (vb) If you ask someone to tea or to a party, you invite them to come.

asleep (adj) When you are asleep, your eyes are closed, you are completely relaxed and not conscious.

aspect aspects (n) An aspect is just one of many ways of seeing or thinking about a thing. *The only aspect of the work that interests me is acting in the play.*

aspirin aspirins (n) This is a drug made into a tablet which is used to treat headaches and minor pains.

ass asses (n) An ass is a type of donkey.

assassinate assassinates assassinating assassinated (vb) If someone plans to kill an important person, they plan to assassinate them. **assassination** (n)

assault assaults assaulting assaulted
1 (vb) A person or group assaults someone if they attack and hurt them physically.
2 (n) An assault is a sudden attack by one person on another.

assemble assembles assembling assembled
1 (vb) If you assemble people or objects, you collect them together in one place.
2 (vb) If you assemble something, you put pieces together to make a complete object.

assembly assemblies (n) An assembly is a group of people gathered together in one place.

assembly line (n) An assembly line is a place in a factory where articles are put together piece by piece as they pass by on a conveyor belt.

assess assesses assessing assessed (vb) If you assess something, you gather all the information you can together to decide on its value or worth, or to see what progress is being made. **assessment** (n)

assignment assignments (n) An assignment is a particular piece of work given to somebody to do.

assist assists assisting assisted (vb) If you assist somebody, you help them. **assistance** (n) **assistant** (n)

associate associates associating associated
1 (vb) If you associate with a particular group of people, you spend a lot of time with them.
2 (vb) If you associate ideas or things, you make a connection between them. *I always associate the idea of oxygen with Humphrey Davy.*
3 (n) An associate is a person you keep company with, or work with.

association associations
1 (n) An association is an organisation of people or companies that have something in common.
2 (n) If you make an association between ideas or people, you discover that they are connected in some way.

assortment assortments (n) An assortment is a collection of things, usually having something in common, but also with differences. *There was a good assortment of biscuits in the tin.*

asteroid asteroids (n) Asteroids are very small planets which orbit the sun.

asthma (n) is a condition which makes breathing difficult. **asthmatic** (n)

astonish astonishes astonishing astonished (vb) If something astonishes you, it surprises or amazes you. **astonishment** (n)

astrology (n) If you believe in astrology, you think that the way you live is controlled by the movement of the stars and the planets. **astrologer** (n)

astronaut astronauts (n) An astronaut is a person who travels in space.

astronomy (n) is the study of planets, stars, comets and space. **astronomer** (n)

atheist atheists (n) An atheist is a person who does not believe in any form of God. **atheism** (n)

athletics (n) are organized competitions of track and field sporting activities such as running, jumping, vaulting and throwing. *The most important athletics meeting is the Olympic Games.* **athlete** (n)

athletics

jumping
(high jump)

running

throwing (shot-put)

Atlantic

Atlantic (n) The Atlantic is the ocean separating the Americas and Europe and Africa.

atlas atlases (n) An atlas is a book of maps which shows different countries, oceans, towns, roads and other geographical information.

atmosphere atmospheres
1 (n) The atmosphere is made up of gases and vapours which surround and protect the earth. **atmospheric** (adj)
2 (n) The atmosphere in a place can be the feeling generated by a group of people. *Everyone was happy until the sad news changed the atmosphere.*

atom atoms
1 (n) An atom is the smallest part of anything. Everything is made from atoms.
2 (n) An atom is a tiny amount of something. *An atom of dust blew in my eye.*

atom bomb atom bombs (n) An atom bomb is a very powerful bomb that uses the energy stored in atoms. It kills with radiation as well as explosives.

atomic (adj) If anything is atomic, it uses the energy contained in atoms.

attach attaches attaching attached
1 (vb) If you attach something, you join it to something else.
2 (adj) If somebody is attached to a group, they belong to it.
3 (vb) If you are attached to someone, you are fond of them. **attachment** (n)

attack attacks attacking attacked
1 (vb) If you attack someone, you hurt them physically.
2 (vb) If a player attacks in a game, they try to score a goal or a point.
3 (vb) You attack someone when you criticise them strongly.
4 (n) An attack is an assault on a person or group of people.
5 (n) An attack is a sudden illness. *She had a bad attack of asthma at school.*

attempt attempts attempting attempted
1 (vb) If you attempt something, you have a try at it. *He attempted to climb the wall, but fell back .*
2 (n) An attempt is a try at something. It may or may not be successful.

attend attends attending attended
1 (vb) If you attend to something, you concentrate on it. **attention** (n)
2 (vb) If you attend a meeting, you are present at it. **attendance** (n)

attendant attendants (n) An attendant is a person who is employed to give information and directions to visitors at places like museums and exhibitions.

attic attics (n) An attic is a room or space in a house just under the roof.

attitude attitudes (n) Your attitude is the way you approach a task or a person. *He has a very poor attitude towards his work.*

attract attracts attracting attracted
1 (vb) If a magnet attracts something, it pulls it towards it.
2 (vb) If you attract someone's attention, you make them notice you.
3 (adj) If someone or something attracts you, they have certain qualities which you like. **attraction** (n)

attractive
1 (adj) An attractive person is good looking or has an exciting personality.
2 (adj) An attractive thing is interesting.

aubergine aubergines (n) A vegetable with a smooth, dark skin and soft, white flesh.

auburn (adj) is a red-brown hair colour.

auction auctions (n) An auction is a sale where customers bid for goods, property or animals. Whoever offers the most money buys the item. **auctioneer** (n)

audible (adj) If something is audible, you can hear it. **audibility** (n) **audibly** (adv)

audience audiences (n) An audience is a group of people who go to hear or see a performance of a play or concert.

audio-visual aids (n) are a variety of apparatus such as tape-recorders, videos and slide projectors used by teachers.

audition auditions (n) An audition is a test for actors, musicians, singers, dancers, etc. to see if they are suitable to take part in a performance of some kind.

aunt aunts (n) Your aunt is the sister of your mother or father, or the wife of your uncle.

author authors (n) Authors write books.

authorise authorises authorising authorised (vb) If you authorise something, you allow it to happen officially. *He is the one person who can authorise payment.*

authority authorities
1 (n) Authority is the right to tell other people what to do. *I have the authority to stop this building work.*
2 (n) An authority is an expert on a particular subject. *She was an authority on the life of Mozart.*
3 (n) An authority is an organisation which controls public interests. *The education authority.*

autobiography autobiographies (n) The writers of autobiographies tell the story of their own lives. **autobiographical** (adj)

autograph autographs (n) An autograph is someone's signature.

automatic (adj) machines perform a series of tasks without a person having to do very much. **automatically** (adv)

autumn (n) Autumn is the season in the year between summer and winter.

avalanche avalanches (n) A fall of rocks or snow from a mountain is called an avalanche.

average averages
1 (adj) Average means normal or usual.
2 (adj) The average is a mathematical term for the result you get when you add a group of numbers together and divide the total by the number of items. The average of 3, 9, 12 is 8. $(3 + 9 + 12 = 24; 24 \div 3 = 8)$

avenue avenues (n) An avenue is a wide road or path often lined with trees.

aviary aviaries (n) An aviary is a large outdoor cage for keeping birds.

aviation (n) is the name for the science of flying aircraft.

avid (adj) If a person does something in an avid way, they do it with great enthusiasm. *Simon was an avid reader.* **avidly** (adv)

avoid avoids avoiding avoided (vb) If you avoid a person or a situation, you decide not to see that person or to take part in the event. **avoidance** (n)

awake (adj) If you are awake, you are not asleep.

award awards awarding awarded
1 (vb) You award a prize to someone or something that does something well.
2 (n) An award is a prize or certificate for a good achievement.

aware
1 (adj) If you are aware of someone or something, you sense their presence. *I was aware of someone else in the room before I switched on the light.*
2 (adj) If you are aware of a problem, you sense what it is without having been told about it directly. *My mother was aware of my difficult position at school and made time to talk to me.* **awareness** (n)

away
1 (adv) If you have been away, you have been somewhere else.
2 (adv) If you look away from a person, you no longer look at them.
3 (adv) If you move away from where you live, you move to another town or country.
4 (adv) If you put an item away, you put it somewhere carefully.
5 (adj) If you play an away match, you do not play on your home ground.

awe (n) Awe is a feeling of respect mixed with fear.

awful (adj) If you say something is awful, you think it is very unpleasant.

awkward
1 (adj) If you find yourself in an awkward situation, you feel embarrassed and uncomfortable.
2 (adj) An awkward movement is one that is clumsy, and an awkward position is one that is, or looks, uncomfortable. **awkwardly** (adv) **awkwardness** (n)

awning awnings (n) An awning is a piece of thick material attached to a building, tent or caravan that protects those under it from the weather.

axe axes (n) An axe is a tool with a sharp metal blade and a strong handle usually used to chop wood.

axle axles (n) An axle is the rod that passes through, or is fixed to, the centre of a wheel around which it turns.

Bb

babble babbles babbling babbled (vb) If you babble, you talk quickly so that you are difficult to understand.

baby babies (n) A baby is a new-born child or animal. **babyish** (adj)

skeleton p273

backbone backbones (n) The backbone or spine is the set of bones that supports a back.

background backgrounds
1 (n) If you enquire about somebody's background, you ask about their life.
2 (n) If you prefer to stay in the background, you do not like to be the centre of attention.
3 (n) The background of a picture is the scene or colour behind the main people or objects.

backstage
1 (n) Backstage is the area behind the stage which the audience cannot see.
2 (adv) If you work backstage in the theatre, you help with the props, lighting and special effects. You do not act.

backstroke (n) is a swimming movement where the swimmer swims on their back.

backwards (adv) If you move backwards, you move to a place behind you.

bacon (n) is cured meat from a pig.

bacteria (n) are tiny organisms with only one cell. Some can cause disease.

bad worse worst (adj) If you call someone or something bad, you are saying that the person or thing is unpleasant or harmful.

Baden-Powell (1857–1941) was a British General best known as the man who founded the Boy Scouts (1908) and later, with his sister, the Girl Guides (1910).

badge badges (n) A badge is a sign worn to show you belong to a special group or to give a message. *He pinned his anti-smoking badge on his coat.*

badger badgers (n) A badger is the largest British mammal. It is black and white and lives underground in a sett and comes out at night to feed.

badminton (n) is a game like tennis, but it is played with a shuttlecock instead of a ball, and with a lighter racquet.

bagpipes (n) are a musical instrument with a leather bag and a pipe that wind is forced through to make sound.

bail bails
1 (n) When someone is arrested for a crime, they can be set free until their trial by paying a sum of money called bail.
2 (n) Bails are the two small pieces of wood laid across the stumps in cricket.

bait baits
1 (n) Bait is a small amount of food you put on a hook or in a trap to attract fish or animals you want to catch.
2 (vb) If you bait someone, you tease them.

baker bakers (n) A baker makes, cooks and sells cakes, pastries and bread.

balance balances balancing balanced
1 (vb) When you balance, you try to keep steady.
2 (n) A balance is a pair of scales with two pans hanging from a central pivot.

balcony balconies
1 (n) A balcony is a platform which is built outside a room on an upstairs floor.
2 (n) The balcony is the upstairs part of a theatre.

bald balder baldest (adj) If you are bald, you have little or no hair on your head. **baldness** (n)

bale bales (n) A bale is a bundle of hay, cotton or cloth which has been tightly bound.

ballad ballads (n) A ballad is a long song or poem which tells a story.

ballet ballets (n) A ballet tells a story using dance and music.

balloon balloons
1 (n) A balloon is a thin rubber container filled with air which children play with.

2 (n) A balloon is an aircraft which has a huge sack filled with hot air or gas and a basket to carry passengers.

bamboo bamboos (n) This is a tropical plant with a hollow, woody stem.

ban bans banning banned (vb) If you ban something, you forbid it to happen.

banana bananas (n) A banana is a long, curved fruit with a yellow skin and firm, cream-coloured flesh.

band bands banding banded
1 (n) A band is a thin strip of material, for instance, that is put round something else to hold it together.
2 (vb) If some people band together, they form a group to get something done.
3 (n) A band is a group of people who play music together.

bandage bandages bandaging bandaged
1 (n) A bandage is a long piece of thin cloth which is wound around an injured part of the body.
2 (vb) If you bandage a wound, you cover it and bind it around for protection.

banish banishes banishing banished
1 (vb) If you banish a person from a place, you send them away and never allow them to return.
2 (vb) If you banish something from your mind, you push it out of your thoughts.

banjo banjos or banjoes (n) A banjo is a small, round, stringed musical instrument with a long neck.

bank banks banking banked
1 (n) A bank is a place where people or companies can keep their money safe and can take it out when required. Banks offer many other services that deal with money.
2 (vb) If you bank your money, you put it in the bank.
3 (n) A bank is a mound of grass, sand, snow or mud.
4 If you bank on something happening, you rely on it taking place.

bank holiday bank holidays (n) A bank holiday is a public holiday when the banks and many businesses are closed.

banner banners (n) A banner is a long piece of material that is put up to advertise something, or to decorate a place.

banquet banquets (n) A banquet is a large special meal often held to celebrate a special occasion.

baptism baptisms (n) Baptism is a ceremony when a person is sprinkled with water or goes under water to show that they have become a Christian.

bar bars barring barred
1 (n) A bar is a long, solid piece of wood or metal.
2 (vb) If someone bars your way, they make it impossible for you to pass.
3 (n) A bar is a place where you can buy alcoholic and other drinks.
4 (n) A bar on an electric fire is a metal piece that glows and gives off heat when the electricity supply is turned on.

barbecue barbecues
1 (n) A barbecue is a metal grill that is used out of doors to cook food.
2 (n) It is also the name for an outdoor party with food cooked on a barbecue.

barber barbers (n) A barber is a men's hairdresser.

bare bares baring bared; barer barest
1 (adj) If a person is bare they have no clothes on.
2 (vb) If you bare a part of your body, you take off part of your clothing.
3 (adj) If a place is bare, it is empty.

barely (adv) If someone barely manages to do something, they only just succeed.

bargain bargains bargaining bargained
1 (n) A bargain is an item in a shop which is sold at a lower price than the usual value. *The sales had many bargains.*
2 (n) A bargain is an agreement where each person decides what they will do. *I knew what I should do to keep the bargain.*
3 (vb) If you bargain with someone over something, you talk over what each of you will do.

barge barges barging barged
1 (n) A barge is a large boat used to carry goods or for living in on canals.
2 If you barge into someone or something, you push them forcefully.

bark

tree p313

b

bark barks barking barked
1 (vb) When a dog barks, it makes a sudden, loud noise.
2 (n) Bark is the protective outer covering on a tree.

barley (n) is a cereal crop with long, spiky hairs. It is used to make beer and whisky.

bar mitzvah bar mitzvahs (n) A bar mitzvah is a Jewish ceremony on a boy's thirteenth birthday to mark his entry into adulthood.

barn barns (n) A barn is a large farm building where animals are kept and crops are stored.

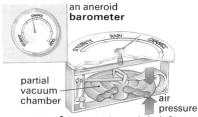

acorn **barnacle**   goose **barnacle**

barnacle barnacles (n) A barnacle is a small shellfish that fixes itself firmly to rocks and boats.

Barnardo, Thomas John (1845–1905) was a man who raised money to open homes for destitute children.

an aneroid barometer

partial vacuum chamber

air pressure

barometer barometers (n) A barometer is an instrument that measures the air pressure, so that by reading it you can have some idea of what the weather will be like.

barrel barrels
1 (n) A barrel is a round, wooden container which is wider at the middle than at the top or the bottom.
2 (n) The barrel of a gun is the part the bullet goes through when the gun is fired.

barricade barricades (n) A barricade is a wall or a line of objects that is set up to stop people going through. *Barricades divided the city.*

barrier barriers (n) A barrier is a fence to keep things apart.

barrister barristers (n) A barrister is a lawyer who works in the law courts.

barrow barrows
1 (n) A barrow is a small cart with wheels which can be used for collecting garden rubbish.
2 (n) A barrow is a stall in a street market which can be filled with fruit and vegetables or other goods to sell.
3 (n) A barrow is an ancient burial ground.

base bases basing based
1 (n) The base of something is the part on which it rests.
2 (n) If you make a place your base, you use it as a centre from which to work or travel.
3 (vb) If you base your ideas on someone else's, you use their ideas to work out your own.

baseball (n) is a team game played with a bat and ball. It is popular in the U.S.A.

basement basements (n) A basement is a room or a group of rooms below the level of the street.

basic basics
1 (adj) Something basic is simple and straightforward. **basically** (adv)
2 (n) If you give someone the basics of a subject, you give the most important details.

BASIC is a simple computer language. It is short for Beginner's All-purpose Symbolic Instruction Code.

basin basins
1 (n) A basin is a round, deep container for keeping or mixing food.
2 (n) A basin is the area of low-lying land which is drained by a river.
3 (n) A basin is a bowl fixed to a wall in a bathroom where people can wash.

basket baskets (n) A basket is a container usually made from thin sticks woven together. It can be any shape and has handles.

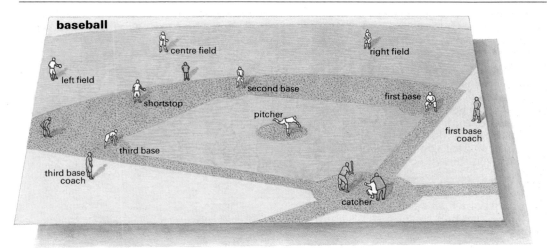

baseball

centre field

right field

left field

shortstop

second base

first base

pitcher

third base

first base coach

third base coach

catcher

bass (adj) drums, guitars or voices give the lowest musical notes.

bassoon bassoons (n) A bassoon is a deep sounding woodwind instrument which has a double reed to blow through to make a note.

bath baths bathing bathed
1 (n) A bath is a large container that a person can sit in to wash their whole body.
2 (vb) If you bath someone, you wash them.

bathe bathes bathing bathed
1 (vb) When you go swimming you bathe.
2 (vb) If you bathe a cut, you clean it with water or antiseptic.

baton batons
1 (n) A baton is a short, thin, light stick used by a conductor to show the orchestra the pace of the music.
2 (n) A baton is the short stick passed by runners in a relay race.

battalion battalions (n) A battalion is a large group of about 500 to 1000 soldiers.

batter batters battering battered
1 (n) Batter is a covering of fat, egg and flour on certain foods, especially fried fish. Batter is also used to make pancakes and Yorkshire Pudding.
2 (vb) If you batter a person, you beat them about very badly.

battery batteries
1 (n) A battery produces electricity.
2 (n) A battery of guns is a large number of guns which fire from the same spot.
3 (adj) In battery farming, egg-laying chickens are kept shut in cages.

battle battles (n) A battle is a fight between groups of armed forces.

battlement battlements (n) The battlements are the top part of a castle or fort wall where there are openings through which weapons could be fired.

castle p41

battleship battleships (n) A battleship is a large fighting ship carrying powerful guns.

bayonet bayonets (n) A bayonet is the dagger which is fixed to the end of a rifle.

bazaar bazaars (n) A bazaar is a large market or sale.

beach beaches (n) A beach is a sandy or stony strip of land which is by the sea.

beacon beacons
1 (n) A beacon is a warning light.
2 (n) A radio signal used to guide aeroplanes is called a beacon.

beam beams beaming beamed
1 (vb) If you beam, you smile broadly.
2 (n) A beam is is a piece of metal, concrete or wood which supports heavy weights. Every house has beams to hold up the floors.
3 (vb) If you beam a signal, you send it out for someone to receive.
4 (n) A beam is a ray of light.

bean

bean beans (n) A bean is a plant which produces seeds (also called beans) that you can eat. *Runner beans, broad beans, kidney beans, mung beans, soya beans...*

bear bears bearing bore borne
1 (n) A bear is a large animal living in many parts of the world. There are many different species of bear. The Polar bear lives in the Arctic; the Grizzly bear lives in North America. Most are dangerous.
2 (vb) If you bear something, you put up with it, even though you do not like it.

beard beards
1 (n) A beard is the hair that grows on the lower part of a man's face.
2 (n) The long hair under a goat's chin is called a beard.

beat beats beating beaten
1 (vb) If you hit someone several times, you beat them.
2 (vb) If you win a game, you beat the other players.
3 (vb) When you beat eggs, you whisk them up until they are light and frothy.
4 (n) Beat is the rhythm of music.

beautiful (adj) things or people are attractive to look at. **beauty** (n)

Beatles, The (1961–70): was an English pop group from Liverpool. John Lennon, Paul McCartney, George Harrison and Ringo Starr made a major contribution to pop music in the Sixties.

Beaufort Scale, The (n) is a measure of wind strength named after Admiral Beaufort who devised it. *A severe gale, force ten on the Beaufort Scale, is blowing in the North Sea.*

beaver beavers (n) A beaver is an animal like a large rat with a big flat tail that lives in and beside rivers and lakes. It fells trees by gnawing them to make dams for its lodge.

because is a word often used in answering a question which asks why? It means 'for the reason that'. *'Why are you out so late?' 'Because my bike broke down.'*

become becomes becoming became (vb) If something becomes something else, it changes in some way. *A tadpole becomes a frog.*

bumble **bee**

bee bees (n) A bee is an insect which lives in large groups in a hive. Some people keep swarms of bees for the honey they make.

beech beeches (n) A beech is a tree with a smooth, grey trunk and branches that spread outwards.

beef (n) is meat from cattle.

beer beers (n) This is an alcoholic drink made from malt, barley, hops and yeast.

Beethoven, Ludwig van (1770–1827) was a famous German composer who, even though he became deaf, continued to compose music.

male stag **beetles** fighting

The **ladybird** is a kind of **beetle**.

beetle beetles (n) A beetle is a crawling insect which has a hard casing covering its wings.

before (prep) If something happens before, it happens earlier. *You go to primary school before secondary school.*

beg begs begging begged
1 (vb) You beg if you ask for money or food because you are very poor. **beggar** (n)
2 (vb) If you beg someone to do something, you ask for it very seriously.

begin begins beginning began (vb) When you begin to do something, you start to do it. **beginner** (n)

behave behaves behaving behaved
1 (vb) The way you behave is how you act. **behaviour** (n)
2 (vb) If someone tells you to behave, they ask you to stop doing something wrong.

behind
1 (prep) If something is behind something else, it is at the back of it. *The ball was hidden behind the wall.*
2 (adv) If you are behind with work, you are late in finishing it.

belated (adj) If something is belated, it comes late. *I forgot her birthday so I sent a belated greetings card.*

belch belches belching belched
1 (vb) If you belch, you make a noise when gases are forced up your throat from your stomach and out through your mouth.
2 (vb) A volcano belches lava when it throws out liquid, rocks, ash and fire.

believe believes believing believed
(vb) If you believe that something is true, you are sure that it is, even though it cannot be proved. **belief** (n)

Belisha beacon
Belisha beacons (n) The orange lights which flash at a zebra crossing are called Belisha beacons after Hore-Belisha, who was the Minister of Transport when they were introduced.

belong belongs belonging belonged
1 (vb) If something belongs to you, it is yours.
2 (vb) If you belong to an organisation or group, you are a member of it.

below (prep) If something is below something else, it is in a lower position.

belt belts belting belted
1 (n) A belt is a strip of material or leather you wear around your waist to hold up trousers or skirts, or for decoration.
2 (n) A belt is a continuous band used in machinery to carry power or articles.

bench benches
1 (n) A bench is a long, narrow seat usually without a back which has enough room for several people to sit down.
2 (n) A bench is a place where a craftsman works and keeps his tools.

bend bends bending bent
1 (n) A bend is a curve in a piece of wood, metal, a river or a road.
2 (vb) If you bend something, you put a curve into it.

beneath (prep) If you describe an object as being beneath something, it is under it.

benefit benefits benefiting benefited
1 (n) A benefit is something that makes life better or easier.
2 (vb) If you benefit from something, your life is made easier because of it. *He benefited from the air at the sea-side which made him feel healthier.*

benevolent (adj) means kind and helpful.

bereaved (adj) If you are bereaved, it means that someone in your family has just died. **bereavement** (n)

berry berries (n) A berry is a very small fruit that grows on trees and bushes. Some berries are poisonous.

berth berths berthing berthed
1 (n) A berth is a bed on a ship or a train.
2 (n) A berth is the place in a harbour or a marina where a ship can stay.
3 (vb) If a ship berths, it is brought into harbour and tied up.
4 If you give someone a wide berth, you keep well away from them.

beside (adv) When someone is beside you they are next to you.

besides
1 (prep or adv) Besides means as well as something. *Besides being a good swimmer he could dive and water ski.*
2 (adv) Besides can mean in any case. *The film isn't suitable for you to see; besides you're too young to stay up so late.*

best

best
1 (adj) If you say that something or someone is best, they are better than anyone or anything else.
2 If you do your best at something, you do it as well as you possibly can.
3 The best man at a wedding looks after the bridegroom.
4 A best-seller is a book that is very popular and sells a great many copies.

bet bets betting betted (vb) If you bet on a race, you risk some of your money on the result. If you pick the winner you win some money; if not, you lose your original bet.

betray betrays betraying betrayed
1 (vb) If you betray a secret, you tell someone else so that it is not a secret any more.
2 (vb) If you betray a friend, you do something that is disloyal. **betrayal** (n)

better
1 (adj) Better means that something is of a higher quality or standard than something else. *You did better than me in the maths test.*
2 (adj) If you say that you're feeling better, it means that you have been ill but now you are well again.
3 If you are better off than someone else, you have more money or more advantages than they have.

between
1 (prep) Something that has two things on either side of it is between them. *The house stood between the church and the pub.*
2 (prep) If someone or something moves between two places, they go to and from one to another. *Her job meant that she had to travel between London and York weekly.*
3 (prep) If you divide sweets or money between people, you share them out.
4 (prep) If you say you go to school between 8.30 and 8.45, you set out sometime after 8.30 but before 8.45.
5 (prep) Between is a word used for comparing things. *There are a lot of differences between English and Chinese food.*

beware (vb) If you tell someone to beware of something it means that the thing is dangerous so they must be careful.

beyond
1 (prep) If a house is beyond the town, it is on the far side or outside of it.
2 (prep) When something is beyond you, you cannot do it or understand it.
3 (prep) An article which is beyond repair cannot be mended.

bhindi (n) is a vegetable of green pods. It is also known as okra or ladies' fingers.

biased (adj) If someone is biased, they like or prefer some people or things and dislike others so much that they can be unfair in their thinking.

Bible Bibles (n) The Bible is the sacred or holy book of the Christian church.

bibliography bibliographies (n) A bibliography is a list of books dealing with a particular subject. *He made a detailed bibliography about space travel for his project.*

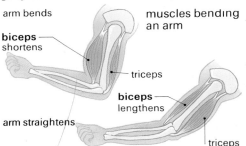

muscles bending an arm
arm bends
biceps shortens
triceps
biceps lengthens
arm straightens
triceps

biceps (n) are the large muscles in the upper arms.

bicycle bicycles (n) A bicycle is a two-wheeled vehicle; you ride it by pedalling with your feet.

big bigger biggest
1 (adj) If something is big, it is large.
2 (adj) Big means important. *The big match of the season was played at Wembley.*

bikini bikinis (n) A bikini is a brief two-piece swimsuit for girls and women.

bilingual (adj) If you are bilingual, you can speak two languages well.

bill bills billing billed
1 (n) A bill is a piece of paper showing how much money you owe. *The waiter brought the bill at the end of the meal.*

2 (vb) If you bill someone, you send them a piece of paper to say how much they owe.
3 (n) A bill is another name for an advertising poster.
4 (n) A bill in Parliament is a list of new plans which have to be voted on before they can become law.
5 (n) A bird's beak can be called a bill.

billiards (n) is a game played on a snooker table but using only 3 balls.

billion billions (n) A billion is a thousand million: 1,000,000,000.

billow billows billowing billowed (vb) If smoke billows, it swells up in large clouds. If curtains, skirts or sails billow they fill out with the wind.

binary
1 (n) The binary system is a number system used when working with computers. It has only two numerals: 0 and 1.
2 (adj) Something that has two parts is binary.

bind binds binding bound
1 (vb) If you bind someone, you tie them up.
2 (vb) If you bind a wound, you wrap bandages around it.
3 (vb) If you bind a book, you join the pages together and put a cover on it.
4 (vb) If you bind food, you make the ingredients stick together. *He added a beaten egg to bind the mixture.*

bingo (n) is a gambling game where each player has a card with numbers on. As the numbers are called out the players mark them. The first person to mark all their numbers is the winner.

binoculars (n) are like two small telescopes joined up. You look through them to see things far away.

biography biographies (n) A biography is a book about someone's life, written by another person.

biology (n) is the study of plants and animals. **biologist** (n)

bionic (adj) characters appear in stories and are supposed to be superhuman. Parts of their body have been replaced by machine parts so that they can see, hear and run better than an ordinary person.

birch birches (n) A birch tree is a tall tree with thin, peeling bark.

Biro Biros (n) The Biro was the first ball-point pen which was invented by the Biro brothers in Hungary in 1938.

birth births
1 (n) Your birth was when you were born.
2 (n) A woman gives birth at the time she has a baby.
3 (n) Someone's country of birth is the place where they were born.
4 (n) The birth of an idea is the beginning of it.

birthday birthdays (n) Your birthday is the date you were born. Most people celebrate their birthday.

biscuit biscuits (n) A biscuit is a small flat piece of baked cake mixture which is sweet or savoury.

bishop bishops
1 (n) A bishop is a senior clergyman who is in charge of other priests.
2 (n) A bishop is a piece used in the game of chess which can only move diagonally.

bison bison (n) A bison is a wild ox or buffalo found in North America.

bit bits
1 (n) A bit is a small piece of something.
2 (n) A bit is the small piece of metal which is put between a horse's teeth to control it.
3 (n) A bit is the smallest unit of information in a computer memory.

bite bites biting bit bitten (vb) If you bite something, you cut into it with your teeth.

black blacker blackest
1 (adj) If something is black it is of the darkest colour, the colour of coal.
2 (adj) Black is a way in which some people describe themselves. Sometimes the word black is used for political reasons.
3 If you are in the black, you have money in your bank account.

blackboard blackboards (n) A blackboard is a large board in a classroom which is painted black for a teacher to write on with chalk.

blackbird blackbirds (n) A blackbird is a wild bird common in the United Kingdom.

blackberry blackberries (n) The blackberry or bramble is the small edible fruit of the bramble often found growing wild.

black box black boxes (n) A black box is a special instrument used in an aircraft to record everything that happens on a flight.

black hole black holes (n) A black hole is the empty space made by the collapse of a star.

blacksmith blacksmiths (n) A blacksmith works with metal, making such things as horseshoes, gates and fire irons.

bladder bladders (n) The bladder is like a bag in the lower part of the body where waste water is stored.

blade blades
1 (n) The blade of a knife or a sword is the part with a sharp edge.
2 (n) A blade is a shoot of grass.

blame blames blaming blamed (vb) If you blame someone for something, you say that they have done something wrong.

blank blanks
1 (adj) If a piece of paper is blank, it has nothing on it.
2 (adj) A blank bullet has an empty cartridge. It makes a noise but causes no harm.
3 If you draw a blank, you find no solution to a problem.

blanket blankets (n) A blanket is a warm bed covering.

blare blares blaring blared (vb) If a car horn, siren or radio blares, it makes a loud, harsh noise.

blast blasts (n) A blast is a loud sound, particularly the noise of an explosion.

blaze blazes blazing blazed
1 (vb) A fire blazes when the flames are high and it gives out a great heat.
2 (n) A blaze is a roaring fire.

blazer blazers (n) A blazer is a school or uniform-style jacket.

bleach (n) is a chemical used to lighten the colour of materials, and to kill germs.

bleak bleaker bleakest
1 (adj) A place that is bleak is cold, bare and miserable.
2 (adj) A bleak situation is bad and unlikely to improve.

bleat bleats bleating bleated (vb) If an animal bleats, it makes a noise like a sheep or a goat.

bleed bleeds bleeding bled (vb) If you bleed, you lose blood.

blend blends blending blended (vb) If you mix various things together, you blend them.

blind blinds
1 (n) A blind is a flat or gathered window covering.
2 (adj) A blind person cannot see.

blink blinks blinking blinked (vb) When you blink, you move your eyelids up and down very quickly.

blister blisters (n) A blister is a small bubble of skin filled with liquid; it is caused by rubbing or burning.

blizzard blizzards (n) A blizzard is a bad snow storm.

bloated (adj) Something bloated is swollen and puffed up.

block blocks blocking blocked
1 (n) A block is a large lump of wood or stone with rectangular sides.
2 (vb) If you block something, you stop it from happening.
3 (n) A block of flats is a tall building where many people live.

blood (n) is the red fluid in your veins and arteries which carries oxygen around your body.
artery p15

blood-donor blood-donors (n) A blood-donor is a person who gives some blood so that it may be used in an operation on another person.

bloodthirsty (adj) If a person is bloodthirsty, they show great interest in violence or killing.

bloom blooms blooming bloomed
1 (n) A bloom is a flower on a plant.
2 (vb) If a plant blooms in the spring, it has flowers at this time of year.

blossom blossoms blossoming blossomed
1 (n) A blossom is the flower on a plant.
2 (vb) If a plant blossoms, flowers appear.

blot blots blotting blotted
1 (vb) If you blot something, you remove liquid from it with a piece of soft paper or cloth.
2 (n) A blot is a drop of liquid that is spilled onto a surface.

blotting paper (n) is a special kind of soft, thick paper used to dry up wet ink.

blouse blouses (n) A blouse is a garment similar to a shirt worn by women and girls.

blow blows blowing blew
1 (vb) When the wind blows, air moves.
2 (vb) If you blow something, you move it from one place to another, by sending out air from your mouth. *We blew the dust off the table.*
3 (vb) If you blow a musical, instrument you make a noise by blowing air into it.
4 (n) If you give someone or something a blow, you hit them sharply.

blow up
1 (vb) If you blow up something, you destroy it with an explosive device.
2 (vb) If you blow up in an argument, you lose your temper.

blue bluer bluest
1 (adj) If something is blue it is the colour of the sky when the weather is bright and clear.
2 (adj) If someone looks blue with cold, their skin is a purple-red colour.

bluebell bluebells (n) A bluebell is a plant that grows in the wild and in gardens in spring. It has a long stem and blue bell-shaped flowers.

bluebottle bluebottles (n) A bluebottle is a large fly. It has a shiny, blue body and buzzes loudly.

blue tit blue tits (n) A blue tit is a small garden bird found in Europe that has blue, white and yellow colouring to its feathers.

bluff bluffs bluffing bluffed
1 (vb) If you bluff your way through something, you pretend to know more or to be more capable than you really are. *I had to bluff my way through the test.*

2 If you call someone's bluff, you tell them to carry out a threat, believing that they will not do so.

blunder blunders blundering blundered
1 (vb) If you blunder into a situation, you do so with little thought and in an awkward way. *Mr. Jones had blundered his way into the meeting and was forced to leave.*
2 (n) A blunder is a mistake.

blunt blunter bluntest
1 (adj) A blunt knife will not cut.
2 (adj) If a person is blunt, they speak as they think, without trying to be polite.

blur blurs blurring blurred (vb) If something is blurred, it has a hazy outline so you cannot see it clearly.

blurt blurts blurting blurted (vb) If someone blurts out information, they do it suddenly, without thinking.

blush blushes blushing blushed (vb) If you blush, your face goes red. This is caused usually by embarrassment.

boa boas (n) A boa is a large snake that lives in hot countries and kills other animals to eat by wrapping itself around them, suffocating them before eating them.

Boadicea was the Queen of the British tribe, the Iceni, who fought against the Romans and won many victories. She died in 62 AD.

boar boars (n) A boar is a male pig.

board boards boarding boarded
1 (vb) If you board a plane or a ship, you get on it.
2 (vb) If you board in someone else's house, you live in a room there, usually paying money for it.
3 (n) A board is a thin, flat piece of wood or other material.
4 (n) The board of a company is the group of people who direct it.

boarder boarders (n) A boarder is a student who lives in a school during term-time. A boarding school is the place where they stay.

boast boasts boasting boasted (vb) If someone boasts about something, they try to show how clever or how proud they are.
boastful (adj) **boastfully** (adv)

boat

boat boats
1 (n) A boat is a small water craft.
2 If people are in the same boat, they are worrying about the same thing.
3 (n) The Boat Race is the annual rowing race between Cambridge and Oxford Universities.

body bodies
1 (n) Body is the word used to mean all the parts of a person or animal that can be touched, such as bones, organs, skin, etc.
2 (n) A body is the body of a dead person.

bodyguard bodyguards (n) A bodyguard is a person who protects other people, especially important and famous ones.

boil boils boiling boiled
1 (vb) If a liquid like water or milk boils, it reaches a high temperature and bubbles and steams.
2 (n) A boil is a sore, red lump on your skin containing pus.
3 (vb) If a person boils with anger, they are very angry.

boiler boilers (n) A boiler burns a fuel to make heat and hot water for a building.

fahrenheit
p105
boiling point (n) If water reaches boiling point, it bubbles and has a temperature of 100 °C. Other liquids boil at different temperatures.

boisterous (adj) people act in a loud and lively way.

bold bolder boldest
1 (adj) If someone acts in a bold way, they do so with determination and no fear.
boldly (adv) **boldness** (n)
2 (adj) If something is printed in bold print, it stands out more clearly.

bollard bollards (n) A bollard is a post used to stop traffic going into a particular area.

bolt bolts bolting bolted
1 (n) A bolt is a metal bar that slides across to lock a door or window tightly.
2 (vb) If you bolt a door, you lock it.
3 (n) A bolt of lightning is a sudden flash.
4 (n) A bolt is a metal cylinder with a thread, used to fix things together, often used with a nut.
5 (vb) If you bolt your food, you eat it very quickly.

bomb bombs bombing bombed
1 (n) A bomb is made from explosives, so that when it is dropped, thrown or touched it goes off.
2 (vb) If you bomb something, you attack it with a bomb.

bombshell bombshells (n) A bombshell is news which is unexpected, sudden and often unwelcome. *The news that he had been left out of the team was a bombshell.*

bond bonds bonding bonded
1 (n) A bond between people is a strong feeling of friendship. *As the boys grew up together they felt a special bond develop between them.*
2 (vb) If two things bond together, they stick together with glue.

bone bones boning boned
1 (n) A bone is one of the hard parts of a person's body which all together make up a skeleton.
2 (vb) If you bone a chicken, for example, you take out all the bones.
3 If you work your fingers to the bone, you work extremely hard.

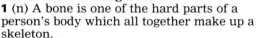

skeleton
p273

bonfire bonfires (n) A bonfire is a fire out of doors often using a mixture of wood and rubbish.

bonnet bonnets
1 (n) A bonnet is a type of hat which ties under the chin.
2 (n) The bonnet of a car or a lorry is the cover over the engine.

bonus bonuses (n) A bonus is any sort of extra reward. *The men were pleased with their £50 Christmas bonus.*

book books booking booked
1 (n) A book is a number of pieces of paper fixed together along one side. If the pages are printed the book can be read. If the pages are blank, the book can be used for writing or drawing.
2 (vb) If someone books a holiday, they arrange in advance for their hotel and transport.
3 (vb) If a referee books a player in a game, he writes down his name because he has broken the rules of the game.

booklet booklets (n) A booklet has paper covers and a small number of pages of information.

bookstall bookstalls (n) A bookstall is a small shop, open at the front, where magazines, papers and books are sold, often on railway stations.

bookworm bookworms (n) A bookworm is a person who spends a lot of time reading and enjoying books.

boomerang boomerangs (n) A boomerang is a weapon which returns to the thrower if it misses its target.

boot boots
1 (n) A boot is a heavy shoe which covers the ankle and sometimes part of the leg.
2 (n) The part of a car that holds luggage is called the boot.

border borders
1 (n) A border is the line where one country is divided from another.
2 (n) A border is an edging used for decoration.
3 (n) Borders are flowerbeds around the edges of a garden.

bore bores boring bored
1 (vb) If you bore a hole, you use a drill to make it.
2 (vb) You bore people when you do not interest them. **boredom** (n)
3 (n) A bore is an uninteresting person.

borrow borrows borrowing borrowed (vb) If you borrow something from someone, you take it with their permission for a time. **borrower** (n)

boss bosses bossing bossed
1 (n) A boss is the leader or person in charge of a group of people.
2 (vb) If you boss people about, you order them about.

both (adj or pro) When you say both, you mean two together. *Both the children had red hats.*

bother
1 (vb) If you bother to do something, you take trouble over it.
2 (n) If someone is a bother, they are troublesome.

bottle bottles
1 (n) A bottle is a narrow-necked container which can be filled with liquid.
2 If you bottle things up, you keep your feelings to yourself.

bottleneck (n) A bottleneck is where a road becomes narrower and can cause a traffic jam.

bottom bottoms
1 (n) Your bottom is the part of your body you sit on.
2 (n) The bottom is the lowest part of something.

bough boughs (n) A bough is a heavy branch on a tree.

bought see buy.

boulder boulders (n) A boulder is a very large rock.

bounce bounces bouncing bounced (vb) If something bounces, it springs up and down like a ball.

bound bounds bounding bounded (vb) If someone or something bounds, they spring up into the air.

boundary boundaries (n) The boundary is the limit of an area.

bouquet bouquets (n) A bouquet of flowers is a bunch of flowers in an attractive arrangement.

bout bouts (n) A bout is a short length of time. *His bout of flu lasted a week... The boxing match was the third bout that week.*

bow bows bowing bowed
1 (n) A bow is a curved piece of wood used for shooting arrows.
2 (n) A bow is a decorative knot in ribbon or string.
3 (n) A bow is a long piece of wood with horsehair strings attached. It is used to play stringed instruments.
4 (vb) You bow when you bend forward from the waist to greet someone formally.
5 (n) The bow of a ship is the front part.

bowel bowels (n) The bowel is the part of the body which carries undigested food away from the stomach.

bowl bowls bowling bowled
1 (n) A bowl is a dish for serving or mixing food.
2 (vb) When you bowl in cricket or rounders, you throw the ball for the batsman to hit.

bowling alley (n) A bowling alley is a place where people play ten pin bowling.

box

box boxes boxing boxed
1 (n) A box is a container of any size which has a lid.
2 (vb) When you box someone, you fight them with your fists.

Boxing Day (n) is the day after Christmas Day when boxes of gifts were traditionally given to tradesmen.

boxer boxers
1 (n) A boxer is someone who boxes.
2 (n) A boxer is also a type of dog.

Boy Scout Boy Scouts (n) A Boy Scout is a member of the Scouts Organisation founded by Baden-Powell.

bra bras (n) A bra is part of a woman's underwear which supports her breasts. It is short for brassiere.

brace braces bracing braced
1 (vb) If you brace yourself, you get ready for a shock.
2 (n) A brace is a support for something which is weakened. *A brace supported his leg . . . The brace on the wall stopped it from collapsing.*
3 (n) Braces are elastic straps worn over the shoulders to hold trousers up.

bracelet bracelets (n) A bracelet is a piece of jewellery you wear on your wrist or arm.

bracken (n) is a common type of fern found on moorlands, hillsides and woodlands.

bracket brackets
1 (n) A bracket is a support for a shelf or cupboard.
2 (n) You can put brackets around words in a sentence to show they are not quite so important. *He went to the shops (which were not very far away) and got very wet.*

brag brags bragging bragged (vb) If you brag, you boast about something in an unpleasant way.

Braille (n) is a system which uses raised dots on paper for blind people to read by touch. It was devised in the 19th century by Louis Braille, who was blind from the age of three.

brain brains (n) The brain is an organ inside the skull. It controls the body.

brake brakes braking braked
1 (vb) If a vehicle brakes, it goes slower or stops.
2 (n) Brakes stop any moving vehicle.

bramble brambles (n) Brambles are prickly, rambling plants that produce blackberries.

bran (n) refers to the small brown flakes left after the wheat for white flour has been removed from wheat grains. It can be added to cereals and bread to increase fibre in the diet.

branch branches branching branched
1 (n) A branch is a part of a tree.
2 (vb) If a road branches, it divides and goes two ways.
3 (n) An office or shop can be a branch of a large organisation.

brand brands branding branded
1 (vb) When you brand an animal, you mark it to show who owns it.
2 (n) A type of product made by one particular company is a brand.
3 (adj) If something is brand new, it has never been used before.

brandy brandies (n) This is a very strong alcoholic drink made from wine.

brawl brawls brawling brawled
1 (vb) If you brawl, you fight roughly.
2 (n) A brawl is a rough fight.

brave braver bravest (adj) Brave people or animals show courage at a difficult or dangerous time. **bravery** (n)

bread breads (n) Bread is a food made from flour, water and, often, yeast. It is made into a soft dough and baked in an oven.

break breaks breaking broke broken
1 (vb) When you break something, you destroy it or stop it from working.
breakable (adj) **breakage** (n)
2 (vb) If you break a promise, you do not keep your word.
3 (n) A break in something happens when it stops for a short time then begins again.

breakdown breakdowns
1 (n) A car breakdown happens when it stops working during a journey.
2 (n) When a person can no longer cope with the pressures on them, they may have a breakdown.

breaker breakers (n) A breaker is a big wave that crashes onto the rocks and the sea shore.

breakfast breakfasts (n) Breakfast is the first meal of the day.

breast breasts (n) A woman's breasts are the soft lumps on her chest that can fill with milk to feed a baby.

breath breaths (n) Breath is the air taken into your body and let out again.

breathalyser breathalysers (n) A breathalyser is the equipment used by the police to see if a car driver has been drinking too much alcohol.

breathe breathes breathing breathed (vb) When you breathe, you take air into your body and let it out again.

breed breeds breeding bred
1 (vb) If a human or an animal breeds, it gives birth to its young.
2 (vb) People breed animals and plants to control and improve their quality.
3 (n) A breed is a particular type of animal.

breeze breezes (n) A breeze is a light wind.

brewery breweries (n) A brewery is a place where beer is made.

bribe bribes bribing bribed (vb) If you bribe someone, you persuade them to do something for you by giving them a gift. That gift is called a bribe. **bribery** (n)

brick bricks
1 (n) A brick is a block of hard, baked clay used for building.
2 If you come down like a ton of bricks on someone, you are very angry.

bricklayer bricklayers (n) A bricklayer is a person who builds walls by cementing bricks together.

bridegroom bridegrooms (n) A man is called a bridegroom on his wedding day.

bridesmaid bridesmaids (n) A bridesmaid helps the bride on her wedding day.

bridge bridges (n) A bridge is built across a road, river or railway to help people to cross from one side to the other.

bridle bridles (n) A bridle is a harness for controlling a horse.

bridge

Tower Bridge in London is a **bascule bridge**. It can open to let ships through.

The Forth Railway Bridge is a **cantilever bridge**.

The Clifton Bridge is a **suspension bridge**.

Richmond Bridge is a **stone-arch bridge**.

brief

brief briefs briefing briefed
1 (adj) Brief is another word for short.
2 (vb) If you brief someone, you give them information about a task or job you want them to do.
3 (n) Briefs are small pants or knickers.

briefcase briefcases (n) A briefcase is a small hand case for carrying papers and documents.

bright brighter brightest
1 (adj) When a light or colour is bright, it is clear and strong.
2 (adj) If you are bright, you are clever.
3 (adj) A bright idea is a good one.

brilliant
1 (adj) A brilliant jewel or light shines very brightly. **brilliantly** (adv)
2 (adj) A brilliant person is extremely clever.

bring brings bringing brought
1 (vb) When you bring something, you take it with you. *Bring your mac in case it rains.*
2 (n) A bring–and–buy sale is where you bring something to sell and buy something else. The money usually goes to charity.

brink brinks
1 (n) The brink is the edge of a deep hole, cliff or ravine.
2 If you are on the brink of something, you are about to do it. *They were on the brink of finding a cure for colds.*

brisk brisker briskest (adj) If you are brisk, you are quick and energetic.

bristle bristles (n) Bristles are short, strong hairs on animals such as pigs sometimes used to make brushes.

brittle (adj) things are easily broken.

broad broader broadest
1 (adj) A broad river is wide.
2 (adj) Broad daylight is in the full light of day. *The robbery happened in broad daylight.*
3 (adj) The broad outline of a story gives the main points but no details.

broadcast broadcasts broadcasting broadcasted
1 (vb) If you broadcast a programme, you send it out by radio or television.
2 (n) A broadcast is a programme seen on television or heard on the radio.

bronchitis (n) is an illness that affects your throat and lungs.

brontosaurus brontosauruses or **brontosauri** (n) A brontosaurus was a plant-eating dinosaur.

dinosaurs p83

bronze bronzes
1 (n) Bronze is a metal made of copper and tin.
2 (n) Bronze is a brownish-red colour.
3 (n) The Bronze Age was the time in history between the Stone Age and Iron Age in Britain when tools and weapons were made of bronze.
4 (adj) The bronze medal in sports competitions is awarded to the third prize winner.

brooch brooches (n) A brooch is a piece of jewellery with a fastening on the back so that it can be pinned to a coat, jacket or dress.

brood broods brooding brooded
1 (vb) When a bird broods it sits on its eggs and waits for them to hatch.
2 (vb) A person who broods on something thinks deeply or worries about it.
3 (n) A brood is a large family of baby birds.

brook brooks (n) A brook is a small stream.

broom brooms (n) A broom is a large floor brush with stiff bristles and a long handle.

broomstick broomsticks (n) A broomstick is a broom with a bundle of sticks at the sweeping end.

brother brothers (n) Your brother is a boy or man who has the same mother and father as you.

brought see **bring**

brown (n) is the colour of earth and wood.

Brownie Brownies (n) A Brownie is the youngest sort of Girl Guide.

Bruce, Robert the (1274–1329) was the King of Scotland who defeated the English at the Battle of Bannockburn and gained recognition of Scotland's independence in 1328.

bruise bruises (n) A bruise is the purple mark made on your skin when you are hit.

Brunel, Isambard Kingdom (1806–59) was a great designer of bridges such as the Clifton Suspension Bridge, and steamships such as The Great Britain. He also designed railways.

brush brushes brushing brushed
1 (n) A brush is a piece of wood with bristles in it that is used for sweeping, brushing or scrubbing. Brushes can be all sorts of sizes.
2 (vb) When you brush something, you clean it by using a brush.

bubble bubbles bubbling bubbled
1 (vb) When something bubbles, lots of air pockets move about in it.
2 (n) A bubble is a ball of gas enclosed in a thin film of liquid.

bucket buckets (n) A bucket is a container with a handle for carrying water.

buckle buckles buckling buckled
1 (n) A buckle is a metal fastener on a belt.
2 (vb) When you buckle a belt, you fasten it.
3 (vb) If metal buckles, it crumples up.

Buddha, the (about 563–483 BC) was the founder and teacher of Buddhism.

Buddhism (n) teaches that the right way to live is not to attach importance to material things. It is practised mainly in eastern and central Asia. **Buddhist** (n)

budgerigar
budgerigars (n) A budgerigar is a small, brightly-coloured bird the size of a sparrow. It is often kept in a cage as a pet.

budget budgets budgeting budgeted
1 (vb) If you budget your money, you work out what you will spend it on in advance.
2 (n) A budget is a plan for how you will spend your money.

buffalo buffaloes (n) A buffalo is a large ox-type animal which lives in North America and Africa.

buffet buffets
1 (n) A buffet is a snack bar, particularly at a railway station.
2 (n) A buffet meal is one where people serve themselves from many dishes.

buggy buggies (n) A buggy is a small vehicle. A beach buggy is a small car; a push-chair can be called a buggy.

build builds building built
1 (vb) If you build something, you make it by joining things together.
2 (n) A building is a structure that is built such as a house, block of flats or a church.

bulb bulbs
1 (n) A bulb is shaped like an onion and is the root of a plant.
2 (n) A bulb is a glass lamp that lights up when electricity is switched on.

bulge bulges bulging bulged
1 (vb) If something bulges, it swells.
2 (n) A bulge is a lump in something that is normally flat.

bulldozer bulldozers (n) A bulldozer is a powerful tractor with a blade in front used for pushing earth and clearing space.

bullet bullets (n) A bullet is a small cylindrical-shaped piece of metal that is fired from a gun.

bulletin

bulletin bulletins (n) A bulletin is a short statement of news which can be spoken or written.

bullion (n) is gold or silver bars.

bullock bullocks (n) A bullock is a male of the cattle family bred for its meat.

bully bullies bullying bullied
1 (n) A bully is a person who frightens someone weaker than themselves.
2 (vb) If you bully someone, you use your strength to frighten someone weaker than yourself.

bulrush bulrushes (n) A bulrush is a tall reed found near rivers.

bumper bumpers (n) A bumper is a strip of rubber or plastic on the front and back of a vehicle which protects it if it is in an accident.

bunch bunches (n) A bunch is a group of things together. *A bunch of flowers; a bunch of keys.*

bundle bundles (n) A bundle of things is several things tied loosely together. *A bundle of wood.*

bungalow bungalows (n) A bungalow is a house built on one level only.

bunk bunks (n) A bunk is a place to sleep. Bunk beds are usually stacked one above the other.

buoy buoys (n) A buoy is a floating marker at sea or in a river.

burgle burgles burgling burgled (vb) If you burgle a property, you break in and steal things. **burglar** (n) **burglary** (n).

burn burns burning burned
1 (vb) If you burn something, you destroy it with fire.
2 (n) A burn is a mark on someone or something made by fire.

burrow burrows burrowing burrowed
1 (n) A burrow is a hole in the ground that an animal such as a rabbit digs for its home.
2 (vb) If you burrow into a pile of things, you dig around in it to search for something.
3 (vb) If you burrow under blankets, for example, you get underneath them for warmth.

burst bursts bursting burst
1 (vb) If something bursts, it suddenly breaks, splits or explodes.
2 (n) A burst is the place where something has split or exploded.

business businesses
1 (n) A business is a place of work.
2 (n) Your business consists of matters which concern you only.

busker buskers (n) A busker sings or plays a musical instrument on the street for money.

busy busier busiest (adj) If you are busy, you have a lot of things to do.

butcher butchers (n) A butcher is someone who prepares and sells meat.

butter (n) is the yellow fat made from cream, used for spreading and cooking.

buttercup buttercups (n) A buttercup is a common, yellow wild flower.

butterfly

the life cycle of the peacock **butterfly**

eggs laid on stinging nettles

caterpillars hatch and feed on nettles

adult **butterfly** emerges from **chrysalis** and flies off after wings have expanded

mature **caterpillar** forms chrysalis

some other common British **butterflies**

hedge brown | small tortoiseshell | common blue | large white | Essex skipper

butterfly butterflies (n) A butterfly is an insect with large wings which are often beautifully-coloured and patterned.

insect p149

buttocks (n) are the part of your body between your back and your legs that you sit on.

button buttons buttoning buttoned
1 (n) A button is a small disc sewn onto clothes for fastening.
2 (vb) If you button your clothes, you fasten them with buttons.
3 (n) A button is something you press to ring a bell or to operate machinery.

buttress buttresses (n) A buttress is a support, usually of brick, that keeps up a wall of a building.

buy buys buying bought (vb) When you buy something you get it by paying for it.

buzz buzzes buzzing buzzed
1 (vb) If something buzzes, it makes a humming sound like a wasp or a bee.
2 (vb) If an aircraft buzzes a building or other planes, it flies very close to them in a dangerous way.

buzzard buzzards (n) A buzzard is a large bird of prey.

by-pass by-passes by-passing by-passed
1 (vb) If you by-pass a town, you travel around it instead of going through it.
2 (n) A by-pass is a road built to take traffic around the edges of a town so that the town centre isn't too busy.
3 (n) A by-pass operation redirects the blood away from diseased areas of the heart.

cabbage

Cc

cabbage cabbages (n) A cabbage is a round, leafy, green, white or red vegetable.

cabin cabins
1 (n) A cabin is a small house usually made of wood.
2 (n) A cabin is a small room on a boat or an aeroplane.

cabinet cabinets
1 (n) A cabinet is a piece of furniture like a cupboard used to store things.
2 (n) The Cabinet is the committee of ministers who govern the country.

cable cables

hydro
electricity
p142

1 (n) A cable is a thick wire rope used to suspend or pull heavy objects.
2 (n) Cables are lengths of wire used for electricity or telephone systems.

cactus cacti or cactuses (n) A cactus is a plant which lives in hot, dry places. It stores water in its stem and it has sharp spines.

cadet cadets (n) A cadet is a young person who is being trained to join an organisation like the army or the police.

Caesar, Julius (100-44 BC) was the Roman general who invaded Britain in 55 BC.

café cafés (n) A café is a place where you can buy snacks and drinks.

caffeine or caffein (n) is a chemical substance found in coffee, tea and cocoa which makes your brain and body more active.

cagoule cagoules (n) A cagoule is a waterproof nylon jacket with a hood.

calculate calculates calculating calculated (vb) If you calculate something, you use information that you have, to work out a number or an amount.
calculation (n)

calculator calculators (n) A calculator is an electronic machine that works out the answers to sums.

calendar calendars (n) A calendar is a chart showing the days, weeks and months of the year.

calf calves
1 (n) A calf is a young cow, elephant, whale, giraffe, buffalo or seal.
2 (n) The calf is the fleshy part at the back of the lower leg.

calm calmer calmest
1 (adj) A calm person does not get upset easily.
2 (adj) When the sea is calm, there are no big waves.

calorie calories (n) The amount of energy that food supplies is measured in calories. *Bread has about 100 calories a slice.*

camel camels (n) A camel is a large animal with humps that carries people and goods in desert areas. A Bactrian camel has two humps and a dromedary has one.

camera cameras (n) A camera is a device used to take photographs. Cameras are also used to make films, videos and television pictures.

camouflage (n) Camouflage is colouring that hides animals, vehicles or people by blending them into their background.
camouflages camouflaging camouflaged (vb)

canal canals (n) A canal is a man-made waterway.

canary canaries (n) A canary is a yellow songbird.

cancel cancels cancelling cancelled (vb) If you cancel an appointment or an order, you call it off.

cancer cancers (n) Cancer is a serious disease in which abnormal growth appears somewhere in the body and may spread.

candidate candidates (n) A candidate is a person who offers to be elected for public office or applies for a job.

candle candles (n) A candle is a stick of wax with a wick through the middle. It is burned to give light.

mouth p186

canine canines
1 (adj) Canine means belonging to or to do with the dog family.
2 (n) Canines are the pointed teeth near the front of the mouths of humans and animals. Humans have four canines.

cannibal cannibals (n) Cannibals are people who eat human flesh.

cannon cannons (n) A cannon is a large, heavy gun on a mount which fires iron balls or explosive shells.

canoe canoes (n) A canoe is a small, narrow boat which is moved with paddles.

canteen canteens (n) A canteen is a large dining room in a school or factory.

canvas canvases (n) Canvas is strong coarse cloth.

capable (adj) If you are capable, you are able to do something or many things well.

capacity capacities
1 (n) The capacity of a container is the largest amount it can hold.
2 (n) The capacity to do something is the power to do it.

capital capitals
1 (n) The capital city is the main city of a country.
2 (n) A capital letter is a large letter. *A B C*
3 (n) Capital is a large amount of money you use to start a business or to invest.

capsize capsizes capsizing capsized (vb) If a boat capsizes it turns over in the water.

capsule capsules
1 (n) A capsule is a small container of medicine which can be swallowed.
2 (n) A capsule is the part of a rocket which contains the crew.

captain captains (n) A captain is the person in charge of a group of people: the leader of a team; the commander of a ship; or an officer in the army.

captive captives (n) A captive is someone who is locked up and kept prisoner.

capture captures capturing captured (vb) If you capture someone, you take them prisoner. **captor** (n).

caravan caravans
1 (n) A caravan is a vehicle that people live in or use for holidays.
2 (n) A caravan is a group of people and animals who travel together for safety.

carbohydrate carbohydrates (n) Carbohydrates are the sugars and starches found in food which give energy.

carbon (n) is the chemical found in coal, diamonds and graphite. All organic substances contain carbon.

cardboard (n) is very thick, stiff paper.

cardigan cardigans (n) A cardigan is a knitted jacket.

care

care cares caring cared
1 (vb) If you care about someone, you like them and are interested in them.
2 If children are in care, they live in a children's home because their own parents are not able to look after them.
3 If you take care of someone, you look after them.

career careers (n) A person's career is the series of jobs they do.

caretaker caretakers (n) A caretaker looks after a large building such as an office block or school.

cargo cargoes (n) A cargo is the load of goods that a ship, plane or lorry carries.

carnation carnations (n) A carnation is a plant with thin leaves which has scented, colourful flowers.

carnival carnivals (n) A carnival is a lively public celebration.

carpenter carpenters (n) A carpenter works with wood making furniture, window frames and doors, etc.

carriage carriages
1 (n) A carriage is the part of a train that passengers travel in.
2 (n) A carriage is a horse-drawn vehicle.

carriageway carriageways (n) There are two carriageways on a road, each of which may be divided into two or three lanes.

carrot carrots (n) A carrot is an orange-coloured root vegetable.

carton cartons (n) A carton is a thick paper or plastic container that can be closed to carry and store food and drinks.

cartoon cartoons
1 (n) A cartoon is an amusing drawing or series of drawings that tell a story or a joke.
2 (n) A cartoon is a film, usually funny, with characters who are drawn, not real.

cartridge cartridges
1 (n) A cartridge is the a case which contains a bullet and explosive.
2 (n) A cartridge is a small tube filled with ink for a cartridge pen.

carve carves carving carved (vb)
If you carve something, you shape it with a knife.

cash-and-carry (n) A cash-and-carry is a very big shop where people buy things in large quantities at lower prices than in ordinary shops.

cashier cashiers (n) A cashier is a person who takes or gives you money in a bank, shop or cinema.

cashpoint cashpoints (n) A cashpoint is a machine at a bank where people can get money at any time using a cash card.

cassava (n) is a tropical plant with starchy roots from which tapioca is extracted. Tapioca is a food consisting of white grains, rather like rice.

casserole casseroles
1 (n) A casserole is a stew made from vegetables, meat or fish.
2 (n) A casserole is a dish with a lid used for cooking.

cassette cassettes (n) A cassette is an audio or video tape inside a flat plastic box.

cast casts casting cast
1 (vb) When a fisherman casts his line, he throws the baited end into the water.
2 (n) The cast of a play is all the actors in it.
3 (n) A cast is the plaster support for a broken limb.

castaway castaways (n) A castaway is someone who is shipwrecked but survives on a lonely shore or island.

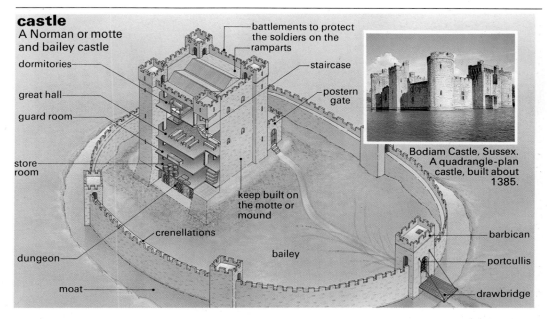

castle
A Norman or motte and bailey castle

- dormitories
- great hall
- guard room
- store room
- dungeon
- moat
- crenellations
- bailey
- battlements to protect the soldiers on the ramparts
- staircase
- postern gate
- keep built on the motte or mound
- barbican
- portcullis
- drawbridge

Bodiam Castle, Sussex. A quadrangle-plan castle, built about 1385.

castle castles (n) A castle is a large fortified building that was built to withstand enemy attacks.

casual
1 (adj) A casual meeting is unplanned.
2 (adj) A casual acquaintance is someone you know slightly.

cat cats
1 (n) A cat is a small, furry, domestic pet.
2 (n) A cat is any animal that belongs to the family that includes lions and tigers.
3 If you let the cat out of the bag, you tell a secret.
4 If people are fighting like cat and dog, they are fighting violently.

catalogue catalogues (n) Catalogues are books which list things. They can be used for shopping or as guides to museums. A library catalogue is an alphabetical list of books.

catapult catapults
(n) A catapult is a small weapon made from a forked stick and a piece of elastic, which shoots small stones.

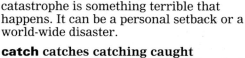

catarrh (n) is the thick substance that blocks your nose when you have a cold.

catastrophe catastrophes (n) A catastrophe is something terrible that happens. It can be a personal setback or a world-wide disaster.

catch catches catching caught
1 (vb) If you catch a ball or anything that is coming towards you, you take hold of it with your hands.
2 (vb) If something runs away from you and you catch it, you chase and capture it.
3 (vb) When you catch a bus or train, you get on it to go somewhere.
4 (vb) If you catch a disease, you get it.

category categories (n) A category is a group or set of things that have something in common. *That book belongs to the history category.*

caterpillar caterpillars (n) A caterpillar is the grub of a butterfly or moth.

butterfly p37

cathedral cathedrals (n) A cathedral is a large and important church which has a bishop as the chief clergyman.

Catholic Catholics (n) A Catholic is a person who belongs to a part of the Christian church which has the Pope as its leader.

Goyden Pot, Yorkshire

Smoo **Cave** near Durness in the Scottish Highlands

cat's eyes (n) are the pieces of glass set in the centre or sides of roads to reflect car headlights.

cattle (n) are cows, bulls and oxen.

cattle grid cattle grids (n) Cattle grids are sets of metal bars put over a hole in a road to stop farm animals from straying.

cauldron cauldrons (n) A cauldron is a large cooking pot used for cooking over an open fire.

cauliflower cauliflowers (n) A cauliflower is a green, leafy vegetable with a white centre.

cause causes (n) A cause is a reason for something to happen. *The cause of the fire was a smouldering cigarette end.*

causeway causeways (n) A causeway is a raised path higher than the surrounding land, water or marsh. It may be covered when the tide comes in.

cautious (adj) People who take care to avoid making mistakes are cautious.

Cavalier Cavaliers (n) A Cavalier was a supporter of King Charles I in the English Civil War.

cavalry (n) were soldiers who fought on horseback. In Britain today the cavalry regiments use armoured vehicles and only use horses for special occasions.

cave caves (n) A cave is a tunnel or hole in a cliff or underground which has been made by water or wind action.

cavity cavities (n) A cavity is a hole. It can be tiny like a hole in a tooth or enormous like a crater.

Celsius (n) is a scale used to measure temperature. Water freezes at 0° Celsius and boils at 100° Celsius. The symbol for Celsius is C.

 fahrenheit p105

ceiling ceilings (n) A ceiling is the roof inside a room.

celebrate celebrates celebrating celebrated (vb) You celebrate when you enjoy yourself on a special occasion. **celebration** (n)

celebrity celebrities (n) A celebrity is someone famous.

celery (n) is a vegetable with long, green, crisp stems eaten in salads or cooked.

cell cells
1 (n) A cell is a small room in a prison or a monastery.
2 (n) A cell is the smallest part of any living thing that can survive on its own.
3 (n) A cell is a hole in a honeycomb where the queen bee lays her eggs.

cellar cellars (n) A cellar is a room below ground level where wine or coal can be stored.

cello cellos (n) A cello is a large, stringed musical instrument.

cement (n) is a grey powder which is mixed with sand and water and hardens when dry.

cemetery cemeteries (n) A cemetery is where the dead are buried.

census censuses (n) A census is an official count of all the people living in a country.

centenary centenaries (n) A centenary is the year exactly 100 years after a special event.

centigrade (n) is a scale to measure temperature where water freezes at 0° and boils at 100°.

ahrenheit
105

centimetre centimetres (n) A centimetre is a unit of measurement which equals 10 millimetres.

centipede centipedes (n) A centipede is a small, crawling creature with many legs.

central
1 (adj) Something central is in the middle.
2 (adj) A place that is central is easy to reach from all places.
3 (adj) An idea that is central is the main idea.

central heating (n) is a system used to keep a building warm. Air or water is heated in one place and goes through pipes and radiators around the building.

centre centres
1 (n) The centre of a thing is its middle.
2 (n) A centre is a place for particular activities. *Youth Centre... Sports Centre.*
3 (n) The centre of gravity of a thing is the point at which it balances. *The motorbike had a very low centre of gravity.*

century centuries
1 (n) A century is one hundred years.
2 (n) In cricket, a century is 100 runs scored by a player in one innings.

cereal cereals
1 (n) A cereal is any kind of grain like wheat or rice.
2 (n) Cereal is a breakfast food.

ceremony ceremonies (n) A ceremony is a formal set of actions on an occasion like a wedding or a prize-giving.

certain
1 (adj) If you are certain about something, you are sure it is true.
2 (adj) If you visit a certain part of a country, you go to a particular area.

certificate certificates (n) A certificate is an official piece of paper that proves that something took place. *Birth certificate; marriage certificate; examination certificate.*

chaffinch chaffinches (n) A chaffinch is a small, brightly-coloured European bird.

chain chains (n) A chain is a series of metal rings linked together.

chain mail (n) is armour made of many small rings linked together.

chain store chain stores (n) A chainstore is one of a group of shops owned by the same firm.

chair chairs
1 (n) A chair is a piece of furniture with a back and legs for one person to sit on.
2 If someone is in the chair at a meeting, they are in charge.

chairlift chairlifts (n) A chairlift consists of many chairs linked together on a cable to take people up and down mountains.

chalet chalets (n) A chalet is a small, wooden house like a bungalow.

chalk chalks (n) Chalk is a soft, white rock. It can be made into small, hard sticks for writing on a blackboard.

challenge challenges challenging challenged
1 (n) A challenge is an invitation to compete at something such as a fight or a competition.
2 (vb) If you challenge someone, you demand to know who they are and what they are doing.
3 (n) A challenge is something you find difficult to do but you try your best.

chameleon chameleons (n) A chameleon is a small, lizard-like creature that can change colour to match its surroundings.

champion champions (n) A champion is the winner of a contest.

chance chances
1 (n) A chance is a happening without an obvious cause. *They met by chance.*
2 (n) A chance is a risk or an opportunity. *The motorcyclist took a chance when he cornered at 70 mph.*

The Chancellor of the Exchequer is the British government minister who is in charge of finance.

change changes changing changed
1 (vb) When something changes it becomes different. *He changed his mind... The wind changed direction... She changed trains... He changed his clothes.*
2 (n) Change is the money you receive when you pay with a larger amount than the item costs.

changeable (adj) Changeable people or things are unpredictable; you don't know what will happen next. *Changeable weather... changeable moods.*

channel channels
1 (n) A channel is a stretch of water that joins two seas.
2 (n) A channel is a ditch for water drainage.
3 (n) A channel is a television or radio wavelength.

chaos (n) is complete confusion.

chapel chapels (n) A chapel is a small church.

chapped (adj) If your skin is chapped, it is cracked and sore.

chapter chapters (n) A chapter is a section of a book.

character characters
1 (n) Your character is what you are like. It's all the things that make up your personality. **characteristic** (adj or n)
2 (n) A character is a person in a story.

charades (n) is a party game where one team guesses what the other team is acting out.

charcoal (n) is made by slowly burning down wood into small, black lumps which can be used for barbecue fuel and for drawing.

charge charges charging charged
1 (n) If there is a charge for admission, people have to pay to go in.
2 (vb) When you charge at something, you rush at it with force.

chariot chariots (n) A chariot was a form of two-wheeled vehicle pulled by horses in ancient times.

charity charities
1 (n) A charity is an organisation that helps to raise money for those in need.
2 (n) Charity is kindness and generosity.

charm charms
1 (n) A charm is a magic spell.
2 (n) A charm is something you can wear for good luck.
3 (n) If you have charm, you attract and please others.

chart charts
1 (n) A chart is a map of the seas used by sailors.
2 (n) A chart is a graph or a drawing which gives information.
3 (n) The Charts are the weekly lists of pop records which have sold the most copies.

chase chases chasing chased (vb) If you chase someone, you run after them and try to catch them or to make them go away.

chat show chat shows (n) A chat show is a television or radio programme where the presenter has a friendly talk with his or her guests.

chatter chatters chattering chattered (vb) When people chatter, they talk a lot about unimportant things.

chauffeur chauffeurs (n) A chauffeur's job is to drive a car.

chauvinist chauvinists (n) A chauvinist is a person who believes that their country, group or sex is better than anyone else's.

cheap cheaper cheapest
1 (adj) If something is cheap, it does not cost much.
2 (adj) Cheap can mean of poor quality.

cheat cheats cheating cheated
1 (vb) If you cheat, you are dishonest by tricking or lying to get what you want.
2 (n) A cheat is a dishonest person.

check checks checking checked
1 (vb) When you check something, you make sure it is correct.
2 (vb) If you check something, you stop it from moving or spreading.
3 (n) Checks are square patterns on fabric or paper.
4 If your king is under attack in the game of chess, you are in check.

checkout checkouts (n) A checkout is the place in a supermarket where you pay for goods you have bought.

cheerful (adv) If you are cheerful, you are happy.

cheese cheeses (n) Cheese is a solid food made from milk curds.

cheesecake cheesecakes (n) This is a pudding made of soft cheese, sugar and eggs on a biscuit base.

cheetah cheetahs (n) A cheetah is a large, spotted, cat-like animal found mainly in Africa.

chef chefs (n) A chef is a cook in a hotel or restaurant.

chemical chemicals (n) A chemical is a substance used in chemistry.

chemist chemists
1 (n) A chemist is a person who studies chemistry.
2 (n) A chemist is a person who sells drugs and medicines.

chemistry (n) is the study of substances, what they are made of and how they affect each other.

cheque cheques (n) A cheque is a written order for a bank to pay a certain amount of money to someone from your account.

cherry cherries (n) A cherry is a small, round, red or black fruit with a stone.

chess (n) is a game for two players on a board of 64 squares with 16 pieces for each player.

chest chests
1 (n) A chest is a large, strong box.
2 (n) The chest is the upper part of the body at the front.

chestnut chestnuts
1 (n) A chestnut is a large, shiny, brown nut that grows on the sweet chestnut tree. It can be eaten roasted or as a purée. It should not be confused with the inedible conker which grows on the horse chestnut tree.
2 (n) The chestnut is a tall tree with narrow, oblong leaves with pointed tips.

chew chews chewing chewed (vb) When you chew your food, you bite and crush it as you turn it over in your mouth.

chewing gum (n) Chewing gum is a sweet which is chewed but not swallowed.

chicken chickens (n) A chicken is a bird which is kept for its meat and eggs.

chicken-pox (n) is an infectious disease which causes a fever and itchy red blisters on the skin.

chidwa (n) is a savoury party snack made of a mixture of split peas, peanuts, small bits of potato chips, etc which have been fried and salted.

chief chiefs
1 (n) The chief is the head or the leader of something.
2 (adj) The chief person or idea is the main and most important one.

chilblain chilblains (n) A chilblain is a painful swelling on your hands or feet caused by the cold.

child children (n) A child is a young boy or girl, or a son or daughter.

childminder childminders (n) A childminder is paid to look after children while their parents are at work.

childproof (adj) things are designed to stop children from undoing or breaking them.

childhood (n) is the time of being a child.

chill chills chilling chilled
1 (vb) If you chill something you make it cold.
2 (n) A chill is a shivery sickness or cold.

chilli chillies (n) A chilli is a small, red or green pepper which is very hot to taste.

chime chimes chiming chimed (vb) When bells chime they ring.

chimney chimneys (n) A chimney is a tall column which takes smoke or fumes out of the top of a building into the open air.

chimpanzee chimpanzees (n) A chimpanzee is a large African ape.

china (n) is a delicate type of pottery.

chip chips chipping chipped
1 (n) A chip is a long, thin piece of potato deep fried in oil.
2 (vb) If you chip something, you break something off it.

electronic p96
3 (n) A chip is a very small piece of silicon used in computers.

chiropodist chiropodists (n) A chiropodist cares for people's feet.

chisel chisels (n) A chisel is a sharp tool used by carpenters or sculptors. It is hit with a mallet to remove pieces of wood or stone.

chlorine (n) is a strong, chemical liquid used to disinfect swimming pools and make cleaning liquids.

chocolate chocolates (n) Chocolate is a sweet, hard, brown food made from cocoa beans. It is eaten as a sweet or used in cooking or for hot drinks.

choice choices (n) If you make a choice, you decide between several different things.

choir choirs (n) A choir is a group of people who sing together. In a church building it is the area where the choir sits.

choke chokes choking choked
1 (vb) If you choke, you cannot breathe properly because something blocks your throat.
2 (n) The choke on a car engine controls the amount of air going into it.
3 (adj) If a road is choked with cars, it is blocked and filled with traffic.

cholesterol (n) is a substance that is found in the body. Too much of it may cause heart disease.

choose chooses choosing chose chosen
1 (vb) If you choose something, you select the one you prefer from several things.
2 (adj) Your chosen profession is the job you select from several.

chopstick chopsticks (n) Chopsticks are a pair of thin sticks used to eat Chinese food.

chord chords (n) A chord is two or more notes in music played together to make a pleasant sound.

chore chores (n) A chore is a boring job you have to do.

chorus choruses
1 (n) A chorus is a group of people who sing or dance together in a show.
2 (n) A chorus in a song is the part you repeat in each verse.

Christ (n) is a name for Jesus. Christians believe that Jesus is the Son of God.

christen christens christening christened (vb) When a clergyman christens a baby, he puts water on its head and names it.

Christianity (n) is a religion that is based on the teachings of Jesus Christ and the belief that He is the Son of God.
Christian (n)

Christmas Christmases (n) Christmas is the Christian festival which is celebrated on and around December 25th to honour Christ's birth.

chromosome chromosomes (n) A chromosome is the part of a cell in a living thing that gives it its particular characteristics.

chronological (adj) If things are arranged in chronological order, they are put in the order in which they actually happened.

chrysalis chrysalises (n) A chrysalis is a butterfly or moth at the stage between larva and adult, when it is in a cocoon with a hard outer shell.
butterfly p37

chrysanthemum chrysanthemums (n) A chrysanthemum is a garden flower with many thin petals. Its blooms come in a variety of colours.

chuckle **chuckles chuckling chuckled**
(vb) When you chuckle, you laugh quietly
to yourself.

chuni (n) is a Punjabi woman's head
covering. It is like a scarf and is worn
loosely. It has to be worn in holy places.

church **churches** (n) A church is a
building where Christians go to worship
God.

Church (n) A Church is one of the
different branches of the Christian religion,
for example, the Catholics.

Church of England (n) The Church of
England is the main Church in England,
which has the Queen as its head.

Churchill, Sir Winston (1874–1965) was
noted for his leadership during the Second
World War. He was a great statesman,
speaker and writer.

churchyard **churchyards** (n) A
churchyard is the land surrounding a
church. It often contains graves.

churn **churns** (n) A churn is a metal
container for making milk or cream into
butter.

chute **chutes** (n) A chute is a slide, at a
swimming pool, for example, or for sending
rubbish down.

chutney **chutneys** (n) Chutney is a
strong-tasting mixture of fruit, vegetables,
vinegar and spices.

cider (n) is an alcoholic drink made from
apples.

cigar **cigars** (n) A cigar is a fat roll of
dried tobacco leaves that some people
smoke.

cigarette **cigarettes** (n) A cigarette is
dried tobacco rolled up in thin paper that
some people smoke.

cinder **cinders** (n) Cinders are the little
grey or black lumps that are left after wood
or coal has been burned.

cinema **cinemas** (n) A cinema is a place
where you go to see films.

circle **circles circling circled**
1 (n) A circle is a round, flat shape.
2 (vb) If you circle something, you move
around it.
3 (vb) If you circle a word or picture, you
draw a ring around it.

4 (n) If people stand in a circle, they stand
in a ring.
5 (n) The circle in a theatre or a cinema is
the upper floor.

circuit **circuits**
1 (n) A circuit is a pathway for electricity
to flow along.
2 (n) A racing circuit is a track where races
for cars, motorbikes, or cycles are held.

circulation
1 (n) The circulation is the movement of
blood around the body.
2 (n) The circulation of a newspaper or
magazine is the number of copies sold each
time it is issued.

circumference **circumferences**
1 (n) The circumference is the distance all
around a circle.
2 (n) The circumference is the distance
around the edge of a piece of land or water.

circumstance **circumstances** (n) The
circumstances are the conditions or ways
in which something happens. *The unhappy
circumstances in which their mother died
made life difficult.*

circus **circuses** (n) A circus is a travelling
show, performed in a large tent, in which
there may be acrobats, clowns and
performing animals.

cistern **cisterns**
1 (n) A cistern is a tank which stores water
to flush the toilet.
2 (n) A cistern is a tank for storing liquids.
It is often used to store water in a roof.

citizen **citizens** (n) A citizen is a person
living in a town, city or country who has all
the rights that are allowed to such people.

citrus fruit **citrus fruits** (n) Citrus fruits
are juicy, sharp-tasting fruits such as
oranges and lemons.

city **cities** (n) A city is a very large or
important town.

civil (adj) Someone civil is polite.

Civil Engineer **Civil Engineers** (n) A
Civil Engineer's job is to design and build
roads, bridges, large buildings, etc.

civilian

civilian civilians (n) A civilian is someone who is not a member of the army, navy or airforce.

civilisation civilisations (n) A civilisation is a large group of people who live in an organised society with its own special laws, art, customs, etc.

civilized
1 (adj) Someone who is civilised behaves in an organised, calm and polite way.
2 (adj) A civilised country is one that is highly-developed and well-organised so that its citizens should have a good standard of living, and good government.

civil rights (n) are the claims that all people in a society have to equal opportunity and fair treatment regardless of sex, religion or race.

civil servant civil servants (n) A civil servant is someone who works in the civil service.

Civil Service (n) The Civil Service is all the people who work for the government.

civil war civil wars (n) A civil war is fought by different groups of people who live in the same country.

claim claims claiming claimed
1 (vb) If you claim a thing, you ask for it because you have a right to it.
2 (vb) If you claim something, you say that it is true.

clamber clambers clambering clambered (vb) If you clamber somewhere, you climb using your hands to help you.

clammy (adj) things feel damp, sticky and unpleasant.

clamp clamps (n) A clamp holds two things tightly together.

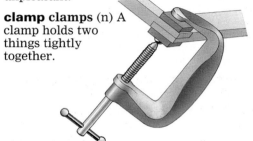

clan clans (n) A clan is a family group or tribe.

clarify clarifies clarifying clarified (vb) If you clarify something, you make it clear or easier to understand.

clarinet clarinets (n) A clarinet is a wind instrument.

clash clashes clashing clashed
1 (vb) If you clash with someone you argue, disagree or fight with them.
2 (vb) If colours clash, they do not look pleasing to the eye.

class classes
1 (n) A class is a group of children who are taught together in school.
2 (n) A class of people or things have something in common.

classic classics (adj) Something that is classic is thought to be important or of high quality. *Classic books . . . classic horse race . . . classic film.*

classify classifies classfying classfied (vb) If you classify things, you sort them into groups that have something in common.

clatter clatters clattering clattered (vb) When someone clatters they make lots of short, sharp, loud sounds.

claustrophobia (n) is a feeling of fear someone has when shut in a small space.

clay (n) is a smooth, heavy earth which is used to make pottery or bricks.

clean cleans cleaning cleaned; cleaner cleanest
1 (vb) If you clean something, you wash or dust it to get rid of the dirt.
2 (n) A cleaner is a person who is paid to clean a house, office or building.

clear clearer clearest
1 (adj) If the meaning of something, spoken, written or seen is clear it is easy to understand.
2 (adj) If writing is clear, it is easy to read.
3 (adj) Clear water is not polluted.

cleft clefts
1 (n) A cleft is a crack between rocks.
2 (adj) A cleft chin has a dimple in it.
3 (adj) A cleft palate is a narrow opening in the roof of a person's mouth which makes speaking difficult unless it is repaired by an operation.

clench clenches clenching clenched (vb) If you clench something, you hold it tightly. *He clenched the stick in his hand.*

clergyman clergymen (n) A clergyman is a minister, vicar or priest who works for the Church.

clerk clerks (n) A clerk is a person who works in an office, filing and looking after the records.

clever cleverer cleverest (adj) Clever people are able to think and learn quickly.

cliché clichés (n) A cliché is a word or phrase which is used so often that it loses its effect.

click clicks clicking clicked (vb) If something makes a short, sharp but quiet sound, it clicks. *When you fasten your seat belt it clicks.*

client clients (n) A client is a customer of a shop or a business.

cliff cliffs (n) A cliff is a vertical drop on the side of high land, often down to the sea.

climate climates (n) Climate is the kind of weather a country has. *India has a hot climate.*

climax climaxes (n) The climax is the most exciting or important and often final part of an event.

climb climbs climbing climbed (vb) If you climb something, you move to the top. You can climb stairs or a mountain.

cling clings clinging clung (vb) When someone clings to something or someone, they hold them tightly.

clinic clinics (n) A clinic is a place where specialist doctors give advice to their patients.

clipboard clipboards (n) A clipboard is a piece of stiff board with a clip at the top to keep papers in place.

clique cliques (n) A clique is a small group of people who spend time or work together closely and do not like others to join in.

cloak cloaks (n) A cloak is a piece of clothing with no sleeves that hangs from the shoulders.

clock clocks
1 (n) A clock measures the time in hours, seconds and minutes.
2 If you work around the clock, you work very long hours.

clockwise (adj) If you move in a clockwise direction, you move in the same direction as the hands of a clock.

clockwork
1 (n) Clockwork is the machinery in some clocks and toys that works when wound up with a key.
2 (n) If something works like clockwork, it works very well.

close closes closing closed
1 (vb) If you close anything, you shut it.
2 (vb) When a shop or bank closes, it stops doing business for a period of time.
3 (adj) A close friend is someone whom you know very well.
4 (adj) If the weather is close, it feels uncomfortably hot.

closed-circuit television (n) A closed-circuit television is used to show what is happening close by. It is used in shops to prevent theft.

close-up close-ups (n) A close-up in a film is a photograph or shot that focuses on a particular person or object to show them in detail.

clot clots clotting clotted
1 (vb) If liquid clots it thickens and forms lumps.
2 (n) Clots in a liquid are thick patches or lumps: blood clots, for example.

cloth cloths
1 (n) Cloth is a material made by weaving natural or man-made fibres together.
2 (n) A cloth is a piece of material used to clean or cover objects.

clothes (n) are the things you wear such as dresses, trousers and shirts.

clotted cream (n) is very rich, thick cream.

cloud clouds (n) A cloud is a white or grey mass of water vapour which can be seen in the sky.

clover

clover (n) is a small, pink or white meadow plant.

clown clowns (n) A clown is someone who works in a circus making people laugh.

club clubs
1 (n) A club is an organised group of people who share the same interest or hobby.
2 (n) A club is a weapon made from a heavy stick with one end heavier than the other.
3 (n) Clubs are one of the four suits in a pack of cards.

clue clues
1 (n) A clue is something that is heard or found that helps to solve a puzzle or a mystery. *They searched all around the place where the UFO was seen but found no clues.*
2 (n) If you say you haven't a clue about something, you know nothing about it.

clumsy clumsier clumsiest (adj) A clumsy person is awkward, bumping into things and knocking things over.

cluster clusters (n) A cluster is a group of similar things growing or found close together. *He noticed a cluster of stars in the night sky.*

clutch clutches clutching clutched
1 (vb) If you clutch something, you hold it tightly.
2 (n) A clutch is a group of bird's eggs.
3 (n) The clutch on a car or other vehicle is the control which disconnects the wheels from the engine so that the vehicle can change gear.

cluttered (adj) If a table, a desk or a room is cluttered, it is covered untidily with odds and ends.

coach coaches coaching coached
1 (n) A coach is a large, single-decker bus for carrying people on long journeys.
2 (n) A coach is a person who trains people to do something well.
3 (vb) If someone coaches you, they teach you how to do something well.
4 (n) A coach is a horse-drawn vehicle.

coal coals (n) Coal is a black rock-like substance mined from the ground. It is used for fuel and to make coke and coal gas.

coal-miner coal-miners (n) A coal-miner's job is to mine coal out of the ground. A miner may work above ground or underground.

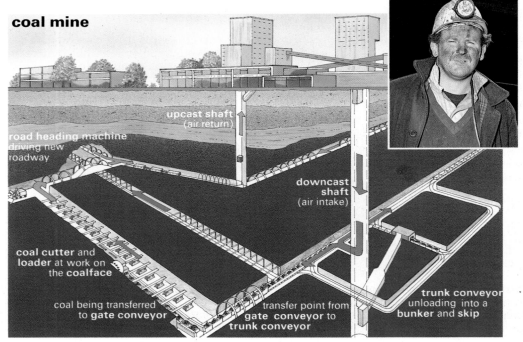

coal mine

upcast shaft
(air return)

road heading machine driving new roadway

downcast shaft
(air intake)

coal cutter and loader at work on the coalface

coal being transferred to gate conveyor

transfer point from gate conveyor to trunk conveyor

trunk conveyor unloading into a bunker and skip

coat of arms
Full achievement of Royal coat of arms

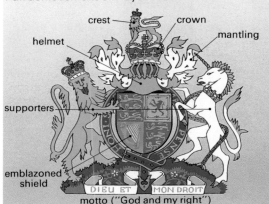

crest   crown

helmet   mantling

supporters

emblazoned shield

motto ("God and my right")

A complete **coat of arms** including the shield and outer decorations is called an **achievement**.

The **crest** is an object at the top of the coat-of-arms, originally worn on the knight's helmet.

The **helmet** shows the rank of the owner of the arms. A sovereign's helmet is gold and faces to the front.

The **supporters** are figures of animals or persons placed on either side of the shields of important persons or towns.

The **motto** is usually a short sentence or phrase to serve as a rule.

The **mantling** represents the cloth originally protecting the crusading knight from the sun.

coarse coarser coarsest
1 (adj) Something that is coarse is rough. *Coarse cloth... coarse skin.*
2 (adj) If a person is coarse, they are rude and ill-mannered.

coast coasts
1 (n) The coast is where the sea and the land meet.
2 (n) The coast is the area of land by the sea.

coastguard coastguards (n) A coastguard's job is to watch an area of coast for trouble at sea, or for smugglers.

coat of arms coats of arms (n) A coat of arms is a special symbol, usually in the shape of a patterned shield, that is used to represent noble families, towns or organisations.

coax coaxes coaxing coaxed (vb) If you coax someone, you try to persuade them gently to do something.

cobble cobbles (n) A cobble is a smooth round stone that was once used to make road surfaces. A cobbled street is made up of cobblestones.

cobra cobras (n) A cobra is a poisonous snake found in India and Africa.

cobweb cobwebs (n) A cobweb is a pattern of fine threads spun by a spider to catch insects.

cockle cockles (n) A cockle is a soft-bodied, edible shell-fish.

cockroach cockroaches (n) A cockroach is a large, brown beetle found in dirty places and where food is kept.

cocoa (n) is a hot, chocolate drink made with powder (also called cocoa) ground from the seeds of the cacao tree.

coconut coconuts (n) A coconut is a large fruit which has a hard, hairy shell. It contains a sweet, milky liquid you can drink and white flesh that you can eat.

cocoon

cocoon cocoons (n) A cocoon is a silken case spun by some insects to protect their grubs while they develop into adults.

cod (n) A cod is a white-fleshed, edible sea-fish.

code codes
1 (n) A code is a series of letters or symbols used for a secret message.
2 (n) A code is a set of rules shared by a group of people.

co-education (n) is when boys and girls are taught together at the same school.

coffee coffees (n) is a drink made from the ground beans of the coffee plant.

coffin coffins (n) A coffin is a wooden box in which dead bodies are buried or cremated.

cog cogs
1 (n) A cog is a tooth on the edge of a wheel.
2 (n) A cog is a wheel with teeth which turn another wheel or part.

cog

coil coils coiling coiled
1 (vb) If you coil rope or wire, you wind it in loops.
2 (n) A coil is a device to carry an electrical current which is made by winding a piece of wire into a connected series of loops.

coin coins (n) A coin is a metal disc used as money.

coincidence coincidences (n) A coincidence is a chance meeting or happening.

coke (n) is a solid fuel made from coal which is burned in boilers.

colander colanders (n) A colander is a dish with holes used to drain water from vegetables.

cold-blooded
1 (adj) Cold-blooded animals such as fish and reptiles have a blood temperature the same as their surroundings.
2 (adj) If you are cold-blooded, you are cruel.

coleslaw (n) is chopped raw vegetables in mayonnaise.

coley (n) is an edible sea fish.

collaborate collaborates collaborating collaborated (vb) If people collaborate, they work together on a project.

collage collages (n) A collage is a picture made by sticking pieces of fabric, paper etc onto a backing.

collapse collapses collapsing collapsed
1 (vb) If something collapses, it falls down.
2 (vb) If a person collapses, they fall down because they are hurt or suddenly taken ill.
3 (vb) An organisation or business collapses when it fails completely.

collapsible (adj) things are designed to fold up when not in use.

colleague colleagues (n) Your colleague is someone who works with you.

collect collects collecting collected
1 (vb) If you collect things, you gather them together in one place.
2 (vb) If you collect a person or item, you fetch them and take them somewhere.
3 (vb) If you collect stamps, coins or something else, you spend time getting a large number of these things together because you are interested in them.
collection (n) **collector** (n)

college colleges (n) A college is a place where students go after leaving school to study for further qualifications.

collide collides colliding collided (vb) If things collide, they bang or hit together usually with some damage. **collision** (n)

colliery collieries (n) A colliery is a place where coal is mined.

colon colons
1 (n) The colon is part of the large intestine.
2 (n) A colon is a punctuation mark used before a list of items. *The boy emptied his pockets: two mice, a catapult and a tooth fell out!*

intestine
p152

colonel colonels (n) A colonel is a senior army officer.

colony colonies (n) A colony is a group of people, animals or insects that live together.

colossal (adj) things are huge.

colour

The colour pictures in this book are made from a combination of three separate colours: **yellow, magenta** and **cyan**. Black is added to give extra sharpness. The diagram below shows how the colours combine.

yellow

+magenta

+cyan

+black

yellow + magenta = red
yellow + cyan = green
cyan + magenta = blue

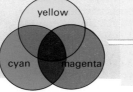

A beam of ordinary 'white' light can be broken into the colours of the rainbow by being passed through a **prism**.

prism

red orange yellow green
blue
indigo
violet

colour colours colouring coloured
1 (n) Colour is the appearance of something when light reflects on it. Red, blue, green and yellow are all colours.
2 (vb) If you colour a picture, you put different colours on it with pencils, crayons or paints.

colour blind (adj) If someone is colour blind, they have problems seeing the difference between certain colours.

colt colts (n) A colt is a young, male horse.

Columbus, Christopher (1451–1506) was an Italian explorer in the service of Spain who discovered America.

column columns
1 (n) A column is a tall, narrow support for part of a building, often made of stone.
2 (n) A column in a newspaper is a section of print going down the page.
3 (n) If people line up in a column, they form a straight line.

coma comas (n) If someone is in a coma, they are unconscious.

comb combs combing combed
1 (n) A comb is a piece of plastic or metal with a fine row of points along one side, used for tidying hair.
2 (vb) If you comb your hair, you use a comb to make it tidy.
3 (vb) If the police comb an area, they search it very carefully.

combat combats combatting combatted
1 (n) If you take part in armed combat, you are involved in fighting.

2 (vb) If you combat anything, you fight against it in a determined way.

combine combines combining combined (vb) If you combine things, you mix them together.

combustible (adj) substances catch fire easily.

comedian comedians (n) A comedian is an entertainer who tells jokes.

comedy comedies (n) A comedy is a play, film or book which is meant to amuse you.

comet comets (n) A comet is an object that travels around the sun leaving a bright trail behind it. *Halley's comet.*

comfort comforts comforting comforted
1 (vb) If you comfort another person, you help them and try to relieve their sadness.
2 (adj) Comforting news makes you feel better when you hear it.

comfortable
1 (adj) A comfortable chair is relaxing to sit in.
2 (adj) If you feel comfortable with another person, you feel at ease with them.
3 (adj) If someone is comfortable after an operation, they are recovering as well as can be expected.
4 (adj) If you are comfortable, you feel settled and relaxed.

comic comics
1 (n) A comic is a picture magazine.
2 (adj) If a person tells a comic story, they make you laugh.

comma commas (n) A comma is a punctuation mark which shows a short pause in a longer sentence. It is also used in lists. *I need butter, eggs, sugar and tea. Go to the shop, then come home please.*

command commands commanding commanded
1 (n) A command is an order.
2 (vb) If you command someone to do something, you order them to do it.
3 (vb) If an officer commands a part of the army, they are in charge of that part.

commendable (adj) If something is commendable, it is worth praising.

comment comments commenting commented
1 (vb) If you comment on something, you make a remark about it.
2 (n) Comments are brief written or spoken words about something.

commentary commentaries (n) A commentary is a spoken description of something as it happens, especially in sport, on radio and television.

commentator commentators (n) A commentator is a person whose job is to give commentaries on television or radio.

commerce (n) is the buying and selling of things especially in business operations.

commit commits committing committed
1 (vb) If you commit a crime, you do it.
2 (vb) If you commit something to memory, you learn it by heart.
3 (vb) If you commit yourself to something, you promise that you will do it.
commitment (n)
4 (vb) If you commit someone to prison you send them there.

committee committees (n) A committee is a group of people who meet to discuss and organise something.

common commons
1 (n) A common is an area of open land where everyone can go to walk and play.
2 (adj) If something is common there are a lot of them. *Daisies are common plants.*
3 If you have something in common with someone else, you share the same interests or you have a similar characteristic.
4 If something is common knowledge, everyone knows about it.

Common Market (n) The Common Market is a group of European countries, including Britain, which have joined together to support and trade with each other.

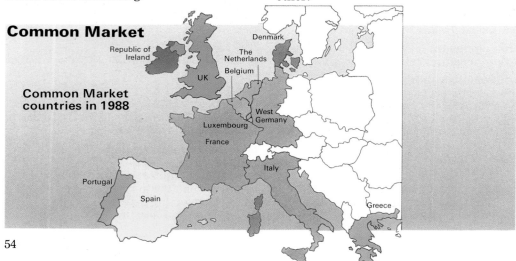

Common Market

Common Market countries in 1988

Denmark
Republic of Ireland
The Netherlands
Belgium
UK
West Germany
Luxembourg
France
Italy
Portugal
Spain
Greece

common sense (n) is knowing how to behave sensibly in any situation.

Commonwealth (n) The Commonwealth is a group of countries which were once ruled by Britain, but still have political and other links.

communicate communicates communicating communicated (vb) If you communicate with a person or an animal, you try to make them understand you. **communication** (n)

communion communions
1 (n) Holy Communion is a Christian service of sharing holy bread and wine.
2 If people are in communion with each other, they share the same feelings and thoughts.

community communities
1 (n) Community is friendship or cooperation between a group of people who live or work together. *The Business community.*
2 (n) The community in an area, town or village is the group of people who live there.

commuter commuters (n) A commuter is a person who has to travel far from home each day to work.

compact disc compact discs (n) A compact disc is a small silver-coloured disc on which music is recorded in high-quality form.

companion companions (n) A companion is someone who spends time with you either because you are friends or because you travel together.

company companies (n) A company is a group of people who work together. *A ship's company ... a company of actors ... a business company.*

compare compares comparing compared (vb) If you compare two things or two people, you look carefully at them to try to see their differences and similarities.

compartment compartments
1 (n) The small sections in a railway carriage are compartments.
2 (n) Compartments are sections in suitcases, bags and wallets or refrigerators, for example.

compass compasses
1 (n) A compass is an instrument with a magnetic needle that always points north. People use it to find their way.
2 (n) A compass is a hinged V-shaped instrument used for drawing circles.

compassion (n) is a feeling of sympathy towards someone who is unhappy or in trouble.

compel compels compelling compelled (vb) If you compel someone to do something, you force them to do it.

compensation (n) is payment that you claim from a person or organisation that is responsible for something unpleasant that has happened to you.

compete competes competing competed (vb) If you compete, you try to do better than others.

competent (adj) If you are competent, you are able to do something well.

competition competitions (n) A competition is a contest to find out who is the best at something. Those who take part are called competitors.

compile compiles compiling compiled (vb) When you compile something you collect information and put it together.

complain complains complaining complained (vb) If you complain, you write a letter or say that you are not satisfied with something. **complaint** (n)

complete completes completing completed (vb) If you complete something, you finish it or make it whole. **completion** (n)

complex complexes
1 (n) A complex is a group of similar buildings. *A shopping complex.*
2 (adj) If something is complex, it is difficult to do or understand.

complexion (n) Your complexion is the colour and condition of your skin, especially your face.

complicated (adj) If something is complicated, it is hard to understand.

compliment compliments (n) A compliment is praise or an admiring remark.

component

component components (n) A component is one of the parts that something is made of.

compose composes composing composed
1 (vb) If you compose a piece of music, you make it up.
2 (adj) If something is composed of particular things or people, it is made up of them.
3 (adj) If you are composed, you are calm.

comprehension (n) is the ability to understand something.

comprehensive (adj) Something that is comprehensive includes all things. A comprehensive school is for the education of pupils of all abilities and backgrounds.

compulsory (adj) If something is compulsory, you have to do it.

computer computers (n) A computer is an electronic machine which stores information and can help solve problems.

A **concave** satellite receiver dish.

lens p165

concave (adj) surfaces curve inwards.

conceal conceals concealing concealed (vb) If you conceal something or someone, you hide them.

conceited (adj) people are too proud of their abilities.

conceive conceives conceiving conceived
1 (vb) If you can conceive of something, you can imagine what might happen or might be possible.
2 (vb) If a woman conceives, she becomes pregnant.

concentrate concentrates concentrating concentrated
1 (vb) If you concentrate on something, you think about it very hard. **concentration** (n)
2 (adj) A substance is concentrated if it is strong and needs to be diluted before it is used.

concentric circles on an archery target

concentric (adj) circles or spheres have the same centre.

concept concepts (n) A concept is a complete idea about a particular project or plan. *My concept for these buildings is totally new.*

conception (n) takes place at the moment when an egg is fertilised.

concern concerns
1 (n) Concern is the feeling of worry that you have about a situation.
2 (n) A concern is something you are worried about or that you have a responsibility for. *My main concern is the safety of the passengers.*

concert concerts (n) A concert is a performance of music or singing by a band, group or orchestra.

concerto concertos (n) A concerto is a long piece of orchestral music, featuring one or more instruments.

concession concessions (n) A concession is something given to another person when bargaining, in order to reach a solution. *The government made concessions to the trade unions to end the dispute.*

concise (adj) If an order, letter or description is concise it is short but clear.

conclude concludes concluding concluded
1 (vb) If you conclude something, you finish it.
2 (vb) If you conclude that something has happened, you reach a decision after considering all the facts.
conclusion (n)

concoction concoctions (n) A concoction is a mixture of things which are rather unusual. *What is that concoction you're eating?*

concrete
1 (n) Concrete is a mixture of sand, stones, cement and water which is used for building.
2 (adj) If something is concrete, it is definite rather than just an idea. *You will need to give me some concrete evidence to support your plans.*

concussion (n) is dizziness and sickness caused by a blow to the head.

condemn condemns condemning condemned
1 (vb) If you condemn an action, you say it is wrong to do it.
2 (vb) If a judge condemns a person, he sentences them to a particular punishment.
3 (adj) If a building is condemned, it will be pulled down because it is dangerous.

condense condenses condensing condensed
1 (vb) If you condense something, you shorten it or make it more concentrated.
2 (vb) Steam condenses when water vapour meets a cold surface and turns back to water. **condensation** (n)

condescending (adj) If you are condescending, you treat people as if you are better than they are.

condition conditions
1 (n) The condition of something is the state that it is in.

2 (n) A condition is a term of agreement to something. *She agreed to the plan on condition that her husband could go too.*

conditioner conditioners (n) A conditioner is a liquid used to soften something when it is washed. *Hair conditioner . . . fabric conditioner.*

condolence condolences (n) As a mark of sympathy, you offer your condolences to someone whose friend or relative has died.

conduct conducts conducting conducted
1 (vb) If you conduct a task, you carry it out.
2 (vb) If you conduct an orchestra, you stand in front of it and direct it.
3 (vb) Metals such as copper and iron conduct electricity, that is electricity can pass along them.
4 (n) Your conduct is your behaviour.

conductor conductors
1 (n) A conductor takes fares from passengers on some buses.
2 (n) A conductor directs an orchestra.
3 (n) A conductor is a metal which will allow electricity to pass along it.

cone cones
1 (n) A cone is a solid shape with a point at the top and a circular or oval base.
2 (n) Anything shaped like a cone is called a cone. *Volcanic cone . . ice-cream cone . . . traffic cone.*

conference

conference conferences (n) A conference is a large meeting with discussions and lectures which can last several days.

confess confesses confessing confessed (vb) If you confess that you have done something, you admit to having done it. **confession** (n)

confetti (n) Confetti consists of tiny pieces of coloured paper. It is often thrown over a newly-married couple at their wedding.

confide confides confiding confided (vb) If you confide in someone, you trust them with a secret.

confidence confidences
1 (n) If you have confidence in someone, you trust them.
2 (n) If you have confidence in yourself, you are sure you can do something.

confident (adj) people believe that they can manage things successfully.

confidential (adj) information is private.

confirm confirms confirming confirmed
1 (vb) If you confirm something you say it is true.
2 (vb) When you confirm an appointment, you say you will be there. **confirmation**(n)
3 (vb) If you are confirmed, you are accepted into the Christian Church.

confiscate confiscates confiscating confiscated. (vb) If you confiscate something, you take it away for a short time, usually as a punishment.

conflict conflicts conflicting conflicted
1 (n) A conflict is a disagreement between two people or groups of people.
2 (adj) If two people or groups have conflicting ideas, they do not agree.
3 (vb) If two or more people, ideas, interests, etc, conflict, their differences are so great that there seems no chance of settling them.

conform conforms conforming conformed (vb) If you conform, you behave in the way that you are expected to.

confront confronts confronting confronted
1 (vb) When you confront someone, you meet them face to face.
2 (vb) If you confront something, you have to face up to a difficult situation. **confrontation** (n)

confuse confuses confusing confused
1 (vb) When you confuse two people or two things, you are not sure which is which.
2 (adv) If you feel confused, you are not sure how to behave in a situation.
3 (adj) Something that is confusing is difficult to understand. **confusion** (n)

congeal congeals congealing congealed (vb) If a liquid congeals, it becomes thick.

congested (adj) If something is congested, it is blocked. *The road was congested with traffic... His nose was so congested, he had difficulty in breathing.* **congestion** (n)

congratulate congratulates congratulating congratulated (vb) When you congratulate someone on their success, you tell them how pleased you are for them. **congratulations** (n)

congregation congregations (n) A congregation is a large gathering of people who come together for the same reason, usually a church service.

conifer conifers (n) A conifer is a tall, usually evergreen tree with needle-like leaves and cones.

tree p313

conjunction conjunctions (n) A conjunction is a word that joins two parts of a sentence. Examples are 'and', 'but', 'although'.

conjunctivitis (n) is a disease which makes your eyes red and sore.

conjuror conjurors (n) A conjuror performs magic tricks to entertain other people.

conker conkers (n) A conker is the round, brown seed of the horse-chestnut tree.

connect connects connecting connected
1 (vb) If you connect one thing to another, you join them in some way.
2 (adj) If ideas are connected, they are linked in some way.

connection connections (n) A connection is the point where two things join. *A railway connection . . . a telephone connection.*

connoisseur connoisseurs (n) A connoisseur is someone who enjoys and is an expert on a subject such as wine or paintings or antiques, etc.

conquer conquers conquering conquered
1 (vb) If one country conquers another, it takes control of it.
2 (vb) If a person conquers a handicap, they fight off the problems it brings for them.

conqueror conquerors (n) A conqueror is the person who takes over a country or completes a difficult task successfully. *The conquerors of Everest were delighted to reach the summit successfully.*

conscientious (adj) people work thoughtfully and carefully.

conscious (adj) If you are conscious, you are aware of what is happening around you.

consecutive (adj) Things which are consecutive follow one after another in the order that they usually occur. Monday, Tuesday and Wednesday are consecutive days.

consent consents consenting consented (vb) If you consent to do something, you agree to do it.

consequence consequences
1 (n) The consequence is the result of something that happens. *He didn't attend school on Thursday and the consequence is that he has to see the head teacher.*

2 (n) If you suffer the consequences of an action, you find yourself in an unpleasant situation because of something you have done.

conservation (n) is the care and protection of things against neglect and damage.

conservative conservatives (adj) A conservative person is one who does not like changes in fashion or ideas.

Conservative (n) A Conservative is a member of the Conservative Party, which is one of the main political parties in Britain.

conservatory conservatories (n) A conservatory is a room with glass walls and roof built onto a house. Plants may be grown in it.

consider considers considering considered
1 (vb) If you consider something, you think about it very carefully before you make up your mind about it.
2 (vb) If someone considers other people, they think about their needs and try to help them.

considerable (adj) A considerable amount of something is a large amount. *Her work has shown considerable improvement this term.*

considerate (adj) people are thoughtful towards others.

consideration (n) is careful thought that you give to something or someone.

consignment consignments (n) A consignment is a load of goods.

consistent (adj) Someone or something that is consistent does not change. *She was consistent in her attendance at school as she went every day.*

console consoles consoling consoled
1 (vb) If you console someone, you comfort them in a time of loss.
2 (n) A console is a panel with dials and switches used to control a machine.

consolation prize consolation prizes (n) A consolation prize can be given to someone who does not win a competition but who has tried very hard.

consonant

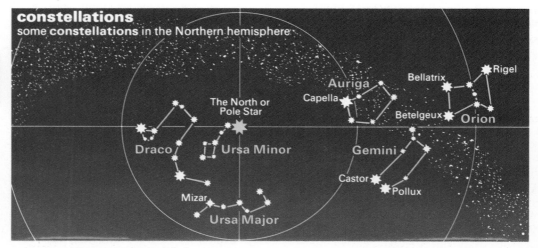

constellations
some **constellations** in the Northern hemisphere

The North or Pole Star

Draco

Ursa Minor

Mizar

Ursa Major

Auriga

Capella

Bellatrix

Rigel

Betelgeux

Orion

Gemini

Castor

Pollux

consonant consonants (n) A consonant is any letter of the alphabet that is not one of the vowels A E I O or U.

conspicuous (adj) people or things stand out and can be seen very easily. *She was conspicuous in her scarlet cloak.*

conspiracy conspiracies (n) A conspiracy is a plot by a group of people to do something against the law.

constable constables (n) A constable is a policeman of the lowest rank.

constant (adj) If something is constant, it is always there or always the same.

constellation constellations (n) A constellation is a group of stars that form a pattern and has been given a name. *The constellation of Orion forms the shape of a hunter with a belt, club and shield.*

constipated (adj) If a person or animal is constipated, they are unable to empty their bowels easily.

constitution constitutions
1 (n) The constitution of a country is the system of laws, rules and principles by which it is governed.
2 (n) A person's constitution is their state of health. *She had a strong constitution and was never ill.*

constraint constraints (n) A constraint is something that holds you back or stops you from doing something.

construct constructs constructing constructed (vb) If you construct something, you make it or build it. **construction** (n)

consult consults consulting consulted (vb) If you consult someone, you ask their advice about something. **consultation** (n)

consultant consultants (n) A consultant is someone who has special knowledge and skills. *An eye consultant... a tax consultant.*

consume consumes consuming consumed (vb) If you consume something, you eat, drink or use it. *The car consumed petrol... We consumed paper writing our notes.*

consumer consumers (n) A consumer is a person who buys something.

contact contacts contacting contacted
1 (vb) If you contact someone, you get in touch with them.
2 (n) A contact is a person you know, who will help you to do something you want to do.

contact lens contact lenses (n) A contact lens is a small plastic disc you can put on your eye to help you to see instead of wearing glasses.

contagious (adj) If something is contagious, it is catching. *Contagious disease... contagious laughter.*

contain contains containing contained
1 (vb) If something contains another object, it has this inside it. *The room contains several antiques.* **container** (n)
2 (vb) If you try to contain your anger, you try not to show how angry you feel.

contaminate contaminates contaminating contaminated (vb) If you contaminate food or liquid, it is unfit to eat or drink. **contamination** (n)

contemporary
1 (adj) If something is contemporary, it is happening now.
2 (adj) A contemporary account is one that was written at the time of the events that it describes.

 content contents
1 (adj) If you are content, you are happy.
2 (n) The contents of something are what is inside it.

contest contests contesting contested
1 (n) A contest is a competition. **contestant** (n)
2 (vb) If you contest a result or decision, you object to it.

continent continents
1 (n) A continent is a large land mass, often containing several countries, surrounded, or almost surrounded, by water.
2 (n) The Continent is the mainland of Europe. *They enjoyed their holiday on the Continent, camping in France and Spain.* **continental** (n)

continue continues continuing continued (vb) If you continue to do something, you go on doing it.

continuous (adj) If something is continuous, it does not stop.

contour contours
1 (n) The contour of something is its outline.
2 (n) The contours on a map are lines which link places of the same height.

contract contracts contracting contracted
1 (vb) If you contract your muscles, you tighten them.
2 (vb) If something contracts, it gets smaller in size.
3 (vb) If you contract a disease, you catch it.
4 (n) A contract is a legal and binding agreement between two people or groups.

contradict contradicts contradicting contradicted (vb) If you contradict another person, you say the opposite to what they have just said. **contradiction** (n)

contrast contrasts contrasting contrasted
1 (vb) If one thing contrasts with another, they are very different.
2 (n) A contrast is a difference between two or more things.

contribute contributes contributing contributed (vb) If you contribute your money or time to something, you give it to help to pay for something. **contribution** (n)

control controls controlling controlled
1 (vb) If you control a group of people or a business, you make all the important decisions so that things run as you wish.
2 (n) The controls of a machine are the switches and levers that make it work.

controversial
1 (adj) If something is controversial, it will be talked about and argued over by many people. **controversy** (n)
2 (adj) If a person is controversial, they hold views which are unacceptable to many people.

convalescence (n) is the time you spend recovering after an illness. **convalescent** (n)

convenience conveniences
1 (n) If something is done at your convenience, it is done at a time that suits you. **convenient** (adj)
2 (n) A convenience is another name for a public lavatory.

convenience food (n) is food that is tinned, frozen or dried, that can be cooked in a short time with little preparation.

convent convents (n) A convent is a group of buildings where nuns live as a community.

conventional (adj) people do things in the usual, accepted way.

converge converges converging converged (vb) If roads converge, they meet in a particular place.

conversation conversations (n) If you have a conversation with someone, you talk with them about various things.

convert converts converting converted
1 (vb) If you convert something, it becomes different in some way. *She has a sofa which converts to a bed.*
2 (vb) If one person converts another person, they make them change their ideas, especially religious ideas.

convex (adj) Something that is convex curves outwards in the centre.

coal mine
p50

conveyor belt conveyor belts (n) A conveyor belt is a long band that is always moving. It is used in factories to move items along while they are being assembled.

convict convicts convicting convicted
1 (vb) When a jury convicts a person, this person is found guilty of a crime.
2 (n) A convict is a person who has been sent to prison.

convince convinces convincing convinced
1 (vb) If you convince another person of something, you make them believe you.
2 (adj) If someone is convinced about something, they feel sure that this thing is right.

Cook, Captain James (1728–79) was an English navigator and explorer who discovered parts of Australia.

convulsion convulsions (n) A convulsion is a series of sudden, violent and uncontrollable movements.

cool cools cooling cooled; cooler coolest
1 (vb) If you cool something, you lower the temperature.
2 (adv) If something is cool, it is low in temperature.

co-operate co-operates co-operating co-operated (vb) If you co-operate, you work willingly with other people to do something.

co-operative co-operatives (n) A co-operative is a business jointly owned by the people who run it.

copier copiers (n) A copier is a machine that reproduces documents.

copper (n) is a red-brown metal.

copy copies copying copied (vb) If you copy something, you write or draw or use a machine to produce the same thing again.

copyright (n) is the legal right of writers, composers and other artists to be the only person allowed the use of their work.

coral (n) is a hard substance formed in the sea from the skeletons of small creatures.

cordon cordons (n) A cordon is a temporary barrier used to control crowds.

corduroy (n) is a heavy, ribbed cotton fabric.

cork corks corking corked
1 (vb) If you cork a bottle, you block up the hole at the top to stop liquid escaping.
2 (n) Cork is a very light material which floats. It comes from the bark of a tree and is used for floor and wall coverings and for stoppers for bottles.
3 (n) A cork is a stopper for a bottle.

corkscrew corkscrews (n) A corkscrew is a device for taking corks out of bottles.

cormorant cormorants (n) A cormorant is a large, dark-coloured sea bird.

corn corns
1 (n) Corn is the name for cereal crops such as wheat or barley.
2 (n) Corn is the seeds from wheat and barley, ground to make flour and animal feeds.
3 (n) A corn is a painful, area of hard skin on someone's foot.

corner corners cornering cornered
1 (n) A corner is a place where two roads, walls or lines meet.
2 (vb) If you corner an animal, it is trapped with no way of escape.

cornet cornets
1 (n) A cornet is a wafer cone that ice-creams are served in.
2 (n) A cornet is a type of trumpet.

Cornish pasty Cornish pasties (n) A Cornish pasty is an individual pie filled with meat and vegetables.

coronary coronaries
1 (n) A coronary is a kind of heart attack.
2 (adj) Coronary is to do with the heart. The coronary artery takes blood away from the heart.

coronation coronations (n) A coronation is the occasion when a new king or queen is crowned.

coroner coroners (n) A coroner is an official whose job is to investigate sudden or unexpected deaths.

corporal corporals (n) A corporal serves in the army, at a junior level of command.

corporal punishment (n) is punishment by beating or caning.

corporation corporations
1 (n) A corporation is responsible for running a town and organising its services.
2 (n) A corporation is a large company or group of companies that are run together as one organisation.

corpse corpses (n) A corpse is a dead body.

corpuscle corpuscles (n) Corpuscles are the red and white cells in the blood. The red cells carry oxygen, the white cells help fight diseases.

correct corrects correcting corrected
1 (vb) If you correct something, you put it right. **correction** (n)
2 (adj) If something is correct, it has no mistakes in it.

correspond corresponds corresponding corresponded
1 (vb) When you correspond with someone, you write to them and they reply.
2 (vb) Things correspond to one another if they are similar to each other. *His job in Aberdeen corresponds to my mother's job in Dublin.*

correspondent correspondents
1 (n) A correspondent is a person who writes a letter.
2 (n) A correspondent is a person who writes for a newspaper, radio or television especially from another country.

corridor corridors (n) A corridor is a long, narrow passage in a building or train.

corrode corrodes corroding corroded (vb) If something corrodes, it is eaten away or wears down something else. *Rust corrodes metal. Iron corrodes in water.* **corrosion** (n)

corrugated (adj) If something is corrugated, it is ridged and grooved. Corrugated iron, for example.

corrupt corrupts corrupting corrupted
1 (vb) If you corrupt someone, you make them behave in a dishonest way.
2 (adj) Someone who is corrupt is dishonest.

cosmetics (n) consist of lipstick, powder, eyeshadow and other make-up for the body.

cosmonaut cosmonauts (n) A cosmonaut is a Russian astronaut.

cosmopolitan
1 (adj) A cosmopolitan city is where people from all over the world live and where things from many different cultures can be seen.
2 (adj) A cosmopolitan person has travelled widely and lived in many different cultures.

cosmos (n) is another name for the universe.

cost of living (n) The cost of living is the amount it costs for food, clothes and somewhere to live over a period of time.

costume costumes
1 (n) A costume refers to the clothes worn by actors or other performers to help them to look the part they are playing.
2 (n) Costume also describes the clothes people wore in the past. *Roman costume... medieval costume... Victorian costume.*

cottage cottages (n) A cottage is a small house which is usually old and often in the country or by the sea.

cotton cottons
1 (n) Cotton is a plant grown in warm countries which is used in making cotton fabric.
2 (n) Cotton is fabric made from the fibres of the cotton plant. It is used to make dresses, shirts, curtains, etc.
3 (n) Cotton is thin thread used for sewing, made of cotton fibres.

C

cotton wool (n) is very soft cotton, fluffed up and often used for putting creams and liquids onto the skin as well as for cleaning them off and mopping up liquids.

couch couches (n) A couch is a long seat for several people to sit on.

cougar cougars (n) A cougar is a large member of the cat family. It lives in the mountains of North and South America.

cough coughs coughing coughed (vb) If you cough, you make a short, loud, choking noise in your throat.

could
1 (vb) If you say you could do something, it means that in the past you were able to do it. *When I was six I could climb like a monkey.*
2 (vb) If you say something could happen, it means that you think it might be possible. *By the look of the sky it could rain later.*
3 (vb) Could is also used politely to ask permission. *Could I have a cake, please?*

council councils
1 (n) A council is a group of people who are elected to run a certain area, town or county in Britain. It is responsible for the housing, roads, education and other services. *Town Council ... County Council.*
2 (n) A council is a group of people who are brought together to give advice on certain things; to certain people; or to organise something. *The Advisory Council for Mathematics ... The Council for Civil Liberties ... The Arts Council.*

count counts counting counted
1 (vb) If you count a set of things, you find out how many there are.
2 (n) A count is a foreign nobleman.
3 If you count on someone, you rely on them to help you.

countdown (n) A countdown is the counting downwards before an important beginning, for example, a space launch. *10, 9, 8, 7, 6, 5, 4, 3, 2, 1, Blast Off!*

counter counters
1 (n) A counter is a small, coloured disc that is used for learning to count or for marking your place in a board game.
2 (n) A counter is a long, flat-topped table in a shop or café.

counterfeit (adj) Something that is counterfeit is a copy of something valuable, made to deceive people into thinking it is the real thing.

country countries
1 (n) A country is a large area of land which has its own government.
2 (n) The country is the land outside of towns and cities which is not built up.

countryside (n) is the land outside of the towns and cities.

county counties (n) A county is a large area of the country which has its own local government. *The counties of Berkshire ... Gwent ... Suffolk.*

couple couples coupling coupled
1 (n) A couple is two of anything.
2 (vb) If you couple two things together, you join them up.

courageous (adj) people are brave in the face of danger. **courage** (n)

courgette courgettes (n) A courgette is a small, green vegetable from the marrow family.

courier couriers
1 (n) A courier looks after people on a holiday tour.
2 (n) A courier takes deliveries by motorbike or van from one place to another.

course courses
1 (n) A course is a series of lessons or lectures about a particular subject.
2 (n) A course is one part of a meal. *The ice-cream was the final course of the meal.*
3 (n) A course of injections, for example, is medical treatment you take over a period of time.
4 (n) A course can be a piece of land where certain sports such as racing and golf take place.

court courts courting courted
1 (n) A court is where legal matters are decided.
2 (n) You play tennis on a court.
3 (adj) A couple who are courting are going out together and intend to marry.

courteous (adj) people are polite and pleasant. **courtesy** (n)

courtyard courtyards
(n) A courtyard is a flat, open area surrounded by buildings or walls.

cousin cousins (n) Your cousin is your uncle's or your aunt's child.

cover covers covering covered
1 (n) A cover is a layer of something on top of something else. *Book cover... bed cover.*
2 (vb) If you cover an object, you put something over it to protect it or to hide it.

coward cowards (n) A coward is afraid in times of danger.

crab crabs (n) A crab is a shell-fish with five pairs of legs. Some have large front claws.

crack cracks cracking cracked
1 (vb) If something cracks, it breaks without falling apart completely.
2 (vb) If you crack a joke, you tell one.
3 (n) A crack is a small space between two surfaces.

cracker crackers
1 (n) A cracker is a plain, dry, thin biscuit.
2 (n) A cracker is a decorated tube of cardboard and paper, popular at Christmas. When it is pulled apart it bangs. It often contains a small toy or paper hat and joke.

cradle cradles
1 (n) A cradle is a baby's bed which can be rocked.
2 (vb) If you cradle someone in your arms, you hold them carefully.

craft crafts crafting crafted
1 (n) A craft is an activity that involves a person using their hands in a creative way. *Pottery, needlework and woodwork are crafts.*
2 (n) A craft is another name for a small boat. *A pleasure craft... a fishing craft.* Several boats are also referred to as craft.

craftsman craftsmen (n) A craftsman makes things with his hands in a skilful way. **craftswoman (fem. n).**

cramp cramps cramping cramped
1 (n) If you have cramp in a part of your body, you get a strong pain in the muscle there.
2 (vb) If you cramp a person's ideas or movements, you do not allow them to express themselves fully.
3 (adj) If you live in cramped conditions, you have little space.

crane cranes craning craned
1 (n) A crane is a large piece of machinery which lifts heavy items.
2 (n) A crane is a large bird with a long beak and long legs.
3 (vb) If you crane your neck to see something, you stretch your neck so that you can see more easily.

crash crashes crashing crashed
1 (vb) If someone crashes into another person or thing, they hit it noisily.
2 (n) A crash is an accident in which motor vehicles or aeroplanes are involved.
3 (n) A crash is a loud, unexpected noise.

crate crates crating crated
1 (vb) If you crate something, you put it into a container for safety.
2 (n) A crate is a strong container made of wood, metal or plastic used to carry items.

crater

crater craters (n) A crater is a large hole in the ground. There are craters on the moon.

crave craves craving craved (vb) If you crave for something, you want it very badly.

crawl crawls crawling crawled
1 (vb) If you crawl along the ground, you move on your hands and knees.
2 (n) Crawl is a type of swimming stroke.

crayon crayons (n) A crayon is a coloured pencil.

crazy crazier craziest
1 (adj) Someone who behaves in a crazy way acts strangely or foolishly.
2 (adj) When you are crazy about something or someone, you are very keen on them.

creak creaks creaking creaked (vb) If something creaks, it makes a squeaking noise when it moves.

cream creams creaming creamed
1 (n) Cream is a fatty liquid taken from milk. It is used in cooking and poured on puddings.
2 (vb) If you cream two or more ingredients when cooking, you mix them together thoroughly to make them smooth.

crease creases creasing creased
1 (n) If material or paper has creases it is crumpled.
2 (n) A crease is a straight line that is pressed into trousers.

create creates creating created (vb) If you create something, you invent it or design it or make it happen.

creation creations
1 (n) Creation is the act of making something exist or happen.
2 (n) Creation is the whole of the universe and everything that exists in it.
3 (n) The Creation in religion is the making of all things in the universe by a God.

creative (adj) people produce imaginative and exciting ideas.

creature creatures (n) A creature is any living thing that can move.

crèche crèches (n) A crèche is a place where young children can be left safely while their parents are working.

credit credits
1 (n) Credit is praise given to you for good work.
2 If you pay for something on credit, you pay for it in small amounts regularly over a period of time.
3 If your bank account is in credit, you have money in it.

creek creeks (n) A creek is a narrow inlet which allows the sea to flow inland.

creep creeps creeping crept (vb) If you creep, you move slowly and quietly, trying not to be seen or heard.

cremate cremates cremating cremated (vb) If you cremate someone you burn their body after they die, usually as part of a funeral service. **cremation** (n) **crematorium** (n)

creosote (n) is a dark, oily, strong-smelling liquid used for preserving wood.

crescent crescents
1 (n) A crescent is a curved shape which is wider in the middle than at the ends.
2 (n) A crescent is the name given to a row of houses built in a curved shape.

cress (n) is a small salad plant.

crest crests
1 (n) A crest is the special sign of a family, school, town, etc.
2 (n) The crest of a wave or the crest of a hill is the top of it.

coat of arms p51

crevice crevices (n) A crevice is a small crack in rocks.

crew crews
1 (n) A crew is a group of people who sail a ship or fly an aircraft under the orders of the captain.
2 (n) A crew is a group of people who work together on one job. *A film crew.*

cricket crickets
1 (n) Cricket is a game played between two teams with bats, a ball, and two pairs of stumps. The object of the game is for one team to score more runs than the other.
2 (n) A cricket is an insect like a small grasshopper.

crime crimes (n) A crime is any act which is against the laws of a country.

criminal criminals (n) A criminal is someone who breaks the law.

crimson (adj) is a dark red colour.

cripple cripples crippling crippled
1 (vb) If you cripple someone, you injure them so that they cannot move part of their body.
2 (adj) A crippled person is unable to use their body normally because of illness or injury. **cripple** (n)

crisis crises (n) A crisis is a turning point when a situation seems particularly dangerous, or when something disastrous could happen.

crisp crisps
1 (n) A crisp is a very thin slice of deep fried potato.
2 (adj) If something is crisp, it is brittle and hard.
3 (adj) If the weather is crisp, it is cold and frosty.

critical
1 (adj) If you are critical about an idea or a plan, you can see its good and bad points.
2 (adj) A critical time or situation is a very important point when things must be done correctly.

criticism criticisms
1 (n) A criticism of something is spoken or written disapproval of it.
2 (n) A criticism of a book, film or play, etc is an examination of its good and bad points. **critic** (n)

criticise criticises criticising criticised
1 (vb) If you criticise someone or something, you point out all the things that you think are wrong with them.
2 (vb) If you criticise something, you look at it very carefully so that you can make intelligent remarks about it.

croak croaks croaking croaked
(vb) If an animal or bird croaks, it makes a loud, harsh sound. Crows and frogs croak.

crochet crochets crocheting crotcheted
1 (n) Crochet is a kind of knitting done with a hooked needle and cotton or wool.
2 (vb) If you crochet, you use a hooked needle and wool or cotton to make lacy garments and furnishings.

crockery (n) consists of cups, plates, saucers, bowls and other dishes made from pottery.

crocodile crocodiles (n) A crocodile is a large, flesh-eating reptile that lives in the rivers and swamps of Africa, India and Australia.

crocus crocuses (n) A crocus is a small, bright, yellow, white or purple flower that blooms in early spring.

croft crofts (n) A croft is a small farmhouse in Scotland with a small piece of farmland.

crook crooks
1 (n) Crook is an everyday word for someone dishonest or a criminal.
2 (n) A crook is a long stick with a hook which shepherds use to catch their sheep.
3 (n) The crook of your arm is the inside of your elbow.

crooked
1 (adj) If something is crooked, it is not straight. *A crooked path.*
2 (adj) Someone who is crooked is dishonest and not to be trusted.

crop

crop crops cropping cropped
1 (n) Crops are the plants that farmers grow in large quantities such as wheat, barley, oats etc.
2 (n) A crop is the harvested produce from a field, garden or orchard.
3 (vb) If you crop something, you cut it short.
4 (n) A crop is a short whip used by some horse riders.
5 If something crops up, it appears unexpectedly and may cause problems.

croquet (n) is a game played on grass where the players hit coloured balls through hoops, using long wooden mallets.

cross crosses crossing crossed; crosser crossest
1 (vb) If you cross a road, you go from one side to the other.
2 (vb) If roads or railways cross, they meet and go over or under each other by means of a bridge.
3 (vb) If you cross something out, you put a line through what you have written.
4 (vb) If you cross someone, you have a disagreement with them.
5 (n) A cross is a shape like + or x.
6 (adj) If you are cross with someone, you are angry with them.

cross-country (adj) A cross-country race is a running race which takes place across open countryside and little-used roads.

cross-examination cross-examinations (n) A cross-examination happens when someone is questioned in a very detailed way.

crossing crossings (n) A crossing is a place where people can cross a road or railway track safely. *Level crossing... zebra crossing.*

cross-section (n) A cross-section of something is made by slicing through it so that you can see how it is formed inside.

crossword crosswords (n) A crossword is a word puzzle where you have to fill in answers to questions to fit in a grid.

crotchet crotchets (n) A crotchet is a musical note which has the value of one beat. ♩

crouch crouches crouching crouched (vb) If a person or an animal crouches, they bend their legs and get close to the ground without actually sitting down.

crowbar crowbars (n) A crowbar is a heavy iron bar used for levering things apart.

crowd crowds crowding crowded
1 (n) A crowd is a large number of people gathered together in one place.
2 (vb) If people crowd around something, they gather round in large numbers.
3 (vb) If you crowd people into a space, you squeeze in as many as you can
4 (adj) A crowded place is full of people.

crown of Queen Maria Leczinska from the imperial collection of French jewels

crown crowns crowning crowned
1 (vb) If a king or queen is crowned, they are officially declared king or queen by the placing of a crown on their head.
2 (vb) When a dentist crowns a tooth, he fits a false top on it.
3 (n) A crown is the head-dress usually made of precious metals and jewels that is worn by a king or queen.
4 (n) The Crown refers to the monarchy of a country, not to any particular king or queen.
5 (n) The crown of your head, the crown of a hat and the crown of a hill is the top.

coat of arms p51

crucial (adj) If something is crucial, it is very important indeed. *The exam was crucial to her future success in becoming an engineer.*

crucify crucifies crucifying crucified (vb) To crucify someone is to kill them by tying them or nailing them to a cross and leaving them to die. *Jesus was crucified by his enemies.*

crude cruder crudest
1 (adj) If something is crude, it is roughly and simply made.
2 (adj) If a person is crude, they are loud, bad-mannered and offensive.
3 (adj) If an idea or plan is crude, it is not thought out very well.

cruel crueller cruellest
1 (adj) A cruel person deliberately causes pain and suffering to other people or to animals.
2 (adj) If a situation is described as cruel, it means that it causes hardship and suffering. *It was a cruel winter and many wild creatures died.*

cruise cruises cruising cruised
1 (vb) If you cruise, you travel at a comfortable speed.
2 (n) A cruise is a holiday on a ship which allows the passengers to visit many places.

cruise missile cruise missiles (n) A cruise missile is a weapon that carries a nuclear warhead.

cruiser cruisers
1 (n) A cruiser is a fast-moving warship.
2 (n) A cruiser is a fast motor-boat with a cabin.

crumb crumbs (n) A crumb is a tiny piece of bread, cake or biscuit.

crumble crumbles crumbling crumbled
1 (vb) If you crumble something, you break it up into small pieces in your hands.
2 (vb) When buildings crumble, they fall into ruins because they have been neglected.
3 (n) A crumble is a pudding made of fruit with a crumbly mixture of flour, fat and sugar baked on the top.

crumple crumples crumpling crumpled
1 (vb) If you crumple something like a piece of paper or material, you crush it until it is full of creases.
2 (vb) If someone's face crumples, it falls into lines of sadness or shock.
3 (vb) If someone's body crumples, it collapses because of a shock of some kind.

crunch crunches crunching crunched
1 (vb) If you crunch when you are eating, you eat noisily.
2 (vb) If you crunch something, you crush it so that it makes a noise.

crusade crusades
1 (n) The Crusades were wars fought by the Christians against the Muslims in the 11th, 12th and 13th centuries.
2 (n) Nowadays, a crusade is a campaign for something you really believe in.

crush crushes crushing crushed
1 (vb) If you crush something, you squash it or press it so hard that it is forced out of shape and broken.
2 (vb) If you crush an army or a rebellion you defeat it.
3 (n) A crush is a crowd of people squashed together.

crust crusts
1 (n) The crust on a loaf of bread or a cake is the harder outside layer.
2 (n) A crust can be any hard layer on top of or surrounding something soft. *There was a hard crust on the surface of the muddy ditch.*
3 (n) The crust of the planet earth is the thin outer layer containing the land and the ocean.

crutch crutches (n) A crutch is a long stick with padding at the top which is used for leaning on when you need help to walk.

cry cries crying cried
1 (vb) When you cry, tears fall from your eyes, usually because you are sad.
2 (vb) If you cry out, you shout loudly because you need help or are in pain.
3 If a pack of hounds, wolves or dogs are in full cry, they are eagerly chasing their prey.

crypt crypts (n) A crypt is an underground room beneath a church or cathedral.

crystal

crystal crystals
1 (n) A crystal is a mineral with a symmetrical shape.
2 (n) A crystal is a rock which is transparent and catches the light.
3 (adj) If something is crystal clear, it is very easy to understand.

cub cubs
1 (n) A cub is a young, wild animal. *Lion cub... wolf cub... bear cub.*
2 (n) The Cubs is an organisation for boys aged 8 and above, before they join the Scouts.

cube cubes (n) A cube is a solid object with 6 equal square surfaces.

cubicle cubicles (n) A cubicle is a very small room used for dressing and undressing in a clothes shop or at a swimming pool, for example.

cuckoo cuckoos (n) A cuckoo is a grey bird that lays its eggs in other birds' nests. Its call sounds like its name.

cucumber cucumbers (n) A cucumber is a long, green salad vegetable.

cud (n) When a cow or sheep chews the cud, they chew their food many times.

cuddle cuddles cuddling cuddled (vb) If you cuddle someone, you put your arms around them and hold them close to you to show you like them or to comfort them.

cul-de-sac cul-de-sacs (n) A cul-de-sac is a short road with one end blocked.

culprit culprits (n) The culprit is the person who is to blame for doing something wrong.

cult cults (n) A cult is a particular group, especially an unusual religious group, that becomes popular, often for a short time.

cultivate cultivates cultivating cultivated
1 (vb) If you cultivate land, you prepare it and grow crops on it. **cultivation** (n)
2 (adj) Cultivated plants are suitable for farms and gardens, not for growing in the wild.
3 (adj) A cultivated person is well-educated and has a wide range of cultural interests.

culture cultures
1 (n) The culture of a group of people is made up of their ideas, their arts and the way they live their lives.
2 (n) Culture can be used to refer to the arts (music, literature, painting etc).
cultural (adj)

cunning (adj) If a person or animal is cunning, they are clever and get what they want by deceiving others.

cupboard cupboards (n) A cupboard is a piece of furniture usually made of wood with doors at the front and shelving for storage inside.

curator curators (n) A curator is a person in charge of a museum or art gallery.

curb curbs curbing curbed
1 (n) A curb is the edge of a path or a pavement where it is raised up (also spelled kerb).
2 (vb) If you curb your feelings, you control them.
3 (vb) If you curb a child who is acting badly, for example, you act firmly to control them.

curdle curdles curdling curdled
(vb) If milk is curdled, it is sour and has started to separate.

cure cures curing cured
1 (vb) If a doctor cures someone of an illness, they help them to get better.
2 (vb) If you cure meat or fish, you smoke it to give it flavour and preserve it.
3 (n) A cure is something which heals or helps someone to get better.

curfew curfews (n) A curfew is a law which forbids people to be out of their houses after a certain time, usually after nightfall.

curious
1 (adj) If you are curious, you want to find things out. **curiosity** (n)
2 (adj) Something that is curious is unusual or strange.

curl curls curling curled
1 (vb) If you curl hair or paper, you twist it around into a tight curve.
2 (n) A curl is a rounded twist of hair or paper.
3 (n) A curl is also a curved, spiral shape.

curlew curlews (n) A curlew is a moorland bird with long legs and a curved bill.

currant currants (n) A currant is a small, black, dried, seedless grape, often used in cooking.

currency currencies (n) The currency of a country is its money.

current currents
1 (n) A current is the strong flow of water in the sea or a river.
2 (n) A current is the flow of electricity.
3 (adj) Current affairs are news events which are happening now.

curriculum curricula (n) The curriculum is the collection of subjects that you study at school.

curry curries (n) A curry is a spicy dish of vegetables, meat or fish often served with rice.

curse curses cursing cursed
1 (vb) If you curse someone, you swear at them.
2 (n) A curse is an evil spell.

cursor cursors (n) A cursor is a flashing light on a computer monitor which shows where the next letter or symbol is.

curtain curtains (n) A curtain is a piece of fabric often hanging at a window on the inside.

curtsey curtseys (n) A curtsey is a little bobbing bow of respect made by girls and women on formal occasions.

curve curves curving curved
1 (vb) If something curves, it bends. *The road curves to the right.*
2 (n) A curve is a bend.

cushion cushions
1 (n) A cushion is a soft pad on a chair.
2 (vb) If you cushion something or someone, you protect them from a blow or from problems.

custard custards (n) Custard is a yellow sauce made with eggs, milk and sugar. It can be eaten with puddings.

custody (n) If someone is in custody, they are kept by the police until it is time for their appearance in court.

customary (adj) If something is customary, it is usual. *He was sitting at his customary place at the table.*

customer customers (n) A customer is a person who goes into a shop to buy something, or who buys goods or services from another sort of business.

customise customises customising customised (vb) If you customise something such as a car or a motorbike, you change it according to your own personal design.

Customs and Excise (n) is the Government department responsible for collecting taxes on things brought into this country from abroad. They also deal with smugglers.

cutting cuttings
1 (n) A cutting is an item cut out of a newspaper.
2 (n) A cutting is a gap in a hill for a railway line.

cutlery (n) is the collection of knives, forks and spoons etc that you use as instruments for eating or cooking.

cutlet cutlets (n) A cutlet is a small portion of meat on the bone.

cycle cycles cycling cycled
1 (n) A cycle is a push-bike. It is short for bicycle.
2 (vb) If you cycle, you ride a push-bike. **cyclist** (n)
3 (n) A cycle is a series of events which repeat over and over again in the same order.

cyclone cyclones (n) A cyclone is a very strong wind which blows in a spiral like a corkscrew.

cygnet cygnets (n) A cygnet is a young swan.

cylinder cylinders
1 (n) A cylinder is a hollow or solid shape with circular faces at each end and straight sides. *A drainpipe is a cylinder.*
2 (n) The cylinder is the part of the engine that the piston travels in.

cymbal cymbals (n) A cymbal is a percussion instrument. It is a large metal plate that is hit to make a crashing sound.

C

Dd

dabble dabbles dabbling dabbled
1 (vb) If you dabble in something, you take an interest, but are not an expert. *He dabbled in astronomy as a hobby.*
2 (vb) If you dabble your fingers in water, you get the tips wet.

dachshund dachshunds (n) A dachshund is a small dog with short legs and a long body.

dagger daggers (n) A dagger is a short, pointed weapon used for stabbing.

daily dailies
1 (adv) Something which happens daily happens every day.
2 (n) A daily is something published each day, a newspaper, for example.

dainty daintier daintiest (adj) If something is dainty it is light and delicate.

dairy dairies
1 (n) A dairy is a shop or company that sells milk and milk products.
2 (n) A dairy is a room on a farm where milk is stored and milk products are made.
3 (adj) Dairy products are foods made from milk, such as cheese, yoghurt and butter.

daisy daisies (n) A daisy is a small, white, wild flower often seen in grass.

daisywheel daisywheels (n) A daisywheel is a circular device with letters at the end of thin stalks. It is the part of an electric typewriter or printer which produces the letter.

dal or dhal (n) is the name given to pulses in Indian cooking. Lentils or chick peas are the most commonly used.

Dalmatian Dalmatians (n) A Dalmatian is a large, white dog with black spots.

damage damages damaging damaged
1 (n) Damage is harm done to someone or something.
2 (vb) If you damage something or somebody, you cause them physical harm.
3 (n) Damages is the money awarded by a court as compensation for some harm done to a person.

damson damsons (n) A damson is a small, dark plum with a sharp taste.

dance dances dancing danced
1 (vb) If you dance, you move your body and feet in time to a rhythm. **dancer** (n)
2 (n) A dance is a series of rhythmic movements that people can do in time to music.
3 (n) A dance is a social event where people meet to dance together.

dance studio dance studios (n) A dance studio is a place where you go for dancing lessons.

dandelion dandelions (n) A dandelion is a yellow, wild flower with many petals. Its seeds form a fluffy ball which easily blows away.

dandruff (n) refers to the small, white pieces of dead skin found in some people's hair.

danger dangers (n) Danger is the risk or chance that someone may be hurt, or that something might go wrong. **dangerous** (adj) **dangerously** (adv)

danger money (n) is an extra payment made to someone for doing a dangerous job.

dangle dangles dangling dangled (vb) If you dangle something or if something dangles, it hangs down loosely.

dank (adj) A dank place is cold and damp.

dappled
1 (adj) A dappled animal has irregular spots on its coat.
2 (adj) Dappled is used to describe patches of light and shade. *Dappled sunlight came through the trees.*

dare dares daring dared
1 (vb) If you dare to do something, you have the nerve or courage to do something.
2 (n) A dare is a challenge you make to someone.

daredevil daredevils (n) A daredevil is a person who takes risks and does dangerous things.

daring (adj) people take risks.

darkroom (n) A darkroom is a small room with minimal light used for developing photographs.

darn darns darning darned (vb) If you darn a hole in something, you fill it with thread or wool.

dart darts darting darted
1 (n) A dart is a small, pointed object that you throw in a game of darts.
2 (vb) If someone or something darts away, they move quickly and unexpectedly.
3 (n) A dart is a kind of pleat used in sewing to make a garment fit properly.

Darwin, Charles Robert (1809–1882) developed the theory of evolution, which states that some species have evolved, and survived, because they are better adapted to their natural environment than other weaker species.

dash dashes dashing dashed
1 (vb) If you dash somewhere, you go very fast.
2 (n) A dash is a short, straight line used in writing to show a pause.
3 (n) If you use a dash of something, you use a very small quantity. *A dash of salt.*

dashboard dashboards (n) A dashboard in a vehicle is the panel where most of the instruments are found.

data (n) is information. *The girl collected all the data and completed her project.*

database databases (n) A database or databank is a lot of data brought together in a computer, so that it can be accessed quickly.

data processing (n) is a series of processes using data, usually in computers, carried out so that information can be presented, interpreted or found.

daub daubs daubing daubed (vb) If you daub something like paint, you spread it quickly and carelessly.

daughter daughters (n) A daughter is someone's female child.

daughter-in-law daughters-in-law (n) A daughter-in-law is the wife of a person's son.

dawdle dawdles dawdling dawdled (vb) If you dawdle, you are slow about doing something or going somewhere. **dawdler** (n)

dawn dawns dawning dawned
1 (n) Dawn is sunrise.
2 (vb) When the day dawns, the sun rises.
3 If something dawns on you, you become aware of it.

dawn chorus (n) This is the sound of the birds singing as dawn breaks.

daydream daydreams daydreaming daydreamed (vb) If you daydream, you think about something you wish would happen and forget what you should be doing.

daylight (n) is when it is not dark.

day release (n) is a system where people who are working can have one day a week free to study at college.

day return (n) A day return is a bus or travel ticket that allows you to go somewhere and return on the same day.

daze dazed
1 (n) If someone is in a daze, their mind is muddled and confused.
2 (adj) If you are dazed, you can't think clearly, either because you've been knocked on the head or because you are confused.

d

dazzle

dazzle dazzles dazzling dazzled
1 (adj) Dazzling lights are so bright that they hurt your eyes.
2 (adj) A dazzling smile is a big smile.
3 (adj) Someone who looks dazzling looks extremely attractive.
4 (vb) If the sun dazzles you, it shines in your eyes so that you can't see.
5 (vb) If someone dazzles you, you are very impressed with them.

deactivate deactivates deactivating deactivated (vb) If you deactivate anything, you prevent it from working. *They deactivated the bomb.*

dead
1 (adj) A person, creature or plant is dead when it stops living.
2 (adj) When a part of your body goes dead, it is numb and has no feeling in it.
3 (adv) When a vehicle stops dead, it stops suddenly.
4 (adj) If any electrical equipment is dead, it has no electric power.

deadlock deadlocks (n) An argument or discussion reaches a deadlock when there is no agreement.

deadly deadlier deadliest (adj) A deadly illness or poison is likely to cause death.

deaf deafer deafest
1 (adj) A person who is deaf has great difficulty in hearing.
2 (adj) If someone is deaf to something, they choose to take no notice although they can hear.

deaf aid deaf aids (n) A deaf aid is a small device which helps a deaf person to hear.

deal deals dealing dealt
1 (vb) When you deal a pack of cards, you share them out between the players.
2 (n) A deal is a business agreement.
3 A good deal or a great deal of something is a lot.
4 If you deal with something, you see to it or organise it.

dealer dealers
1 (n) A dealer is someone whose business is to buy and sell things. *A car dealer . . . a scrap dealer . . . an antique dealer.*
2 (n) The dealer in a game of cards is the person who shares the cards out.

death deaths (n) Death is when the life of a person or creature ends.

death trap death traps (n) A death trap is a place or a vehicle or a piece of equipment that is so dangerous it could cause someone's death.

death watch beetle death watch beetles (n) A death watch beetle bores its way into wood causing a great deal of damage.

debate debates debating debated
1 (n) A debate is a discussion about something between people who have different opinions. *There was a debate in Parliament about raising the school leaving age.*
2 (vb) When people debate, they take turns to give their views.

debris (n) is the scattered remains of something large that has been destroyed.

debt debts (n) A debt is an amount of money that you owe to someone. **debtor** (n)

debug debugs debugging debugged (vb) If you debug a computer program, you remove the faults which stop it running properly.

debut debuts (n) Someone's debut is their first appearance or performance in public.

decade decades (n) A decade is a period of ten years.

decaffeinated (adj) If coffee or tea is decaffeinated, it has most of the caffeine removed from it.

decathlon (n) A decathlon is an athletic competition in which athletes take part in ten separate events.

decay decays decaying decayed (vb) If something decays, it rots.

deceased (adj) If someone is deceased, they are dead.

deceive deceives deceiving deceived (vb) If you deceive someone, you try to make them believe something that is not true. **deceit** (n) **deceitful** (adj) **deceitfully** (adv)

decent (adj) means acceptable or proper. *We expect decent behaviour . . . Have a decent meal before the journey.* **decency** (n)

decide decides deciding decided (vb) If you decide to do something, you make up your mind to do it.

deciduous (adj) trees or bushes lose their leaves each year during winter.

ee p313

decimal decimals (adj) A decimal number system has a base of ten and uses units, tens, hundreds, thousands etc. *Decimal coins are based on 100p = £1.00; decimal measurement is based on 10mm = 1cm; 100cm = 1m; 1000m = 1km.*

decimal point decimal points (n) The decimal point in maths separates the whole numbers on the left, from the tenths, hundredths etc on the right. *3.7 means 3 whole ones and seven tenths; 4.25 means 4 whole ones and twenty five one hundredths.*

decipher deciphers deciphering deciphered (vb) If you decipher a piece of writing or a message, you work out what it means even if it is hard to understand. *The spy deciphered the secret message.*

decision decisions (n) A decision is the choice you make about several courses of action you have.

deck decks (n) A deck on a vehicle such as a ship or a bus is a downstairs or upstairs area on it.

deckchair deckchairs (n) A deckchair is a lightweight, collapsible chair.

declare declares declaring declared
1 (vb) If you declare something, you say firmly that it is true. **declaration** (n)
2 (vb) If you declare goods at customs, you tell the officers what goods you have bought while you were abroad.

decline declines declining declined
1 (vb) If you decline something, you refuse it. *He declined my offer of help.*
2 (vb) If something declines it grows smaller, weaker or poorer in quality.

decode decodes decoding decoded (vb) If you decode a piece of writing, or a message, you change it from a code to an ordinary language.

decompose decomposes decomposing decomposed (vb) If something decomposes, it rots after it dies. **decomposition** (n)

decompression (n) is a process where the weight or pressure of air on something is gradually lessened. *Deep sea divers must go through decompression before being allowed back into the air.*

decongestant decongestants (n) A decongestant is a medicine which unblocks your nose.

decorate decorates decorating decorated
1 (vb) If you decorate a room, you paint or wallpaper it.
2 (vb) If you decorate something like a tree, you put ornaments on it to make it look attractive.
3 (vb) If you decorate someone, you give them an award for bravery. **decoration** (n)

decoy decoys (n) A decoy is something which lures a person or animal into a trap.

decrease decreases decreasing decreased (vb) If something decreases, it gets smaller in size or number.

decrepit (adj) means old and worn out.

dedicate dedicates dedicating dedicated
1 (adj) If you are dedicated to your work or your hobby, you spend a lot of time and effort on it.
2 (vb) If you dedicate a book or other piece of work to someone, their name appears on it to show respect, affection or thanks. **dedication** (n)

deduct deducts deducting deducted (vb) If you deduct an amount, you take it away from a total amount. **deduction** (n)

deed deeds
1 (n) A deed is something that you do with a particular purpose in mind. *Brave deeds... wicked deeds.*
2 (n) A deed is an important piece of paper or document that an agreement is written on.

deep deeper deepest
1 (adj) If something is deep, it goes down or is a long way from a surface.
2 (adj) A deep sound is a very low note.
3 (adj) A deep colour is dark and rich.
4 (adj) You use deep to show how serious your feelings are. *She felt deep concern when she saw the state of the dog.*

deep freeze deep freezes (n) A deep freeze is a large chest or cabinet used for freezing food so that it can be kept for some time.

deer deer (n) A deer is a large wild animal found in Britain and other countries. It lives on plants and the male has large branching antlers on its head.

deface defaces defacing defaced (vb) If you deface something, you damage its appearance in some way. *The posters were defaced with spray paint.*

defeat defeats defeating defeated (vb) If you defeat someone, you beat them at a game, contest or battle.

defect defects defecting defected
1 (n) A defect is a fault in someone or something. **defective** (adj)
2 (vb) A person defects if they leave a country, political organisation or any group to join one which has opposite views. **defector** (n)

defend defends defending defended
1 (vb) If you defend yourself, you protect yourself against attack.
2 (vb) If a country defends itself against attack, it uses its armed forces.
3 (vb) A lawyer defends someone in court by arguing that they are not guilty.
4 (vb) If you defend your goal in sport, you try to stop the other team from scoring. **defence** (n) **defensive** (adj)

defendant defendants (n) A defendant is a person in a court of law accused of a crime.

defer defers deferring deferred (vb) If you defer something, you put it off until a later date.

defiance (n) If you show defiance, you show that you will not obey someone, or will not behave as expected. **defiant** (adj) **defiantly** (adv)

deficiency deficiencies (n) A deficiency is something that is lacking. *The disease is caused by a deficiency in her diet.*

define defines defining defined (vb) If you define a word, you explain its meaning. **definition** (n)

definite
1 (adj) If you are definite about something, you are certain about it.

2 (adj) If something is definite, it is certain and not likely to be altered. **definitely** (adv)

deflate deflates deflating deflated
1 (vb) If you deflate something, you let the air out of it.
2 (vb) If you deflate someone, you make them feel less important than they think they are. **deflation** (n)

deformed (adj) If someone or something is deformed they are misshapen. **deformity** (n)

defrost defrosts defrosting defrosted
1 (vb) If you defrost a fridge or freezer, you switch it off so that the ice melts.
2 (vb) If you defrost frozen food, you take it out of the freezer to thaw.

defuse defuses defusing defused
1 (vb) If you defuse a bomb, you take out the fuse so that it cannot explode.
2 (vb) If you defuse a tense situation, you calm people down.

defy defies defying defied (vb) If you defy an order, you challenge it or disobey it.

degrade degrades degrading degraded (vb) If you degrade someone, you make them seem worthless.

degree degrees
1 (n) A degree is a unit of measurement. Angles and temperature are measured in degrees. The symbol for degree is °. *The temperature reached 28°C . . . A right angle is 90°.*
2 (n) A degree is an academic qualification awarded by a university or other institute of higher education.
3 (n) Degree can mean the amount to which you do something. *I agree with Wendy to a degree, but I doubt some of her facts.*

fahrenheit 105

dehydrated (adj) Something dehydrated is dried out. **dehydration** (n)

de-ice de-ices de-icing de-iced (vb) When you de-ice something, you remove the ice from it.

deity deities (n) A deity is a god or goddess.

dejected (adj) If you are dejected, you are sad and gloomy. **dejection** (n)

delay delays delaying delayed
1 (vb) If you delay someone, you make them late.
2 (n) A delay is when something cannot or does not happen on time.
3 (vb) If you delay, you put something off till later.

delegate delegates (n) A delegate is someone sent to represent others at a conference or·meeting. *Delegates from all countries arrived at the conference.*
delegation (n)

delete deletes deleting deleted (vb) If you delete something, you cross it out in writing, or remove it from a computer screen or file. **deletion** (n)

deliberately (adj) If something is done deliberately, it is done on purpose.

delicacy delicacies (n) A delicacy is something delicious to eat but expensive.

delicate
1 (adj) Something delicate is fragile or easily broken.
2 (adj) A delicate person is often ill.

delicatessen delicatessens (n) A delicatessen is a shop selling cheeses, cold meats and foods imported from other countries.

delicious (adj) food is very good to eat.

delight delights delighting delighted
1 (vb) If you delight someone, you please them.
2 (n) Delight is great pleasure and enjoyment. **delightful** (adj)
delightfully (adv)

delinquent delinquents (n) A delinquent is a young person who often commits crimes.

delirious
1 (adj) If you are delirious when you are ill, you are feverish and confused.
2 (adj) If you are delirious, you are wildly excited. *He was delirious with joy.*

deliver delivers delivering delivered
1 (vb) If you deliver a letter or parcel, you take it to the person's house.
2 (vb) If you deliver a lecture or a speech, you give it to an audience.
3 (vb) When someone delivers a baby, they help the mother to give birth. **delivery** (n)

delta deltas (n) A delta is triangular piece of land at the mouth of a river where the river divides into separate streams.

deluge deluges (n) A deluge is sudden, heavy rain.

demand demands demanding demanded
1 (vb) If you demand something, you ask in a forceful way.
2 (n) A demand is a firm request for something.

demist demists demisting demisted (vb) When you demist a car window, you blow warm air over it to clear the condensation.

democracy democracies (n) A democracy is a system of government in which representatives are voted for by all the people over a certain age, in regular elections. **democrat** (n) **democratic** (adj) **democratically** (adv)

demolish demolishes demolishing demolished (vb) If you demolish something, you destroy it. *The old building was demolished before it collapsed.*
demolition (n)

demon demons
1 (n) A demon is an evil spirit.
2 Someone who works like a demon works with all their energy and force.

demonstrate demonstrates demonstrating demonstrated
1 (vb) If you demonstrate something to someone, you show them how to do it or to use it.
2 (vb) If people demonstrate, they take part in a march or a meeting to show their support of or objection to something.
demonstration (n)

denim

denim (n) is a very strong cotton cloth, usually blue, and is used to make jeans, jackets and skirts, etc.

dense denser densest
1 (adj) If something is dense, it is closely packed with people or things. *The crowds were dense at the sales.*
2 (adj) Dense fog or smoke is thick and difficult to see through. **density** (n)

dentist dentists (n) A dentist is a person who examines and treats people's teeth.

deny denies denying denied
1 (vb) If you deny something that someone says about you, you say it is not true.
2 (vb) If you deny someone something, you refuse to let them have it.

deodorant deodorants (n) A deodorant is a spray or liquid you put on your body to hide or prevent your body smell.

depart departs departing departed
1 (vb) If you depart, you go away.
2 (n) When people talk about the 'departed' they mean someone who has died.

department departments (n) A department is one section of a large organisation such as a hospital, college, company or government.
departmental (adj)

department store department stores (n) A department store is a very large shop, divided into departments, each selling different types of goods.

departure departures
1 (n) Departure is the act of going away from somewhere.
2 (adj) The departure time of a train, aircraft or boat is the time it sets out on a journey.

depend depends depending depended
1 (vb) If you depend on something, you need it in order to survive.
2 (vb) If you depend on someone or something, you trust them to help you because they are reliable.

dependable (adj) If someone is dependable, you can trust them to be helpful, sensible and reliable.

dependant dependants (n) A dependant is someone who has no money of their own and who relies on other people to feed and clothe them.

deport deports deporting deported (vb) If you deport someone from a country you send them away, either because they have no right to be there or because they have done something wrong.

deposit deposits depositing deposited
1 (n) A deposit is an amount of money paid into a bank or savings account.
2 (n) A deposit is the first payment you make for something you have agreed to buy such as a car or a house.
3 (vb) If you deposit someone or something somewhere, you put them down there or leave them there.
4 (n) A deposit or deposits are minerals, rocks, etc that have been laid down on the earth's surface over thousands of years.

depot depots
1 (n) A depot is a place where supplies of food or equipment are stored until they are needed.
2 (n) A bus depot is a bus station.

depress depresses depressing depressed
1 (adj) If you are depressed, you feel very sad and nothing cheers you up.
2 (vb) If something depresses you, it makes you feel miserable and hopeless.
3 (adj) Depressed areas are places where there are no jobs because there are no businesses or factories.

depression depressions
1 (n) Depression is a deep feeling of sadness and despair that is difficult to overcome.
2 (n) A depression is a hollow in the ground or any other surface.
3 (n) A depression is a time when businesses and the industrial activity of a country slow down and many people lose their jobs.
4 (n) A depression is an area of low air pressure that usually brings rain.

deprive deprives depriving deprived
1 (vb) If you deprive someone of something, you take it away from them.
2 (adj) If someone is deprived, they don't have things like good housing, good food and good education. **deprivation** (n)

depth depths
1 (n) The depth of something is the distance between its top and bottom surfaces.
2 (n) The depth of a situation or of emotion is how serious or worrying it is.
3 If you are out of your depth, you are in a situation that you cannot cope with.

depth charge depth charges (n) A depth charge is an explosive that works under water.

deputy deputies (n) A deputy stands in for another person.

derail derails derailing derailed (vb) If a train is derailed, it comes off the tracks in an accident.

derelict (adj) If something is derelict, it has been left uncared for. *The derelict building was falling down.*

derive derives deriving derived (vb) If something derives from something else, it comes from it. *The word telephone derives from Greek words which mean to speak over a long distance.* **derivation** (n)

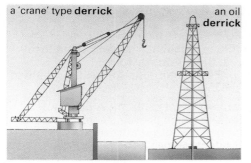

a 'crane' type **derrick**   an oil
                                 derrick

derrick derricks
1 (n) A derrick is a type of crane used for loading and unloading ships.
2 (n) A derrick is a steel tower above an oil well which holds the drill during boring.

descant descants (n) A descant is a tune sung at the same time but higher than the main tune.

descend descends descending descended (vb) If you descend, you go down. *They descended the stairs.*

describe describes describing described (vb) When you describe something, you say exactly what it is like. **description** (n)

desert deserts deserting deserted
1 (n) A desert is a dry, waste land where few things grow.
2 (vb) If you desert someone or something, you abandon them.
3 (vb) If someone deserts from the army, they run away from it. **desertion** (n)

deserve deserves deserving deserved (vb) If you deserve a reward or punishment, you have earned it.

design designs designing designed
1 (vb) When you design something, you create and plan it in your mind. You may make a detailed drawing of it to show what the real thing will be like. **designer** (n)
2 (n) A design is a drawing or a pattern.

desire desires desiring desired
1 (vb) If you desire something, you want it very much.
2 (n) A desire is a strong wish for something.

desolate
1 (adj) Desolate places are lonely and empty.
2 (adj) If you feel desolate, you are lonely and sad. **desolation** (n)

despair despairs despairing despaired
1 (vb) If you despair, you feel that everything has gone wrong and will never be right.
2 (n) Despair is hopelessness. *He was in despair when he lost his job.*

desperate
1 (adj) If you are desperate, you are ready to do anything to make your situation better.
2 (adj) A desperate person or act has no hope of success. *A desperate attempt was made to rescue the dog as it slid below the ice.* **desperation** (n)

despise despises despising despised (vb) If you despise someone or something, you have a very low opinion of them.

despite (prep) If you do something despite some difficulty, you do it anyway.

despondent (adj) If you feel despondent, you feel miserable and low-spirited.

dessert desserts (n) A dessert is a sweet or a pudding eaten after the main course.

destination

destination destinations (n) Your destination is where you want to be at the end of your journey.

destiny destinies
1 (n) Your destiny is your fate; the things that will happen to you in the future.
2 (n) Destiny is the force that some people believe controls your life.

destitute (adj) A person who is destitute has no home and no belongings.

destroy destroys destroying destroyed
1 (vb) If you destroy something, you ruin it so completely that it cannot be repaired. **destruction** (n) **destructive** (adj)
2 (vb) If you destroy an animal, you kill it either because it is in pain or it is a danger to people.

destroyer destroyers (n) A destroyer is a small and fast warship, often used to hunt submarines.

detach detaches detaching detached
1 (vb) If you detach something, you separate it from something else. *The engineer detached the exhaust from the engine.* **detachable** (adj)
2 (adj) A detached house or building stands on its own and is not joined to any other building.
3 (adj) If you behave in a detached way, you show that you have no particular interest in something or someone. **detachment** (n)

detail details detailing detailed
1 (n) Details are facts, items of information or visual features that you remember about something when you think about it carefully.
2 (vb) If you detail things, you list them giving precise information about each thing on the list.

detain detains detaining detained (vb) If you detain someone, you keep them from going somewhere or doing something. *The police detained him overnight.*

detect detects detecting detected
1 (vb) If you detect something, you notice it. *I detect a smell of burning toast.*
2 (vb) If you detect someone or something, you find them. *The boys detected an intruder and phoned the police.*

detective detectives (n) A detective is a plain clothes policeman or investigator who gathers information to solve crimes.

detector detectors (n) A detector is a machine which can notice the presence of something and give warning of it. *Smoke detector . . . radiation detector.*

detention detentions
1 (n) A detention is a punishment given in some schools when a pupil has to stay in school for extra time.
2 (n) If a person is held in detention, they are held prisoner by the police or armed forces.

deter deters deterring deterred
(vb) If you deter someone from doing something, you persuade them not to do it, or try to stop them in some way.

detergent detergents (n) Detergent is a substance, usually a liquid or powder, used for washing things.

deteriorate deteriorates deteriorating deteriorated (vb) If something deteriorates, its condition becomes worse.

determine determines determining determined
1 (adj) If you are determined to do something, you make up your mind firmly to do it. **determination** (n)
2 (vb) If you determine something, you find out the facts.

deterrent deterrents (n) A deterrent is something which prevents someone doing something because it makes them afraid of what might happen as a result. *Prison acts as a deterrent to criminals.*

detest detests detesting detested (vb) If you detest something or someone, you hate them or dislike them intensely.

detonate detonates detonating detonated (vb) If you detonate a bomb, you set it off. **detonation** (n) **detonator** (n)

detour detours (n) A detour is an indirect route or diversion to get around an obstacle.

detract detracts detracting detracted (vb) If one thing detracts from another, it makes it seem less attractive or valuable. *The graffiti detracted from the elegant appearance of the building.*

detrimental (adj) If something has a detrimental effect on another thing, it harms it. *Salt and water have a detrimental effect on the metal parts of cars.*

devalue devalues devaluing devalued (vb) If you devalue something, you make it seem to be worth less in some way.

devastation (n) is severe damage caused by something. *The storm left a trail of devastation.*

develop develops developing developed
1 (vb) If something or someone develops, they grow bigger.
2 (vb) If you develop photographs, you make negatives or prints from a photographic film.
3 (vb) If you develop an idea, you give it more detail.
4 (vb) If someone develops land, they build on it.

development developments
1 (n) A development in something or someone is a gradual change or growth in them.
2 (n) A housing development is an area of houses which have been built by property developers.

device devices
1 (n) A device is an object or mechanism intended for a particular purpose.
2 (n) If you leave someone to their own devices, you let them get on without any help.

devil devils
1 (n) In Christianity, the Devil represents evil.
2 (n) A devil is something or someone evil and against good.

devious (adj) people behave in an underhand and secretive way.

devise devises devising devised (vb) If you devise something, you plan it, invent it and check how it will work.

devoted (adj) If you are devoted to another person, you love and care for them.

dew (n) Dew refers to the tiny drops of water that can be found outside in the early morning.

dhoti dhotis (n) A dhoti is a long, loose garment that covers the lower part of the body and is worn by men in India.

diabetic diabetics (adj) If a person is diabetic, they have too much sugar in their blood. **diabetes** (n)

diagnose diagnoses diagnosing diagnosed (vb) If you diagnose an illness or a problem, you discover and identify what is wrong. **diagnosis** (n)

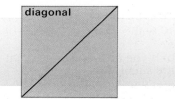

diagonal

diagonal diagonals (adj) A diagonal line slopes in one direction.

diagram diagrams (n) A diagram is a basic line drawing often used to show how something works.

dial dials dialling dialled
1 (n) A dial on a telephone is the circle on the front that shows the numbers 0 to 9.
2 (vb) If you dial a telephone number, you push buttons or turn the dial to phone the number you want.
3 (n) A dial is a device on the front of a machine or instrument that shows the speed or temperature, for instance.

dialect dialects (n) A dialect is a particular form of language that is spoken in one area. *The foreigners found the Yorkshire dialect hard to understand.*

dialogue dialogues
1 (n) A dialogue is a conversation between two people in a play or a book.
2 (n) If there is dialogue between two countries or groups of people, communication takes place.

diameter diameters (n) The diameter of a circle is the distance straight across its widest part.

diamond

diamond diamonds
1 (n) A diamond is a sparkling, colourless, precious stone of great value.
2 (n) Diamonds are one of the four suits of playing cards, with red symbols.
3 (n) A diamond jubilee is the 60th anniversary of a significant event.
4 (n) A diamond wedding is the celebration of 60 years of a couple's marriage.

diaphragm diaphragms (n) The diaphragm is the muscle between the lungs and the stomach which moves during breathing.

diary diaries (n) A diary is a book with spaces for each day where you can note appointments or daily events.

dice dices dicing diced
1 (n) Dice are more than one die. The word dice is often used to mean just one. A die is a cube with small dots on each of its six faces.
2 (vb) If you dice vegetables, you cut them up into small cubes.
3 If you dice with death, you do something that is very dangerous.

Dickens, Charles (1812–70) was a great writer who showed Victorian life very clearly through his novels.

dictionary dictionaries (n) A dictionary is a book in which words are listed in alphabetical order and their meanings are explained.

die dies dying died
1 (vb) When a person, creature or plant dies they stop living.
2 (vb) When someone is dying, they are so ill that there is no hope of their getting better.
3 If you're dying to see someone or to do something, you long for the event. *I'm dying to go to America to see Disneyland.*

diesel diesel (n) Diesel is a fuel used in diesel engines.

diet diets
1 (n) A person's or animal's diet is the food they eat.
2 (n) If you are on a diet, you eat particular foods either to improve your health or to lose weight.

dietitian dietitians (n) A dietitian is a person whose job it is to advise people on their nutrition during illness and also in health.

difference differences
1 (n) A difference is something that makes one thing unlike another. *One difference between oranges and lemons is that oranges are sweet and lemons sour.*
2 (n) The difference between two numbers or two quantities is the amount that one is less or more than the other. *The difference between 5p and 20p is 15p.*
3 (n) If people have a difference, they disagree about something.

different
1 (adj) People or things that are different are unlike each other in various ways.
2 (adj) Someone or something that is different can also be unusual or strange.

difficult
1 (adj) If something is difficult, it is hard to do or to understand.
2 (adj) If a person is difficult, they are hard to get on with. **difficulty** (n)

dig digs digging dug
1 (vb) When a person or animal digs, they make a hole in the ground or move earth from one place to another.
2 (n) A dig is an excavation where archaeologists and their helpers carefully uncover remains of old buildings and other things so that they can study the past.
3 (vb) If something digs into something else, it pushes in quite hard. *Her finger dug into my back.*

digest digests digesting digested (vb) When food is digested, it passes through the stomach where it is broken down to provide energy. **digestion** (n)

digit digits
1 (n) A digit is the written symbol for any number from 0–9. *0 1 2 3 4 5 6 7 8 9 are digits.*
2 (n) Digit is a formal word for a finger or thumb.

figure p109

number p194

digital
1 (adj) Digital watches and clocks give the time in numbers only. *09:45 or 21:15*
2 (adj) Digital computers use a binary system to represent processed information.

dignified (adj) people are calm and serious and behave in a way that other people would admire and respect.

dilapidated (adj) If something is dilapidated, it is broken down and in very bad condition.

dilemma dilemmas (n) If you are in a dilemma, you are in a situation where you have to make a very difficult choice.

diligent (adj) people work very hard at a task and do it with care. **diligence** (n)

dilute dilutes diluting diluted (vb) If you dilute a liquid, you mix it with another liquid so that it is not so strong.

dimension dimensions
1 (n) The dimensions of something are its size.
2 (n) A dimension is measurement in space such as length, width or height.

dimple dimples (n) A dimple is a small round hollow in someone's chin or cheek which shows when they smile.

dinghy dinghies (n) A dinghy is a small open boat for rowing or sailing.

dinner dinners (n) Dinner is a main meal, eaten either at midday or in the evening.

dinosaur dinosaurs (n) Dinosaurs were large reptiles that lived in prehistoric times.

diplomat diplomats (n) A diplomat is a person who works for their government liaising with governments of other countries. **diplomacy** (n)

dinosaur

pterosaur

brontosaurus

diplodocus

plesiosaur

human drawn to same scale

tyrannosaurus rex

stegosaurus

diplomatic

diplomatic (adj) If you are diplomatic, you are tactful and say and do things without offending people.

direct directs directing directed
1 (vb) If you direct someone to a place , you show them how to get there.
2 (adv) If you go direct to a place, you go straight there.
3 (adj) If you talk in a direct way, you talk in an open, honest manner.
4 (vb) If you direct a play or a scheme, you organise it and are responsible for what happens.

direction directions (n) If you give directions, you explain how to get to a place or how to do something.

director directors
1 (n) A director decides how films and plays should be produced.
2 (n) A director is a manager of a business or company.

directory directories (n) A directory is a book of information, often names and addresses, arranged in alphabetical order.

dirty dirtier dirtiest (adj) Something dirty needs to be cleaned.

disabled (adj) A disabled person has a handicap which means their everyday life may be restricted in various ways.

disadvantage disadvantages
1 (n) A disadvantage is something which causes problems.
2 If someone is at a disadvantage, they have particular problems that make it difficult for them to succeed.

disagree disagrees diagreeing disagreed
1 (vb) If you disagree with what someone says, you do not accept their ideas. **disagreement** (n)
2 (vb) If certain foods or drinks disagree with you, they make you ill.

disappear disappears disappearing disappears (vb) If something disappears, you cannot see it anymore. **disappearance** (n)

disappoint disappoints disappointing disappointed (vb) If you disappoint someone, you let them down by not doing what they expected. **disappointment** (n)

disapprove disapproves disapproving disapproved (vb) If you disapprove of something or someone, you do not think much of them. **disapproval** (n)

disarm disarms disarming disarmed
1 (vb) If a country disarms, it gives up using weapons. **disarmament** (n)
2 (vb) If you disarm someone who is angry, you are so pleasant and tactful that they stop feeling angry.

disaster disasters (n) A disaster is a large-scale accident: an aircrash, an earthquake, a famine in which, for example, many people die. **disastrous** (adj)

disc discs
1 (n) A disc is a flat circular shape.
2 (n) Records are sometimes called discs.

discard discards discarding discarded (vb) If you discard something, you throw it away.

discharge discharges discharging discharged
1 (vb) If someone is discharged from a hospital, they are allowed to go home.
2 (vb) If you discharge a gun, you fire it.
3 (n) A discharge is something which comes out from something else. *The river was polluted by a discharge from the factory.*

disciple disciples
1 (n) A disciple is a person who believes strongly in someone else's religious or political teaching.
2 (n) The earliest followers of Jesus were the twelve disciples.

discipline disciplines disciplining disciplined
1 (n) Discipline is the process of making people or animals obey orders, or behave in a reasonable way.
2 (n) A discipline is a particular branch of study. *The university was known for its work in the discipline of medicine.*
3 (n) Self-discipline is being able to control yourself.

disco discos
1 (n) A disco is a place where records are played for people to dance to.
2 (adj) Disco dancing is a style of dancing usually done to pop records.

discomfort discomforts (n) Discomfort is an unpleasant feeling but not bad enough to be called pain.

disconnect disconnects disconnecting disconnected
1 (vb) If you disconnect something, you separate it from the main part.
2 (vb) If you disconnect your gas or electricity, you cut it off.
3 (adj) If your ideas are disconnected, they do not make sense.

discontented (adj) If you are discontented, you are not satisfied with the things you have or the way you are treated.

discontinue discontinues discontinuing discontinued
1 (vb) If you discontinue something, you stop doing something that you have previously done.
2 (vb) If a shop discontinues an item, they no longer sell it.

discount discounts (n) A discount is a saving in the price of something.

discourage discourages discouraging discouraged (vb) If you discourage someone from doing something, you try to persuade them not to do it by pointing out all the difficulties

discover discovers discovering discovered
1 (vb) If you discover a fact, you find out something that you did not know before.
2 (vb) If someone discovers a place, they find a place that no one has found before. **discoverer** (n)

discreet (adj) If you are discreet, you keep private things to yourself and can be trusted with a secret. **discretion** (n)

discriminate discriminates discriminating discriminated
1 (vb) If you discriminate between people, you prefer one group to another and treat them better - often unfairly.
2 (vb) If you discriminate between things, you choose one in preference to another.
3 (adj) If you are discriminating, you can use good judgement in making choices. **discrimination** (n)

discus discuses (n) A discus is the flat circular weight which athletes throw in field sports.

discuss discusses discussing discussed (vb) If you discuss a subject, you talk about it with other people or write about it. **discussion** (n)

disease diseases (n) A disease is an illness caused by infection.

disfigured (adj) If someone is disfigured, their appearance has been spoiled, possibly by an accident.

disgrace disgraces disgracing disgraced
1 (vb) If you disgrace yourself, you do something which others regard as very bad.
2 If you are in disgrace, people disapprove of something you have done and no longer respect you. **disgraceful** (adj)

disguise disguises disguising disguised
1 (vb) If you disguise something, you try to hide it by making it look like something else.
2 (vb) If people disguise themselves, they try to alter their appearance using make-up, wigs, clothes, etc.

disgusting (adj) If someone or something is disgusting, they are very unpleasant.

disheartened (adj) If you feel disheartened, you feel unhappy and disappointed.

dishonest (adj) If a person is dishonest, they cannot be trusted. **dishonestly** (adv)

dishwasher dishwashers (n) A dishwasher is a machine that washes crockery, cutlery and pans.

disinfectant disinfectants (n) Disinfectant is a strong substance used to kill germs.

disintegrate disintegrates disintegrating disintegrated (vb) If something disintegrates it falls to pieces.

Disney, Walt (1901–66) was an American film producer who first devised cartoon characters and films such as Mickey Mouse, Donald Duck and Fantasia.

disk disks (n) Computers store information on floppy disks or hard disks.

dislike

dislike dislikes dislikes disliking **disliked** (vb) If you dislike a person or something, you do not like them.

dislocate dislocates dislocating **dislocated** (vb) If you dislocate a bone in your body, you put it out of its usual position, usually in an accident. **dislocation** (n)

dismal (adj) means depressing and bleak.

dismiss dismisses dismissing dismissed
1 (vb) If you dismiss someone, you send them away.
2 (vb) If you dismiss an idea or thought, you put it out of your mind.
3 (vb) If someone is dismissed from a job, they are sacked.

disobedient (adj) If you are disobedient, you do not do as you are told. **disobedience** (n)

disobey disobeys disobeying disobeyed (vb) If you disobey the rules, you break them. If you disobey a person, you refuse to do as they tell you.

disorderly (adj) If people act in a disorderly way, they are rowdy and badly behaved.

disorganised (adj) If someone is disorganised, they do not plan ahead or arrange things with the result that they get into a muddle.

dispensary dispensaries (n) A dispensary is the place in a hospital where medicines are made up and given out.

display displays displaying displayed
1 (vb) If you display something, you put it on show where everyone can see it.
2 (vb) If you display emotions or feelings such as anger or interest, you show them.
3 (n) A display is a collection of things put on show where people can see it, in a museum or shop window for example.
4 (n) A display is also a performance or event that people can watch. *A firework display... an air display... a gymnastic display.*

disposable (adj) things can be thrown away after use.

dispose disposes disposing disposed (vb) If you dispose of something you get rid of it. *We disposed of our litter carefully.*

disposition dispositions (n) Your disposition is the way you are, how you think and how you behave. *He was of a nervous disposition.*

disprove disproves disproving **disproved** (vb) If you disprove something you show that it is not true.

dispute disputes disputing disputed
1 (n) A dispute is a disagreement or a quarrel about something.
2 (vb) If you dispute something you say that it's not true.
3 Something beyond dispute is so clearly true that nobody can argue about it.

disqualify disqualifies disqualifying **disqualified** (vb) If you disqualify someone from a race or an exam, you stop them from taking part in it, usually because they have done something wrong.

disregard disregards disregarding disregarded
1 (vb) If you disregard someone or something, you take no notice of them.
2 (n) If you show disregard for something, you show that you don't care about it.

disrespect (n) If you show disrespect, you behave rudely or in a way that shows that you have no respect. **disrespectful** (adj)

disrupt disrupts disrupting disrupted (vb) If you disrupt a meeting or a lesson, you disturb or upset it. **disruption** (n)

dissatisfied (adj) When you are dissatisfied with something, you are not satisfied with it.

dissect dissects dissecting dissected (vb) When you dissect a plant or the body of an animal you cut it up so that you can examine it closely.

dissolve dissolves dissolving dissolved
1 (vb) If you dissolve something such as a powder in a liquid, you put it in liquid so that the two substances mix.
2 (vb) If an organisation or a business partnership dissolves, it breaks up.
3 (vb) When Parliament is dissolved, its work ends until a new parliament is elected.
4 (vb) When a marriage is dissolved, it is ended officially.

distance distances
1 (n) The distance between one thing and another is the amount of space between them.
2 (n) The distance is somewhere far away from where you are.

distant
1 (adj) If something is distant, it is very far away.
2 (adj) A distant relative is a member of your family but not a close relative.
3 (adj) A person who is distant is rather cold and unfriendly to other people, or doesn't listen to what you say to them.

distend distends distending distended
(adj) If part of a person's or animal's body is distended, it is swollen and stretched out of its usual shape.

distillery distilleries (n) A distillery is a place where whisky or other strong alcoholic drinks are made by the distilling process. Liquid is heated until it becomes steam and cooled again: the liquid formed is said to be distilled.

distinct
1 (adj) If something is distinct, it is clear. *A distinct voice . . . a distinct outline.*
2 (adj) If something is distinct from something else, it is clearly different.

distinction
1 (n) A distinction between two things is a difference between them.
2 (n) A distinction is an award for great achievement in something.

distinguish distinguishes distinguishing distinguished
1 (vb) If you distinguish one thing from another, you see the difference between them.
2 (vb) If you distinguish yourself at an activity, you do very well at it.

distort distorts distorting distorted
1 (vb) If you distort something you twist it out of shape.
2 (vb) If you distort an argument or the truth you twist the facts to suit yourself. **distortion** (n)

distract distracts distracting distracted
(vb) If you distract someone you take their attention away from what they should be doing. **distraction** (n)

distress (n) is the state of being extremely worried or upset about something.

distribute distributes distributing distributed (vb) If you distribute things, you share them between a number of people. **distribution** (n)

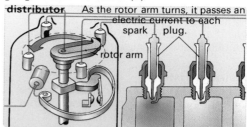
distributor As the rotor arm turns, it passes an electric current to each spark plug. rotor arm

distributor distributors
1 (n) A distributor is a person or company that sells goods to other businesses.
2 (n) A distributor in a motor vehicle spreads the electric current to all the spark plugs in turn to make sure the vehicle runs smoothly.

district districts (n) A district is an area within a town, city or country with definite boundaries.

distrust distrusts distrusting distrusted (vb) If you distrust someone, you do not trust them.

disturb disturbs disturbing disturbed (vb) If you disturb a person or an animal, you interrupt them or wake them up. **disturbance** (n)

disuse (n) If something falls into disuse, it is no longer used.

ditch ditches (n) A ditch is a small channel at the edge of fields or roads for water to drain into.

divan divans (n) A divan is a type of bed with a thick base under the mattress.

diver divers
1 (n) A diver is a person who uses breathing apparatus to swim or work under water.
2 (n) A diver is a person who takes part in diving competitions.
3 (n) A diver is a bird that catches its food by diving into water.

diverse (adj) If things are diverse they show a wide range of differences.

diversion

diversion diversions (n) A diversion is an alternative road you can use if the main one is blocked.

divide divides dividing divided
1 (vb) If you divide a number, you split it into smaller equal parts. *9 ÷ 3 = 3*
2 (vb) If you divide something between several people, you share it out equally.
3 (vb) If an issue divides people, it makes them take sides and argue against each other.

division divisions
1 (n) Division is the mathematical process where one number is divided into another.
2 (n) A division is a group of teams of roughly the same standard who play against one another in a league.
3 (n) A division can be a part of a larger organisation responsible for one aspect or area of activities. *He worked for the sales division of the company.*

divorce divorces divorcing divorced
(vb) When a couple divorce their marriage is legally ended. **divorce** (n)

Diwali (n) is the Hindu festival of light .

dizzy dizzier dizziest (adj) If you are dizzy, you lose your sense of balance.

docile (adj) A docile person or animal is calm and unlikely to cause any trouble.

docker dockers (n) A docker is a person who works in the docks, loading and unloading ships.

doctor doctors
1 (n) A doctor is a person who works in a hospital or at a surgery, caring for people's health.
2 (n) A doctor is a person with a doctoral degree (Ph.D., D.Phil., etc.) which can be in any subject, not necessarily medicine.

document documents documenting documented
1 (n) A document is an official or legal form or piece of paper.
2 (vb) If you document an event, you keep an official and written record of it.

documentary documentaries (n)
1 (n) A documentary is a film, or radio or T.V. programme which is about real events or people rather than imaginary ones.
2 (adj) Documentary evidence is written proof of something.

dodge dodges dodging dodged
1 (vb) You dodge to get out of the way of something or someone that could hit you or harm you.
2 (vb) If you dodge something, you avoid doing something you don't want to do.
3 (n) A dodge is a trick to get something you want or to avoid doing something you don't want to do.

dodgem dodgems (n) Dodgems are the electric cars at fairgrounds which you deliberately bump into other cars.

dodo dodos (n) The dodo was a flightless bird which lived on the island of Mauritius. It is now extinct, hence the expression 'dead as a dodo'.

doe does (n) A doe is a female deer.

dog dogs
1 (n) A dog is a common, four-legged animal which can be kept as a pet or as a working animal.
2 If you say someone has a dog's life, you mean it is an unpleasant and miserable one.
3 If you treat someone like a dog, you treat them badly.

dog-eared (adj) If a book is dog-eared, the corners of the pages are curled up or bent over.

dogmatic (adj) A dogmatic person refuses to believe that they could be wrong in their opinions.

dogsbody dogsbodies (n) A dogsbody is a person who is given all the odd jobs that nobody else wants to do.

dole doles doling doled
1 (vb) If you dole out food or money, you share it out between people.
2 (n) The dole is an everyday word for payments to unemployed people in the U.K.

dollar dollars (n) A dollar is a unit of money in the U.S.A., Canada, Hong Kong, etc.

dolphin dolphins (n) A dolphin is a large, intelligent sea mammal like a fish with a pointed mouth.

dome domes (n) A dome is a rounded roof on buildings.

domestic
1 (adj) If you enjoy domestic activities, you like your home and family life.
2 (adj) A domestic animal is tame, not wild.

dominate dominates dominating dominated
1 (vb) If you dominate a person or a group, you show that you have influence over them in some way. **domineering** (adj)
2 (vb) If a building dominates an area, it is bigger or taller than any other.

domino dominoes (n) A domino is a small rectangular piece of wood or plastic with sets of spots or blanks on each end, and is used to play a game called dominoes.

donate donates donating donated (vb) If you donate something to a charity, you give it as a gift. **donation** (n)

donkey donkeys (n) A donkey is an animal like a horse, but smaller with long ears.

donor donors (n) A donor is a person who gives something to someone else. *After the accident many more blood donors were needed.*

doodle doodles doodling doodled (vb) If you doodle, you draw little patterns as you think.

dormant (adj) If something is dormant, it is not active, but may be at a later date. *Dormant volcano ... dormant plant.*

dormitory dormitories (n) A dormitory is a large room with many beds in it usually found in youth hostels or boarding schools.

dormouse dormice (n) A dormouse is a small, long-tailed mouse found in Europe.

dorsal (adj) means relating to the back of a fish or an animal. *Fish have a dorsal fin.*

dose doses (n) A dose is a measure of medicine.

double doubles doubling doubled
1 (vb) If you double something, you make it twice as much, or twice as big.
2 (vb) If someone is doubled up, they are bent over.
3 (n) Your double is someone who looks exactly like you.

double bass (n) A double bass is a very large, stringed instrument.

double-glazing (n) is an extra layer of glass fitted to windows, which makes a house or building warmer and quieter.

doubt doubts doubting doubted
1 (vb) If you doubt something, you are not sure whether it's true.
2 (n) A doubt is a feeling of uncertainty about something.

dough (n) is the uncooked mixture of flour and water, and sometimes fat and yeast, which is baked into bread, pastry, etc.

doughnut doughnuts (n) A doughnut is a cake made by frying pieces of dough in deep fat.

downcast (adj) If you are downcast you feel sad and without hope.

downfall (n) Someone's downfall is the thing that causes their ruin or failure. *Laziness was his downfall.*

downhearted (adj) Someone who is downhearted feels sad and dejected.

Downing Street The Prime Minister of Great Britain lives at 10, Downing Street, in London.

downpour downpours (n) A downpour is a very heavy shower of rain.

downwind (adv) If a person or an animal is downwind of something, the smell of it is brought to them on the wind.

dowry dowries (n) A dowry is the gift of money or goods that, in some cultures, a woman's father gives to the man she marries. *Part of Ajeet's dowry was a carved, golden box.*

doze dozes dozing dozed (vb) When someone dozes, they go into a short, light sleep.

dozen dozens
1 (n) A dozen is twelve of something.
2 (n) Dozens can mean several or many. *I've told you dozens of times to tidy up.*

drab

drab (adj) things are unattractive.

drag drags dragging dragged
1 (vb) If you drag something, you pull it along the ground with difficulty.
2 (vb) If time drags, it passes slowly.
3 (n) Someone or something that is a drag is boring.

dragon dragons (n) A dragon is a monstrous creature in children's stories and legends. It has large wings and claws, and breathes fire.

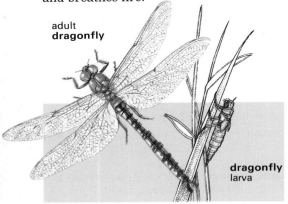

adult
dragonfly

dragonfly
larva

insect
p149 **dragonfly** dragonflies (n) A dragonfly is a highly-coloured insect with a long body and two pairs of wings.

drain drains draining drained
1 (vb) If you drain something containing liquid, for example, a glass or a pond, you empty it.
2 (n) A drain is a a sewer or a ditch that takes liquid away from a place.

Drake, Sir Francis (1540–1596) was the first Englishman to sail round the world, and led a section of the English fleet to defeat the Spanish Armada in 1588.

drama dramas
1 (n) A drama is a play for the television, radio or stage.
2 (n) Drama describes anything connected with the theatre. *Drama school . . . drama workshop.*
3 (n) A drama can be anything exciting. *There was a great drama over who should be in the school netball team.*

drastic
1 (adj) If you make a drastic change to something, you change it very noticeably. *The red hair dye made a drastic change to his appearance.* **drastically** (adv)
2 (adj) Drastic action is forceful and usually done quickly to prevent a disaster.

draught draughts
1 (n) A draught is the cold current of air coming into an area through cracks.
2 (n) Draughts is a board game for two players using twenty-four pieces.
3 (n) A draught is a round piece used by players in the game of draughts.
4 (adj) Draught beer comes from a barrel, not bottles.

draw draws drawing drew drawn
1 (vb) If you draw, you use a pencil, pen, etc to make a picture.
2 (vb) When you draw water from a well, you take it using a bucket.
3 (vb) If you draw in a game, you finish in the same position as your opponent.
4 (vb) If you draw a gun or knife, for example, you take it out to use.
5 (vb) If you are drawn to another person, you are attracted to them.

drawback drawbacks (n) A drawback is a problem which upsets a plan.

drawbridge drawbridges (n) A drawbridge can be let down or pulled up over a moat.

castle p41

drawer drawers (n) A drawer is the compartment in a table or chest that slides in and out, where you can keep things.

dread dreads dreading dreaded (vb) If you dread something happening, you are afraid about it.

dreadful (adj) Something dreadful is very bad or unpleasant.

dreadlocks (n) is a hairstyle where hair is grown long and twisted into strands.

dream dreams dreaming dreamed dreamt (vb) If you dream, you imagine various pictures and ideas while you are asleep.

dredge dredges dredging dredged (vb) When you dredge a river, canal or harbour, you scrape mud or sand away from the bottom to make deeper water.

dregs (n) are the last drops of liquid left in a container.

drench drenches drenching drenched (vb) If you drench something you soak it in liquid.

dressing dressings
1 (n) A dressing is a bandage or a plaster to put on a wound.
2 (n) A dressing is a mixture of oils and spices which can be added to salads and other dishes to heighten the flavour.

dressing gown dressing gowns (n) A dressing gown is a long, warm garment usually worn over nightclothes.

dressmaker (n) A dressmaker is a person who makes women's clothes.

drew see draw.

dribble dribbles dribbling dribbled
1 (vb) If a person dribbles, saliva drops out of their mouth.
2 (vb) When you dribble a ball in sport, you move it along by tapping it with your foot or a stick, or by bouncing it with your hand.

dried see dry

drift drifts drifting drifted
1 (vb) If a boat drifts it is moved by the wind, sea or current with nobody in control.
2 (vb) If snow drifts, it is blown by the wind into deep piles.

3 (n) A drift is a heap of snow or something else that has built up because of the action of wind or water.
4 If you get the drift of an argument, you understand the main points.

driftwood (n) is wood which is washed up on the beach.

drill drills drilling drilled
1 (n) A drill is a tool used to bore holes.
2 (vb) If you drill holes in something, you use a tool to make them.
3 (vb) If you drill people, you train them to do a particular thing, usually by repetition.

drink drinks drinking drank drunk
1 (vb) If you drink, you swallow liquid.
2 (n) A drink is an amount of liquid which is suitable for drinking.
3 (n) A drunk is someone who has had too much alcohol to drink.
4 (adj) If someone is drunk, they have had too much alcohol to drink.

drip dry (n) Drip dry clothes dry without creases when they are hung out wet.

drive drives driving drove driven
1 (vb) If you drive a vehicle or an animal, you are in charge of it and control it.
2 (vb) If you drive somewhere, you travel there in a vehicle.
3 (n) A drive is a pathway that leads through a garden to a house or building.
4 (vb) If you drive something in, you hammer or push it into place.
5 (n) If you have drive, you have a strong desire to succeed.

drivel (n) is talk which is nonsense.

driver drivers (n) A driver is a person who controls and steers a vehicle of some sort, usually on a road.

driving licence (n) A driving licence shows that you have passed a driving test and are legally allowed to drive.

drizzle drizzles drizzling drizzled
1 (n) Drizzle is a light fall of rain.
2 (vb) If the weather drizzles, the rain comes down very lightly.

drone

drone drones droning droned
1 (n) A drone is a low monotonous noise.
2 (vb) If someone drones on and on, they talk for a long time in a boring way.
3 (n) A drone is a male bee.

droop droops drooping drooped (vb) If something droops, it hangs down without the strength to hold itself up.

drought droughts (n) A drought is a serious water shortage.

drove see drive

drown drowns drowning drowned (vb) If a person or animal drowns, they die because they have so much water in their lungs that they cannot breathe.

drowsy drowsier drowsiest (adj) If you feel drowsy, you feel sleepy.

drug drugs drugging drugged
1 (n) A drug is a chemical substance used to make medicines.
2 (n) Drugs can be illegal and dangerous substances which some people take to make them feel good for a short time.
3 (vb) If you drug someone, you give them a chemical which makes them fall asleep.

druid druids (n) A druid was one of the priests of a Celtic pre-Christian religion.

drum drums drumming drummed
1 (n) A drum is a musical instrument with a round frame and skin stretched across it. It is played with hands or sticks.
2 (vb) If you drum your fingers you make a regular beating noise on a hard surface.

drunk see drink

dry dries drying dried; drier driest
1 (vb) If you dry something, you remove moisture from it.
2 (adj) If the weather is dry, there is no rain.
3 (adj) If your mouth feels dry, you have no saliva in it.

dual (adj) If something is dual, it has two parts which are exactly the same. *The driving instructor was glad that he had dual controls on his car.*

dual carriageway dual carriageways
(n) A dual carriageway is a road with two lanes on each side and a piece of ground to separate them.

dub dubs dubbing dubbed (vb) If a film is dubbed, the original voices are not used and different voices in another language are put on the soundtrack instead.

dubious
1 (adj) If you are dubious about something, joining a club for example, you are doubtful whether you should or not.
2 (adj) If someone makes a dubious decision, it is not a good or a trustworthy one.

duchess duchesses (n) A duchess is the wife or widow of a duke.

due dues
1 (n) If you pay your dues, you pay regular sums of money to a club or organisation that you belong to.
2 (adj) If a bus is due at a particular time, it is expected to arrive then.
3 (adj) If your pocket money is due to you, it is owed to you.
4 (adv) If you walk due west or north, you walk exactly in that direction.

duel duels (n) A duel is an organised fight between two people with guns, swords, etc as weapons.

duet duets (n) A duet is a piece of music for two instruments or singers.

duffel-coat duffel-coats (n) A duffel coat is a loose-fitting, warm, hooded overcoat that fastens with toggles.

duke dukes (n) A duke is a nobleman of rank, just below the rank of prince.

dull duller dullest
1 (adj) Someone or something that is dull is not very interesting.
2 (adj) A dull colour or dull light is not very bright.
3 (adj) A dull pain is an ache, not a sharp pain.

dumb dumber dumbest
1 (adj) Someone who is dumb is unable to speak.
2 (adj) If you say that someone is dumb, you mean they are silly or stupid.

dumbfounded (adj) If you are dumbfounded, you are so shocked or surprised about something that you can't speak.

dummy dummies
1 (n) A dummy is a model of a human used for displaying clothing in shops.
2 (n) A dummy can be a model or a copy of anything. It looks real but it's a fake.
3 (n) A dummy is a teat you give to babies to suck so that they are comforted and don't cry.

dump dumps dumping dumped
1 (n) A dump is a place where rubbish is thrown away.
2 (vb) If you dump something, you take it to the rubbish dump and throw it away because you don't want it anymore.
3 (n) A dump is a very unattractive place.
4 (vb) If you dump things you throw them down carelessly.
5 (vb) If you dump computer data, you copy it from one kind of storage system to another.

dune dunes (n) A dune is a hill of dry sand near the sea or in the desert.

dung (n) is animal excrement or manure.

dungarees (n) Dungarees are trousers with a bib front and straps over the shoulder.

castle p41 **dungeon** dungeons (n) A dungeon is an underground prison.

duplicate duplicates duplicating duplicated
1 (vb) If you duplicate something, you make copies of it.
2 (n) A duplicate is an exact copy of something.
duplication (n)

durable (adj) things are very strong and last a long time.

duration (n) The duration is the time that something lasts.

during
1 (prep) During means all through a particular period of time. *During the war food was rationed.*
2 (prep) During can also mean at some point in a period of time. *She woke up during the night.*

dustbin dustbins (n) A dustbin is a container for rubbish usually kept outdoors.

duty duties
1 (n) Your duty is what you should do because it's part of your job or because it's expected of you.
2 (n) When doctors or firemen, for example, are on duty they are at work.
3 (n) Duty is a tax paid to the government for certain things you buy. *Dad had to pay duty on the extra wine we brought back from France.*

duvet duvets (n) A duvet is a bag filled with feathers or other material which you use as a bed cover.

dwarf dwarfs dwarfing dwarfed
1 (n) In fairy stories a dwarf is a very small man who sometimes digs underground for gold and precious stones.
2 (n) A dwarf is a person who has not grown to normal size.
3 (adj) Dwarf plants or animals are very small.
4 (vb) If one thing dwarfs another, it makes it look very small in comparison. *The huge oak dwarfed all the other trees.*

dwindle dwindles dwindling dwindled
(vb) If something dwindles it gradually gets smaller in size, weight or quantity.

dye dyes dying dyed
1 (vb) If you dye something, you change its colour by soaking it in a dying liquid.
2 (n) A dye is a substance which, when mixed with water, will change the colour of cloth, hair etc.

dyke dykes (n) A dyke is a barrier put up to stop a river, a lake or the sea from flooding low-lying land.

dynamic (adj) people are full of energy, life and ideas.

dynamite (n) is a very powerful explosive.

dynamo dynamos (n) A dynamo is a machine which produces electricity. Small ones are fitted to bicycles to provide light and large ones provide power for towns.

dynasty dynasties (n) A dynasty is a series of rulers who all belong to one family. It's sometimes used to mean family control of a business for many generations.

dyslexia (n) is a persistent difficulty in reading, spelling and writing.
dyslexic (adj)

Ee

each is every one of a group.

eager (adj) If you are eager, you are keen to do something. **eagerly** (adv)

eagle eagles (n) An eagle is a large bird of prey with a sharp, curved beak and keen eyesight.

ear ears (n) The ear is the organ used for hearing.

senses p264

early (adv) If you are early, you are in good time for something.

earn earns earning earned (vb) When you earn money, you work for it and deserve it.

earnest (adj) If you are earnest, you are very serious about things. **earnestly** (adv)

earth

solar system p278

1 (n) The earth is the planet we live on.
2 (n) Earth is another word for soil.

earthquake earthquakes (n) An earthquake is a violent shaking of part of the earth's crust.

earwig earwigs (n) An earwig is an insect with tail pincers.

easel easels (n) An easel is a stand for a painting or for a blackboard.

east (n) This is one of the points of the compass. The sun rises in the east.

Easter (n) is the Christian festival to remember the resurrection of Jesus Christ.

easy (adj) Things that are easy are not difficult. **easily** (adv)

eat eats eating ate eaten (vb) When you eat you chew and swallow food. **eater** (n)

eaves (n) The eaves are the edges of a roof which overhang the walls.

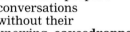

eaves

eavesdrop (n) If you eavesdrop, you listen in on other people's conversations without their knowing. **eavesdropper** (n)

ebb ebbs ebbing ebbed (vb) When the tide ebbs, it goes out.

ebony (n) is a hard, black wood.

eccentric (adj) If a person is eccentric, they behave in an odd way. **eccentricity** (n)

echo echoes echoing echoed
1 (n) An echo is a sound which bounces back so that you hear it again.
2 (vb) If a sound echoes, you hear it repeat again and again.

eclair eclairs (n) An eclair is a long, thin pastry filled with cream.

eclipse eclipses (n) An eclipse of the sun happens when the moon comes between the sun and the earth, blocking the sunlight. An eclipse of the moon happens when the earth comes between the sun and the moon.

ecology (n) is the study of the way in which all living things exist in relation to one another. **ecologist** (n)

economy (n) The economy is the way in which the industries, banks, businesses, etc of a country or region are organised to produce wealth. **economist** (n)

economical (adj) If you are economical, you are careful with your money. **economise** (vb)

ecstasy ecstasies (n) Ecstasy is a feeling of great happiness. **ecstatic** (adj)

edge edges edging edged
1 (n) The edge of a knife is the sharp, cutting side.
2 (vb) If you edge towards something, you move nearer slowly.

edible (adj) If something is edible, you are able to eat it.

edit edits editing edited
1 (vb) If you edit books or papers, you read them to correct or alter parts of them.
2 (vb) Someone who edits a newspaper or magazine is in charge of it. **editor** (n)

edition editions (n) An edition of a book or newspaper is one or all the copies printed at any one time.

educate educates educating educated (vb) If you educate someone, you teach them in a school, college, or university, so that they learn about many things.
education (n)

eel eels (n) An eel is a long, thin fish.

eerie eerier eeriest (adj) If a place is eerie, it is mysterious, and makes you nervous.

effect effects (n) An effect is the change in something or someone that is caused by someone or something else. *When his cat died, the effect on the boy was very noticeable.*

efficient (adj) If you are efficient, you do things in a well-organised way.
efficiently (adv) **efficiency** (n)

effort efforts
1 (n) When someone makes an effort they try hard, physically or mentally.
2 (n) If something is an effort, it is difficult to do.

egg eggs (n) An egg is an oval or round object containing a baby bird or reptile which hatches by breaking the shell.

Eid-ul-Fitr or **Id-al-Fitr** (n) is the festival when Muslims give thanks and celebrate at the end of Ramadan.

Einstein, Albert (1879–1955) was an important mathematician and scientist whose theories enriched our knowledge of the way the universe works.

eisteddfod eisteddfods (n) An eisteddfod is a Welsh arts festival with competitions for singing, dancing, poetry, etc.

either
1 (conj) If you have two or more things to choose between, you put either before the first of them. *You can have either cheese, ham, or peanut butter on your sandwiches.*

2 (adv) Either shows that you and another person are in the same position. *I cannot play the piano either.*

eject ejects ejecting ejected (vb) If you eject something or someone, you push them out of something with force. **ejection** (n)

elaborate
1 (adj) If you do something in an elaborate way, you do it in great detail.
2 (adj) Something elaborate is richly decorated. **elaboration** (n)
elaborately (adv)

elapse elapses elapsing elapsed (vb) When time elapses, it goes by. *Two weeks elapsed before I saw my uncle again.*

elastic (n) is a material that stretches when you pull it and then goes back to its original size when you let go.

elated (adj) When someone is elated they are very happy and excited. **elation** (n)

elbow elbows (n) The elbow is the joint which connects the upper and lower arm.

elderly (adj) refers to a person or people who are old.

eldest (adj) The eldest person in a group is the oldest.

elect elects electing elected
1 (vb) When people elect someone, they choose them as their representative, for example in parliament or on a committee. **election** (n)
2 (vb) If you elect to do something, you choose to do it. *She elected to do science rather than art.*

electrician electricians (n) An electrician is a person whose job is to install and repair electrical equipment.

electricity (n) is a form of energy used for heating, lighting and working machinery. It is generated in power stations and can be produced by batteries. **electric** (adj)

electrocute electrocutes electrocuting electrocuted (vb) If you electrocute yourself, you are accidentally killed or badly injured because you have touched a strong electric current. **electrocution** (n)

electronic

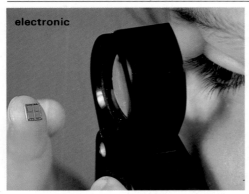

electronic

a silicon chip being viewed through a magnifying glass

electronic electronics
1 (n) Electronics is the technology which uses transistors, silicon chips, etc. to produce radios, computers, etc.
2 (adj) An electronic device is one which is powered by electricity passing through silicon chips, transistors, etc.

elegant (adj) means very smart and pleasing. **elegance** (n)

element elements
1 (n) In chemistry an element is something made up of only one type of atom. *Oxygen and carbon are elements.*
2 (n) The elements can refer to the weather especially when it is bad. *We were protected from the elements by a good roof.*
3 (n) The element is the part of an electric kettle or heater that changes the electric current into heat.

elephant elephants (n) An elephant is a very large animal found in Africa or India. It has a long, flexible nose called a trunk. The adult elephant has large, ivory tusks at either side of its mouth.

elf elves (n) An elf is a tiny, mischievous creature in fairy stories.

eligible (adj) Someone who is eligible for something is qualified to do it or receive it. *Students are eligible for cheap rail fares.* **eligibility** (n)

eliminate eliminates eliminating eliminated (vb) If you eliminate something, you get rid of it. *The new head teacher quickly eliminated bullying.* **elimination** (n)

elite (n) The elite of a community are those who are richer, more powerful or more influential than anyone else.

Elizabethan (adj) Someone or something Elizabethan lived or was made in the reign of Queen Elizabeth I, who ruled from 1558–1603.

elk elks (n) An elk is a large deer that lives in North America and parts of Northern Europe.

ellipse

ellipse (n) An ellipse is an oval shape.

elm elms (n) An elm is a tree with a rough bark, which produces heavy, hard wood.

else
1 (adj) If someone else does something, it is another person that does it.
2 (adj) If you know something else about a thing, you know more about it.
3 If you say 'or else' you suggest that you will punish someone if they do not do as you wish. *Do what I say, or else!*

elsewhere (adv) If you do something elsewhere, you do it in another place.

elusive (adj) People or things that are elusive are hard to find.

embankment embankments (n) An embankment is a wide wall of earth which stops river water overflowing, or which carries a road or railway over low ground.

embark embarks embarking embarked
1 (vb) If you embark on a ship, you get on board a ship. **embarkation** (n)
2 (vb) If you embark on an activity, you start something new and possibly difficult. *He embarked on a career as an actor after leaving school.*

embarrass embarrasses embarrassing **embarrassed** (vb) If you embarrass someone, you make them feel anxious or shy. **embarrassment** (n)

embassy embassies (n) An embassy is the group of officials of a particular government that live and work in a foreign country, and look after their country's business there.

emblem emblems (n) An emblem is a badge or a symbol which represents a country, a group of people, a sport, a club or a society.

embroider embroiders embroidering **embroidered** (vb) If you embroider, you sew a design onto fabric. **embroidery** (n)

embryo embryos
1 (n) An embryo is the name given to the early stages of the development of an unborn baby person or animal.
2 If a plan is in embryo, it is at a very early stage of development.

emerald emeralds
1 (n) An emerald is a bright green, precious stone.
2 (adj) Emerald is a bright green colour.

emerge emerges emerging emerged
1 (vb) If you emerge from somewhere, you come out from it. *The potholers emerged from the cave.*
2 (vb) If you emerge from a difficult experience, you come to the end of it.

emergency emergencies
1 (n) An emergency is a sudden and dangerous situation that needs prompt action.
2 (adj) Emergency services or supplies are organisations and goods sent to help those in an emergency.

emigrate emigrates emigrating **emigrated** (vb) If someone emigrates, they leave their own country, and go to live in another one. **emigrant** (n) **emigration** (n)

eminent (adj) An eminent person is one who is very important in their own subject field. *An eminent scientist . . . an eminent judge.* **eminence** (n)

emir emirs (n) An emir rules over a Muslim country called an emirate.

emit emits emitting emitted (vb) Something emits sound, heat, light or smell, if it produces it or lets it out. *The old car emitted a wheeze.* **emission** (n)

emotion emotions (n) Emotion refers to the feelings of happiness, sadness, anger, love, etc. which you feel at different times. **emotional** (adj) **emotionally** (adv)

emperor emperors (n) An emperor is a person who rules over an empire. **empress** (fem. n)

emphasise emphasises emphasising **emphasised** (vb) If you emphasise something you make it look or sound more important than the things around it. *He emphasised the word by underlining it in red.* **emphasis** (n)

empire empires (n) An empire is a group of countries which are conquered and ruled by another country.

employ employs employing employed (vb) If you employ someone, you pay them to work for you. **employer** (n) **employment** (n)

employee employees (n) An employee is a person who works for a someone else.

empty empties emptying emptied; emptier emptiest.
1(vb) If you empty something, you take all the contents out of it.
2 (adj) If something is empty, it has nothing inside it.
3 (adj) An empty threat or promise is one which cannot be carried out or kept.

emu emus (n) An emu is a large, flightless bird which lives in Australia.

emulsion emulsions
1 (n) Emulsion is a type of paint.
2 (n) Emulsion is also a chemical used in photography to make film sensitive to light.

enable enables enabling enabled (vb) Something which enables you to do something allows you to do it.

enchanted

enchanted (adj) If someone in a fairy story is enchanted, they are put under a spell. **enchantment** (n)

enclose encloses enclosing enclosed
1 (vb) If you enclose something in a letter or parcel, you put it in with the thing being sent.
2 (vb) If you enclose a space, you put up a barrier to separate it from another area. **enclosure** (n)

encore encores (n) An encore is an extra item by a performer at the end of his or her act.

encounter encounters encountering encountered
1 (vb) If you encounter someone or something, you meet them.
2 (n) An encounter is a meeting with someone or something.

encourage encourages encouraging encouraged (vb) If you encourage someone, you praise them to make them carry on trying hard at something. **encouragement** (n)

encyclopaedia encyclopaedias (n) An encyclopaedia is a reference book containing information in alphabetical order about a wide variety of subjects.

endanger endangers endangering endangered (vb) If you endanger something, you put it in a dangerous situation where it might be damaged.

endeavour endeavours endeavouring endeavoured
1 (vb) If you endeavour to do something, you try hard to do it.
2 (n) An endeavour is a scheme or plan which will take time or effort to achieve.

endorse endorses endorsing endorsed
1 (vb) If your driving licence is endorsed, it is stamped to show you have committed a driving offence. **endorsement** (n)
2 (vb) If you endorse someone or something, you say publicly that you approve of them.

enemy enemies
1 (n) If someone is your enemy, they totally oppose you, and may even wish to harm you.
2 (n) In a war the enemy is the force or country you are fighting against.

energy
1 (n) Energy is the strength you have to do physical activities. **energetic** (adj)
2 (n) Energy is the power from various sources such as coal or electricity which makes other things work.

enforce enforces enforcing enforced
(vb) If you enforce a rule, you ensure that it is obeyed. **enforcement** (n)

engage engages engaging engaged
1 (vb) If you engage someone to do something, you agree to pay them to do it.
2 (vb) If you engage in a particular activity, you take part in it.
3 (adj) If two people are engaged, they have decided to get married. **engagement** (n)
4 (adj) If a telephone number is engaged, the people whom you rang are already speaking on the 'phone.

engine engines
1 (n) An engine is the machine that makes a car, aeroplane, ship, etc. move.
2 (n) An engine is that part of a train which pulls the carriages.

engineer engineers engineering engineered
1 (n) An engineer is a person who has studied how to plan and build machines, buildings, roads, etc.
2 (vb) If you engineer something, you plan and scheme to make it happen.

engrave engraves engraving engraved
1 (vb) If you engrave something, you cut a pattern or words into the surface.
2 (n) An engraving is a picture made by cutting lines into a piece of metal called a plate and printing from it.

engross engrosses engrossing engrossed
1 (adj) If you are engrossed in something, you are concentrating only on that thing.
2 (vb) If you engross someone, you fascinate them with what you have to say.

enjoy enjoys enjoying enjoyed (vb) If you enjoy doing something, you like doing it. **enjoyment** (n)

enlarge enlarges enlarging enlarged
(vb) If you enlarge something, you make it bigger. **enlargement** (n)

enlist enlists enlisting enlisted
1 (vb) If a person enlists, they join the armed forces.
2 (vb) If you enlist a person's help, you ask them to help.

enormous (adj) means extremely large.

enough (n) If you have enough of something, you have just the right amount of it. *There was enough money left to buy a ticket home.*

enquire enquires enquiring enquired
1 (vb) If you enquire about something you ask for information about it. **enquiry** (n)
2 (adj) Someone with an enquiring mind seeks information and is keen to learn new things.

enrich enriches enriching enriched (vb) If you enrich something you improve the quality and make it better in some way. **enrichment** (n)

enrol enrols enrolling enrolled (vb) If you enrol or are enrolled for something you put your name on a list to take lessons, or to join something. **enrolment** (n)

ensure ensures ensuring ensured (vb) If you ensure that something happens you make certain that it does happen. *He ensured his privacy by living behind high walls.*

enter enters entering entered
1 (vb) If you enter a place you go in.
2 (vb) If you enter a race, competition or exam, you take part in it.
3 (vb) If you enter something in a book or diary, you write it down in the book.

enterprise enterprises
1 (n) An enterprise is something new and exciting you try to do. **enterprising** (adj)
2 (n) An enterprise is a large business or company.

entertain entertains entertaining entertained
1 (vb) If you entertain someone you do something to interest and amuse them.
2 (vb) If you entertain you invite people to your house for a meal or to visit. **entertainment** (n)

enthusiastic (adj) If you are enthusiastic about something, you are excited and eager when you talk about it or do it. **enthusiasm** (n)

entrance entrances
1 (n) An entrance is a way in.
2 (n) An entrance is the place and the manner in which an actor comes onto the stage.

entrant entrants (n) An entrant is someone who enters a race, competition, or exam.

entrepreneur entrepreneurs (n) An entrepreneur is a person who is always looking for new ways to make profitable business deals.

entry entries
1 (n) An entry is a way into a place.
2 (n) An entry is a short note put into a diary, computer, etc.
3 (n) An entry in a dictionary or encyclopaedia is information about a word or a subject.

envelop envelops enveloping enveloped (vb) If you envelop someone or something, you cover them completely. *The coat was so big that it enveloped Darren.*

envelope envelopes (n) An envelope is the paper cover that letters are put into before being posted.

environment environments
1 (n) Your environment is the area, people and events that influence your life.
2 (n) The environment is the natural world: all the land, sea, plants and animals that live in the world. **environmental** (adj)

envy envies envying envied (vb) If you envy someone you long to have what they have, or to be like them. **envious** (adj) **enviously** (adv)

enzyme enzymes (n) This is a word used in biology for a substance found in living creatures that can change other things without being changed itself. *The stomach contains enzymes to break down food.*

e

epidemic

epidemic epidemics (n) An epidemic is a large number of cases of an infectious disease. *An epidemic of 'flu broke out.*

epilepsy (n) is a disease that may cause a person to lose consciousness and have convulsions. **epileptic** (adj)

episode episodes (n) An episode is one part of a book or play that is serialised. *Did you see the last episode of the thriller?*

equal (adj) Things that are equal are of the same size, quantity or value.

equator (n) The equator is an imaginary line making a circle around the middle of the earth. The North and South Poles are the same distance from it. **equatorial** (adj)

equestrian (adj) things are to do with riding horses.

equinox equinoxes (n) The equinox is one of the two days in the year when day and night are the same length.

equip equips equipping equipped (vb) If you equip yourself, you collect all the tools you need. **equipment** (n)

erratic (adj) Something erratic happens without any predictable pattern. *Erratic rainfall... erratic behaviour.*

error errors (n) An error is a mistake.

erupt erupts erupting erupted
1 (vb) When a volcano erupts, it throws out molten lava and rocks. **eruption** (n)
2 (vb) If a fight erupts, it breaks out.
3 (vb) If someone erupts, they become angry suddenly.

escalator escalators (n) Escalators are moving stairways which carry people from one place to another.

escape escapes escaping escaped
1 (vb) If you escape, you break free and run away from someone or from somewhere.
2 (vb) If something escapes your attention, you do not notice it.
3 (n) If you plan an escape, you decide how to get away from someone or somewhere.

4 (n) If you enjoy something as an escape you like it because you forget about other, less pleasant things.

escort escorts escorting escorted
1 (vb) If you escort someone, you accompany them.
2 (n) An escort is a person who guides or protects you when you go somewhere.

especially (adv) This is a word used to stress the importance of something or someone. *He was especially pleased to pass his exam.*

espionage (n) is the activity of finding out the secrets of other countries by spying.

essay essays (n) An essay is a short piece of writing on a certain subject.

essential
1 (adj) If something is essential, it is necessary.
2 (n) The essentials of a situation or argument are the main points.

establish establishes establishing established
1 (vb) If you establish something, you set it up and get it going. *I established the new laboratory at Henley.*
2 (vb) If you establish a fact you confirm that it is definitely correct.
3 (vb) If you establish a reputation for something, you prove to other people that you are good at it. *He established a reputation for his fine woodwork.*

estate estates
1 (n) An estate is an area of land attached to one particular house or owner.
2 (n) An area of land used for one purpose is an estate. *Factory estate... trading estate... housing estate.*
3 (n) A person's estate is the money and property that they leave when they die.

estate agent estate agents (n) An estate agent is in business to enable people to buy and sell their houses.

estimate estimates estimating estimated
1 (vb) If you estimate something like cost, size or distance, you work it out roughly without taking careful measurements. **estimation** (n)

2 (n) An estimate is a rough calculation of cost, distance, time, etc. *We got an estimate from a builder to put up the garage.*

estuary estuaries (n) An estuary is the mouth of a river, where it joins the sea.

eternal (adj) Something which is eternal lasts for ever. **eternally** (adv)

ethnic (adj) Something which is ethnic is connected with a particular racial group, especially a minority group.

euthanasia (n) is the killing of animals or people to save them from suffering through painful and incurable illnesses. It is illegal to practise it on human beings in Britain.

evacuate evacuates evacuating evacuated (vb) If you evacuate an area, you move all the people away because of some danger. *We were evacuated to the country in case London was bombed.* **evacuation** (n)

evaluate evaluates evaluating evaluated (vb) If you evaluate someone or something you judge carefully how good they are or what they are worth. **evaluation** (n)

evaporate evaporates evaporating evaporated (vb) If a liquid evaporates, it changes from a liquid to a vapour, and seems to vanish. **evaporation** (n)

even evens evening evened
1 (adj) If a surface is even it is smooth.
2 (adj) An even number is one that can be divided by two and leave no remainder.
3 (adv) Even can be used to compare things or states. *I am even worse off than I was before.*
4 (adj) If a person is even-tempered they are calm and not very excitable.
5 You can even things out, debts for example, by spreading out the payments regularly. **evenly** (adv)

evening evenings (n) Evening is the period between afternoon and nightfall.

event events (n) An event is an occurrence or happening. *On my way here I saw a most unusual event.*

evergreen evergreens (n) An evergreen plant is one which does not lose its leaves during winter.

tree p313

every (adj) means all the objects or people in a group. **everybody** (n) **everyone** (n) **everything** (n)

everyday (adj) Everyday items or events are common ones. *We were shopping for everyday things such as soap and bread.*

everywhere (n) This means in many or most places. *I've looked everywhere for my keys but I can't find them.*

evict evicts evicting evicted (vb) If you evict someone, you force them to leave their home. **eviction** (n)

evidence
1 (n) If you give evidence in court, you tell the facts as you know them to help the court find out the truth.
2 (n) Anything which proves that something is correct, or makes matters clearer, is evidence.

evident (adj) If something is evident, it can be seen easily. *From her smile, it was evident that she was delighted with her new bike.*

evil
1 (n) Evil is the strong force which many people believe works against good.
2 (adj) If someone or something is evil they are wicked or cruel.

evolve evolves evolving evolved (vb) If an animal evolves it changes gradually into another form. *Human beings are believed to have evolved from ape-like creatures.*

evolution (n) is the gradual process whereby an animal or plant changes its form over thousands or millions of years.

ewe ewes (n) A ewe is a female sheep.

exact
1 (adj) If something is exact, it is very accurately measured or made. **exactly** (adj)
2 (adj) An exact person is very careful about details.

exaggerate exaggerates exaggerating exaggerated (vb) If a person exaggerates, they add a great deal to the facts of a story, to make it seem better or more important. **exaggeration** (n)

examine

examine examines examining examined
1 (vb) If you examine something you look at it very closely.
2 (vb) If a doctor examines you, he checks carefully to find out if you are well.
examination (n) **examiner** (n)

example examples
1 (n) If you give an example, you choose something which makes your meaning clearer. *This house is an example of a brick building.*
2 (n) If someone is an example to others their way of life is seen as a good one to follow.
3 (n) If you make an example of someone you punish them so that others will not behave in the same way.

excavate excavates excavating excavated (vb) If you excavate you dig in the ground, either to put up a building, or to uncover remains. **excavator** (n) **excavation** (n)

exceed exceeds exceeding exceeded
1 (vb) If one number exceeds another, it is greater. *78 exceeds 68 by 10.*
2 (vb) If you exceed the speed limit, you drive faster than the law allows.

excel excels excelling excelled (vb) If you excel at something you do it very well.

excellent (adj) If a thing is excellent it is very good indeed. **excellence** (n)

except (prep or conj) You say except when you want to leave out one thing or certain things when you are talking about a group. *We went to all the places that you mentioned except Harlech Castle.*

excerpt excerpts (n) An excerpt is a short piece of writing or music, etc. which is taken from a longer piece.

excess excesses (n) An excess is too much of something. **excessive** (adj) **excessively** (adv)

exchange exchanges exchanging exchanged
1 (vb) If you exchange something you give it to someone and get something in return.
2 (vb) If you exchange addresses with someone, you give them yours in return for theirs.

Exchequer (n) The Exchequer is the part of the government in Britain that deals with the country's money.

excite excites exciting excited (vb) If someone or something excites you, it makes you happy and nervous at the same time. **excitable** (adj) **excitement** (n)

exclaim exclaims exclaiming exclaimed (vb) If you exclaim you speak in a loud and excited way. *"Fancy meeting you here!"* he exclaimed. **exclamation** (n)

exclamation mark (n) An exclamation mark (!) is used to show that a speaker is shocked, surprised or upset. *"That was awful!" said the boy as he got off the ghost train.*

exclude excludes excluding excluded
1 (vb) If you exclude someone, you do not allow them to take part in an activity.
2 (vb) If you exclude something, you do not put it in. **exclusion** (n)

exclusive
1 (adj) Something that is exclusive is only available to a few people.
2 (adj) An exclusive is a news story which is only reported by one paper.

excrement (n) is solid waste matter passed out of the bowels of humans and animals.

excursion excursions (n) An excursion is an organised trip of some kind.

excuse excuses excusing excused
1 (vb) If you excuse yourself from doing something, you ask not to do it.
2 (vb) If you excuse a person's bad behaviour, you find reasons for them to have behaved in this way. *Please excuse his bad language as he is very upset.*
3 (n) An excuse is a reason you give to explain why you have done or not done something which is wrong.

execute executes executing executed
1 (vb) If a person is executed they are killed by the state for crimes they have committed. **execution** (n)
2 (vb) If you execute an order, you carry it out.

executive executives (n) An executive is a man or a woman who works at a senior level in a company.

exempt exempts exempting exempted
1 (vb) If you exempt someone from something, you say officially that they do not have to do it.
2 (adj) If you are exempt from something you are excused from doing it. *She was exempt from paying taxes.* **exemption** (n)

exercise exercises exercising exercised
1 (vb) If you exercise your body you play sports, jog, etc. in order to keep fit and healthy.
2 (vb) If you exercise power or control over something, you use your authority to do something. *He exercised his authority to stop the plane and have it searched.*
3 (vb) If something exercises your mind you have to think a lot about it.
4 (n) Exercises are physical movements you do in order to stay fit.

exert exerts exerting exerted
1 (vb) If you exert yourself, you make a great deal of effort to do something.
2 (vb) If you exert your influence or power, you use them to change events. *She exerted her influence to get the best seats.* **exertion** (n)

exhaust exhausts exhausting exhausted
1 (vb) If you exhaust something such as supplies, energy, etc. you use it all up.
2 (adj) If you are exhausted, you have no energy left. **exhaustion** (n)
3 (n) The exhaust of a vehicle is both the waste gas which is blown out, and the pipe from the engine along which the gas travels.

exhibit exhibits exhibiting exhibited
1 (vb) If you exhibit something you put it on show to the public.
2 (vb) If you exhibit certain feelings or qualities you show that you have them. *He was exhibiting signs of fear and anger.*
3 (n) An exhibit is something that is put on public show. **exhibition** (n)

exhilarate exhilarates exhilarating exhilarated
1 (vb) Something that exhilarates you makes you feel very excited.
2 (adj) Anything which you find exhilarating makes you feel excited and thrilled. **exhilaration** (n)

exile exiles (n) An exile is a person who is forced to live outside their own country.

exist exists existing existed
1 (vb) Anything that exists is alive, real or has a form which you can understand.
2 (vb) If you just exist, you live on a very low income or have just enough food to keep you alive. **existence** (n)

exit exits
1 (n) An exit is the way out of a public place.
2 (n) If you make an exit you leave a place in a dramatic way.
3 (n) A motorway exit is the place where traffic can leave the motorway.

exotic (adj) Something is exotic if it is unusual and interesting because it comes from another country.

expand expands expanding expanded
1 (vb) If something expands it becomes larger in size or amount. *My waistline is expanding and my clothes don't fit me.*
2 (vb) If a business expands it becomes bigger and more successful. **expansion** (n)

expanse (n) An expanse is a large area of something such as the sky, grass, etc.

expect expects expecting expected
1 (vb) If you expect something you believe it will happen. **expectation** (n)
2 (vb) If you expect someone to do something you believe they should do it. *We all expected Jonie to win her race.*
3 (vb) If a woman is expecting, she is going to have a baby. **expectant** (adj)

expedition expeditions
1 (n) An expedition is an organised journey to explore or climb mountains, etc.
2 (n) An expedition can also be a short trip or outing.

expel expels expelling expelled (vb) If you expel someone from a place, you force them to leave usually because of their bad behaviour. **expulsion** (n)

expense expenses
1 (n) The expense involved in something is the amount it costs you. *Was your American holiday worth the expense?* **expensive** (adj)
2 (n) If you do something at someone else's expense, they have to pay for it. *I visited Paris at my grandmother's expense.*
3 (n) The same expression can be used when you do something which harms others.

experience

experience experiences experiencing experienced
1 (n) Experience is knowledge and skill gained over a long time.
2 (n) An experience is something that happens to you or that you do. *Seeing the accident was a very upsetting experience.*
3 (vb) If you experience something, it happens to you. *I experienced a sharp pain in my back.*

experiment experiments experimenting experimented
1 (vb) If a scientist experiments, he does tests in order to find out information, or to test a theory.
2 (n) An experiment is a scientific test done to test new ideas.
3 (vb) If you experiment, you try something new. **experimental** (adj)
experimentally (adv)

expert experts (n) An expert is a person who is very skilled at something.
expertise (n)

expire expires expiring expired
1 (vb) If a document expires, its time has run out and you can no longer use it.
expiry (n)
2 (vb) If a person or animal expires, they die.

explain explains explaining explained
1 (vb) If you explain something to somebody you tell them how to do it or what it means.
2 (vb) If you explain, you give reasons why something has happened or will happen.
explanation (n)

explode explodes exploding exploded
1 (vb) If something explodes it bursts with a loud bang, often causing injury and damage. **explosion** (n)
2 (vb) If someone explodes with anger they show their feelings in a sudden or violent way. **explosive** (adj) **explosively** (adv)
3 (vb) If you explode an idea, you show it to be utterly wrong.

exploit exploits exploiting exploited
1 (vb) If you exploit something, you use it to your advantage. *The people were upset because the man exploited his power and closed the shopping centre to build a car park.*

2 (adj) People who are exploited are treated very unfairly, and get very little reward for their ideas or work.
3 (n) An exploit is something adventurous, brave or amusing that someone has done.

explore explores exploring explored
1 (vb) If you explore a place or a country you go there to travel about and find out about it.
2 (vb) If you explore an idea, you think about it or discuss it with others.
exploration (n)

export exports exporting exported
1 (n) Exports are goods which are sent for sale abroad.
2 (vb) If you export something, you send it for sale in a foreign country.

expose exposes exposing exposed
1 (vb) If you expose something, you uncover it so that it can be seen. **exposure** (n)
2 (vb) If you expose a criminal, you make the truth known about them.

express expresses expressing expressed
1 (vb) If you express a point of view, you talk about it or write it down.
2 (adj) Express describes a service which is very fast. *Express cleaning ... express mail.*

expression expressions
1 (n) Your expression is the look on your face.
2 (n) An expression is a certain way of saying things. *She was always using slang expressions.*

exquisite (adj) Something exquisite is particularly delicate and beautiful.

extend extends extending extended
1 (vb) If you extend something you make it bigger or longer. **extension** (n)
2 (vb) If certain rules extend to several groups of people, they include all of these groups.
3 (vb) If a job extends you, it makes you work hard, using all your skills.

extensive (adj) Something extensive covers a wide area.

extent extents (n) The extent of something is its length or the area it covers.

exterior exteriors (n) The exterior of anything is its outside.

exterminate exterminates
exterminating exterminated (vb) When
people exterminate other people or
animals, they kill them ruthlessly in large
numbers. **extermination** (n)

external (adj) This describes anything
outside a person or a place. *The external
features of the house were damaged by the
storm.*

extinct (adj) If a species of an animal or
plant is extinct, it has died out or been
destroyed and there are none left alive.
extinction (n)

extinguish extinguishes extinguishing
extinguished (vb) If you extinguish
something that is alight or on fire, you put
it out.

extra (adj) describes something which is in
addition or more than usual. *Extra
children... extra food... extra money.*

extract extracts extracting extracted
1 (vb) If a person or animal extracts
something, they pull it out forcefully.
2 (vb) If you extract ideas from a book, you
select those that suit your needs.
3 (n) An extract is part of a piece of music,
writing, etc. that is taken out for some
purpose.

extraordinary (adj) People or things that
are extraordinary have unusual and
striking qualities. **extraordinarily** (adv)

extravagant (adj) People who are
extravagant spend their money very freely.
extravagance (n)

extreme extremes (adj) Something that is
extreme is far away from the normal.
Extreme cold... extreme behaviour.

extrovert extroverts (n) An extrovert is a
person who is outgoing and who likes being
with other people.

exuberant (adj) people are high-spirited.

eye eyes (n) The eye is an organ that living
creatures see with. see p264

eyewitness eyewitnesses (n) An
eyewitness is someone who has seen
something happen and can describe it.

eyrie eyries (n) An eyrie is the nest of an
eagle or other bird of prey.

fabric fabrics (n) Fabric is cloth woven
from materials such as cotton, wool, etc.

fabulous
1 (adj) If you say something is fabulous you
think it is marvellous.
2 (adj) Fabulous creatures, people or places
are those that occur in fables, legends and
fairy tales. **fable** (n)

face faces facing faced
1 (n) A face is the front part of a head.
2 (vb) If a person or animal faces you they
are looking at you.
3 (vb) If something faces in a certain
direction its front is pointing that way. *Our
house faces North.*
4 If you face up to problems you deal with
them and don't run away.

facetious (adj) people try to be funny by
making rather silly remarks.

fact facts (n) A fact is something that can
be proved to be true. **factual** (adj)

factory factories
(n) A factory is a
building or several
buildings where
goods are made in
large quantities,
usually with the use
of machines.

Fahrenheit (n) is a
temperature scale
which has the
freezing point for
water at 32° and the
boiling point at 212°.

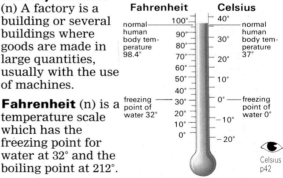

temperature

Celsius
p42

faint faints fainting fainted; fainter
faintest
1 (vb) If you faint you lose consciousness
suddenly.
2 (adj) A colour, sound, idea or feeling
which is faint lacks strength. *They could
hear the faint sound of the sea in the
distance.*

fair

fair fairs
1 (n) A fair is a large market, often with amusements, which is held for a fixed period of time.
2 (adj) If you are fair, you are honest and reasonable.

fairy fairies (n) A fairy is an imaginary creature in children's stories. They are imagined in human form and often with wings. **fairyland** (n)

faith faiths
1 (n) Faith is trust in someone or something.
2 (n) Faith is a religious belief.

false falser falsest
1 (adj) If a statement is false, it is not true.
2 If you do something under false pretences, you do it deceitfully.

famous (adj) If you are famous, you are well-known by a large number of people. **fame** (n)

family families
1 (n) A family is a group of people related to each other.
2 (n) A family is a group of people living together in a household.
3 (n) A family is a group of related species of plants or animals. *The lion belongs to the cat family.*

famine famines (n) A famine is a serious shortage of food in an area or country.

fan fans fanning fanned
1 (n) If you are a fan of a particular sport or a pop group, you are an enthusiastic supporter.
2 (n) A fan is a mechanical device with large, flat blades for cooling the air.
3 (n) A fan is a small flat object to move the air as you wave it about.
4 (vb) If you fan yourself, you cool the air around you with a fan.

fancy fancies fancying fancied; fancier fanciest
1 (vb) If you fancy doing something, you want to do it.

2 (adj) Something fancy is highly decorated or special. *Fancy food . . . fancy hats.*

fanfare fanfares (n) A fanfare is a short, rousing piece of music often played on a trumpet at a special occasion.

fang fangs (n) An animal with fangs has long sharp teeth.

fantasy fantasies (n) A fantasy is an imaginative story that is unlikely to happen in real life. **fantastic** (adj)

far farther farthest or further furthest
1 (adv) If something or someone is far away from you, they are a long distance from you.
2 (adv) If you ask someone how far they have got with their work, you want to know what point they have reached.
3 (adv) If you say you have worked far too hard, you mean you have overworked.
4 (adj) If you live at the far end of the street, you live at the other end from where you are standing.

fare fares (n) A fare is the money you pay to travel on a bus, train, plane, etc.

farm farms farming farmed
1 (vb) If you farm land, you plant crops or keep animals there. **farmer** (n)
2 (n) A farm is land where crops are grown or animals are kept for their meat, milk, wool, etc.

fascinate fascinates fascinating fascinated (vb) If someone or something fascinates you, they occupy many of your thoughts. **fascinating** (adj) **fascination** (n)

fashion fashions
1 (n) A fashion is the style of clothes, hair, make-up, etc that is popular for a time.
2 If someone does something after a fashion, they do not do it very well.

fast faster fastest; fasts fasting fasted
1 (adj) If you do something fast, you do it quickly.
2 (adj) If you own a fast vehicle, it will go very quickly.
3 (adj) If your watch is fast, it shows a time ahead of the real time.
4 (adj) If you are fast asleep, you are completely asleep.
5 (vb) If you fast, you deliberately eat no food for a time.

fasten fastens fastening fastened (vb) If you fasten something, you close it so that it cannot come apart.

fatal (adj) If someone has a fatal accident, they are killed in it.

father fathers (n) A father is a male parent.

fatigue (n) is great tiredness.

fault faults faulting faulted
1 (n) A fault is a mistake.
2 (vb) If you fault someone, you find things wrong with them. **faulty** (adj)
3 (n) If something goes wrong and it is your fault, you are to blame.
4 (n) A fault is a crack in the earth's surface.

favour favours favouring favoured
1 (vb) If you favour someone or something, you prefer them to others. **favourite** (n)
2 If you do someone a favour, you help them.

fawn fawns
1 (n) A fawn is a young deer.
2 (adj) Fawn is a light brown colour.

fax faxes (n) Fax is short for facsimile which means an exact copy. You can send a fax of a document electronically by telephone link.

fear fears fearing feared
1 (vb) If you fear someone or something, you are afraid of them.
2 (n) A fear is a feeling you have when you think you are in danger.

feast feasts (n) A feast is a large meal for a special occasion to which many people are invited.

secondary **feathers**

primary **feathers**

feather feathers (n) A feather is one of the light growths which form the covering of a bird's body.

feel feels feeling felt
1 (vb) If you feel something, you touch it to find out what it is like.
2 (vb) If someone feels pain, they are actually hurt in some way.
3 (vb) If you say that you feel like something, you want that thing. *I feel like a cool drink.*
4 (vb) If you feel happy, sad, or angry, you have those emotions. **feelings** (n)

feeler feelers (n) Feelers are long, thin, thread-like objects on the heads of some insects.

feline
1 (adj) Feline means belonging to or to do with the cat family.
2 (adj) If you describe someone as feline, you mean that they look, move or behave like a cat.

felon felons (n) A felon is someone who has committed a serious crime. **felony** (n)

felt felts (n) Felt is a firm, thick material made from wool or other fibres, often used to make hats.

female females
1 (n) A female is a woman or girl.
2 (n) The female of any species is the one which lays eggs or can produce babies.

feminine (adj) If something is described as feminine, it has to do with women. *In the past engineering was not considered a feminine career.*

feminist feminists (n) A feminist is someone who believes that women should have the same rights and opportunities as men.

fen fens (n) A fen is very low, flat and wet land.

fence fences fencing fenced
1 (n) A fence is a barrier made from wood, wire or both, used to separate one piece of land from another.
2 (vb) If you fence a piece of land, you put up a fence around it.
3 (n) In horse racing, or show jumping, a fence is a barrier for the horse to jump over.

feral (adj) animals were once pets but have gone to live in the wild.

ferment ferments fermenting fermented (vb) When beer, wine, cider, etc ferment they fizz and bubble because a chemical change happens.

fern ferns (n) A fern is a green plant with feathery leaves.

ferocious (adj) means very fierce or savage. *The ferocious dog was chained up.*

ferret ferrets (n) A ferret is a small and fierce animal kept for hunting rabbits.

ferry ferries ferrying ferried
1 (n) A ferry is a boat which takes people or goods across short stretches of water.
2 (vb) If you ferry people or objects, you transport them, usually on a regular basis.

fertilise fertilises fertilising fertilised
1 (adj) When a female is fertilised the male sperm joins with the egg, and reproduction begins. **fertile** (adj)
2 (adj) When a plant is fertilised, pollen comes into contact with it so that seeds and fruit can be formed. **fertilisation** (n)
3 (vb) If you fertilise land, you spread manure or chemicals over it to make the soil richer. **fertiliser** (n)

festival festivals
1 (n) A festival is an occasion or time in the year when something special is celebrated, often in public. **festive** (adj) **festivity** (n)
2 (n) A festival can be a lot of events such as plays, concerts, ballets, taking place at one period of time. *Edinburgh has an arts festival every year.*

fetch fetches fetching fetched
1 (vb) If you fetch something, you go to get it and bring it back.
2 (vb) If you are selling something and you ask, 'What will it fetch?', you are wondering how much you will get for it.

fête fêtes (n) A fête is an event with stalls and side shows, organised to raise money.

fetid (adj) A fetid smell is a very unpleasant smell as if something is stale or rotting.

feud feuds (n) A feud is a very bitter quarrel which carries on for a long time.

fever fevers (n) If you are ill and your temperature rises and your heart beats faster than normal, you have a fever.

few fewer fewest (adj) A few things means not many or a small number.

fiancé fiancés (n) A woman's fiancé is the man to whom she is engaged.
fiancée (fem. n)

fiasco fiascos (n) Something which fails completely is a fiasco.

fibre fibres
1 (n) A fibre is a thin thread of material either natural or man-made.
2 (n) Fibre is a part of food found in bran, etc which your body cannot digest.

fickle (adj) If someone is fickle they are likely to change their minds often about what they like or want.

fiction (n) Stories that are made up or imaginary are fiction. **fictitious** (adj)

fiddle fiddles fiddling fiddled
1 (vb) If you fiddle, you keep touching or meddling with things because you are nervous or bored.
2 (n) Fiddle is another word for the violin. **fiddler** (n)

fidget fidgets fidgeting fidgeted (vb) If you fidget, you keep shuffling, twiddling your fingers or changing your position.

field fields fielding fielded
1 (n) A field is a large, open space used for growing crops or grazing animals.
2 (n) A field is a place used for sports.
3 (n) A field is a particular area of study. *My field is biology.*
4 (vb) When you field in a game like cricket or rounders you try to catch and stop the ball.

fiend fiends
1 (n) A fiend is an imaginary creature like a devil.
2 (n) A fiend is an evil and horrible person.

fierce fiercer, fiercest (adj) Something or someone fierce is either very aggressive or frightening.

fiery
1 (adj) Something which burns strongly is fiery.
2 (adj) Somebody with a quick temper or who is easily angered is fiery.
3 (adj) A very hot food or drink can be described as fiery.

fig figs (n) A fig is a fruit, very sweet and full of seeds, which is often eaten dried at Christmas time.

fight fights fighting fought
1 (n) A fight is a struggle between two or more people or sides, trying to injure each other.
2 (vb) If you try to hurt an opponent while they try to hurt you, you fight.

figure figures
1 (n) Figure is another word for number. *471 is a three-figure number.*
2 (n) Your figure is your shape or the outline of your body.
3 (n) A figure is a drawing used to help explain a piece of writing.

digit p82
number p194

filament filaments
1 (n) A filament is a very thin thread.
2 (n) A filament is the coiled wire which glows in a light bulb.

film films filming filmed
1 (n) A film is the moving pictures and sounds on a screen.
2 (n) A film is a roll of treated plastic used in cameras to take pictures.
3 (n) Film is a very thin layer of something. *A film of oil lay on the puddle.*
4 (vb) If you film something or someone, you use a camera to take moving pictures.

filter filters filtering filtered
1 (vb) If you filter a substance, you pass it through a device which removes tiny particles from it.
2 (n) A filter is a fine mesh which allows liquids to pass through leaving the solids behind.
3 (n) Some filters block out or reduce certain lights and sounds in cameras or stereos.
4 (n) A traffic filter allows one lane of vehicles to move but stops others.

filth (n) is dirt of a nasty kind. **filthy** (adj)

fin fins (n) A fin is a flat object like a wing that sticks out of a fish's body. It helps the fish to swim and to keep its balance.

fish p110

final finals
1 (n) The final of a competition is the last round or game that decides the winner. **finalist** (n)
2 (adj) In a series the final one is the last. *This is my final year at school.* **finally** (adv)

finale finales (n) The finale is the last part of a stage show when the whole cast comes onto the stage to take part.

finance finances (n) This is a general word for anything to do with money. **financial** (adj)

find finds finding found (vb) If you discover something you have been searching for, you find it.

findings (n) The findings of an enquiry are the results and conclusions that are reached. *Our findings show an increase in road accidents during the summer.*

finger fingers (n) A finger is one of the four long parts of your hand that you use to feel and hold things.

skeleton p273

finish finishes finishing finished
1 (vb) If you finish something you are doing, you come to the end of it.
2 (vb) When something such as a film, match, etc finishes it comes to an end.
3 (adj) When something that is being built is finished, it is complete.
4 (n) The finish of something is the end. *We came to the finish of the race.*

fiord see **fjord**

fir firs (n) A fir is an evergreen tree which produces cones.

fire fires firing fired
1 (n) A fire is the flames, smoke and heat produced when something is burned.
2 (n) In a house a fire is the wood or coal burning in a fireplace to heat a room.
3 (n) A gas or electric fire is a device which produces heat to keep a room warm.
4 (vb) If you fire a gun, you shoot a bullet.
5 (vb) When potters fire a pot, they put it into a kiln to bake and harden.
6 (vb) If an employer fires someone, he dismisses them from their job.
7 (n) If something is on fire, it is burning.

fire extinguisher

fire extinguisher fire extinguishers (n)
A fire extinguisher is a device containing
foam or water which can be carried around
and used to put out small fires.

fire fighter fire fighters (n) A fire fighter's
job is to put out fires, or to help people or
animals who are trapped in some way.

firm firmer firmest
1 (adj) Something that is firm feels solid
and does not squash when you touch it.
2 (adj) If an object is firm, it is standing
solidly and does not wobble.
3 (adj) People who are firm mean what they
say and are not easily persuaded to change
their mind.
4 (n) A firm is a business company.

firth firths (n) A firth is an inlet of sea,
especially in Scotland.

fish fishes fishing fished
1 (n) Fish are water creatures with fins and
tails.
2 (vb) When people fish they use rods, lines,
nets, etc. to catch fish for food or sport.
fisherman (n)

fishmonger fishmongers (n) A
fishmonger is a person who sells fresh fish
in a shop or market.

fissure fissures (n) A fissure is a deep
crack in the ground or in rock.

fjord or **fiord** fjords or fiords (n) Fiords
are narrow inlets of sea between high
mountains in Scandinavia.

flag flags flagging flagged
1 (n) A flag is a piece of cloth with a special
design on it to show nationality, club, etc.
2 (vb) If you flag, you get tired or weak.

flair (n) If you have flair, you have a
natural talent for doing something.

flake flakes flaking flaked
1 (n) A flake is a small thin piece of
something such as pastry or chocolate.
2 (vb) If something such as paint flakes, it
peels off in small pieces.

flamboyant (adv) Someone or something
flamboyant is very showy.

flame flames
1 (n) A flame is a tongue of fire which
comes from something which is burning.
2 If something is in flames, it is on fire.

flamingo flamingos or flamingoes (n) A
flamingo is a bird with pink feathers, a long
neck, long legs and a curved beak. It lives
near water in warm countries.

flannel flannels
1 (n) Flannel is a thick, soft, woollen fabric.
2 (n) A flannel is a small piece of towelling
for washing the face or body.

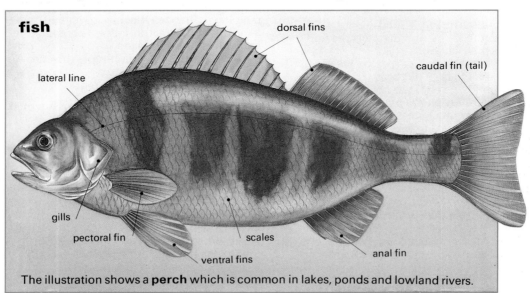

fish

dorsal fins

caudal fin (tail)

lateral line

gills

pectoral fin

ventral fins

scales

anal fin

The illustration shows a **perch** which is common in lakes, ponds and lowland rivers.

flare flares flaring flared
1 (n) A flare is a sudden bright light.
2 (vb) When a fire flares it burns with a bright, unsteady flame.

flash flashes flashing flashed
1 (n) A flash of light is a sudden, brief burst of light.
2 (vb) If a light flashes or you flash a light, it shines briefly.
3 (n) Flash is the name for artificial light for photography.

flask flasks
1 (n) A flask is a small bottle or container. It is often used for holding an alcoholic drink that you carry with you.
2 (n) Flask is an informal word for a vacuum or Thermos flask.

flat flats; flatter flattest
1 (n) A flat is a set of rooms for living in on one floor of a building.
2 (adj) Something that is flat is level.
3 If an event falls flat, it is unsuccessful.
4 If you work flat out, you work as hard as you can.

flatter flatters flattering flattered (vb) If you flatter someone, you praise them without really meaning it. **flattery** (n)

flaunt flaunts flaunting flaunted (vb) If you flaunt yourself, you show off.

flavour flavours flavouring flavoured
1 (vb) If you flavour food or drink with something you give it that particular taste.
2 (n) A flavour is the special taste of a food or drink.

flaw flaws (n) A flaw is a fault in something. *The new carpet had a flaw in it so we sent it back.*

flea fleas (n) A flea is a tiny, jumping insect which lives on the blood of people and animals.

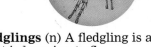

fledgling fledglings (n) A fledgling is a young bird that is learning to fly.

fleece fleeces (n) The woolly coat cut from a sheep is called a fleece.

fleet fleets (n) A fleet is a group of ships.

flesh
1 (n) The flesh of a person or animal is the soft part between the skin and the bones.
2 Your flesh and blood is your family.

flex flexes flexing flexed
1 (vb) If you flex your muscles, you tighten them up.
2 (n) Flex is a pliable, plastic-covered wire which carries electricity.

flexible
1 (adj) Something that is flexible is easily bent.
2 (adj) Someone who is flexible is adaptable and easy to please.

flicker flickers flickering flickered
1 (vb) If a light flickers, its brightness comes and goes.
2 (n) A flicker is a faint trace of something. *A flicker of happiness . . . a flicker of light.*

flight flights
1 (n) A flight is a journey made by flying.
2 If you take flight, you run away.

flimsy flimsier flimsiest
1 (adj) Something that is flimsy falls apart easily.
2 (adj) If you give a flimsy excuse, it is not a very good one.

flinch flinches flinching flinched (vb) If you flinch, you make a small, sudden movement usually because you are startled or frightened.

fling flings flinging flung
1 (vb) If you fling something, you throw it hard and perhaps without aiming it.
2 (vb) If you fling yourself into something, you do it with great enthusiasm.

flint flints
1 (n) Flint is a very hard, grey-black stone which is used for building.
2 (n) A flint is a small piece of stone that can be struck with metal to make a spark to light a fire or to cause a gun to fire.

float floats floating floated
1 (vb) If someone or something floats in liquid they lie on the surface.
2 (vb) Something that floats is light enough to rest on air, a balloon for example.
3 (n) A fisherman uses a float to keep the hook off the bottom of the river or lake.
4 (n) A float is an amount of money that a shop or stall keeps for change.

flock

flock **flocks flocking flocked**
1 (n) A flock of birds or sheep is a group of them together.
2 (vb) If people flock to someone or something, they come in large numbers.

flood **floods flooding flooded**
1 (n) A flood is a great deal of water which covers land which is normally dry. It is usually caused by heavy rainfall.
2 (adj) If land is flooded, it is covered with water.
3 (vb) If a memory floods back, it comes back suddenly and powerfully.

floor **floors** (n) The floor of a room is the part that you walk on.

floppy disk see **disk**

florist **florists** (n) A florist is a person who sells flowers. Their shop is also called a florist.

flotilla **flotillas** (n) A flotilla is a group of small ships.

flotsam (n) is the rubbish left in the sea by accident and which is washed up onto the shore.

flounce **flounces flouncing flounced**
1 (vb) If someone flounces somewhere, they hurry off in a dramatic and offended way.
2 (n) A flounce is a frill around the bottom of chairs, dresses, etc.

flour (n) is the fine white or brownish powder that is ground from wheat and used for baking bread, cakes, etc. **floury** (adj)

flourish **flourishes flourishing flourished**
1 (vb) If a person, plant or animal flourishes, they grow strong and healthy.
2 (vb) If a country or an organisation flourishes, it does well and is strong.
3 (vb) If you flourish something, you wave it about excitedly.

flout **flouts flouting flouted** (vb) If you flout rules or laws of any kind, you deliberately disobey them.

flow **flows flowing flowed**
1 (vb) If something flows, it moves along smoothly. *The river flowed south to the sea.*
2 (vb) When traffic flows, it moves easily with no hold-ups.

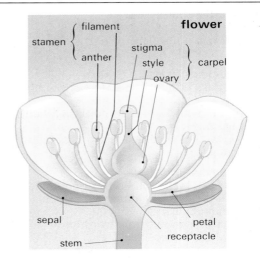

flower

stamen { filament / anther } stigma / style / ovary } carpel

sepal

petal

receptacle

stem

flower **flowers flowering flowered**
1 (n) A flower is the part of a plant usually made up of coloured petals.
2 (vb) When plants flower it means that their flowers are open and in bloom.
3 (adj) A flowering plant is one that flowers.

'flu see **influenza**

fluctuate **fluctuates fluctuating fluctuated** (vb) If something fluctuates, it changes quickly. *Her feelings towards the new girl fluctuated between friendship and dislike.*

flue **flues** (n) A flue is a pipe that takes smoke away from a fire or boiler.

chimney

flue

fire in hearth

fluent
1 (adj) If you are a fluent reader, you read easily.
2 (adj) If you are fluent in a language, it means that you can speak it perfectly. **fluently** (adv)

fluff (n) is small bits of soft, woolly waste material or thread bunched together.

fluid **fluids**
1 (n) A fluid is a liquid.
2 (adj) A fluid movement is an easy flowing movement, not jerky or clumsy but graceful.

fluke flukes
1 (n) A fluke is something which happens by accident. *He had never played football before, but by a fluke he scored a goal.*
2 (n) The curved fin-like ends of a whale's tail are called flukes.

fluorescent
1 (adj) If something is fluorescent, it shines very brightly, especially when a light shines onto it in the dark.
2 (adj) A fluorescent light is usually in the form of a long tube or strip which shines with a very hard, bright light.

fluoride (n) is a chemical mixture that is added to some drinking water and toothpastes because it is thought to be good for teeth.

flush flushes flushing flushed
1 (vb) If your face flushes, you go red because you are embarrassed or too hot.
2 (vb) If you flush the lavatory, you pull the handle and the bowl fills with water and then empties.
3 (vb) If you flush somebody or something out, you force them out of hiding.

flute flutes (n) A flute is a musical instrument like a pipe with holes in it. You blow through it to make music.

flutter flutters fluttering fluttered
1 (vb) When a bird flutters its wings, it makes small, quick movements with them.
2 (vb) If flags or curtains move about when the wind blows gently on them, they flutter.

fly flies flying flew flown
1 (n) A fly is a small flying insect with two wings.
2 (vb) Birds and aircraft fly to move through the air.
3 (vb) When people fly, they travel through the air in an aircraft.
4 If you fly into a temper, you get angry very quickly.

flyover flyovers (n) A flyover is a bridge-like construction which carries one road over the top of another.

foal foals (n) A foal is a baby horse.

foam foams foaming foamed
1 (n) Foam is a mass of tiny bubbles.

2 (vb) If a liquid foams, a mass of bubbles rises to the top and makes it frothy.

focus focuses focusing focused
1 (vb) If you focus a camera, telescope or microscope you adjust the lens by moving it until you get a clear picture of what you want to see.
2 (vb) If you focus your eyes on something, you look at it very carefully.
3 (vb) If you focus your mind on something, you give all your attention to it and concentrate on it.

fodder (n) is the food given to horses and cattle.

foetus foetuses (n) A foetus is an unborn baby, either human or animal.

fog fogs (n) A fog is a very thick mist made up of tiny drops of water. **foggy** (adj)

foghorn foghorns (n) A foghorn is a very loud horn that is used in foggy weather to warn ships of other approaching craft and dangerous coastlines.

foil foils foiling foiled
1 (n) Foil is paper-thin metal which is used to wrap food and other goods.
2 (vb) If you make plans to do something and your plans are foiled, it means that you are prevented from carrying them out.
3 (n) A foil is a sword with a very thin blade used for the sport of fencing.

folk folks
1 (n) Folk is an old-fashioned word for people in general.
2 (n) Your folks are your close relations.

folk music (n) is the popular music of ordinary people that has been handed down for many generations.

folklore (n) is all the old stories and customs that have been handed down, usually by word of mouth, and preserved by people of a particular country or community.

follow follows following followed
1 (vb) If you follow someone or something, you go after them.
2 (vb) If someone is explaining something to you and says, 'Do you follow?' It means 'Do you understand?'.
3 (vb) If you follow someone's advice, you do as they suggest.

folly

folly follies
1 (n) Folly is a very foolish or silly act. *It was pure folly to go out in that weather.*
2 (n) A mock castle or ruin built to decorate a piece of land is called a folly.

fond fonder fondest (adj) If you are fond of someone or something, you like them a lot.

fondle fondles fondling fondled (vb) If you touch and cuddle someone or something in an affectionate way, you fondle them.

font fonts (n) A font is the stone bowl in a church which holds water baptisms.

food (n) is the general term for the things we eat.

fool fools (n) A fool is a person who acts in a stupid or silly manner.

foot feet
1 (n) The foot is the part of the body which is at the end of the leg and is used for walking or standing.
2 (n) A foot is a measure of length of 12 inches, which is about 30 centimetres.

football footballs
1 (n) Football is a game played by two teams of 11 players who kick a ball around a field to try to score goals. **footballer** (n)
2 (n) A football is a large, inflated, round ball.

forage forages foraging foraged
1 (vb) An animal forages when it searches an area for food.
2 (vb) If somebody searches for something, they are foraging for it.

forbid forbids forbidding forbade forbidden
1 (vb) If you forbid somebody to do something, you order them not to do it. **forbidden** (adj)
2 (adj) A forbidding person or place is threatening.

force forces forcing forced
1 (n) Force is the amount of power used to move something.
2 (vb) If you force somebody to do something, you make them do it even if they don't want to. **forceful** (adj)

forceps (n) is the term for an instrument used to pick things up. They are like pincers or tongs.

ford fords (n) A ford is a place where a road goes through a shallow part of a river.

forecast forecasts (n) A forecast tells us something that is expected to happen. *The weather forecast was for rain.*

foresight (n) If you use foresight, you look forward in your plans to things that could happen.

foreign (adj) Something or someone foreign does not come from your own country or the country you are in. **foreigner** (n)

forest forests (n) A forest is a large area covered closely with trees.

forever (adv) Something which goes on forever never ends. *The road seemed to go on forever.*

forfeit forfeits forfeiting forfeited
1 (n) A forfeit is a penalty you have to pay if you lose at certain games.
2 (vb) If you forfeit something, you give it up, either willingly or as a penalty.

forge forges forging forged
1 (n) A forge is a place where a metalworker shapes metal.
2 (vb) If you forge something out of metal, you heat it and beat it or bend it into a shape you want.
3 (vb) If you forge something, you make false copies of it. **forger** (n) **forgery** (n)

forget forgets forgetting forgot forgotten
1 (vb) You forget skills and things you have learned and people if you can no longer remember them.
2 (adj) If something is forgotten, it is no longer remembered.

forgive forgives forgiving forgave forgiven (vb) If you forgive someone for a crime or for something else that they have done, you are no longer cross with them or want them punished.

forlorn (adj) If a person is without hope, sad or despairing, you can say they are forlorn.

114

format formats formatting formatted
1 (n) The format of something is the way in which something is arranged.
2 (vb) If you format a computer disk, it is prepared by the computer to receive and store information.

formidable (adj) A formidable task is frightening and daunting.

formula formulae
1 (n) A formula is the recipe for making certain substances.
2 (n) In maths, a formula is a set of symbols which make a rule.
3 (n) Formula is used followed by a number to show the type of car or motorbike used in various kinds of racing. *Formula 1 cars compete in Grand Prix races.*

fort forts (n) A fort is a building like a castle.

castle p41

fortress fortresses (n) A fortress is a very strong and large castle.

fortified (adj) If something is fortified, it is made stronger in some way.

fortnight fortnights (n) A fortnight is two weeks.

fortune fortunes
1 (n) Fortune is good luck and prosperity in life. Bad fortune is the opposite.
fortunate (adj) **fortunately** (adv)
2 (n) A fortune is a large amount of money.

fortune teller fortune tellers (n) A fortune teller is someone who tells what might happen in the future.

fossil fossils (n) A fossil is the hardened remains of a prehistoric plant or animal found inside a rock.

foster fosters fostering fostered
1 (vb) If someone fosters a child, they look after it for a time in their own family.
2 (vb) If you foster an idea, you encourage it.

foul fouls fouling fouled; fouler foulest
1 (adj) Something foul is very dirty.
2 (vb) If you foul in a game, you break the rules.

found founds founding founded
1 (vb) If someone founds an organisation, company, etc. they start it off.
2 (adj) If an idea is founded on something, then it is based on it. **foundation** (n)

foundry foundries (n) A foundry is a workshop where metal or glass is melted and shaped by casting it in a mould.

fountain fountains
1 (n) A fountain is an ornamental pool with water spouting up into the air continuously from one or more jets.
2 (n) A fountain is a powerful jet or spray of water going up into the air.

fowl (n) are birds, particularly poultry.

fox foxes foxing foxed
1 (n) A fox is a red-brown, dog-like animal with a pointed face and a bushy tail.
2 (vb) If something foxes you, you can't make sense of it.
3 If you call someone an old fox, you mean they are cunning or deceitful.

foyer foyers (n) A foyer is an entrance hall in a theatre, cinema or hotel.

fraction fractions
1 (n) A fraction is a small piece of something.
2 (n) A fraction is an exact division of a figure that is used in mathematics such as $\frac{1}{2}$ or $\frac{3}{4}$.

fragile (adj) A fragile thing is easily broken.

fragment fragments fragmenting fragmented
1 (n) A fragment is a very small piece broken from something.
2 (vb) If something fragments, it breaks into tiny pieces.

fragrant (adj) Something that is fragrant smells pleasant. **fragrance** (n)

frail frailer frailest
1 (adj) A frail person is weak and unhealthy.
2 (adj) Something that is frail is weak.

frame

frame frames framing framed
1 (n) A frame is the edge of a door, window, picture, etc.
2 (n) A frame is a piece of apparatus used by old or sick people to help them to walk.
3 (vb) If you frame a picture, you make a surround for it.
4 Your frame of mind is your mood.

frank franker frankest (adj) A frank person speaks to others openly and with honesty.

frankincense (n) is gum from a tree. It gives out a sweet smell when it is burned as incense.

frantic
1 (adj) If a person or animal is frantic, they are desperate with fear or worry and behave wildly. **frantically** (adv)
2 (adj) Frantic can mean chaotic and disorganised.

fraud frauds
1 (n) Fraud is a crime where money or property is obtained from other people by tricking them.
2 (n) A fraud is someone who cheats or deceives others.

fraught
1 (adj) If you are fraught, you are tense through worry or anxiety.
2 (adj) A fraught situation is full of potential dangers or problems.

frayed (adj) If something made of cloth is frayed, the edges of it are worn and the threads are coming loose.

freak freaks (n) A freak is a person who behaves in an unusual way. **freaky** (adj)

free frees freeing freed
1 (vb) If you free someone or something, you let any restraints on them go. **freedom** (n)
2 (adj) If someone or something is free, they are not under any control or limits.
3 (adj) If something is free, you do not have to pay for it.

freeze freezes freezing froze frozen
1 (vb) If you freeze something, you put it in a place at a very low temperature so that it becomes solid. **frozen** (adj)

2 (vb) If you say that it will freeze, you mean that the weather will be very cold; the temperature will be below freezing point.
3 (vb) If you freeze, you stop moving completely.

freezer freezers (n) A freezer is an appliance that keeps foodstuffs frozen.

freezing point freezing points (n) The freezing point of a liquid is the temperature at which it becomes a solid. *The freezing point of water is 0°C.*
fahrenheit
p105

freight (n) is goods carried on ships, boats and trains.

frenzy frenzies (n) If someone is in a frenzy, they behave in an uncontrolled, wild way.

frequent (adj) If something is frequent, it happens often. **frequently** (adv)

fresh fresher freshest
1 (adj) If something is fresh, it has been made or experienced recently.
2 (adj) Fresh water is water that is not salty.

fret frets fretting fretted
1 (vb) If you fret over someone or something, you are worried about them.
2 (n) The fret on a stringed instrument is one of the metal bars where you place your fingers over the strings to make the notes.

friction
1 (n) Friction happens when two surfaces rub against each other.
2 (n) There is friction between two people when they argue.

fridge fridges (n) A fridge is a cold appliance, box or room where food can be stored. It is short for refrigerator.

friend friends (n) People who you know and like a lot are your friends.
friendly (adv) **friendship** (n)

frighten frightens frightening frightened
1 (vb) If you frighten someone, you make them nervous and upset.
2 (adj) Something frightening upsets and worries you. **fright** (n)

fringe fringes
1 (n) A fringe is the hair which hangs over your forehead.
2 (n) The fringes of a town are the outer edges of it.

frisk frisks frisking frisked (vb) If you frisk someone, you search them thoroughly to make sure that they are not carrying anything illegal.

frivolous (adj) If someone or something is frivolous, they are not serious but light-hearted and rather silly.

frog frogs
1 (n) A frog is a small animal with strong back legs to jump with, that lives on land and water.
2 If you have a frog in your throat, you cannot speak properly.

frolic frolics frolicking frolicked (vb) If a person or animal frolics, they move and jump about in a happy, playful way.

front fronts
1 (n) The front of something is the side that usually faces you.
2 (n) The front of a building is the side which faces the road.
3 (adj) The front seats in a theatre or cinema are those nearest the screen or stage.
4 (n) In a battle the front line is where the two armies are facing each other.
5 (n) At the seaside the front is the road that runs alongside the beach.
6 (n) In weather forecasting a front is a line where warm and cold air meet.

frontier frontiers (n) A frontier is a border between two countries.

frost frosts (n) Frost is the powdery white ice that covers everything outside when the temperature is freezing.

frostbite (n) is a damaging condition which happens when a part of your body gets so cold that blood cannot reach it. *The mountaineer's fingers turned black with frostbite.*

frosty frostier frostiest
1 (adj) If the weather is frosty, the temperature is freezing, and a frost forms.

2 (adj) If a person is frosty, they are unfriendly.

froth (n) is a mass of tiny bubbles that can collect on the surface of liquids. **frothy** (adj)

frown frowns frowning frowned (vb) If you frown, you wrinkle your forehead and lower your eyebrows. People usually frown when they are cross or worried.

frozen see **freeze**

frugal (adj) people who are frugal spend their money very carefully.

fruits fruits (n) A fruit is the part of a plant that contains the seeds. Many fruits can be eaten, but some cannot.

frustrate frustrates frustrating frustrated
1 (vb) If you frustrate someone or something, you prevent them from doing what they wish to do.
2 (adj) Someone or something that is frustrating is annoying because they hold you up, or stop you doing something that you want to do. **frustration** (n)

fry fries frying fried (vb) If you fry something, you cook it in hot oil or fat.

fudge (n) is a sweet made from sugar and cream.

fuel fuels fuelling fuelled
1 (n) Fuel is anything that is burned to produce heat or power.
2 (vb) When you fuel a vehicle, you supply it with fuel.

fugitive fugitives (n) A fugitive is someone who is running away, or hiding from something.

fulfil fulfils fulfilling fulfilled
1 (vb) If you fulfil a promise or a duty to do something, you actually do it. *He fulfilled his promise to play at the concert.*
2 (adj) If you are fulfilled, you are happy and satisfied with your life.
3 (vb) If something fulfils you, it gives you pleasure and satisfaction. **fulfilment** (n)

fumble fumbles fumbling fumbled
1 (vb) If you fumble, you are clumsy with your hands.
2 (vb) If you fumble for words, you cannot think what to say next, or what words to use.

fume

fume fumes fuming fumed
1 (vb) If something fumes, it produces smoke or gases.
2 (n) Fumes are gases and smoke given off by things burning.
3 (vb) If someone fumes, they are very angry indeed, but keep themselves under control.

function functions functioning functioned
1 (vb) If a thing functions, it works as it should.
2 (n) The function of someone or something is the work they are supposed to do. *Your function is to look after the engines.*
3 (n) In computing the function is the set of operations the computer performs when you press a certain key.
4 (n) A function is also a rather grand party or gathering held on special occasions.

fund funds funding funded
1 (n) Funds are the supply of money for spending on a certain thing. *The repair funds are used up.*
2 (vb) If you fund something, you provide the money to pay for it. *The millionaire funded the research.*

fundamental
1 (adj) If something is fundamental, it is a basic necessity. *Good food is fundamental to good health.*
2 (adj) A fundamental change is one that will change things completely.

funeral funerals (n) A funeral is the religious service when a person who has died is buried or cremated.

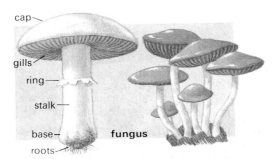
cap
gills
ring
stalk
base
roots
fungus

fungus fungi or funguses (n) A fungus is a leafless and flowerless plant. *Mushrooms, toadstools, mildew and mould are all fungi.*

funnel funnels
1 (n) A funnel is a chimney on a ship.
2 (n) A funnel is a tube, wide at one end and narrow at the other, used to pour liquids into containers.

funny funnier funniest
1 (adj) If someone or something is funny, they make you laugh.
2 (adj) Funny can also mean strange or peculiar.

fur furs
1 (n) Fur is the soft hair of a mammal.
2 (n) A fur is a coat made from real or synthetic fur.
3 If the fur flies, there is an argument.

furlong furlongs (n) A furlong is a measure of distance, about 200 metres.

furnace furnaces (n) A furnace is a very hot oven used to melt metal, etc.

furnish furnishes furnishing furnished (vb) If you furnish a room or a house, for example, you put tables, chairs, beds, etc. in it. **furniture** (n)

furore (n) A furore is a great amount of fuss and anger.

furrow furrows (n) A furrow in a field is a shallow, straight channel dug by a plough.

further see **far**

furtive (adj) If you do something in a furtive way, you act suspiciously, and try to stop others seeing what you are doing.

furious (adj) If you are furious, you are very angry. **fury** (n)

fuse fuses fusing fused
1 (n) A fuse is a device which protects electrical equipment from damage by too much electricity.
2 (vb) If two things fuse, they join and become one thing.
3 (n) A fuse is used to set off fireworks or bombs, giving the person time to get clear.

futile (adj) If a plan or action is futile, it has no chance of succeeding.

future (n) The future is the time which is yet to come.

fuzz (n) The soft hair on your skin or on the skin of a peach, for example, is called fuzz.

Gg

gable gables (n) A gable is the triangular piece of wall at the end of a building where the wall meets the roof.

gadget gadgets (n) A gadget is a mechanical device which does a useful job.

Gagarin, Yuri (1934–1968) was the first man to travel in space. He was a Russian and orbited Earth in the spaceship Vostock in 1961. He was killed in a plane crash.

gain gains gaining gained
1 (vb) If you gain something such as weight, money, etc, you increase the amount you have.
2 (vb) A clock or watch gains time if it starts to tell a later time than it really is.

gala galas (n) A gala is a public celebration: sports, concerts, etc.

galaxy galaxies (n) A galaxy is a huge group of stars and planets, occupying millions of miles of space.

gale gales (n) A gale is a very violent wind.

gallant (adj) people are brave and honourable.

galleon galleons (n) A galleon was an old type of sailing ship used during the 15th, 16th and 17th centuries.

gallery galleries
1 (n) A gallery is a place where exhibitions are held.
2 (n) A gallery is a balcony inside a building.
3 (n) In a coal mine a gallery is a long tunnel.

galley galleys
1 (n) A galley is a kitchen on a ship or plane.
2 (n) A galley is an old type of ship moved by oars and sails.

gallon gallons (n) A gallon is a measure of liquid equal to 8 pints or 4.55 litres.

gallop gallops galloping galloped (vb) A horse gallops when it runs fast.

gallows (n) This is a framework on which criminals were hanged.

gamble gambles gambling gambled
1 (vb) People who gamble bet money on the results of card games or horse races for example, hoping to make money. **gambler** (n)
2 (vb) If you gamble, you take risks in the hope of gaining wealth, success etc.
3 (n) A gamble is a risk you take in order to improve your situation.

game games
1 (n) A game is an activity played according to rules.
2 (n) Games are activities that children invent such as playing with cars and dolls.
3 (n) Game is a term for wild birds and animals which are hunted for sport or for food. **gamekeeper** (n)

gander ganders (n) A gander is a male goose.

Gandhi (1869–1948), known as Mahatma Gandhi, was a famous Indian leader and man of peace.

gang gangs (n) A gang is a group of people who do things together.

gangster gangsters (n) A gangster is one of a group of criminals.

gangway gangways
1 (n) A gangway is a space left between rows of seats, for example in a train or cinema, for people to walk through.
2 (n) A gangway is a short movable passenger bridge between a ship and the shore.

g

gantry

gantry gantries (n)
A gantry is a tall,
strong metal frame
for supporting
cranes, railway
signals, etc.

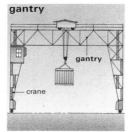

gaol or **jail gaols** or
jails (n) A gaol is a
prison. **gaoler** (n)
jailer (n)

garage garages
1 (n) A garage is a building where one or
more cars are kept.
2 (n) A garage is a place where you can buy
petrol and where sometimes cars and other
vehicles are serviced and repaired.

garbage (n) is another name for rubbish.

garbled (adj) Information that is garbled is
muddled and confused.

garden gardens gardening gardened
1 (n) A garden is a piece of land next to a
house where people grow flowers,
vegetables, trees, etc.
2 (vb) When people garden they work in the
garden digging, weeding, planting, etc.
gardener (n)

gargle gargles gargling gargled (vb) If
you gargle, you hold liquid in the back of
your mouth, tilt your head back and gurgle
the liquid around.

gargoyle gargoyles
(n) A gargoyle is a
stone decoration on
an old building, often
in the shape of a head
with an open mouth,
which drains water
from the roof.

garlic (n) is an onion-like plant whose
strongly flavoured root is used in cooking.

garrulous (adj) people talk a lot.

gas gases; gasses gassing gassed
1 (n) Gas is a substance like air, neither
liquid nor solid.
2 (n) Gas is used as fuel in homes for
cookers, heating, etc.
3 (n) Certain kinds of gas are used as
anaesthetics so that operations can be
carried out.

4 (vb) If somebody gasses another person,
they kill them by making them breathe in a
poisonous gas.

gateau gateaux (n) A gateau is a large
rich cake with cream or fruit or both.

gather gathers gathering gathered
1 (vb) If you gather information, you collect
details from various places.
2 (vb) If some people gather together, they
form a group.
3 (n) A gathering of people is a coming
together of various people for some reason.

gauge gauges gauging gauged
1 (n) A gauge is a device for measuring.
Fuel gauge... wind gauge.
2 (vb) If you gauge how much is needed for
something, you work out the amount you
require.

gauze (n) This is a thin cotton cloth, often
used for bandages.

gaze gazes gazing gazed (vb) If you gaze
at someone or something, you look at them
for some time because they attract your
attention.

gazelle gazelles (n) A gazelle is a small,
delicate African or Asian antelope with
large eyes.

gazump gazumps gazumping gazumped
(vb) If you gazump someone who has
agreed to buy a house at a certain price,
you make a higher offer than theirs and the
seller lets you buy it instead.

gear gears
1 (n) The gears in a car or other vehicle are
a set of cog wheels that carry the engine
power to the wheels.
2 (n) Gear is the special clothes or
equipment you need for any activity.

Geiger counter Geiger counters (n) A
Geiger counter is an instrument that
detects and measures radioactivity.

gel gels (n) This is thick, jelly-like
substance that you can put on your hair to
style it.

gelatine or **gelatin** (n) This is a fine
powder or crystals that you mix with
liquids to make them set like jelly.

gelignite (n) is an explosive like dynamite.

gem gems
1 (n) A gem is a jewel or a precious stone.
2 (n) If you say someone is a gem, you mean they are very precious and you value them.

gender genders (n) If you want to know what gender a person or animal is, it means that you want to know whether they are male or female.

gene genes (n) Genes are those parts of living things that control what a person or an animal will look like, and how they will grow and develop. Genes are passed on from parents to children through the generations.

genealogy genealogies (n) Genealogy is the study of families and their history.

general generals
1 (adj) Something general is to do with most people or things. *General knowledge ... general interest.*
2 (n) A general is a senior officer in the armed forces.

generate generates generating generated
1 (vb) If you generate something, you start it happening. *The committee generated a lot of good ideas for the Christmas show.*
2 (vb) If you generate electricity, for example, you make it from another source of power such as coal. **generator** (n)

generation generations
1 (n) If you say people are of the same generation, they are about the same age.
2 (n) A generation is a period of about 30 years.

generous (adj) people are kind and give a lot of their time or possessions to others.

genie genies (n) In magical stories, genies have to obey or grant the wishes of the person who controls them.

genitals (n) These are the sex organs of the body.

genius geniuses (n) A genius is someone who shows exceptional talent, skill or intelligence in a particular activity.

gentle gentler gentlest
1 (adj) A gentle person is quiet and kind.
2 (adj) A gentle voice is soft and pleasant.
3 (adj) A gentle touch is light.

gentleman gentlemen
1 (n) Gentleman is a polite word for a man.
2 (n) A gentleman is a person who has good manners and thinks of other people's feelings and comfort before his own.

genuine (adj) Things that are genuine are real. *Genuine jewels ... genuine feelings.*

geography (n) is the study of the countries of the world: the land, seas and rivers and how they are formed; the climate and the peoples of the world and where and how they live.

geology (n) is the study of soil and rocks.

geometry (n) is the part of mathematics that studies lines, curves, angles and shapes.

George, Saint is the patron saint of England. His feast day is April 23rd.

Georgian (adj) This is the term used to describe buildings, literature, etc. of the 18th Century.

geranium geraniums (n) A geranium is a bright, colourful, flowering plant.

gerbil gerbils (n) A gerbil is a small rodent with long back legs that is often kept as a pet.

geriatric (adj) describes very old people and their illnesses.

germ germs (n) A germ is a microscopic living thing which can cause disease.

German measles (n) is a common illness which causes a skin rash. It can have serious effects on unborn babies.

German shepherd German shepherds (n) This dog is large, wolf-like and often fierce. It is also known as an Alsatian.

germinate germinates germinating germinated (vb) When a seed starts to grow, it germinates. **germination** (n)

gestation (n) This is the time it takes for a baby to develop inside its mother.

gesticulate gesticulates gesticulating gesticulated (vb) If you gesticulate, you use your hands and arms rapidly to emphasise what you are saying.

g

gesture gestures
1 (n) A gesture is any movement that conveys a meaning. *His gesture made her sit down.*
2 (vb) If you gesture, you make a movement with part of your body or your hands to draw someone's attention to something.

geyser geysers
1 (n) A geyser is a fountain of hot water which occurs naturally.
2 (n) A geyser is a water heater in a house.

ghastly (adj) things are horrible or very unpleasant.

ghetto ghettos or ghettoes (n) A ghetto is an area of a town or country where one particular group of people live.

ghost ghosts (n) A ghost is the spirit of a dead person which is supposed to appear after they die.

Giani Gianies (n) A Giani is a priest of the Sikh religion.

giant giants (n) a giant is an imaginary person of enormous size.

gibbet gibbets (n) A gibbet is a framework where the bodies of executed criminals were hung as a warning to others in days gone by.

giblets (n) are the insides of poultry that you remove before cooking.

giddy giddier giddiest (adj) If you are giddy, you become dizzy and lose your balance.

gift gifts
1 (n) A gift is a present.
2 (n) A gift is a talent that someone has.

giggle giggles giggling giggled (vb) If you giggle, you laugh in a quiet way.

gill gills (n) The gills are the part of a fish that allow it to breathe under water.

fish p110

gimmick gimmicks (n) A gimmick is something unusual or clever.

gin gins (n) An alcoholic drink made from malt or grain flavoured with juniper berries.

ginger (n) is a spice made from the root of the ginger plant.

gingerly (adv) If you do something gingerly, you do it very carefully and cautiously, because it may be dangerous.

Gipsy see **Gypsy**

giraffe giraffes (n) A giraffe is a large African animal with a long neck and legs. It has dark patches on its yellowish skin.

girder girders (n) A girder is a strong beam usually made of concrete or steel.

Girl Guide Girl Guides (n) The Girl Guides is an organisation that girls can join where they learn self-sufficiency skills.

girth girths
1 (n) The girth of something is the measurement around it.
2 (n) A girth is a leather strap fastened around a horse's body which keeps the saddle in place.

glacier glaciers (n) A glacier is a mass of ice and snow which moves slowly and gradually, often down the sides of a mountain.

glade glades (n) A glade is an open grassy space in a wood or forest.

gladiator gladiators (n) A gladiator was a man in Roman times who was forced to fight against other men and wild animals for public amusement.

glamorous (adj) people are fashionable, elegant, charming and exciting. **glamour** (n)

glance glances glancing glanced
1 (n) A glance is a very quick look.
2 (vb) If you glance at someone or something, you look at them briefly.

gland glands (n) Glands are cells or organs in the bodies of humans, animals or plants that make substances for the body to use or that allow unwanted substances to be removed.

glare glares glaring glared
1 (vb) If you glare at something or somebody, you give them a hard, angry stare.
2 (n) A glare is an angry look.
3 (n) Glare is bright, dazzling light.

glass glasses
1 (n) Glass is a hard, transparent substance, easily broken, and used to make windows, bottles, drinking tumblers, ornaments, etc.
2 (n) A glass is a container for drinking made from glass.
3 (n) A glass, or looking glass, is a mirror.
4 (n) Glasses are spectacles used by people who cannot see well.

glaze glazes glazing glazed
1 (vb) If someone glazes a window, they put glass in it.
2 (vb) When pottery is glazed, it is painted with a special liquid that, when fired, produces a hard, shiny surface.
3 (n) A glaze is a mixture of beaten egg or milk, etc. painted onto the surface of food before it is baked to give a shiny appearance or a special flavour.

gleam gleams gleaming gleamed
1 (vb) If a light gleams, it shines.
2 (adj) If a surface is gleaming, it is shining and light reflects from it.
3 (n) A gleam is a ray of light.
4 (vb) If your eyes or your face gleam, they light up with pleasure and excitement.

glen glens (n) A glen is a valley, especially in Scotland or Ireland.

Glendower, Owain (1350–1461) was a great Welsh leader who fought the invading English and led a revolt against Henry V.

glide glides gliding glided
1 (vb) If someone or something glides, they move along very smoothly.
2 (n) Gliding is the sport of flying a glider.

glider gliders (n) A glider is an aircraft with no engine which floats on air currents.

glimmer glimmers
1 (n) A glimmer is a faint, flickering light.
2 (vb) If something glimmers it gives off a soft, unsteady light.
3 (n) A glimmer of something, such as hope, interest or excitement, is a very faint trace of it.

glimpse glimpses glimpsing glimpsed
1 (vb) If you glimpse something or someone, you see them very briefly.
2 (n) A glimpse is a very short look at something.

glint glints glinting glinted (vb) If something glints, it shines with flashes of light.

glisten glistens glistening glistened (vb) Something that glistens, shines.

glitter glitters glittering glittered (vb) If something glitters, it sparkles.

gloat gloats gloating gloated (vb) If you gloat, you delight in your own good fortune or success in a very selfish way, or you are pleased at the misfortunes of others.

global (adj) things concern the whole world.

globe globes
1 (n) A globe is an object shaped like a sphere: a ball, for example.
2 (n) The globe is the Earth.
3 (n) A globe is a sphere showing the map of the world.

globule globules (n) A globule is a round drop of liquid.

gloomy gloomier gloomiest
1 (adj) If you feel gloomy, you are sad and depressed.
2 (adj) If the weather is gloomy, there is little light and it is cloudy. **gloom** (n)

glory glories glorying gloried
1 (n) Glory is the great success and fame you gain by doing something extraordinary.
2 (vb) If you glory in doing something, you enjoy it very much. *She gloried in her new-found freedom.*

glossary glossaries (n) A glossary is an alphabetical list of specialist words or expressions and their explanations, often found at the back of a textbook.

glossy

glossy **glossier glossiest**
1 (adj) If something is glossy, it is smooth and shiny.
2 (adj) If a magazine is glossy, it has a shiny cover and many coloured pictures inside.

glove **gloves** (n) A glove covers your hand and each finger for protection or warmth.

glower **glowers glowering glowered** (vb) If you glower at someone or something, you scowl at them.

glue **glues gluing glued**
1 (n) Glue is a sticky substance used to join things together.
2 (vb) If you glue two things together, you fix them together securely with a sticky substance.

glut **gluts** (n) A glut is a very large amount of something, much more than is needed.

glutton **gluttons** (n) A glutton is a greedy person who eats too much. **gluttony** (n)

gnarled (adj) Something gnarled, a tree for example, is twisted with age.

gnash **gnashes gnashing gnashed** (vb) If you gnash your teeth, you make a noise with your teeth because you are angry or upset.

gnat **gnats** (n) A gnat is a small, flying insect that can bite people.

gnaw **gnaws gnawing gnawed**
1 (vb) If you gnaw something you keep biting and chewing it.
2 (vb) If a feeling gnaws at you, it keeps worrying you and won't go away.

gnome **gnomes** (n) A gnome is a small, imaginary old man with a beard and pointed hat that appears in some children's stories.

goad **goads goading goaded**
1 (vb) If you goad someone, you irritate them so that they will react.
2 (n) A goad is a sharp, pointed stick for driving cattle.

goal **goals**
1 (n) If you score a goal in a game like hockey or football, you get the ball into a particular space.
2 (n) If you set yourself goals in your life, you give yourself particular aims to achieve.

goalkeeper **goalkeepers** (n) A goalkeeper is the person who tries to stop the opposing team from scoring goals.

goat **goats** (n) A goat is an animal with horns, a short tail and a beard, found in mountain areas and on farms; the female gives milk.

gobble **gobbles gobbling gobbled** (vb) If you gobble your food, you eat it very quickly.

god **gods**
1 (n) God, in the Christian and other faiths, is the creator of everything.
2 (n) A god is a being or spirit in various religions who is worshipped as powerful.

goggles (n) are glasses that fit tightly round the eyes as protection against water, dirt, etc.

go-kart **go-karts** (n) A go-kart is a small, motorised vehicle that can be raced.

gold
1 (n) Gold is a very valuable, yellow metal that is used for coins, jewellery, etc.
2 (adj) Gold is a dark yellow colour.
3 Someone who has a heart of gold is thoughtful and kind.

goldfish **goldfish** (n) A goldfish is a small, orange fish often kept as a pet.

golf (n) is a game played with a small, hard, white ball that is hit with long sticks called clubs into holes over a wide grassy area.

gondola **gondolas** (n) A gondola is a long, narrow boat used on the canals of Venice. It is moved through the water by a man called a gondolier using a long pole.

gong **gongs** (n) A gong is a round piece of metal that makes a loud, deep, ringing sound when you hit it.

good better best
1 (adj) If you say something is good, you like it or enjoy it.
2 (n) Good is the strong force of right which works against evil.
3 (adj) A good person is kind to others.
4 (adj) A good idea is a clever one.
5 (adj) If someone is good at something, they do it well.

goodbye or **good-bye** You say goodbye to someone when you or they are leaving.

goose geese
1 (n) A goose is a large water bird with a long neck. Geese are sometimes kept by people for their eggs, for eating and also to guard their property.
2 A wild goose chase is a useless journey.

gooseberry gooseberries (n) A gooseberry is a small, green fruit that grows on bushes.

gore gores goring gored
1 (n) Gore is what we call the messy blood from an accident or a killing. **gory** (adj)
2 (vb) If an animal gores you it wounds you by sticking a tusk or horn into you.

gorge gorges gorging gorged
1 (n) A gorge is a narrow, steep-sided river valley between high cliffs or mountains. It can be a dry gorge.
2 (vb) If you gorge yourself you eat so much that you can't eat any more.

gorgeous (adj) Something gorgeous is wonderful or beautiful.

gorilla gorillas (n) A gorilla is a large, strong, monkey-like animal. It is the largest of the African apes and it lives in family groups.

gorse (n) is a very prickly bush with yellow flowers that grows on heathland.

gosling goslings (n) A gosling is a baby goose.

gospel gospels (n) A gospel is one of the first four books of the New Testament of the Bible.

gossamer
1 (n) Gossamer is the fine thread spiders spin to make their webs.
2 (n) Something, such as material, that is like gossamer is thin and delicate.

gossip gossips gossiping gossiped
1 (n) Gossip is talk between two or more people, usually about other people.
2 (n) A gossip is a person who goes around telling stories about everyone else's business.
3 (vb) If you gossip, you tell stories about other people's activities.

gouge gouges gouging gouged (vb) If you gouge something out, you scoop it out forcefully with a sharp tool or your finger.

gourd gourds (n) A gourd is a melon-like fruit that is often left to dry out. Its empty shell is often used to store liquid.

gourmet gourmets (n) A gourmet is a person who is very interested in good food and wine.

gout (n) is a very painful disease that causes swelling in the joints especially in the feet.

govern governs governing governed (vb) People who govern a country make or change the laws of the land and manage the country. **government** (n)

governor governors
1 (n) A governor is someone who governs an area of land or a group of people.
2 (n) A governor is someone who represents the Queen in a foreign country.
3 (n) A governor of a school or a hospital is a member of a committee that meets to discuss the running of the place.

graceful (adj) people move in an elegant, smooth way. **grace** (n) **gracefully** (adv)

gracious (adj) people are polite and pleasant.

grade grades grading graded
1 (n) A grade is a mark given for a piece of work
2 (vb) When you grade something, such as a piece of work, you make a judgement about its quality.
3 (vb) If you grade things, such as eggs, you sort them according to quality or size.

gradient

gradient gradients
1 (n) A gradient is a slope.
2 (n) The gradient is the measure of how steep a slope is.

gradually (adv) If something happens gradually, it happens slowly, over a period of time. **gradual** (adj)

graduate graduates graduating graduated
1 (n) A graduate is someone who has a degree.
2 (vb) When you graduate from a course, you finish it and obtain a qualification.
3 (vb) If a person graduates from one level to another in work or sport, they move up a stage.

graffiti (n) is writing or drawing that is seen on walls in public places.

graft grafts grafting grafted
1 (n) A graft is a piece of skin taken from one part of the body to cover a wound on another part.
2 (n) A graft is a piece of one plant placed so that it will grow on another.
3 (vb) If you graft something, you make something grow on something else.

grain grains
1 (n) A grain is a single seed.
2 (n) Grain is corn.
3 (n) The grain of wood is the way the fibres lie to make the patterns in wood.

gram or **gramme** grams or grammes (n) A gram is a small unit of weight. *1000 grams = 1 kilogram.* The abbreviation for gram is g.

grammar (n) is that part of the study of language which describes the way that words are put together into sentences.

granary granaries (n) A granary is a place where grain is stored.

grand grander grandest (adj) Something that is grand, a building for example, is large, important and imposing.

grandchild grandchildren (n) A grandchild is the child of a person's son or daughter. **granddaughter** (fem. n) **grandson** (n)

grandeur (n) is magnificence; the quality which makes something look spectacular.

grandparent grandparents (n) Your grandparents are the parents of your mother and father. **grandmother** (fem. n) **grandfather** (masc. n)

Grand Prix Grands Prix (n) A Grand Prix is one of a series of races for cars, motorbikes, etc.

granite (n) is a hard, strong rock often used for building.

grant grants granting granted
1 (vb) If you grant someone something, you allow them to have it or to do it. *I granted him permission to leave.*
2 (n) A grant is an allowance given to a person or an organisation by the government, *etc. Housing grants... education grants*

Granth Sahib (n) The Granth Sahib is the holy book of the Sikh religion.

grape grapes (n) Grapes are the sweet, green or purple fruits that grow in bunches on vines.

grapefruit grapefruits (n) Grapefruit is a bitter-sweet, yellow citrus fruit.

graph graphs (n) A graph is a diagram or chart which gives information.

grapple grapples grappling grappled
1 (vb) If you grapple with a person or animal, you grab them and struggle to overpower them.
2 (vb) If you grapple with a problem or difficulty, you try to solve it or deal with it.

grasp grasps grasping grasped
1 (vb) If you grasp something, you seize it and hold it firmly in your hand.
2 (n) A grasp is a strong hand grip.
3 (vb) If you grasp something, you are being taught, you understand it.
4 (n) If something is within your grasp, you are capable of doing it.
5 (adj) A grasping person is greedy for money.

grass grasses (n) Grass is the very common plant with narrow, green leaves which grows in fields and in gardens as lawns.

grasshopper grasshoppers (n) A grasshopper is an insect with long back legs. It can jump long distances.

insect p149

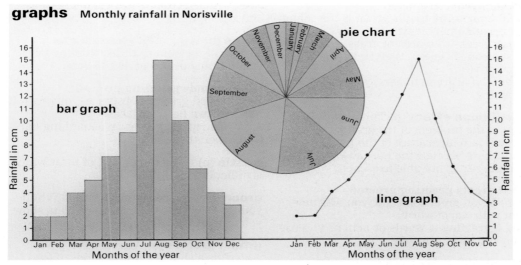

graphs Monthly rainfall in Norisville

bar graph

pie chart

line graph

grass snake grass snakes (n) A grass snake is a small, harmless, greeny-brown snake.

grate grates grating grated
1 (vb) If you grate cheese or vegetables, you shred them using a grater.
2 (vb) If something grates, it makes a harsh, unpleasant noise.
3 (n) A grate is the metal framework of bars which holds coal or logs in a fire-place.

grateful (adj) If you are grateful to someone, you are thankful for their kindness or their help. **gratitude** (n)

grave graves; graver gravest
1 (n) A grave is the place where a dead body has been buried.
2 (adj) Something that is grave is very serious and worrying.
3 (adj) A grave person behaves quietly and seriously.

gravel (n) is a mixture of tiny stones and rock fragments deposited on river beds and other places, and used for covering paths, yards, etc.

gravity (n) is the force that causes things to fall towards the surface of the earth, and other planets, and to stay there instead of floating off into space.

gravy gravies (n) Gravy is a sauce made from the juices of cooked meat.

graze grazes grazing grazed
1 (vb) When animals graze, they eat grass and other growing plants.
2 (vb) If you graze your knee, for example, you scrape the skin from it when you have a fall.
3 (n) A graze is a wound where the skin is scraped off.

grease greases greasing greased
1 (n) Grease is a thick, oily substance, used for lubricating moving parts of engines and machines. **greasy** (adj)
2 (n) When you cook meat, the fat left over is called grease.
3 (vb) If you grease a car engine, for example, you put grease on it to make it work smoothly.

great greater greatest
1 (adj) Something that is great is very large. *A great tree... a great building.*
2 (adj) A great amount of something is a large amount.
3 (adj) Someone or something great is famous and important. *A great writer... Great achievements.*
4 (adj) A great friend is a very good friend.
5 (adj) If you feel great, you feel happy and healthy.
6 (adj) If something is great, it is excellent.

greedy greedier greediest (adj) A greedy person wants and often takes more than they need of something. **greed** (n)

green

green greener greenest
1 (adj) Something that is green is the colour of grass and many leaves.
2 (n) A green is an area of grass.
3 If someone is green, they lack experience in an activity.
4 If you have green fingers, you are good at gardening.

greenhouse effect (n) This is the term given to the problem of the gradual increase in temperature of the Earth's atmosphere because the heat absorbed from the sun is not able to escape.

greet greets greeting greeted
1 (vb) If you greet someone, you welcome them with warm words.
2 (n) A greeting is words or actions you use when you meet someone.

grenade grenades (n) A grenade is a small bomb that can be thrown by hand or fired from a gun.

grey greyer greyest (adj) Grey is the colour of clouds when it is raining.

greyhound greyhounds (n) A greyhound is a dog that can run very fast and which is sometimes used for racing.

grid grids
1 (n) A grid is a set of straight lines regularly crossing each other.
2 (n) The national grid in the United Kingdom is the network of wires for distributing electricity.
3 (adj) Maps have a system of regular numbered lines on them so that places can be found more easily by grid references.

grievance grievances (n) If you have a grievance against someone, you feel that you have been unfairly treated by them.

grieve grieves grieving grieved (vb) If you grieve, you feel great sadness. **grief** (n)

grill grills grilling grilled
1 (vb) When you grill food, you cook it with the heat directly under or over it.
2 (n) The grill is the part of an oven where you cook food with the heat above it.

grim grimmer grimmest
1 (adj) If someone is in a grim situation, they are in serious difficulties.

2 (adj) A place that is grim is depressing and gloomy.

grime (n) is dirt that goes below the surface of the skin or collects on the fabric of a building over a period of time.

grind grinds grinding ground
1 (vb) If you grind a substance, you crush it between two hard surfaces.
2 (vb) You grind knives on something hard to sharpen them.

gristle (n) is the tough part of meat which is difficult to eat.

groan groans groaning groaned (vb) If you groan, you make a deep sound to show you are upset or disapproving.

grocer grocers (n) A grocer is a person who runs a shop selling all kinds of food and household goods. **grocery** (n)

groove grooves (n) A groove is a deep, narrow cut in the surface of something.

grope gropes groping groped (vb) You grope for something when you have to feel for it in the dark.

gross gross; grosser grossest
1 (n) A gross of something is twelve dozen.
2 (adj) The gross amount is the total weight or value of something. *Gross weight . . . gross pay.*
3 (adj) Gross behaviour or language is bad.

grotesque (adj) things look strange and ugly.

grotto grottos or **grottoes** (n) A grotto is a small cave, made beautiful by coloured rocks or by rocks with interesting shapes.

ground grounds
1 (n) The ground is the surface of the earth.
2 (n) The grounds of a house are the lawns and gardens surrounding it.
3 (n) A ground is a piece of land used for a particular activity like a sports ground.
4 (n) Grounds can be reasons. *What are your grounds for thinking that I broke the window?*

group groups (n) A group is a collection of things or people with something in common.

grouse grouses grousing groused
1 (n) Grouse are small game birds.
2 (vb) If you grouse about something, you complain about it.

grove groves (n) A grove is a group of trees that have been planted together.

grovel grovels grovelling grovelled (vb) If you grovel to somebody, you behave humbly towards them because you want something from them or because you are afraid of them.

grow grows growing grew
1 (vb) When a person or an animal grows, their body gets bigger.
2 (vb) When things such as hair, nails or beards grow, they get longer.
3 (vb) If an idea grows, it develops.
4 (vb) If a problem grows, it gets worse.
5 (vb) If you grow plants, you plant seeds or cuttings and wait for them to develop.
growth (n)

growl growls growling growled (vb) Dogs growl by making a deep, rumbling noise in their throat when they are angry.

grub grub grubs
1 (n) A grub is the larva of an insect. It hatches from an insect egg and looks like a tiny, fat worm.
2 (n) Grub is an everyday word for food.
3 (vb) If you grub something up, you dig it out of the ground.

grubby grubbier grubbiest (adj) Grubby means dirty and scruffy.

grudge grudges (n) If you have a grudge against someone, you have bad feelings about them for a long time because of some harm they have done to you.

gruelling (adj) journeys or jobs are difficult and exhausting.

gruesome (adj) Something which is gruesome, a film for example, is unpleasantly full of gory details of murder and violent death.

gruff gruffer gruffest (adj) voices are hoarse and deep, and sometimes angry.

grumble grumbles grumbling grumbled (vb) If you grumble, you complain and moan about something.

grumpy (adj) people are bad-tempered and cross a lot of the time.

grunt grunts grunting grunted (vb) If you grunt, you make a low, snorting noise.

guarantee guarantees guaranteeing guaranteed
1 (n) A guarantee is a promise.
2 (n) A guarantee is a paper you may get when you buy something that promises, in writing, to repair or replace it within a certain time if it goes wrong.
3 (vb) If you guarantee something, you promise that it is good.

guard guards guarding guarded
1 (vb) If you guard a prisoner, you stay close to them so they cannot escape.
2 (vb) If you guard someone or something, you protect it.
3 (n) A guard is a wire cage that you put in front of an open fire for safety.
4 (n) Some sportspeople and people who do dangerous jobs wear guards on different parts of their bodies for protection.

guardian guardians (n) A guardian is a person appointed to look after the interests of another person, usually a child, who cannot look after themselves.

guerilla guerillas (n) A guerilla is a fighter belonging to a small group or army, fighting against the regular armed forces of a country.

guess guesses guessing guessed (vb) If you guess the answer to something, you give an answer that you hope is right.

guest guests (n) A guest is a visitor.

guide guides guiding guided
1 (n) A guide is a person who shows people the way around places such as cities and towns; museums and galleries.
2 (vb) If you guide someone, you help them and show them how to do something.
guidance (n)

guild guilds (n) A guild is an organised group of people who do the same jobs or who share a similar interest. *The Townswomen's Guild ... The Goldsmiths' Guild.*

guillotine guillotines (n) A guillotine was a device used until recently in France, for beheading criminals.

g

guilty

guilty guiltier guiltiest (adj) You are guilty if you are responsible for a crime. **guilt** (n)

guinea pig guinea pigs (n) A guinea pig is a small, South American rodent often kept as a pet.

guitar guitars (n) A guitar is a stringed instrument which can be plucked or strummed. **guitarist** (n)

gulf gulfs
1 (n) A gulf is a large inlet of sea into a land mass.
2 (n) A gulf in opinion is a wide difference in opinion between groups of people.

gull gulls (n) A gull is a sea-bird.

gullible (adj) people are easily fooled or tricked.

gulley gullies (n) A gulley is a channel used to carry water.

gulp gulps gulping gulped
1 (n) A gulp is the noise you make when you swallow.
2 (vb) You gulp your food if you swallow quickly or swallow a large amount at a time.

gun guns (n) A gun is a weapon which fires bullets or larger shells.

gunpowder (n) is an explosive powder used in the past to fire guns and cannons. It is now used in fireworks.

guru gurus (n) A guru is a Sikh teacher.

Guru Nanak's Birthday (n) is the holiest festival of the Sikh religion. Guru Nanak founded the religion in the 15th century.

gust gusts (n) A gust is a short rush of strong wind.

gut guts
1 (n) The gut is a tube inside the body which food passes through while it is digesting.
2 (n) The guts of a person or animal are all the inside organs.
3 (n) Gut is made from animal's stomachs and is used for stringing some instruments and rackets.

gutter gutters
1 (n) The gutter is the area where the road meets the kerb. Water runs down the gutters to the drains.
2 (n) The gutters on a roof carry rain water away from the building.
3 (n) The gutter press are newspapers which report scandal and gossip rather than factual news.

gym gyms (n) A gym is a hall or room equipped for sports and exercises. It is short for gymnasium.

gymkhana gymkhanas (n) A gymkhana is a competition involving horse riding.

gymnastics (n) This is the sport of exercises using bars, mats, ropes, etc to develop coordination. **gymnast** (n)

Gypsy Gypsies (n) A Gypsy is a member of an ethnic group living in most countries of Europe, the Middle East and the Americas. The Gypsies are believed to have originated in India in the 9th century.

gyrate gyrates gyrating gyrated (vb) If something gyrates, it spins around very fast.

Hh

habit habits
1 (n) A habit is something that you do regularly. *She was trying to break her nail-biting habit.*
2 (n) A habit is a garment worn by nuns and by monks.

habitat habitats (n) The habitat of a plant or animal is its natural home.

habitually (adv) If you do something habitually, you do it regularly.

hacksaw hacksaws (n) A hacksaw is a small saw used to cut metal.

haemorrhage haemorrhages (n) A haemorrhage is heavy bleeding inside the body.

haggard (adj) If someone looks haggard, they look tired through illness or worry.

haggis haggises (n) Haggis is a Scottish dish made from offal, cereal and spices cooked in a bag.

haggle haggles haggling haggled (vb) If you haggle over the price of something, you argue about it.

hail hails hailing hailed
1 (n) Hail is frozen rain.
2 (vb) When it hails, tiny balls of ice fall from the sky.
3 (n) A hail is a shower of something. *A hail of bullets fell on them.*

hair hairs (n) A hair is one of many fine threads that grow all over the body. A person's hair is the mass of hairs that grows on their head.

hairdresser hairdressers (n) A hairdresser washes, cuts and styles hair.

halal (adj) Halal meat is meat prepared according to Muslim custom.

half halves (n) A half is one of two equal parts of something.

hallmark hallmarks (n) A hallmark is a special mark on a precious metal object to show its purity and the place where it was made.

halo halos or **haloes** (n) A halo is the ring of light shown around the heads of holy people in paintings.

halt halts halting halted (vb) If someone or something halts, they stop.

halter halters (n) A halter is a leather or rope strap used to lead a horse.

hamburger hamburgers (n) A hamburger is a flat disc of minced meat which can be fried or grilled and is often eaten in a bun.

hamlet hamlets (n) A hamlet is a very small village.

hammer hammers hammering hammered
1 (n) A hammer is a tool used for hitting nails, etc.
2 (vb) When you hammer something, you hit it with a hammer.
3 (vb) If you hammer on a table or a door, you beat on it with your fists.

hammock hammocks (n) A hammock is a hanging bed usually made from strong rope or cloth.

hamper hampers hampering hampered
1 (n) A hamper is a basket with a lid for carrying food.
2 (vb) If something hampers you, you are held back or prevented from doing what you want to do. *The long skirt hampered her as she tried to climb the ladder.*

hamster hamsters (n) A hamster is a small rodent often kept as a pet.

hand hands handing handed
1 (n) Your hand is at the end of your arm; it has four fingers and a thumb.
2 (vb) If you hand something to someone, you pass it to them.
3 (n) A hand of cards is the set of cards dealt to each player in a game of cards.

handcuff

handcuff handcuffs (n) Handcuffs are strong, metal rings joined by a chain that can be locked onto a person's wrists.

handicap handicaps
1 (n) A handicap is a disability either of the body or the mind caused by illness or accident, or that some people are born with.
2 (n) A handicap can be something that makes it difficult for you to do what you want to do. *Her shyness was a handicap in making friends.*
3 (n) A handicap is a deliberate penalty or disadvantage taken by sportsmen to enable them to compete with others on level terms.

handicraft handicrafts (n) A handicraft is a skill such as embroidery, pottery, weaving, etc.

handkerchief handkerchiefs (n) A handkerchief is a small square of soft cloth for wiping your nose.

handle handles handling handled
1 (n) The handle on a door or a window is the knob or lever that you move to open or close it.
2 (n) A handle is the part of a mug, cup, bag, etc that you hold to pick them up or to carry them.
3 (vb) If you handle something, you pick it up and feel it with your hands to examine it carefully.
4 (vb) If you handle a horse, car or a machine you control it or use it.

handsome (adj) people are good-looking.

handwriting (n) is writing done by hand with a pencil or pen. **handwritten** (adj)

hang hangs hanging hanged hung
1 (vb) If you hang something, you attach it to a hook or nail, etc on a wall or elsewhere above the ground.
2 (vb) If something hangs, it is attached at the top but loose at the bottom so that it can swing.
3 (vb) If you hang wallpaper, you paste it onto the walls of a room.
4 To hang someone means to kill them by tying a rope around their neck and taking away the support.
5 If you hang around, you wait in the same place for a long time.

hangar hangars (n) A hangar is a large shed where aircraft are kept.

hanger hangers (n) A hanger is a piece of shaped wood, plastic or wire for hanging up clothes.

hang-glider hang-gliders (n) A hang-glider is a glider for one or two people who hang below the frame in a harness. **hang-gliding** (n)

Hanukkah (n) is the Jewish festival of lights which celebrates the cleansing of the temple in Jerusalem.

haphazard (adj) Something haphazard is without order. *The pictures were laid out in a haphazard way.*

happen happens happening happened (vb) If something happens, it takes place.

happy happier happiest (adj) If you are happy, you are enjoying yourself, and feel pleasure from what is going on around you. **happiness** (n)

harbour harbours harbouring harboured
1 (n) A harbour is a place where ships stop to load and unload and where they shelter from storms.
2 (vb) If you harbour someone, you shelter and hide them from danger.

hard harder hardest
1 (adj) If a surface is hard, it is not easily damaged or scratched.
2 (adj) If a person is hard, they are not easily moved by other people's problems.
3 (adj) If a job is hard, it is difficult.

hardboard (n) is a kind of thin, wooden sheet made by pressing together small wood fibres.

hardly (adv) If you can hardly do something, you can only just do it.

hardship hardships (n) refers to an experience that causes you suffering in some way. *On their journey across the desert the explorers endured many hardships.*

hardware
1 (n) Hardware is the name for tools for the home and garden, such as spades, screwdrivers, cooking equipment, etc.
2 (n) Hardware refers to the mechanical parts of a computer system: disk drive, monitor, etc.

hardwood hardwoods (n) Hardwood comes from deciduous trees which grow slowly and produce dense, strong wood. Oak, beech and elm are hardwoods.

hare hares
1 (n) A hare is a wild animal that looks like a large rabbit with long ears.
2 If you hare off somewhere, you run very fast.

harem harems (n) A harem is the women's part of the house in Muslim society.

harm harms harming harmed (vb) If you harm someone or something, you hurt or damage them in some way. **harmful** (adj)

harmonica
harmonicas (n) A harmonica is a mouth organ, played by moving it across the lips and blowing or sucking air through it.

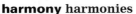

harmony harmonies
1 (n) Harmony is the pleasing, musical sound made by two or more musicians producing different notes at the same time. They are said to **harmonise**.
2 (n) If people or animals live in harmony, they live together in peace and happiness. **harmonious** (adj)

harness harnesses harnessing harnessed
1 (vb) If you harness an animal, you put a set of straps on it so that you can control it or so that it can pull machinery, etc.
2 (vb) If you harness power or energy, you control it so that it works for you.
3 (n) A harness is the set of straps used to fasten or to keep people secure. *The parachutist buckled on his harness.*

harp harps (n) A harp is a stringed instrument played by plucking with the fingers.

harpoon harpoons (n) A harpoon is like a spear and is used for hunting fish or whales.

harsh harsher harshest
1 (adj) If someone says something harsh, they say something hurtful or scolding.
2 (adj) If a judgement is harsh, it is strict or severe.

harvest harvests harvesting harvested
1 (n) Harvest is the time of year when farmers gather in their crops.
2 (vb) If you harvest a crop, you gather it and prepare it for selling.

hassle hassles hassling hassled
1 (vb) If you hassle someone, you annoy them and cause trouble by constantly asking or demanding that they should do something.
2 (n) A hassle is a task that is difficult and a nuisance to do.

hasty hastier hastiest (adj) If someone is hasty or does something hasty, they do it in a rush. **hastily** (adv) **haste** (n)

hatch hatches hatching hatched
1 (vb) When a young bird or other animal hatches from an egg, it breaks its shell and comes out.
2 (vb) If you hatch a plot with someone, you make plans with them.
3 (n) A hatch is an opening in a wall where food can be passed through.

hatchback hatchbacks (n) A hatchback is a car with a door at the back which opens upwards.

hate hates hating hated (vb) If you hate someone or something, you dislike them very much.

haul hauls hauling hauled
1 (vb) If you haul something, you pull it as strongly as possible because it is so heavy or awkward.
2 If a piece of work or a journey is a long haul, it is particularly difficult to complete.

haunt haunts haunting haunted
1 (vb) If a ghost haunts a place or a house, it appears there regularly.
2 (vb) If unpleasant thoughts haunt you, they stay with you and make you worry.
3 (n) If a place is a favourite haunt, you like to visit it often.

havoc

havoc (n) If there is havoc in a place, there is much confusion and damage. *The autumn storms created havoc.*

hawk hawks (n) A hawk is a large bird with talons, which catches small birds and animals for food.

hawthorn (n) is a small tree with sharp thorns which grows white flowers and red berries.

hay-fever (n) is an allergy to pollen or dust which causes a runny nose and sore throat.

haystack haystacks (n) A haystack is a large pile of hay stored in a field until it is required.

hazard hazards hazarding hazarded
1 (n) A hazard is a danger to a person or an animal. *She was a aware of the hazards of the weather conditions.* **hazardous** (adj)
2 (vb) If you hazard a guess about something, you make a guess which you know could be wrong.

haze (n) A haze is a light mist caused by heat, or smoke, so that it is difficult to see clearly.

hazel hazels
1 (n) A hazel is a tree with edible nuts.
2 (adj) Hazel eyes are a green-brown colour.

hazy hazier haziest
1 (adj) If you have a hazy view, you cannot see clearly because of dust or clouds in the air.
2 (adj) Hazy ideas are vague and not clear.

skeleton p273 **head heads heading headed**
1 (n) The head is the top part of the body with eyes, nose, brain, etc in it.
2 (n) Your head is your mind and mental abilities. *He does difficult sums in his head.*
3 (n) The head of something is the top part or the most important part. *Head of the queue... head of the company.*
4 (n) If a meal costs £5 a head, it costs £5 each.
5 (vb) If you head in a particular direction, you go that way.

6 (vb) When you head a ball, you strike it with your head.
7 If you cannot make head or tail of something, you cannot understand it at all.
8 If you say something off the top of your head, you say it without thinking much about it.

headache headaches
1 (n) A headache is a pain in the head.
2 (n) A headache is a problem that you worry about.

headline headlines
1 (n) The headlines are at the top of the page in large lettering in a newspaper, especially on the front page.
2 (n) The headlines are the main news points read out on radio or television.

headphone headphones (n) Headphones are pads containing small loudspeakers which fit over each ear, so that you can listen to tapes, radio, T.V. etc without others hearing.

headquarters (n) The headquarters of a company or a business are the buildings or offices where the leaders work.

headteacher headteachers (n) The headteacher is the man or woman who is in charge of a school.

heal heals healing healed
1 (vb) When a cut or some other injury heals, it gets better.
2 (vb) If someone heals another person, they help them to recover their health.
health (n) **healthy** (adj)

heap heaps heaping heaped
1 (n) A heap is a mass of things piled up on top of each other.
2 (vb) If you heap things up, you put them in an untidy pile.

hear hears hearing heard
1 (vb) When you hear something, you pick up sounds through your ears.
2 (vb) If you hear from someone, you receive a letter or a telephone call from them.

senses p264

hearse hearses (n) A hearse is a special car used to carry a coffin to a funeral.

heart hearts
1 (n) The heart is the organ in the chest that pumps blood around the body.

hem

2 (n) The heart of something is its centre.
3 (n) The heart is thought of as the centre of feelings. *She has a warm heart.*

heat heats heating heated
1 (vb) If you heat something, you warm it.
2 (n) A heat is one of several races in which the winners qualify for the final.
3 (adj) If you are heated about something, you are angry.

heath heaths (n) A heath is a large open area of rough grass with very few trees.

heather heathers (n) Heather is a plant with white, pink or purple flowers. Wild heathers grow on open hills and moors.

heaven heavens (n) In many religions, heaven is a place of never-ending happiness where good people are believed to go after they die.

heavy heavier heaviest (adj) If something is heavy, it weighs a lot and is often difficult to move.

heckle heckles heckling heckled (vb) If you heckle a speaker at a public meeting, you interrupt them with unpleasant comments.

hectic (adj) If an activity is hectic, it is very busy.

hedge hedges (n) A hedge is a line of bushes or small trees that border a garden, road, etc.

hedgehog hedgehogs (n) A hedgehog is a small, nocturnal animal covered with spines. It rolls up into a ball when frightened.

heel heels
1 (n) The heel is the back part of the foot.
2 (n) The heel of a shoe or sock is the part that covers the back part of the foot.
3 If you drag your heels, you do not make an effort.

heifer heifers (n) A heifer is a young cow which has not yet had calves.

height heights
1 (n) The height of something or someone is the measurement from top to bottom.
2 (n) If an aeroplane, for example, reaches a certain height, it is this distance above the ground.
3 When something is at its height, it is at its best or most serious.

heir heirs (n) An heir is a boy or man who inherits money, goods, etc when someone dies. **heiress** (fem. n)

helicopter helicopters (n) A helicopter is an aircraft which flies using a set of large rotating blades. It can take off and land in a small space. aircraft p5

hell (n) In some religions hell is believed to be a place of punishment where wrong-doers go after death.

helm helms (n) The helm of a boat is the wheel or tiller from which it is steered. **helmsman** (n)

helmet helmets (n) A helmet covers the head to protect it. *Safety helmets.* coat of arms p51

help helps helping helped
1 (vb) If you help someone, you make things easier for them in a practical way. *I helped by cleaning up before friends came.*
2 (vb) If you help someone who is in trouble, you do what you can to comfort them and try to solve their problems.
3 (vb) If you say you can't help doing something, you mean that you can't stop yourself from doing it.
4 (n) If you give help to someone, you advise them in some way or give them something they might need.
5 If someone calls 'Help', it means they are in trouble and need assistance.

helpless (adj) people or animals cannot protect or look after themselves.

hem hems hemming hemmed
1 (n) The hem of a garment is the edge of it that has been folded up and stitched in place.
2 (vb) If you hem a garment or piece of material, you fold the edges over and sew them down to stop them fraying.
3 If someone or something is hemmed in, they are closely surrounded by something. *The houses were hemmed in on all sides by high fences.*

heraldry

coat of arms p51 **heraldry** (n) is the study of the coats of arms of old noble families.

herb herbs (n) A herb is a plant that can be used for making medicines or for flavouring in cooking. **herbal** (adj)

herbivore herbivores (n) A herbivore is an animal that eats only plants. **herbivorous** (adj)

herd herds herding herded
1 (n) A herd is a collection of certain animals of the same kind that live together in a group.
2 (vb) If you herd people or animals together, you gather them into a group.

hereditary (adj) Something that is hereditary is passed down from parents to children through many generations.

heretic heretics (n) A heretic is someone who belongs to a certain religion but who then comes to disagree with many of its beliefs. **heresy** (n)

heritage (n) A country's heritage is all the traditions, customs, arts and architecture that have been passed down through the centuries.

hermit hermits (n) A hermit is a person who prefers to live alone and far away from other people. **hermitage** (n)

hero heroes
1 (n) A hero is a boy or man who has done something very brave or good and who is admired by many people. **heroic** (adj)
2 (n) The hero in a play, film or book is the leading male character.
3 (n) If you say someone is your hero, you admire them very much.
heroine (fem. n)

heron herons (n) A heron is a large, long-legged, wading bird.

herring herrings also **herring** (n) Herrings are edible sea fish that live in large shoals.

hesitate hesitates hesitating hesitated (vb) If you hesitate, you stop for a little while before you do something, either because you are unsure or because you are afraid. **hesitation** (n)

hexagon hexagons (n) A hexagon is a six-sided shape.

a regular **hexagon**

hibernate hibernates hibernating hibernated (vb) Animals which hibernate do so by spending the winter in a state like a deep sleep so that they need no food. **hibernation** (n)

hiccup hiccups (n) A hiccup is a spasm of the chest that produces short, sharp sounds from the throat.

hide hides hiding hid hidden
1 (vb) When you hide, you put yourself in a place where no one can find you.
2 (vb) If you hide something, you put it where no one can find it.
3 (vb) If you hide your feelings, you do not show how happy, sad, excited, etc. you feel.
4 (adj) If something is hidden, it can't be seen.
5 (n) A hide is a concealed shelter made from branches, grass, etc. used for bird or animal watching.
6 (n) A hide is the skin of an animal used for making leather.

hideous (adj) Things or people that are hideous are very ugly and unpleasant.

high higher highest
1 (adj) If you say that a thing is 10 metres high, it measures 10 metres from the bottom to the top.
2 (adj) High mountains and buildings reach a very long way from their bases into the sky.
3 (adj) If something is high, it's a long way above the ground.
4 (adj) High prices are more than you would expect to pay.
5 (adj) High winds are strong.
6 (adj) If someone holds high rank in the police, the civil service or the forces, they are very important.
7 (adj) If you have a high opinion of someone, you admire them.

highway highways (n) A highway is a main road.

hijack highjacks highjacking hijacked (vb) If someone hijacks a plane or other vehicle, they seize control of it by force. **hijacker** (n)

h

hike hikes hiking hiked
1 (vb) You hike when you go for a long
walk across country.
2 (n) A hike is a long, difficult walk.
hiker (n)

hilarious (adj) If something is hilarious, it
is very funny indeed.

Hillary, Sir Edmund (1919-) is a New
Zealand mountaineer and explorer. He and
Norgay Tenzing were the first two men to
reach the summit of Mt. Everest in 1953.

hilt hilts (n) The hilt of a knife or sword is
its handle.

hind hinds
1 (n) A hind is a female deer.
2 (adj) The hind legs of an animal are the
back legs.

hinder hinders hindering hindered (vb)
If you hinder someone or something, you
get in the way and slow things up.

Hinduism (n) is an Indian religion with
many gods. It teaches that people will live
again after they die. **Hindu** (n)

hinge hinges (n) A hinge is a piece of
metal, wood or plastic that holds two things
together so that they can swing freely.

hint hints hinting hinted (vb) If you hint,
you suggest something in a secretive way.

hip hips
1 (n) The hip is the joint at the top of the
thigh.
2 (n) Hips are the fruit of some kinds of
rose bush.

hippie hippies (n) A hippie is a person
who has chosen to live a life based on love
and peace and who has rejected
conventional ideas, dress and values. The
hippie movement began in the 1960's.

hippopotamus hippopotamuses or
hippopotami (n) A hippopotamus is a large
animal with short legs and hairless,
wrinkled skin. It lives in the lakes and
rivers of Africa.

hire hires hiring hired
1 (vb) If you hire something, you pay to use
it for a while.
2 (vb) If you hire a person, you pay them to
work for you to do a particular job.

history histories (n) History is the study
of past events. **historical** (adj)

hitch hitches hitching hitched
1 (vb) If you hitch something, you tie it up
by using a loop.
2 (n) A hitch is an upset in your plans.

Hitler, Adolf (1889–1945) was the leader of
the Nazi party in Germany. His army's
invasion of Poland brought about World
War II and by his orders millions of Jews,
Gypsies and other peoples were killed.

hive hives
1 (n) A hive is a structure for keeping bees.
2 If a place is a hive of industry, it is very
busy.

hoard hoards hoarding hoarded
1 (n) A hoard is a secret store of valuable
things.
2 (vb) If you hoard things, you collect them
and keep them.

hoarse hoarser hoarsest (adj) If your
voice is hoarse, it is husky and rough.

hoax hoaxes (n) A hoax is a nasty trick.

hob hobs (n) A hob is the surface on top of
a cooker or stove which can be heated and
used for boiling or frying.

hobble hobbles hobbling hobbled (vb) If
you hobble, you walk awkwardly and
lamely.

hobby hobbies (n) A hobby is a favourite
activity that you enjoy in your spare time.

hockey (n) is a game played between two
teams of 11 players. Long curved sticks are
used to hit a small, hard ball into a net.

hoe hoes (n) A hoe is a long-handled stick
with a short, metal blade, used by
gardeners to loosen soil.

Hogmanay (n) In Scotland Hogmany is
New Year's Eve and its celebrations.

hoist hoists hoisting hoisted
1 (vb) If you hoist something heavy, you
pull it up to a high position.
2 (vb) If you hoist a flag, you raise it up.
3 (n) A hoist is a machine for lifting heavy
things.

h

holder

holder holders
1 (n) A holder is someone who owns, looks after or has control of something. *Holders of driving licences, premium bonds, etc.*
2 (n) A holder is a container for something. *A pen holder ... a plant holder.*

hole holes
1 (n) A hole is a space inside something solid. *A hole in the ground.*
2 (n) A hole can be a home for a small animal like a mouse or rabbit.
3 If you pick holes in someone's ideas, you comment on all the bad points.

holiday holidays
1 (n) A holiday is time off from work or school.
2 (n) A holiday is time spent away from home visiting other places and people.

hollow hollows hollowing hollowed
1 (vb) If you hollow something out, you take out material from inside, leaving an empty space.
2 (adj) If something is hollow, it has empty space inside it.

holly (n) This is a small, evergreen tree with red berries in winter and prickly, shiny leaves.

holocaust holocausts (n) A holocaust is widespread destruction of people by war or fire.

hologram holograms (n) A hologram is a three-dimensional picture made by laser beams.

holster holsters (n) A holster holds a gun and is worn round the waist or strapped under the arm.

holy holier holiest
1 (adj) Something holy is linked with God or to a particular religion. *Holy Bible ... Holy Spirit.*
2 (adj) A holy person leads a good life, dedicated to God or to a particular religion.

homesick (adj) If you feel homesick, you are away from home and wish to return there. **homesickness** (n)

honest (adj) people can be trusted to tell the truth. **honesty** (n) **honestly** (adv)

honey (n) is a yellow, sticky, sugary substance made by bees.

honeycomb honeycombs (n) A honeycomb is made by bees from wax; honey is stored in it in six-sided cells.

honeymoon honeymoons (n) A honeymoon is a holiday for a newly-married couple after their wedding.

honour honours honouring honoured
1 (n) Honour is a feeling of pride about something you belong to or that you represent. *Family honour ... honour of the regiment.*
2 (vb) If you honour someone, you praise or reward them in public because of some particularly brave or noteworthy action.
3 (vb) If you honour an agreement, you keep it.
4 (n) If you receive an honour, you get a special award for bravery, leadership, etc.

hood hoods (n) A hood is a covering for the head and neck, often fastened to the back of a coat or jacket.

hoof hoofs or **hooves** (n) A hoof is the hard part of an animal's foot.

hook hooks hooking hooked
1 (n) A hook is a curved piece of plastic, metal or wood, used to hang things on. *Coat hook ... cup hook.*
2 (vb) If you hook a fish, you catch it.
3 If you do something by hook or by crook, you do it despite obstacles.

hooligan hooligans (n) A hooligan is a noisy, often destructive person, usually in a group of other, similar people. *The football hooligans smashed the shop windows when their team lost the match.*

hope hopes hoping hoped
1 (vb) If you hope something will happen, you want it to take place. **hopefully** (adv)
2 (vb) If you hope to do something, you plan to do it. *We hope to paper the walls next week.*
3 (n) Hope is a feeling that things will go as you wish in the future.
4 (n) A hope is something that you want.
5 If you hope for the best, you hope all will go well. **hopeful** (adj)
6 If you do not hold out much hope, you think things are unlikely to work out well for you. **hopeless** (adj)

horde hordes (n) A horde of people is a very large crowd.

horizon horizons (n) The horizon is the line in the distance where land and sky seem to meet.

horizontal (adj) If someone or something is horizontal, they are parallel to the ground or level with it.

horn horns
1 (n) A horn is a hard, pointed growth on the heads of certain animals.
2 (n) Horn is the hard substance that animals' horns are made from; it is used to make other objects.
3 (n) A horn is a musical instrument that is played by blowing into it.
4 (n) A horn is a device on a vehicle that is sounded as a warning.

hornet hornets
1 (n) A hornet is a large wasp that can give a painful sting.
2 If you stir up a hornet's nest, you cause trouble between people.

horoscope horoscopes (n) A horoscope is information about what may happen to you in the future. It is based on the positions of the stars and planets when you were born.

horror horrors
1 (n) Horror is a powerful feeling of fear and shock, which is brought on by someone or something very unpleasant.
2 (adj) A horror film is made to frighten you with monsters or ghosts, for instance.

horrible
1 (adj) When you dislike someone or something, you say they are horrible.
2 (adj) If you are shocked or very upset by some event, you describe it as horrible.

horse horses
1 (n) A horse is a large animal which is used for riding, racing or for work.
2 (n) A horse is a piece of equipment which gymnasts use for exercises and jumping.
3 A dark horse is someone who has abilities that few people know about.

horse chestnut (n) The horse chestnut is a large tree with flowers and shiny brown nuts usually known as conkers.

horsepower (n) is a way of measuring the power of an engine.

horticulture (n) describes anything to do with gardening. **horticultural** (adj)

hose hoses hosing hosed
1 (n) A hose is a long plastic or rubber tube. Water is sent down it to water the garden, clean a car, etc.
2 (vb) If you hose something, you clean it using water through a hose.

hospital hospitals (n) A hospital is a place where people who are ill or who have had an accident can be treated and cared for.

host hosts
1 (n) A host is a man who gives a party and looks after those who are invited. **hostess** (fem. n)
2 (n) The host of a programme on television or radio, introduces it to the audience.

hostage hostages (n) A hostage is a person who is taken prisoner by an individual or group and who is threatened with harm unless people do what they demand.

hostel hostels (n) A hostel is a large building where people can stay quite cheaply for a limited time.

hostile
1 (adj) If you are hostile to someone, you act in an unfriendly way. **hostility** (n)
2 (adj) If a situation is hostile, it is difficult and unpleasant.

hot hotter hottest
1 (adj) If the weather is hot, the temperature is high.
2 (adj) If you are hot, you feel uncomfortable because your body temperature is high.
3 If someone is hot on a subject, they know a lot about it.
4 Someone who is hot-tempered gets angry quickly.
5 If you are in hot water, you are in trouble.

hotel hotels (n) A hotel is a building where people pay to sleep in the rooms and often to eat meals.

hound hounds hounding hounded
1 (n) A hound is a breed of dog used for hunting or racing.
2 (vb) If you hound someone, you pursue them in an unpleasant, threatening way.

h

hour hours
1 (n) An hour is made up of 60 minutes and there are 24 hours in one day.
2 (n) If someone is an hour away from a place, it will take 60 minutes to get there.
3 If you keep late hours, you go to bed late.
4 If someone works all hours, they work very hard and at all times.

house houses
1 (n) A house is a building where people, sometimes of the same family, live.
2 (n) A house is the name sometimes given to a particular group of school pupils.
3 (n) A house can be a building for a special purpose. *The White House... hen house.*
4 If you get on with another person like a house on fire, you get on very well with them.
5 If you are given something on the house, you get it free.

household households (n) A household is all the people who live in one house.

housekeeper housekeepers (n) A housekeeper is a person whose job it is to look after someone else's house.

housewife housewives (n) A housewife is a married woman who looks after the home.

hover hovers hovering hovered (vb) When a bird hovers, it stays at the same place above ground for some time without changing its position.

hovercraft hovercrafts (n) A hovercraft is a machine that can move across land or water, as it floats on a cushion of air beneath it.

however
1 However can mean even so or nevertheless. *She looked bad-tempered, however, she was an excellent baby-sitter.*
2 However can also mean no matter how or to whatever extent. *However much she ate she never got fat.*

howl howls howling howled
1 (vb) When a wolf or dog howls, it makes a long series of crying sounds.
2 (vb) When a person howls, they cry and moan loudly, either because they are very sad or because they are in great pain.

3 (vb) When the wind howls, it moans in the trees or around buildings.
4 (n) A howl is a long, drawn-out, crying sound.

hub hubs (n) The hub is the centre of a wheel.

huddle huddles huddling huddled
1 (vb) If humans or animals huddle together, they crowd very close to each other, for warmth or comfort.
2 (vb) If you huddle somewhere, you lie or crouch with your body curled up and your legs and arms pulled in close.

huge (adj) means very big.

hulk hulks
1 (n) A hulk is the remains of a large, wrecked ship.
2 (n) A hulk is a very large person, building or object.

hull hulls (n) The hull of a boat is its main framework.

hum hums humming hummed
1 (n) A hum is a low, continuous noise such as the distant sound of traffic, conversation or machinery.
2 (vb) If you hum, you sing a tune with your lips closed.

human humans
1 (n) A human is a man, woman or child.
2 (adj) Human means belonging to or relating to all people.

humane (adj) people believe that all living creatures should be treated kindly and sympathetically.

humanity
1 (n) Humanity means the human race.
2 (n) If someone has humanity, they are kind and care deeply about the feelings and problems of other people.

humble humbles humbling humbled; humbler humblest
1 (adj) Someone who is humble feels that they are not interesting enough or clever enough for other people to take much notice of them.
2 (adj) Humble can mean low in rank.
3 (adj) A humble cottage is very small and poorly furnished.

h

4 (vb) If you humble someone, you make them feel inferior.

humid (adj) If a place is humid, it is warm and damp.

humiliate humiliates humiliating humiliated
1 (vb) If you humiliate someone, you do or say something that makes them feel ashamed or very silly.
2 (adj) If something is humiliating, it embarrasses you and makes you feel ashamed. **humiliation** (n)

humour humours humouring humoured
1 (n) If you have a good sense of humour, you are able to see the funny side of things and be cheerful.
2 (vb) If you humour someone, you try to please them and put them in a good mood.
3 (n) Humour is another word for mood.
She was in good humour today.
humorous (adj)

hump humps humping humped
1 (n) A hump is a fleshy lump on the back of an animal or human.
2 (n) A hump is a very small hill or piece of raised ground.
3 (vb) If you hump something, you carry it on your back.

hunch hunches hunching hunched
1 (vb) If you hunch your shoulders, you raise them and push them forward and bend over slightly.
2 (vb) If someone hunches themselves, they bend their shoulders over and lower their head because they are cold or miserable.
3 (n) A hunch is an idea you have about something that you think will happen.

hungry hungrier hungriest (adj) If you are hungry, your stomach feels empty and uncomfortable because you need to eat.
hunger (n)

hunt hunts hunting hunted
1 (vb) Animals hunt other animals for food; people hunt animals for food and fur and some hunt for sport.
2 (n) A hunt is a group of people who meet together to hunt animals such as foxes.
hunter (n)
3 (vb) If you hunt for something, you look for it because you have lost it.

hurdle hurdles
1 (n) A hurdle is a kind of fence used for jumps in horse racing.
2 (n) A hurdle is a difficulty that you have to overcome in order to do or gain something.

hurl hurls hurling hurled
1 (vb) If you hurl something, you throw it with as much force as you can.
2 (vb) If you hurl abuse at someone, you say nasty things about them in a loud voice.

hurricane hurricanes (n) A hurricane is a violent, storm-force wind.

hurry hurries hurrying hurried
1 (vb) If you hurry, you go somewhere or do something as quickly as you can.
2 (vb) If you hurry something, you make it happen faster than it would normally.
3 If you do something in a hurry, you do it quickly.

hurt hurts hurting hurts
1 (vb) If you hurt yourself, you have an accident of some kind.
2 (vb) If part of your body hurts, it is painful.
3 (vb) If you hurt someone's feelings you say or do something that makes them feel sad or upset. **hurtful** (adj)
4 (n) A hurt is the damage done to someone's feelings when they have been badly treated.

husband husbands (n) A husband is the man who is married to a woman.

husk husks (n) A husk is the hard, outer layer of a seed.

hustle hustles hustling hustled (vb) If you hustle someone, you push them roughly.

hutch hutches (n) A hutch is a cage for keeping small pets such as rabbits.

hydrant hydrants (n) A hydrant is a pipe that is connected to the main water supply of a town or a city and is only used for emergencies such as drought or fire.

hydraulic (adj) Something that is hydraulic involves or is operated by water, oil or another fluid under pressure.

ḣ

hydro-electric

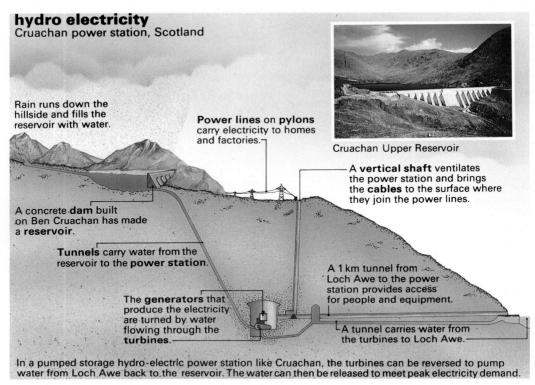

hydro electricity
Cruachan power station, Scotland

Rain runs down the hillside and fills the reservoir with water.

Power lines on pylons carry electricity to homes and factories.

Cruachan Upper Reservoir

A **vertical shaft** ventilates the power station and brings the **cables** to the surface where they join the power lines.

A concrete **dam** built on Ben Cruachan has made a **reservoir**.

Tunnels carry water from the reservoir to the **power station**.

A 1 km tunnel from Loch Awe to the power station provides access for people and equipment.

The **generators** that produce the electricity are turned by water flowing through the **turbines**.

A tunnel carries water from the turbines to Loch Awe.

In a pumped storage hydro-electric power station like Cruachan, the turbines can be reversed to pump water from Loch Awe back to the reservoir. The water can then be released to meet peak electricity demand.

hydro-electric (adj) This kind of power is electricity made from the energy of running water.

hydrofoil hydrofoils (n) A hydrofoil is a boat that travels above the surface of the water by resting on a pair of fins.

hyena hyenas (n) A hyena is a dog-like, wild animal that hunts in a pack. It is found in Africa.

hygienic (adj) Something that is hygienic is clean and free from germs.

hymn hymns (n) A hymn is a song of praise.

hyphen hyphens (n) A hyphen is a dash - which is used to join two words to make a single, new word with a meaning of its own. *Letter-box.*

hypnotise hypnotises hypnotised hypnotised (vb) When you hypnotise someone, they seem to be asleep but will respond to suggestions that you make. **hypnosis** (n) **hypnotist** (n) **hypnotism** (n)

hypochondriac hypochondriacs (n) A hypochondriac worries about their health all the time. **hypochondria** (n)

hypocrite hypocrites (n) A hypocrite is someone who pretends to be good or to have particular beliefs when this is not so.

hypothermia (n) is a condition in which a person is ill because they have been extremely cold for some time.

hysteria (n) is a nervous state in which people cannot stop laughing or crying.

Ii

ice ices icing iced
1 (n) Ice is frozen water.
2 (vb) If you ice a cake, you cover it with a paste made of icing sugar. **icing** (n)

Ice Age (n) The Ice Age was a time lasting thousands of years, when a lot of the world was covered in ice.

iceberg icebergs (n) Icebergs are huge lumps of ice which float in the sea.

ice cream ice creams (n) Ice cream is a frozen mixture of sugar and cream.

ice-skate ice-skates ice-skating ice-skated
1 (n) An ice-skate is a shoe or boot with a metal blade that you wear when you skate on ice.
2 (vb) If you ice-skate, you move about on ice wearing ice-skates. **ice-skater** (n)

icicle icicles (n) An icicle is a pointed stick of ice that hangs from roofs, window ledges, etc in freezing weather.

icy icier iciest
1 (adj) If roads are icy, they are covered with ice.
2 (adj) If the weather is icy, it is extremely cold.

idea ideas (n) An idea is a plan or a thought in your head. *I had a great idea about how we could raise money for charity.*

ideal ideals
1 (n) An ideal is something that you think is perfect and might like to achieve or copy.
2 (adj) If you say that something is ideal, you think that it's perfect.

identical (adj) If things are identical, they are exactly the same.

identify identifies identifying identified (vb) If you identify someone or something, you recognise and name them.

identification (n) **identity** (n)

idiot idiots (n) If you call someone an idiot, you think they are very stupid or have done something very silly.

idle
1 (adj) If someone is idle, they are lazy or have nothing to do.
2 (adj) If machines are idle, they are not being used.
3 (adj) Idle can also mean useless or worthless. *Idle chatter . . . idle gossip.*

idol idols
1 (n) An idol is a statue that is worshipped as a god.
2 (n) An idol is a person who is admired by a lot of people.

igloo igloos (n) An igloo is a small, temporary house made of snow blocks used by the Inuit or Eskimo people.

ignite ignites igniting ignited (vb) If something ignites, it starts to burn.
ignition (n)

ignorant
1 (adj) Someone who is ignorant has had very little education and does not know much.
2 (adj) If you are ignorant of certain things, you know little or nothing about them.
ignorance (n)

ill (adj) When someone is ill, they are in poor health or are suffering from a disease.

illegal (adj) If something is illegal, it is against the law.

illegible (adj) If writing is illegible, it is so badly done that you cannot read it.

illiterate (adj) people cannot read or write.

illness illnesses (n) An illness is a disease or infection that makes people unwell.

illogical

illogical (adj) If you are illogical, you do not act sensibly or think things out reasonably. *He went to the bathroom to get the tea, which seemed illogical.*

illuminate illuminates illuminating illuminated
1 (vb) If you illuminate something, you shine light on it. **illumination** (n)
2 (adj) If someone or something is illuminating, they make things easy to understand.

illusion illusions
1 (n) An illusion is an idea that you think is true, but isn't really.
2 (n) An illusion is a clever trick, performed by a magician, which deceives your eyes.

illustrate illustrates illustrating illustrated (vb) If you illustrate something, you help explain its meaning by using pictures, diagrams, etc. **illustration** (n)

image images
1 (n) Your image is your reflection in a mirror.
2 (n) The pictures on film, television or photographs, or those created by a piece of writing are called images.
3 (n) If you are the image of someone, you look very like them.

imagine imagines imagining imagined (vb) If you imagine something or someone, you make a picture of them in your mind. **imagination** (n) **imaginary** (adj) **imaginative** (adj)

imam imams (n) An imam is an official of a mosque in the Islam religion.

imitate imitates imitating imitated (vb) If you imitate another person, you copy what they do or say. **imitation** (n)

immediately (adv) If you do something immediately, you do it at once.

immense (adj) Something that is immense is very large.

immerse immerses immersing immersed
1 (vb) If you immerse something, you cover it completely with liquid.
2 (vb) If you immerse yourself in an activity, you become completely occupied with it. **immersion** (n)

immigrant immigrants (n) An immigrant is someone who has left their own country and come to settle in a new one. **immigration** (n)

immortal
1 (adj) Something which is immortal will live or last for ever.
2 (adj) If someone or something is said to be immortal, they are famous and likely to be remembered for a long time.

immunise immunises immunising immunised (vb) If doctors immunise you against a disease, they give you an injection so that you cannot catch the disease. **immune** (n) **immunisation** (n)

impact impacts
1 (n) If something makes an impact upon you, it has a noticeable effect. *The new teacher made a big impact on the class.*
2 (n) When one object hits another object, there is an impact.

impatient (adj) An impatient person is not prepared to wait and is easily irritated. **impatience** (n)

impede impedes impeding impeded (vb) If you impede somebody's movement, you make it difficult for them to move.

imperfect (adj) Something that is imperfect has faults in it.

impersonate impersonates impersonating impersonated (vb) If you impersonate someone, you pretend to be that person. **impersonation** (n)

impertinent (adj) If you are impertinent, you are rude to someone in authority. **impertinence** (n)

impetuous (adj) An impetuous person does things without thinking.

implore implores imploring implored (vb) If you implore someone to do something, you beg them very strongly. *I implore you to sack the man.*

imply implies implying implied (vb) If you imply something, you suggest it but do not actually say it. *By searching David's bag, the policeman implied that he was the thief.* **implication** (n)

import imports importing imported
1 (vb) If a country imports goods, it buys them from another country.
2 (n) Imports are the goods brought into a country from another country.

important (adj) Something important is very serious, valuable or has great consequences. **importance** (n)

impose imposes imposing imposed (vb) If you put a burden or an unwanted problem onto a person, you impose it upon them. *The headteacher imposed very strict rules on the whole school.* **imposition** (n)

imposing (adj) If someone or something is imposing, they are large and impressive.

impossible (adj) If something is impossible, it cannot be done under any circumstances.

impostor (n) An impostor is a person who pretends to be someone they are not, usually for devious reasons.

impregnable (adj) Something impregnable cannot be broken into or captured. *The army found the castle was impregnable.*

impress impress impressing impressed
1 (vb) If you impress someone, you cause them to admire you. **impressive** (adj)
2 (vb) If you impress something on someone, you make sure that they understand and remember it.

impression impressions
1 (n) An impression is a vague idea or feeling you have about people or situations.
2 (n) The impression of an object is the mark that is left when something has been pressed into its surface.

impressionable (adj) A person is impressionable if they are too easily impressed by other people.

imprison imprisons imprisoning imprisoned (vb) If you put someone, or keep someone in prison, you imprison them. **imprisonment** (n)

improbable (adj) If something is improbable, it is unlikely to happen. *I think it improbable that our team will win the cup this year.*

improve improves improving improved (vb) If you get better after being ill, or do better at sports, work, etc, you improve. **improvement** (n)

improvise improvises improvising improvised (vb) If you improvise something, you make it up as you go along. **improvisation** (n)

impudent (adj) If you are impudent, you are cheeky, rude or insolent. **impudence** (n)

impulse impulses (n) An impulse is an urge to do something immediately and without thinking. **impulsive** (adj)

inability (n) The inability to do something is not being able to do it.

inaccessible (adj) If someone or something is inaccessible, it is impossible or very difficult to reach them.

inaccurate (adj) Something is inaccurate if it is not correct. **inaccuracy** (n)

inadequate (adj) If something is inadequate it is not sufficient, not good enough, or not satisfactory in some way. **inadequacy** (n)

inanimate (adj) Something inanimate is without life. *Rocks, furniture, etc. are inanimate.*

inappropriate (adj) Something inappropriate is not suitable for a particular occasion, or purpose. **inappropriately** (adv)

inarticulate (adj) People who are inarticulate cannot express themselves well in speech.

inaudible (adj) If something is inaudible, it is not loud enough to be heard.

inborn (adj) abilities are natural abilities or attitudes rather than learned ones.

incapable (adj) If you are incapable of doing something, you are not able to do it.

incendiary (adj) An incendiary device is something designed to start fires.

incessant (adj) Something which is incessant goes on without stopping.

inch

inch inches (n) An inch is a unit of measurement. There are 12 inches in 1 foot. 1 inch measures the same as about 25 millimetres.

incidence (n) The incidence of something is the frequency with which it happens.

incident incidents (n) An incident is an occurrence, an event or a happening.

incinerate incinerates incinerating incinerated (vb) If you incinerate something, you burn it until only ashes are left. **incinerator** (n)

incision incisions (n) An incision is a cut made deliberately and carefully.

incite incites inciting incited (vb) If you incite somebody to do something, you encourage them to do it by making them excited or angry.

incline inclines inclining inclined
1 (n) An incline is a slope of some sort.
2 (vb) If you incline towards an idea or side, you agree with it or support it.

include includes including included (vb) If you include someone or something, you put them in as part of the whole. *The list included all the people living in the house.* **inclusion** (n) **inclusive** (adj)

income incomes (n) Your income is all the money you have paid to you.

income tax (n) is a percentage of a person's income that the government takes to pay for national services such as health, education and defence.

incompetent (adj) Someone who is incompetent does not have the skills to do a job properly. **incompetence** (n)

inconspicuous (adj) If someone or something is inconspicuous, it is difficult to see them because they are small or hidden away.

inconvenient (adj) Something that is inconvenient is awkward and makes difficulties for you at the time.

increase increases increasing increased
1 (vb) If something increases, it gets bigger in number or size.

2 (n) An increase is a rise in the level, amount, etc. of something. *An increase in pay... an increase in temperature... an increase in water level.*

incredible (adj) If something is incredible, it is so amazing that it is difficult to believe.

incriminate incriminates incriminating incriminated (vb) If you incriminate someone, you say or do something to suggest that they are guilty of a crime.

incubate incubates incubating incubated
1 (vb) When eggs incubate, or a bird incubates them, they are kept warm until they hatch.
2 (vb) If ideas or plans incubate, they develop slowly after a great deal of thought and discussion.

incubator incubators
1 (n) An incubator is a special machine which helps to keep babies alive if they are very small or weak.
2 (n) An incubator is a device which keeps eggs at the correct temperature for them to hatch.

incurable (adj) If someone has an incurable disease, they will not recover.

indebted
(adj) If you are indebted to someone, you are grateful to them for something they have done for you.

indecent (adj) Something or someone indecent is rude.

indeed
1 You use indeed to agree with something that has been said. *I do indeed!*
2 You can use indeed to give extra force to what you are saying. *Thank you very much indeed.*

indefinite (adj) If something is indefinite, information about it is not clear.

indelible
1 (adj) A mark or a stain which is indelible cannot be removed.
2 (adj) An indelible memory of something is not forgotten.

independent
1 (adj) If you are independent, you are able to do things for yourself without needing help from others.
2 (adj) Something that is independent is set apart from everything else.
3 (adj) An independent school, broadcasting company, etc receives no money from the government.
4 (adj) Independent countries are those which used to be ruled by other countries but which now have their own governments.
5 (n) An independent is a politician who does not represent any political party.

index indexes (n) An index is an alphabetical list. It is usually found at the back of books to help you find information.

indicate indicates indicating indicated (vb) If you indicate something to someone, you show it to them. **indication** (n)

indicator indicators
1 (n) An indicator is a mechanism that can give information.
2 (n) The indicators on a car are the lights that show if it is turning left or right.
3 (n) An indicator is a chemical which changes colour if an acid or an alkali is added to it.

indifferent (adj) If you are indifferent to someone or something, you have no feelings about them. **indifference** (n)

indigestion (n) is the discomfort you feel when you cannot digest your food properly.

individual individuals
1 (n) An individual is a person, considered separately from every other person.
2 (adj) If you behave in an individual way, you act differently from most others.
3 (adj) If something is for individual use, it is for one person to use. *The class had individual projects to complete.*
individually (adv)

indulge indulges indulging indulged (vb) If you indulge in something, you do it because you enjoy it. **indulgence** (n)

industrious (adj) An industrious person works very hard.

industry industries
1 (n) Industry is all the work of factories in making and producing things.

2 (n) An industry is one particular type of work, including all the people and products. *The computer industry is expanding rapidly.* **industrial** (adj)

inefficient (adj) If someone or something is inefficient, they do not work as well as they might. **inefficiency** (n) **inefficient** (adj)

inert (adj) If something is inert, it does not move.

inevitable (adj) If something is inevitable, it will happen and cannot be prevented. **inevitability** (n)

inexcusable (adj) If something is inexcusable, it is so bad that no excuse can be made for it.

inexpensive (adj) Something inexpensive costs very little.

infamous (adj) An infamous person or thing is well known for their bad qualities.

infant infants
1 (n) An infant is a small child or baby.
2 (adj) Infant describes anything for small children. *Infant clothes . . . infant class.*

infantry (n) The infantry are soldiers who fight on foot.

infatuated (adj) If you are infatuated with someone, you feel such a strong love for them that you cannot think reasonably about them.

infect infects infecting infected
1 (vb) If someone or something infects a person or an animal, they cause them to catch a disease of some kind. **infection** (n)
2 (vb) If a certain mood infects a group of people, it spreads through them very quickly. **infectious** (adj)

infer infers inferring inferred (vb) If you infer that something is correct, you decide it is true by using details you already know. **inference** (n)

inferior inferiors
1 (adj) Something that is inferior is of poorer quality than something of a similar kind.
2 (n) If you feel someone is your inferior, you think this person has a lower status than yourself. **inferiority** (n)

infertile
1 (adj) Infertile soil does not produce crops.
2 (adj) A person, animal or plant that is infertile is unable to reproduce. **infertility** (n)

infested (adj) If plants, animals or places are infested, they are full of pests such as slugs, fleas, rats etc.

infiltrate infiltrates infiltrating infiltrated (vb) If people infiltrate an organisation, for example, they gradually enter it secretly to spy on it or to find out its secrets. **infiltrator** (n) **infiltration** (n)

infinite (adj) Something that is infinite is endless or so big that you cannot imagine it. **infinity** (n)

infirm (adj) A person who is infirm is very weak and ill, usually because they are old.

inflammable (adj) Something inflammable catches fire easily.

inflate inflates inflating inflated (vb) If you inflate something, you fill it with air or gas. *He inflated the football.*

inflation (n) is a general increase in the cost of living.

inflict inflicts inflicting inflicted (vb) If you inflict something unpleasant on someone, you make them suffer it.

influence influences influencing influenced
1 (n) Influence is a power which helps you to persuade other people to do something the way you want it done. **influential** (adj)
2 (vb) If you influence something, you have an effect on the way it happens.

influenza (n) is an illness causing a high temperature, aches and pains and a running nose.

inform informs informing informed
1 (vb) If you inform someone about something, you tell them about it.
2 (vb) If you inform on someone, you tell the authorities about them. *She had evidence of his crime so she informed on him.*

informal (adj) You use the word informal to describe a way of behaving or a situation that is relaxed and casual.

information (n) is something you know about, news, facts, etc.

infuriate infuriates infuriating infuriated (vb) If you infuriate someone you make them angry.

ingenious (adj) An ingenious device involves new ideas. An ingenious person is clever.

ingot ingots (n) An ingot is a block of metal.

stamping refined gold **ingots**

ingratitude (adj) is a lack of care or thanks for something that has been done for you.

ingredient ingredients (n) Ingredients are all the separate things you need for making something, a cake, for example.

inhabit inhabits inhabiting inhabited (vb) If you inhabit a place, you live there.

inhale inhales inhaling inhaled (vb) If you inhale something, you breathe it in. **inhalation** (n)

inherit inherits inheriting inherited
1 (vb) If you inherit something such as property or money, you receive it when someone dies. **inheritance** (n)
2 (vb) If you inherit a characteristic or quality, you are born with it because your ancestors had it.

inhospitable (adj) If a place or a person is inhospitable, they are unwelcoming and unpleasant.

inhuman (adj) An inhuman act is cruel and without feeling.

initial initials
1 (n) Your initials are the first letters of each of your names. *Mary Jane Cole's initials are M.J.C.*
2 (adj) Initial describes the first stage of something.

initiative initiatives
1 (n) Initiative is the ability to see what must be done and to act upon it.
2 If you use your initiative, you do something without being told to do it.
3 If you take the initiative, you make the first move.

inject injects injecting injected (vb) If a doctor, for example, injects you with a drug or a medicine, he or she puts it into your body using a hollow needle. **injection** (n)

injure injures injuring injured (vb) If you injure someone, you hurt or damage them in some way. **injury** (n)

injustice injustices (n) Injustice is unfairness.

ink inks (n) Ink is the coloured liquid used for writing or printing.

inland (adj) Inland areas are the part of a country away from the sea.

inlet inlets (n) An inlet is a narrow channel of the sea which goes inland.

inmate inmates (n) An inmate is a person who lives in an institution, prison etc.,

inn inns (n) An inn is a public house, with bedrooms which can be rented.

inner
1 (adj) Something which goes inside something else can be called inner. *A bike tyre has an inner tube… The inner ring road is nearer the city centre.*
2 (n) The inner is the part of a dart board or target nearest the bull or centre.

innocence (n) is the state of being harmless, blameless and free from guilt. **innocent** (adj).

innovation innovations (n) An innovation is a completely new idea or invention.

inoculate inoculates inoculating inoculated (vb) If a doctor inoculates a person, or a vet inoculates an animal, they inject a weak solution of a disease into them which prevents them from catching it. **inoculation** (n)

input inputs inputting inputted
1 (n) Input is a contribution to an argument, discussion or sequence of ideas.
2 (n) Input is the information fed into a computer.
3 (vb) If you input information on a computer, you put it in.

inquest inquests (n) An inquest is an enquiry into the cause of a person's death.

inquisitive (adj) If you are inquisitive, you are eager to find out about things.

insane (adj) A person who is insane is mentally ill. They may act strangely or believe things that are not true or possible. **insanity** (n)

inscribe inscribes inscribing inscribed (vb) If you engrave or cut a mark into a surface, you inscribe it. **inscription** (n)

insect insects (n) An insect is a small creature with six legs and its skeleton on the outside. Ants, flies, beetles, etc. are insects.

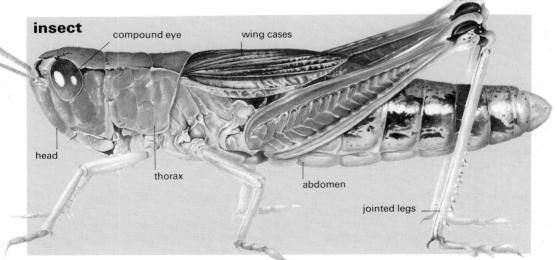

insect

compound eye

wing cases

head

thorax

abdomen

jointed legs

insecticide insecticides (n) An insecticide is a chemical which kills insects.

insecure
1 (adj) If a thing is insecure, it is not fixed properly and could move or fall.
2 (adj) If you feel insecure, you feel unsafe and worried about your situation. *Johnson is not very confident and seems insecure in his new job.* **insecurity** (n)
3 (adj) If a building is insecure, it means that it is easy to break into.

insert inserts inserting inserted
1 (n) An insert is an extra part put into something. *With this week's magazine there is a special insert on badgers.* **insertion** (n)
2 (vb) If you insert something, you put it inside something else, usually carefully. *You insert your bank card into the machine to get cash.*

inshore (adj) If you are inshore, you are at sea, but close to the coastline.

inside (adj) If someone or something is inside something, they are in it. *She was inside the house... The book was inside the desk.*

insignia insignia (n) An insignia is a badge or something similar which shows rank.

insignificant (adj) If something or someone is insignificant, they are not important.

insist insists insisting insisted (vb) If you insist on something, you demand it strongly. *I insist on seeing Mr. Thomas now.* **insistent** (adj) **insistence** (n)

insolent (adj) If you are insolent, you are rude or cheeky. **insolence** (n)

insomnia (n) is a difficulty in getting to sleep.

inspect inspects inspecting inspected (vb) If you inspect something you check it to see if it is correct or safe. **inspection** (n)

inspector inspectors
1 (n) An inspector is a person whose job it is to check things.
2 (n) Inspector is the rank in the police force above sergeant.

inspire inspires inspiring inspired
1 (vb) If you cause someone to do something good and worthwhile, you inspire them. *He was inspired to write a book about his grandfather's exciting life.*
2 (adj) If you are inspired, you have a sudden good idea. **inspiration** (n)

install installs installing installed (vb) If you install a machine, you fit it into its correct place in working order. **installation** (n)

instalment instalments
1 (n) An instalment is one of several parts of a story, film etc. *The T.V. serial was shown in four instalments.*
2 (n) Instalments are part payments for something paid at regular intervals.

instance instances
1 (n) An instance is a particular event or occurrence. *We usually charge for this service but in this instance it will be free.*
2 For instance means for example. *For instance, oranges are citrus fruits.*

instant (adj) If something is instant, it happens straight away. **instantly** (adv)

instead (prep) You use instead when you want to show that something happens as an alternative to something else. *She walked to the shops instead of taking the car.*

instinct instincts
1 (n) The instinct of a person or an animal is the natural feeling that they should behave in a particular way.
2 (n) Instinct is the feeling that you have that something is the case without really knowing the truth.

institution institutions
1 (n) An institution is a large important organisation, such as a university, bank, etc.
2 (n) An institution is something such as a custom which has gone on for a very long time.

instruct instructs instructing instructed
1 (vb) If you instruct someone to do something, you order them to do it. **instructions** (n)

2 (vb) If you instruct someone in something such as horse-riding, you teach them how to do it. **instructor** (n)

instrument instruments
1 (n) An instrument is a tool or device for doing something.
2 (n) An instrument is an object you use to produce music.

insufficient (adj) Something that is insufficient is not enough.

insulate insulates insulating insulated
1 (vb) If you insulate an object, you cover it with material that will protect it against heat loss or from electricity passing through it. **insulation** (n)
2 (vb) If you insulate a person from something unpleasant, you protect them from it.

insult insults insulting insulted (vb) If you insult someone, you say something to them that upsets them.

insurance (n) is a fixed amount of money you pay each year to a special company as a way of protecting yourself in the case of an emergency.

intact (adj) If something is intact, it is complete.

intake intakes (n) Your intake of food or drink is the amount you consume.

integer integers (n) An integer is a mathematical term for a whole number such as 1, 7 or 9.

integrate integrates integrating integrated (vb) If a person or a group integrates with others, they mix in and become part of them.

integrity (n) is the quality of being honest and trustworthy.

intellect intellects (n) Your intellect is your ability to understand and deal with ideas and information.

intelligence (n) is the ability a person or animal has to understand, learn and think.

intelligible (adj) If something is intelligible, it can be understood.

intend intends intending intended (vb) If you intend to do something, you plan to do it. **intention** (n) **intent** (n)

intense (adj) Something that is intense is very great in amount, strength or degree. *Intense feelings . . . intense colour.*

intercept intercepts intercepting intercepted (vb) If you intercept someone or something as it travels from one place to another, you stop them before they get to their destination.

interchange interchanges (n) An interchange is a junction on a motorway where it meets a main road or another motorway.

intercom intercoms (n) An intercom is a device that people use to talk to each other if they are in different rooms or vehicles.

interest interests interesting interested
1 (vb) If something interests you, it attracts your attention.
2 (n) If you have an interest in someone or something, you want to know more about them.
3 (n) Interest is a sum of money that is paid as a proportion of a larger sum of money, which has been borrowed or invested. You receive interest on money that you invest and pay interest on money that you borrow.

interface interfaces (n) An interface is a device used to connect two different computers.

interfere interferes interfering interfered
1 (vb) If you interfere with something or somebody, you meddle with something that does not concern you.
2 (vb) If something interferes with a plan, it often stops it from happening.
3 (adj) An interfering person gets involved with other people's lives when it does not concern them.
4 (vb) When sound or radio waves interfere with each other, they get too close together and people cannot receive programmes or messages clearly.

interior interiors (n) The interior of something is the inside. *The interior of the room was decorated beautifully.*

intermediate (adj) An intermediate stage or position in something, is one that comes between other stages, positions, sizes, or times.

i

internal

internal (adj) describes anything inside a person, animal or thing.

international internationals
1 (adj) International is the term used to describe something to do with more than one country.
2 (n) An international is a sporting match between two countries. *Many thousands watched the England-Scotland rugby international.*

interpret interprets interpreting interpreted
1 (vb) If you interpret a foreign language, you put the spoken words into another language. **interpreter** (n)
2 (vb) If you interpret what a person does or says, you decide on what this means. *She interpreted the girl's rudeness as a sign of unhappiness.* **interpretation** (n)

interrogate interrogates interrogating interrogated (vb) If you interrogate someone, you question them in great detail to find out information. **interrogation** (n)

interrupt interrupts interrupting interrupted (vb) If you interrupt someone, you start talking when they are talking. **interruption** (n)

interval intervals
1 (n) An interval is a short break in a play, concert, performance, etc.
2 (n) An interval is the time between two particular dates or moments.
3 (n) If something happens at intervals, it occurs several times but not regularly.

interview interviews
1 (n) An interview is a formal meeting where an applicant for a job or position is asked questions to see if they are suitable for it.
2 (n) An interview is a conversation in which a reporter for the radio, press or television talks to a person about the interesting and important things that they do.

intestine intestines (n) Your intestine is the tube carrying food from your stomach.

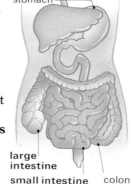

stomach

large intestine

small intestine   colon

intimidate intimidates intimidating intimidated (vb) If you intimidate someone, you frighten them by threatening them.

intolerable (adj) An intolerable situation is almost impossible to bear.

intolerant (adj) An intolerant person is unable to accept views and behaviour different from theirs. **intolerance** (n)

intricate (adj) An intricate piece of work has many small details which may be complicated to make. *Intricate carving ... intricate needlework.*

intriguing (adj) If someone or something is intriguing, they arouse your curiosity or hold your interest.

introduce introduces introducing introduced
1 (vb) If you introduce someone to someone else, you give their names so that they can get to know each other.
2 (vb) If you introduce something, you bring it to people's attention for the first time.

introduction introductions
1 (n) An introduction in a book is the first part where the writer gives brief details of its contents.
2 (n) An introduction to a subject is a book, talk or guide outlining the main ideas on the subject.

introvert introverts (n) An introvert is someone who spends much of their time absorbed in their own thoughts, rather than being friendly with other people. **introverted** (adj)

intrude intrudes intruding intruded (vb) If you intrude on someone, you disturb them when they do not wish this to happen. **intrusion** (n) **intruder** (n)

intuition intuitions (n) Your intuition is your ability to feel convinced about something without definite proof.

invade invades invading invaded
1 (vb) When one country invades another, they take it over by force.
2 (vb) If people or animals invade a place, very many come in.

invalid invalids
1 (n) An invalid is someone in poor health who needs someone else to care for them.

2 (adj) If a result is invalid, it is unacceptable because mistakes have been made.

invaluable (adj) Someone or something that is invaluable is very useful or cannot be replaced. *She was an invaluable member of the expedition.*

invent invents inventing invented
1 (vb) If you invent something, you are the first person to have thought of it, designed it or built it. **inventor** (n) **invention** (n)
2 (vb) If you invent an excuse or an explanation, you make up something untrue.

invest invests investing invested (vb) If you invest money, you put it into a bank or into a business where it will earn interest. **investment** (n)

investigate investigates investigating investigated (vb) If you investigate someone or something, you try to find out something about them. **investigation** (n) **investigator** (n)

invincible (adj) If something is invincible, it cannot be defeated. *Our team is invincible this season.*

invisible (adj) Something that is invisible cannot be seen.

invite invites inviting invited
1 (vb) If you invite someone to a party or to stay at your home, you ask them if they would like to come. **invitation** (n)
2 (adj) Something that is inviting is tempting and attractive. *That cream cake looks inviting.*

involve involves involving involved
1 (vb) If a situation involves certain activities, they are a necessary part of it. *Passing exams involves a lot of hard work.*
2 (vb) If someone or something is involved in a situation or activity, they take part in it. *Many vehicles were involved in the accident.*
3 (adj) Something that is involved is very complicated. *These instructions are so involved I can't understand them...*

irate (adj) Someone who is irate is very angry about something. *Irate passengers were complaining bitterly about late trains.*

iris irises
1 (n) The iris is the coloured part of your eye.
2 (n) An iris is an early summer flower with spiky leaves.

senses (eye) p264

iron irons ironing ironed
1 (n) Iron is a metal found in rocks.
2 (n) An iron is a flat piece of metal used for pressing clothes.
3 (vb) If you iron something, you press out the creases using a hot iron.
4 (n) An iron is a golf club.

Iron Age (n) The Iron Age was a period of time, about three thousand years ago, when people started to make tools from iron.

irrational (adj) A person who is irrational behaves illogically.

irregular
1 (adj) An irregular surface is not smooth and even.
2 (adj) An irregular shape or pattern is not balanced and symmetrical.
3 (adj) Irregular behaviour does not conform to the usually accepted patterns.

irrelevant (adj) An irrelevant remark or comment has nothing whatever to do with what is being said or discussed. **irrelevance** (n)

irresponsible (adj) If you are irresponsible, you act in a thoughtless, careless way. *It was irresponsible to leave your baby brother alone in the house* **irresponsibility** (n)

irrigate irrigates irrigating irrigated (vb) When you irrigate dry land you supply it with water through ditches and pipes so that crops can be grown. **irrigation** (n)

irritable (adj) An irritable person is very easily annoyed.

irritate irritates irritating irritated
1 (vb) When someone or something irritates you, they annoy you and make you feel cross.
2 (vb) Something that irritates your skin makes it itch and become sore. **irritation** (n)

Islam

Islam
1 (n) Islam is the Muslim religion. Its sacred book is the Koran and it teaches that there is one God whose word must be obeyed. Mohammed is Islam's most important prophet.
2 (n) Islam is the name sometimes given to the countries where Islam is the main religion.

island islands (n) An island is a piece of land surrounded by water.

isolate isolates isolating isolated
1 (vb) If you isolate yourself, you separate yourself from others.
2 (vb) If you isolate a sick person or animal, you keep them away from others so that disease does not spread.
3 (adj) An isolated house is far away from others. **isolation** (n)

issue issues issuing issued
1 (n) An issue is an important topic for debate.
2 (n) An issue is a specific edition of a paper or magazine.
3 (vb) If you issue a statement, you make public what you want to say. *The police issued a statement about the murder hunt.*

italic italics (n) Italics are letters that are written so that they slope in one direction. The example sentences in this dictionary are written in italics.

itch itches itching itched
1 (vb) When you itch, a place on your skin makes you want to scratch it.
2 (n) If you have an itch to do something, you are keen to do it.

item items (n) An item is one in a group of things.

ivory ivories (n)
Ivory is the hard, creamy- white material which makes up an elephant's tusks and is used for making ornaments.

ivy ivies (n) is a leafy, evergreen plant which climbs walls and creeps along the ground.

Jj

jack jacks
1 (n) A jack is a device for raising heavy objects, a car for example, up from the ground.
2 (n) A jack is one of the picture cards in a pack of cards.

jackal jackals (n) A jackal is a small dog-like animal of Africa and Asia.

Jacuzzi Jacuzzis (n) A Jacuzzi is a large round bath with swirling water.

jagged (adj) A jagged edge or rock has many sharp points along it.

jaguar jaguars (n) A jaguar is a large South American animal like a leopard.

jail see gaol

jamboree jamborees (n) A jamboree is a large party or celebration with much noise and excitement.

jargon (n) This is a term used for language that contains lots of specialist words. *Clyde found it hard to understand the computer jargon that his sister and her friend were using.*

jaundice (n) is a liver disease that makes your skin and eyes yellow.

javelin javelins (n)
A javelin is a long, light spear that is thrown in sporting competitions to see who can throw farthest.

skeleton
p273

jaw jaws (n) The jaw is one of the two bones in the mouth that hold teeth.

jazz (n) is a type of popular music with strong rhythms and some improvisation.

jealous
1 (adj) A jealous person is envious of others, wanting what they have or wishing to be like them.
2 (adj) If you feel jealous of a thing or a person, you do not want to share them with anyone else. **jealousy** (n)

jeans (n) are strong cotton trousers, often made of blue denim.

jeep jeeps (n) A jeep is a car designed for travelling over rough ground.

jeer jeers jeering jeered (vb) If you jeer at someone, you make fun of them in a rude, loud way.

Jehovah (n) Jehovah is the name for God in the Old Testament of the Bible.

jelly jellies (n) A jelly is a soft food made with gelatine.

jellyfish jellyfishes (n) A jellyfish is a sea animal with a jelly-like body.

jerk jerks jerking jerked (vb) If you jerk something, you tug it suddenly.

jersey jerseys (n) A jersey is a knitted pullover.

Jesus Christ (n) is the name of the man who Christians believe is the son of God and whose teaching is the basis of Christianity.

aircraft p5
jet jets
1 (n) A jet is a rush of air, steam or liquid escaping from a small outlet.
2 (n) A jet is an aeroplane which is propelled by streams of hot gases.
3 (n) Jet is a hard, black mineral used for making ornaments.

jetlag (n) is a feeling of confusion and tiredness that people have after very long aeroplane journeys.

jetsam (n) is rubbish that has been thrown from a ship and which floats on the sea or is washed up on the shore.

jettison jettisons jettisoning jettisoned(vb) If you jettison something, you throw it overboard or abandon it.

jetty jetties (n) A jetty is a small pier.

Jew Jews (n) A Jew is a person whose religion is Judaism.

jewel jewels (n) A jewel is a precious stone. **jeweller** (n) **jewellery** (n)

jigsaw-puzzle jigsaw-puzzles (n) A jigsaw-puzzle is a puzzle made of odd-shaped pieces that must be fitted together to make a picture.

jingle jingles jingling jingled
1 (vb) When something jingles, it makes a gentle ringing sound.
2 (n) A jingle is a catchy rhyme often used in advertising.

jockey jockeys (n) A jockey is a person who rides horses in races.

jocular (adj) Someone who is jocular is inclined to be cheerful and tries to make people laugh.

join joins joining joined
1 (vb) If you join two things, you fix them together.
2 (vb) If you join a club, you become a member of it.

joiner joiners (n) A joiner is a person who works with wood, making window frames, door frames, etc.

joint joints
1 (n) A joint is the place where two or more things join.
2 (n) A joint is a large piece of meat.

joist joists (n) A joist is a beam which supports the floors and ceilings of a house.

joke jokes joking joked
1 (n) A joke is a short funny story told to make people laugh.
2 (vb) If you joke, you fool around to make people laugh.

jolly jollier jolliest (adj) people are full of fun.

j

jolt

jolt jolts jolting jolted
1 (vb) If something jolts, it briefly moves very suddenly and violently.
2 (vb) If you jolt someone, you bump into them clumsily.
3 (n) A jolt is a sharp, sudden movement, or a sudden and nasty surprise.

jostle jostles jostling jostled (vb) If people or animals jostle, they push and bump into each other roughly, usually because they are in a crowd.

journal journals
1 (n) A journal is a kind of diary in which you write down all you do each day.
2 (n) A journal is another name for a magazine or newspaper.

journalism (n) is the job of collecting news and writing articles for newspapers, magazines and radio and television news programmes. **journalist** (n)

journey journeys (n) If you go on a journey, you travel from one place to another.

joust jousts jousting jousted (vb) In medieval times two knights jousted by trying to knock each other from their horses with lances.

jovial (adj) people are very good tempered and jolly.

jubilant (adj) If you are jubilant, you are very excited and happy because something wonderful has happened.

jubilee jubilees (n) A jubilee is a very special celebration, usually of an anniversary.

Judaism (n) Judaism is the religion of the Jews. It is based on their history and their special relationship with God.

judge judges judging judged
1 (n) A judge is someone whose job it is to preside over law courts and decide what punishment to give to people who are found guilty of crimes.
2 (vb) If you judge a competition, you decide who should win.
3 (vb) If you judge a person, you decide what their character is like.
judgement (n)

judo (n) is a form of wrestling where two people use various holds and movements to force each other onto the ground and hold them there.

juggernaut juggernauts (n) A juggernaut is an extremely long and heavy lorry.

juggle juggles juggling juggled (vb) A person who juggles throws several objects in the air at the same time and keeps them there without dropping them. **juggler** (n)

juice juices (n) Juice is the liquid squeezed from fruit or vegetables. **juicy** (adj)

jukebox jukeboxes
(n) A jukebox is a machine that will play your chosen record if you put some coins into it and press some buttons.

jumble jumbles jumbling jumbled
1 (vb) If you jumble things, you mix them together until they are in a muddle, usually because you are in a hurry.
2 (n) A jumble of things is a lot of objects all mixed together.

jumbo
1 (adj) Jumbo is used to describe something that is much larger than usual. *Jumbo sausages . . . jumbo box of tissues.*
2 (n) A jumbo jet is a huge aeroplane that can carry hundreds of passengers.

junction junctions
1 (n) A junction is a place where railway lines or roads meet.
2 (n) A junction on a motorway is an entrance or an exit to or from other roads.

jungle jungles (n) A jungle is a very thick forest in a hot country, where the air is hot and wet and where many plants and trees grow closely together.

junior juniors
1 (adj) Junior means younger or lower in rank.
2 (n) In Britain, juniors are school children of about 7 to 11 years old.

jumper jumpers (n) A jumper is a warm garment that covers the top part of your body.

junk junks
1 (n) Junk is anything that you think is useless and you don't need any more.
2 (n) A junk is a Chinese boat with square sails.

junk shop junk shops (n) A junk shop sells second-hand goods.

junk food junk foods (n) Junk food is quick and easy to prepare but not all that good for you.

jury juries (n) A jury is a group of twelve people who are chosen and required by law to listen to evidence at a trial and to decide if the accused person is guilty or innocent.

justice
1 (n) Justice is fairness.
2 (n) Justice is the system of law created by communities to ensure that people obey laws and to punish those who do not.
3 A Justice of the Peace is a person who is authorised to act as a judge in local courts and to deal with minor crimes.

justify justifies justifying justified (vb) If you justify something, you have done or said you give good reasons for doing it or saying it.

jute (n) is a fibre from a plant grown mostly in South-east Asia. It is used to make ropes, sacking, etc.

juvenile juveniles
1 (n) A juvenile is a child or young person not yet considered to be adult.
2 (adj) Juvenile matters are those concerned with children and young people. *Juvenile court . . . juvenile behaviour.*

Kk

kaleidoscope kaleidoscopes (n) A kaleidoscope is a closed tube with a hole at one end. If you look through the hole and turn the tube, you see patterns of colours and shapes.
kaleidoscopic (adj)

kangaroo kangaroos (n) A kangaroo is a large Australian animal with very powerful back legs. It carries its young in a pouch at the front.

karate (n) is a system of unarmed combat that is also practised as a sport.

kayak kayaks (n) A kayak is a type of canoe, originally used by the Inuit or Eskimo people.

kebab kebabs (n) A kebab is made of small pieces of meat and vegetables grilled on a skewer.

Kennedy, John Fitzgerald (1917–1963) was the youngest person to be elected President of the United States. He was assassinated in 1963.

kennel kennels
1 (n) A kennel is a small hut for a dog to sleep in.
2 (n) Kennels are also places where dogs are bred, or where they can stay while their owners are away.

kerb

kerb kerbs (n) The kerb is the raised edge of a pavement.

kernel kernels (n) A kernel is the middle part of a nut that you eat.

kestrel kestrels (n) A kestrel is a small kind of falcon.

ketchup ketchups (n) Ketchup is a thick sauce, often made from tomatoes.

kettle kettles (n) A kettle is a container used to boil water.

key keys keying keyed
1 (n) A key is a piece of shaped metal used to open locks or wind up clocks and toys.
2 (n) A key is a button on a computer or typewriter.
3 (n) A key is an explanation of symbols on a map. *We found the symbol for a windmill in the key.*
4 (n) A key is the part of a piano that you press to make a sound.
5 (vb) If you key information into a computer, you type it in.

keyboard keyboards (n) A keyboard is the panel on a computer, typewriter or piano which has all the keys on it.

khaki (adj) is a yellowish-brown colour.

kibbutz kibbutzim (n) A kibbutz is an Israeli community where people share work and the money they earn.

kick kicks kicking kicked
1 (vb) If you kick anything, you strike it with your foot.
2 If you kick up a fuss, you make a fuss.
3 A kick-off is the start of a game of football.

kidnap kidnaps kidnapping kidnapped (vb) If a person kidnaps someone, they take them away by force and release them only when they get what they demand in return. *The kidnappers demanded £50,000 for the boy's release.*

kidney kidneys (n) The kidneys are the organs which produce urine from the waste matter in the blood.

kill kills killing killed (vb) When you kill something living, you end its life. **killer** (n)

kiln kilns (n) A kiln is an oven used for baking clay or bricks, to make them hard.

kilogram kilograms (n) A kilogram is a unit of weight weighing 1000 grams. The word can be shortened to kg.

kilometre kilometres (n) A kilometre is a unit of distance, measuring 1000 metres. The word can be shortened to km.

kilt kilts (n) A kilt is a type of skirt, usually in a tartan pattern, traditionally worn by Scotsmen. It is also worn by women.

kimono kimonos (n) A kimono is a long, silk dress traditionally worn by Japanese women.

kin (n) Your kin are your relatives.

kind kinder kindest
1 (adj) A person who is kind is gentle and helpful to other people.
2 (n) A kind is a type or sort of thing. *What kind of dog is that?*

kindle kindles kindling kindled (vb) If you kindle a flame, you light wood, paper, etc. to start it burning.

king kings
1 (n) A king is a man who is the head of a country.
2 (n) A king is a chessman, and one of the picture cards in a pack of cards.

kingdom kingdoms
1 (n) A kingdom is a country ruled by a king or queen.
2 (n) The living world is divided into the plant kingdom and the animal kingdom.

King, Martin Luther (1929–1968) was the black American minister who became a great civil rights leader. He was against the segregation of black and white people. He was assassinated in 1968.

k

kingfisher
kingfishers (n)
The kingfisher is a very brightly coloured bird which lives near water and catches fish.

kiosk kiosks
1 (n) A kiosk is a small booth or shop, where you can buy tickets, ice-creams, etc.
2 (n) Kiosk is another name for telephone box.

kipper
kippers (n) A kipper is a smoked herring, a fish that is dried in smoke to preserve it and give it a special taste.

kiss kisses kissing kissed
(vb) If you kiss someone, you touch them with your lips as an affectionate gesture.

kitchen
kitchens (n) A kitchen is the room where food is prepared, dishes are washed, etc.

kite kites
1 (n) A kite is a frame covered with fabric or paper and flown on the end of a string on a breezy day.
2 (n) A kite is a small kind of vulture.

kitten
kittens (n) A kitten is a young cat.

kiwi
kiwis (n) A kiwi is a flightless bird which lives in New Zealand.

kiwi fruit
kiwi fruits (n) A kiwi fruit is an oval fruit with green flesh and brown fuzzy skin.

knack
(n) A knack is a skill or way you have of doing something. *She really has the knack of getting on with people.*

knead kneads kneading kneaded
(vb) If you knead something, you squash it, pull it and push it with your fingers.

skeleton p273

knee
knees (n) The knee is the joint half way down the leg, which allows the leg to move backward and forward.

kneel kneels kneeling knelt
(vb) If you kneel, you bend so that one or both knees touch the floor.

knickers
(n) Knickers is an informal word for women's underpants.

knife
knives (n) A knife is a tool with a handle and sharp blade used for cutting.

knight knights knighting knighted
1 (vb) If the Queen knights a man, she honours him for some important service he has done. He is allowed to put 'Sir' in front of his name. **knighthood** (n)
2 (n) In medieval times, a knight was a nobleman, who would fight in armour on horseback.

knit knits knitting knitted
1 (vb) When you knit, you use wool and needles to make clothes, etc.
2 (vb) When broken bones knit, they heal and join together.

knob
knobs (n) A knob is a round handle on doors, furniture, or machinery.

knock knocks knocking knocked
1 (vb) If you knock something, you hit it or bump it, sometimes accidentally.
2 (vb) If you knock at a door, you rap or tap on it so the people inside will hear.

knocker
knockers (n) A knocker is a metal door fitting which you use to make a noise and attract the people inside.

knot knots knotting knotted
1 (n) A knot is the part of a piece of string, cloth, etc where two ends have been tied together.
2 (vb) If you knot something, you fasten it by tying it.
3 (n) A knot of people is a small group, very close together.
4 (n) A knot in a piece of wood is a hard round spot where a branch grew on the tree.
5 (n) A knot is a unit of measurement of speed for ships and aircraft. *The boat was doing 5 knots.*

know knows knowing knew
1 (vb) If you know something, it is fixed in your mind and you are sure that it is true. **knowledge** (n)
2 (vb) If you know a person, you recognise them, and have met them before.

knuckle knuckles (n) Your knuckles are the hard joints where your fingers meet your hands.

koala koalas (n) A koala is a small, furry, grey Australian animal that looks like a bear.

kohl (n) is a cosmetic used to darken the edge of a person's eyelids.

Koran or **Qur'an** (n) The Koran is the sacred book of the Islamic religion.

kosher (adj) Something that is kosher is approved by the laws of Judaism. It usually describes the foods that Jews are allowed to eat and is also applied to anything that is right or honest

Kung-Fu (n) is a system of fighting, originally from China, in which you use both your hands and your feet.

kurta or **khurta pyjamas** (n) are the tight trousers and tunic worn by Hindu men and women.

Ll

label labels labelling labelled
1 (vb) If you label something, you attach to it a small notice with information on it.
2 (n) A label is a small note which is attached to something, giving information about it.

laboratory laboratories (n) A laboratory is a room where scientists work and perform experiments.

labour labours labouring laboured
1 (vb) If you labour, you work hard at something. **laborious** (adj)
2 (n) Labour is another name for work.
3 The Labour Party is one of the main political parties in Britain.

Labrador Labradors (n) A Labrador retriever is a powerfully built black or yellow coated dog.

labyrinth labyrinths (n) A labyrinth is a complex set of passages which are difficult to find your way around.

lace laces lacing laced
1 (n) A lace is a long string used to fasten shoes.
2 (vb) If you lace something up, you fix it together by tying a lace.
3 (n) Lace is a very delicate material used for curtains and for decoration. **lacy** (adj)

lack lacks lacking lacked
1 (vb) If you lack something, you do not have it. *She lacked sense.*
2 (n) A lack of something is a shortage of it. *There is a lack of sugar in the shops at the moment.*

lacquer lacquers (n) Lacquer is a varnish.

ladder ladders
1 (n) A ladder is a long narrow frame with steps that can be used for climbing up walls, the sides of ships, trees etc.
2 (n) A ladder is a long, narrow tear in a woman's stockings or tights.

ladle ladles ladling ladled
1 (n) A ladle is a large spoon with a long handle used for serving soups and other liquids.
2 (vb) If you ladle a liquid, you spoon it out with a ladle.

lady ladies
1 (n) You use the word lady when you are referring to a woman in a polite way.
2 (n) A lady is a woman who behaves in a polite and gracious way.
3 (n) Lady is the title used before the name of some female members of the nobility.
Lady Jane Grey.

ladybird ladybirds (n) A ladybird is a small, red beetle with black spots.

lager lagers (n) Lager is a light beer.

lagging (n) is the material wrapped around water pipes and tanks to stop them freezing in winter.

mangrove **lagoon**, Venezuela

lagoon lagoons (n) A lagoon is an area of sea inside a reef or sand bank.

lair lairs (n) A lair is the home of a wild animal.

lake lakes (n) A lake is an area of inland freshwater.

lamb lambs (n) A lamb is a young sheep.

lame (adj) A person or animal that is lame cannot walk properly.
lameness (n)

lament laments (n) A lament is a sad poem or song.

laminate laminates laminating laminated
1 (n) A laminate is a material built up of many layers.
2 (vb) If you laminate something, you cover it with a layer of something.

lamp lamps (n) A lamp is a light.

lance lances lancing lanced
1 (n) A lance is a long spear which was caried by knights when fighting on horseback.
2 (vb) If you lance a boil, you make a small cut in it to let the pus out.

land lands landing landed
1 (n) Land is the solid part of the world on which we live.
2 (vb) If you land somewhere, your plane or ship arrives and you get out onto land.
3 (n) A landing is the part of a building at the top of stairs.

landmark landmarks (n) A landmark is a feature, a building or a hill, for example, which stands out from its surroundings.

landscape landscapes landscaping landscaped
1 (n) Landscape is the land you can see from a particular spot.
2 (vb) If you landscape an area, you move soil and plant trees, shrubs, etc to make it look attractive.
3 (n) A landscape is a painting of a country scene.

lane lanes
1 (n) A lane is a narrow road, especially in the country.
2 (n) A lane is one of the marked divisions of a motorway or major road. *Lorries must not use the outside lane on a motorway.*

language languages (n) Language refers to the words we use when speaking or writing.

lank (adj) hair is greasy and dull.

lantern lanterns (n) A lantern is an old-fashioned word for lamp.

lap laps lapping lapped
1 (vb) If water laps, it breaks very gently in waves against the shore.
2 (vb) If an animal laps, it drinks by collecting the liquid on its tongue.
3 (n) Your lap is the part of your body between your knees and hips when you are sitting down.
4 (n) A lap in a race is one circuit of the course.

lapel lapels (n) The lapel is the part of the collar which folds over at the front of a jacket or coat.

lapse

lapse lapses lapsing lapsed
1 (n) A lapse is a moment of bad behaviour or forgetfulness.
2 (n) A lapse of time is a period of time which has passed.
3 (vb) If you lapse you make a mistake through forgetfulness.
4 (vb) If something, such as a promise or agreement lapses, it is no longer valid.

larch larches (n) A larch is a tall, coniferous tree which grows to about 40m in height. It is the only coniferous tree to lose its needles in winter.

lard (n) is a solid, white cooking fat, made from pigs' fat.

larder larders (n) A larder is a small, cool cupboard or room where food is kept.

large larger largest
1 (adj) Something large is bigger in size or amount than usual.
2 If someone or something seems larger than life, they seem more important or noticeable than usual.

lark larks larking larked
1 (n) A lark is a small, brown bird with a pleasing song.
2 (vb) If you lark around, you play about in a silly way.
3 If you are up with the lark, you get up very early.

larva larvae (n) A larva is a very young insect, after being hatched from an egg and before becoming a pupa.

larynx larynxes (n) The larynx is the top part of the windpipe where the vocal cords are.

lasagne (n) is an Italian dish made with layers of pasta, meat or vegetables and a tomato sauce.

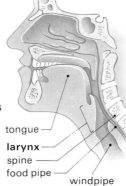

tongue
larynx
spine
food pipe
windpipe

laser lasers (n) A laser is a very powerful, thin beam of light produced by a special machine. It is used for cutting very hard materials and in surgery.

lash lashes lashing lashed
1 (vb) If you lash things together, you tie them together firmly.
2 (vb) If rain lashes down, it beats down powerfully.
3 (vb) If you lash out at someone, you speak to them harshly or strike at them uncontrollably.
4 (n) A lash is one of the small hairs that grow from your eyelids.

lasso lassoes (n) A lasso is rope looped at one end with a slip-knot used to catch cattle and horses.

last lasts lasting lasted
1 (vb) If something lasts for a particular time, it goes on this long. *The party lasted six hours.*
2 (n) If someone is the last to do something, no one follows them.
3 (adv) If someone or something was last seen on a particular day, they have not been seen since then.
4 (adj) The last part of anything is the very end.
5 (adj) The last person or thing is the most recent one. *Their last meeting was in July . . . The last person to see Mr. Jones alive was Susan.*
6 If you leave something until last, you do everything else before it.
7 If something happens at last, it happens after a long wait.

late later latest
1 (adj) If you are late for an appointment, you arrive after the arranged time.
lateness (n)
2 (adj) If you go shopping in the late afternoon, you go at the end of the afternoon.
3 If you do something late in the day, it is left to the last moment.

lately (adv) If something has happened lately, it has taken place recently.

lathe lathes (n) A lathe is a machine that is used to shape wood or metal by turning it against a sharp cutting tool.

lather lathers (n) A lather is a white mass of bubbles made from mixing soap and water.

Latin
1 (n) Latin is the language of the ancient Romans.
2 (adj) Latin peoples and cultures are those of countries like France, Spain, Italy and South America whose languages developed from Latin.

latitude latitudes (n) Latitude is a position measured in degrees North or South of the equator.

laugh laughs laughing laughed
1 (vb) When you laugh, you make a sound to express your amusement. **laughter** (n)
2 If you do something for a laugh, you do it for fun.
3 If you laugh your head off, you laugh a great deal.

launch launches launching launched
1 (vb) If you launch a ship or a boat, you put it into the water for the first time.
2 (vb) If you launch a new activity, you start it.
3 (n) A launch is a large motor boat.

launderette launderettes (n) A launderette is a shop fitted with washing machines and driers where you can go to do your washing.

laurel laurels
1 (n) A laurel is a small, evergreen tree with shiny leaves.
2 If you rest on your laurels, you are contented with your achievements and stop trying for more.

lava (n) Lava is a volcanic rock which is red hot at first then cools and solidifies.

lavatory lavatories (n) A lavatory is a toilet.

lavender (n) is a bushy plant with purple, fragrant flowers on long stems.

law laws
1 (n) A law is a rule made by government that people have to obey.
2 (n) The law is all the rules together that a society or government agrees on to deal with crime, business agreements and social relationships.
3 (n) A law is a rule in sport, for example.
4 If you lay down the law, you give orders bossily and believe yourself to be right.

lawn lawns (n) A lawn is a piece of well-kept grass usually in a park or a garden.

lawyer lawyers (n) A lawyer is someone who is trained in the law and speaks for people in court.

lay lays laying laid
1 (vb) If you lay something or someone down, you put them down carefully.
2 (vb) If you lay a table, you set out the cutlery, plates, etc for a meal.
3 (vb) If a bird lays an egg, it produces one.
4 If you lay claim to something, you say it belongs to you.

layer layers (n) A layer is a quantity of a substance underneath or above another quantity of the same or a different substance. *She put on another layer of make-up to hide her spots.*

layoff layoffs (n) A layoff takes place when people are told to leave their jobs because there is no work for them.

laze lazes lazing lazed (vb) If you laze, you relax and make no effort to do anything. **lazy** (adj) **laziness** (n) **lazily** (adv)

lead leads leading led
1 (vb) If you lead someone, you guide them by going on in front of them.
2 (vb) If you lead in a race, you are at the front.
3 (vb) If a path, road, etc. leads to a particular place, it goes in that direction.
4 (vb) If you lead a team, an expedition or a group of people, you are in charge of them. **leader** (n)
5 (n) The lead in a play or a film is the main part.
6 (n) A lead is a strap for controlling a dog.
7 (n) Lead is a heavy, grey metal.
8 (n) The lead in a pencil is the part that makes marks on paper.

leaf leaves
1 (n) A leaf is one of the green, flat growths on trees or plants. **leafy** (adj)
2 (n) The leaves of a book are its pages.

tree p313

leaflet leaflets (n) A leaflet is a piece of paper or a very thin booklet containing information.

league

league leagues
1 (n) A league is a group of countries or people who have joined together because they share common interests. *The League of Friends... The League of Nations.*
2 (n) A league is a group of sports clubs which play in competition against each other. *The Football League.*
3 If you are in league with someone, you are working closely with them, usually secretly.

leak leaks leaking leaked
1 (n) A leak is a hole or crack in something that allows liquids or gas to escape.
2 (vb) If a container leaks, it is damaged and its contents seep out. **leaky** (adj)
3 (vb) If a liquid or gas leaks, it escapes through a hole or a crack.
4 (vb) If secret information is leaked, it is made known to the public.

lean leans leaning leaned leant
1 (vb) If something leans it is not upright, but in a sloping position.
2 (vb) If you lean in a particular direction, you move your body that way.
3 (vb) If you lean against something, you rest against it so that it supports you.
4 (adj) Someone who is lean is slim.
5 (adj) Lean meat is meat with no fat.

learn learns learning learned learnt (vb) If you learn something, you gain knowledge of it or become skilled at it either by practice or by being taught. **learner** (n)

least (adj) The least of something is the smallest amount. *The least sound will wake her.*

leather leathers
1 (n) Leather is animal skin specially treated so it can be used as a material. **leathery** (adj)
2 (n) Leathers are the protective leather clothing worn by some motorcyclists.

leave leaves leaving left
1 (vb) If you leave a place or a person, you go away from them.
2 (vb) If you leave something somewhere, you put it in a particular place where it stays while you are away.
3 (vb) If you leave something behind, you forget it.
4 (vb) If something is left after the main part of it has been used or taken away, it remains.

5 (vb) If you leave something to somebody, you say that you want them to have it when you die.
6 (n) Leave is a time when you are on holiday from your job, or time off when you are ill.

lecture lectures lecturing lectured
1 (n) A lecture is a formal talk about something given by an expert.
2 (vb) A person who lectures gives talks on a special subject. **lecturer** (n)
3 (n) A lecture is a telling-off for doing something wrong.
4 (vb) If someone lectures you, they speak to you at length for doing something wrong.

ledge ledges (n) A ledge is a narrow shelf on a window, wall or mountainside.

leek leeks (n) A leek is a long vegetable, white at the root end and green at the other, that tastes like an onion.

left see also **leave**
1 (adj) The left-hand side of a page is the side where English writing begins. The left hand is the hand which most people do not write with.
2 (n) Left is the left side, position or direction.
3 (adv) Left describes the direction in which someone moves. *He turned left.*

leg legs
1 (n) The leg is the part of the body that a person or animal uses to walk with.
2 (n) The leg of a table or chair is one of several that supports the weight.
3 (n) A leg of a journey is one part of it.

legacy legacies (n) A legacy is an amount of money or some property left to someone in a will.

legal
1 (adj) The word legal is used to describe anything that is to do with the law. *Legal aid... legal advice.*
2 (adj) A situation or act that is legal is allowed by law. **legally** (adj) **legality** (n)

legend legends (n) A legend is a very old story passed down from generation to generation that may or may not be true. **legendary** (adj)

legible (adj) If writing is legible, it has been written neatly and is easy to read. **legibly** (adj)

legion legions
1 (n) A legion is a large group of soldiers that form part of an army.
2 (n) Legions of people are large numbers of people.

legislate legislates legislating legislated (vb) If a government legislates, it passes new laws. **legislator** (n) **legislation** (n)

legitimate
1 (adj) If something is legitimate, it is allowed by law. **legitimately** (adv)
2 (adj) Something that most people agree is fair can be called legitimate. *We felt we had a legitimate complaint against our noisy neighbours.*

leisure (n) is time when you don't have to work but can relax and do what you like.

lemon lemons (n) A lemon is a citrus fruit with a thick, yellow skin and sharp-tasting juice.

lemonade (n) is a lemon-flavoured drink.

lend lends lending lent (vb) If you lend something to somebody, you let them have it for a while.

length lengths
1 (n) The length of something is the measurement of its longest side.
2 (n) The length of a river or a road is the whole measurement from one end to the other.
3 (n) The length of a book is how many pages it has.
4 (n) The length of an activity is how much time it takes to do it.
5 (n) A length of rope, string, cloth, etc is a certain amount needed for a purpose.

Lenin, Vladimir Ilyich (1870–1924) was the Russian revolutionary who became the first president of the Soviet Union.

lens lenses
1 (n) A lens is a thin piece of glass or plastic with a curved surface that make things look larger or smaller when you look through it. Lenses are used in cameras, telescopes, microscopes and spectacles.
2 (n) The lens in your eye is the part that focuses light and makes you see clearly.

senses
(eye)
p264

Lent (n) is the forty-day period before Easter when some Christians fast or give up something they enjoy.

lentil lentils (n) Lentils are small orange, yellow or brown pea-like seeds that are used in cooking, especially in Eastern dishes.

leopard leopards (n) A leopard is a wild animal that looks like a large cat. It has yellow fur with black spots.

leotard leotards (n) A leotard is a garment you wear for dancing or exercising to music. It looks like a swim-suit.

leprosy (n) is a painful, infectious disease affecting the skin and nerves causing toes and fingers to drop off.

less lesser least
1 (adj) Less means not as much as before or a smaller amount. *As I am not hungry, give me less food*
2 (adj) In maths, less means minus or take-away. *12 less 6 is 6.*

lens

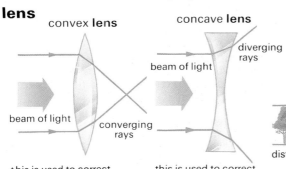

convex **lens**

concave **lens**

beam of light

beam of light

converging rays

diverging rays

this is used to correct long-sighted eyes.

this is used to correct short-sighted eyes

The lens in your eye works the same way as a camera lens: light rays pass through the lens and are bent so that an image is formed on the retina at the back of the eye or on the film in the camera. The upside-down image in the eye is turned upright by the brain.

distant object

small, upside-down image

lesson

lesson lessons
1 (n) A lesson is a period of time in which something is taught.
2 (n) A lesson is something to be learned especially an experience that teaches you smething.
3 (n) A lesson is a short piece read out from the Bible in the Christian Church.

lethal (adj) If something is lethal, it can kill people or animals.

letter letters
1 (n) A letter is one of the symbols that make up words. *a, g, and p are letters.*
2 (n) A letter is a written message usually sent by post in an envelope.

lettuce lettuces (n) A lettuce is a leafy salad plant.

leukaemia (n) is a serious disease of the blood.

level levels levelling levelled
1 (adj) If something, a field for instance, is level, it is flat.
2 (adj) When scores are level, they are equal.
3 (adj) If things are level with each other, they are the same height.
4 (vb) If you level something, you make it flat.

lever levers levering levered
1 (n) A lever is a handle attached to a machine that has to be pulled or pushed to make the machine work.
2 (n) A lever is a strong bar. You place one end under something very heavy in order to lift it.
3 (vb) When you lever something, you use a lever to move it. **leverage** (n)

liable
1 (adj) If something is liable to happen, it is likely to happen.
2 (adj) If you are liable for something, you are responsible for it. **liability** (n)

liar liars (n) A liar is a person who says or writes things that are not true.

liberal
1 (adj) A liberal person is generous and tolerant.
2 (adj) A liberal amount of something is a lot.

liberty liberties (n) Liberty is freedom.

library libraries (n) A library is a place where books are kept and where people can go to read or borrow them. **librarian** (n)

licence licences (n) A licence is an official document which gives you permission to own something or to do something. *TV licence... driving licence.*

license licenses licensing licensed (vb) If you are licensed to do something or to use something, you have official permission to do so. **licencee** (n)

lichen lichens (n) Lichen is a mass of tiny plants looking like moss that grow in clumps on rocks, walls, trees, etc.

lick licks licking licked (vb) If a person or animal licks something they rub their tongue along the surface of it to taste it, clean it or wet it.

lie lies lying lied; lay lain
1 (n) A lie is an untruth.
2 (vb) If you lie, you say something which is untrue. **liar** (n)
3 (vb) If a person or animal lies, they do not stand or sit but they rest their body flat on a surface.

lieutenant lieutenants (n) A lieutenant is a junior officer in the army, navy or air force.

life lives
1 (n) Life is the quality of being alive that people, animals and plants have but objects do not.
2 (n) The life of a person or animal is the time between birth and death.

lifeboat lifeboats (n) A lifeboat is a boat for rescuing people who are in difficulties at sea.

lift lifts lifting lifted
1 (n) A lift is a device, normally in tall buildings, that carries people or goods from floor to floor.
2 (vb) If you lift something, you take it in your hands and raise it to a higher place.
3 (vb) If you lift your voice, you make it sound louder.
5 (n) If you give someone a lift, you give them a ride on or in a vehicle.

light lights lighting lighted lit; lighter lightest
1 (n) Light is brightness that comes from the sun, moon, lamps, fire, etc and allows us to see things.
2 (n) A light is something, a torch, a candle, for example, that gives brightness in the dark so that you can see.
3 (vb) If you light something, you make it burn.
4 (vb) When something is lit, it shines with light or burns.
5 (adj) Something light is not heavy.
6 (adj) A light colour is pale.

lightning (n) is a bright flash of electricity in the sky seen during thunderstorms.

like likes liking liked
1 (vb) If you like someone or something, you find them pleasing.
2 (vb) If you say you would like something, you are saying you want it in a polite way.
3 (vb) If one thing is like another, they are similar.
4 If you want to know what something is like, you want a description of it.

likely likelier likeliest
1 (adj) If something or someone is likely to do something, they will probably do it.
2 (adv) If something is likely to happen, it probably will. **likelihood** (n)

lilac lilacs (n) A lilac is a small tree with sweet-smelling flowers which may be white, pink, or purple.

lily lilies (n) A lily is an elegant, tall white flower.

limb limbs
1 (n) The limbs of a body are the arms and legs.
2 (n) The limbs of a tree are its branches.

lime limes
1 (n) A lime is a citrus fruit like a lemon but smaller and with a green skin.
2 (n) Something that is lime is a pale but bright green colour.

limerick limericks (n) A limerick is an amusing rhyming poem with five lines.

limit limits limiting limited
1 (vb) If you limit something, you restrict it to a certain amount or number.
limitation (n)
2 (n) The limit of something is the largest or the smallest amount of it.
3 (n) The limit of an area is its boundary.

limp limps limping limped
1 (vb) If a person or an animal limps, they walk in an uneven way because a leg or foot is hurt in some way.
2 (adj) If something is limp, it is soft and bends easily.

limpet limpets (n) A limpet is a small, shelled sea animal which attaches itself very firmly to rocks.

Lincoln, Abraham (1809–1865) was the 10th president of the United States, famous for saving the Union in the American Civil War and for freeing the slaves.

line lines lining lined
1 (vb) If you line something, you put an extra layer on the inside of it to protect it or to make it warm. **lining** (n)
2 (n) A line is a long, thin mark on a surface.
3 (n) A line of people is a row of people.
4 (n) Lines in a play are the words an actor has to speak.

linen linens (n) Linen is a cloth made from a plant called flax. It is used to make sheets, tablecloths, teacloths, etc.

liner liners
1 (n) A liner is something put inside a container to protect it in some way.
2 (n) A liner is a large passenger ship used for cruises.

linger lingers lingering lingered (vb) If you linger over something, you take a long time doing it.

linguist linguists (n) A linguist is a person who is good at learning and speaking foreign languages.

link links linking linked
1 (vb) If you link things, you join them together.
2 (n) A link is a piece in a chain.
3 (n) Golf links are a golf course.

lint (n) is a cotton material often used to make medical dressings.

1

lintel

lintel lintels (n) A lintel is a piece of wood, stone or brick over a door or window, which supports the building above it.

lion lions (n) A lion is a large member of the cat family that lives in Africa. The female is called a lioness.

lip lips
1 (n) Your lips are the soft, red parts at the edge of your mouth.
2 (n) The lip of a jug or other container for liquid is the part you pour from.

liquid liquids (n) A liquid is a substance which is not solid and can flow. Milk, water, petrol and juice are all liquids.

liquidise liquidises liquidising liquidised (vb) If you liquidise food, you make it into a liquid using a machine called a liquidiser.

liquorice (n) is a firm, black substance with a strong taste which is used to make chewy sweets.

lisp lisps (n) If you have a lisp, you have difficulty in saying your S sounds, which you sound like TH.

list lists listing listed
1 (n) A list is a set of objects or ideas written one below the other, or spoken one after the other.
2 (vb) If you list things, you say or write many items one after the other.
3 (vb) If a ship lists, it leans over to one side.

listen listens listening listened (vb) If you listen, you pay attention to what is being said. **listener** (n)

literate (adj) If you are literate, you are able to read and write. **literacy** (n)

literature (n) is everything we read, especially novels, plays and poetry.

litre litres (n) A litre is a measure of volume. It is 1000 cubic centimetres or 1.75 pints. l is the short form of litre.

litter litters littering littered
1 (n) Litter is the rubbish that people leave behind them.
2 (vb) If you litter a place with things, you leave rubbish or other items scattered around.
3 (n) A litter is a group of new-born animals born to the same mother.

little (adj) Something little is small.

live lives living lived
1 (vb) Something which lives is alive, like a plant or animal.
2 (vb) If you live in a particular place, that is where your home is.
3 (vb) If you live by doing something, that is how you earn your living.
4 (adj) Something live is alive.
5 (adj) A live performance or broadcast is not a recording.

lively livelier liveliest (adj) A lively person or animal has lots of energy. **liveliness** (n)

liver livers (n) The liver is the organ in the body which helps to clean the blood.

lizard lizards (n) A lizard is a small, dry-skinned reptile with short legs and a long tail.

load loads loading loaded
1 (n) A load is an amount to be carried somewhere.
2 (vb) If you load a car or a person, you put things on or into them to take them elsewhere.
3 (n) A load of something means a lot of it.
4 (vb) If you load a camera or a computer, you put a film or a disk into it.

loaf loaves (n) A loaf is bread that is shaped into one piece.

loan loans loaning loaned
1 (n) A loan is money borrowed, sometimes from a bank, which must be paid back, often with interest.
2 (vb) If something is on loan to you you are allowed to have it for a while.

loathe loathes loathing loathed (vb) If you loathe someone or something, you dislike them very much.

lobe lobes (n) The lobe of the ear is the round, fleshy part that hangs at the bottom.

lobster lobsters (n) A lobster is an edible shellfish with a segmented body, eight legs and two strong claws.

local locals
1 (adj) If someone or something is local, they belong to a particular place or area.
2 (n) A local is someone who lives in a particular area.
3 (n) Your local is the pub that you go to regularly. *My local is The Bear at Colyton.*

location locations
1 (n) A location is a place where something happens.
2 (n) If a film is made on location, it is not made in a studio.

loch lochs (n) A loch is a lake in Scotland.

lock locks locking locked
1 (n) A lock is a device used to keep a door or window securely shut. It can only be opened by using a key.
2 (vb) If you lock something, you use a key to close it securely.
3 If something is left under lock and key, it is locked away.

locker lockers (n) A locker is a small lockable cupboard where things can be kept safely.

locust locusts (n) A locust is a winged insect like a large grasshopper found in hot countries. Locusts fly in swarms and sometimes destroy crops.

lodge lodges lodging lodged
1 (vb) If you lodge in someone's house, you pay to stay there for a while. **lodger** (n)
2 (vb) If something lodges somewhere, it gets stuck there.
3 (vb) If you lodge a complaint, you make it officially.
4 (n) A lodge is a small house near the entrance of a big one.
5 (n) A lodge is a beaver's home.

loft lofts (n) A loft is a room under the roof of a building.

log logs logging logged
1 (n) A log is a piece of a thick part of a tree trunk or branch.
2 (n) A log is an official written record of a journey by sea, air, etc. **logbook** (n)
3 (vb) If you log events, you record them officially.

4 If you sleep like a log, you sleep soundly.
5 If you log onto a computer system, you enter it by giving a password.

logical (adj) If an argument is logical, each point follows on and makes sense.
logically (adv)

loiter loiters loitering loitered (vb) If you loiter in a place, you move around slowly and without going very far.
loiterer (n)

lollipop lollipops (n) A lollipop is a hard sweet or fruit-flavoured ice on a stick.

lonely
1 (adj) A lonely person feels sad because they are on their own. **loneliness** (n)
2 (adj) A lonely place is visited by few people.

long longs longing longed
1 (adj) Long is a way of describing time or measurement. *We waited four hours in the queue, which was a long time ... The dress was too long as it reached to the ground.*
2 (vb) If you long for someone or something, you want them very much.

longitude longitudes (n) Longitude is a position measured as a distance from East or West of a set line.

loofah loofahs (n) A loofah is a long, sponge-like dried plant used for scrubbing your body.

look looks looking looked
1 (vb) If you look somewhere, you move your eyes there so that you can see what is happening.
2 (vb) If you look at television, for example, you watch it.
3 (vb) If someone looks ill, they appear to be so.
4 (n) If someone has good looks, they have an attractive appearance.
5 (vb) If you look after something for someone, you keep it safe.

loom looms looming loomed
1 (vb) If something looms, it shows as a large shape, often frightening.
2 (vb) If problems loom, they dominate your thoughts.
3 (n) A loom is a machine that weaves threads into cloth.

l

loop

loop loops
1 (n) A loop is a circular shape made by a piece of string, rope, etc.
2 (n) A loop is a series of tasks in a computer program that must be completed before it can move to the next series.

loose loosens loosening loosened; looser loosest
1 (adj) If something is loose, it isn't held firmly in place.
2 (adj) Loose clothes are not tight fitting.
3 (adj) If animals are loose, they are roaming free.
4 (adj) If a rope, string, shoelace, etc. is loose, it is not tied tightly.
5 (vb) If you loosen something, you make it less tight.
6 (vb) If something loosens, it becomes less tight.

loot loots looting looted
1 (n) Loot is stolen property.
2 (vb) When people loot shops, homes, etc. they steal things from them, usually during a riot or other disturbance.

lord lords
1 (n) In Britain, a lord is a member of the aristocracy.
2 (n) The Lords is short for The House of Lords which is one of the Houses of Parliament in London.
3 (n) In the Christian church Our Lord or The Lord refers to God or to Jesus Christ.

lorry lorries (n) A lorry is a large vehicle used for transporting goods by road.

lose loses losing lost
1 (vb) If you lose something you can't find it.
2 (vb) If you lose someone who is close to you, they die.
3 (adj) If you are lost, you don't know where you are.
4 (vb) If you lose a game, match, etc you do not win. **loser** (n)
5 (vb) If a clock or watch loses time, it goes slower than it should.

loss losses
1 (n) Loss is when you no longer have something or when you lose something.
2 Loss of life is when people die.
3 If you say someone is a great loss, it means that they have left or died and that they are greatly missed.

4 If a business makes a loss, it spends more money than it earns and is not doing well.

lost see **lose**

lotion lotions (n) A lotion is a liquid that is used to soothe, protect, clean or soften your skin or hair.

loud louder loudest
1 (adj) A loud sound is a large amount of sound.
2 (adj) Loud colours are very bright and patterned and may not look pleasant.

loudspeaker loudspeakers (n) A loudspeaker is a piece of electrical equipment that produces the sound in a radio, record player, telephone, etc.

lounge lounges lounging lounged
1 (vb) If you lounge, you lie around or lean against something in a lazy way.
2 (n) A lounge is a room with comfortable chairs where you can relax.
3 (n) A lounge in an airport is a large room where passengers can sit and relax while waiting for their planes.

louse lice (n) A louse is a small insect that lives on the bodies of humans and animals and bites them to feed on their blood.

lout louts (n) A lout is a boy or a man who is bad-mannered and anti-social.

love loves loving loved
1 (vb) If you love someone, you like them very much and you want to be with them and make them happy because they are important to you.
2 (vb) If you love something, you are very fond of it and it is important to you.
3 (vb) If you say you love doing something, you enjoy doing it very much.
4 (n) Love is a very strong feeling of affection that you have for someone or something.
5 (adj) A loving person is someone who is full of love and affection.
loveable (adj)

lovely lovelier loveliest
1 (adj) Something that is lovely is pleasing because it is beautiful to look at, listen to, touch, etc.
2 (adj) A lovely person can be beautiful to look at or have a loving, generous nature.

low lower lowest
1 (adj) If something is low, it is close to the ground.
2 (adj) If a river, pond, lake, etc is low, it contains much less water than usual.
3 (adj) Low can mean small in amount. *Low wages... low prices.*
4 (adj) If you speak in a low voice, you speak quietly.
5 (adv) If you feel low, you feel miserable and depressed.

lower lowers lowering lowered
1 (vb) If you lower something, or if something is lowered, it is moved downwards.
2 (vb) If you lower your eyes, you look down.
3 (vb) If you lower your voice you speak more quietly.
4 (adj) If something is lower than something else, it is below it.
5 (adj) If something is lower it is less advanced. *A lower standard... a lower grade.*

loyal (adj) A loyal person or animal is faithful and friendly no matter what happens. **loyalty** (n)

lubricate lubricates lubricating lubricated (vb) If you lubricate a machine you put oil or grease on its parts so that they move smoothly. **lubrication** (n)

luck (n) Luck is something that seems, for no apparent reason, to cause good things to happen to some people and bad things to happen to others. **lucky** (adj)

luggage (n) Your luggage is all the bags and cases that you take with you when you travel.

lukewarm
1 (adj) Something, usually a liquid, that is lukewarm is only just warm.
2 (adj) If someone is lukewarm in their attitude to you or to something, they are not very friendly or enthusiastic. *The audience gave the play a lukewarm reception.*

lull lulls lulling lulled
1 (vb) If you lull someone, you soothe them and make them feel relaxed and sleepy.
2 (n) A lull is a time of quiet when nothing is happening between times of great activity.

lullaby lullabies (n) A lullaby is a sweet, gentle song sung to small children to help them go to sleep.

lumber lumbers lumbering lumbered
1 (vb) If a person or animal lumbers from place to place, they move clumsily and slowly.
2 (adj) A lumbering person or animal is one that moves heavily and clumsily.
3 (n) Lumber is the word for trees that have been cut down for their wood.

luminous (adj) If something is luminous it shines in the dark.

lump lumps
1 (n) A lump is a piece of something of any shape or size. *A lump of pastry... a lump of coal.*
2 (n) A lump is a growth or swelling on the body. *He had a lump on his head after the rounders ball hit him.*

lunar (adj) means to do with to the moon.

lunar month lunar months (n) A lunar month is the time the moon takes to orbit the earth, which is 29 days.

lunch lunches lunching lunched
1 (vb) If you lunch you eat a meal in the middle of the day.
2 (n) Lunch is a midday meal.

lung lungs (n) The lungs are the two organs inside the chest that fill up with air during breathing.

lurch lurches lurching lurched
1 (vb) If you lurch you make sudden uncontrolled movements, usually forward.
2 If someone leaves you in the lurch, they leave you when you most need help.

lure lures luring lured (vb) If you lure a person or an animal you lead them astray or into a trap by tempting them in some way.

lurk lurks lurking lurked (vb) If a person or an animal lurks somewhere, they wait, keeping out of sight.

lush lusher lushest (adj) Plants and trees that are lush are growing strongly and healthily.

lustre (n) is a shine that is reflected from polished surfaces on some metals.

l

lute lutes (n) A lute is an old-fashioned stringed instrument rather like a guitar.

luxury luxuries
1 (n) Luxury is great comfort, especially beautiful and expensive possessions, surroundings, etc. **luxurious** (adj)
2 (n) A luxury is something, usually expensive, that you would like to have but which you do not need.

lynch lynches lynching lynched (vb) If a group of angry people lynch a person, they hang them without a proper trial.

lynx lynxes (n) A lynx is a wild animal of the cat family with a short tail and tufted ears.

lyric lyrics
1 (n) The lyrics are the words of a popular song.
2 (n) A lyric is a poem usually about love or other emotions.

Mm

mac macs (n) Mac is short for mackintosh.

macaroni (n) is a tube-shaped pasta.

Mach (n) is a unit used to measure very high speeds of aircraft. Mach 1 is the speed of sound, Mach 2 is twice the speed of sound, etc.

machine machines (n) A machine is a piece of equipment designed to do a particular job, usually using power from an engine or electricity. **machinery** (n)

machine gun machine guns (n) A machine gun is a type of gun that automatically fires a continuous stream of bullets very quickly.

macho (adj) A man who tries to look macho or act in a macho manner, is aggressively masculine.

mackintosh mackintoshes (n) A mackintosh is a waterproof coat.

mad madder maddest
1 (adj) Someone who is mad is extremely angry.
2 (adj) A mad person is insane. **madness** (n)
3 If you are mad about someone or something, you like them very much.

madden maddens maddening maddened
1 (vb) If you madden someone, you annoy them or make them angry.
2 (adj) If someone or something is maddening, they are very irritating.

Mafia (n) The Mafia is a large criminal organisation that operates largely in Sicily and in the United States of America.

magazine magazines
1 (n) A magazine is a publication containing stories, articles, photographs, etc. usually published weekly or monthly.
2 (n) In a gun, the magazine is the part that holds the ammunition.
3 (n) A magazine is the secure area used for storing ammunition and explosives in buildings and ships.

maggot maggots (n) Maggots are the larvae of some kinds of fly. They look like small, fat worms. **maggoty** (adj)

Magi (n) The Magi were the three wise kings who visited the infant Jesus at Bethlehem.

magic
1 (n) Magic is the so-called art of using supernatural force to make the impossible happen. *The wizard raised his staff and, by magic, the boy disappeared.*
2 (adj) A magic show is an entertainment where someone performs clever tricks and illusions. **magician** (n)

magistrate magistrates (n) Magistrates are people who act as judges in law courts that deal with less serious crimes.

magnet magnets (n) A magnet is a piece of metal which has the power to pull iron towards it. **magnetic** (adj) **magnetism** (n)

magnificent (adj) Something magnificent is very grand or beautiful.

magnify magnifies magnifying magnified
1 (vb) If you magnify an object, you make it look bigger by looking at it through a microscope or magnifying glass. **magnification** (n)
2 (vb) If you magnify a situation, you make it seem more important or greater than it really is.

magpie magpies (n) A magpie is a long-tailed, black and white bird about the size of a crow.

mahogany (n) is a dark, reddish-brown hardwood.

maid maids (n) A maid is a female servant in a house or hotel.

maiden maidens
1 (n) Maiden is an old-fashioned word for girl.
2 (adj) Maiden can describe the first time something happens. *The ship's maiden voyage was across the Atlantic.*
3 (adj) A woman's maiden name is the name she had before she married.
4 A maiden over in cricket is one where no runs are scored.

mail
1 (n) Mail is the name for all letters and parcels sent by post.
2 (n) Mail or chain mail is a type of armour made from small metal rings.

maim maims maiming maimed (vb) If you maim someone, you injure them so badly that parts of their bodies will not work.

main mains
1 (adj) The main part or thing is the largest or most important. *The main entrance was closed.*
2 (n) The mains are large pipes for carrying water to buildings.
3 (n) The mains is the name for the gas or electricity supply to a building.

maintain maintains maintaining maintained
1 (vb) If you maintain something, you keep it going. *They maintained their friendship for many years.*
2 (vb) If something such as a building or machine is maintained, it is kept in good condition. **maintenance** (n)
3 (vb) If you maintain someone, you provide money for their needs.
4 (vb) If you maintain something, you believe it to be true and say so. *I maintain that it was his fault I lost the job.*

maize (n) is a tall plant which produces the cobs of sweet, yellow corn. It is a basic food crop in many countries.

majesty majesties
1 (n) Your Majesty is a polite way of addressing a queen or king.
2 (n) Majesty is the quality of being dignified and impressive. **majestic** (adj)

major majors
1 (n) Major is an officer's rank in the army.
2 (adj) If something is major, it is greater or more important than something else.

majority

majority majorities
1 (n) A majority is the greater part of a group.
2 (n) In an election the person who gets the majority of the votes is the winner.
3 (n) When you reach your majority, you are officially an adult. In Britain this is at 18 years of age.

make up (n) refers to the creams, powders, lipsticks etc. that people put on their faces to make themselves more attractive, or when acting in a play or film.

maladjusted (adj) A maladjusted person has psychological or behaviour problems.

malaria (n) is a serious disease which is caught through mosquito bites.

male males
1 (n) A male is the person or animal which does not give birth to children.
2 (adj) Something described as male refers to men, not women.

malicious (adj) A malicious person intends to hurt others by words or action.

mallet mallets (n) A mallet is a wooden hammer, used to hit chisels, etc.

malnutrition (n) is a condition resulting from unhealthy food or lack of food.

mammal mammals (n) A mammal is an animal that gives birth to live babies, which are fed on the mother's milk.

mammoth mammoths
1 (n) A mammoth was a huge, hairy elephant, which is now extinct.
2 (adj) Someone or something mammoth is huge.

man men; mans manning manned
1 (n) A man is an adult male human being.
2 (n) Man refers to both men and women. *Man has been on the planet for a long time.*
3 (vb) If you man something, you are responsible for, or take part in it. *Parents manned the fête stalls.*

manage manages managing managed.
1 (vb) If you manage to do something, you do it successfully, but usually after some problems.
2 (vb) If you manage a company, you control and organise it.
management (n) **manager** (n)

mane manes (n) The mane is the long hair that grows on a horse's neck or around a lion's face.

manger mangers (n) A manger is a food box for horses and cows.

mangle mangles mangling mangled
1 (vb) If you mangle something, you twist it with much force.
2 (adj) Something which is mangled is twisted out of shape.

mania mania
1 (n) If you have a mania for something, you are very keen on it.
2 (n) Mania is madness. **maniac** (n)

mankind (n) means all human beings.

manner manners
1 (n) The manner in which you do something is the way in which you do it.
2 (n) Your manners are the way you behave with others. *Her table manners were disgusting.*

manoeuvre manoeuvres manoeuvering manoeuvred (vb) If you manoeuvre something, you steer and guide it.

manor manors (n) A manor is a large, country house with land.

mansion mansions (n) A mansion is a large house.

manslaughter (n) is the crime of killing a person by someone who intended to hurt but not kill them.

manual manuals
1 (n) A manual is a book giving information on how to use or work something.
2 (adj) Manual work is usually unskilled work done with your hands.

manufacture manufactures manufacturing manufactured
1 (vb) If you manufacture something, you make it using machinery.
manufacturer (n)
2 (vb) If you manufacture a story, you make it up.

manure manures manuring manured
1 (n) Manure is animal dung which is used to help plants grow.
2 (vb) If you manure the ground, you spread manure to help plants grow.

manuscript manuscripts
1 (n) A manuscript is a handwritten copy of a book, story or piece of music, before it is published.
2 (n) A manuscript is a piece of very old writing.

many (adv) Many things means a large number of them.

map maps mapping mapped
1 (n) A map is an accurate drawing showing the shape and features of an area of land.
2 (vb) If you map out something, you plan it.

maple maples (n) A maple is a type of tree with broad, five-pointed leaves. It grows in cool climates.

marathon marathons (n) A marathon is a running race, over 26 miles long.

marble marbles
1 (n) Marble is a very hard, cold stone, with different-coloured patterns in it.
2 (n) A marble is a small, glass ball, sometimes used in a game of marbles.

march marches marching marched
1 (vb) If you march, you walk with regular steps and arm movements.
2 (vb) If an army marches, it moves from one place to another. *The German armies marched into Poland in 1939.*

mare mares (n) A mare is a female horse.

margarine (n) is a yellow substance made from vegetable oil, animal fat and water. It is used for spreading on bread and for cooking.

margin margins (n) A margin is a gap left down the side of a page.

marijuana (n) is a kind of drug.

marina marinas (n) A marina is a place where small boats can moor.

marine marines
1 (adj) Anything which is marine is connected with the sea. *Marine animals... marine plants.*
2 (n) A marine is a special type of soldier who serves with the navy.

mark marks marking marked
1 (vb) If you mark something, you scratch or stain it. *I marked my skirt when I walked into the wet paint.*
2 (vb) You can also mark things deliberately, with your name, for example, to show that they are yours.
3 (vb) If teachers mark your work, they comment on it in various ways.

market markets (n) A market is a place with stalls where people buy and sell things.

marksman marksmen (n) A marksman is a person who is an expert shot with a rifle or pistol.

marmalade (n) is a jam made from a citrus fruit such as oranges.

maroon maroons
1 (adj) Maroon is a very deep, red colour.
2 (n) A maroon is a flare which ships fire as a signal for help if they are in trouble.

marquee marquees (n) A marquee is a very large tent, often used for large groups of people to eat in.

marrow marrows
1 (n) A marrow is a vegetable, like a large, fat cucumber.
2 (n) Marrow is the substance that fills the space at the centre of human and animal bones.

marry marries marrying married
(vb) If a man and woman marry, they promise at an official ceremony to spend the rest of their lives together. **marriage** (n)

marsh marshes (n) A marsh is an area of land which is very wet and boggy.

marshmallow marshmallows (n) A marshmallow is a very soft, sugary, sticky sort of sweet.

marsupial marsupials (n) A marsupial is a mammal which carries its growing young in a pouch.

martial (adj) Anything which is described as martial is to do with the army, fighting or war. *The bands played martial music all through the parade.*

martyr martyrs (n) A martyr is a person who suffers or is killed, rather than change their religious or political beliefs.

m

marvel

marvel marvels marvelling marvelled
1 (vb) If you marvel at something, you are filled with awe and admiration for it. *We marvelled at the way she drove the car.*
2 (n) A marvel is something wonderful.
marvellous (adj) **marvellously** (adv)

marzipan (n) is a paste of almond, sugar and egg used on top of cakes or as sweets.

mascara (n) is a dark paste which people use to lengthen and thicken their eyelashes.

mascot mascots (n) A mascot is a toy, doll, etc. which people believe is lucky.

masculine (adj) Anything which is masculine is to do with being male.
masculinity (n)

mask masks masking masked
1 (n) A mask is something you wear over your face to cover it.
2 (vb) If you mask something, you cover it up in some way. *Her perfume masked the smell of garlic.*

masonry (n) is the brick or stone which make up buildings.

mass masses
1 (n) The mass of an object is the amount of physical matter it is made up of.
2 (adj) Masses of something are large amounts. *He has masses of red hair.*
3 (adj) Mass is used to describe something which affects a lot of people. *The earthquake caused mass destruction.*
4 (n) A Mass is a religious service in the Christian church, especially Roman Catholic.

massacre massacres massacring massacred
1 (vb) If people massacre others, they kill large numbers of them at the same time in a cruel way.
2 (n) A massacre is the killing of large numbers of people at one time.

massage massages massaging massaged
1 (vb) If you massage someone, you rub a part of their body to relieve pain or to help them relax.
2 (n) When part of a person's body is rubbed to ease pain or to help them relax they are having a massage.

massive (adj) Something massive is very large.

mass media (n) The mass media are all the ways of giving news and information to many people at the same time. *Newspapers, television, radio and the cinema are all types of mass media.*

mast masts
1 (n) A mast is the tall pole to which sails or flags are attached.
2 (n) A mast can also hold a radio or T.V. aerial.

master masters mastering mastered.
1 (n) A master is a man who controls other people or animals.
2 (n) If you are a master of something, you can do it very well.
3 (vb) If you master a skill, you learn how to do it well.

masterpiece masterpieces (n) A masterpiece is the very best piece of work which someone, usually an artist, has done.

match matches matching matched
1 (n) A match is a small stick, tipped with a chemical which catches fire when rubbed on a rough surface or along the side of the box.
2 (n) A match is a sporting contest in football, netball, etc.
3 (vb) If colours match, they go together.
4 (vb) If you match up things in a puzzle, you find the connections.
5 If you meet your match, you meet your equal at something. *I played the game as best I could, but I had met my match in Peter.*

material materials
1 (n) Material is the fabric and cloth from which clothes, etc. are made.
2 (n) Material is anything from which something else can be made or put together. *We had all the materials we needed to make a raft.*
3 (adj) The material world is the world of physical things that we can touch, see, hear, etc.

maternal (adj) is used to describe things relating to motherhood.

maternity (adj) is used to describe things to do with a woman's pregnancy.

m

mathematics (n) is the study of numbers, shapes, etc. **mathematical** (adj) **mathematician** (n)

matrix matrices (n) A matrix is a rectangular arrangement of numbers, lines, etc. used to solve some mathematical problems.

matter matters mattering mattered
1 (n) Matter is every substance that occupies space.
2 (n) A matter is a situation that needs attention.
3 (vb) If something matters to you, it is important.
4 If something is no laughing matter, it is very serious.

mattress mattresses (n) A mattress is a thick covered pad of feathers, hair, straw, etc. on which to sleep.

mature matures maturing matured
1 (vb) When an infant matures it becomes an adult.
2 (vb) If good wine, cheese etc matures, it ages until it is ready to be eaten.
3 (adj) A mature person is adult and has an adult approach to life.

maul mauls mauling mauled (vb) If an animal mauls you, it attacks you savagely.

maximum
1 (adj) The maximum amount or number is the most that is possible.
2 (n) A maximum is the largest amount possible.

mayhem (n) describes a very confused and sometimes violent situation.

mayonnaise (n) is a cold sauce made from eggs, oil, etc and used on salads.

mayor mayors (n) A mayor is a person elected by a town to represent the people at official functions. **mayoress** (fem n)

maze mazes (n) A maze is a puzzle of many tracks or pathways which is difficult to find your way through because some are dead ends.

meadow meadows (n) A meadow is a grassy field where animals may graze.

meagre (adj) Anything meagre is very small.

meal meals (n) A meal is the food that you eat at certain times, lunch, tea, etc.

mean means meaning meant; meaner meanest
1 (adj) If someone is mean, they do not share with others or are unkind to them.
2 (adj) A mean person is unwilling to spend much money or use much of something. **meanness** (n)
3 (vb) If you mean to do something, you intend to do it.
4 (vb) If you want to know what someone or something means, you are asking for an explanation. **meaning** (n)
5 (n) If you find the means to do something, you find a way or the money to achieve it.
6 (n) The mean is a number that is the average of a set of numbers.
7 If something means a lot to you, it is important.

meander meanders meandering meandered
1 (vb) When a river or road meanders, it winds from side to side.
2 (n) A meander is a bend in a river.
3 (vb) If you meander, you move along slowly and aimlessly.

meanwhile (adv) is used to show that two separate events are happening at the same time. *The builders worked on the walls; meanwhile the plumbers put in the boiler.*

measles (n) is an infectious illness which causes a high temperature and spots.

measure measures measuring measured
1 (vb) If you measure something, you find out its height, width, weight, etc.
2 (n) A measure of something is a certain amount of it.
3 (n) A measure is something such as a ruler or a tape measure you use for measuring.
4 If you take measures, you take certain actions to achieve something.
5 If clothes are made to measure, they are made to your size. **measurement** (n)

meat meats (n) Meat is the animal flesh that is eaten.

m

mechanic

mechanic mechanics (n) A mechanic is someone who services and repairs machines.

mechanical
1 (adj) Anything mechanical is worked by machinery.
2 (adj) If you are mechanical, you understand how machines work.

medal medals (n) A medal is a small metal badge awarded for bravery, sporting achievement,or doing well in a competition. **medallist** (n)

meddle meddles meddling meddled (vb) If you meddle, you interfere in things which are not your business. **meddler** (n)

media (n) The word media refers to radio, television and newspapers.

medical medicals
1 (n) A medical is an examination of your body by a doctor.
2 (adj) Anything medical is to do with the treatment of people who are ill.

medicine medicines
1 (n) Medicine is the care and treatment of ill people.
2 (n) Medicines are tablets, drugs, etc that people take when they are ill.

medieval (adj) Medieval times were roughly between AD 1100 and AD 1500. This period is also called the Middle Ages.

Mediterranean
1 (n) The Mediterranean is the sea between Europe and North Africa.
2 (adj) Anything Mediterranean is concerned with the area around the Mediterranean sea.

medium mediums or **media**
1 (adj) Medium means half way between two extremes. *He was of medium height and medium weight.*
2 (n) A medium is a person who claims to be able to contact the dead.

meek meeker meekest (adj) If you are meek, you are very gentle, quiet and timid.

meeting meetings
1 (n) A meeting takes place when a group of people gather together for a purpose.
2 (n) A meeting is a coming together of people by accident or by arrangement.

megaphone megaphones (n) A megaphone is a trumpet-like device that makes your voice sound very loud when you speak through it. *She called the names of the runners through the megaphone.*

melancholy (adj) If someone is melancholy, they are very sad.

melodramatic (adj) If you are melodramatic, you behave in a showy and emotional way.

melody melodies (n) A melody is a tune.

melon melons (n) A melon is a large, round or oval, juicy fruit with a hard, green or yellow skin.

melt melts melting melted
1 (vb) When something melts, it changes from solid to liquid because it has been heated.
2 (vb) If something melts away, it gradually disappears.

member members
1 (n) A member of a group is one of that group. *She was a member of a large family.*
2 (n) If you join a club or a society, you are a member of it. **membership** (n)

Member of Parliament Members of Parliament (n) A Member of Parliament is a person who has been elected by the people of a particular town or district to represent them in the House of Commons.

membrane membranes (n) A membrane is very thin skin.

memorable (adj) Something memorable is so interesting or exciting that you cannot forget it.

m

the Victoria **Memorial** outside Buckingham Palace, London

memorial memorials (n) A memorial is an object placed somewhere to remind people of a famous person or event.

memory memories
1 (n) Your memory is your ability to remember things.
2 (n) A memory is something that you remember.
3 (n) A computer's memory is the part where the information is stored.

men see **man**

menace menaces menacing menaced
1 (vb) If someone menaces you, they threaten to harm you.
2 (n) A menace is something that could harm you.
3 (adj) If something is menacing, it frightens you because it could be dangerous.

menagerie menageries (n) A menagerie is a collection of birds or animals.

mental (adj) Anything described as mental is to do with the brain. *You must make a great mental effort to understand.*

mention mentions mentioning mentioned (vb) If you mention something, you talk or write about it very briefly.

menu menus
1 (n) A menu is a list of foods from which you can order at a restaurant or a list of food eaten at a special meal.
2 (n) A menu is a computer list which tells you how to find the information in your computer.

mercenary mercenaries
1 (n) A mercenary is a person who will fight for any country which pays them.
2 (adj) Someone who is mercenary is mainly interested in getting money.

merchant merchants
1 (n) A merchant is a person who imports and exports large quantities of goods.
2 (adj) Merchant ships are ships that carry goods around the world.
3 Merchant seamen are sailors who work on merchant ships.

mercury
1 (n) Mercury is a silver-coloured, liquid metal.
2 (n) Mercury is a planet.

mercy mercies
1 (n) If you show mercy, you are forgiving and don't want to punish someone for doing something wrong. **merciful** (adj)
2 If you are at the mercy of someone or something, you are in their power.

merit merits meriting merited
1 (n) The merits of something are its good points.
2 (vb) If you merit something, you deserve it.

mess messes messing messed
1 (n) A mess is an untidy or dirty situation.
2 (n) A mess is a room where servicemen eat.
3 (vb) If you mess something up, you make it untidy, or do it very badly.
4 If you are in a mess, you have problems.

message messages (n) A message is information or a request for information, either spoken or written, from one person to another. **messenger** (n)

metal metals (n) A metal is a hard substance such as iron, steel, silver, etc. **metallic** (adj)

meteor meteors (n) A meteor is a piece of rock or metal that burns briefly as it enters the earth's atmosphere.

meteorite meteorites (n) A meteorite is a piece of rock from space which has landed on the earth.

meteorology (n) is the study of the weather. **meteorologist** (n)

m

meter

meter meters
1 (n) A meter is a device which measures how much gas, electricity, etc has been used.
2 (n) A parking meter is a device which shows how long a vehicle has been parked.

method methods (n) A method is a certain way of doing something.

Methodist Methodists (n) Methodists are Christians who follow the teachings of John Wesley and who have particular ways of worship. **Methodism** (n)

metre metres (n) A metre is equal to 100 centimetres; m is short for metre.

metric system The metric system is a measuring system with a base of 10 and multiples of 10 using litres, metres, grams, kilograms, etc.

miaow miaows miaowing miaowed
1 (n) A miaow is the noise a cat makes.
2 (vb) When a cat miaows, it makes a crying noise.

micro micros (n) A micro is a small computer.

microbe microbes (n) A microbe is a very small, living thing that can only be seen under a microscope.

electronic
p96
microchip microchips (n) A microchip is a very small piece of silicon inside a computer, which can store large amounts of information, and perform mathematical and logical calculations.

microfilm microfilms microfilming microfilmed
1 (n) A microfilm is film which is used for photographing information so that it can be stored. The information is made very small and can be looked at by using a special machine.
2 (vb) If you microfilm something, such as a document or a map, you put them on microfilm.

microlight microlights (n) A microlight is a very small and light aeroplane.

microphone microphones (n) A microphone is a device which is used to help record sounds or make them louder.

microscope microscopes (n) A microscope is a device which, when you look through it, makes small objects look larger.

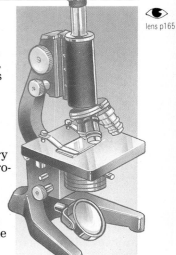
lens p165

microwave oven microwave ovens (n) A microwave oven cooks food very quickly using electro-magnetic waves rather than heat.

midday (n) is at 12 o'clock in the middle of the day.

middle middles
1 (n) The middle of a line, book, etc is the part that is the same distance from the beginning as it is from the end.
2 (n) If you are in the middle of doing something, you are involved with doing it at that time.
3 (n) The middle of a road or river is the part furthest from both sides.

Middle Ages see **medieval**

midnight (n) is 12 o'clock at night.

midwife midwives (n) A midwife is a nurse trained to help women during pregnancy and at the birth of their babies.

might
1 (vb) If you might do something, it is possible you will do it.
2 (vb) If you believe something might happen, it is possible that it will.
3 (vb) If you feel someone might have done something, you believe they should have done so. *You might have 'phoned to say you weren't coming!*
4 If you do something with all your might, you do it with all your strength and energy.

migrate migrates migrating migrated (vb) When animals or people migrate, they move to another part of the world for a season. **migrant** (n) **migration** (n)

mild milder mildest
1 (adj) Mild weather is not very hot or very cold.
2 (adj) A mild food is not strong tasting.
3 (adj) If you have a mild infection you are not very ill.

mildew (n) is a fungus which grows on things in damp conditions.

mile miles
1 (n) A mile is a distance of 1760 yards and equals 1.6 kilometres. **mileage** (n)
2 If you are miles away, you are daydreaming, or not aware of what is happening around you.
3 If something stands out a mile, it is very noticeable. *He wants to be captain of the football team, it stands out a mile.*

milk milks milking milked
1 (n) Milk is the white liquid which mammals produce for their young to drink.
2 (vb) If you milk an animal, you get milk from it by squeezing its teats.

mill mills milling milled
1 (n) A mill is a building where grain is ground into flour, or a factory where certain materials such as paper or wood are prepared for use. **miller** (n)
2 (n) A mill is a small device for grinding peppercorns, sea-salt, etc.
3 (vb) If you mill something, you grind it to powder or small pieces.

millilitre millilitres (n) A millilitre is a small quantity of liquid: 1/1000th of a litre. ml is short for millilitre.

millimetre millimetres (n) A millimetre is a small unit of length. There are 1000 millimetres in one metre. mm is short for millimetre.

millionaire millionaires (n) A millionaire is a very rich person who has money and property worth at least a million in currency.

mime mimes miming mimed (vb) If you mime something, you act it out without speaking.

mimic mimics mimicking mimicked (vb) If you mimic somebody or something, you copy them.

minaret minarets (n) A minaret is a tall, thin tower, often part of a mosque.

mince minces mincing minced
1 (vb) If you mince something, you grind it into very small pieces.
2 (n) Mince is usually beef which has been ground into very small pieces.

mincemeat (n) is a sweet mixture of fruits, used to make mince pies.

mind minds minding minded
1 (n) Your mind is that part of you which thinks and feels emotions, but is not a physical object.
2 (vb) If you mind something, you look after it for somebody else. *Will you mind my baby while I go shopping?* **minder** (n)

mine mines mining mined
1 (n) A mine is a place where coal, gold, etc are dug out from deep under the ground. **miner** (n)
2 (vb) If you mine something, you dig it out from the earth.
3 (n) A mine is an exploding device used to sink ships in wartime, or buried in the earth to kill soldiers and destroy vehicles.
4 (pro) Mine means belonging to me. *That book is mine.*

mineral minerals (n) A mineral is a substance which is found naturally in rocks and earth.

mingle mingles mingling mingled
1 (vb) You mingle when you mix and talk with other people.
2 (vb) If sounds or flavours mingle, they get mixed up together.

m

miniature

miniature miniatures
1 (adj) If something is miniature, it is very small.
2 (n) A miniature is a small version of a much larger object.

minibus minibuses (n) A minibus is a van with passenger seats in the back and windows along the sides.

minimum (n) The minimum is the smallest amount of anything you can have for a particular purpose.

minister ministers
1 (n) A minister is a clergyman.
2 (n) A minister is someone in charge of a government department. *The Minister for Transport . . . Minister for Health.*

mink minks (n) Mink is an animal bred or trapped for its valuable fur.

minnow minnows (n) A minnow is a very small freshwater fish.

minor minors
1 (adj) Something which is minor is smaller or less important than something else. *He was only a minor painter.*
2 (n) A minor is a person who is still legally a child.

minority minorities (n) The minority of a group of things or people is the group that is less than half the number. *Most football fans are all right, it is the minority that causes the trouble.*

mint mints minting minted
1 (n) In Britain, the official place where coins are made is called the Mint.
2 (vb) If you mint coins or medals, you make them. *The government is the only organisation allowed to mint coins.*
3 (n) Mint is a strong-smelling plant. The leaves are used for flavouring in cooking.
4 (adj) If something is in mint condition, it is perfect.

minus minuses
1 (n) A minus is the sign $-$. It is used in maths to show that one number is being subtracted from another. $15-7=8$
2 (prep) Minus can mean something is missing. *He came in, minus his bag.*

minute minutes
1 (n) A minute is sixty seconds long, and sixty minutes make one hour.
2 (adj) Something minute is very small.

miracle miracles
1 (n) A miracle is something marvellous which people believe only God could have caused.
2 (n) A miracle is something which is very surprising. *It's a miracle he wasn't killed in the accident.* **miraculous** (adj)

mirage mirages (n) A mirage is an illusion caused by heat haze in hot places such as deserts.

mirror mirrors (n) A mirror is a piece of glass or plastic which reflects light and images. *I used the mirror to see how I looked in my new dress.*

misbehave misbehaves misbehaving misbehaved (vb) If you misbehave, you behave badly.

miscellaneous (adj) A miscellaneous group of things or people are not connected to one another in any way. **miscellany** (n)

mischief (n) is behaviour which will cause other people trouble. **mischievous** (adj)

miser misers (n) A miser loves to hoard money but hates to spend it. **miserly** (adj)

miserable
1 (adj) People who are miserable are very unhappy. **misery** (n)
2 (adj) If the weather is miserable, it is very unpleasant.

misfire misfires misfiring misfired
1 (vb) If a gun misfires, it does not go off properly.
2 (vb) A car misfires when the engine does not run smoothly.

misfortune misfortunes (n) Misfortune is something unlucky that happens to you. *I had the misfortune to lose my purse on the way to school.*

miss misses missing missed
1 (vb) If you miss someone, you feel sad because they are not with you.
2 (vb) If you miss a ball, you do not hit or catch it.
3 (vb) If you miss an appointment, for example, you fail to be there on time.
4 Miss is used before a woman's name if she is not married or does not use her husband's name.

missile missiles
1 (n) A missile is a weapon that can be aimed at a distant target.
2 (n) A missile is any object which is thrown to harm someone or something.

misspell misspells misspelling misspelled misspelt (vb) If you misspell a word, you spell it wrongly.

mist mists misting misted
1 (n) A mist is a cloud of very small water droplets, which makes it difficult to see.
2 (vb) If the windows mist up, they are covered with water droplets so that it is difficult to see out.

mistake mistakes mistaking mistook mistaken
1 (n) A mistake is something you do wrongly by accident.
2 (vb) If you mistake something or someone you are confused about them.

mistletoe (n) is a parasitic plant growing on trees. It has white berries and is used for Christmas decorations in Britain.

mixture mixtures (n) A mixture is two or more things or groups combined together.

moan moans moaning moaned
1 (vb) If you moan about something you complain about it.
2 (n) A moan is a low cry of pain or unhappiness.

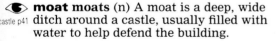 **moat** moats (n) A moat is a deep, wide ditch around a castle, usually filled with water to help defend the building.
castle p41

mob mobs (n) A mob is a large, angry crowd of people, often behaving violently.

mobile mobiles
1 (adj) If you are mobile, you are able to move around freely. **mobility** (n)
2 (n) A mobile is an ornament made up of several parts, which is hung up and moves in a breeze.

mock mocks mocking mocked
1 (vb) If you mock someone, you make fun of them.
2 (adj) Something which is mock is not real. *Mock leather ... mock jewellery.*
3 (n) Mocks are practice exams.

model models modelling modelled
1 (n) A model is a small copy of an object which shows how it works, or what it looks like.
2 (vb) If you model yourself on someone, you try to be like them.
3 (n) A model is someone who displays clothes, makeup, etc for people to look at and buy.

moderate (adj) A moderate amount of something is neither too large nor too small. **moderation** (n)

modern (adj) Modern describes things made or happening at the present time.

Mohammed or **Muhammad** (?590–632) was the prophet of the Islamic faith which is set out in the Koran. He was born in Mecca, which has become a sacred place to Muslims.

moist (adj) Something which is moist is slightly wet. **moisture** (n)

mole moles
1 (n) A mole is a small, black animal which burrows undergrond. It makes molehills.
2 (n) A mole is a brown spot on a person's skin.

molecule molecules (n) A molecule is a collection of atoms; the smallest part of a substance which can exist alone without changing or breaking.

periwinkles and mussels are **molluscs**

mollusc molluscs (n) A mollusc is any soft-bodied animal without a backbone. Many molluscs have shells and live in water.

molten (adj) Rock or metal which is molten is melted into a very hot liquid.

moment moments
1 (n) A moment is a short period of time.
2 (n) If you have your moments, you have times of particular activity or success.

monarch

monarch monarchs (n) A monarch is a king or queen. **monarchy** (n)

monastery monasteries (n) A monastery is a place where monks live and work.

money monies (n) Money is the coins and banknotes used to pay for goods and services.

mongoose mongooses (n) A mongoose is a small African or Asian animal which kills snakes.

mongrel mongrels (n) A mongrel is a dog whose parents are of different breeds.

monitor monitors monitoring monitored
1 (vb) If you monitor something, you check its progress regularly. *They monitored his health at the clinic.*
2 (n) A monitor is a television screen used with a computer.
3 (n) A monitor is a machine used to record and check things.
4 (n) A monitor is a school pupil chosen to do special jobs.

monk monks (n) Monks are men who belong to a religious community usually separate from the rest of society.

monkey monkeys
1 (n) A monkey is an agile, long-tailed animal that lives in trees.
2 If you monkey around, you behave in a playful and silly way.

monopolise monopolises monopolising monopolised (vb) If you monopolise something, you have a very large share of it. **monopoly** (n)

monorail monorails (n) A monorail is a train which moves on a single rail, often high above the ground.

monotonous (adj) Something monotonous is boring because it has no variety. *Mr Brown's voice was deep and monotonous.* **monotony** (n)

monsoon monsoons (n) The monsoon is the wind which brings a season of very heavy rain to South East Asia.

monster monsters
1 (n) A monster is a grotesque and frightening creature in films and stories.
2 (n) If you call a person a monster, it is because they behave in a very cruel and evil way.

monstrous
1 (adj) If you say that someone's behaviour is monstrous, you mean it is shocking. *His treatment of the child is monstrous.*
2 (adj) If you say that something looks monstrous, you mean that it is ugly. *The trees had been twisted into monstrous shapes.*
3 (adj) If you say that something is monstrous in size, you mean it is very big. *The cliffs were full of monstrous caverns.*

month months (n) A month is one of the twelve parts of the year and lasts about four weeks.

monument monuments
1 (n) A monument is a large statue or building erected as a memorial to a person or event. For example, Nelson's Column in Trafalgar Square.
2 (n) Monuments are castles, bridges, houses, etc which represent a country's history.

mood moods (n) Your mood is the way you feel. *A good mood ... a bad mood.* **moody** (adj)

moon moons
1 (n) The moon is the round, bright planet seen in the night sky that orbits the earth once every four weeks.
2 (n) A moon is an object like a small planet that travels round another planet.
3 If you are over the moon about something, you are very pleased about it.

solar syste p278

m°

moor moors mooring moored
1 (n) A moor is an area of open land often covered with grass or heather.
2 (vb) If you moor a boat, you tie it up to something so that it cannot drift away.
3 (n) A mooring is a place where a boat can be tied up.

mope mopes moping moped (vb) If you mope, you sit around feeling sorry for yourself.

moral morals
1 (n) Morals are standards of behaviour that a society in general agrees are good. **morality** (n)
2 (adj) A moral problem is one concerned with right or wrong.
3 (adj) A moral story is one which shows that good behaviour is best.

morale (n) Your morale is the way you feel. If your morale is high you are happy and optimistic; if it is low, then you are depressed and unhappy.

morbid (adj) A morbid person is concerned too much with death and illness.

more
1 More can mean a greater amount of things than before. *There are more apples on the trees this year.*
2 More can mean an extra amount. *Would you like some more cake?*
3 More can also mean once again. *Shall we swim once more?*
4 Something which is more or less right is roughly correct.

morning mornings (n) Morning is the part of the day between dawn and noon.

morse (n) Morse or morse code is a code using dots and dashes or short and long sounds to stand for a letter of the alphabet. It was devised by Samuel Morse (1791–1872).

morsel morsels (adj) A morsel is a very small piece of something, especially food.

mortal mortals
1 (adj) A mortal wound causes death.
2 (n) A mortal is an ordinary person.
3 (adj) Mortal means bound to die. *All people are mortal.*
4 (adj) A mortal enemy is one that you hate very much.

mortar mortars
1 (n) Mortar is the mixture used to hold bricks together.
2 (n) A mortar is a small cannon which fires bombs high into the air.
3 (n) A mortar is a bowl, used with a pestle, to grind spices or chemicals.

mortgage mortgages (n) A mortgage is a loan from a building society or a bank, which you use to buy a house.

mortuary mortuaries (n) A mortuary is a place where dead bodies are kept.

mosaic mosaics (n) A mosaic is a pattern or picture made up from small pieces of coloured glass or stone.

Moslem see **Muslim**

mosque mosques (n) A mosque is a building in which Muslims worship.

mosquito mosquitoes (n) A mosquito is a small, blood-sucking insect, which bites animals and people.

moss mosses (n) Moss is a tiny, green plant which grows on damp ground, wood or stone.

most
1 Most means the greatest amount. *You have the most sweets out of all of us.*
2 Most means more than any other of its kind. *The most important discovery, the most precious jewel.*
3 Most means above all else. *Her health concerned us most of all.*

motel motels (n) A motel is a hotel where motorists can park their cars close to their rooms.

moth

moth moths (n) A moth is an insect that flies at night.

mother mothers (n) Your mother is your female parent.

motif motifs (n) A motif is a design or part of a pattern.

motive motives (n) Your motives are your reasons for doing something.

motor motors (n) A motor is the part of a machine that uses fuel to make the machine work.

motorcycle motorcycles (n) A motorcycle is a heavy two-wheeled vehicle similar to a bicycle. It is also known as a motorbike.

motorway motorways (n) A motorway is a two or three-laned road where vehicles can travel quickly for long distances.

coat of arms p51 **motto mottoes** or **mottos** (n) A motto is a phrase used as a rule for good behaviour, or appearing as part of a badge. *The motto of the Scouts is 'Be Prepared'.*

mould moulds moulding moulded
1 (vb) If you mould clay, for example, you make it into a shape.
2 (n) A mould is a hollow shape into which liquid can be poured and left to set to take on the shape of the mould.
3 (n) Mould is a growth found either on food which has gone off or in damp places. **mouldy** (adj)

moult moults moulting moulted (vb) When an animal moults, it sheds old fur or feathers to be replaced by new growth.

mound mounds
1 (n) A mound is a small hill.
2 (n) A mound is an untidy pile.

mount mounts mounting mounted
1 (vb) If you mount a horse, bicycle, etc you get on to it.
2 (vb) If problems mount, they increase.

mountain mountains (n) A mountain is a raised part of the earth's surface with steep sides that are usually difficult to climb. **mountainous** (adj)

mourn mourns mourning mourned (vb) If you mourn the loss of someone you are sad because they have died. **mournful** (adj)

mouse mice (n) A mouse is a small, furry, long-tailed rodent.

moustache moustaches (n) A moustache is the hair growing on a man's upper lip.

mouth mouths
1 (n) The mouth is the opening in the face that is used for eating.
2 (n) A mouth is the opening of a bottle, jar, cave, etc. or where a river joins the sea.
3 If you keep your mouth shut about something, you say nothing.

mouth

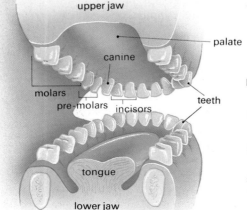

upper jaw

palate

canine

molars

pre-molars   incisors

teeth

tongue

lower jaw

a taste map of the tongue

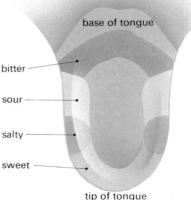

base of tongue

bitter

sour

salty

sweet

tip of tongue

move moves moving moved
1 (vb) If you move something, you change its position. **movable** (adj)
2 (vb) If you move or move house, you go to live in a different area or house.
3 (adj) If you find something moving, a film or a book, for example, it stirs your emotion.

movement movements
1 (n) A movement is the action of moving from one place to another.
2 (n) A movement is a group of people who act together to try to make something happen. *He was very active in the peace movement.*

Mozart, Wolfgang Amadeus
(1756–1791) was a famous Austrian composer who began his professional career at the age of six.

much
1 Much can be used to stress strong feelings, actions, etc. *We are looking forward to the holidays very much.*
2 Much can tell you more about how often something happens. *She doesn't talk much about it.*
3 You can use much to refer to an amount of money or amount of information. *How much money have you got? How much do you know?*

mucus (n) is thick fluid produced by some parts of the body, for example, the nose.

mud muds (n) is a thick mixture of earth and water. **muddy** (adj)

muddle muddles
1 (vb) If you muddle things, you confuse them.
2 (n) A muddle is a confused mess of things.

muesli (n) is a breakfast cereal made of mixed grain, fruit, etc.

mug mugs mugging mugged
1 (n) A mug is a large drinking cup without a saucer.
2 (vb) If you mug someone, you attack them and steal their belongings.
3 (n) If you call someone a mug, you mean they are easily tricked.

mule mules (n) A mule is an animal whose parents were a horse and a donkey.

multilingual (adj) If you are multilingual, you can speak many languages.

multinational (adj) A multinational company has branches in many countries.

multiple multiples
1 (n) A multiple is a number which can be divided by a smaller number an exact number of times. *21 is a multiple of 7 and 3; 10 is a multiple of 5 and 2.*
2 (adj) Something which is multiple has many parts or many uses.

multiply multiplies multiplying multiplied
1 (vb) If you multiply a number, you add the same number together a certain number of times. *2 multiplied by 4 or 2 × 4 is the same as 2 + 2 + 2 + 2.*
multiplication (n)
2 (vb) If animals multiply, they breed and increase in number.

multiracial (adj) Something which is multiracial involves people from many different nationalities and cultures. *Britain is a multiracial society.*

multitude multitudes (n) A multitude is a very large number of people or things. *There is a multitude of reasons why you can't go out tonight.*

mumble mumbles mumbling mumbled (vb) A person who mumbles speaks very quietly and is difficult to hear.

mummy mummies
1 (n) Mummy is a way of saying Mother.
2 (n) A mummy is a dead body which has been preserved by being rubbed in oils and wrapped in a cloth. Usually mummies are associated with ancient Egypt.

mumps (n) is a disease which causes painful swelling of the glands in the neck.

munch munches munching munched (vb) If you munch something, you chew it noisily and thoroughly.

mural murals (n) A mural is a wall painting.

murder murders murdering murdered (vb) Someone who murders another person kills them unlawfully.
murderer (n) **murder** (n)

m

murky murkier murkiest (adj) Something is murky if you cannot see clearly through it, water or fog for example.

murmur murmurs murmuring murmured
1 (vb) If people murmur, they speak very quietly so that no one else can hear.
2 (n) A murmur is a very low, quiet noise.

muscle muscles (n) Muscles are the bundles of fibres connected to the bones of the body which enable people or animals to move. **muscular** (adj)

museum museums (n) A museum is a place where things of historical interest are kept.

mushroom mushrooms (n) A mushroom is a type of fungus. Some are edible but some are poisonous.

music (n) is a series of sounds arranged by a composer which seem pleasant to the listener. **musician** (n)

musket muskets (n) A musket is a type of gun, used before rifles were invented.

Muslim Muslims (n) A Muslim is a person who believes in Islam and follows its laws.

mustard (n) is a hot, yellow or brown paste used to flavour food.

mutant mutants (n) A mutant is an animal or plant which is different from others of the same species because its genes have been altered.

mute (adj) If a person or animal is mute, they cannot speak or make a sound.

mutilate mutilates mutilating mutilated
1 (vb) If you mutilate something, you damage it very badly.
2 (adj) A mutilated body is very badly injured or damaged.

mutiny mutinies mutinying mutinied
(vb) Soldiers or sailors mutiny if they refuse to obey their officers, and try to take over themselves. **mutineer** (n)

mutter mutters muttering muttered
(vb) A person mutters if they speak quietly so that other people find it difficult to understand.

mutton (n) is the meat from older sheep, usually tougher than lamb.

mutual (adj) Something which is mutual affects or is shared by more than one person or group. *We have a mutual love of dogs.*

muzzle muzzles muzzling muzzled
1 (vb) If you muzzle an animal, you fit a strap over its jaws so that it cannot bite.
2 (n) An animal's muzzle is its nose and jaws.
3 (n) The muzzle of a gun is the hole from which the bullet or shell is fired.

mystery mysteries
1 (n) A mystery is a strange happening which cannot be explained. **mysterious** (adj)
2 (n) A mystery is a type of story where the reader has to try and solve a puzzle in the story.

mystify mystifies mystifying mystified
(vb) Something which mystifies you cannot be explained or understood. *I am mystified as to where she went after the shop shut.*

myth myths (n) A myth is a story that people have made up in the past to explain how the world began, the way people lived and what people believed.

m

Nn

nail nails nailing nailed
1 (n) A nail is a short, metal pin usually flat at one end which can be hammered into wood to join two pieces together.
2 (vb) If you nail things together, you join them using nails and a hammer.
3 (n) Your nails are thin, horny discs on the upper side of your fingers and toes.

naked (adj) A naked person wears no clothes. **nakedness** (n)

name names naming named
1 (n) The name of a person, animal, place, etc. is the word by which they are known. *Her name was Payal.*
2 (vb) If you name something or someone, you give them a name.
3 (vb) If someone names a person or a thing, they identify them by saying their name.

nan or **naan bread** (n) is made with yeast and baked in a clay oven. It is eaten with spicy foods.

nanny nannies
1 (n) A nanny is a person whose job is to live with a family and look after the children.
2 (n) Nanny is another name for grandmother.

napalm (n) is a substance used in bombs that destroys animals, people and plants by fire.

napkin napkins
1 (n) A napkin is a small square of cloth or paper, used to protect your clothes when you eat.
2 (n) A napkin can also be a baby's nappy.

narcotics (n) are drugs which kill pain and make you sleepy. They are often highly addictive.

narrate narrates narrating narrated
(vb) If you narrate something, you say it out loud, either to tell a story or to accompany a play, film, etc. **narrator** (n)

narrow narrower narrowest (adj) If something is narrow, it is thin, not wide.

narrow boat narrow boats (n) A narrow boat is a long, thin boat built especially for use on canals.

nasty nastier nastiest (adj) Someone or something nasty is very unpleasant.

nation nations
1 (n) A nation is a country and all the people who live there.
2 (n) A nation is all the people who share the same history and language.
national (n) **nationality** (n)

native natives
1 (n) A native of a country is a person who was born there.
2 (adj) Your native language is the one you learn to speak as a child.

Nativity (n) In the Christian religion, the Nativity is the birth of Jesus Christ.

natural history (n) is the study of animals and plants. **naturalist** (n)

natural science (n) is the study of biology, physics and chemistry.

nature
1 (n) Nature refers to all those things in the world not made by man.
2 (n) A person's nature is all the qualities that make up their character.
3 If something is second nature to you, you can do it easily.
natural (adj) **naturally** (adv)

naughty naughtier naughtiest (adj) A naughty child is badly behaved. **naughtily** (adv)

nausea (n) is a feeling of sickness.

nautical (adj) Nautical describes anything to do with ships and sailing.

nautical mile nautical miles (n) A nautical mile is a measurement at sea. 1 nautical mile equals 1,852 metres.

navel navels (n) The navel is the small hollow in the stomach where the umbilical cord was cut at birth.

navigate navigates navigating navigated (vb) If you navigate, you use maps, compass, etc. to plot your journey, particularly on water. **navigable** (adj) **navigation** (n)

n

navy navies (n) A navy is all the ships, sailors, etc. used by a country for its defence at sea. **naval** (adj)

Nazi Nazis (n) A Nazi was a follower of Adolf Hitler.

near nearer nearest
1 (prep, adv, adj) If someone or something near to a place, thing or person, it is only a short distance away.
2 (prep) If you are near to someone, you are close friends.

nearly (adv) If you nearly do something, you almost do it, but not quite.

nebula nebulas or **nebulae** (n) A nebula is an area of pale light in the night sky.

necessary (adj) If something is necessary, it is needed, or it must be done.

necessity necessities (n) A necessity is something you must have or do.

neck necks
1 (n) The neck is the part of the body between the head and shoulders.
2 (n) The neck of a bottle is the narrow part at the top.
3 If you risk your neck, you put your life in danger.

necklace necklaces (n) A necklace is jewellery to wear around your neck.

nectar (n) is a sweet liquid produced by flowers and collected by bees and other insects.

need needs needing needed
1 (vb) If you need something, it is important that you have it.
2 (vb) If you need something or you need to do something, you must have it or do it.
You need to repair the car before it is safe to drive.
3 If a person is in need, they want help of some sort.

needle needles needling needled
1 (n) A needle is a thin piece of metal used in sewing or in knitting.
2 (n) A needle is the sharp part of a syringe used for injections.
3 (n) Pine needles are the sharp, thin, pointed leaves of the pine tree.

negative negatives
1 (adj) A negative answer is 'No'.
2 (adj) A negative feeling or experience is a bad one.
3 (adj) In mathematics, a negative number is one that is less than 0: $-1 -2 -3$
4 (n) A negative is the image produced on film when you take a photograph, in which the areas of light and dark are reversed.

neglect neglects neglecting neglected
1 (vb) If you neglect someone or something, you do not look after them properly.
2 (vb) If you neglect to do something, you fail to do it.

negligent (adj) People who are negligent fail to take proper care in their work. **negligence** (n)

negotiate negotiates negotiating negotiated
1 (vb) When people negotiate, they discuss things until they come to an agreement. **negotiation** (n)
2 (vb) If you negotiate an obstacle, you steer your way around it.

neigh neighs neighing neighed (vb) When a horse neighs, it makes a loud sound, through its nose.

neighbour neighbours (n) Your neighbour lives next door to you. **neighbourly** (adj)

neighbourhood neighbourhoods (n) Your neighbourhood is the area in which you live.

neither (conj) You use neither in front of the first of two alternatives. *He drank neither coffee nor tea.*

Nelson, Horatio Viscount (1758–1805) He was the British naval commander who became a hero to the British people because of his victories over the French in the Napoleonic wars. He was killed at the Battle of Trafalgar.

neon (n) Neon is a gas used in glass tubes to make lights.

nephew nephews (n) Your nephew is your brother's or sister's son.

nerve nerves (n) A nerve is a long, thread-like fibre which carries messages between the brain and other parts of the body.

nervous (adj) A nervous person worries a lot and may show it by fidgeting.
nervously (adv)

nest nests nesting nested
1 (vb) If a bird nests, it makes a place to lay its eggs.
2 (n) A nest is a place made by birds and some insects in which to lay their eggs.

nestling (n) A nestling is a bird which is too young to fly and cannot leave the nest.

netball (n) is a game for two teams of seven players. The aim is to score by putting a ball through the opponents' net.

nettle nettles nettling nettled
1 (n) A nettle is a plant whose leaves can give a painful sting.
2 (vb) If you nettle someone, you irritate them.

network networks networking networked
1 (vb) If a T.V. or radio programme is networked, it is broadcast by several companies at once.
2 (n) A network is a system of roads, lines, wires, etc that cross each other and look like a net.
3 (n) A network can be an organisation that has many branches or covers a large area.

neutral
1 (adj) A person or country which is neutral in an argument or contest does not support either side.
2 (adj) Neutral colours are pale and unexciting.
3 (n) Neutral is a position in a gear box where none of the gears is engaged.
4 (adj) The neutral wire in an electric plug is neither live nor earthed.

never (adv) If you say never, you mean at no time.

new newer newest
1 (adj) Something new has been made or bought recently and has not been used.
2 (adj) If you are new at a school or a job you have not been there long.
3 (adj) The New Year is the time right at the start of the year.
4 (n) News is all the information about current events and current affairs.

newsagent (n) A newsagent is a person who sells newspapers, magazines, etc.

newspaper newspapers (n) A newspaper is several sheets of paper with news, advertisements, etc. which is published daily or weekly.

newt newts (n) A newt is a small, amphibious creature that looks like a lizard.

amphibian
p8

next
1 (adj) The next day, minute, etc is the one immediately after the present one.
2 (adj) The next person to you in a line is the one nearest you.
3 The next thing that happens will happen immediately following this moment.
4 (prep) If you place something next to something else, you put it beside it.

nibble nibbles nibbling nibbled (vb) If you nibble at something, you take very small bites at it.

nickname nicknames (n) A nickname is an informal name used instead of your real one.

nicotine (n) is the chemical in tobacco which smokers find addictive.

niece nieces (n) Your niece is your brother's or your sister's daughter.

night nights (n) Night is the time between sunset and sunrise when it is dark.

nightdress nightdresses (n) A nightdress is a loose garment worn by girls in bed.

nightingale nightingales (n) A nightingale is a small, brown, European bird famous for its beautiful song.

n

Nightingale, Florence

Nightingale, Florence (1820–1910) was famous for organising and improving the conditions of the nursing of soldiers wounded during the Crimean War. She founded training schools for nurses in London.

nightmare nightmares (n) A nightmare is a frightening dream.

nimble nimbler nimblest (adj) A nimble person is able to move quickly and lightly.

nimbus nimbuses (n) A nimbus is a dark cloud which brings rain and snow.

nitrogen (n) is a gas without smell or colour. It makes up about 75% of the earth's atmosphere.

Nobel Prize Nobel Prizes (n) A Nobel Prize is awarded annually to someone who has made a major contribution to science, literature, peace, etc.

noble nobler noblest (adj) A noble person is unselfish, honest and admirable.

nobody nobodies
1 (pro) Nobody is used to mean not anyone.
2 (n) A nobody is a person of no importance to anyone.

nocturnal (adj) A nocturnal animal is normally active only at night.

no-go area no-go areas (n) A no-go area is a place which some people control, and will stop other people entering.

noise noises
1 (n) A noise is a sound that a thing or person makes.
2 (n) Noise is irritating, loud sound.
3 (n) If you make a noise about something, you complain to get something done.

nomad nomads (n) A nomad is a member of a tribe that travels from one place to another. **nomadic** (adj)

no man's land (n) is the area between two opposing armies, or land which no one owns.

nominate nominates nominating nominated (vb) If you nominate someone, you put their name forward as a candidate in an election. **nomination** (n)

none (pro) None means not one or not any.

non-existent (adj) If something is non-existent, it is not there or does not exist.

nonsense
1 (n) Nonsense is any writing or words which do not make sense.
2 (n) Nonsense is writing or speech which is funny or entertaining without making much sense.

noodle noodles (n) Noodles are long strips of pasta used in soups, etc. They are used mostly in Italian and Chinese cooking.

noon (n) is 12 o'clock midday.

noose nooses (n) A noose is a loop in a piece of rope which tightens up when it is pulled.

normal (adj) If you say someone or something is normal, you mean they are usual or typical.

north
1 (n) North is the direction on your left as you face the rising sun.
2 (adj) A north wind comes from the north.

North Pole (n) The North Pole is the most northerly point on the earth's surface.

nose noses nosing nosed
1 (n) The nose is the part of the face used for breathing and smelling.
2 (n) Your nose can mean your sense of smell. *My nose told me that he had been drinking.*
3 (n) The nose of a car or an aeroplane is the part at the front.
4 (vb) If a person, animal or vehicle noses in a certain direction, it moves slowly and carefully in that direction.
5 If a person noses around, they sneak around other people's belongings. *Stop nosing around my room.* **nosey** (adj)

nostalgia (n) is a feeling of longing for happy times you have had in the past.

nostril nostrils (n) Your nostrils are the holes in the end of your nose.

note notes noting noted
1 (n) A note is a short written message to yourself or someone else to remind you of facts or to do something.
2 (vb) If you note something down, you write it down.
3 (n) A note is a single sound in music.

n

4 (n) A note can be a sound in a person's voice. *There was a note of anger in her voice.*

5 (n) A note is a piece of paper money.

nothing

1 (pro) If you eat nothing, you don't eat at all.

2 (pro) If there is nothing in a box or bottle, it is empty.

3 (pro) If something costs you nothing, it is free.

4 (pro) If a quarrel is over nothing, it is caused by something very small.

5 (pro) If you say that someone or something means nothing to you, you do not care about them.

notice notices noticing noticed

1 (vb) If you notice someone or something you see, hear or smell them.

2 (n) A notice is a written message placed so that many people can read it.

3 (n) A notice is a letter sent out to a large number of people to tell them about something.

4 (n) If you hand in your notice, you resign from your job. If you are given notice, you are told to leave your job.

notify notifies notifying notified (vb) If you notify someone of something, you tell them about it in a formal way, often by letter.

notion notions (n) A notion is an idea or an opinion. *He hadn't a notion how to work the machine.*

notorious (adj) If someone or something is notorious, they are well known because they are shocking or bad.

nought (n) is the number 0 or zero.

noun nouns (n) A noun names a person, place or thing. *Mary, Dublin, happiness* and *table* are all nouns.

nourish nourishes nourishing nourished (vb) If you nourish someone or something, you keep them healthy by feeding them well. **nourishment** (n)

nova novas or novae (n) A nova is a star that explodes and becomes very bright.

novel novels

1 (adj) Anything novel is new and different.

2 (n) A novel is a long story which fills a book. **novelist** (n)

novice novices

1 (n) A novice is someone who is just beginning to learn to do something.

2 (n) A novice is a person who is training to be a monk or a nun.

nowhere

1 (adv) Nowhere means no place. *There was nowhere to hide.*

2 If you say a place is in the middle of nowhere, you mean that it is out in the wilds far from houses or shops.

3 If someone or something appears from nowhere, they appear very suddenly.

4 If you say you're getting nowhere with a problem or job, you are not making progress.

nozzle nozzles (n) A nozzle is a small, cone-shaped piece fitted to a pipe to control the flow of liquid or gas.

prototype AGR **nuclear** reactor, Windscale, Cumbria

nuclear

1 (adj) Anything nuclear refers to power produced from the energy released by atoms when they are split. *Nuclear energy . . . nuclear industry . . . nuclear power.*

2 (adj) Nuclear describes the use of weapons that explode by using energy released by atoms splitting. *Nuclear weapons . . . nuclear war.*

nugget

nugget nuggets
1 (n) A nugget is a small piece of something, often gold.
2 (n) A nugget is a small piece of valuable information. *Where did he learn that little nugget?*

nuisance (n) Something which is a nuisance annoys you and causes you problems.

numb numbs numbing numbed
1 (adj) If a part of your body is numb, it is unable to feel anything.
2 (vb) If a doctor or dentist numbs part of your body, you cannot feel anything there.
3 (adj) If you are numbed through shock, then you are unable to react normally.

numbers numbers numbering numbered
1 (n) Any of the words or figures used for counting are numbers.
2 (vb) If you number something, you give it a number, usually in a sequence. *She numbered the samples 1–10.*
3 (n) The word number can be used when you don't know the exact quantity. *There are a number of colours to choose from.*
4 (n) Your number can be your telephone number.
5 (n) The word number can be used by musicians to refer to a song or piece of music.

numeral numerals (n) A numeral is a symbol used to represent a number. *1,2,3,4,5 etc are Arabic numerals; in Roman numerals they are written as I,II,III,IV,V.*

numerate (adj) Someone who is numerate understands and can work with numbers.

nun nuns (n) A nun is a woman who has taken religious vows and lives in a community with other nuns.

nurse nurses nursing nursed
1 (vb) If you nurse someone, you look after them when they are ill.
2 (n) A nurse is a person who cares for sick people or for very young children.
3 (vb) If you nurse something, you hold it gently and carefully.

nursery (n) A nursery is a special room or school for very young children.

nurture nurtures nurturing nurtured
(vb) If you nurture a plant or animal, you care for it while it is growing.

nut nuts
1 (n) A nut is the hard fruit from certain trees which grows inside a very hard shell.
2 (n) A nut is a metal fastener which screws onto a bolt.

nutrition (n) is the process of absorbing food into the body.

nutritionist nutritionists (n) A nutritionist is a person who specialises in nutrition and the values of various foods.

nuzzle nuzzles nuzzling nuzzled (vb) If an animal or person nuzzles, they affectionately rub their nose and mouth against you.

nylon nylons
1 (n) Nylon is an artificial fibre used for making cloth.
2 (n) Nylons are stockings or tights.

nymph nymphs
1 (n) A nymph is the larva of an insect which changes into an adult without going through the pupal stage.
2 (n) In myths a nymph is a spirit of nature, a type of elf or fairy.

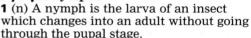
insect p149

n

Oo

oak oaks (n) An oak is a large tree that produces acorns.

oar oars (n) An oar is a pole with a flat blade used to row a boat through the water.

oasis oases (n) An oasis is a place in a desert where there is water and plants and trees grow.

oath oaths
1 (n) An oath is a solemn promise.
2 If you take an oath in a courtroom, you promise to tell the truth.

oat oats (n) Oats are cereal grains used for feeding animals and making porridge.

obese (adj) Someone or something that is obese is extremely fat.

obey obeys obeying obeyed (vb) If you obey instructions, you do as you are told. **obedience** (n) **obedient** (adj) **obediently** (adv)

object objects objecting objected
1 (vb) If someone objects to something, they say that they disagree with it.
objection (n) **objector** (n)
2 (n) An object is a thing that you can see or touch, but that is not living.
3 (n) The object of doing something is the purpose or reason for doing it.

objectionable (adj) Someone or something that is objectionable is unpleasant.

oblige obliges obliging obliged
1 (vb) If you are obliged to do something, you have to do it. **obligation** (n)
2 (vb) If you oblige someone, you help them in some way. *He obliged me by giving me a lift.*
3 (adj) If you are obliged to someone, you feel grateful to them for their help.
4 (adj) An obliging person is helpful.

oblique (adj) An oblique line slants.

oblong oblongs (n) An oblong is a four sided shape with opposite sides of equal length and all its angles are right angles.

rectangle p240

obnoxious (Adj) If someone or something is obnoxious they are most unpleasant.

oboe oboes (n) An oboe is a musical instrument. It is played by blowing through a double reed down a wooden tube.

obscene (adj) Someone or something that is obscene is indecent and very offensive. **obscenity** (n)

obscure obscures obscuring obscured
1 (vb) If something obscures your view, it gets in the way of what you are looking at.
2 (adj) Something that is obscure is not very well known.
3 (adj) If a book, play, etc is obscure, it is difficult to understand.

observe observes observing observed
1 (vb) If you observe something, you notice it. **observant** (adj) **observer** (n)
2 (vb) If you watch someone or something carefully, you observe them. **observation** (n)
3 (vb) If you observe a religious festival or law, you are careful to follow it.

obsession obsessions (n) An obsession is something you think about all the time. *His obsession is racing cars.* **obsessive** (adj)

obsolete (adj) If something is obsolete, it is out of date and no longer used.

obstacle obstacles (n) An obstacle is something that gets in your way.

obstinate (adj) People stubbornly refuse to change their ideas or opinions.

obstruct obstructs obstructing obstructed
1 (vb) If you obstruct someone or something, you block their path.
2 (vb) If something obstructs a road, it is in the way. **obstruction** (n)
3 (vb) If you obstruct a person you stop them from doing what they wish to do.

195

obtain

obtain obtains obtaining obtained. (vb)
If you obtain something, it comes into your
possession.

obtuse
1 (adj) An obtuse
angle is one that is
greater than 90
degrees.
2 (adj) If someone is
obtuse they are slow
to understand
anything.

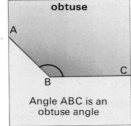

obtuse

Angle ABC is an
obtuse angle

obvious (adj) Something obvious is easily
seen or understood. **obviously** (adv)

occasion occasions
1 (n) An occasion is a time when something
happens. **occasionally** (adv)
2 (n) An occasion is a special event. *The
wedding was a great occasion.*

occupation occupations (n) Your
occupation is your job.

occupy occupies occupying occupied
1 (vb) If you occupy a house, etc you live in
it.
2 (vb) If one country occupies another,
their armies invade and take control of it.
3 (vb) If something occupies your time, it
takes up much of it.

occur occurs occurring occurred
1 (vb) If something occurs, it happens.
occurrence (n)
2 (vb) If an idea occurs to you, it suddenly
comes to you.

ocean oceans (n) An ocean is one of the
large expanses of water on the earth's
surface.

o'clock (adv) You use o'clock to show the
time of the hours for 1–12. *1 o'clock.*

octagon octagons (n) An octagon is an
eight-sided shape.

odd odds odder oddest
1 (adj) If someone or something is odd they
are unusual in some way.
2 (adj) Odd numbers such as 3, 7 and 9 do
not divide exactly by two.
3 (adj) Odd socks do not belong together.
4 (adj) If you are the odd one out in a
situation, you do not fit in with the others.
5 (n) The odds are the probability of
something happening or not.
6 If something happens against the odds, it
happens despite great problems.

odour odours (n) An odour is a smell.

offence offences
1 (n) If you commit an offence, you break
the law or the rules of a game.
2 (n) If you cause offence, you embarrass or
upset someone.
3 (n) If you take offence, you feel that
someone has been rude or hurtful to you.

offend offends offending offended
1 (vb) If you offend someone, you upset
them.
2 (vb) If you offend, you break the law.
offender (n)

offensive offensives
1 (adj) Someone or something that is
offensive, upsets others.
2 (n) If you take the offensive, you criticise
or attack other people.

offer offers offering offered
1 (vb) If you offer to do something, you say
that you are willing to do it.
2 (vb) If you offer something to someone,
you ask whether they would like it.
3 If someone makes you an offer, you can
accept it or reject it. *She made an offer to
help with the maths homework.*

office offices
1 (n) An office is a place or room where you
work.
2 (n) An office is a government department.
Tax office ... Home Office.
3 If you hold office, you have a position of
some importance in an organisation. *He
held the office of President.*

officer officers.
1 (n) An officer is someone who has a
position of authority in the armed forces.
2 (n) An officer is anyone who holds a
position of importance in an organisation.
Health and safety officer ... prison officer.

official officials
1 (adj) If something is official, it is approved
by those in authority. *The official
explanation was published today.*
2 (n) An official is someone in authority in
an organisation.

often
1 (adv) If something happens often, it
happens frequently.
2 (adv) If you ask how often something
happens, you want to know how many
times it happens.

O

ogle ogles ogling ogled (vb) If you ogle someone, you stare at them rudely.

ogre ogres
1 (n) An ogre is a large, frightening, imaginary creature in children's stories.
2 (n) Someone who behaves in a very cruel way can be called an ogre.

oil oils oiling oiled
1 (vb) If you oil a machine, you put oil on it to make it run smoothly.
2 (n) Oil is the slippery liquid that is used to make machines run smoothly.
3 (n) Oil is also used as a fuel.

oilfield oilfields (n) An oilfield is an area at sea or on land, where oil is drilled.

oil production platform, Ninian Field, North Sea

oil rig oil rigs (n) An oil rig is a platform used to drill for oil.

oilskin oilskins (n) An oilskin is a piece of clothing made from thick, waterproof cotton.

oil slick oil slicks (n) An oil slick is a large patch of oil on the surface of water.

oil well oil wells (n) An oil well is a deep hole drilled in the ground to obtain oil.

oily oilier oiliest (adj) Something oily is covered with oil.

ointment ointments (n) An ointment is a smooth paste used to help soothe and heal scratches or injuries.

okra see bhindi

old older oldest
1 (adj) Someone or something that is old has been alive or existing for a long time.
2 (adj) If you say that something is a particular age, you say it is so many months or years old.
3 (adj) An old friend is one you have known for a long time.
4 (adj) Something can be called old if it has been replaced by a newer version. *My old car was a wreck.*

old-fashioned (adj) Someone or something that is old-fashioned is out of date.

Old Testament The Old Testament is the first part of the Bible which deals mainly with Jewish history.

olive olives
1 (n) An olive is the black or green fruit of the olive tree.
2 (adj) Anything olive is light greeny-brown in colour.

olive branch olive branches. (n) An olive branch is the traditional symbol of peace.

Olympic Games (n) The Olympic Games are a group of athletic and sporting contests, held in a different country every four years.

ombudsman ombudsmen (n) An ombudsman is a person, appointed by the government, who investigates complaints made by people against public organisations.

omelette omelettes (n) An omelette is a dish made from whisked eggs cooked in a frying pan.

omen omens (n) An omen is a a sign that suggests something will happen. *The expression on the teacher's face was an omen of trouble to come.* **ominous** (adj)

omit omits omitting omitted (vb) If you omit something, you leave it out. **omission** (n)

O

once
1 (adv) If something existed once, it existed on one occasion only.
2 (adv) If something happened once, it happened sometime in the past. *There were once wolves in Britain.*
3 (adv) If something happens once a week, it happens regularly every seven days.
4 (adv) Once can mean as soon as. *Once we have finished tea we'll go for a walk.*
5 If something happens at once, it happens immediately.

onerous (adj) An onerous task or job is difficult and tiring.

onion onions (n) An onion is a round vegetable with a very strong taste.

onlooker onlookers (n) An onlooker is someone who watches as something happens.

only
1 (adj) If you are the only person, there is no one else.
2 (adv) If there is only a certain amount of time, there is no more than that.
3 If you are only too pleased to do something, you are very pleased to do it.
4 (conj) Only can mean however. *I would like to come, only I am busy.*
5 (adj) An only child has no brothers or sisters.

ooze oozes oozing oozed (vb) If something such as a liquid oozes, it moves slowly. *The syrup oozed out of the sandwich.*

opaque (adj) If something is opaque, you cannot see through it.

open opens opening opened
1 (vb) If you open a door, window, etc you move it so that air or a person can get through.
2 (vb) If you open a tin, packet, etc you remove the packaging so that you can get at what is inside.
3 (vb) If you open a book, you fold back the cover so that you can read it.
4 (adj) If a shop, office, etc. is open, the public are allowed in to do business.
5 (adj) If you are open to new ideas, you are willing to think about them.
6 (adj) If a job is still open, the post has not been filled.

opening openings
1 (n) An opening is the first part of a performance, book, etc.
2 (n) An opening is a hole where air can pass through.
3 (adj) Your opening remarks are the ones you make when you start to speak.

opera operas (n) An opera is a play where most of the words are sung to music.

operate operates operating operated
1 (vb) If you operate a business or a machine, you run it. **operator** (n)
2 (vb) When surgeons operate, they open a patient's body to help heal disease or repair damage. **operation** (n)

opinion opinions
1 (n) An opinion is a statement of a person's ideas or beliefs.
2 (n) If public opinion is strong about something, many people share the same feelings and ideas.

oppose opposes opposing opposed.
1 (vb) If you oppose something or someone, you are against them.
2 (adj) If two people are on opposing sides, they have different points of view.
opponent (n) **opposition** (n)

opposite opposites
1 (adv) If one thing is opposite another, it is on the other side of a space. *My house is opposite your house.*
2 (n) People or things that are opposites are completely different from each other.

oppress oppresses oppressing oppressed (vb) If you oppress people, you treat them cruelly and prevent them from having freedom. **oppression** (n)

opt opts opting opted (vb) If you opt for something, you choose it. **option** (n)

optician opticians (n) An optician is a person who tests your eyes and sells contact lenses and glasses.

optimist optimists (n) An optimist is a person who looks on the bright side of things. **optimistic** (adj)

option options
1 (n) An option is a choice. *You have the option of this job, or that one.*
2 If you keep your options open, you do not take a decision.

oral orals
1 (adj) An oral test is spoken not written.
2 (n) An oral is a spoken examination.

orange oranges
1 (adj) Something that is orange is a colour between red and yellow.
2 (n) An orange is a round, juicy fruit with a thick skin.

orbit orbits (n) An orbit is the path an object takes around a planet or star.

orchard orchards (n) An orchard is a place where fruit trees are grown.

orchestra orchestras (n) An orchestra is a large group of musicians who play music together.

Showy Lady's Slipper **Orchid**

orchid orchids (n) An orchid is a beautiful, exotic flower that grows in many different parts of the world. There are many varieties.

ordeal ordeals (n) An ordeal is a difficult, unpleasant and sometimes dangerous experience.

order orders ordering ordered
1 (vb) If you order someone to do something, you tell them they must do it and you expect them to do it. *The headteacher ordered everyone to sit.*
2 (vb) If you order something from a restaurant or a shop, you ask for what you want and pay for it when it arrives.
3 If you put things in order, you arrange them according to a set plan.
4 (n) An order is a command.
5 If a machine or an engine is in good order, it is working smoothly.
6 If you keep order, you make sure that other people behave themselves and obey the law.

ordinary
1 (adj) Ordinary things are common place and not particularly interesting.
2 (adj) Ordinary can also mean dull or unexciting. *I was surprised that such a famous person could look so ordinary.*

ore ores (n) Ore is rock or mineral from which metals are produced.

organ organs
1 (n) An organ is a part of the body that performs a particular function for example, the heart, the liver, etc.
2 (n) An organ is an instrument with a keyboard like a piano and long pipes through which air is forced to produce its musical sound. **organist** (n)

organic (adj) is used to describe methods of farming and gardening that use only natural animal and plant products.

organism organisms (n) An organism is a living plant or animal, particularly those so small they can be seen only with a microscope.

organisation organisations
1 (n) An organisation is a large business or group with particular aims and objectives. *The World Health Organisation . . . The Organisation of African Unity.*
2 (n) Organisation is the act of planning and arranging something so that it runs smoothly and efficiently.
3 (n) The organisation of something like a school or business is the way all the various parts are connected and work together.

organise organises organising organised
1 (vb) If you organise something, you plan and make arrangements so that everything happens smoothly.
2 (vb) When people organise, they form a group to protest or to fight for something.
3 (adj) If you are organised, you are efficient and orderly in your daily life.

Orient (n) The Orient is the Far East. It is the part of the world that includes India, Japan, China, etc. **oriental** (adj)

orienteering (n) is a sport in which runners find their way by stages across country using maps and compasses.

O

origami

origami (n) is the Japanese art of folding paper into interesting shapes.

origin origins (n) The origin of something is its beginning and how and why it began. *There are various theories about the origin of the universe.*

original originals
1 (adj) Something that is original is the very first or the earliest. *This house was built on the ruins of the original one.*
2 (adj) An original painting is not a copy.
3 (adj) An original thinker is an imaginative person who produces new ideas.
4 (adj) Something original is unusual and different. *She wore a very original hat.*

ornament ornaments
1 (n) An ornament is an attractive object you display on a shelf or a table.
2 (n) An ornament is something worn as decoration, jewellery for example.

ornithology (n) Ornithology is the study of birds. **ornithologist** (n)

orphan orphans (n) An orphan is a child whose parents are both dead.
orphaned (adj)

orthodox
1 (adj) Something that is orthodox is believed or accepted by most people.
2 (adj) A person who is orthodox believes in established and traditional values and ideas of their religion, or the political party they support.

ostrich ostriches
(n) An ostrich is a very large, African bird. It can run very fast but it cannot fly.

other others
1 (adj) Other people or things are different from those already mentioned.
2 (pro) The other can mean the second of two things.
3 The other day means a few days ago.

otherwise
1 (conj) Otherwise can mean or else, or if not. *Eat your tea otherwise you cannot come.*
2 (adv) Otherwise can mean differently. *I think you are right, but he thinks otherwise.*
3 (conj) Otherwise can mean in other respects, apart from that. *It rained the first day, otherwise it was fine.*

otter otters (n) The otter is a furry, web-footed animal, which eats fish and lives near water.

ought (vb) If you ought to do something, you feel obliged to do it.

ounce ounces
1 (n) An ounce is a unit of weight equal to 28.3 grams.
2 (n) Ounce also means a very small amount. *He didn't do an ounce of work.*

our ours Our means belonging to us.

ourselves (pro) We use ourselves when we talk about a group of people which includes the speaker. *We made ourselves some tea.*

outback (n) The outback is the vast, unpopulated area of Australia.

outbreak outbreaks (n) An outbreak is a sudden occurrence of something such as a disease, fighting, etc.

outcome outcomes (n) The outcome of an activity is its result.

outing outings (n) An outing is an organised visit to a particular place.

outlaw outlaws outlawing outlawed
1 (n) An outlaw is a criminal.
2 (vb) If you outlaw something, you ban it.

O

outlet outlets
1 (n) If you look for an outlet for your feelings, you try to find a way of expressing them.
2 (n) An outlet is the shops, customers, etc. who buy things from a business.
3 (n) An outlet is a place or pipe where water can flow away.

outline outlines outlining outlined
1 (n) An outline is the shape of something.
2 (n) If you give an outline of your plan you give brief details.
3 (vb) If you outline something you draw the shape of it.

outlook outlooks
1 (n) Your outlook is your general attitude to life.
2 (n) The outlook is the weather forecast for the next few days.

output outputs
1 (n) A company's output is the amount it produces.
2 (n) Output is the information sorted out and produced by a computer program.
3 (vb) When a computer outputs something, it sorts and produces information as a result of a certain program.

outrage outrages outraging outraged
1 (vb) If something outrages you, it upsets you very much.
2 (n) An outrage is an act or event which people find very shocking.
outrageous (adj) **outrageously** (adv)

outright
1 (adj) If someone is the outright winner, they win with no close competition.
2 (adv) If a person or animal is killed outright, they are killed instantly.

outside outsides
1 (n) The outside of a building or object is the part that is exposed.
2 (adv) If you go outside, you go out of a building.
3 (adj) If there is an outside chance of something happening, there is little chance of it happening.

outskirts (n) The outskirts of a town are the outer edges.

outspoken (adj) An outspoken person gives their views openly, even though it may upset others.

outstanding
1 (adj) Something which is outstanding is particularly good.
2 (adj) An outstanding bill has yet to be paid.

oval ovals (n) An oval is a shape like a slightly flattened circle.

oven ovens (n) An oven is a box-shaped part of a cooker which can be heated to cook food.

over overs
1 (prep) Something which is over another thing is above it.
2 (prep) If a person is over other people, they are in charge of them, or are more important.
3 (adv) Over can be used to mean more than. *There were over 10,000 people there.*
4 (adv) If an amount of something is left over, it is extra, and not needed.
5 (n) In cricket, an over is a series of six balls bowled by one bowler.

overall overalls
1 (n) Overalls are a one-piece garment worn to protect your clothes when you do a messy job.
2 (adv) Overall is used to describe a whole situation. *Overall, we would be better off in Preston.*

overbalance overbalances
overbalancing overbalanced (vb) If you overbalance, you stumble and may fall.

overbearing (adj) An overbearing person is one who tries to dominate other people.

overboard
1 (adv) If someone or something goes over the side of a ship, it goes overboard.
2 If you go overboard about something, you get over-enthusiastic about it.

overcast (adj) If the weather is overcast, the sky is covered with grey clouds and rain seems likely.

O

overcome

overcome overcomes overcoming overcame
1 (vb) If you overcome difficulties, you manage to cope and achieve something despite the problems.
2 (adj) If you are overcome, you are affected by strong emotions.
3 (adj) If you are overcome by fumes, smoke, etc you are made unconscious by them.

overdraw overdraws overdrawing overdrawn (vb) If you overdraw at the bank, you take out more money than there is in your account.

overdue (adj) Something overdue is late.

overflow overflows overflowing overflowed
1 (vb) If a liquid overflows, it runs over the top of its container.
2 (n) An overflow is a pipe or container which gathers or drains excess liquid from another container. *The bathwater ran down the overflow.*

overgrown (adj) If a place is overgrown, it is covered with weeds.

overhaul overhauls overhauling overhauled
1 (vb) If you overhaul a machine, you check and repair it to ensure that it runs properly.
2 (n) An overhaul is a a detailed check on a piece of machinery when any faults are corrected.

overhead overheads
1 (n) In business overheads are the costs, such as rent, heating and lighting, you have to keep paying.
2 (adj) Anything overhead is directly above you.

overhear overhears overhearing overheard (vb) When you overhear something you hear a conversation or comment between other people.

overjoyed (adj) If you are overjoyed you are very happy and excited.

overlap overlaps overlapping overlapped (vb) If one thing overlaps another it lies partly on top of it.

overloads overloads overloading overloaded
1 (vb) If you overload something, you put more weight on to it than it can carry.
2 (vb) If you overload a piece of electrical equipment you use more electricity than it was designed for and as a result it breaks down.
3 (vb) If you overload a person you give them more work than they are capable of doing.

overlook overlooks overlooking overlooked
1 (vb) If you overlook something you forget to do something you should do, or do not notice something that you should see.
2 (vb) If you overlook something you ignore it. *That was stupid behaviour, but I'll overlook it this time.*
3 (vb) If a house overlooks a place, it has a view of it from above.

overpower overpowers overpowering overpowered (vb) If you overpower someone you defeat them because you are stronger than they are.

overrated (adj) If something is overrated, it is made to seem better than it is.

overreact overreacts overreacting overreacted (vb) If you overreact to something, you react in an extreme way. *She overreacted to his questions and got very angry.*

overrule overrules overruling overruled (vb) If you overrule someone, you use your authority to cancel their decisions.

overseas (adj) Someone living overseas lives abroad, across the sea.

oversimplify oversimplifies oversimplifying oversimplified (vb) If you oversimplify a problem you make it seem simpler than it really is.

oversleep oversleeps oversleeping overslept (vb) If you oversleep you sleep on past the time at which you intended to get up.

overtake overtakes overtaking **overtook** (vb) If you overtake something, you go past it.

overtime (n) is an extra period of time which you can work to earn more money.

overture (n) The overture is the opening piece of music at a show, opera, etc.

overweight (adj) people or animals are too heavy for their size.

overwork overworks overworking **overworked** (vb) If you overwork you work too hard.

overwrought (adj) A person who is overwrought is very upset.

owe owes owing owed (vb) If you owe money or a favour to someone, you are in debt to them or grateful to them.

owl owls (n) An owl is a nocturnal bird with large eyes and a flat face.

own owns owning owned
1 (vb) If you own something it is legally yours. **owner** (n)
2 If you are on your own, you are alone.

ox oxen (n) An ox is a large bull used in many countries to pull carts and ploughs.

oxygen (n) is a gas which we need to breathe and which fires need in order to burn.

oyster oysters (n) An oyster is a shellfish which lives in the sea. One type can be eaten, another produces pearls.

ozone (n) is a gas which forms a layer around the earth and helps protect us from the harmful rays of the sun.

Pp

pace paces pacing paced
1 (n) A pace is the distance of a single walking step.
2 (vb) If you pace up and down, you walk about, usually because you are worried.
3 (vb) If you pace out a distance, you measure it out in strides.
4 (n) Your pace is your walking or running speed.

pacemaker pacemakers
1 (n) A pacemaker is a tiny device put into a person's body, which helps to regulate the heart beat.
2 (n) A pacemaker is a runner in a race who sets the speed for the other runners.

Pacific Ocean (n) The Pacific Ocean lies between the west coasts of the Americas and the east coasts of Asia and Australia.

pacifist pacifists (n) A pacifist believes that war and violence is always wrong and does not take part in wars. **pacifism** (n)

pacify pacifies pacifying pacified (vb) If you pacify someone or something, you make them feel calm and peaceful.

package packages
1 (n) A package is a small parcel.
2 (n) A package is an arrangement for a holiday, for example, that includes all the travel, accommodation, etc.

packet packets (n) A packet is a container made of paper, cardboard or plastic in which things are packed to be sold.

pact pacts (n) A pact is an agreement between people or governments.

paddle paddles paddling paddled
1 (n) A paddle is a pole with a flat blade at one end or at each end, used to propel small boats through the water.
2 (vb) If you paddle a small boat, you make it move by using paddles.
3 (vb) If you paddle, you walk in shallow water with bare feet.

p

paddock

paddock paddocks (n) A paddock is a small field for horses or donkeys.

padlock padlocks (n) A padlock is a lock for fastening two things together. It has a curved metal loop at one end that can be locked into place and released by using a key.

paediatrician paediatricians (n) A paediatrician is a doctor who specialises in the treatment of children.

pagan pagans (n) A pagan is someone who does not believe in any of the main religions.

page pages
1 (n) A page is one side of a sheet of paper in a book, magazine, etc.
2 (n) In medieval times, a page was a young boy who was a servant to a knight.

pageant pageants
1 (n) A pageant is an outdoor entertainment where people dress up and act out scenes from history.
2 (n) A pageant is a grand public ceremony or display. **pageantry** (n)

pagoda in Kew Gardens, London

pagoda pagodas (n) A pagoda is a beautiful, sacred building used by Buddhists.

pail pails (n) A pail is a bucket.

pain pains (n) Pain is the unpleasant feeling that hurts when you are ill or have injured yourself. **painful** (adj) **painfully** (adv)

paint paints painting painted
1 (n) Paint is a coloured liquid or paste used for colouring, protecting or making pictures and designs on surfaces.
2 (vb) If you paint something, you cover it with paint.
3 (vb) If you paint a picture, you make a picture of something using paint.
painter (n)

pair pairs pairing paired
1 (n) A pair is two things that are meant to go together. *A pair of earrings.*
2 (n) A thing with two similar and joining parts is called a pair. *A pair of trousers.*
3 (vb) If you pair things you put them together in pairs.

pajamas see **pyjamas**

palace palaces (n) A palace is the home of a king, queen or ruler of a country or the home of a bishop. **palatial** (adj)

palaeontology (n) is the study of fossils. **palaeontologist** (n)

pale paler palest
1 (adj) If your face is pale, it is a lighter colour than usual because you are ill or scared.
2 (adj) A pale colour is a light colour.
3 (adj) A pale light is dim and doesn't shine brightly.

palette palettes (n) A palette is a board on which an artist mixes colours.

Pali Canon (n) The Pali Canon is the sacred book containing the teachings of the Buddha.

palm palms
1 (n) A palm is a tree which usually grows in hot climates. It can have dates or coconuts as fruits.
2 (n) Your palm is the flat area on the inside of your hand.

Palm Sunday (n) is the Sunday before Easter in the Christian year.

pampas grass (n) is a tall, feathery grass.

pamper pampers pampering pampered (vb) If you pamper a person or an animal, you spoil them.

pamphlet pamphlets (n) A pamphlet is a very small booklet of only a few pages.

p

pan pans
1 (n) A pan is a container used in cooking.
2 (n) Pan was an ancient Greek god.

pancake pancakes (n) A pancake is a round, flat cake made from fried batter.

panda pandas (n) The giant panda is a rare, black and white, bear-like animal which lives in the bamboo forests of China.

pane panes (n) A pane is a sheet of glass in windows or doors.

panel panels
1 (n) A panel is a flat piece of wood or other material used to cover a surface.
2 (n) A panel is a group of people who meet to make decisions or interview people for jobs.

panic panics panicking panicked (vb) If you panic, you stop thinking clearly and act in a frightened way. **panicky** (adj)

Pankhurst, Emmeline (1858–1928) was the leader of the British Suffragette movement, whose work aimed at giving women the vote.

pannier panniers (n) A pannier is a bag which is carried on the side of an animal, bicycle or motor bike.

panorama panoramas (n) A panorama is a very wide view of a landscape.

panther panthers (n) A panther is a large, wild member of the cat family which is usually black in colour.

pantomime pantomimes (n) A pantomime is a comic play for children, usually based on a well-known fairytale.

paper papers papering papered
1 (n) Paper is thin sheets of material used for making books, newspapers, wrapping things, etc.
2 (vb) If you paper a room, you cover the walls with wallpaper.

pâpier maché (n) is bits of damp paper mixed with glue which can be shaped into various objects.

parable parables (n) A parable is a short story with a religious or moral point.

parachute parachutes parachuting parachuted
1 (n) A parachute is a large circle of material, folded up and secured to a person, who can open it when they jump from an aeroplane so that they land safely.
2 (vb) When you parachute, you jump from an aeroplane using a parachute.
parachutist (n)

parade parades parading paraded
1 (n) A parade is an official procession of people for a special occasion or for an inspection.
2 (vb) If you parade, you walk around so that others can admire you.

paradise
1 (n) Paradise is heaven.
2 (n) Paradise can be any beautiful place. *The island was a tropical paradise.*

paragraph paragraphs (n) A piece of writing can be divided into paragraphs, each one dealing with an aspect of the main subject and starting on a new line.

parallel (adj) Lines that are parallel run side by side at the same distance apart.

paralyse paralyses paralysing paralysed (vb) If a disease or an accident paralyses part of a person or an animal, they cannot feel or move that part. **paralysis** (n)

paraphernalia (n) are all the bits and pieces that belong to you. *The girls collected up their coats, shoes and other paraphernalia.*

paraplegic paraplegics (n) Someone who is a paraplegic is paralysed in the lower part of the body.

parasite

parasite parasites (n) A parasite is a plant or animal that lives on another and takes its food from it. **parasitic** (adj)

paratha (n) is a deep-fried Indian bread.

paratroops (n) are soldiers trained to drop from an aircraft by parachute. **paratrooper** (n)

parcel parcels (n) A parcel is one or more things wrapped around with paper.

pardon pardons
1 (n) If someone who has been punished for a crime is given a pardon, they are shown to be not guilty and are set free.
2 If you say 'Pardon?' you want something said again.

parent parents (n) A parent is the mother or father of a person or an animal. **parental** (adj)

parish parishes (n) A parish is a small area, usually a village or town, in the care of one church.

parking meter parking meters (n) A parking meter is a machine beside a parking space where you put coins to pay for parking.

parliament parliaments (n) The parliament of a country is a group of people who meet to make or to change the laws of the land and to arrange the management of the country.

parole (n) Prisoners who are on parole are allowed out of prison early on condition that they behave well.

parquet floor parquet floors (n) A parquet floor is made of blocks of wood fitted in patterns.

parrot parrots (n) A parrot is a tropical bird sometimes kept as a pet. Some parrots can be taught to imitate voices.

parsley (n) is a green herb used to flavour and decorate food.

parsnip parsnips (n) A parsnip is a long, pale-coloured root vegetable.

parson parsons (n) A parson is a clergyman.

partial
1 (adj) A partial amount is only a part of a whole.
2 (adj) If you are partial to something, you like it very much.

participate participates participating participated (vb) If you participate in something you take part in it or join in. **participation** (n)

particle particles (n) A particle is a very tiny piece or amount of something.

particular
1 (adj) If you refer to a particular person or thing, you mean nobody or nothing else. **particularly** (adv)
2 (adj) A particular person, place or thing is special or important.
3 (adj) Someone who is particular is rather fussy and not easily pleased.

partition partitions (n) A partition is a dividing wall or screen.

partly (adv) Partly means not completely.

partner partners (n) A partner is one of a pair who share things. *Marriage partners; business partners; dancing partners.*

partridge partridges (n) A partridge is a short-tailed, brown game bird.

part-time (adj) Something that is part-time happens only for part of a day or a week.

party parties
1 (n) A party is a happy social occasion when people meet to enjoy themselves or to celebrate something.
2 (n) A political party is a group of people with the same beliefs. They may have representatives in parliament.
3 (n) A party is a group of people who travel or do things together.
4 (n) In law, the guilty party is the person who commits a crime.

passage passages
1 (n) A passage is a long, narrow space inside or outside a building with walls on either side. It connects one place to another.
2 (n) A passage is a boat journey from one place to another.
3 (n) A passage is a short section in a book or in a piece of music.

p

passenger passengers (n) A passenger is a person who travels in any kind of vehicle or aeroplane.

passion passions (n) If you have a passion for a person, a belief or a cause you feel very strongly about them. **passionate** (adj) **passionately** (adv)

passive (adj) A passive person does not react strongly to anything. **passively** (adv)

Passover (n) The Passover is a Jewish religious festival lasting for eight days.

passport passports (n) A passport is an official document that you must show when you enter a foreign country.

password passwords
1 (n) A password is a secret word which only a few people know. It allows people on the same side to recognise a friend.
2 (n) A password may be needed to get into some private computer files.

past (n) Time that has already gone by is the past.

pasta (n) is a food made of flour and is used to make spaghetti, noodles, etc. This is a staple food in Italy.

paste pastes pasting pasted
1 (n) A paste is any thick, smooth mixture.
2 (n) Paste is a thick glue used for putting up wallpaper.
3 (vb) If you paste something, you cover it with glue or paste in order to stick it to something else.

Pasteur, Louis (1822–1895) was a French chemist, who studied bacteria. His work resulted, for example, in milk being pasteurised.

pasteurised (adj) milk has been heated to kill any germs.

pastime pastimes (n) A pastime is something you enjoy doing in your free time.

pastry pastries (n) Pastry is a mixture of flour, fat and other ingredients which is usally baked and used as a case for other food. *The steak pie had a lovely pastry case.*

pasty pasties (n) A pasty is a pastry case filled with meat or vegetables.

patch patches patching patched
1 (n) A patch is a small piece of material used to cover a hole in something else. *We repaired the tube with a rubber patch.*
2 (vb) If you patch something, you repair a hole by putting a patch over it.
3 (n) A patch of something is a small area of that thing.

patchy (adj) If something is patchy it is uneven in quality or quantity. *The fog was very patchy.*

pâté pâtés (n) Pâté is a paste made from meat, fish or vegetables and eaten with bread or biscuits.

paternal
1 (adj) is used to describe things relating to fatherhood.
2 (adj) If a person feels paternal, they have fatherly feelings towards someone.

path paths
1 (n) A path is a narrow way along which you can walk or ride.
2 (n) The path of an object is the direction in which it travels. *We followed the path of the rocket as it fell to earth.*

pathetic
1 (adj) Anything pathetic is weak, sad, or causes pity. **pathetically** (adv)
2 (adj) Pathetic is also used to describe something worthless.

patient patients
1 (n) A patient is a person who is being treated by a doctor.
2 (adj) If you are patient you are prepared to wait for something. **patience** (n) **patiently** (adv)

patio patios (n) A patio is a paved area outside a house where people can sit.

patka patkas (n) A patka is the small piece of white cloth that Sikh boys wear on their topknots.

p

Patrick, Saint

Patrick, Saint (?385–?461) was a bishop who went to Ireland and became Ireland's patron saint. His feast day is March 17th.

patriot patriots (n) A patriot is a person who supports their own country very strongly. **patriotic** (adj) **patriotism** (n)

patrol patrols patrolling patrolled
1 (n) A patrol is a group of people, usually policemen or soldiers, who together move around an area to make sure that it is safe.
2 (n) A patrol is a group of scouts or guides.
3 (vb) If you patrol an area, you move around it to keep watch and to keep it safe.

patron saint patron saints (n) A patron saint is believed to protect a particular country, church, trade, etc. *St Andrew is the patron saint of Scotland.*

patter patters pattering pattered (vb) If something patters, rain for example, it continually makes a tapping sound.

pattern patterns
1 (n) A pattern is an arrangement of lines, colours and shapes which can be repeated.
2 (n) A pattern is a drawing which can be copied to make something such as a dress.

pause pauses pausing paused
1 (n) A pause is a short break in an activity or in speaking.
2 (vb) If you pause before doing something, you wait a moment before you go ahead.

pavement pavements (n) A pavement is a raised pathway alongside a street.

cricket **pavilion**, Oxford University

pavilion pavilions (n) A pavilion is a building on a sports field where players can prepare for play.

pawn pawns (n) A pawn is the smallest and least important piece in the game of chess.

pay pays paying paid
1 (vb) If you pay someone, you give them money in exchange for something.
2 (n) Your pay is the money you receive for working. **payment** (n)
3 If you pay attention, you listen to what is being said.
4 If something you do pays off, it is successful.

pea peas (n) A pea is a small, round, green vegetable that grows in a pod on a climbing plant.

peace
1 (n) is a time when there is no fighting or wars.
2 If a person has peace they are quiet and undisturbed. **peaceful** (adj) **peacefully** (adv)

peach peaches (n) A peach is a round fruit with furry skin, sweet, pale orange flesh and a large stone.

peacock peacocks (n) A peacock is a large bird which can spread out its tail to show magnificent, brightly-coloured feathers. The female is called a peahen.

peak peaks
1 (n) The peak of a mountain is its highest point.
2 If you reach your peak in fitness, for example, you are at your fittest.

peal peals pealing pealed
1 (n) When bells peal, they ring one after another.
2 (vb) A peal of thunder is a loud, rumbling noise heard during a thunderstorm.

peanut peanuts (n) A peanut is a small, hard nut, grown underground.

pear pears (n) A pear is an oval fruit with green or yellow skin and sweet, juicy, white flesh.

pearl pearls (n) A pearl is a hard, shiny, white ball that grows inside an oyster shell.

peasant peasants (n) A peasant is a farm worker who usually earns little money.

peat (n) is decaying plant matter found underground in wet areas and is often used as fuel and in compost.

pebble pebbles (n) A pebble is a rounded stone often found on beaches.

peck pecks pecking pecked
1 (vb) If a bird pecks, it bites with its beak in short, sharp movements.
2 (vb) If you peck at your food, you eat only very small amounts.

peculiar (adj) Someone or something peculiar is strange or unusual.
peculiarity (n)

pedal pedals pedalling pedalled
1 (n) The pedals on a bicycle are the two parts you push around with your feet to make it go.
2 (vb) When you pedal your bicycle, you work the pedals with your feet to make it move.

pedestrian pedestrians (n) A pedestrian is someone who walks instead of travelling in a vehicle.

pedigree pedigrees
1 (n) A pedigree is a list of ancestors of a person or an animal.
2 (adj) A pedigree animal is bred from known ancestors of good reputation.

peel peels peeling peeled
1 (n) Peel is the skin of a fruit or vegetable.
2 (vb) If you peel a fruit or vegetable, you take its skin off.
3 (vb) If your skin peels, the top layer of your skin comes off.

peer peers peering peered
1 (vb) If you peer at something you look at it closely, usually because you can't see it very clearly.
2 (n) A peer is a nobleman.
3 (n) Your peer is your equal in age, interests or background.

peevish (adj) A peevish person is irritable and complaining.

peewit peewits (n) The peewit or lapwing is a medium-sized bird with a crest. It is liked by farmers because it eats harmful insects.

pekinese pekineses (n) A pekinese is a small, long-haired dog with a flat face.

pelican pelicans (n) A pelican is a large water bird which catches fish and keeps them in the bottom part of its beak which is shaped like a big bag.

pellet pellets
1 (n) A pellet is something pressed together to make a small ball.
2 (n) A pellet is a small ball of metal fired from air-pistols.
3 (n) A pellet is a lump of undigested bones, fur and feathers, regurgitated by owls and other birds of prey.

pelt pelts pelting pelted
1 (vb) If you pelt someone or something, you throw lots of things at them very fast.
2 (vb) If rain pelts down, it rains very hard.
3 (n) An animal's pelt is its skin and fur used for making clothes, etc.

penalise penalises penalising penalised
1 (vb) If you are penalised in a game or competition, you lose marks or points.
2 (adj) If someone feels penalised, they feel that they are being treated unfairly.

penalty penalties
1 (n) A penalty is a legal punishment for crimes committed. *The penalty for smuggling drugs is severe.*
2 (n) In sport, a penalty is an advantage awarded to a team if their opponents break the rules.
3 (n) If you pay the penalty for doing something wrong or foolish, you have to live with the unpleasant results of your actions.

pence see **penny**

pencil pencils (n) A pencil is a thin stick of wood containing a piece of graphite, used for drawing and writing.

pendant pendants
(n) A pendant is a piece of jewellery that hangs from a chain round the neck.

pendulum pendulums (n) A pendulum in a clock is a piece of metal or cord with a weight at the end which swings from side to side.

pendulum

p

penetrate penetrates penetrating penetrated
1 (vb) If you penetrate a particular area that is difficult to get into, you succeed in getting into it.
2 (adj) A penetrating look is one that makes you feel uncomfortable.

penguin penguins (n) Penguins are black and white Antarctic birds that do not fly but swim very well.

penicillin (n) is an antibiotic used to treat bacterial infections.

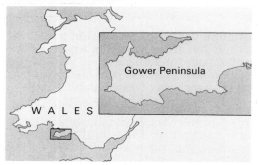

Gower Peninsula

WALES

peninsula peninsulas (n) A peninsula is a long piece of land jutting out from the mainland and almost surrounded by water.

penis penises (n) The penis is the male sex organ.

pen name pen names (n) A pen name is a false name used by writers instead of their own.

penny pennies or **pence** (n) A penny is the smallest value coin in Britain. 100 pennies or pence equal £1.

penny farthing (n) A penny farthing was a type of bicycle of the 19th century. It had a large front wheel and a small back wheel.

pension pensions (n) A pension is money paid regularly to a person who no longer works. **pensioner** (n)

pensive (adj) If you are pensive, you are thoughtful.

pentagon pentagons
1 (n) A pentagon is a five-sided shape.
2 (n) The Pentagon is the building where the defence of the United States of America is organised.

pentathlon pentathlons (n) A pentathlon is a competition in which athletes take part in five different events.

penultimate (adj) The penultimate thing is the last but one in a series of things.

peony peonies (n) A peony is a plant with large flowers.

people peoples
1 (n) People are men, women and children.
2 (n) A people are the inhabitants of one particular country. *The American people, the Russian people.*

pepper peppers
1 (n) Pepper is a hot spice made from ground peppercorns.
2 (n) A pepper is a hollow vegetable with an uneven, round shape. It can be red, yellow or green.

peppermint peppermints
1 (n) A peppermint is a type of sweet which has a minty taste.
2 (n) Peppermint is a herb.

per If you use the word per it means in or each. 70 miles per hour means 70 miles in each hour, per annum means each year. It can be abbreviated to p.a.

percentage percentages (n) A percentage is a fraction of something if the whole is divided into a hundred parts.

perceive perceives perceiving perceived (vb) If you perceive something you notice and understand it.

perch perches perching perched
1 (n) A perch is a thin piece of wood for birds to stand on.
2 (vb) If you perch, you sit on the edge of something.
3 (n) A perch is a freshwater fish.

percolator percolators (n) A percolator is a special jug for making fresh coffee.

percussion (adj) instruments are those which are played by hitting or shaking them, such as drums, tambourines and triangles.

perennial
1 (n) A perennial is a flower which blooms year after year.
2 (adj) A perennial problem is one which keeps occurring.

p

perfect perfects perfecting perfected
1 (adj) Something which is perfect has no faults at all. **perfection** (n)
2 (vb) If you perfect something, you succeed in making something which works very well. *After years of work, scientists perfected a vaccine for smallpox.*

perforate perforates perforating **perforated** (vb) If you perforate something, you make a small hole or holes in it. **perforations** (n)

perform performs performing **performed**
1 (vb) If you perform an act or a duty, for example, you do it. *She performed a good deed by helping with the shopping.*
2 (vb) If an entertainer or actor performs, they do their act for an audience. **performer** (n) **performance** (n)

perfume perfumes
1 (n) Perfume is a liquid with a pleasant smell used by people to put on their skin
2 (n) A perfume is a pleasant smell.

peril perils (n) Peril is a serious danger, or a dangerous situation.

perimeter perimeters (n) The perimeter is the outside edge or the measurement of the outside edge of an enclosed area.

period periods (n) A period is a certain length of time. *We were in Africa for a period of 6 months.*

periodical periodicals (n) A periodical is a magazine which appears at regular intervals.

periscope periscopes (n) A periscope is a tube with mirrors placed in it so that you can see things which are otherwise out of sight.

perish perishes perishing perished
1 (vb) If people, animals or plants perish, they die.
2 (vb) If food perishes it goes bad.
3 (vb) If rubber, etc perishes, it rots away. **perishable** (adj)

permanent (adj) If something is permanent, it lasts for a very long time or for ever. **permanently** (adv) **permanence** (n)

permit permits permitting permitted
1 (vb) If you permit something to happen, you allow it. **permission** (n)
2 (n) A permit is an official paper that allows the holder to do something.

permutation permutations (n) A permutation is a variation in the way a group of things can be arranged.

perpendicular
1 (adj) If something is perpendicular, it stands up straight from the ground.
2 (adj) If something is perpendicular to something else, it is at an angle of 90°.

perpetual (adj) If something is perpetual, it never stops. **perpetually** (adv)

perplexing (adj) If something is perplexing, it is confusing or puzzling.

persecute persecutes persecuting **persecuted** (vb) If you persecute someone, you treat them cruelly and make them suffer. **persecution** (n)

persevere perseveres persevering **persevered** (vb) If you persevere at something, you keep on trying, even though it is difficult.

persist persists persisting persisted
1 (vb) If something persists, it will not stop.
2 (vb) If you persist at something, you continue to do it, despite problems. **persistent** (adj)

person persons
1 (n) A person is a male or female human being.
2 If you do something in person, you do it yourself rather than send someone else.

personal
1 (adj) Anything personal belongs or refers to one particular person. *Personal belongings... personal stereo.*
2 (adj) Personal problems are private and discussed only with people you trust.

personality personalities
1 (n) Your personality is your complete character.
2 (n) If you are a personality, you are well-known.

p

personnel
1 (n) The personnel of an organisation are all the people it employs.
2 (n) The personnel department of a company looks after its staff.

perspective perspectives
1 (n) If you have an unusual perspective on something, you see it in a different way from other people.
2 If an object in a picture is in perspective, it has the correct size in relation to the other objects in the picture, and so looks realistic.
3 If you see things in perspective, you think about them in a sensible, careful way.

perspire perspires perspiring perspired (vb) When you perspire, you sweat. **perspiration** (n)

persuade persuades persuading persuaded (vb) If you persuade someone to do something, you convince them that they should do it even though they are unwilling. **persuasion** (n) **persuasive** (adj)

pessimistic (adj) A pessimistic person always believes that bad things will happen. **pessimism** (n)

pest pests (n) A pest is an insect, rat or other small creature that damages crops or food supplies.

pester pesters pestering pestered (vb) If you pester someone, you keep annoying them.

pesticide pesticides (n) A pesticide is a chemical used by farmers and gardeners to kill small animals and insects.

petal petals (n) Petals are the coloured or white, leaf-like parts of a flower that grow out from the centre.

flower
p112

petition petitions (n) A petition is a written request signed by a lot of people asking the government or other official body to do or not to do something.

petrify petrifies petrifying petrified
1 (vb) If you petrify someone, you frighten them severely.
2 (adj) If a substance is petrified, it has gradually changed over thousands of years into stone. **petrification** (n)

petrol (n) is a carbon fuel used for driving motor vehicles.

petty
1 (adj) Petty things are unimportant and trivial.
2 (adj) A petty person is someone who fusses too much about small things.

petulant (adj) Someone who is petulant is sulky and bad-tempered in a childish way.

pew pews (n) A pew is a long, wooden seat with a back, used in most churches.

phantom phantoms (n) A phantom is a ghost.

pharmacist pharmacists (n) A pharmacist is someone qualified to prepare and sell medicines.

phase phases (n) A phase is a stage in the development of something or somebody.

pheasant pheasants (n) A pheasant is a game bird. The male has long, colourful tail feathers.

phenomenal (adj) Something that is phenomenal is exceptionally amazing or remarkable. **phenomenon** (n)

philatelist philatelists (n) A philatelist is a stamp collector. **philately** (n)

philosophy (n) is the creation and study of ideas about man and his relationship to the universe. **philosopher** (n)

phobia phobias (n) A phobia is a deep, irrational fear or dislike of something.

phoenix phoenixes (n) The phoenix is a legendary bird that, every hundred years, burns itself and then rises from the ashes.

phone phones phoning phoned
1 (n) Phone is short for telephone.
2 (vb) If you phone someone, you telephone them.

phosphorescent (adj) Something that is phosphorescent glows with light in the dark. **phosphorescence** (n)

photo photos (n) Photo is short for photograph.

photocopy photocopies (n) A photocopy is a photographed copy of a page of writing or a picture. **photocopier** (n)

photograph photographs photographing photographed
1 (vb) If you photograph something you use a camera to take a picture of it.
2 (n) A photograph is a picture taken by a camera using film which is then developed and printed on special paper.
photographic (adj)

phrase phrases (n) A phrase is a small group of words or musical notes.

physical
1 (adj) Physical refers to things connected with the body and its functions but not the mind and emotions.
2 (adj) The physical characteristics of something are the parts that can be seen and touched.
3 (n) A physical is a medical examination for fitness.

physical education (n) is sport, gymnastics, athletics, etc at school.

physician physicians (n) A physician is a doctor.

physics (n) is the scientific study of the forces and property of matter, for example, magnetism, electricity, sound, heat, etc.

physiotherapy (n) is a medical treatment for people who cannot move very well and involves exercise, massage and heat.
physiotherapist (n)

physique physiques (n) Your physique is the size and shape of your body.

pianist pianists (n) A pianist is someone who plays the piano.

piano pianos (n) A piano is a large musical instrument with a row of black and white keys. When the keys are pressed, hammers strike the strings and produce notes.

piccolo piccolos (n) A piccolo is a small wind instrument rather like a flute.

pickaxe pickaxes (n) A pickaxe is a heavy tool used for breaking up hard ground.

picket pickets picketing picketed (vb) If you picket a workplace during a strike, you stand outside and try to persuade other workers not to go in.

pickle pickles pickling pickled
1 (vb) If you pickle vegetables, you preserve them in vinegar.
2 (n) Pickle is a spicy mixture of vegetables, fruit and vinegar, served with food.

pickpocket pickpockets (n) A pickpocket is a thief who steals things from your pockets or bags.

picnic picnics picnicking picnicked
1 (n) A picnic is a meal which you eat outdoors, often in the countryside or at the seaside.
2 (vb) If you picnic, you eat out of doors.

picture pictures picturing pictured
1 (n) A picture is a drawing, photograph or painting of something or somebody.
2 (n) If you go to the pictures, you go to the cinema.
3 (vb) If you picture something, you imagine it.

picturesque (adj) Something that is picturesque is attractive to look at. *The thatched cottage was very picturesque.*

pidgin (n) is a language that is a mixture of two other languages.

pie pies (n) A pie is a pastry case with a sweet or savoury filling.

piebald (adj) A piebald animal is one which has patches of any two colours on its skin.

piece pieces piecing pieced
1 (n) A piece of something is one part of it. *He had a piece of the chocolate cake.*
2 (n) A piece can mean one of a set of objects. *We had a 72 piece dinner service.*
3 (n) A piece can be something you have made or written. *I wrote this piece of music myself.*
4 (vb) If you piece something together, you use all the small bits of information you have to try to get a complete idea.

piecework (n) If you are paid for doing piecework, you are paid according to how much work you do, rather than how long you work.

p

pier piers (n) A pier is a long platform on legs which stands in the sea and is joined to the shore. It often has entertainments on it.

pierce pierces piercing pierced
1 (vb) If you pierce something, you make a hole in it.
2 (adj) A piercing noise is a very loud, shrill noise.

pig pigs (n) A pig is a large farm animal kept for its meat; pork, bacon, ham, gammon, etc.

pigeon pigeons (n) A pigeon is a bird, usually grey in colour, which has a fat body and makes long, low cooing sounds.

pike pikes
1 (n) A pike is a large, freshwater fish, which will attack other fish and even small birds such as ducklings.
2 (n) A pike is an old-fashioned weapon: a long pole with a spike on the end.

pile piles piling piled
1 (vb) If you pile something up, you make a heap of it. *He piled sand outside the back door.*
2 (n) A pile is a heap of anything.
3 (n) Piles are concrete or metal supports for buildings driven into the ground.

pilfer pilfers pilfering pilfered (vb) If a person pilfers, they steal small things or small amounts of money.

pilgrim pilgrims A pilgrim is a person who goes on a journey to a holy place. **pilgrimage** (n)

pill pills (n) A pill is a medicine in the form of a tablet.

pillar pillars (n) A pillar is a column which supports a roof, arch, etc.

pillar box pillar boxes (n) A pillar box is a round metal box where letters are posted.

pillion (n) When you ride pillion on a motorbike, you sit behind the driver.

pillow pillows (n) A pillow is a large, soft cushion that supports the head in bed.

pilot pilots piloting piloted
aircraft p5
1 (n) A pilot is a person trained to fly an aeroplane.
2 (n) A pilot is the person who guides a ship safely into harbour.

3 (vb) If you pilot a boat or an aeroplane, you control it.
4 (vb) If you pilot a new examination or course, you try it out.

pimple pimples (n) A pimple is a small, red spot on the skin.

pinch pinches pinching pinched
1 (vb) If you pinch someone or something, you catch a part of them between your thumb and first finger.
2 (adj) A pinch of salt, spice, etc is a very small amount.
3 If you take a remark, for example, with a pinch of salt, you do not take it seriously.

pine pines pining pined
1 (n) A pine is a tall, evergreen tree with long, very thin leaves called needles.
2 (vb) If you pine for someone when they go away, you are sad because they are not there.

pineapple pineapples (n) A pineapple is a large, oval fruit that is sweet and juicy. It has a thick, woody skin.

pink (adj) is a colour between red and white.

pint pints (n) In Britain, a pint is a measurement of liquid. One pint is the same as 0.57 litres.

pioneer pioneers pioneering pioneered
1 (n) A pioneer is the first person to do something new.
2 (n) If you pioneer something, you are one of the first to try it.

pipe pipes
1 (n) A pipe is a long, narrow, hollow tube to carry gas or liquids.
2 (n) A pipe is a small object used for smoking tobacco.
3 (n) A pipe is a musical instrument.

pipeline pipelines
1 (n) A pipeline is a long line of pipes for carrying liquids or gas.
2 If something is in the pipeline, it is being worked on and thought about.

pirate pirates pirating pirated
1 (n) A pirate is a sailor who robs ships at sea.
2 (vb) If you pirate videos, you copy them illegally.

p

pistol pistols (n) A pistol is a small, hand-held gun.

piston pistons (n) A piston is the part of an engine that moves under pressure inside a cylinder.

pit pits pitting pitted
1 (n) A pit is a hole in the ground such as a sand pit or gravel pit.
2 (n) A pit is a coal mine.
3 (adj) If a surface is pitted, it has small holes in it.
4 If you pit your wits against someone else, you compete against them.

pitch pitches pitching pitched
1 (vb) If you pitch a tent, you put it up.
2 (vb) If you pitch a ball, you aim and throw it at something.
3 (vb) If something pitches forward it falls.
4 (vb) If a ship pitches, it moves sharply up and down in a rough sea.
5 (n) In music, the pitch of a note is the level of it, high or low.
6 (n) A pitch is an area where a game is played. *Football pitch... hockey pitch.*
7 (n) Pitch is a black substance painted onto ends of roofs and boat bottoms to waterproof them.

pitcher pitchers
1 (n) A pitcher is a large jug.
2 (n) In baseball, the pitcher is the player who throws the ball to the batsman.

pitchfork pitchforks (n) A pitchfork is a large two-pronged fork with a long handle, used for moving hay, grass, etc.

piteous (adj) Something piteous makes you feel full of pity and sadness.

pitfall pitfalls (n) A pitfall is an unsuspected problem or danger.

pitta (n) is a flat rounded bread, hollow inside, that can be filled with savoury or sweet food.

pity pities pitying pitied
1 (vb) If you pity someone, you feel sorry for them.
2 (n) Pity is a feeling of sadness and concern for someone or something.
3 If you say it's a pity that something happened, you mean that it was unfortunate that it happened.
4 If you take pity on a person or an animal, you help them when they need it.

pivot pivots (n) A pivot is a point on which something balances or turns.

pizza pizzas (n) A pizza is a flat, round of dough covered with a savoury mixture of tomatoes, cheese, mushrooms, etc and baked in an oven.

placard placards (n) A placard is a large notice written on card and carried by demonstrators or put up in public.

placate placates placating placated (vb) If you placate someone you soothe them and stop them from being angry or upset.

place places placing placed
1 (vb) If you place something you put it carefully onto a particular spot.
2 (n) A place is a particular area, spot or position.
3 (n) A place in a race or competition is first, second, third, etc.
4 (n) A place at a table is somewhere to sit.
5 (n) Your place is where you live. *Come to my place for a coffee.*
6 If something takes place, it happens.

placid
1 (adj) A placid person or creature is calm, even-tempered and not easily angered.
2 (adj) If water is placid it is flat and calm; if a place is placid it is peaceful and quiet.

plague plagues plaguing plagued
1 (n) A plague is a dangerous disease that spreads very fast.
2 (n) The plague is a fatal disease spread by rats and fleas. It causes severe fever and swellings on the body.
3 (vb) If you plague someone you keep pestering them.
4 (vb) If something plagues you it bothers you or worries you.
5 (n) A plague of insects or unpleasant things is a very large number of them.

p

plaice (n) are flat, saltwater fish that are good to eat.

plaid plaids
1 (n) Plaid is a tartan patterned material.
2 (n) A plaid is a large piece of tartan material worn over the shoulder by someone wearing Scottish Highland dress.

plain plainer plainest
1 (n) A plain is a large, flat area of grassland.
2 (adj) Something that is plain has no pattern or design on it.
3 (adj) Plain food is simple food.
4 (adj) Plain writing or plain speech is clear, frank and easy to understand.
5 (adj) A person who is plain to look at is unattractive.

plaintive (adj) A plaintive sound is mournful and sad. **plaintively** (adj)

plait plaits plaiting plaited
1 (vb) If you plait hair, ribbon or cord, you take three strands or more and twist them into one thick length.
2 (n) A plait is a length of plaited hair, ribbon, rope, etc.

plan plans planning planned
1 (vb) If you plan something, you organise it and make arrangements for it to happen.
2 (n) A plan is a series of ideas in your head; a written list of ideas; or a detailed diagram showing your main ideas about something you intend to do or write about.
3 (n) The plan of a building, street, town, etc, is a detailed drawing or diagram of it as seen from above.

plane planes
1 (n) A plane is a tool for smoothing wood.
2 (n) Plane is short for aeroplane.
3 (n) A plane tree is a tall tree often grown in towns.

planet planets (n) A planet is a large sphere in space that orbits a sun.

solar system p278

planetarium planetariums (n) A planetarium is a building where you pay to see special picture shows about the planets and space.

plank planks (n) A plank is a long, flat slice of wood cut lengthways from a tree trunk.

plankton (n) is a mass of minute animals and plants that live on the surface of the sea.

plant plants planting planted
1 (n) A plant is a living thing which grows with its roots in the earth.
2 (vb) If you plant something, you put its roots into soil to make it grow.

plantation plantations (n) A plantation is an area where crops or trees are grown.

plaster plasters plastering plastered
1 (n) Plaster is a thick paste which hardens and is used to cover walls.
2 (vb) If you plaster a wall, you cover the bricks with plaster.
3 (n) A plaster is a dressing used to cover cuts.

plastic plastics (n) Plastic is a material made from oil or chemicals. It has many uses.

Plasticine (n) is a soft, coloured material like clay, that children use to make models.

plate plates plating plated
1 (n) A plate is a flat dish.
2 (n) A plate can be anything flat. *A plate of glass . . . a metal plate.*

plateau plateaux (n) A plateau is a flat top on a hill or mountain.

platform platforms
1 (n) A platform in a railway station is the place where you wait to get on and off trains.
2 (n) A platform is a flat-topped structure. *An oil platform . . . a helicopter platform.*

platinum (n) is a rare metal, more valuable than gold.

platoon platoons (n) A platoon is a small group of soldiers, led by a lieutenant.

platypus platypuses (n) A platypus is an Australian egg-laying mammal with a bill like a duck.

plunge

plausible (adj) If something is plausible it could be true.

play plays playing played
1 (vb) If you play at something, you have fun doing it. **playful** (adj)
2 (vb) You play when you take part in a game.
3 (vb) If you perform on an instrument, you play it.
4 (vb) If you have a part in a performance, you play a part. *I played the part of Captain Hook in the pantomime.*
5 (vb) If you play a part in some event, you are involved in it.
6 (n) A play is a performance by actors on a stage, radio or television.

playground playgrounds (n) A playground is a special area for children to play in.

playwright playwrights (n) A playwright is a person who writes plays.

plea pleas (n) A plea is an appeal or request to someone. *We delivered a plea for mercy for the condemned man.*

plead pleads pleading pleaded (vb) If you plead, you ask or beg for something strongly or desperately.

pleasant (adj) Something pleasant is attractive or nice in some way.
pleasantly (adv)

please pleases pleasing pleased
1 (vb) If you please someone, they like what you do or say.
2 If you ask politely for something, you say please.

pleasure pleasures (n) Pleasure is the feeling you have when you are enjoying yourself. **pleasurable** (adj)

pleat pleats (n) A pleat is a regular fold in a piece of fabric.

pledge pledges (n) A pledge is a promise to do something.

plenty (n) If you have plenty of something, you have more than enough for your needs.
plentiful (adj)

pliable (adj) Something pliable is easily bent.

pliers (n) A pair of pliers is a tool used to pull out nails, etc or to cut wire.

plimsoll plimsolls (n) A plimsoll is a flat, rubber-soled, canvas shoe.

plot plots plotting plotted
1 (n) The plot of a story, book, film, etc is its story.
2 (n) A plot of ground is an area of land for building, growing vegetables, etc.
3 (vb) If you plot against someone, you make a secret plan to harm them.
4 (vb) If you plot points on a graph, you make marks on it.

plough ploughs ploughing ploughed
1 (n) A plough is a tool used by farmers to dig up the ground.
2 (vb) If you plough land, you dig it over.
3 (vb) If you plough money into a company, you put in a great deal of money.

pluck plucks plucking plucked
1 (vb) If you pluck a guitar, violin, etc you move your fingers across the strings to make the sound.
2 (vb) If you pluck a flower, you pick it.
3 (n) Pluck is courage.
4 If you pluck up courage, you prepare yourself to do something difficult.

plug plugs plugging plugged
1 (n) A plug is a piece of rubber used to block a hole in the bath when full of water.
2 (n) A plug is a plastic device used to connect an electrical appliance such as a lamp to the main electricity supply.
3 (vb) If you plug a hole, you fill it.
4 (vb) If you plug something in, you connect it to the main electricity supply using a plug.

plum plums (n) A plum is an oval-shaped purple, red or yellow fruit. It has juicy flesh with a stone in the middle.

plumage (n) is the feathery covering on a bird.

feather p107

plumber plumbers (n) A plumber is a person who fits and mends water pipes of all kinds.

plunge plunges plunging plunged
1 (vb) If you plunge into a swimming pool, for example, you throw yourself in.
2 If you take the plunge, you go ahead with something despite possible problems.

plural

plural plurals The plural of a word is given when reference is made to two or more things. *Mice is the plural of mouse.*

plus
1 (prep) Plus shows that one number is added to another. *Six plus ten equals sixteen. 6 + 10 = 16*
2 If something is a plus for you, it is an advantage, and extra for you.

plywood (n) is wood made up of several layers of wood stuck together.

pneumatic
1 (adj) Pneumatic describes something worked by air pressure, such as a pneumatic drill.
2 (adj) Pneumatic describes something filled with air, such as a pneumatic tyre.

pneumonia (n) is a lung disease which makes breathing difficult.

poach poaches poaching poached
1 (vb) If you poach eggs or fish, you cook them gently in boiling water.
2 (vb) If you poach fish, animals, etc you take them from other people's property without permission. **poacher** (n)
3 (vb) If you poach a member of an opposing football team, you secretly arrange for them to play in your team.

pocket pockets pocketing pocketed
1 (n) A pocket is a flat bag sewn into clothing for carrying small items.
2 (vb) If you pocket the profits of something, you take the money for yourself.
3 (vb) When players pocket a ball in a game of snooker, they push it into one of the six bags round the edge of the table.
4 If people live in each other's pockets, they spend a lot of time with each other.
5 If you are out of pocket after spending some money, you have less money than you planned.

pocket money (n) is spending money given to children by their parents.

pod pods (n) A pod is a container for seeds that grows on some plants such as beans and peas.

poem poems (n) A poem is a piece of writing with words chosen carefully for their sound or impact and with lines usually short but rhythmical. Poems do not always rhyme. **poet** (n) **poetry** (n)

point points pointing pointed
1 (vb) If you point, you stretch your index finger in the direction of something to show where it is.
2 (vb) If you point a gun, you aim it.
3 (n) A point is the sharp end of something.
4 (n) In maths, a point is a decimal point marked with a dot.
5 (n) In games or competitions, a point is a unit of scoring.
6 (n) A point can be a certain place or spot.
7 (n) In a lecture, discussion or argument the point is the most important part of what is said.
8 (n) The point of something is the reason why it's done.
9 (n) Points on a railway line are junctions where rails can be moved to direct a train from one line to another.

point-blank (adv) If you shoot at point-blank range you shoot very close to the target.

poised
1 (adj) If you are poised you are ready and waiting to do something.
2 (adj) If part of your body is poised you hold it still but ready to move.
3 (adj) If you are poised you are self-confident and graceful. **poise** (n)

poison poisons poisoning poisoned
1 (n) Poison is a substance that causes illness or death, **poisonous** (adj)
2 (vb) If you poison an animal or a human, you make them ill or kill them by giving them poison.
3 (adj) If food or drink is poisoned, it has had poison added to it.
4 (adj) If land, water or air is poisoned, it has been contaminated by dangerous chemicals.

poky pokier pokiest (adj) A poky house or room is uncomfortably small and cramped.

polar (adj) Anything polar is to do with the area around the North or South poles. *Polar regions . . . polar ice.*

p

polar bear polar bears (n) Polar bears are huge white bears living near the North Pole.

Polaroid camera Polaroid cameras (n) The Polaroid camera can take, develop and print photographs in seconds.

pole poles
1 (n) A pole is a long piece of wood or metal.
2 (n) The poles are the most northerly and southerly points on the earth.

pole vault pole vaults (n) A pole vault is a jump an athlete makes over a very high bar, using a pole to help.

police
1 (n) The police is the organisation responsible for keeping law and order.
2 (n) The police refers to the men and women who are members of the police force.

policy policies (n) A policy is a plan of action made, for example, by managers of businesses, local or national government.

polio (n) This is short for poliomyelitis, a serious disease that can cause paralysis.

polish polishes polishing polished
1 (n) Polish is a substance you put onto things such as shoes, furniture, etc to clean, shine and preserve them.
2 (vb) If you polish something, you put polish onto it and rub it until it shines.
3 If you polish off some food, you eat it all up very quickly.
4 (adj) If something is polished, it is shining and smooth.
5 (adj) A person who is polished has excellent manners and is confident and sophisticated.

polite (adj) Someone who is polite has good manners, knows how to behave and considers other people's feelings.
politely (adv)

political (adj) Something described as political is to do with the governing of a country and the organising of its affairs.
politician (n) **politics** (n)

pollen (n) is fine powder produced by flowers as part of the reproductive cycle.

pollen count pollen counts (n) This is the measure of how much pollen is in the air.

polling station polling stations (n) A polling station is the place where you vote when there is a general election.

pollute pollutes polluting polluted (vb) If you pollute water, land or air you spoil it by making it unclean or dangerous.
pollution (n)

polo (n) is a game played between two teams riding ponies. The aim is to score goals as in hockey.

poltergeist poltergeists (n) A poltergeist is believed to be a type of ghost or spirit which causes noises and throws objects around.

polygon polygons (n) A shape which has three or more straight sides is a polygon.

polythene (n) is an artificial material used to make large waterproof sheets and bags.

pompous (adj) A pompous person is self-important.

pond ponds (n) A pond is a small area of water enclosed by land.

ponder ponders pondering pondered (vb) If you ponder, you think carefully about something for a time.

pony ponies (n) A pony is a small horse.

ponytrekking (n) Ponytrekking is a leisure activity in which you ride across country on a pony.

poor poorer poorest
1 (adj) A poor person or country has very little money.
2 (adj) A poor design or performance is very bad in quality.
3 (adj) A poor result is a bad one.

Pope Popes (n) The Pope is the head of the Roman Catholic Church.

poplar poplars (n) A poplar tree is tall and narrow with upswept branches.

poppadom poppadoms (n) Poppadoms are thin, crisp, round pieces of bread served with Indian meals.

p

poppy

poppy poppies (n) A poppy is a bright red flower which grows in cornfields and meadows.

popular (adj) Popular describes things enjoyed by many people. *The popular press... popular television... popular science.*

populated (adj) If a place is populated, people or animals live there.

population (n) A populated place has people or animals living there. **population** (n)

porcelain (n) is very fine china.

porch porches (n) A porch is a shelter around a doorway.

porcupine porcupines (n) A porcupine is an animal with hard, sharp quills on its back.

pore pores poring pored
1 (n) Pores are tiny holes in your skin which allow you to sweat.
2 (vb) If you pore over something, you study it closely. *He pored over the dusty books.*

pork (n) is the meat from a pig.

porous (adj) If something is porous, it lets water through.

porpoise porpoises (n) A porpoise is a sea mammal very similar to a dolphin.

porridge (n) is a thick food made from boiled oats and eaten with salt or sugar and milk.

port ports
1 (n) A port is a town by the sea with a harbour.
2 (adj) The port side of a ship is the left side facing towards the front.
3 (n) Port is a strong wine sometimes drunk at the end of a meal.

portable (adj) Something that is portable can be carried easily, for example, a portable television.

portcullis portcullises (n) A portcullis is castle p41 a strong criss-cross of bars that can be brought down to defend a castle, fort, etc.

porter porters
1 (n) A porter is a person employed to carry luggage and other goods at railway stations.
2 (n) A porter is a person employed to do general duties in a hotel, etc.

porthole portholes (n) A porthole is a small, round window in a ship or an aeroplane.

portion portions
1 (n) A portion of food is the amount served to one person.
2 (n) A portion is one of several equal parts which something is divided into.

portrait portraits (n) A portrait is a drawing or painting of someone, usually only of their head and shoulders.

pose poses posing posed
1 (vb) If you pose for a photograph, you sit or stand in a particular way for it.
2 (vb) If you pose as someone else, you deceive others by pretending to be that person.
3 (vb) If you pose a question, you ask it.

position positions positioning positioned
1 (n) A position is a particular place.
2 (n) If you apply for a position in a company, you apply for a job.
3 (vb) If you position something, you put it in a particular place.
4 If you are in position at the beginning of a race, you are ready to start.

positive
1 (adj) Something that is positive is certain. *Positive results... positive response.*
2 (adj) If someone is positive about something, they are confident in it.

possess possesses possessing possessed
1 (vb) If you possess something, you own it. **possession** (n)
2 (vb) If you possess certain qualities, you have these characteristics.

possessive (adj) If you are possessive, you keep things for yourself.

possible possibles
1 (adj) If something is possible, it can be done.
2 (n) If something or someone is a possible, they may well be chosen for a particular purpose. **possibility** (n)

p

post posts posting posted
1 (n) A post is any strong vertical piece of wood, metal, etc.
2 (n) The post is the whole system of carrying letters, parcels, etc and delivering them.
3 (n) Your post is all the letters, parcels, etc delivered to you by the postman.
4 (vb) If you post a letter, you put it in a postbox or take it to a post office.
5 (vb) If your employers post you to another country, they send you there as part of your job.

postage (n) is the charge made for the carrying of a letter, parcel, etc.

postcode postcodes (n) A postcode is the small group of numbers and letters at the end of an address, used to speed up postal deliveries.

poster posters (n) A poster is a large notice, picture or advertisement.

posthumously (adv) If a person receives an award posthumously, they get it after they have died.

postmortem postmortems (n) A postmortem is an examination by a doctor of a dead body to find out how they died.

postpone postpones postponing postponed (vb) If you postpone an activity, you put it off until later.

potato potatoes (n) A potato is a round, starchy, root vegetable which grows below the ground.

potential (n) If someone has the potential to do something, they have the ability to do it.

pothole potholes
1 (n) A pothole is a hole in a road that should not be there.
2 (n) A pothole is a hole that goes deep into the ground often leading to caves.
potholer (n)

potion potions (n) A potion is an old-fashioned word for a medicine. It can also mean a magic liquid.

potter potters (n) A potter is a person who makes pottery.

pottery potteries
1 (n) Pottery is all the articles, jugs, bowls, dishes, etc made of baked clay.
2 (n) A pottery is a factory or workshop where pottery is made.

pouch pouches
1 (n) A pouch is a small bag.
2 (n) Kangaroos and some other animals have skin bags on the outside of their bodies called pouches, to keep their babies safe.
3 (n) Hamsters and some other rodents have food pouches inside their mouths.

poultice poultices (n) A poultice is a pad with ointment on it that soothes sore and inflamed parts of the body.

pounce pounces pouncing pounced (vb) If an animal or a person pounces on something, they leap on and take hold of it.

pound pounds pounding pounded
1 (vb) If you pound something you crush it by beating it with something hard.
2 (vb) If your heart pounds, it beats very fast.
3 (adj) Pounding footsteps are heavy, running footsteps.
4 (n) A pound in Britain is a coin worth one hundred pence.
5 (n) A pound is a unit of weight worth 0.454 kilograms.
6 (n) A pound is a place where stray dogs and cats are kept.

pour pours pouring poured
1 (vb) When you pour liquid from a container, you tilt the container until the liquid comes out.
2 (vb) When liquid pours, it moves rapidly and in large quantities.
3 (vb) When rain pours, it rains heavily.

pout pouts pouting pouted (vb) If you pout you push out your lips because you're cross or displeased.

poverty (n) is the condition of being very poor.

powder powders powdering powdered
1 (n) Powder is very small particles of something as fine as dust. **powdery** (adj)
2 (vb) If you powder something, you cover it with powder.

p

power

power powers
1 (n) A person or people with power have control over other people and their activities.
2 (n) If you have the power to do something, you have the ability or the authority to do it.
3 (n) Power is physical strength.
4 (n) Power is energy, generated by the wind, the sun or by burning fuel.
5 (n) Electricity is often called power. *Turn off the power, please.*
powerful (adj) **powerless** (adj)

power boat power boats (n) A power boat is a large, extremely fast motor boat.

power cut power cuts (n) When there is a power cut, the electricity supply stops.

power station power stations (n) A power station is where electricity is generated.

hydro electricity p142

practical
1 (adj) Practical means concerned with the actual doing of something, rather than theories or ideas about it.
2 (adj) A practical person is efficient and good at getting things done.
3 (adj) A practical gift is one that will be useful.

practical joke practical jokes (n) A practical joke is a trick you play on someone.

practice practices
1 (n) The practice of something such as religion, is the following of its teachings and beliefs.
2 (n) A practice is something done over many years so that it becomes a tradition. *There is a practice of lighting bonfires on November 5th.*
3 (n) Practice is the doing of something over and over again in order to improve.
4 (n) A doctor's or lawyer's practice is their business and all the people who consult them.

practise practises practising practised
1 (vb) If you practise, you do something over and over again so that you become very good at it.
2 (vb) If you practise something, you do it because it's traditional or because you believe in it. *The village still practised the ancient ceremony of crowning a May Queen.*

3 (vb) If you practise medicine, you work as a doctor; if you practise law, you work as a lawyer.

prairie prairies (n) A prairie is a vast area of grassland in North America.

praise praises praising praised
1 (vb) If you praise someone, you tell them how good or clever or kind or attractive they are.
2 (n) Praise is what you say or write about someone or something to show your approval.

praiseworthy (adj) If someone or something is praiseworthy, they deserve to be praised.

pram prams (n) A pram is a small, four-wheeled carriage for a baby.

prance prances prancing pranced
1 (vb) If you prance, you leap about because you are excited or showing off.
2 (adj) A prancing horse moves quickly, lifting its legs high.

prank pranks (n) A prank is a practical joke or a trick.

prawn prawns (n) A prawn is an edible shell-fish like a large shrimp.

pray prays praying prayed
1 (vb) If you pray, you talk to your God.
2 (vb) If you pray that something will happen, you really want it to happen.
prayers (n)

prayer book prayer books (n) A prayer book is a book of prayers.

prayer rug prayer rugs (n) A prayer rug or prayer mat is a small carpet on which Muslims kneel to pray.

prayer shawl prayer shawls (n) A prayer shawl or tallit is a white shawl worn by Jewish men during religious ceremonies.

prayer wheel prayer wheels (n) A Buddhist prayer wheel contains prayers or has them written on it. Each turn of the wheel counts as one prayer said.

preach preaches preaching preached
1 (vb) If a person preaches they talk to a group of people about religious things.
2 (vb) A person who preaches tries to tell others how to behave.

p

precarious (adj) Something or someone in a precarious position is not safely fixed and is liable to fall. **precariously** (adv)

precaution precautions (n) If you take precautions, you try to stop something unpleasant or unwanted happening.

precede precedes preceding preceded (vb) If one thing precedes another, it comes before it. *Band music preceded the match.*

precinct precincts
1 (n) A precinct is an area of land with a special purpose. *Shopping precinct... sports precinct.*
2 (n) Precinct can mean the area around a certain place. *I am in the precincts of the temple.*

precious
1 (adj) If something is precious, it is valuable.
2 (adj) If a person is precious, they are well loved.

precipice precipices (n) A precipice is a steep or sheer cliff face.

precise
1 (adj) If something is precise, it is very accurate.
2 (adj) If a person is precise, they are careful, neat and accurate in their work. **precisely** (adj) **precision** (n)

predator predators (n) A predator is an animal which hunts another for food.

predecessor predecessors (n) Your predecessor is the person who did your job before you took over.

predicament predicaments (n) A predicament is an awkward situation.

predict predicts predicting predicted (vb) If you predict something, you say that it will happen some time in the future. **predictable** (adj)

predominant (adj) Something that is predominant is more important or noticeable in the group of people or things. **predominantly** (adv)

predominate predominates predominating predominated (vb) If one group predominates, they outnumber others or have more power than other groups.

preen preens preening preened
1 (vb) Animals or people preen when they groom themselves. *The bird preened its feathers with its beak.*
2 (vb) If people preen, they are pleased with themselves after doing something well.

preface prefaces (n) The preface is the introduction at the beginning of a book which gives brief details about it.

prefect prefects (n) A prefect is a pupil in a school who has been given some authority by the staff over other pupils.

prefer prefers preferring preferred (vb) If you prefer one thing or person to another, you like that thing or person better. **preferable** (adj) **preferably** (adj) **preference** (n)

pregnant (adj) A woman or female animal is pregnant if they are carrying an unborn baby or young animal inside them. **pregnancy** (n)

prehistoric (adj) Animals and plants which come from the very earliest times, before written records were kept, are prehistoric.

prejudiced (adj) A prejudiced person has opinions not based on fact or experience.

preliminary (adj) Anything which is preliminary comes at the start of something.

premature (adj) Anything premature happens too early.

premeditated (adj) If some action such as a crime is premeditated, it has been carefully planned or thought about, and does not happen on the spur of the moment.

premier premiers (n) The premier is the Prime Minister or President of a country.

premiere premieres (n) A premiere is the first performance of a piece of music, a play, etc.

premises (n) Premises are the buildings where a shop or a business is located.

premium premiums (n) A premium is the amount of money paid regularly for insurance.

p

Premium Bonds

Premium Bonds (n) are savings certificates which give the owner a chance of winning prize money in a monthly lottery.

premonition premonitions (n) If you have a premonition, you have a feeling that something - usually unpleasant - will happen before it actually does.

pre-occupied (adj) If you are pre-occupied, you are totally involved with your thoughts and do not notice anything else.

prepare prepares preparing prepared
1 (vb) If you prepare someone or something, you get them ready for an occasion later on.
2 If you prepare yourself for a new situation, you get yourself used to the change that will occur.

preposition prepositions (n) A preposition is a word put before a noun to show such things as position, direction, method or time. *On, to, by* and *after* are prepositions.

prep school prep schools (n) A prep school is a fee-paying private school for 7–12 year old boys and girls.

prescription prescriptions (n) A prescription is a written order to a chemist from your doctor to supply you with the medicine you need.

present presents presenting presented
1 (n) You give something as a present to someone on a special occasion.
2 (n) A present is a gift.
3 (adj) Present describes people and things happening now. *The present headteacher ... the present problems.*
4 (adj) If you are present at a talk, you are there in the audience.
5 (vb) When chat show hosts, for example, present programmes, they introduce them.

presently (adv) If something is due to happen presently, it will happen soon.

preserve preserves preserving preserved
1 (vb) If you preserve something, you try to keep it as it is, without any changes.
2 (n) A preserve is a jam.
preservative (n) **preservation** (n)

president presidents
1 (n) The president of a country without a king or queen is the person who holds the highest political office.
2 (n) The president of a company is the person in charge of it.

Presley, Elvis (1935–1977) was the American rock 'n' roll, ballad singer and film star who became world famous.

press presses pressing pressed
1 (vb) If you press clothes, you iron them.
2 (vb) If you press someone to do something, you try to make them do it.
3 (vb) If you press a switch, you push your finger against it to make it work.
4 (n) The Press is a term used for all the magazines and newspapers that are published.
5 (n) The Press is all the journalists who write for newspapers and magazines.

pressure pressures pressuring pressured
1 (vb) If you pressure someone to do something, you try hard to make them do it.
2 (n) Pressure is the force you create when you press down on something.

presume presumes presuming presumed (vb) If you presume something is true, you think it may be so, even though you have no definite proof. **presumption** (n)

pretend pretends pretending pretended (vb) If you pretend, you make out that something is true when it is not. **pretence** (n)

pretty prettier prettiest
1 (adj) A pretty person is attractive.
2 If you do something pretty well, you do it fairly well.

prevent prevents preventing prevented (vb) If you prevent something, you stop it from happening. **prevention** (n)

previous (adj) The previous time or event is one that happened some time before a similar one occurred. **previously** (n)

prey (n) The animals hunted by other creatures as food are called prey.

price prices
1 (n) The price of something is the money that you pay to buy it.
2 If you want to do something at any price, you will do all you can to succeed.

priceless (adj) Something that is priceless is extremely valuable.

prick pricks pricking pricked
1 (vb) If you prick something you make tiny holes in it with something sharp and pointed.
2 (vb) If something sharp pricks you, it gives you a small stinging pain.
3 If you prick up your ears, you listen carefully.

prickle prickles
1 (n) A prickle is a thorn.
2 (n) Prickles are the sharp spikes on the backs of some creatures such as hedgehogs and sticklebacks.

pride prides priding prided
1 (n) Pride is the feeling of being happy and satisfied when you have done something well.
2 (n) Pride is a feeling of being better than other people.
3 (vb) If you pride yourself on something, you are proud of it.
4 (n) A pride of lions is a group of lions that live together.

priest priests (n) In many religions a priest is a person who leads the worship and advises the congregation.

prim primmer primmest (adj) Someone who is prim behaves very correctly and finds improper behaviour and language shocking.

primary (adj) Something that is primary is most important.

primary colours (n) The primary colours are red, yellow and blue.

colour p53

primary school primary schools (n) In Britain, a primary school is for children from 5 to 11 years old.

prime primes priming primed
1 (vb) If you prime wood, you put a layer of paint called primer on it to make it ready for painting.
2 (vb) If you prime a gun, you prepare it for firing.

3 (n) Your prime is the time of your life when you are at your peak of fitness and ability.

Prime Minister Prime Ministers (n) The Prime Minister is the leader of the government.

prime number prime numbers (n) A prime number is any number greater than one that cannot be divided exactly by any other whole number except for itself and one. *2, 3, 5 and 7 are prime numbers.*

primeval or **primaeval** (adj) Primeval things are extremely old, belonging to the earliest times on our planet.

primitive
1 (adj) A primitive society has no industries but lives very simply by hunting or by growing food.
2 (adj) Something primitive belongs to a very early stage of development.
3 (adj) If you say a house or a hotel is primitive it is rather old-fashioned and without modern conveniences.

primrose primroses (n) A primrose is a small, yellow, sweet-smelling spring flower.

prince princes (n) A prince is a son of a king or queen.

Prince of Wales (n) The title Prince of Wales is given to the eldest son of a British monarch.

princess princesses (n) is the daughter of a king or queen or the wife of a prince.

Princess Royal (n) Princess Royal is a title sometimes given by the King or Queen to their eldest daughter.

principal principals
1 (adj) The principal means the most important. *The principal character in a play . . . his principal interest.*
2 (n) The principal of a school or college is the head or the person in charge.

principle principles
1 (n) Your principles are the things you believe in and the rules that you try to live by.
2 (n) A principle is a general law or rule about how something works.

p

print

print prints printing printed
1 (vb) When words are printed, they are produced in books, magazines, etc in large numbers by a printing machine.
2 (vb) If you print, you write in letters that are not joined up.
3 (n) A print is a machine-made or hand-made copy of a painting.
4 (n) A print is a foot or finger mark.
6 (adj) Something that is printed has a pattern or design on it.

print-out print-outs (n) A print-out is a paper copy of information from a computer.

prior (prep) If something happens prior to something else, it happened before it.

prism prisms (n) A prism is a solid piece of glass or plastic that separates white light into the colours of the rainbow.

colour p53

prison prisons (n) A prison is a building where people who have broken the law are locked up as punishment. **prisoner** (n)

private privates
1 (n) A private is a soldier of the lowest rank in the army.
2 (adj) A private place belongs to a particular person or group and is not open to the public.
3 (adj) Private letters, conversations, discussions, etc are confidential and not for everyone to hear.
4 (adj) A private person is quiet and shy.
5 (adj) Your private life is the life you lead away from your work. **privately** (adv)
privacy (n)

private enterprise (n) is business or industry owned by one person or a group of people and not aided by the government.

privilege privileges (n) A privilege is a right to do something which only certain people are allowed to do.

prize prizes prizing prized
1 (n) A prize is a reward for winning or doing well at something.
2 (vb) If you prize something you value it highly.
3 (adj) You can use prize to emphasise the value or quality of something. *A prize pig . . . a prize idiot.*

probable (adj) If something is probable it is likely to happen. **probably** (adv)
probability (n)

probation
1 (n) If you are on probation you spend a certain time being supervised because you have committed a crime.
2 (n) A person's probation can be a period when they are being tried out to see if they are suitable to continue in a particular job.
probationary (adj)

probe probes probing probed
1 (vb) When doctors or dentists probe they use a sharp instrument to prod and examine their patient.
2 (n) A probe is a long, thin, metal instrument used by doctors and dentists to examine delicate parts of the body.
3 (vb) If you probe you ask questions to discover something.

problem problems (n) A problem is a difficulty.

procedure procedures (n) A procedure is the correct way to do something.

proceed proceeds proceeding proceeded
1 (vb) If you proceed to do something, you go on to do it after you have completed another task.
2 (vb) If you proceed, you move in a particular direction or you continue to do something.
3 (n) Proceeds are the profits made from an event.

process processes processing processed
1 (n) A process is a series of actions which end in one result. *The process of constructing a building is complicated.*
2 (vb) If you process something, you put it through a series of actions to achieve a result.
3 (vb) A computer processes data.

procession processions (n) A procession is a group of people or vehicles moving along a road, usually to mark a special occasion or event.

proclaim proclaims proclaiming proclaimed (vb) If you proclaim something, you announce it publicly.
proclamation (n)

p

produce produces producing produced
1 (vb) If you produce something, you make
it. **production** (n)
2 (vb) If you produce a film, opera or play,
you are responsible for seeing that it is
made or performed.
3 (n) Produce is something which is made
or produced, often vegetables.

producer producers (n) A producer is the
person in charge of putting on a show or
making a film.

product products
1 (n) A product is something which a
country or factory manufactures or grows.
2 (n) A product is the answer to a
multiplication sum. *The product of 4 and 3
is 12.*

profession professions (n) A profession
is a job for which special training and study
are necessary, such as being a lawyer, a
doctor, a teacher or a nurse.
professional (n)

professor professors (n) A professor is a
senior teacher at a university.

proficient (adj) If you are proficient at
something, you are good at it.

profile profiles
1 (n) A person's profile is the side view of
their face.
2 (n) A profile is a description of a person's
character.

profit profits profiting profited
1 (vb) If you profit from something, you
gain an advantage from it.
2 (n) Profit is the money you make when
you trade or buy and sell things.

profound (adj) Something profound is
deep and serious. *This is a profound poem.*

program programs (n) A program is a set
of instructions for a computer which make
it perform certain functions.

programme programmes
1 (n) A programme is an item on television
or radio such as a play, news, etc.
2 (n) A programme is a booklet which tells
you the order of events at a concert, play,
football match, etc.

progress progresses progressing
progressed
1 (n) Progress is a movement forward.
2 (vb) If you progress in your work at
school, you improve. **progression** (n)

prohibit prohibits prohibiting
prohibited (vb) If you prohibit something,
you forbid it. **prohibition** (n)

project projects projecting projected
1 (n) A project is a plan for future activity.
2 (n) A project is a detailed study of
something.
3 (vb) If something projects, it juts out.
4 (vb) If you project your voice, you speak
out clearly so that you can be heard easily.

projector projectors (n) A projector is a
machine used to show films and slides on a
screen or wall.

prolific (adj) If something is prolific, there
is a large amount of it. *She was a prolific
writer; she wrote over a hundred books.*

prolong prolongs prolonging prolonged
(vb) If you prolong something, you make it
last longer.

prominent
1 (adj) If you are a prominent person, you
are very important.
2 (adj) If something is prominent, it is
easily noticed.
prominently (adv) **prominence** (n)

promise promises promising promised
1 (vb) If you promise to do something, you
say you will definitely do it.
2 (n) If you show promise in an activity,
you are likely to become very good at it.
3 (adj) Promising weather, for example,
looks as if it will be sunny.

promote promotes promoting promoted
1 (vb) If a company promotes a product, it
is advertised widely so that it sells well.
2 (vb) If someone promotes you at work,
you move to a better job. **promotion** (n)

prompt prompts prompting prompted
1 (adj) If you are prompt, you do things on
time.
2 (vb) If someone prompts you to do
something, they make you get on and do it.
3 (vb) If you prompt an actor, you tell them
their words if they forget them.

p

prone (adj) If you are prone to colds, you are likely to catch them.

pronoun pronouns (n) A pronoun stands in place of a noun. *She, we and it are pronouns.*

pronounce pronounces pronouncing pronounced
1 (vb) If you pronounce a word, you say it. **pronunciation** (n)
2 (vb) If judges pronounce verdicts in court cases, they give them in a formal way.
3 (adj) If someone has a pronounced accent, it is easily noticed.

proof proofs
1 (n) If you want proof of something, you want facts to show it is true.
2 (n) A proof is a first printed copy of a book, etc so that errors can be put right.

prop props propping propped
1 (vb) If you prop up an object you put it against something for support.
2 (n) A prop is an object or piece of furniture that is used in the theatre or on a film set.

aircraft p5
propeller propellers (n) A propeller on a boat or an aeroplane is two or more blades fixed to a central bar. When the engine starts, the propeller turns round and the boat or plane can move forward.

properly (adv) If you do something properly, you do it correctly. **proper** (adj)

property properties
1 (n) Your property is all the things you own.
2 (n) A property is a house and the land around it.

prophet prophets (n) A prophet is someone who is believed to speak for God.

proportion proportions (n) A proportion of something is part of it.

propose proposes proposing proposed
1 (vb) If you propose a plan, you suggest it. **proposition** (n)
2 (vb) If you propose to someone, you ask them to marry you.
3 (vb) If you propose a toast at a social function, you ask those present to drink to the success of someone or something. **proposal** (n)

prose proses (n) Prose is continuous writing in sentences and paragraphs and contrasts with poetry.

prosecute prosecutes prosecuting prosecuted (vb) If you prosecute someone, you charge them with an offence and make them stand trial. **prosecutor** (n) **prosecution** (n)

prospect prospects prospecting prospected
1 (vb) If you prospect, you search for precious metals.
2 (n) A prospect is a wide view.
3 (n) A prospect is something which may happen in the future. *She was not pleased at the prospect of another spelling test.*

prospectus prospectuses (n) A prospectus is a booklet which describes a business or college.

prosper prospers prospering prospered (vb) If you prosper, you do well at your business and make money. **prosperous** (adj) **prosperity** (n)

protect protects protecting protected (vb) If you protect something, you try to stop it from coming to harm. **protection** (n) **protective** (adj)

protein proteins (n) Protein is an essential part of food, which helps to build up your body.

protest protests protesting protested
1 (vb) If you protest about something, you publicly show your disagreement with it.
2 (n) A protest is a disagreement or objection to something.

Protestant Protestants (n) The Protestants belong to the branches of the Christian church which separated from the Catholic church in the sixteenth century.

prototype prototypes (n) A prototype is the first model of a new machine built to test new ideas.

protractor protractors (n) A protractor is an instrument used to measure and draw angles.

protrude protrudes protruding protruded (vb) Something that protrudes sticks out.

p

proud
1 (adj) If you are proud of something or someone, you are pleased with them.
2 (adj) If someone is proud they are independent and dignified.
3 (adj) A proud person can be arrogant and conceited. **pride** (n)

prove **proves proving proved**
1 (vb) If you prove something, you show that it is true. **proof** (n)
2 (vb) When dough proves, it rises when it is put in a warm place.

proverb **proverbs** (n) A proverb is a short saying which gives advice or tells you something. *Every cloud has a silver lining.*

provide **provides providing provided**
1 (vb) If you provide something, you supply it.
2 If you provide for someone, you make sure they have enough money to live on. **provider** (n)

province **provinces**
1 (n) A province is a part of a country that has its own boundaries and its own administration.
2 (n) The provinces are the parts of the country away from the capital. **provincial** (n)

provisional (adj) If something is provisional, it is temporary.

provisions (n) are supplies of food, water, fuel, etc.

provoke **provokes provoking provoked** (vb) If you provoke someone, you taunt them into an argument or fight. **provocative** (adj) **provocation** (n)

prow **prows** (n) The prow is the front end of a ship.

prowess (n) is skill at anything.

prowl **prowls prowls prowling** (vb) If a person or animal prowls, they creep about in a sinister way trying not to be noticed. **prowler** (n)

proximity (n) The proximity of something is its closeness to something else.

proxy **proxies** (n) If you do something by proxy, you allow someone else to stand in for you.

prudent (adj) A prudent person is careful. **prudence** (n)

prune **prunes pruning pruned**
1 (n) A prune is a dried plum.
2 (vb) If you prune a tree or bush, you shape it to help it to grow well.

pry **pries prying pried** (vb) If you pry, you look inquisitively into other people's business.

psalm **psalms** (n) A psalm is a poem in the old testament of the bible.

psychiatry (n) is the study and treatment of illnesses of the mind. **psychiatrist** (n)

psychic (adj) A person who is psychic claims to have unusual powers to be able to see into the future, know what others are thinking, etc.

psychology (n) is the study of the human mind and the way people behave.

pterodactyl **pterodactyls** (n) A pterodactyl was a flying reptile in prehistoric times.

puberty (n) is the time when children develop into adults.

public
1 (n) People in general are the public.
2 (adj) Public describes anything which belongs to or can be used by people in general. *Public library . . . public baths.*
3 If information is made public, it is announced to everyone, not kept secret.
4 If you are in the public eye, you are a well-known person.

publication **publications** (n) A publication is a book, magazine, etc.

publicity (n) is the business of attracting attention to people, products, etc.

public school **public schools** (n) A public school is a secondary school where students pay fees to attend.

publish **publishes publishing published** (vb) If you publish something, it is printed and put on sale.

pudding **puddings** (n) A pudding is the sweet part of a meal. *Apple pie, ice cream and treacle tart are all puddings.*

p

puddle

puddle puddles (n) A puddle is a small area of liquid, often water, on the surface of the ground.

puff puffs puffing puffed
1 (vb) If you puff, you breathe out air in short, sharp bursts.
2 (n) A puff of air is a short burst.

pugnacious (adj) A pugnacious person is quick to start fighting.

pullet pullets (n) A pullet is a young hen starting to lay eggs.

pulley pulleys (n) A pulley is a piece of machinery with a wheel and chain or rope over it, used for lifting heavy items.

pullover pullovers (n) A pullover is a woollen, long-sleeved jumper put on over the head.

pulpit pulpits (n) A pulpit is a small place above the congregation in a church where the minister or others can talk or pray.

pulse pulses pulsing pulsed
1 (n) The pulse is the regular beat of blood as it moves round the body. You can feel it at points called pulses.
2 (n) A pulse is a series of regular vibrations in a sound wave, etc.
3 (n) Pulses are certain edible seeds such as lentils, red kidney beans, chick peas, etc.

pump pumps pumping pumped
1 (n) A pump is a machine that forces air, gas or liquid out of or into something.
2 (vb) If you pump, you use a pump to force liquid, gas or air out of or into something.
3 (n) Pumps are canvas shoes like plimsolls.

pumpernickel (n) is dark brown bread made from rye.

pumpkin pumpkins (n) A pumpkin is a large, yellow fruit good for making pies and lanterns.

pun puns (n) A pun is a clever way of using words that sound the same but have different meanings. *What did the big 'phone say to the little 'phone? You're too young to be engaged.*

punch punches punching punched
1 (vb) If you punch someone you hit them hard with your fist.
2 (vb) If you punch holes in something, you do it with a punching tool or machine.
3 (n) A punch is a blow with the fist.
4 (n) A punch is a device for making holes in paper, leather, cloth, etc.
5 (n) Punch is a hot drink made from wine or spirits mixed with water, fruits and spices.

punctual (adj) If you are punctual, you arrive at appointments exactly on time.

punctuation (n) refers to all the marks you make to divide a piece of writing into phrases, sentences, etc. Commas, full stops, question marks, etc are punctuation marks.

puncture punctures (n) A puncture is a hole in a tyre or air-bed.

pungent (adj) Something that is pungent has an unpleasantly sharp smell or bitter flavour.

punish punishes punishing punished (vb) If you punish someone, you make them suffer for doing wrong. **punishment** (n)

punk punks
1 (n) Punk is loud rock music that often protests against conventional attitudes in an aggressive way.
2 (n) A punk is someone who likes punk music and who dresses in a way that will shock people.

punt punts punting punted
1 (n) A punt is a long, flat boat moved along by pushing on the river bottom with a long pole.
2 (vb) When you punt, you travel along a river in a punt.

puny punier puniest (adj) Someone who is puny is small and weak.

p

pupa pupae (n) A pupa is an insect that is in the stage of development between a larva and a fully grown adult.

pupil pupils
1 (n) A pupil is someone who goes to a place where they can be taught.
2 (n) The pupil is the small black hole in the centre of the eye.

puppet puppets (n) A puppet is a doll that can be made to move by pulling strings attached to it or by putting your hand inside it.

puppy puppies (n) A puppy is a young dog.

purchase purchases purchasing purchased
1 (vb) If you purchase something you buy it.
2 (n) A purchase is something you buy.

pure purer purest
1 (adj) A substance that is pure is not mixed with anything else.
2 (adj) Pure water or pure air is clean.

puree purees (n) Puree is a food that has been blended or mashed to a very thick liquid.

purify purifying purified (vb) If you purify a substance, you remove the harmful substances from it.

puritan puritans
1 (n) The Puritans were very strict English protestants who opposed the Roman Catholics in the 16th and 17th centuries.
2 (adj) If someone is described as a puritan, they are very strict and disapprove of pleasure and luxury.

purple purples (n) Something purple is a dark, reddish-blue colour.

purpose purposes
1 (n) The purpose of something is the reason for doing it.
2 (n) Your purpose is the thing you are determined to do.
3 If you do something on purpose, you do it deliberately and not by accident.

purr purrs purring purred
1 (vb) When a cat purrs, it makes a low, rumbling sound in its throat to show it is contented.
2 (vb) When a car engine purrs, it makes a low, continuous sound.

purse purses (n) A purse is a small bag for keeping money safe.

pursue pursues pursuing pursued
1 (vb) If you pursue someone, you chase them and search for them.
2 (vb) If you pursue an ambition, you try hard to achieve it.

pus (n) is the thick, yellow liquid that forms in boils or infected wounds.

putrid (adj) If something is putrid it is rotting and smells disgusting.

putt putts putting putted (vb) When you putt in golf, you hit the ball gently towards the hole from a short distance away.
putter (n)

putty (n) is a thick paste used to fix glass into window frames.

puzzle puzzles puzzling puzzled
1 (n) A puzzle is a question, a problem or a game that is difficult to answer or solve.
2 (vb) If you puzzle over something, you think carefully and try to understand it.
3 (adj) If you are puzzled by something or someone, you are slightly confused because you can't understand them.

pyjamas (n) are thin, loose trousers and a jacket for sleeping in.

pylon pylons (n) Pylons are high, metal towers that carry electricity cables.

pyramid pyramids
1 (n) A pyramid is a solid shape with a square or triangular base and sloping sides which meet in a point.
2 (n) The Pyramids are huge, ancient stone monuments built as the tombs of Egyptian kings and queens.

pyre pyres (n) A pyre is a pile of wood on which dead bodies are burned.

pyrotechnics (n) is the making and displaying of fireworks.

python pythons (n) a python is a large snake that kills its prey by coiling around it and crushing it.

p

Qq

quack quacks quacking quacked
1 (vb) Ducks quack when they make a noise.
2 (n) A quack is a person who pretends to be a doctor but is not qualified.

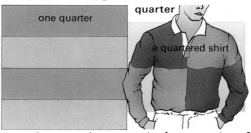
castle p41 **quadrangle** quadrangles (n) A quadrangle is a lawn or yard with buildings on each side.

quadrilateral quadrilaterals (n) A quadrilateral is a flat shape with four straight sides.

quadruped quadrupeds (n) A quadruped is an animal with four legs.

quadruplet quadruplets (n) Quadruplets are four babies born to the same mother at the same time. They are called quads for short.

quagmire quagmires (n) A quagmire is a very boggy, marshy area of land.

quail quails quailing quailed
1 (vb) If you quail, you show fear. *He quailed at the sight of the snarling dogs.*
2 (n) A quail is a small bird of the partridge family.

quaint quainter quaintest (adj) Someone or something that is quaint is old fashioned but charming. **quaintly** (adv) **quaintness** (n)

quake quakes quaking quaked (vb) If you quake, your body shakes with fear.

qualify qualifies qualifying qualified
1 (vb) If you qualify, you successfully complete a training course or you pass exams that enable you to go on to further training.
2 (adj) Someone who is qualified is trained to do a particular job. **qualification** (n)

quality qualities
1 (n) If you talk about the quality of something, you say whether it's good or bad.
2 (n) Your qualities are the characteristics that show what kind of person you are, for example, kindness, a sense of humour, honesty, etc.

qualm qualms (n) A qualm is a feeling of uneasiness and doubt. *I had qualms about inviting all my friends without permission.*

quantity quantities (n) A quantity is an amount of something or a number of things.

quarantine (n) is a period of time which a person or animal has to spend alone to stop the possible spread of disease.

quarrel quarrels quarrelling quarrelled
1 (vb) If you quarrel with someone you have an angry disagreement with them.
2 (n) A quarrel is a row or a violent argument.

quarry quarries
1 (n) A quarry is a place where stone, slate or minerals are dug from the ground.
2 (n) A quarry is a hunted animal. *The leopard stalked its quarry.*

quart quarts (n) A quart is a unit of measurement for liquid. It is the equivalent of 1.14 litres or 2 pints.

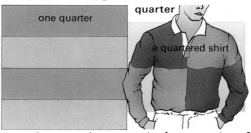

quarter
one quarter
a quartered shirt

quarter quarters quartering quartered
1 (vb) If you quarter something, you divide it into four equal parts.
2 (n) A quarter ($\frac{1}{4}$) is one of four equal parts that something has been divided into.
3 (n) Quarters is a name for living accommodation for the armed forces.

quarterly quarterlies
1 (n) A quarterly is a magazine published four times a year.
2 (Adj) If something happens quarterly, it happens once every three months.

q

quilt

quartet quartets (n) A quartet is a group of four musicians or singers who perform together.

quartz (n) is a hard mineral in crystal form used to make electronic equipment.

quaver quavers quavering quavered
1 (vb) If your voice quavers, it shakes because you are nervous or frightened.
2 (n) A quaver is a musical note ♪. It is half the value of a crotchet.

quay quays (n) A quay is a wall of a harbour which forms a platform by the water. Boats tie up at a quay to unload and load cargo.

queen queens
1 (n) A queen is a woman crowned as the sovereign of a country.
2 (n) A queen is the wife of a crowned king.
3 (n) The queen is a piece in a chess set.
4 (n) The queen is the large ant, bee, or wasp that lays eggs in an insect colony.

queer queerer queerest
1 (adj) Something or somebody that is queer is strange, curious or odd.
2 If you feel queer you feel unwell.

quell quells quelling quelled
1 (vb) If you quell a disturbance or a riot, you stop it.
2 (vb) If you quell feelings of anger, excitement, etc, you try not to show them.

quench quenches quenching quenched
1 (vb) If you quench your thirst, you have a drink to stop yourself being thirsty.
2 (vb) If you quench a fire, you put it out.

query queries querying queried
1 (vb) If you query something, you question whether it's true or not.
2 (n) A query is a question or an enquiry.

quest quests (n) A quest is a long and often difficult search for something that you value.

question questions questioning questioned
1 (vb) If you question someone, you ask them a lot of questions.
2 (vb) If you question something, you are not sure that it is correct.
3 (n) A question is something that you ask about in words or writing.

question mark question marks (n) A question mark (?) is the punctuation mark at the end of a sentence that asks a question. *Are you coming home?*

questionnaire questionnaires (n) A questionnaire is a list of questions to be answered by people taking part in a survey or census.

queue queues queuing queued
1 (n) A queue is a line of people or vehicles waiting for something.
2 (vb) If you queue, you wait in a line for something.

quiche quiches (n) A quiche is a savoury open tart of eggs, cheese, bacon, etc.

quick quicker quickest (adj)
1 (adj) If someone or something is quick they move with speed. **quickly** (adv)
2 (adj) If something is quick, it is soon finished. *A quick meal.*
3 (adj) A quick person is mentally bright or clever.

quicksand quicksands (n) A quicksand is dangerously soft, wet sand which you can sink into if you walk on it.

quiet quieter quietest
1 (adj) Someone or something that is quiet makes very little noise.
2 (adj) If a place such as a cinema or shop is quiet, then few people are using it.
3 If you keep quiet, you say nothing.
4 If you do something on the quiet, you do it without anyone knowing.

quill quills
1 (n) A quill is a long, strong feather, once used to make pens.
2 (n) A quill is a long spine on an animal such as a porcupine.

quilt quilts (n) A quilt is a soft, warm bed cover, filled with feathers, down, etc.

q

quintuplet quintuplets (n) Quintuplets are five babies born to the same mother at the same time. They are called quins for short.

quintet quintets (n) A quintet is a group of five musicians.

quit quits quitting quit
1 (vb) If you quit, you give up.
2 If two people are quits, they are even and owe each other nothing.

quite
1 (adv) Quite means rather. *Quite a lot of apples were rotten.*
2 (adv) Quite can also mean completely. *I quite agree.*
3 If someone says 'quite', they agree with you.

quiver quiver quivering quivered
1 (vb) If someone or something quivers, they shake slightly but quickly.
2 (n) A quiver is a case to hold arrows.

quiz quizzes quizzing quizzed
1 (vb) If you quiz someone about something, you question them closely.
2 (n) A quiz is a competition where people are asked questions to test their knowledge.

Qur'an see **Koran**

quota quotas (n) A quota is a certain amount of something that is allowed. *That is your quota of books for this term.*

quotation mark quotation marks (n) Quotation marks are punctuation marks which show where written speech begins and ends. *'No,' she said, 'I'm not going with you.'*

quote quotes quoting quoted
1 (vb) If you quote someone, you write or repeat exactly what they have said or written. **quotation** (n)
2 (vb) If someone quotes a price for something, they say what it will cost.

Rr

rabbi rabbis (n) A rabbi is a Jewish religious leader or teacher.

rabbit rabbits (n) A rabbit is a furry, wild animal with long ears. Some breeds of rabbit are kept as pets.

race races racing raced
1 (vb) If people or animals race, they compete to see which is the fastest.
2 (n) A race is a competition to see who is fastest.
3 (n) A race is one of the major groups of people who share the same physical characteristics, such as skin colour, facial features, etc.

racism (n) is the treatment of some people as inferior because they belong to a particular race. **racist** (n)

racket rackets
1 (n) A racket is a bat for hitting a ball in squash, tennis, etc.
2 (n) If you make a racket, you make a lot of noise.

radar (n) is a system used by aircraft, ships, etc. for detecting objects and their speeds, by radio waves which leave an image on a screen.

radiant
1 (adj) If something is radiant, it shines and sparkles brightly.
2 (adj) If a person is radiant, they look beautiful because they are so happy. **radiance** (n)

radiate radiates radiating radiated
1 (vb) Things that radiate come out in lines from a central point, for example the spokes of a wheel.
2 (vb) If a light or fire radiates, it gives out light or heat.

radiation
1 (n) Radiation is caused by the very small particles of radioactive substances that can cause illness and death.
2 (n) Radiation is also the heat which comes from a source such as the sun.

q

radiator radiators
1 (n) A radiator is a metal container filled with water, steam, or oil, for heating rooms.
2 (n) A radiator is a device for keeping engines cool.

radio radios radioing radioed
1 (n) A radio is an electrical device used to receive programmes from a radio station.
2 (n) A radio is a piece of equipment that can send out and receive radio signals.
3 (vb) If you radio someone, you send them a message by radio.

radioactive (adj) Something that is radioactive gives off rays which can be harmful.

radiography (n) is X-ray photography, especially for medical use.

the Mark 1A **radio telescope** at Jodrell Bank, near Manchester

radio telescope radio telescopes (n) A radio telescope is a device for receiving radio waves from space.

radish radishes (n) A radish is a small, round, salad vegetable, with a strong, hot taste.

radius radii (n) A radius is a straight line drawn from the centre of a circle to the edge.

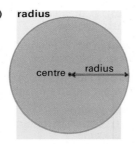

radius

centre ← radius →

raffle raffles (n) A raffle is a competition in which people buy numbered tickets. If their ticket is picked they win the prize.

raft rafts (n) A raft is a flat platform that floats.

rafter rafters (n) A rafter is one of the thick beams which hold up a roof.

rage rages
1 (n) A rage is a violent fit of anger.
2 If something is all the rage, it is very fashionable or popular.

raid raids raiding raided
1 (n) A raid is a sudden attack.
2 (vb) If police raid a place, they enter it by force to search for someone or something.

railing railings (n) Railings are a series of metal bars that make up a fence.

railway railways (n) A railway is a means of carrying passengers and goods using trains running on rails.

rain rains raining rained
1 (n) Rain is water that falls as small drops from the sky.
2 (vb) When it rains, small drops of water fall from the clouds.

rainbow rainbows (n) A rainbow is an arch of different colours that sometimes appears in the sky when the sun shines through rain.

colour p53

raise raises raising raised
1 (vb) If you raise something, you lift it to a higher level.
2 (vb) If you raise money, you find ways of obtaining it.
3 (vb) If you raise a child or an animal, you care for them as they grow up.

raisin raisins (n) A raisin is a dried grape.

r

rally

rally rallies rallying rallied
1 (n) A rally is a large public meeting, often for a political purpose.
2 (n) A rally is a car race.
3 (vb) If someone rallies during an illness they begin to get better.
4 (vb) If people rally round they get together to support each other.

Ramadan (n) During the month of Ramadan, Muslims over the age of ten go without food and drink during the hours of daylight.

ramble rambles rambling rambled
1 (n) A ramble is a long country walk.
2 (vb) If you ramble, you talk for a long time and muddle your ideas.
3 (vb) If plants ramble, they grow in all directions.

ramp ramps
1 (n) A ramp is a slope that joins two different levels.
2 (n) Ramps are small bumps placed in the road used to slow the traffic.

castle p41

rampart ramparts (n) Ramparts are the banks or walls built to protect a castle.

ramshackle (adj) A ramshackle building is badly built or not looked after properly.

ranch ranches (n) A ranch is a farm in America where cattle are reared.

rancid (adj) If butter, milk, etc are rancid, they go bad and taste unpleasant because they are old.

random (adj) Something that is random is done by chance, without any reason or planning.

range ranges ranging ranged
1 (vb) If something ranges, it varies between two limits. *Our prices range from 20 to 200.*
2 (n) A range is a selection or choice of goods of a similar type. *The shop sold a wide range of sports goods.*
3 (vb) If someone ranges, they wander about. *He ranged the desert looking for oil.*
4 (n) A range of hills or mountains is a long line of them.
5 (n) A range is a place where guns can be fired.
6 (n) A range is an old-fashioned cooker.

ranger rangers (n) A ranger is a person who works in a wildlife park, etc.

rank ranks
1 (n) A rank is a position in one of the armed forces, or similar organisation. *He rose to the rank of colonel.*
2 (n) A rank is a place where taxis wait for customers.
3 (adj) Something rank is rotting and smells unpleasant.

ransack ransacks ransacking ransacked (vb) If you ransack a place, you make a mess because you are searching for something.

ransom ransoms (n) A ransom is the money paid to kidnappers so that they release their victim.

rap raps rapping rapped
1 (vb) If you rap something, you tap it sharply.
2 (n) Rap is a style of pop music which involves talking and rhyming to a strong beat.

rapid rapids
1 (adj) Something which is rapid, is fast.
2 (n) Rapids are parts of a river where the water moves very fast, often over rocks.

rapier rapiers (n) A rapier is a thin sword.

rapture raptures
1 (n) Rapture is a state of great excitement and pleasure.
2 If you go into raptures about something, you talk about it with great enthusiasm.

rare
1 (adj) Something rare is very uncommon.
rarity (n)
2 (adj) A piece of meat which is rare is very lightly cooked.

rarely (adv) If something happens rarely, it doesn't happen very often.

rascal rascals (n) A rascal is someone who is naughty or mischievous.

rash rashes
1 (n) A rash is a patch of small spots on your skin.
2 (adj) If someone is rash, they rush into things without thinking properly.
3 (adj) A rash action or decision is one that is done without proper thought.

r

rasher rashers (n) A rasher is a slice of bacon.

rasp rasps rasping rasped
1 (vb) If a cat licks you for example, its tongue is rough and rasps you.
2 (n) A rasp is a tool used to smooth wood.
3 (adj) A rasping noise is harsh and grating.

Rastafarian Rastafarians (n) A Rastafarian is a member of a religious sect which was started in Jamaica.

rat rats (n) A rat is a rodent like a large mouse.

rate rates rating rated
1 (n) The rate is the speed at which something happens.
2 (n) A rate is an amount of money charged for something.
3 (n) Rates were taxes people pay for services such as water, education, roads, etc. The rates have now been replaced with the community charge.
4 (vb) If you rate someone or something, you make a judgement about their quality or ability.

rather
1 (adv) Rather means fairly or to a certain extent. *It is rather cold today.*
2 (adv) If you would rather do or have something, you would prefer to have or do it.
3 Rather than means instead of. *I chose pizza rather than chips.*

ratio ratios (n) The ratio between two things shows how much one is greater than the other. *The pupil/teacher ratio is 25 to 1.*

ration rations rationing rationed
1 (vb) If you ration something, you share it out by giving a very small amount at one time.
2 (n) A ration of something is an allowance of it.

rational (adj) A rational person is sensible and clear thinking.

rattle rattles rattling rattled
1 (n) A rattle is a series of short, clicking noises.
2 (n) A rattle is a baby's toy which makes a noise when it is shaken.
3 (vb) If something rattles, it makes a series of short, sharp noises.

rattlesnake rattlesnakes (n) A rattesnake is a poisonous American snake which can rattle its tail.

raucous (adj) A raucous noise is harsh and loud.

ravage ravages ravaging ravaged (vb) If something or someone ravages something, they cause serious damage and almost destroy it. *Starvation and disease had ravaged the population.*

rave raves raving raved
1 (vb) If you rave about something, you talk very enthusiastically about it.
2 (vb) If someone raves, they talk loudly and angrily.
3 (adj) If you say that someone is raving, you mean they are crazy.

raven ravens (n) A raven is a large, black bird of the crow family.

ravenous (adj) If a person or animal is ravenous, they are extremely hungry.
ravenously (adv)

ravine ravines (n) A ravine is a very narrow valley with steep sides.

raw rawer rawest
1 (adj) Raw food has not been cooked.
2 (adj) Raw substances are in their natural state and have not been processed in any way. *Raw sugar . . . raw timber.*
3 (adj) A raw place on the body is one where the skin has been rubbed or scraped off.
4 (adj) If the weather is raw, it is painfully cold and damp.

ray rays
1 (n) A ray is a narrow band of heat or light.
2 (n) A ray is a very large, flat sea fish with a long tail.

rayon (n) is a smooth, silky fabric made from cotton, wool or synthetic materials.

raze razes razing razed (vb) If people raze forests or buildings, they totally destroy them.

razor razors (n) A razor is an instrument used for shaving areas of skin.

r

reach

reach reaches reaching reached
1 (vb) If you reach for something, you stretch out your arm to get it.
2 (vb) If someone or something reaches a place, they arrive there.
3 (vb) If you reach a decision, you decide to do something.
4 (n) The reach of someone or something is the distance they are able to stretch or travel.

react reacts reacting reacted
1 (vb) If a person reacts to something, they behave in a certain way because of it. *He reacts to criticism by getting angry.*
2 (vb) If a person reacts to a medicine or drug, they are allergic to it, and may become ill. **reaction** (n)

reactionary reactionaries (n) A reactionary is a person who is against change, and tries to stop it.

read reads reading read
1 (vb) If you can read, you can look at written or printed words and understand them.
2 (vb) When someone reads a measuring device, for example a gas meter, they look at it and note the figure it shows.

reader readers.
1 (n) A reader is someone who reads.
2 (n) A reader is a machine that can read a text so that it can be stored in a computer.

ready readier readiest
1 (adj) If someone or something is ready, they are prepared to do or begin something.
2 (adj) If you keep something ready, you keep it close to use quickly.

real
1 (adj) Someone or something real actually exists. **reality** (n)
2 (adj) If something is real, it is genuine and not a fake.

realistic (adj) Something realistic is like the real thing.

realise realises realising realised.
1 (vb) If you realise something, you become aware of it or understand it.
2 (vb) If you realise an ambition, you achieve it. **realisation** (n)

really (adj) or (adv) Really is used to emphasise a point. *She was really beautiful. I wanted to know if he was really joking.*

reap reaps reaping reaped (vb) When farmers reap corn, etc they cut it and collect it.

rear rears rearing reared
1 (n) The rear of something is the back of it.
2 (vb) If you rear animals, etc you look after them as they grow up.
3 (vb) If an animal rears, it raises its front legs off the ground.

reason reasons reasoning reasoned
1 (n) A reason is an explanation or cause for something happening.
2 (vb) If you reason, you think things out carefully.
3 (n) If you see reason, you decide to behave in a sensible way.

reasonable
1 (adj) A reasonable person behaves in a sensible way.
2 (adj) If something is reasonable, it is fair and moderate.

reassure reassures reassuring reassured (vb) If you reassure someone, you try to calm their fears and comfort them. **reassurance** (n)

rebel rebels rebelling rebelled
1 (n) A rebel is a person who fights against authority.
2 (vb) If you rebel, you fight against the authority of those who are governing you.

recall recalls recalling recalled (vb) If you recall something you remember it.

recede recedes receding receded (vb) If something recedes, it moves backwards or away from you.

receipt receipts (n) A receipt is a slip of paper given to you as proof that you have paid for something.

receive receives receiving received
1 (vb) If you receive something, you get it when it is given or sent to you.
2 (vb) A radio or television receives signals and changes them into sounds or pictues.

recent (adj) A recent event is something which happened a short while ago.
recently (adv)

receptacle receptacles (n) A receptacle is a container of some sort.

reception receptions
1 (n) Reception in a public building is the area where enquiries are made.
2 (n) A reception is a formal party to welcome guests or to celebrate something important.
3 (n) The reception on your radio or television is the quality of the sound or picture.

recipe recipes (n) A recipe is a list of instructions and ingredients to make a particular dish.

recite recites reciting recited (vb) If you recite something, you say it aloud from memory.

reckless (adj) A reckless person behaves with little care and takes risks.

recline reclines reclining reclined (vb) If you recline, you lie or lean backwards.

recluse recluses (n) A recluse is a person who is rarely seen and does not like company.

recognise recognises recognising recognised (vb) If you recognise someone or something, you realise that you know them or have seen them before.
recognition (n)

recoil recoils recoiling recoiled (vb) If you recoil, you draw back from something or someone in shock or horror.

recollect recollects recollecting recollected (vb) If you recollect something, you remember it. **recollection** (n)

recommend recommends recommending recommended (vb) If you recommend someone or something, you praise them to other people.
recommendation (n)

reconcile reconciles reconciling reconciled
1 (vb) If you reconcile two people, you help them to be friends again after an argument.
reconciliation (n)
2 (vb) If you reconcile yourself to something, you accept it even though you do not totally agree with it.

recondition reconditions reconditioning reconditioned (vb) If you recondition something, you put it back into good working order.

reconnaissance (n) is the gathering of information about an enemy using small groups of soldiers, planes or satellites, etc.

reconnoitre reconnoitres reconnoitring reconnoitred (vb) If you reconnoitre a place, you check it carefully before going into it.

reconsider reconsiders reconsidering reconsidered (vb) If you reconsider an idea, you think again about it.

reconstruct reconstructs reconstructing reconstructed (vb) If you reconstruct something that has been damaged, you build it again.
reconstruction (n)

record records recording recorded
1 (vb) If you record something, you write it down so that it is not forgotten.
2 (vb) If you record something, you make a copy of it on audiotape, videotape, C.D. etc.
3 (n) A record is a written account of things that have happened.
4 (n) A record is a flat disc used to record music and sound.
5 (n) A record is an achievement, in athletics for example, which is the best of its type.
6 (n) A recording is a tape, disc, etc which contains music, pictures, information, etc.

recorder recorders
1 (n) A recorder is a wind instrument.
2 (n) A recorder is any machine which copies music, pictures, information, etc.
3 (n) A recorder is a person who writes accounts of events.

recount recounts recounting recounted
1 (vb) If you recount a story, you tell it to someone.
2 (n) A recount is a second counting of something, especially votes in an election.

recover recovers recovering recovered
1 (vb) If you recover something, you get it back after having it stolen or losing it.
2 (vb) You recover when you get better after an illness. **recovery** (n)

r

recreation

recreation recreations (n) Recreation is all the things you do in your free time for enjoyment.

recruit recruits recruiting recruited
1 (vb) If you recruit someone, you persuade them to join an organisation.
2 (n) A recruit is a new member of an organisation.

rectangle rectangles (n) A rectangle is a four sided shape with opposite sides of equal length, and four right angles.

recuperate recuperates recuperating recuperated (vb) If you recuperate, you recover after an illness. **recuperation** (n)

recur recurs recurring recurred (vb) Something which recurs keeps happening. **recurrence** (n)

red reds (n) Something red is the colour of blood. Red is one of the primary colours.

Red Cross (n) The Red Cross is an organisation which aims to help people who are suffering as a result of wars, disasters, etc.

redeem redeems redeeming redeemed
1 (vb) If you redeem an item, you claim it back from someone.
2 (adj) A redeeming feature is something that makes up for the bad things about a person or thing.

reduce reduces reducing reduced
1 (vb) If you reduce something, you make it smaller in size.
2 (vb) If you reduce prices, they are cheaper than they were.
3 (vb) If something reduces you to a certain state, it brings you to that state. *She reduced the boy to tears by cruel jokes.*
reduction (n)

redundant
1 (adj) If someone is redundant, they have lost their job.
2 (adj) Something that is redundant is no longer needed.

reed reeds
1 (n) Reeds are plants which grow near water.
2 (n) A reed is the thin piece of cane or metal which makes the sound in woodwind instruments.

reef reefs (n) A reef is a line of rocks, coral, etc just below or above the sea's surface.

reel reels reeling reeled
1 (n) A reel is a cylinder onto which things such as film or fishing line can be wound.
2 (n) A reel is a Scottish dance.
3 (vb) If you reel, you move in a very unsteady way.
4 (vb) If your mind reels, you feel muddled and confused.

refer refers referring referred
1 (vb) If you refer to something, you mention it when you are speaking or writing.
2 (vb) If you refer to something such as an encyclopaedia, you look in it for information.
3 (vb) If a doctor refers you to a hospital etc., they send you there for treatment.
4 (vb) If something refers to something else, they are connected in some way. *The letters NZ refer to New Zealand.*

referee referees refereeing refereed
1 (vb) Someone who referees a match, supervises it to ensure that the rules are kept.
2 (n) A referee is a person who gives you a reference when you apply for jobs, etc.

reference references
1 (n) A reference is a document written by someone who knows you, which describes your character and abilities.
2 (n) A reference is a mention of someone or something in a speech or piece of writing.
3 (n) A reference book is a book which contains factual information.

refill refills refilling refilled
1 (vb) If you refill something, you fill it up again.
2 (n) A refill is a container filled with a substance to replace an empty one.

refine refines refining refined
1 (vb) If you refine a raw material such as oil or sugar, you process it in order to remove impurities.
2 (adj) A refined person is very polite and well mannered.

reflect reflects reflecting reflected
1 (vb) When rays of light or heat reflect, they bounce back from an object. *The sea reflects the light from the sun.*
2 (vb) When something such as a mirror reflects something, it shows images of it.
3 (vb) When you reflect on something, you think about it carefully.
reflection (n)

reflex reflexes
1 (n) A reflex is an uncontrollable movement of the body caused by a blow to a particular nerve.
2 (n) If your reflexes are good, you are able to react very quickly to an unexpected situation.

reform reforms reforming reformed
1 (n) A reform is an improvement to such things as the law, the church, etc.
2 (vb) If institutions such as the government reform schools, they improve them.
3 (vb) When someone reforms, they improve their behaviour.

refrain refrains refraining refrained
1 (vb) If you refrain from doing something, you don't do it.
2 (n) A refrain is a chorus of a song.

refresh refreshes refreshing refreshed
1 (vb) Something that refreshes you when you are hot or thirsty makes you feel cool and fresh again.
2 (adj) Something or someone that is refreshing gives you new energy and zest.

refreshments (n) are drinks and snacks.

refrigerate refrigerates refrigerating refrigerated (vb) If you refrigerate food, you store it at a low temperature in order to preserve it. **refrigeration** (n) **refrigerator** (n)

refuel refuels refuelling refuelled (vb) When an aircraft, ship, etc. refuels. Its tanks are filled with more fuel.

refuge refuges
1 (n) A refuge is a place where you go for safety and protection.
2 (n) A refuge is a place such as a hostel where people who are homeless or in trouble can live for a while.

refugee refugees (n) A refugee is a person who has been forced to leave his or her own country due to war, persecution or disaster.

refund refunds refunding refunded
1 (vb) If you refund money, you return it to the person who gave it to you.
2 (n) A refund is money paid back to someone because they have paid too much, or because the goods bought were unsuitable.

refuse refuses refusing refused.
1 (vb) If you refuse to do something, you will not do it.
2 (n) Refuse is all the waste and rubbish from a home, factory, etc.

regatta regattas (n) A regatta is a race meeting for sailing and rowing boats.

reggae (n) is a type of music originally from the West Indies which has a strong and distinctive rhythm.

regiment regiments (n) A regiment is a large group of soldiers under a colonel's command.

region regions
1 (n) A region is a large area of a country with particular features. *A hilly region.*
2 If a price is in the region of £10,000, for example, it is roughly this amount.

register registers registering registered
1 (n) A register is a book for recording names, births, deaths, marriages, etc.
2 (vb) If you register a birth, death, etc you give all the details so that they are recorded officially.
3 (vb) If you register a letter, you pay extra money above the stamp price, to guarantee its delivery.

registrar registrars
1 (n) A registrar is a person whose job is to keep official records of births, marriages, deaths, etc.
2 (n) A registrar is a senior hospital doctor.

registry office registry offices (n) A registry office is a building where official records are kept, and where people can be married.

r

regret

regret **regrets regretting regretted**
1 (vb) If you regret something, you have done, you wish you had not done it.
2 (n) If you have regrets about something, you feel sad about it and wish it had not happened. **regrettable** (adj)

regular
1 (adj) Regular events happen according to a particular pattern. **regularity** (n)
2 (adj) Regular describes something with an even or fixed pattern.

regulate **regulates regulating regulated**
(vb) If you regulate something, you control it.

regulation **regulations** (n) A regulation is a rule or a law.

rehearse **rehearses rehearsing rehearsed** (vb) If you rehearse a play, etc, you practise it. **rehearsal** (n)

reign **reigns reigning reigned** (n) The reign of a king or queen is the time they spend ruling a country.

rein **reins**
1 (n) Reins are thin straps fixed to a horse's bridle, or to a child's harness, in order to control them.
2 If someone gives you free rein, they allow you to make your own decisions.

reindeer (n) are deer that live in cold parts of the northern hemisphere.

reject **rejects rejecting rejected**
1 (vb) If you reject something, you throw it away or refuse to accept it because it is not good enough or not suitable.
2 (n) A reject is an object which has been rejected.

rejoice **rejoices rejoicing rejoiced** (vb) If you rejoice, you show feelings of great happiness about something.

relate **relates relating related**
1 (vb) If you relate a story, you tell it.
2 (vb) If you connect two ideas, you relate them.
3 (adj) People who are related belong to the same family. **relation** (n)

relationship **relationships** (n) A relationship is the way in which two people or groups get along with one another.

relative **relatives**
1 (n) A relative is a member of your family.
2 (adj) You use relative when you compare two people or things according to size or characteristics, for example. *They discussed the relative merits of the new teachers.*

relax **relaxes relaxing relaxed**
1 (vb) When you relax or something relaxes you, you feel more calm and less worried.
2 (vb) If you relax, you stop work and enjoy your free time. **relaxation** (n)
3 (vb) If you relax rules, you make them less strict.

relay **relays relaying relayed**
1 (vb) If you relay something, you pass it from one person to the next.
2 (n) A relay is a race between two or more teams of runners or swimmers, etc. Each member runs or swims one section of the race.

relent **relents relenting relented** (vb) If you relent, you give way on something you have been firm about.

relevant (adj) Something which is relevant has an important connection with something else. *Your experience is quite relevant to this job.* **relevance** (n)

reliable (adj) Someone or something reliable can be trusted and will not let you down.

relic **relics** (n) A relic is something left over from a former time. *Roman relics were found on the sea-bed.*

relief
1 (n) Relief is the ending of pain, discomfort, worry, etc.
2 (n) Relief is the aid that people give to others who are suffering.
3 (adj) A relief map shows hills and valleys.

relieve **relieves relieving relieved.**
1 (vb) If you relieve someone you take away their pain, worry, etc.
2 (vb) If you relieve someone, you take over their job for a while.

religion **religions** (n) Religion is a set of beliefs about God or Gods and the way they should be worshipped.

relish relishes relishing relished (vb) If you relish something you really enjoy it and welcome it. *I relish the chance to get on a bike again.*

reluctant (adj) If you are reluctant to do something you are unwilling to do it. **reluctance** (n)

rely relies relying relied (vb) If you rely on someone or something, you trust and depend on them. **reliance** (n)

remain remains remaining remained
1 (vb) If you remain somewhere, you stay there.
2 (vb) If something remains, it is left over after everything else has gone. **remainder** (n)
3 (n) Remains are the things left over when something is destroyed or dies.

remarkable (adj) Something remarkable is worth noticing or unusual.

remedy remedies remedying remedied
1 (vb) If you remedy something, you put it right.
2 (n) A remedy is a medicine or a cure for an illness.
3 (n) A remedy is a course of action which will put right a mistake.

remember remembers remembering remembered (vb) If you remember someone or something, you keep it in your mind or recall it.

Remembrance Day (n) is held on the Sunday nearest to the eleventh of November to remember the people who died in two world wars.

remind reminds reminding reminded
1 (vb) If you remind someone of something, you help them to remember it.
2 (vb) If something reminds you of something, it seems similar to it in some way.

reminder reminders (n) A reminder is anything which jogs your memory.

remnant remnants (n) A remnant is a piece of anything left over.

remorse (n) is the feeling of regret for some wrong you have done.

remote
1 (adj) Somewhere remote is far away from cities and towns.
2 (adj) Remote can mean far away in time.
3 (adj) A person who is remote keeps apart from other people.
4 (adj) If something is remote controlled, it can be controlled from a distance.

removal removals
1 (n) The removal of something is the act of taking it away from a place. *The removal of the wrecked car.*
2 (n) A removal van is a large van for transporting household goods when people move.

removes removes removing removed
1 (vb) If you remove something, you take it from its place.
2 (vb) If someone removes their clothes, they take them off.
3 (vb) If you remove a stain or blemish on something, you get rid of it.

render renders rendering rendered
1 (vb) If you render someone or something helpless, harmless, etc., they are made helpless or harmless.
2 (vb) If you render someone assistance, you help them.
3 (vb) If you render a wall, you cover it with a protective layer of cement.

rendezvous (n) A rendezvous is an arranged meeting between people, or their meeting place.

renew renews renewing renewed
1 (vb) If you renew something such as a piece of equipment, you replace it with a new one or new parts.
2 (vb) If you renew a library book, membership, etc you arrange for it to be valid for a longer period. **renewal** (n)

renovate renovates renovating renovated (vb) When you renovate something, you restore it to a good condition. **renovation** (n)

renown (n) is fame. *Her renown came from her success as a runner.*

rent

rent rents renting rented
1 (vb) If you rent something, a house, T.V. etc. you pay the owner to use it.
2 (n) Rent is the amount of money you pay to use something belonging to someone else.

repair repairs repairing repaired (vb) If you repair something you mend it.

repay repays repaying repaid
1 (vb) If you repay money, you pay it back to the person who lent it to you.
2 (vb) If someone does you a favour, you repay them by by doing something for them.

repeat repeats repeating repeated
1 (vb) If you repeat something, you say it or do it again. **repeatedly** (adv)
2 (vb) If you repeat something that you have been told as a secret, you tell it to someone else.

repel repels repelling repelled
1 (vb) If something repels you, it disgusts you.
2 (vb) In a battle if one group of fighters repels another group, they drive them back.

repellent repellents
1 (adj) Someone or something repellent is disgusting and loathsome.
2 (n) A repellent is a chemical used to keep away unwanted pests. *Fly repellent, slug repellent, etc.*

repent repents repenting repented (vb) If you repent, you show you are sorry for something you have done wrong. **repentance** (n)

repertory (adj) A repertory theatre performs several plays in a season, using the same group of actors.

repetition repetitions (n) A repetition is a repeat of something said or done.

replace replaces replacing replaced.
1 (vb) If you replace something that is broken or missing, you put another one in its place.
2 (vb) If someone or something replaces another person or thing, they take their place.
3 (vb) If you replace something, you put it back in its place.

replacement replacements (n) A replacement is a person or thing that takes the place of another. **replaceable** (adj)

replica replicas (n) A replica is an exact copy of something.

reply replies replying replied
1 (vb) If you reply when someone speaks to you, you answer them; if you reply to a letter, you write back to answer it.
2 (n) A reply is a spoken or written answer.

report reports reporting reported
1 (vb) If you report something, you inform someone about it.
2 (vb) If you report someone, you complain about them.
3 (vb) If you report to someone, you see them because you have been told to do so.
4 (n) A report is a spoken or written account of something that has happened.
5 (n) A report is a special document drawn up by a group of people appointed to investigate something.
6 (n) A school report is a document written by teachers to inform parents of their child's progress.
7 (n) A report is a loud noise made when a gun is fired.

reporter reporters (n) A reporter is someone whose job is to find out and report what is happening in the world for newspapers, T.V., radio, etc.

represent represents representing represented
1 (vb) If you represent a person or group, you act on their behalf. *He represented the union at the meeting.*
2 (vb) If something represents another thing, it is a symbol or image of it. *His mask represents a dragon.*
3 (vb) If a picture represents something, it gives an image of it. *The picture represented the Battle of Waterloo.*

representative representatives
1 (n) A representative is a person who talks or works on behalf of other people.
2 (adj) A group of people who are representative are typical of a larger group.

repress represses repressing repressed
1 (vb) If you repress emotions, you try hard not to show them.
2 (vb) If you repress other people, you do not allow them to express their views.

reprieve reprieves (n) A reprieve is an official order stopping someone's punishment.

reprimand reprimands reprimanding reprimanded (vb) If you reprimand someone, you speak or write to them disapprovingly about something they have done wrong.

reproduce reproduces reproducing reproduced
1 (vb) If you reproduce something, you make a copy of it.
2 (vb) If people or animals reproduce, they produce young. **reproduction** (n)

reptile reptiles (n) A reptile is a cold-blooded, egg-laying animal. Snakes and lizards are reptiles.

republic republics (n) A republic is a country or state with no king or queen and which elects its government.

repulse repulses repulsing repulsed (vb) If something repulses you, it disgusts you and you want to avoid it. **repulsive** (adj)

reputation reputations (n) Your reputation is the opinion that others have of you.

request requests requesting requested (vb) If you request something, you ask for it.

require requires requiring required (vb) If you require something, you need it. **requirement** (n)

rescue rescues rescuing rescued
1 (vb) If you rescue someone or something, you save them from danger.
2 (n) A rescue is a successful attempt to save someone from danger.

research researches researching researched
1 (vb) If you research something, you study or investigate it carefully.
2 (n) Research is a detailed study of a subject.

resemble resembles resembling resembled (vb) If someone or something resembles another, they are like each other.

resent resents resenting resented (vb) If you resent someone or something, you feel bitter about them. **resentful** (adj)

reserve reserves reserving reserved
1 (vb) If you reserve something, you arrange for it to be kept for you.
2 (n) If you have a reserve of something, you have a stock of it.
3 (n) If you are a reserve in a team, you play if one of the other members cannot.
4 (n) A reserve is a place where animals can roam free and safely breed.
5 (adj) A reserved person does not show their feelings easily.

reservoir reservoirs (n) A reservoir is a natural or artificial lake where water is stored.

hydro electricity p142

reside resides residing resided (vb) If you reside somewhere, you live there.

resign resigns resigning resigned
1 (vb) If you resign from your job, you give it up.
2 (adj) If you are resigned to something unpleasant, you accept it without complaining. **resignation** (n)

resist resists resisting resisted
1 (vb) If you resist something, you try to stop it happening.
2 (vb) If you resist a violent attack, you fight back. **resistance** (n)

resolute (adj) A resolute person is strong and determined.

resolve resolves resolving resolved
1 (vb) If you resolve to do something, you make up your mind firmly to do it.
2 (n) Resolve is the determination to do something.

resort resorts resorting resorted
1 (vb) If you resort to a way of doing things, you do so because you cannot think of any other way of doing it.
2 (n) A resort is a town, usually by the sea, where people go for their holidays.
3 If you do something as a last resort, you do it after all other options have been tried.

resound resounds resounding resounded
1 (vb) If a noise resounds, it echoes loudly, round and round.
2 (adj) A resounding sound is long and loud.
3 (adj) A resounding blow is a very hard blow.
4 (adj) A resounding success, victory, etc is a very definite one.

resource resources
1 (n) An organisation's resources are the things which it uses in its work.
2 (n) A resource is something of value a country has, such as coal or oil which can be utilised to make the country wealthy.
3 (n) A person's resources are their own abilities.

respect respects respecting respected
1 (vb) If you respect someone, you admire them.
2 (vb) If you respect someone's privacy, rights, etc you leave them alone or treat them as they wish to be treated.
3 (vb) If you respect someone's opinion, you listen to them although you may not agree with them.

respectable
1 (adj) A respectable person is one who behaves as society expects.
3 (adj) Clothing which is respectable is neat and clean and suitable.

respiration (n) is the way in which humans and animals breathe.

respirator respirators (n) A respirator is a device which helps you breathe if you are injured, or in gas or smoke-filled rooms.

respite (n) is a rest from something which is difficult or unpleasant.

resplendent (adj) If someone or something is resplendent, they are very grandly dressed or decorated.

respond responds responding responded.
1 (vb) If you respond to something, you react to it. *She responded to the question by bursting into tears.* **responsive** (adj)
2 (vb) If you respond to someone, you answer them.

responsibility responsibilities
1 (n) A responsibility is a duty that you must do, or must supervise others doing.
2 (n) If you take responsibility, you make sure that something is done.
3 (n) Responsibility is the ability to behave in a sensible way and make wise decisions for yourself. **responsible** (adj)

rest rests resting rested
1 (vb) If you rest, you take a break from whatever you were doing and relax.
2 (n) A rest is a quiet time when no work is done or activities take place.
3 (n) The rest means all the other things which have not already been mentioned. *Some of the group went to the river, the rest went home.*
4 (n) A rest is an object which supports something else. *Head rest . . . tool rest.*
5 (n) A rest in music is a pause when an instrument is not played.

restaurant restaurants (n) A restaurant is a place where you buy and eat meals.

restless (adj) A restless person fidgets and finds it difficult to keep still.

restore restores restoring restored
1 (vb) If you restore something, you repair it so that it is as good as new.
2 (vb) If you restore something, you return it to its owner.
3 (vb) If you restore a situation, you return it to its previous state. *He restored order in the building after the flood.*

restrain restrains restraining restrained.
1 (vb) If you restrain someone, you hold them back or control them in some way.
2 (adj) If someone or something is restrained, they act in a very controlled way even when they do not feel calm.

restrict restricts restricting restricted.
1 (vb) If you restrict something, you limit its size.
2 (vb) If you restrict a person or animal, you limit their movements.
3 (adj) Something restricted is limited in some way. **restriction** (n)

r

result results resulting resulted
1 (vb) If something results from an event, it is caused by it. *His absence resulted in the collapse of the talks.*
2 (n) Results are the marks, grades or positions you achieve in tests, exams or competitions.

resume resumes resuming resumed (vb) If you resume an activity, you carry on after a break.

resurrect resurrects resurrecting resurrected (vb) If someone resurrects something such as an attitude or an activity, they cause it to exist again after it has disappeared. *The new teacher resurrected the netball team.*

Resurrection (n) In the Christian religion, the Resurrection occurred when Jesus came back to life three days after He had been killed.

resuscitate resuscitates resuscitating resuscitated (vb) If you resuscitate someone, you make them conscious again after an accident.

retail retails retailing retailed
1 (vb) If you retail something, you sell it to the public.
2 (adj) The retail price of something is the price you pay in the shops.

retain retains retaining retained (vb) If you retain something you keep it.

retaliate retaliates retaliating retaliated (vb) If you retaliate, you try to hurt someone who has hurt you.
retaliation (n)

reticent (adj) If someone is reticent, they are unwilling to talk about what they know or feel.

retinue retinues (n) A retinue is a group of people who travel with an important person.

retire retires retiring retired.
1 (vb) When you retire you stop working for a living. **retirement** (n)
2 (vb) If you retire you go to bed.
3 (vb) If a sportsman or sportswoman retires, they leave the game or competition due to an injury.

retort retorts (n) A retort is a quick, sharp reply.

retrace retraces retracing retraced (vb) If you retrace your steps, you follow them back exactly.

retreat retreats retreating retreated
1 (vb) If you retreat, you move back from something unpleasant or dangerous.
2 (vb) When an army retreats, it moves back to avoid meeting the enemy.
3 (n) A retreat is a quiet and private place you can go to be alone and to think.

retrieve retrieves retrieving retrieved
1 (vb) If you retrieve something, you get it back from the place where you left or hid it.
2 (vb) If you retrieve information from a computer, you get it back from the memory.

return returns returning returned
1 (vb) If you return to a place after being away, you come or go back to it.
2 (vb) If you return something, you give it back or put it back.
3 (n) Your return is your arrival back from a journey.
4 (n) A return or return ticket is one that allows you to make a journey to a place and back again.
5 (n) A return match is a second match between teams who have already played against one another.

reunion reunions (n) A reunion is a meeting between people who have not seen each other for some time.

reveal reveals revealing revealed
1 (vb) If you reveal something, or if something reveals itself, it can be seen when formerly it was hidden.
2 (vb) If you reveal a secret, you tell it to someone else.

revel revels revelling revelled (vb) If you revel in something, you enjoy it very much.

revenge revenges (n) Revenge is something unpleasant you do to someone because of something they did to you.

reverberate reverberates reverberating reverberated (vb) If a sound reverberates, it echoes loudly. **reverberation** (n)

r

reverence

reverence (n) is a feeling of deep respect you have for someone who is particularly admirable.

reverse reverses reversing reversed
1 (n) The reverse of something is the opposite side of it.
2 (vb) If you reverse an object, you turn it around the opposite way.
3 (vb) If you reverse a vehicle you drive it backwards.
4 (vb) If you reverse a plan or a decision, you change it and decide upon something else.
5 (n) A reverse is a setback of some sort.
reversal (n) **reversible** (adj)

review reviews reviewing reviewed.
1 (vb) If you review something you inspect it or examine it. *The Queen reviewed the troops.*
2 (n) A review is an inspection or a close examination of something.
3 (n) A review is a short account of a play book, etc which gives opinions about it.
4 (n) A review is a series of comic sketches and songs performed on a stage or television.

revise revises revising revised
1 (vb) If you revise, you re-read the work you have done, to be sure that you know it prior to an exam.
2 (vb) If you revise your opinions, you change them after careful thought.
3 (vb) If you revise a book or a piece of music, you alter it to improve it.
revision (n)

revive revives reviving revived
1 (vb) If you revive a person or animal, you bring them back to consciousness again.
2 (vb) If you revive old ideas, plays or customs, you bring them into being again.
revival (n)

revolt revolts revolting revolted
1 (n) A revolt is a violent uprising or rebellion against authority. **revolution** (n) **revolutionary** (adj)
2 (vb) When people revolt, they rebel and fight against the system which governs them.
3 (vb) If something revolts you, you find it shocking or disgusting.

revolve revolves revolving revolved.
1 (vb) If something revolves, it moves around a central point like a wheel.
2 (adj) Revolving describes things which turn around a central point.

revolver revolvers (n) A revolver is a hand gun that can fire several bullets quickly.

reward rewards rewarding rewarded
1 (n) A reward is something you receive for good behaviour or being helpful.
2 (adj) A rewarding job is one that you find satisfying.

rheumatism (n) is a disease which makes muscles or joints very painful.

rhinoceros rhinoceroses (n) A rhinoceros is a large, horned African or Asian animal.

rhombus rhombuses (n) A rhombus is a shape with four sides of equal length but is not a square.

rhombus
rhombus
a kite is a **rhombus** shape

rhubarb (n) is a garden plant with edible stems.

rhyme rhymes rhyming rhymed (vb) Words that rhyme sound very similar. The words mat and cat rhyme.

rhythm rhythms (n) Rhythm is a regular beat in music or poetry.

rib ribs (n) A rib is one of the bones that form a cage in your chest.

skeleton p273

ribbon ribbons (n) A ribbon is a long, thin strip of material for tying up presents, decorating hair, etc.

rice (n) is a grass grown in flooded fields called paddy fields. Its seeds, also called rice, are used for food.

rich richer richest
1 (adj) If you are rich, you have a lot of money.
2 (adj) If someone leads a rich life they live a life full of interest and excitement.

Richter scale (n) The Richter scale is used to measure the strength of earthquakes.

rick ricks (n) A rick is a stack of hay.

rickshaw rickshaws (n) A rickshaw is a two-wheeled, passenger vehicle pulled by a man who walks or rides on a bicycle.

ricochet ricochets ricocheting ricocheted (vb) If something ricochets, it hits a surface and bounces off.

riddle riddles riddling riddled
1 (n) A riddle is an amusing but puzzling question to which you must find an answer.
2 (adj) If something like a piece of wood is riddled, it is full of holes.
3 (vb) If you riddle something, you make a lot of holes in it.

ride rides riding ridden rode (vb) If you ride a horse, bike, etc you take control of it and travel on it.

ridge ridges
1 (n) A ridge is a long, narrow, raised piece of ground or other surface.
2 (n) A ridge is an area of high atmospheric pressure. *The weather map shows a ridge of high pressure over the north, so the fine spell will continue.*

ridicule ridicules ridiculing ridiculed (vb) If you ridicule someone, you make fun of them.

ridiculous (adj) If you say someone or something is ridiculous, you mean they are foolish and unreasonable.

rifle rifles (n) A rifle is a long-barrelled gun used for shooting things at a distance.

rig rigs (n) A rig is a large construction used for mining or drilling for oil, gas, etc below the earth's surface.

right rights righting righted
1 (vb) If you right something, you correct it.
2 (vb) A boat rights itself if it comes back to its normal position after capsizing.
3 (n) Your rights are the things the law allows you to do.
4 (adj) If something is right, it is correct or proper.
5 (adj) You have two hands, your right and your left.
6 If you are in the right, you are morally or legally correct.

right angle right angles (n) A right angle is an angle of 90 degrees.

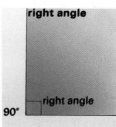

righteous (adj) A righteous person is one who behaves in a morally or religiously correct way of life.

rightful (adj) A rightful owner is the person who has the legal or moral right to own something.

right of way rights of way
1 (n) A right of way is a path or road which the public can use.
2 (n) If you have right of way, other traffic must stop to let you go first.

rigid
1 (adj) Something which is rigid is stiff and unbending, **rigidity** (n)
2 (adj) Rigid laws are strict.
3 (adj) A rigid person is not willing to change the way they think.

rigor mortis (n) is the state of a dead body when it becomes stiff.

ring rings ringing ringed rang rung
1 (n) A ring is a band worn around your finger.
2 (n) A ring is the noise of a bell.
3 (n) A ring is a metal loop for tying things to.
4 (n) A ring is a small electric plate for cooking.
5 (n) A ring is an area where a sporting even happens. *A boxing ring . . . a show jumping ring.*
6 (vb) If a bell rings, it makes a sound.
7 (vb) If you ring someone, you call them on the telephone.

ring leader

ring leader ring leaders. (n) A ring leader of a group is the person who encourages others to do things which are illegal or wrong.

ring master ring masters (n) A ring master is the person at a circus who introduces all the acts.

ring road ring roads (n) A ring road is a large road which takes traffic away from the centre of a town.

rink rinks (n) A rink is a large, indoor area for ice skating or roller skating.

rinse rinses rinsing rinsed (vb) If you rinse something, you wash it in clean water.

riot riots rioting rioted
1 (n) A riot happens when a violent crowd of people damage property and cause fights.
2 (vb) If people riot, they take part in violence which causes damage to people and property. **rioters** (n) **riotous** (adj)

ripe riper ripest
1 (adj) A ripe fruit is ready to eat.
2 (adj) Ripe cheese has a strong flavour.

ripen ripens ripening ripened (vb) If a fruit ripens, it becomes fit to eat.

ripple ripples rippling rippled
1 (vb) A ripple is a little wave on the surface of the water.
2 (n) A ripple of sound is low and quiet.

rise rises rising rose risen
1 (vb) If you rise, you get on to your feet.
2 (vb) If something rises, it goes upwards.
3 (vb) When the sun or moon rises, it appears above the horizon.
4 (vb) If the level of water rises, it gets higher.
5 (vb) When prices rise, they get higher.
6 (vb) When sounds rise, they get louder or more shrill.
7 (vb) When the wind rises, it blows more strongly.
8 (vb) When a group of people rise, they band together to fight against their rulers.
9 (vb) When parliament rises, it finishes a working session.
10 (n) A rise is an upward slope of ground.
11 (n) A rise is an increase in an amount of money. *A pay rise, a rent rise, price rise.*

risk risks risking risked
1 (n) A risk is a chance that something unpleasant or dangerous might happen.
2 (vb) If you risk someone or something, you do something which could lead to danger or distress. *They risked their lives to save others.*

risotto risottos (n) A risotto is an Italian rice dish, which can contain cooked meat, nuts, fish or vegetables.

ritual rituals
1 (n) A ritual is a traditional ceremony, with set actions happening in a set order.
2 (n) A ritual is something you do regularly.

rival rivals rivalling rivalled
1 (n) A rival is someone who is competing with you.
2 (vb) If people or businesses rival one another, they compete. **rivalry** (n)

river rivers (n) A river is a continuous stretch of moving, fresh water, flowing to a larger river, a lake or the sea.

rivet rivets riveting riveted
1 (n) A rivet is a metal pin used to fix pieces of metal together.
2 (vb) If you rivet something, you fix it with rivets.
3 (adj) Something which is riveting is fascinating and holds your attention.

road roads (n) A road is a strip of ground prepared so that vehicles can travel on it.

roam roams roaming roamed (vb) If a person or animal roams, they wander over large areas.

roar roars roaring roared
1 (n) A roar is a loud, rumbling sound.
2 (vb) When someone or something roars, they make a loud rumbling noise.
3 (vb) If you roar with laughter, you laugh loudly for some time.

roast roasts roasting roasted
1 (vb) When you roast food, you cook it in an oven or over an open fire.
2 (adj) Roast meat, potatoes, etc have been cooked by roasting.
3 (n) A roast is a roasted joint of meat.

rob robs robbing robbed (vb) If you rob someone, you steal from them. **robber** (n) **robbery** (n)

r

robin robins (n) A robin is a small British bird with a red breast.

Robin Hood is the legendary popular hero who lived during the reign of Richard I in Sherwood Forest with his band of outlaws. They tried to right wrongs and stole from the rich to give to the poor.

robot robots
1 (n) A robot is a machine programmed to perform mechanical tasks, in a factory, for example.
2 (n) In science fiction, a robot is a machine that can think and perform tasks.

robotic robotics
1 (n) Robotics is the science of designing and building robots.
2 (adj) Robotic movements are short, jerky and mechanical.

robust (adj) Someone or something that is robust is very healthy and strong.

rock rocks rocking rocked
1 (n) Rock is the hard substance of the earth that forms cliffs, mountains, etc.
2 (n) A rock is a large stone sticking up from the sea or ground.
3 (vb) If you rock something, you move it repeatedly to and fro.
4 (n) Rock is a hard sweet in the shape of a stick that you can buy at holiday resorts.
5 (n) Rock is a form of music with a strong rhythm usually played by small groups of musicians.

rock'n'roll (n) is a kind of music with a strong beat that was popular in the 1950's.

rocket rockets (n) A rocket is a device propelled through the air at great speed, by the gasses from fast burning fuel.

rodent rodents (n) A rodent is a small animal with sharp teeth for gnawing.

role roles
1 (n) Your role in an organisation is the particular position you hold, and the job you do.
2 (n) Your role in a play is the part that you act.

roll rolls rolling rolled
1 (vb) If you roll something along the ground you make it turn over and over.
2 (vb) When cameras roll they start to film.
3 (n) A roll is a small, round lump of bread for one person.
4 (n) A roll of paper is a long strip wrapped round many times.

roller skate roller skates (n) Roller skates are shoes or boots with wheels on the bottom.

rolling stock (n) is the engines and carriages on a railway.

Roman numeral Roman numerals (n) Roman numerals were the numbers used by the ancient Romans, and are still used today. I = 1, X = 10, C = 100, etc.

romantic
1 (adj) A romantic story or film is mainly a story about love.
2 (adj) A romantic person is rather emotional and has ideas which are not related to real life.

roof roofs
1 (n) A roof is the covering on a building that protects people and their possessions from the weather.
2 (n) The roof of your mouth is the top part of it.

rook rooks
1 (n) A rook is a large, black, European bird of the crow family.
2 (n) A rook is a piece in chess.

room rooms
1 (n) A room is one of the separate parts into which a building is divided, with its own door, ceiling, windows, etc.
2 (n) Room is space for something.

r

roost

roost roosts roosting roosted
1 (n) A roost is a place where a bird settles or builds a nest.
2 (vb) If a bird roosts it settles in a place for the night.

rope ropes roping roped
1 (n) Rope is a strong line used for climbing, tying things, or holding things.
2 (vb) If you rope things, you tie them together using rope.

rosary rosaries (n) A rosary is a string of beads, used by members of some religions to count prayers.

rose roses
1 (n) A rose is a flower which grows on thorny bushes.
2 (adj) Rose is a reddish-pink colour.
3 If you view the world through rose-coloured spectacles, you only notice the pleasant things around you.
4 (n) A rose is a metal plate with fine holes which fits onto a watering can or hose.

rosette rosettes (n) A rosette is a badge made of ribbon.

roster rosters (n) A roster is a list of people who take turns to do a particular job.

rostrum rostrums or **rostra** (n) A rostrum is a small platform on which a speaker stands to talk to the audience.

rosy rosier rosiest (adj) Something that is rosy is reddish pink in colour.

rot rots rotting rotted
1 (vb) If something rots it decays.
2 (n) Rot is a kind of decay.

rotary (adj) is used to describe things which turn around in a circular motion. *A rotary drier . . . a rotary mower.*

rotate rotates rotating rotated
1 (vb) If a thing rotates it turns with a circular motion.
2 (vb) If you rotate crops, you plant a different crop each year, following a pattern. **rotation** (n)

rote If you do things by rote you do them out of habit rather than because you have thought about them.

roti (n) is a type of flat bread from the Caribbean.

rotor rotors (n) A rotor is a blade on a helicopter which rotates and lifts it.

rotten
1 (adj) If something is rotten, it is decayed.
2 (adj) If you say that something is rotten, you mean it's horrible and useless.
3 (adj) If you feel rotten, you feel ill.

rough rougher roughest
1 (adj) Something rough is not smooth to the touch.
2 (adj) If a person is rough, they are not gentle and may hurt people.
3 (adj) If the weather or sea is rough, it is stormy and unpleasant.
4 (adj) If a machine sounds rough, it is not running smoothly.
5 A rough diamond is a person who seems outwardly tough but is actually kind.

roughage (n) is the substances in bran, fibre etc which help you to stay healthy.

round rounder roundest
1 (adj) Something round is shaped like a ball.
2 (prep) If people gather round something, they form a circle around it.
3 (n) A round is a period of time in a boxing match, etc.
4 (n) A round is a set of games in a competition which happen at the same time.
5 (n) A round of bread is a slice of bread.
6 (n) A round of ammunition is one bullet, or one shell.
7 (n) A round is a song sung by a group of people who all start at different times.

roundabout roundabouts
1 (n) A roundabout is a large, circular, spinning platform with wooden horses, cars, etc on it for children to ride on.
2 (n) A roundabout is a circular obstruction in the road which helps to control traffic.

rounders (n) is a team game played with a bat and ball.

Roundhead Roundheads (n) The Roundheads were the soldiers led by Cromwell in the English civil war.

rouse rouses rousing roused
1 (vb) If you rouse someone, you wake them.
2 (vb) If you rouse yourself, you make yourself get up and do something.
3 (vb) If a subject rouses particular emotions, it makes you feel these emotions.
4 (adj) A rousing song, game, etc is one that is full of energy and excitement.

rout routs routing routed
1 (vb) If you rout your opponents in a game or battle, you defeat them heavily.
2 (n) A rout is total defeat in a game or battle.

route routes (n) A route is the way you decide to take on a journey.

routine routines
1 (n) A routine is a regular pattern of doing things. *My routine was to do my homework before tea.*
2 (adj) Routine occurrences are regular, commonplace happenings.

rowdy rowdier rowdiest (adj) Someone or something that is rowdy is rough and noisy.

royal (adj) Anything royal is connected with a king or queen and their family.

royal family royal families (n) A royal family is the king or queen of a country and their family.

rubber rubbers
1 (n) Rubber is a strong, elastic substance made synthetically, or from the sap of the rubber tree.
2 (n) A rubber is a small piece of rubber used to rub out pencil marks.

rubbish
1 (n) Rubbish is waste things to be thrown away.
2 (n) Rubbish is something of poor quality.
3 (n) If an idea, etc is rubbish, it is nonsense or stupid.

rubble
1 (n) Rubble is small pieces of stone and brick used in building.
2 (n) When a building has been destroyed, the pile of broken bricks, etc is called rubble.

ruby rubies (n) A ruby is a deep red precious stone.

rucksack rucksacks (n) A rucksack is a bag you can carry on your back, when you are walking or climbing.

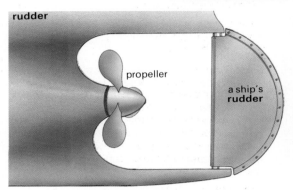

rudder

propeller

a ship's **rudder**

rudder rudders (n) A rudder is a flat piece of wood or metal on a boat or aeroplane used for steering.

aircraft p5

rude ruder rudest
1 (adj) If you are rude, you are impolite.
2 (adj) Rude language or behaviour is likely to offend other people.

rudiments (n) The rudiments of an activity are the basic skills you need to know in order to do it.

ruffian ruffians (n) A ruffian is a violent, criminal person.

ruffle ruffles ruffling ruffled
1 (vb) If you ruffle something, you disturb the surface smoothness.
2 (vb) When a bird ruffles its feathers it fluffs them out to clean them or because it is cold.
3 (n) A ruffle is a small frill used to decorate clothes.

rugby (n) is a game played by teams of 15 or 13 players with an oval ball.

rugged
1 (adj) Rugged countryside is rocky and difficult to walk over.
2 (adj) A rugged piece of equipment is strong and long lasting.

r

ruin

ruin ruins ruining ruined
1 (n) Ruin is the total destruction of something.
2 (n) Ruins are all that is left when something is destroyed.
3 (vb) If you ruin something, you spoil or destroy it.

rule rules ruling ruled
1 (n) A rule is an official order or instruction that should be obeyed or followed.
2 (n) Something that is the rule is the usual thing. *As a rule we stay at home in the holidays.*
3 (n) Rule is the government of a country. *British rule in India ended in 1948.*
4 (vb) The people who rule a country make all the laws.
5 (vb) If you rule a line, you draw it with a ruler.
6 (n) A ruling is a judgement on someone or something. *The judge gave a ruling on the case.*

ruler rulers
1 (n) A ruler is a person who rules a country.
2 (n) A ruler is a flat narrow piece of wood or plastic marked for measuring distances and to draw straight lines.

rum rums (n) Rum is an alcoholic drink made from sugar cane or molasses.

rumbling (adj) A rumbling sound is low and long.

rumour rumours (n)
A rumour is a story or a piece of information which may not be true, but that people are talking about.

rung rungs (n) A rung is one of the bars that make the steps on a ladder.

runner runners
1 (n) A runner is someone who runs in a race.
2 (n) A runner is a track that helps something move smoothly.

runway runways (n) A runway is an area where aeroplanes land.

rural (adj) describes someone or something that is from the country rather than a town.

rush rushes rushing rushed
1 (vb) If you rush somewhere you go there very quickly.
2 (vb) If you rush your work, you do it quickly and carelessly.
3 (n) The rush-hour, when people are going to and from work, is the busiest time for traffic, shops, etc.
4 (n) If there is a rush to buy something, many people are trying to buy it.
5 If you are rushed off your feet, you are very busy.

rust rusts rusting rusted
1 (n) Rust is the reddish-brown substance that covers metal surfaces when they are exposed to water and air.
2 (vb) If something rusts, it corrodes through the action of water and air.
rusty (adj)

rut ruts
1 (n) A rut is a deep, narrow track in the ground caused by heavy wheels.
2 If you feel in a rut, you feel your life lacks excitement and interest.

ruthless (adj) A ruthless person does not care who they hurt as long as they get what they want.
ruthlessness (n)

rye (n) is a cereal crop grown in cold countries and used to make flour.

Ss

Sabbath Sabbaths (n) The Sabbath is the traditional day of rest and prayer for certain religions. Saturday is the Jewish Sabbath; Sunday is the Christian one.

sabotage (n) Sabotage is the deliberate damage or destruction of bridges, railway lines, equipment, etc usually done by small groups against an enemy.

sabre sabres (n) A sabre is a strong sword, sometimes with a curved blade.

sack sacks sacking sacked
1 (n) A sack is a large bag made from rough material for carrying grain, potatoes, etc.
2 (vb) If you sack someone from a job, you tell them to leave.
3 (vb) If soldiers sack a city or town, they destroy it and take its treasures.

sacred (adj) Something that is sacred is thought to be holy.

sacrifice sacrifices sacrificing sacrificed
1 (n) A sacrifice is an offering to a god.
2 (vb) If you sacrifice an animal or a human being, you kill them as an offering to a god.
3 (vb) If you sacrifice something, you give up something important to you, usually to help others.

sacrilege (n) If you are guilty of sacrilege, you show disrespect for holy or sacred things.

saddle saddles saddling saddled
1 (n) A saddle is a seat, fitted onto an animal's back for the rider of the animal to sit on.
2 (n) The seat of a bicycle or motorcycle is called a saddle.
3 (vb) If you saddle a horse, for example, you fasten a saddle on its back.

safari safaris (n) A safari is an expedition to observe or to hunt wild animals.

safe safer safest
1 (adj) If you are safe, you are not in danger.
2 (adj) A safe place is one where nothing can harm you.
3 (adj) If something valuable is safe, it is in a place where it cannot be stolen or damaged.
4 (n) A safe is a very strong metal container with special locks used for storing valuables. **safety** (n)

safeguard safeguards safeguarding safeguarded (vb) If you safeguard something, you protect it.

saga sagas (n) A saga is a very long, often very old story written or told about a hero's travels and adventures.

said see **say**

sail sails sailing sailed
1 (n) A sail is a large piece of material attached to a boat's mast.
2 (vb) When a boat sails it sets off on a voyage.
3 (vb) If you sail, you control a boat that uses sails rather than engines to move it.
4 (n) A sail is the flat arm of a windmill that is propelled by the wind.

sailor sailors (n) A sailor is someone who works on a ship as one of the crew.

saint saints
1 (n) A saint is someone honoured by the Christian Church after their death for being especially good or holy.
2 (n) If you call someone a saint, you think that they are very kind, good and unselfish.

salad salads (n) A salad is a mixture of uncooked vegetables, lettuce, cucumber, tomatoes, etc. or a mixture of fruits served in juice.

salary salaries (n) A salary is the money a person is paid for their work; it is usually paid monthly.

sale sales
1 (n) A sale is a time when shops sell their goods at lower prices.
2 (n) The sale of something is the selling of it for money.
3 Something for sale may be purchased.

saliva (n) is the liquid that is always in the mouth.

S

salt salts (n) Salt is the white powder or crystals that can be used to flavour food. **salty** (adj)

salute salutes (n) A salute is a sign, usually made by raising the hand to the forehead as a greeting or to show respect, especially in the armed forces.

salvage salvages salvaging salvaged (vb) If you salvage materials and goods from shipwrecks and buildings damaged by floods, fire, etc you recover them.

Samaritans (n) The Samaritans is an organisation that tries to help anyone with serious problems. You can phone them any time of day or night.

same (adj) If two things are the same they are exactly like each other.

samosa samosas (n) A samosa is a spicy meat or vegetable snack, deep fried in a triangular case of pastry.

sampan sampans (n) A sampan is a small Chinese boat.

sample samples (n) A sample is a small amount of something that can be tasted or examined for quality or to find out more about it. **sample** (vb)

sanctuary sanctuaries (n) A sanctuary is a place where people, animals or birds can be safe.

sand sands
1 (n) Sand is a substance made up of tiny grains of rock and other materials and found on sea-shores and in deserts.
2 (n) The sands is another name for the beach.

sandal sandals (n) A sandal is a lightweight shoe, not covering the foot completely and worn in hot weather.

sandwich sandwiches sandwiching sandwiched
1 (n) A sandwich is two slices of bread with a savoury or sweet filling.
2 (vb) If you sandwich someone or something, you squash them between two other things.

sane saner sanest (adj) A sane person has a normal and well-balanced mind.

sanitation (n) refers to the drainage, sewerage and cleaning systems that keep buildings clean and germ-free.

Sanskrit (n) is an ancient Indian language now only used for religious writing and ceremonies.

sapling saplings (n) A sapling is a young tree.

sapphire sapphires (n) A sapphire is a precious stone usually bright blue in colour.

sarcastic (adj) Someone who is sarcastic uses words in a way that makes people laugh but that is also rather cruel and hurtful. **sarcasm** (n)

sardine sardines (n) A sardine is a small fish that is good to eat and usually sold in tins.

sari saris (n) The sari is the traditional dress of Indian women. It is a long piece of material wrapped around the body in a special way.

sash sashes (n) A sash is a long strip of cloth worn around the waist as a belt or around the body and over one shoulder as a mark of honour.

Satan (n) (spelled Shaitan by Muslims) In Christianity, Judaism and Islam, Satan is the devil; the enemy of God.

satchel satchels (n) A satchel is a bag with a shoulder strap for carrying books to school.

satellite satellites
1 (n) A satellite is an object in space that orbits another, larger object such as a planet.
2 (n) A satellite is a machine sent into space. It is used to orbit earth or other planets, in communications or to collect information.

satin (n) is cloth which is shiny on the front and dull on the back.

satisfactory (adj) If something is satisfactory it is of an acceptable standard.

satisfy satisfies satisfying satisfied
1 (vb) If something or someone satisfies
you, you are contented and pleased with
them.
2 (vb) If you satisfy someone that what you
say is true, you convince them.
3 (vb) If you satisfy the requirements for
something, you prove that you are capable
of doing it. **satisfaction** (n)

satsuma satsumas (n) A satsuma is a
small, orange fruit which is easy to peel.

saturate saturates saturating saturated
(vb) If you saturate something, you soak it
with water or some other liquid.
saturation (n)

sauce sauces (n) A sauce is a thick, sweet
or savoury liquid that can be poured over
foods to add to their flavour.

saucer saucers (n) A saucer is a shallow
dish for a cup to stand on.

sauna saunas (n) A sauna is a hot steam
bath and also the name of the place where
people go to have one.

sausage sausages (n) A sausage is finely
minced meat mixed with other ingredients
and enclosed in a thin, skin tube.

savage (adj) A savage person or animal is
fierce, violent and wild.

save saves saving saved
1 (vb) If you save someone or something,
you help them when they are in danger or
difficulties.
2 (vb) If you save money, you keep it
instead of spending it. If you save other
things such as stamps, you collect them.
savings (n)
3 (vb) If you save time, energy, electricity,
etc, you are careful not to waste it.
4 (vb) If a goalkeeper saves a goal, he or she
stops the other team from scoring.

saviour saviours
1 (n) A saviour is a person who saves
someone or something from danger or
difficulties.
2 (n) In the Christian Church Jesus is the
Saviour.

savoury (adj) Savoury food is tasty in a
spicy, salty way.

sawdust (n) is the fine, woody powder
that falls when wood is sawn.

saxophone saxophones (n) A saxophone
is a brass musical instrument.

say says saying said (vb) If you say
something, you speak.

scab scabs (n) A scab is the crust that
forms over a wound when it is healing.

scabbard scabbards (n) A scabbard is a
narrow case which is worn to hold a sword
or dagger.

scaffolding (n) is a framework of metal
and wood on which building workers stand
to build or repair high walls.

scald scalds scalding scalded
1 (vb) If you scald yourself, you burn
yourself with boiling liquid or steam.
2 (adj) Something scalding is extremely hot.
3 (vb) If you scald something, you sterilise
it by putting it into boiling water.

scale scales
1 (n) A scale is the set of marks or numbers
used for measuring on a ruler or on any
container or instrument used for
measuring.
2 (n) A scale is a series of notes in music,
played or sung in ascending or descending
order.
3 (n) The scale of something is the extent of
it. Something large scale is very big;
something small scale is very small.
4 (n) The scale of a map, plan, model, etc
shows the relationships between the
measurements represented and those in the
real world.
5 (n) Scales are a machine or piece of
equipment for weighing things.
6 (n) The scales of a fish, snake or other
reptile are the small, thin plates of skin
that cover its body. **scaly** (adj)

fish p110

scalp scalps (n) Your scalp is the skin on
top of your head.

scalpel scalpels (n) A scalpel is a small,
thin, very sharp knife, used by surgeons.

scampi (n) are large, edible prawns.

scan scans scanning scanned
1 (vb) If you scan papers or books, you
glance through them quickly.
2 (vb) A machine, called a scanner, scans
something by moving a beam of light or
electrons over it.

S

scandal

scandal scandals
1 (n) Scandal is talk and gossip that concentrates on the bad or immoral things that people do.
2 (n) Something that is a scandal is shocking or disgraceful. **scandalous** (adj)

scanty scantier scantiest (adj) Something that is scanty is so small that there isn't really enough of it. **scantily** (adv)

scapegoat scapegoats (n) Someone who is made a scapegoat is blamed publicly for something even though it is not their fault.

scar scars scarring scarred
1 (n) A scar is a mark that remains after a wound has healed.
2 (n) A scar is a mark on the surface of something caused by damage.
3 (vb) If you scar something, you damage the surface of it.

scarce scarcer scarcest (adj) If something is scarce, there is very little of it.

scare scares scaring scared
1 (vb) Something that scares you makes you feel afraid.
3 (n) A scare is something that startles or terrifies you.

scarecrow scarecrows (n) A scarecrow is a human figure made from wood, straw, old clothes, etc, put into crop fields by farmers to scare birds away.

scarf scarves (n) A scarf is a strip of material worn around the neck for warmth or for decoration.

scarlet (adj) is a bright red colour.

scatter scatters scattering scattered
1 (vb) If you scatter things, you throw or drop them so they are spread over a large area.
2 (vb) When a group of animals or people scatter, they separate and move off in different directions.

scavenge scavenges scavenging scavenged
1 (vb) If birds or animals scavenge for food, they search for and eat anything they can find including dead creatures.
2 (vb) People or animals who scavenge, search among rubbish and refuse for things they can use or eat. **scavenger** (n)

scene scenes
1 (n) The scene of a particular event, an accident for example, is the place where it happens.
2 (n) A scene can be a view of a particular landscape.
3 (n) A scene is a particular part of a play, film or book where events happen in one place.
4 (n) A scene is a noisy, unpleasant confrontation between two or more people.

scenery
1 (n) If you look at the scenery of a place, you look at its appearance.
2 (n) The scenery of a play, ballet, opera, etc, refers to all the painted cloths and boards and equipment used to make the stage look like a particular place.

scent scents
1 (n) The scent of something is its particular smell. **scented** (adj)
2 (n) Scent is a sweet-smelling liquid.

sceptical (adj) If you are sceptical about something you do not really believe it.

sceptre sceptres (n) A sceptre is the ornamental rod, carried by a queen or king to show their power and authority.

schedule schedules (n) A schedule is a list of things you have to do and the times when you must do them.

scheme schemes scheming schemed
1 (vb) If people scheme, they plot or make secret plans.
2 (n) A scheme is a plan or an idea.
3 (n) A scheme is a large, complex plan produced by an organisation or government.

scholar scholars (n) A scholar is someone who has studied hard and knows a great deal.

scholarship scholarships (n) If you win a scholarship to a school or a college, part or all of your fees are paid for you because you are a promising pupil.

school schools
1 (n) A school is a place where children are educated.
2 (n) The school refers to all the people who teach, work and study there.
3 (n) A school is a large group of fish.

schooner schooners (n) A schooner is a sailing ship with more than one mast.

science sciences
1 (n) Science is the study of nature and the natural world and the use of experiments and observation to gain more knowledge about them. **scientist** (n)
2 (n) A science is one of the many branches of science: chemistry, biology, zoology, for example.

science fiction (n) refers to stories about travelling through space and fantastic happenings in other worlds and other times especially in the future.

scissors (n) A pair of scissors is a device with sharp blades used for cutting paper, cloth, etc.

scold scolds scolding scolding (vb) If you scold someone, you speak angrily to them because they have done something wrong and because they have displeased you.

scoop scoops scooping scooped
1 (n) A scoop is a kitchen tool with a handle and a hollow bowl like a spoon, used for lifting and serving food.
2 (n) A scoop is a huge bucket on an earth moving machine.
3 (vb) If you scoop something up, you lift it using a scoop, or your cupped hands.
4 (n) If a newspaper prints a scoop, it publishes a story before anyone else.

scooter scooters (n) A scooter is a kind of small motorcycle with a low seat.

scope (n) If you have scope, you have the freedom and opportunity to do something.

scorch scorches scorching scorched
1 (vb) If you scorch something, you burn it slightly by putting it too close to or letting it touch something very hot.
2 (n) A scorch is a brown mark made by scorching.

score scores scoring scored
1 (n) The score in a game or competition is the total number of goals, points or runs made by each side.
2 (vb) If someone scores they win a point, goal or run in a competition or a game.
3 (vb) The person who scores in a game keeps a record of all the points, goals or runs. **scorer** (n)
4 (vb) If you score the surface of something, you scratch it with something sharp.
5 (n) The written version of a piece of music is called the score.

scorn scorns scorning scorned
1 (vb) If you scorn someone or something, you treat them as if they were stupid and worthless. **scornful** (adj)
2 (n) Scorn is a feeling of ridicule for someone or something.

scorpion scorpions (n) A scorpion is a creature found in hot countries and may have a dangerous sting in its tail.

scoundrel scoundrels (n) A scoundrel is a wicked person.

scour scours scouring scoured
1 (vb) If you scour a saucepan, for example, you use something rough to clean it and make it shine.
2 (vb) If you scour a place or an area, you search it thoroughly. *They scoured the woods for the lost child.*

scout scouts
1 (n) A scout is someone who is sent out from an army or an expedition to look carefully at the land ahead and report back any difficulties or dangers.
2 (n) A Scout is a member of the Scout Association.

S

scowl

scowl scowls scowling scowled (vb) If you are angry and show it by wrinkling your forehead, you scowl.

scramble scrambles scrambling scrambled
1 (vb) If you scramble, you use your hands to help you over difficult ground, a steep path or rocks, for example.
2 (adj) When phone or radio messages are scrambled, the sounds are mixed up and only those people with special equipment can understand them.
3 (vb) If you scramble eggs, you mix them with a little milk and cook them in a pan.
4 (n) A scramble is a motorcycle race over very rough ground.

scrap scraps scrapping scrapped
1 (n) A scrap is a very small piece of something.
2 (n) Scrap is waste food, material, etc.
3 (vb) If you scrap something, you throw it away.
4 (vb) If you scrap an idea or a plan, you give it up.
5 (n) A scrap is a small fight or quarrel.

scrapbook scrapbooks (n) A scrapbook is a book with blank pages that you can fill with photographs, cuttings, etc. that interest you.

scrape scrapes scraping scraped
1 (vb) If you scrape something, you take off some of the surface using your nails or something sharp.
2 (n) A scrape is a mark on the surface of something caused by a sharp object.
3 People who scrape by live as cheaply as they can in order to save money.
4 If you are in a scrape, you are in trouble of some kind.

scratch scratches scratching scratched
1 (n) A scratch is a small cut or mark on the surface of something.
2 (vb) If you scratch yourself, your skin is damaged by something sharp.
3 (vb) If you scratch, you use your nails to rub a part of your body that itches.
4 (adj) If something is scratched, the surface of it has been damaged by something sharp.

scrawl scrawls scrawling scrawled (vb) If you scrawl, you write in a messy way.

scream screams screaming screamed
1 (n) A scream is a loud, shrill, piercing sound made by a person or an animal usually in pain or danger, but sometimes in excitement.
2 (vb) When a person or animal screams they make a loud, shrill sound.
3 (vb) When something screams, a jet plane, for example, it makes a loud, high-pitched noise.

scree screes (n) Scree is a mass of small, loose stones at the foot of mountains.

screech screeches screeching screeched (vb) If a person, animal, bird or machine screeches they make a harsh, high-pitched sound.

screen screens screening screened
1 (n) A screen is a surface on which a picture can be shown; for example, on televisions or on computers.
2 (n) A screen is a portable, covered framework used to partition off part of a room, to protect people from draughts or to hide something.
3 (vb) If a doctor screens someone they are carefully examined to see if they are healthy.
4 (vb) If you screen someone you question them thoroughly to see if they might be a security risk in their job.

screw screws screwing screwed
1 (n) A screw is a metal pin with a spiral groove cut into it, used to fasten things together.
2 (vb) If you screw something, you fasten it into position with a screw.

scribble scribbles scribbling scribbled
1 (vb) If you scribble, you make squiggly, random marks with a pencil or pen on paper or another surface.
2 (vb) If you scribble, you write very quickly and carelessly.

script scripts
1 (n) A script is the written version of a film, play or television programme.
2 (n) Script is a particular handwriting style.

scripture scriptures
1 (n) A scripture is a collection of sacred or religious writings.
2 (n) The Scriptures refers to the Christian Bible.

S

scroll scrolls (n) A scroll is a roll of parchment, paper or other material with writing on it.

scrounge scrounges scrounging scrounged (vb) If you scrounge, you ask people for money or for food, clothes, etc. instead of buying them. **scrounger** (n)

scrub scrubs scrubbing scrubbed
1 (vb) If you scrub something, you rub it very hard to clean it.
2 (n) Scrub is dry ground covered with small trees and bushes.

scrum scrums (n) A scrum is a pack of rugby players, from each team, who push against each other to get possession of the ball.

scrumptious (adj) Scrumptious food is delicious to eat.

scrupulous (adj) people are careful to be fair and to do things properly.

scrutinise scrutinises scrutinising scrutinised (vb) If you scrutinise something, you look at it and examine it very thoroughly. **scrutiny** (n)

scuba diving (n) is an underwater activity needing special breathing equipment to allow underwater exploration.

scum (n) is a layer of dirty froth that sometimes forms on top of a liquid.

scurry scurries scurrying scurried (vb) If you scurry, you move very quickly.

scurvy (n) is a disease caused by a lack of vitamin C, which is the vitamin found in fresh fruit and vegetables.

scuttle scuttles scuttling scuttled
1 (vb) If a person or animal scuttles, they run quickly but with short steps.
2 (vb) If a captain scuttles his ship, he orders it to be sunk.
3 (n) A scuttle is a metal container for coal, usually kept near to the fire.

scythe scythes (n) A scythe is a long-handled tool with a long curved blade. It is used to cut grass, wheat, oats, etc.

sea seas
1 (n) The sea is the salty water that covers about three quarters of the surface of the earth.
2 (n) A sea is a large area of water, often completely surrounded by land. *The Mediterranean Sea ... The North Sea.*

seal seals sealing sealed
1 (n) A seal is a sea animal that lives partly on rocky coasts and partly in the sea.
2 (vb) If you seal something, you fasten it firmly.
3 (adj) A sealed container has all the openings blocked so that nothing, not even air, can get in.
4 (n) A seal is an official mark of a person or organisation.

seam seams
1 (n) A seam is the line of stitches that joins two pieces of cloth together.
2 (n) A seam is a deposit of coal, iron ore, copper, etc found underground and layered between other rocks.

search searches searching searched
1 (vb) If you search for something, you look carefully for it.
2 (n) A search is an attempt to find someone or something that is hidden.
3 (adj) If a person has a searching look or asks a searching question they try very hard to discover the truth.

seashore seashores (n) The seashore is the land at the edge of the sea.

S

seasick

seasick (adj) If you are seasick, the movement of a boat on the sea makes you feel sick. **seasickness** (n)

seaside (n) The seaside is a place near the sea especially where people go on holiday.

season seasons
1 (n) The seasons are the four parts of the year: Spring, Summer, Autumn, Winter.
2 (n) A season is a period of time during the year when something regularly happens. *The holiday season . . . the football season . . . the nesting season.*
seasonal (adj)

seaweed seaweeds (n) Seaweed is a plant that grows in the sea.

secateurs (n) are a pair of gardening clippers used for cutting and pruning plants and trees.

secluded (adj) A secluded place is a private, quiet place where you are not likely to be disturbed. **seclusion** (n)

second seconds seconding seconded
1 (n) A second is $\frac{1}{60}$th of a minute. There are 60 seconds in one minute.
2 (n) A second is a very short period of time.
3 (n) The second in a series comes after the first and before the third.
4 (n) Seconds are items sold cheaply in shops because they are not top quality.
5 (n) The person who helps and supports a fighter in a boxing match or a duel is called a second.
6 (vb) If you second someone who suggests something in a meeting or a debate, you agree with and support their suggestions.

secondary
1 (adj) Something secondary is of less importance than something else. *My parents think my hobby should be secondary to my school work.*
2 (adj) Secondary schools are for older children between the ages of eleven and eighteen.

second-hand (adj) things are not new and have already been used by someone else.

second-rate (adj) Something second-rate is of a low or inferior quality.

secret secrets
1 (n) A secret is something known only to a very few people.
2 If you do something in secret, you do it without anyone knowing about it.

secret agent secret agents (n) A secret agent is someone whose job it is to find out the secret plans of other governments.

secretary secretaries (n) A secretary is someone employed to type letters and documents, take phone messages and to arrange business meetings, etc.

secretive (adj) people like to keep their business and ideas to themselves.

sect sects (n) A sect is a group of people who separate from a larger religious or political group, because they have formed particular beliefs.

section sections (n) A section is one of the separate parts into which something is divided. *The fence was in six sections.*

secure secures securing secured
1 (vb) If you secure something, you make it safe.
2 (adj) If something is secure, it is safe from danger, damage or harm. **security** (n)

sedate (adj) means calm, quiet and serious.

sedative sedatives (n) A sedative is a drug or a medicine that calms you or makes you sleep.

sedentary (adj) A sedentary job is one that involves a good deal of sitting at a desk, for example.

sediment sediments
1 (n) Sediment is the solid particles that sometimes settle at the bottom of a liquid.
2 (n) Sediment is earth and rocks that have been carried along by rivers, ice or wind, for example, and deposited somewhere.

seductive (adj) Someone or something that is seductive is so attractive that it is difficult to resist. **seduction** (n)

seed seeds
1 (n) A seed is a small, hard part of a plant which can grow if planted.
2 (n) A seed in a sport, such as tennis, is a top player who has been graded according to his or her skill.

S

seep seeps seeping seeped (vb) If liquids or fumes seep, they gradually trickle or move through small openings or cracks.

seethe seethes seething seethed
1 (vb) If liquid seethes, it boils and bubbles.
2 (vb) If you seethe, you are angry but trying to keep your anger under control.
3 (vb) If a place seethes with people or animals, there are great numbers of them all moving around.

segment segments (n) A segment is a section.

segregate segregates segregating segregated (vb) If you segregate two groups of people, animals or things, you keep them apart from each other. **segregation** (n)

seismograph seismographs (n) A seismograph is an instrument for recording earthquakes and measuring their strength.

seize seizes seizing seized
1 (vb) If you seize something, you take hold of it firmly and quickly.
2 (vb) When a group of people or an army seize a place, they take control by force.
3 (vb) If you seize a person, you take them prisoner or arrest them.

seldom (adv) means not very often.

select selects selecting selected
1 (vb) If you select something or someone, you choose them carefully. **selection** (n)
2 (adj) Something that is select is the very best of its kind. *A select group of musicians . . . a select house.*

self selves (n) Your self is your own personality. It is what makes you different from anyone else.

self-centred (adj) people are selfish and think only of themselves.

self-conscious (adj) If you are self-conscious, you are shy and embarrassed when you have to meet people or do anything in public.

self-controlled (adj) people are able to control their feelings.

self-defence (n) is a series of physical skills you can learn in order to protect yourself if you are attacked.

self-employed (adj) A self-employed person works at their own business instead of working and receiving pay from someone else. **self-employment** (n)

selfish (adj) Selfish people care for nobody but themselves.

self-portrait self-portraits (n) A self-portrait is a painting, drawing or written description that you do of yourself.

self-respect (n) is a feeling of pride in your own value and worth.

self-service (adj) If a shop, garage, cafe, etc, is self-service, the customers serve themselves with what they need.

self-sufficient (adj) A country or a group of people that are self-sufficient are able to produce for themselves all the things they need. **self-sufficiency** (n)

semaphore (n) is a signalling system using a flag in each hand. Each position represents a letter of the alphabet.

semicircle semicircles (n) A semicircle is one half of a circle.

semi-colon semi-colons (n) A semi-colon is a punctuation mark. It is used between statements which are linked to each other. *The house was deserted; silence filled every corridor and room.*

semi-detached (adj) A semi-detached house is joined along one side to another house.

semi-final semi-finals (n) In a competition a semi-final is one of two matches played to decide who will compete in the final.

semolina (n) is small grains of wheat used for making milk puddings and also pasta.

senile (adj) If old people become senile, their minds become confused and their bodies weak and feeble. **senility** (n)

senior seniors
1 (adj) If someone is senior to you, they are older than you or in a higher position.
2 (adj) In organisations such as schools and businesses, the senior staff are those that hold the most important jobs.
3 (n) In a school, the seniors are the older pupils. **seniority** (n)

S

senior citizen senior citizens (n) Senior citizens are people old enough to receive an old age pension.

sensation sensations
1 (n) A sensation is a physical feeling experienced by your body. *She woke with a tingling sensation in her foot.*
2 (n) A sensation can be an emotional feeling, or mental impression. *He had the sensation that he was being watched.*
3 (n) A sensation is a happening that causes great public interest and excitement.
sensational (adj)

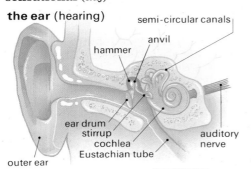

the ear (hearing)
semi-circular canals
anvil
hammer
ear drum
stirrup
cochlea
Eustachian tube
auditory nerve
outer ear

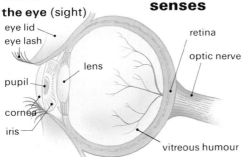

the eye (sight)
eye lid
eye lash
lens
pupil
cornea
iris
retina
optic nerve
vitreous humour

senses

mouth
p186

sense senses sensing sensed
1 (n) Our senses are the five powers that make us aware of the world around us. They are sight, smell, hearing, taste and touch.
2 (vb) If you sense something, you have a feeling it might happen or you become aware of it.
3 (n) A sense is a particular ability to be good or clever at something. *A sense of direction ... clothes sense.*
4 If you have sense, you are level-headed and good at making wise decisions.
5 If something makes sense, it is easy to understand and seems to be a good idea.

sensible (adj) Someone who is sensible is able to make wise decisions and judgements.

sensitive
1 (adj) A sensitive person is aware of beautiful and artistic things and shows great understanding of other people's problems and feelings. **sensitivity** (n)
2 (adj) If you are sensitive to something, your body is affected by it. *My skin is sensitive to sun and comes up in a rash.*
3 (adj) If you are sensitive about something, it embarrasses and worries you.
4 (adj) A sensitive piece of equipment can measure extremely small reactions and changes, for example, in temperature, light rays, etc.

sentence sentences sentencing sentenced
1 (n) A sentence is a group of words that make a statement, question or command. A sentence starts with a capital letter and ends with a full stop, question mark or exclamation mark. *I like vanilla ice-cream. Are you coming to tea? Get out of my sight at once!*
2 (n) In a law court, the sentence is the punishment given to the person found guilty of a crime.
3 (vb) When a judge sentences someone found guilty of a crime, he says what their punishment will be.

sentimental
1 (adj) A sentimental person is rather romantic and emotional.
2 (adj) Books, films, songs, poems, newspaper articles, etc that are sentimental arouse the emotions, especially the tender, romantic and sad ones.

sentry sentries (n) A sentry is a soldier on guard duty, guarding camps, etc.

separate separates separating separated (vb) If you separate people or things you keep them apart from each other. **separation** (n)

septic (adj) If a wound or part of the body is septic, it is infected by bacteria and becomes swollen and painful.

sepulchre sepulchres (n) A sepulchre is a large tomb or vault where bodies are buried.

S

sequel sequels (n) The sequel to a book, film, etc is another that follows later and continues the story.

sequence sequences (n) A sequence is a number of things that follow one after the other in a particular order or pattern. *A sequence of events.*

sequin sequins (n) Sequins are small, shiny discs, sewn onto clothes for decoration.

serene (adj) Someone or something that is serene is calm, quiet and peaceful.
serenity (n)

sergeant sergeants (n) Sergeant is a rank in the army, air-force and police-force.

serial serials (n) A serial is a story told or presented in a number of parts at regular intervals on television, radio or in a magazine.

series
1 (n) A series is a group of similar things in sequence. *We had a series of talks about space this term.*
2 (n) A series on radio or television is a set of programmes each telling a different story but with the same characters. *Dr. Who has been a popular television series.*

serious
1 (adj) Serious ideas and plans are important and need careful thought.
2 (adj) A serious situation or problem is very bad and likely to cause trouble or worry.

sermon sermons (n) A sermon is a talk given by a clergyman as part of a religious service in a church or chapel.

serpent serpents (n) Serpent is an old-fashioned name for a snake.

servant servants (n) A servant is a person employed to do domestic work in someone's house.

serve serves serving served
1 (vb) If you serve in a shop, you work there selling goods to customers.
2 (vb) If you serve someone a meal, you give them food and drink.
3 (vb) If you serve your country, community or a business company, you work for them faithfully for many years.

4 (vb) Someone who serves a prison sentence spends time in prison.
5 (vb) In some games, tennis, for example, one player serves to start the game by throwing up the ball and hitting it to the other players.

service services servicing serviced
1 (n) Service is the activity of serving your country, or doing your duty or just working at a particular job.
2 (n) A service is an organisation that provides people with something they need.
3 (n) If you provide a service, you do a particular job that people need done.
4 (n) The Services are the Army, the Navy and the Air Force.
5 (n) Services are the things paid for by taxes and rates and the community charge: schools, hospitals, roads, for example.

serviette serviettes (n) A serviette is a small square of cloth or paper used to protect your clothing while you eat.

session sessions
1 (n) A session is a period of time used for a particular activity. *Gym sessions... recording sessions.*
2 (n) A session is a meeting of an official group; a parliament, a law court, a council, for example.

setback setbacks (n) A setback is something that delays you or hampers your progress in some way.

settee settees (n) A settee is a long, padded, comfortable seat.

sever severs severing severed (vb) If you sever something, you cut it right through so that it comes away from the main part.

several (adj) is a quantity, not a large number but more than two.

severe severer severest
1 (adj) A severe situation or something that is severe is very unpleasant and difficult.
severity (n)
2 (adj) A severe person is very strict.

sew sews sewing sewed (vb) If you sew, you use a needle and thread to join pieces of material together to make clothes, etc.

sewage (n) refers to all the waste water and human waste products that are carried away from buildings by sewage pipes.

S

sex

sex sexes
1 (n) The sexes are the two groups into which most living things are divided, either male or female.
2 (n) Your sex refers to the bodily characteristics you have which make you male or female.
3 (n) Sex is the activity by which people and animals can produce young, involving the joining of the sex organs.

sexism (n) is the belief that one sex is less intelligent, less able than the other group, or in some other way inferior to it.
sexist (adj)

sextant sextants (n) A sextant is an instrument used on ships or aeroplanes for navigation.

shack shacks (n) A shack is a hut, roughly and quickly made from bits of wood, tin, cardboard, etc.

shackles (n) are two metal rings joined by a chain fixed around someone's wrists or ankles to stop them escaping.

shade shades shading shaded
1 (n) Shade is an area of darkness where the sun does not reach.
2 (vb) If you shade a person or a thing, you protect them from the sun's heat or light.
3 (n) A shade is a cover for a light bulb.
4 (n) The shades of a colour are all the varieties of it from dark to light.

shadow shadows shadowing shadowed
1 (n) A shadow is the dark shape that shows on a surface when something stands between it and a light source.
2 (n) Shadow is an area of darkness caused by lack of light.
3 (vb) If something shadows an area, it shades it from from direct light.
4 (vb) If you shadow someone, you follow them secretly to find out what they are doing.

shaft shafts
1 (n) The shaft of a spear or arrow is the long, thin part to which the head is attached.
2 (n) The handle of a golf club and of certain tools is called a shaft.
3 (n) In a machine a shaft is a rod that turns to transmit power or movement.

4 (n) A shaft is a long, vertical space. *A mine shaft . . . a lift shaft.*

coal mine p50

shaggy shaggier shaggiest
1 (adj) Shaggy hair or fur is long, thick and untidy.
2 A shaggy dog story is an extremely long joke with a rather pointless ending.

shake shakes shaking shook shaken
1 (vb) If you shake something or someone, you hold them and move them quickly up and down, back and forth or from side to side.
2 (vb) If your body shakes, it trembles violently because of fear, cold or illness.
3 (vb) If your voice shakes, it sounds wobbly and strange because you are nervous, angry or upset.

Shakespeare, William (1564–1616) was an English playwright and poet. He wrote more than thirty plays in twenty-one years, most of which are still performed today.

shallot shallots (n) A shallot is a vegetable rather like a small onion.

shallow shallower shallowest
1 (n) Something shallow is not deep.
2 (n) If someone's breathing is shallow, they take in only a little air at a time.

shame shames shaming shamed
1 (n) Shame is the unpleasant guilty feeling you have if you have done something wrong. **shameful** (adj)
2 (vb) If you shame someone, you do something to cause them great embarrassment.

shampoo shampoos shampooing shampooed
1 (n) Shampoo is a liquid for washing hair.
2 (vb) If you shampoo hair, you wash it using shampoo.

shamrock shamrocks (n) The shamrock is a small, green plant which is the national emblem of Ireland.

shandy shandies (n) Shandy is a drink made by mixing beer with lemonade.

shanty shanties
1 (n) A shanty is a hut, roughly made from odds and ends of wood, cardboard, etc. which is not very strong.
2 (n) A shanty is a song that sailors used to sing while they were working on a ship.

shape shapes shaping shaped
1 (n) The shape of something is its outline or external form.
2 (vb) If you shape something, you make it into a particular shape.

share shares sharing shared
1 (vb) If you share something with someone, you each have a part of it, or you can each use it.
2 (n) A share of something is a part of it.
3 (vb) If a group of people share a task, they each do a part of it.
4 (n) A share in a company is one of the many equal parts into which the ownership of the company can be divided. Shares can be bought by people as an investment.

shark sharks (n) A shark is a large sea-fish with extremely sharp teeth.

sharp sharper sharpest
1 (adj) Something that is sharp, a knife or a sword for example, has a fine edge used for cutting, or a finely pointed end, like a needle or pencil.
2 (adj) A sharp person is clever.
3 (adj) A sharp change is a sudden change.
4 (adj) A sharp pain is a strong sudden pain.
5 (adj) A sharp taste is sour.

sharpen sharpens sharpening sharpened (vb) If you sharpen something, a knife or pencil for example, you make it more pointed.

shatter shatters shattering shattered
1 (vb) If you shatter something or it shatters, it breaks into small pieces suddenly and violently.
2 (vb) If news shatters you, you are extremely upset by it.

shave shaves shaving shaved
1 (vb) When a man shaves, he removes hair from his face with a razor.
2 (vb) When someone shaves, they remove hair from parts of their body with a razor.
3 (vb) If you shave something, a piece of wood, for example, you cut thin slices from it with a sharp instrument.

shawl shawls (n) A shawl is a large piece of soft material worn by women around the head or shoulders, or wrapped around babies to keep them warm.

sheaf sheaves
1 (n) A sheaf is a bundle of cut wheat or other grain tied around the middle.
2 (n) A sheaf of papers is a bundle of papers.

shear shears shearing sheared shorn
1 (vb) When someone shears a sheep, they cut off its woolly fleece with a sharp pair of cutters called shears.
2 (vb) If you shear something, you cut it short with a sharp instrument.
3 (n) The scissor-like garden tool used for cutting hedges is called a pair of shears.

sheath sheathes (n) A sheath is a cover for the sharp blade of a knife, sword, etc.

sheathe sheathes sheathing sheathed
1 (vb) If you sheathe a knife or a sword, you put it into a sheath.
2 (vb) If an animal sheathes its claws, it draws them back into their protective sheath.

sheen (n) is the shine on the surface of something.

sheep sheep (n) A sheep is a farm animal, bred for its wool and its meat.

sheepdog sheepdogs (n) A sheepdog is a dog bred and trained to control sheep.

sheer
1 (adj) A sheer mountainside or a sheer drop is almost vertical.
2 (adj) Cloth that is sheer is so thin that you can see through it.
3 (adj) Sheer means complete or absolute. *Sheer nonsense . . . sheer luck.*

sheet sheets
1 (n) A sheet is a large rectangle of cloth used for bed coverings.
2 (n) A sheet of something such as metal or paper is a thin, flat square or rectangular piece of it.
3 (n) A sheet of water or ice, for example, is a large, flat expanse of it.

sheikh sheikhs (n) A sheikh is an Arab ruler or chieftain.

shelf shelves
1 (n) A shelf is a length of wood, metal, glass, etc. fixed to a wall or to the inside of a cupboard and used to keep things on.
2 (n) A shelf is an area of rock sticking out from a cliff or a mountainside.

S

shell

shell shells shelling shelled
1 (n) A shell is the hard outer covering of eggs or nuts, for example.
2 (vb) If you shell nuts, peas or eggs, you take off their covering.
3 (n) Some creatures, such as snails and tortoises, have shells covering parts of their bodies as protection.
4 (n) Shells are the outer coverings of many small sea creatures, often found on beaches.
5 (n) A shell is the metal container for explosives that are fired from guns.
6 (vb) If troops shell a place, they fire explosive shells at it.
7 (n) The shell of a building, boat, etc. is the framework before it is properly built or what is left after most of it has been destroyed.

shellfish (n) are sea creatures with shells. People eat some kinds of shellfish; prawns, crabs, mussels, for example.

shelter shelters sheltering sheltered
1 (n) A shelter is a place, a small building, a cave, etc, where you can hide or be protected from bad weather or danger.
2 (vb) If you shelter, you stay somewhere where you are protected.
3 (vb) If you shelter someone, you protect or help them by providing a place for them to stay.
4 (adj) A sheltered place is protected from very bad weather.
5 Sheltered accommodation is housing where old or handicapped people can live independently but where help and support is available.

shelve shelves shelving shelved (vb) If you shelve a plan, you decide not to carry it out for a while.

shepherd shepherds (n) A shepherd is someone whose job it is to look after sheep.

sheriff sheriffs
1 (n) In America, a sheriff is the law enforcement officer of a county.
2 (n) In Scotland, a sheriff is a senior judge.
3 (n) A sheriff in England or Wales is someone appointed by the Queen to carry out ceremonial duties.

sherry sherries (n) Sherry is a kind of wine usually drunk before meals.

shield shields shielding shielded
1 (n) A shield is a piece of armour carried in one hand to protect the body.
2 (n) Shields of various kinds are used to protect the body. *Eye shield . . . wind shield.*
3 (vb) If someone or something shields you from damage or danger, they protect you.

shift shifts shifting shifted
1 (vb) If something shifts, it moves from one position to another. *The wind shifted to the south.*
2 (n) A shift is a slight change in something.
3 (n) A shift is a group of workers who work for a particular period during the day or the night.

shimmer shimmers shimmering shimmered (vb) If something shimmers, it shines with a soft light that seems to move over the surface.

shin shins (n) Your shin is the front, bony part of your leg between knee and ankle.

skeleton p273

shine shines shining shone shined
1 (vb) When the sun or a light shines, it gives out light.
2 (vb) If you shine a light on something, you light it up by using a torch, candle, etc.
3 (vb) If an object shines, it is bright because light is reflected from its surface.
4 (vb) If you shine something, you rub it with a cloth until its surface is gleaming and bright. **shiny** (adj)

shingle (n) is a mass of pebbles found on some beaches or at the edges of rivers.

ship ships shipping shipped
1 (n) A ship is a large sea-going boat that carries passengers or cargo.
2 (vb) If you ship goods or people somewhere, they are carried there by ship or by some other kind of transport.
3 (n) Shipping is a group of ships.

shipshape (adj) means very neat and tidy.

shipwreck shipwrecks
1 (n) A shipwreck is an accident at sea causing the destruction or sinking of a ship.
2 (n) A shipwreck is the remains of a ship that has been damaged or sunk.

shipyard shipyards (n) A shipyard is a place where ships are built or repaired.

shirk shirks shirking shirked (vb) If you shirk, you get out of doing a job.

shirt shirts (n) A shirt is a piece of clothing worn on the upper part of the body particularly by men.

shiver shivers shivering shivered (vb) When a person or animal shivers they shake all over because they are frightened, ill or cold. **shivery** (adj)

shoal shoals
1 (n) A shoal is a large number of fish swimming together.
2 (n) Shoals are shallow waters with sandbanks or rocks showing at low tide.

shock shocks shocking shocked
1 (n) Shock is a sudden nasty feeling of fear or anxiety when something unpleasant happens.
2 (vb) If something shocks you, it upsets you because it is unpleasant or unexpected.
3 (n) A shock is pain caused by electricity passing through a body.
4 (adj) Something shocking is very bad or unpleasant.

shockproof (adj) watches are very tough and cannot damage easily.

shoddy shoddier shoddiest (adj) Something shoddy is of poor quality and badly made.

shoe shoes shoeing shod
1 (n) A shoe is one of a pair of foot coverings.
2 (vb) When blacksmiths shoe horses, they fix horseshoes onto their hooves.

shoot shoots shooting shot
1 (vb) If you shoot, you fire bullets from a gun.
2 (vb) If you shoot an animal or a person, you wound them or kill them by firing a gun at them.
3 (n) A shoot is a gathering of people who meet to shoot animals or birds for sport.
4 (vb) If someone shoots a goal in a match, they send the ball towards the goal.
5 (vb) When someone shoots a film, they photograph it with a camera.
6 (n) A shoot is a new growth either from a seed or a bulb or on an existing plant.

shooting star shooting stars (n) A shooting star is a meteor that heats up and glows when it enters Earth's atmosphere from space, making a bright streak across the sky for a few moments.

shop shops shopping shopped
1 (n) A shop is a building or part of a building where people can go to buy things.
2 (vb) When people shop they buy things.

shore shores (n) The land at the edge of the sea or a lake is called the shore.

short shorter shortest
1 (adj) If a distance or something you can measure is short, it is not far from one end of it to the other.
2 (adj) Short people are not very tall.
3 (adj) If something lasts for a short time, it does not last long.
4 (adj) If you are short of something, or if it is short, you do not have enough of it.

shortage shortages (n) If there is a shortage of something, there is not enough of it.

shorten shortens shortening shortened (vb) If you shorten something, you make it shorter.

shorthand (n) is a way of writing very quickly by using special signs.

shortly (adv) If something is being done or going to happen shortly, it will happen very soon.

shorts (n) are trousers with shorter legs, usually ending above the knee.

short-sighted
1 (adj) If you are short-sighted, you cannot see far away things very clearly.
2 (adj) If you behave in a short-sighted way, you do not plan ahead for the future.

short-tempered (adj) A short-tempered person gets angry easily.

shot see **shoot**

shotgun shotguns (n) A shotgun is a shoulder gun used mainly for hunting birds and animals.

should If you should do something, you ought to do it.

shoulder shoulders (n) The shoulder is the part of the body where the arm is joined to the main body.

skeleton
p273

shout shouts shouting shouted
1 (n) A shout is a loud call or cry.
2 (vb) If people shout, they make a loud noise to attract attention.

S

shove

shove shoves shoving shoved (vb) If you shove someone or something, you give them a forceful push.

shovel shovels (n) A shovel is a large spade used for moving snow, coal, etc.

show shows showing showed shown
1 (vb) If you show something to someone, you let them see it or you point it out.
2 (vb) If something shows, you are able to see it. *That stain on the carpet shows.*
3 (vb) If you show a feeling or emotion, anger, for example, your looks and behaviour show that you are angry.
4 (n) A show is a form of entertainment which usually includes comedy acts, singing, dancing, etc.
5 (n) Radio or TV programmes can be called shows.
6 (n) A show is an exhibition or a display.

show business (n) refers to all the activities and people involved in the entertainment industry.

shower showers
1 (n) A shower is a short period of rain.
2 (n) A shower is a device which sprays water all over you so you can wash.
3 (n) A shower is a fall of lightweight things, petals or leaves for example.

shrank see **shrink**

shrapnel (n) refers to the pieces of metal that fly from exploding shells and bombs.

shred shreds shredding shredded
1 (vb) If you shred something, you tear or cut it into thin strips.
2 (n) A shred is a thin strip of something.

shrew shrews (n) A shrew is a tiny, fierce, mouselike animal with a long nose.

shrewd shrewder shrewdest
1 (adj) A shrewd person is quick and clever at understanding things and can use their knowledge to their own advantage.
2 (adj) A shrewd idea or decision is a wise one.

shriek shrieks shrieking shrieked
1 (n) A shriek is a loud, sharp, piercing cry.
2 (vb) If someone shrieks, they give a sharp scream of pain, fear or laughter.

shrill shriller shrillest (adj) A shrill sound is high pitched and rather unpleasant.

shrimp shrimps (n) Shrimps are small shellfish, some can be eaten.

shrine shrines
1 (n) A shrine is a place thought to be holy because it is connected with a sacred person or thing. People worship at shrines.
2 (n) A shrine is a container for sacred relics, the bones of saints for example.

shrink shrinks shrinking shrank shrunk
1 (vb) If you shrink something or something shrinks, it becomes smaller in size.
2 (vb) If you shrink from someone or something, you move away because you are disgusted or afraid.

shrivel shrivels shrivelling shrivelled (vb) If something shrivels, it dries up and becomes wrinkled usually because of lack of moisture or exposure to the sun.

shroud shrouds shrouding shrouded
1 (n) A shroud is a cloth used for wrapping a dead body.
2 (vb) If you shroud something, you cover or hide it.
3 (adj) A shrouded place is covered or hidden by fog, heavy rain, darkness, trees, etc.

shrub shrubs (n) A shrub is a bushy plant with woody stems.

shrubbery shrubberies (n) A shrubbery is an area in a garden or park where shrubs grow.

shrug shrugs shrugging shrugged (vb) If you shrug, you lift your shoulders slightly to show you are not sure about something, not interested, or that you do not care.

shrunk see **shrink**

shudder shudders shuddering shuddered
1 (vb) If someone shudders, their body trembles and shakes with strong emotions, fear or disgust for example.
2 (vb) If a vehicle or a machine shudders, it starts to shake violently.

shuffle shuffles shuffling shuffled
1 (vb) If you shuffle, you walk without lifting your feet properly.
2 (vb) When you shuffle a pack of cards, you mix them up before dealing them.

shunt shunts shunting shunted
1 (vb) When a railway engine shunts, it moves carriages from one track to another.
2 (vb) If you shunt things or people, you move them from one place to another.

shutter shutters
1 (n) A shutter is a part of a camera which separates the film from the lens.
2 (n) Shutters are wooden or metal covers for windows or doors.

shuttle shuttles shuttling shuttled
1 (n) A shuttle is a plane or train which does the same journey continually.
2 (n) A shuttle is a type of American spacecraft.
3 (n) A shuttle is a piece of equipment used in weaving. It takes thread backwards and forwards over the other threads to make a piece of material.

shuttlecock shuttlecocks (n) A shuttlecock is the feather-like object you hit in a game of badminton.

shy shies shying shied
1 (adj) A shy person is uncomfortable with people they don't know.
2 (vb) If a person or an animal shies away from something, they jump away because they are surprised.

sibling siblings (n) Your sibling is your brother or sister.

sick sicker sickest
1 (adj) If you are sick, you vomit and bring back up the contents of your stomach.
2 (adj) If you feel sick, you feel ill.
3 (adj) If you are sick of something, you are tired of it.
4 (adj) A sick joke or remark is tasteless and offensive.

side sides
1 (n) The sides of something are the parts other than the back or front of it.
2 (adj) A side road is one which is less important than the main roads.
3 (n) The sides in a war or in a competition are the people opposing each other.

sidecar sidecars (n) A sidecar is a wheeled box, often with a seat, fixed to the side of a motorcycle for a passenger.

sideways
1 (adv) If something moves sideways, it moves towards one side or the other.
2 (adv) If something is positioned so that its sides are where the front and back are usually placed, it is sideways.

siding sidings (n) A siding is a railway track where trains are kept when they are not being used.

siege sieges
1 (n) A siege is a military operation in which a town or castle is surrounded and the attackers try to prevent supplies reaching the defenders.
2 (n) Any situation where a place is surrounded in order to force the people inside to come out is a siege.

siesta siestas (n) In hot countries a siesta is a rest in the middle of the day.

sieve sieves sieving sieved
1 (n) A sieve is a device with small holes used to separate liquids from solids, or small pieces from large pieces.
2 (vb) If you sieve something, you use a sieve to separate its parts.

sift sifts sifting sifted
1 (vb) If you sift a powder, you shake it through a sieve to remove any lumps.
2 (vb) If you sift information or evidence, you go through it to find the important details.

sigh sighs sighing sighed
1 (n) A sigh is a deep breath, loud enough to be heard.
2 (vb) If you sigh, you let out a deep breath when you are tired, depressed or relieved.

sight sights
1 (n) Your sight is your ability to see.
2 (n) The sights are the things worth seeing in a city or country you are visiting.
sightseeing (n)
3 (n) The sights on a gun are the parts you look through in order to aim correctly.
4 If you catch sight of something, you see it or notice it.

senses (eye)
p264

sign

sign signs signing signed
1 (n) A sign is a mark or a symbol which has a particular meaning.
2 (n) A sign is a piece of metal, wood or card which gives information, directions, warnings or instructions.
3 (n) If you make a sign, you use your arms or body to make a gesture.
4 (vb) If you sign something, you write your name on it. **signature** (n)

signal signals signalling signalled
1 (vb) If you signal to someone, you make a gesture to show them what you want.
2 (n) A signal is a gesture, or mechanical device which gives warnings or instructions.

significant (adj) Something significant is important or large enough to be noticed.

signpost signposts (n) A signpost is a post showing the distances and directions to towns, villages, etc.

Sikh Sikhs (n) A Sikh is a follower of the religious teachings of Guru Nanak and his successors. Sikhs believe in one God called Nam.

silage (n) is a crop, stored and fermented to make winter food for farm animals.

silencer silencers
1 (n) A silencer is a part of the exhaust on a motor vehicle which helps to quieten the engine.
2 (n) A silencer can be fitted to a gun to deaden the noise of a shot.

silent
1 (adj) Someone or something that is silent makes no noise at all.
2 (adj) A silent letter in a written word is one that is not sounded when it is spoken. *The k in knife is silent.*

silhouette silhouettes (n) A silhouette is the dark shape of something against a light background. **silhouetted** (adj)

silicon (n) is an element used in computer equipment and glass.

silk silks (n) Silk is a fine material made from fibres spun by silkworms.

silkworm silkworms (n) A silkworm is a caterpillar which produces silk to form its cocoon.

silly sillier silliest (adj) A silly person does not think or behave in a sensible way.

silo silos
1 (n) A silo is a storage tower on a farm for silage, grain, etc.
2 (n) A silo is a concrete bunker where nuclear missiles are kept, ready for launching.

silt silts silting silted
1 (n) Silt is fine sand, mud, etc. which is carried along by a river.
2 (vb) If a river, harbour, etc. silts up, it becomes clogged with silt.

silver silver
1 (n) Silver is a precious metal used for jewellery and ornaments.
2 (adj) Silver is used to describe things which are the same colour as silver.

similar (adj) things are alike in some way. **similarity** (n)

simile similes (n) A simile describes something by comparing it to something else. *He was as fierce as a tiger.*

simple simpler simplest
1 (adj) Something simple is easy to understand.
2 (adj) If food, clothing, etc. is simple it is plain.
3 (adj) A simple person behaves in an honest and straightforward way.

simplify simplifies simplifying simplified (vb) If you simplify something, you make it easier to understand.

simultaneous (adj) events happen at the same time.

sin sins sinning sinned
1 (n) A sin is something you believe to be morally wrong.
2 (vb) If you sin, you do something you believe is morally wrong.

since
1 (conj) Since is used to show that time has gone by. *It's five years since he left.*
2 (conj) Since can mean from the last time. *He is the first man to fall in the lake since Jones did it in 1960.*
3 (conj) Since can mean because. *We suffer from noise since we live near the motorway.*

S

skeleton

sincere (adj) A sincere person is one who says what they mean or believe.

sinew sinews (n) Sinews are the fibres which join muscles and bones in the body.

sing sings singing sang (vb) If you sing you make musical sounds with your voice. **singer** (n)

singe singes singeing singed (vb) If you singe something, you scorch or burn it slightly without it catching fire.

single
1 (adj) A single person is not married.
2 (adj) A single ticket will only take you on a one way journey.
3 (n) A single is a type of record with only one song on each side.

single-minded (adj) If you are single-minded about something, you are determined and will not let anything distract you.

singular
1 (adj) If something is singular, it is highly unusual.
2 (n) In grammar, the singular means one of something.

sinister (adj) Something sinister is threatening or frightening.

sink sinks sinking sank
1 (vb) If something sinks, it moves down below the surface of water, for example.
2 (vb) If a ship sinks, it fills with water and goes under the surface.
3 (vb) If your voice sinks, it gets lower.
4 (n) A sink is a large basin with taps, used for washing things.

siren sirens (n) A siren is a loud warning sound, used on ambulances, police cars, etc. and on buildings.

sister sisters
1 (n) Your sister is a girl who has the same parents as you.
2 (n) A sister is a nun.

sister-in-law sisters-in-law (n) Your sister-in-law is either your brother's wife or your husband's or wife's sister.

skateboard skateboards (n) A skateboard is a small board with wheels, on which you can stand and ride or do tricks.

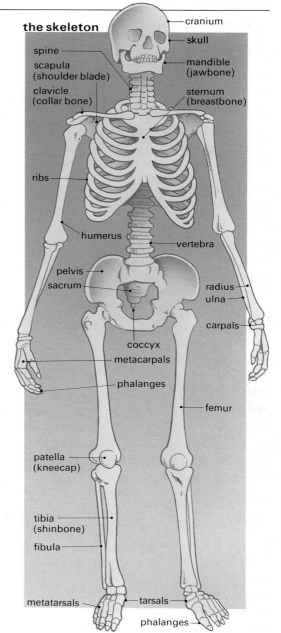

the skeleton

cranium
skull
spine
scapula (shoulder blade)
mandible (jawbone)
clavicle (collar bone)
sternum (breastbone)
ribs
humerus
vertebra
pelvis
sacrum
radius
ulna
carpals
coccyx
metacarpals
phalanges
femur
patella (kneecap)
tibia (shinbone)
fibula
metatarsals
tarsals
phalanges

skeleton skeletons
1 (n) The skeleton is the bony framework inside the body of humans or animals which supports the muscles and organs.
2 A skeleton in the cupboard is something in your past that you wish to keep quiet.

S

273

sketch

sketch sketches sketching sketched
1 (vb) If you sketch, you draw something quickly.
2 (n) A sketch is a quick drawing.
3 (n) A sketch is a short comic piece of acting.

skewer skewers skewering skewered
(n) A skewer is a long, thin piece of metal used to hold meat together.

ski skis skiing skied
1 (n) Skis are narrow pieces of wood, metal or plastic, worn on boots to enable you to glide over snow.
2 (vb) When skiing, you travel over snow on skis. **skier** (n)

skill skills (n) A skill is an ability to do something well. **skilful** (adj)

skim skims skimming skimmed
1 (vb) If you skim a liquid, you remove a thin layer from the surface.
2 (vb) If you skim over something, you pass very close to the surface of it.
3 (vb) If you skim a piece of writing, you read through it quickly.

skin skins skinning skinned
1 (n) Skin is the outer covering of human or animal bodies.
2 (n) Skin is the outer covering of fruit.
3 (vb) If you skin an animal, you remove its skin.

skipper skippers (n) A skipper is the captain of a ship or of a team.

skirt skirts skirting skirted
1 (n) A skirt is a garment worn by women and girls covering from the waist downwards.
2 (vb) If you skirt something, you go around the edges.

skittles (n) Skittles is a game in which players try to knock down as many skittles out of nine as they can with one ball.

skull skulls (n) The skull is the bony structure of the head.

sky skies (n) The sky is the space around the earth.

skyscraper skyscrapers (n) A skyscraper is a very tall building.

slab slabs (n) A slab is a large, solid block of something.

slack slacker slackest
1 (adj) Something which is slack is loose.
2 (adj) A slack period in a business is one when not much business is being done.

slander slanders slandering slandered
(vb) If you slander someone, you say something about them in public which is not true, but that could damage their reputation.

slang (n) is an informal way of writing or speaking. *Quid is slang for one pound.*

slap slaps slapping slapped (vb) If you slap someone or something, you hit it with the palm of your hand.

slash slashes slashing slashed (vb) If you slash something, you make a long deep cut.

slate slates (n) Slate is a type of stone used to tile roofs.

slaughter slaughters slaughtering slaughtered
1 (vb) If you slaughter people or animals, you kill them in large numbers in a cruel way.
2 (vb) If we slaughter animals, we kill them for their meat.

slave slaves slaving slaved
1 (n) A slave is a person who is owned by another person and forced to work without pay. **slavery** (n)
2 (vb) If you slave at something, you work very hard at it.

sledge sledges (n) A sledge is a platform on runners which travels on snow.

sledgehammer sledgehammers (n) A sledgehammer is a large, heavy hammer used for breaking concrete, rocks, etc.

sleek sleeker sleekest (adj) Someone or something that is sleek is well groomed and healthy looking.

sleep sleeps sleeping slept
1 (n) Sleep is the period when you rest with your eyes shut and your mind inactive.
2 (vb) If you sleep, you close your eyes and become inactive and unconscious for a while.

sleeper sleepers (n) A sleeper is a concrete or wooden beam which supports railway tracks.

S

sleet (n) is partly frozen rain.

sleeve sleeves
1 (n) A sleeve is the part of a garment that covers your arm.
2 (n) A sleeve is a close-fitting covering for something. *A record sleeve.*

sleigh sleighs (n) A sleigh is a vehicle with runners for travelling over snow and ice.

slender (adj) Someone who is slender is slim, without too much fat.

slice slices slicing sliced (vb) If you slice something, you cut it into thin pieces.

slick slicks; slicker slickest
1 (n) A slick is a large patch of oil on the surface of water.
2 (adj) Someone who is slick speaks easily and convincingly, but is insincere.
3 (adj) A slick operation or action is one that is done efficiently.

slide slides sliding slid
1 (vb) If someone or something slides, they move smoothly along a slippery surface.
2 (n) A slide is a patch of ice.
3 (n) A slide is a slippery metal ramp.

slight slighter slightest
1 (adj) Someone who is slight, is small and lightweight.
2 (adj) Something slight is small in quantity.

slim slims slimming slimmed; slimmer slimmest
1 (adj) Someone or something that is slim is thin in an attractive way.
2 (vb) If you slim, you try to lose weight.

slime
1 (n) Slime is a clear, sticky liquid on the bodies of snails, slugs, etc. **slimy** (adj)
2 (n) Slime is a thick, sticky, unpleasant substance, for example on the surface of stagnant water.

sling slings slinging slung
1 (n) A sling is a piece of material used to support something. *A baby sling . . . an arm sling.*
2 (vb) If you sling something, you throw it.

slipper slippers (n) A slipper is one of a pair of soft shoes that you wear indoors.

slippery (adj) Something that is slippery is very smooth or greasy and difficult to stand on or to hold.

slipshod (adj) work is inaccurate and poor.

slither slithers slithering slithered (vb) If someone or something slithers, they slide along in a twisting way, like a snake.

sliver slivers (n) A sliver is a small, thin piece of something.

slogan slogans (n) A slogan is a phrase used in advertising or by political parties.

slope slopes sloping sloped
1 (n) A slope is the side of a hill, mountain or valley.
2 (vb) If a thing slopes, it leans with one end higher than the other.

sloth sloths
1 (n) A sloth is a very slow moving animal which lives in trees in South America.
2 (n) Sloth is laziness. **slothful** (adj)

slouch slouches slouching slouched (vb) If you slouch, you stand or walk in a lazy, careless way.

slovenly (adj) Someone or something that is slovenly is dirty and untidy.

slow slows slower slowest slowing slowed
1 (adj) Someone or something that is slow does not move quickly.
2 (vb) If you slow something, you make it happen or travel at a lower speed.

slowworm slowworms (n) A slowworm looks like a small snake but is a reptile, like a lizard without legs.

slug slugs (n) A slug is a garden pest rather like a snail without a shell.

slum slums (n) A slum is a house or collection of houses that are in very poor condition, unfit for people to live in.

slumber slumbers slumbering slumbered (vb) If you slumber, you sleep.

slump slumps slumping slumped
1 (vb) If you slump, you sink down heavily.
2 (n) A slump is a fall in demand for a particular product.

slush (n) is half-melted snow.

S

sly slyer slyest (adj) A sly person is secretive and deceitful.

smack smacks smacking smacked (vb) If you smack someone or something, you hit them with the palm of your hand.

small smaller smallest (adj) Someone or something that is small is not very big.

smart smarter smartest
1 (adj) A smart person is well-dressed.
2 (adj) Someone who is smart is clever.

smash smashes smashing smashed
1 (vb) If you smash something, you break it violently.
2 (n) A smash is a car crash.
3 (adj) If something is smashing, it is very good.
4 (n) A smash or a smash hit is a show, film, record, etc. that is very successful.

smear smears smearing smeared
1 (vb) If you smear something, you spread it over something else.
2 (n) A smear is a dirty mark.
3 (vb) If you smear someone, you try to ruin their reputation by spreading lies about them.

smell smells smelling smelled smelt
1 (n) The smell of something is the effect it has on your nose.
2 (vb) If you smell something, you notice it through the effect it has on your nose.
3 (n) Smell is the sense related to the nose.

smiles smiles smiling smiled
1 (n) A smile is a movement of your lips which shows that you are happy or amused.
2 (vb) If you smile, you turn your lips upwards to show that you are happy or amused.

smirk smirks smirking smirked (vb) If you smirk you smile in an unpleasant way at someone else's troubles or because you think you are very clever.

smithy smithies (n) A smithy is a blacksmith's workshop.

smock smocks (n) A smock is a loose garment covering the top half of the body, sometimes worn over other clothes in order to protect them.

smog smogs (n) A smog is an unhealthy mixture of smoke and fog which may hang in the air, especially over cities.

smoke smokes smoking smoked
1 (n) Smoke is a cloud of gas and tiny particles which is given off when something is burning. **smoky** (adj)
2 (vb) If people smoke, they burn tobacco in a cigarette, cigar or pipe, and inhale the smoke.
3 (vb) If you smoke fish or meat, you hang it over burning wood so that the smoke gives it a particular flavour.

smooth smooths smoothing smoothed; smoother smoothest
1 (adj) A smooth surface is free of holes, lumps and rough patches.
2 (vb) If you smooth something, you get rid of the roughness or creases on it.
3 (adj) A smooth journey, flight, etc. is comfortable and without hold-ups.

smother smothers smothering smothered
1 (vb) If you smother someone, you cover their face so they cannot breathe.
2 (vb) If you smother a fire, you cover it with something which puts it out.

smoulder smoulders smouldering smouldered (vb) If something smoulders, it burns slowly, without producing any flames.

smudge smudges smudging smudged
1 (vb) If you smudge ink or paint, you touch it while it is still wet, and smear it.
2 (vb) A smudge is a smear of ink, paint, dirt, etc.

smug smugger smuggest (adj) A smug person is very pleased with their own achievements and self-satisfied in an unpleasant way.

smuggle smuggles smuggling smuggled (vb) If a person smuggles something, they take it into a country or place where it is not allowed or to avoid paying taxes on it. **smuggler** (n)

snack snacks (n) A snack is a small meal eaten between main ones.

snail snails (n) A snail is a small, slow moving creature with a shell on its back.

S

snake snake (n) A snake is a long, thin, scaly reptile with no legs.

snare snares snaring snared
1 (vb) If you snare someone or something, you trap them.
2 (n) A snare is a trap of some sort.

snarl snarls snarling snarled (vb) If a person or an animal snarls, they make an angry noise like a growl.

snatch snatches snatching snatched (vb) If you snatch something from someone, you take it from them quickly and roughly.

sneak sneaks sneaking sneaked
1 (vb) If someone sneaks on you, they tell someone in authority what you have done.
2 (vb) If you sneak around, you move trying not to be heard or seen.

sneer sneers sneering sneered (vb) If you sneer, you show your scorn or contempt with a look or a remark.

sneeze sneezes sneezing sneezed
1 (n) A sneeze is a sudden rush of air from your nose or mouth, when you have a cold or when something irritates your nose.
2 (vb) If you sneeze, air comes through your nose or mouth suddenly or violently.

sniff sniffs sniffing sniffed (vb) If you sniff, you breathe in sharply through your nose.

snigger sniggers sniggering sniggered (vb) If you snigger, you giggle in an unpleasant way.

sniper snipers (n) A sniper is a person who hides and shoots at people.

snippet snippets (n) A snippet is a small piece of something.

snivel snivels snivelling snivelled (vb) If you snivel, you cry and sniff at the same time.

snob snobs (n) A snob is a person who admires higher social classes, and looks down on lower ones. Informal use.

snooker (n) is a game played with coloured balls on a special table. The object is to hit as many of the balls into pockets as possible, using a cue.

snoop snoops snooping snooped (vb) If a person snoops, they pry into other people's affairs.

snooze snoozes snoozing snoozed (vb) If you snooze, you have a short, light sleep.

snore snores snoring snored (vb) If you snore, you make a noise through your nose and mouth whilst you are asleep.

snorkel snorkels (n) A snorkel is a short tube which allows you to breathe with your face under the water.

snout snouts (n) A snout is the nose of a pig or similar animal.

snow snows snowing snowed
1 (n) Snow is frozen water that falls in white flakes from the sky in cold weather.
2 (vb) If it snows, snow falls from the sky.

snowdrift snowdrifts (n) A snowdrift is a bank of wind-blown snow.

snowdrop snowdrops (n) A snowdrop is a small, white, spring flower.

snub snubs snubbing snubbed (vb) If you snub someone, you ignore them, or treat them rudely.

snuff snuffs snuffing snuffed
1 (vb) If you snuff out a flame, you put it out. *He snuffed out the candle.*
2 (n) Snuff is ground tobacco which some people sniff up their noses.

snug snugger snuggest (adj) A snug place is cosy and comfortable.

snuggle snuggles snuggling snuggled (vb) If you snuggle up to someone or something, you lie or sit very close to them.

soak soaks soaking soaked
1 (vb) If you soak something, you leave it in a liquid for a long time.
2 (adj) If someone or something is soaked, they are wet through.

soap soaps (n) Soap is a substance used with water to get things and people clean.

soap opera soap operas (n) A soap opera is a regular television or radio programme about the daily lives of a particular group of people.

soar soars soaring soared
1 (vb) If something soars, it flies very high.
2 (vb) If prices soar, they increase very quickly.

S

sober

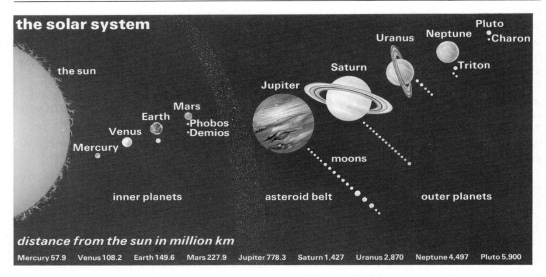

the solar system

the sun

Mercury
Venus
Earth
Mars
•Phobos
•Demios
Jupiter
Saturn
Uranus
Neptune
Pluto
•Charon
•Triton

moons

inner planets   asteroid belt   outer planets

distance from the sun in million km

Mercury 57.9   Venus 108.2   Earth 149.6   Mars 227.9   Jupiter 778.3   Saturn 1,427   Uranus 2,870   Neptune 4,497   Pluto 5,900

sober soberer soberest
1 (adj) A sober person is not drunk .
2 (adj) A sober person is sensible and quiet.
3 (adj) Sober colours are dull.

soccer (n) is the same game as football.

sociable (adj) A sociable person is friendly.

social
1 (adj) Anything social is concerned with how people live together.
2 (adj) Social can mean living together in groups. *Ants are social insects.*
3 (n) A social is a dance or gathering of people purely for pleasure.

socialist socialists (n) A socialist is a person who believes in a political system in which everyone has an equal opportunity to benefit from the country's wealth, usually by having the main industries owned by the state. **socialism** (n)

society societies
1 (n) Society is the name for people in general, and the groups in which they live.
2 (n) A society is an official group of people with the same interests. *A film society . . . A drama society.*

sock socks (n) A sock is clothing to wear on your foot.

socket sockets
1 (n) An electrical socket is a place on a wall or on a piece of electrical equipment that you can fit a plug, bulb, etc. into.
2 (n) A socket is a hollow into which another part fits.

sodden (adj) Anything which is sodden is soaked with liquid.

sofa sofas (n) A sofa is a comfortable seat for two or more people.

soft softer softest
1 (adj) Soft things are smooth and pleasant to touch.
2 (adj) Something soft can be bent or its shape can be changed easily.
3 (adj) A soft sound is quiet and gentle.
4 (adj) A soft person is kind and possibly not strict enough.

soften softens softening softened (vb) If you soften something, you make it softer.

software (n) refers to the programs that control computers.

soggy soggier soggiest (adj) Anything soggy is soaking wet or waterlogged.

soil soils soiling soiled
1 (n) Soil is the earth in which plants grow.
2 (vb) If you soil something, you make it dirty.

solar (adj) Anything solar is concerned with the sun.

solar energy (n) is energy direct from the sun.

solar system (n) Our solar system is the sun and the planets which orbit it.

solder **solders soldering soldered** (vb) If you solder metal things together, you melt a piece of soft metal between them, which holds them together when it cools.

soldier **soldiers** (n) A soldier is a person who serves in the army.

sole soles
1 (n) The sole is the part of your shoe that touches the ground.
2 (n) A sole is a type of flat fish.

solemn (adj) A solemn event or person is quiet and very serious.

solicitor **solicitors** (n) A solicitor is someone qualified in the law, preparing legal documents and cases.

solid
1 (adj) Something solid can be touched and felt and is fairly hard.
2 (adj) A solid structure is strong.
3 (n) A solid is a three dimensional shape.

solitary
1 (adj) A solitary person or thing is all alone.
2 (adj) A solitary activity is done alone.
3 (adj) A solitary place is a lonely place.

solitude (n) is the state of being on your own.

solo solos (n) A solo is a performance, especially of a piece of music, done by one person. **soloist** (n)

soluble
1 (adj) Something soluble dissolves in a liquid.
2 (adj) A problem that is soluble, can be solved.

solution **solutions**
1 (n) A solution is the answer to a problem.
2 (n) A solution is a liquid that has solids or gases dissolved in it.

solve **solves solving solved** (vb) If you solve a problem or a puzzle, you find the answer to it.

solvent **solvents** (n) A solvent is a liquid that will dissolve other substances.

sombre
1 (adj) Someone or something that is sombre is rather sad and serious.
2 (adj) Sombre colours are dark and dull.

some (adv) is used to refer to a number of people or things when you are not stating the number precisely. *Some of you will go swimming.*

somebody see **someone**

somehow (adv) is used to mean in some way. *We will launch the boat somehow.*

someone (pro) is used if you do not know who you are talking about specifically. *Someone is missing.*

somersault **somersaults** (n) A somersault is a movement that you do by rolling head over heels forwards or backwards.

something
1 (pro) Something refers to things when you don't know exactly what they are. *There was something in the cup.*
2 Something is used to contrast with nothing. *We must do something to help.*

sometimes (adv) If something happens sometimes, it happens only occasionally.

somewhere (adv) is used to talk of a place without mentioning it by name. *She went somewhere in the south.*

son sons (n) A person's son is their male child.

sonar (n) is a device which uses sound waves to detect objects under the water, or the depth of water.

song songs (n) A song is a poem or words put to music.

sonic boom **sonic booms** (n) A sonic boom is the noise produced by aeroplanes when they break through the sound barrier.

soon sooner soonest
1 (adv) If something happens soon, it happens in the near future.
2 (adv) If you would sooner do one thing than another, you would prefer to do that thing. *I would sooner go to the pictures than to the football.*

soot (n) is the black powder produced when things burn.

S

soothe

soothe soothes soothing soothed
1 (vb) If you soothe someone who is angry, you make them feel calmer.
2 (vb) If an ointment, for example, soothes an injury, it takes away some of the pain.
3 (adj) Anything which is soothing is restful or relieves pain.

sophisticated
1 (adj) A sophisticated person is experienced in social situations, and is able to talk easily about anything.
2 (adj) A sophisticated machine is complex and uses very modern technology.

soprano sopranos (n) A soprano is a singer with a high singing voice.

sorbet sorbets (n) A sorbet is a frozen dessert made from fruit juice and egg whites.

sorcerer sorcerers (n) A sorcerer is a wizard who performs evil magic in stories. **sorceress** (fem. n)

sordid (adj) A sordid place is dirty, shabby and depressing.

sore sores (n) A sore is a painful place on your body where the skin is raw or infected.

sorrow sorrows (n) Sorrow is a feeling of sadness.

sorry sorrier sorriest
1 Sorry is a word used to apologise to someone for something you have done wrong.
2 If something is in a sorry state it is in poor condition.
3 If you are sorry for someone, you feel sympathy for them.

sort sorts sorting sorted
1 (vb) If you sort things, you arrange them according to some system. *Sort these clothes into those you want and those you don't.*
2 (n) Sort can be used to mean type. *What sort of ice cream do you want?*

soul souls
1 (n) In many religions the soul is the spiritual part of a person that cannot die.
2 (n) Souls can be used to mean people. *200 souls were lost when the ship sank.*

sound sounds sounding sounded
1 (n) A sound is a noise.
2 (vb) If something sounds it makes a noise. *The horn sounded.*
3 (adj) If something is sound, it is in good condition or reliable.

sound barrier (n) The sound barrier is a sudden increase in air pressure at the front of an aircraft as it approaches the speed of sound.

soundproof (adj) A soundproof place does not let any sound out.

soundtrack soundtracks (n) A soundtrack is a recording of music from a film or show.

soup soups (n) A soup is a liquid food containing meat or vegetables.

sour (adj) Anything sour has a sharp, bitter taste.

source sources
1 (n) The source of something is the place it comes from. *The source of this oil is the North Sea.*
2 (n) The source of a river is the place where it starts.

south
1 (n) South is the direction to your right as you look at a rising sun.
2 (n) The south is that part of a country which is in the south. **southern** (adj)

South Pole (n) The South Pole is the southern-most part on the earth's surface.

souvenir souvenirs (n) A souvenir is something you take home from a place to remind you of it.

sovereign sovereigns (n) A sovereign is a king or queen of a country.

soya bean soya beans (n) Soya beans are used to make oil, flour, or soy sauce.

spa spas (n) A spa is a place where water, rich in minerals, comes out of the ground.

space spaces spacing spaced
1 (n) Space is the amount of empty area in a place.
2 (n) Space is the area outside the earth's atmosphere which seems limitless.
3 (n) A space is a gap or unoccupied place in a crowd, etc.

senses p264

space age (n) The space age is the time since space travel began.

space capsule space capsules (n) A space capsule is the part of a space rocket where the astronauts sit.

spacecraft (n) A spacecraft is a machine designed to travel in space.

space station space stations (n) A space station is a base which orbits the earth and is used by scientists to perform experiments in space.

spacious (adj) Somewhere spacious has plenty of open space.

spade spades (n) A spade is a tool used for digging in the ground.

spaghetti (n) is a long, thin form of pasta.

span spans spanning spanned
1 (n) Your span is the distance from the top of your thumb to the top of your little finger when your hand is stretched.
2 (n) The span is the length of anything, from one end to the other.
3 (n) A span can be a length of time. *The time span for this is two years.*
4 (vb) If something spans a gap, distance or time, it stretches across it.

spaniel spaniels (n) A spaniel is a type of long-eared dog.

spanner spanners (n) A spanner is a tool used to tighten and loosen nuts.

spare spares sparing spared
1 (adj) Something that is spare is surplus to your needs.
2 (adj) Something spare is an extra item that you keep in reserve. *The spare wheel.*
3 (vb) If you spare something, you lend it.

spark sparks sparking sparked
1 (n) A spark is a flash of light caused by electricity jumping across a gap.
2 (n) A spark is a tiny piece of burning material which shoots out of a fire.
3 (vb) If something sparks, it shoots out tiny pieces of burning material.

sparkle sparkles sparkling sparkled
(vb) If something sparkles, it glitters and shines.

sparrow sparrows (n) A sparrow is a small, brown bird which is very common in towns.

sparse sparser sparsest (adj) Something that is sparse is small in quantity and spread over a large area. *The trees were very sparse.*

spasm spasms (n) A spasm is a sudden, uncontrollable jerking of the muscles.

spatula spatulas (n) A spatula is like a broad, blunt knife which is used by artists and cooks.

spawn spawns spawning spawned
1 (vb) When fishes spawn, their eggs are laid and fertilised.
2 (n) Spawn is the mass of eggs laid by frogs, toads, fish, etc.

speak speaks speaking spoke spoken
(vb) When you speak, you use your voice to say words.

speaker speakers
1 (n) A speaker is someone who speaks publicly to an audience.
2 (n) A speaker is the part of a radio, stereo, etc. that produces the sound.

spear spears spearing speared
1 (n) A spear is a weapon with a long handle used for stabbing or throwing.
2 (vb) If you spear someone, you push a spear into them.

special
1 (adj) Someone or something that is special, is different or better than others of its type. *It was a special car.*
2 (adj) Something special is made for a distinct purpose. *This is a special tool for woodwork.*

specialise specialises specialising specialised (vb) If you specialise in something you have particular skills in one area. *I specialised in African studies.*
specialist (n)

species (n) A species is a group of animals or plants with the same main features, which are able to interbreed.

specimen specimens
1 (n) A specimen is an example of a type of animal or plant.
2 (n) A specimen is a small amount of something which is a sample of the whole thing. *Soil specimen.*

speck specks (n) A speck is a tiny stain, mark, etc. on something.

S

speckled

speckled (adj) Something that is speckled is covered with small spots.

spectacle spectacles
1 (n) A spectacle is an exciting, public display. **spectacular** (adj)
2 (n) Someone's spectacles are the lenses and frames which allow them to see properly.
3 If you make a spectacle of yourself, you show yourself up in public.

spectator spectators (n) A spectator is a person who watches at a public event.

spectrum (n) The spectrum is the range of colours into which light splits.

speech speeches
1 (n) Speech is the power to talk.
2 (n) A speech is a public talk on some matter that is made by one person.

speed speeds speeding sped speeded
1 (n) The speed of something is the rate at which it travels or happens.
2 (n) Speed is very fast movement.
3 (vb) If you speed, you drive a vehicle over the speed limit.

speedboat speedboats (n) A speedboat is a boat that travels at high speed.

speed limit speed limits (n) A speed limit is the top speed at which you are allowed to travel on a road, river, etc.

speedometer speedometers (n) A speedometer is an instrument which shows the speed at which a vehicle is travelling.

spell spells spelling spelled spelt
1 (vb) If you spell a word, you put the letters of the word into the right sequence.
2 (n) A spell is a rhyme or recipe which witches are supposed to chant.
3 (n) A spell of something is a period of time. *A spell of bad weather.*

spend spends spending spent
1 (vb) If you spend money, you exchange it for goods.
2 (vb) If you spend time or energy on something, you use your time or energy doing it.

sperm sperms (n) A sperm is the male sex cell which fertilises the egg.

sphere spheres
1 (n) A sphere is a shape like a ball.
spherical (adj)
2 (n) A sphere is an area of activity or influence. *Her special sphere is gymnastics.*

sphinx sphinxes (n) A sphinx is one of the huge Egyptian statues to be found near the pyramids. It is a mythological creature with a woman's head and a lion's body.

spice spices (n) Spices are the seeds from plants, whole or powdered, and used for flavouring.

spider spiders (n) A spider is an eight legged creature which spins a web to catch insects for food.

spike spikes spiking spiked
1 (n) A spike is something long and sharply pointed. **spiky** (adj)
2 (vb) If you spike something, you stick something pointed into it.

spill spills spilling spilled spilt
1 (vb) If liquid spills, it accidentally flows out of a container.
2 (n) A spill is a pool of liquid caused by something spilling.
3 (n) A spill is a long, thin stick used for lighting fires, etc.

spin spins spinning spun
1 (vb) If something spins, it turns around quickly.
2 (vb) When someone spins, they turn raw wool or cotton into thread.

spinach (n) is a leafy, green vegetable.

spine spines
1 (n) Your spine is your backbone.
2 (n) A spine is a spike on animals such as porcupines, sea urchins, etc. **spiny** (adj)

skeleton
p273

spinster (n) The term spinster is a rather old-fashioned word for an unmarried woman.

spiral spirals (n) A spiral is a shape with a curve which moves upwards or outwards.

spire spires (n) A spire is a cone-shaped tower on a church.

spirit spirits
1 (n) A spirit is a ghost.
2 (n) A person's spirit is the part supposed to survive after their death.
3 (n) A person's spirit is the amount of energy and determination they put into achieving something.
4 (n) Spirits are feelings. *We were in good spirits.*
5 (n) Spirits are strong alcoholic drinks such as whisky and rum.

spiritual spirituals
1 (adj) Something spiritual is concerned with religious matters and beliefs.
2 (n) A spiritual is a type of religious song originally sung by slaves in America.

spite (n) Spite is a feeling which makes you act in a nasty way, perhaps to get your own back on someone. **spiteful** (adj)

splash splashes splashing splashed
1 (vb) If you splash liquid, you cause drops to fly through the air.
2 (n) A splash is a disturbance in a liquid causing drops of it to be scattered around.
3 (n) A splash of colour or light is a small amount that contrasts with the surrounding areas.

splendid (adj) Something splendid is very well done or impressive.

splint splints (n) A splint is a support for a broken limb.

splinter splinters
1 (n) A splinter is a tiny piece of metal wood, etc. which breaks off a larger piece.
2 A splinter group is a group of people who split from a larger group.

split splits splitting split
1 (vb) If something splits, it tears or divides into two or more parts.
2 (n) A split is a crack or tear.
3 (n) A split is a division of ideas in a group of people.

splutter splutters spluttering spluttered (vb) If someone splutters, they make a series of coughing, spitting noises.

spoil spoils spoiling spoiled
1 (vb) If you spoil something, you damage it in some way.
2 (vb) If you spoil a person, you treat them too well, and they become used to getting everything they want.
3 (vb) If food spoils, it goes bad because it is too old or overcooked.
4 (n) Spoils are the profits made from winning a war or taking power.

spoke spokes (n) A spoke is a piece of metal or wood that joins the hub of a wheel to the rim.

sponge sponges sponging sponged
1 (n) A sponge is a light substance full of holes that absorbs water, it is either man-made or natural.
2 (vb) If you sponge something, you wipe it with a sponge.
3 (n) A sponge is a light cake.
4 (vb) If you sponge, you borrow money and things from people without paying for them.

sponsor sponsors sponsoring sponsored
1 (n) A sponsor is a person who gives money to support a particular activity.
2 (vb) If you sponsor someone or something, you give money to support them.

spontaneous (adj) Something spontaneous happens in an unplanned way.

spool spools (n) A spool is an object shaped like a cylinder which has a larger, round, flat part at each end so that thread, tape, film, etc. can be wound around it.

spoon spoons (n) A spoon is a utensil with a handle and a small bowl used when eating and cooking food.

spoor (n) are the tracks of a bird or animal.

spore spores (n) A spore is a cell from bacteria, plants, etc. that can develop into a new individual.

sporran sporrans (n) A sporran is a large purse worn over his kilt by a Scotsman.

S

sport

sport sports sporting sported
1 (n) Sports are the physical games and competitions such as football, tennis etc. that people play for amusement or money.
2 (adj) If someone is sporting, they play games fairly and good humouredly.

sportsman sportsmen (n) A sportsman is a man who takes part in games.
sportswoman (fem. n)

spotlight spotlights
1 (n) A spotlight is a powerful light used in theatres, etc.
2 If a person is in the spotlight, they are the centre of attention.

spouse spouses (n) A person's spouse is their husband or wife.

spout spouts spouting spouted
1 (n) A spout of liquid is a stream of liquid which shoots out of something.
2 (vb) If a thing spouts flame, water, etc. it shoots flames or water out.
3 (n) A spout is a specially-shaped nozzle on something such as a teapot.

sprain sprains spraining sprained
1 (vb) If you sprain a joint, you injure it by twisting it suddenly.
2 (n) A sprain is an injury to a joint caused by twisting it quickly.

sprawl sprawls sprawling sprawled (vb) If you sprawl, you sit carelessly with your legs and arms stretched out.

spray sprays spraying sprayed
1 (vb) If you spray something, you cover it with a fine mist of liquid.
2 (n) A spray is a cloud of small drops of liquid forced from something at speed.
3 (n) A spray is a device used to spray liquids.
4 (n) A spray is a number of flowers on one stem.

spread spreading spread
1 (vb) If you spread something, you distribute it over an area. *We spread the butter on the bread.*
2 (vb) If you spread your fingers, you open them out.
3 (vb) If a group of people spread out, they move apart from one another.
4 (vb) If something spreads, it covers a wider area or affects more people. *The news spread over the village.*

5 (n) A spread is a paste for sandwiches.
6 (n) A spread is a large, special meal.

sprightly sprightlier sprightliest (adj) A sprightly person is lively and energetic.

spring springs springing sprang sprung
1 (n) Spring is the season when plants start to grow and the weather starts to get warmer.
2 (n) A spring is a coil of metal which helps to absorb shocks, or hold things in place.
3 (n) A spring is a place where water comes out of the ground.
4 (vb) If you spring up, you jump up suddenly.

sprinkle sprinkles sprinkling sprinkled (vb) If you sprinkle something you spread it around in small drops or pieces. *We sprinkled sugar on the cake.*

sprint sprints sprinting sprinted (vb) When you sprint, you run fast for a short distance.

sprout sprouts sprouting sprouted
1 (vb) If a plant sprouts, it shows new growth.
2 (n) A sprout or Brussels sprout is a green vegetable that looks like a small cabbage.

spur spurs spurring spurred
1 (n) A spur is a small metal wheel with spikes worn at the back of a rider's boot and used to make their horse go faster.
2 (vb) If something spurs you on, it encourages you.

spy spies spying spied
1 (n) A spy is a person employed by one country to find out the secrets of another.
2 (vb) If you spy on someone, you watch them without them knowing.

squabble squabbles (n) A squabble is a quarrel about something of little importance.

squad squads
1 (n) A squad is a part of a police force dealing with one particular area of crime such as the murder squad.
2 (n) A squad is a group of sports people from whom a team is picked.

squadron squadrons (n) A squadron is a part of the armed forces, especially the Air Force.

S

squalid (adj) A squalid place is dirty and run down. **squalor** (n)

squander squanders squandering squandered (vb) If you squander money, you waste it.

square squares
1 (n) A square is a shape with four sides of the same length and four corners, each a right angle.
2 (n) A square is an open space in a town or village with houses, etc. round it.
3 (adj) Square describes the total area of something, so a space of 1 square metre is 1 metre wide and 1 metre long.

squash squashes squashing squashed
1 (vb) If you squash something, you press it down forcefully.
2 (n) Squash is an indoor game for two people played with rackets and a small, hard ball in a four walled court.
3 (n) Squash is a fruit drink.

squat squats squatting squatted
1 (vb) If you squat, you balance on your feet with your legs bent and your body close to the ground.
2 (vb) If you squat in a building, you live there illegally, without paying for it.

squaw squaws (n) A squaw is a North American Indian woman.

squawk squawks squawking squawked (vb) If a bird squawks, it makes a short, piercing cry.

squeak squeaks squeaking squeaked (vb) When a person, animal or thing squeaks, it makes a short, high sound.

squeal squeals squealing squealed (vb) If a person, animal or thing squeals, it makes a long, high sound.

squeamish (adj) If you are squeamish, you dislike unpleasant sights; blood, for example.

squeeze squeezes squeezing squeezed
1 (vb) When you squeeze something, you press it together on both sides.
2 (vb) When you squeeze oranges, lemons, etc you force out all the juice.

squid squids (n) A squid is a long-bodied sea-creature with many arms.

squint squints squinting squinted
1 (n) A squint is an eye disorder where your eyes look in different directions.
2 (vb) If you squint at something, you partly close your eyes to see more clearly.

squirm squirms squirming squirmed (vb) When you squirm, you move your body from side to side because you are uncomfortable or anxious.

squirrel squirrels (n) A squirrel is a small, furry, red or grey creature with a bushy tail.

squirt squirts squirting squirted (vb) If you squirt a liquid, it comes out quickly from a narrow opening.

stab stabs stabbing stabbed
1 (vb) If a person stabs someone, they force a knife into them.
2 (adj) A stabbing pain is sharp and sudden.

stable stables
1 (n) A stable is a building where horses are kept.
2 (adj) If a person has a stable character, they are level-headed and dependable.
3 (adj) Stable prices do not change quickly.

stack stacks stacking stacked (vb) If you stack items, you pile them up neatly.

stadium stadiums or stadia (n) A stadium is a big sports ground with rows of seating surrounding it.

staff staffs (n) The staff of a company, etc. are all the people working for it.

stag stags (n) A stag is an adult male deer with large antlers.

stage stages staging staged
1 (n) A stage is a raised area in a theatre, for example, where plays, etc. are performed.
2 (vb) If you stage a play, you put it on for others to watch.
3 (n) If you reach a stage in an activity, you come to a particular point.
4 (n) If you do something in stages, you do it in various parts.

stagger staggers staggering staggered
1 (vb) If you stagger, you walk with great difficulty, as if about to fall down.
2 (adj) If you are staggered by something, you are amazed.

S

stagnant (adj) Stagnant water does not move and is often smelly and unpleasant.

stain stains staining stained (vb) If something stains clothing, a surface, etc. it leaves a mark which is difficult to remove.

stair stairs (n) A stair is one step in a flight or group of stairs.

stake stakes staking staked
1 (n) A stake is a long, pointed stick fixed firmly into the ground for fencing.
2 (n) A stake is money that you place as a bet on a horse or dog race or on a game of cards, etc.

stalactite stalactites (n) A stalactite is a rock, looking like an icicle, hanging down from the roof of a cave.

stalagmite stalagmites (n) A stalagmite is a piece of rock sticking up from a cave's floor.

stale staler stalest (adj) If food, air, etc. is stale, it is not fresh.

stalk stalks stalking stalked
1 (n) The stalk of a plant is the part to which leaves and flowers are joined.
2 (vb) If you stalk a person or an animal, you follow them quietly so that you can observe them or kill them.
3 (vb) If you stalk somewhere, you walk there in a proud or angry way.

stall stalls stalling stalled
1 (n) A stall is a large table where you can display goods for sale at a market or where you can hand out information.
2 (n) A stall is also a place where farm animals are kept.
3 (vb) If a car stalls, it stops suddenly.

stallion stallions (n) A stallion is an adult male horse.

stamina (n) is the strength of mind and body which keeps you going.

stammer stammers stammering stammered (vb) If you stammer, you say words with some difficulty, either with excitement, nerves or because of a speech defect.

stamp stamps stamping stamped
1 (n) A stamp is a small piece of paper sold at Post Offices, and stuck on anything sent by post.
2 (n) A stamp is a device for marking paper by pressing it into an ink pad and then onto the paper.
3 (vb) If you stamp your foot, you put it on the ground very firmly, often in anger.
4 If someone leaves their stamp on a place, they leave a lasting impression.

stampede stampede (n) A stampede is an unexpected rush forward by a large group of animals or people.

stand stands standing stood
1 (vb) If you stand, you put your weight on your legs in an upright position.
2 (vb) If a house stands in a field, for example, that is where it is.
3 (n) A stand is an open-fronted stall where things are sold.
4 (n) A stand is a building at a sports ground with an open front and rows of tiered seating.
5 (vb) If you stand in an election, you are one of the candidates.

standard standards
1 (n) A standard is a level of quality of achievement.
2 (adj) If you are standard size for clothes, you are an ordinary, normal size.
3 (n) A standard is a flag belonging to a particular group of people.

staple staples
1 (n) A staple is a piece of metal pressed through a small machine to clip papers together. **stapler** (n)
2 (adj) A staple food is one that is an important part of our everyday diet, such as rice, bread, etc.

star stars starring starred
1 (n) A star is a ball of burning gas in space. Our sun is a star. We often call all those tiny points of light in the night sky stars. This includes planets, meteors, etc.
2 (n) A star is used to indicate a certain quality. *A five-star hotel . . . a gold star for effort.*
3 (n) A star is a very well-known person in the public eye. *A film star . . . a pop star.*
4 (vb) If you star in a film or a play, you take the leading role.

starboard (adj) describes the right hand side of a ship or aeroplane, as you face the front while on board.

S

stare stares staring stared (vb) If you stare at someone or something, you look at them for a long time with your eyes wide open.

starling starlings (n) A starling is a common garden and city bird with greeny-black plumage.

start starts starting started
1 (vb) If you start something, you begin to do it.
2 (n) The start of anything is the first part of it.
3 (vb) If you start up a new business, you open it.
4 (vb) If you start a car, you turn the ignition key to make it go.
5 (n) A start is a sudden movement that you make because you are surprised or nervous.

startle startles startling startled (vb) If you startle someone, you make them jump by taking them by surprise.

starve starves starving starved
1 (vb) If people starve, they become ill or die because they have no food to eat. **starvation** (n)
2 (adj) If you say you are starving, you feel very hungry.

state states stating stated
1 (n) If someone or something is in a bad state, they are in a poor condition.
2 If you get into a state about something, you become agitated and upset.

statement statements
1 (n) If you make a statement to the police for example, you tell or write down events which have happened.
2 (n) A bank statement is a document informing you about the money you have paid in and taken out of your account.
3 (n) A statement from a person, government, company, etc is an official announcement about a specific situation.

static
1 (adj) If something is static, it does not move.
2 (n) Static is an electrical charge caused by friction.

station stations stationing stationed
1 (n) A station is a building on a railway or a bus route where people can wait for a train or a bus.

2 (n) A station is a large building used as the main office for police, fire services, etc.
3 (adj) If a government stations troops in a country, they send them there.

stationary (adj) A stationary car is not moving.

stationery (n) refers to all the paper, pens, etc used for writing and office work.

statistic statistics (n) Statistics are numbers collected together to produce factual information. *Statistics showed how the August temperatures had varied over a number of years.*

statue statues (n) A statue is a human or animal figure made of wood, clay, etc.

steady steadier steadiest
1 (adj) If something is steady, it does not move or change.
2 (adj) A steady person is stable and dependable.

steak steaks (n) A steak is a firm, juicy piece of beef, fish, etc.

steal steals stealing stole stolen (vb) If you steal something, you take it without the owner's permission.

steam
1 (n) Steam is the hot mist that water turns into when it boils.
2 (n) Steam is the mist made when water in air cools, like your breath on a cold day.
3 If you let off steam, you relax by showing your true feelings in a lively manner.

This vehicle is powered by steam.

steel steels steeling steeled
1 (n) Steel is a very strong metal made mainly from iron.
2 (vb) If you steel yourself before you do something difficult, you prepare yourself for the demanding experience ahead.

S

steelband

steelband steelbands (n) A steelband is a band using upturned oildrums as musical instruments. Steelband music is popular in the Caribbean.

steep steeper steepest
1 (adj) A steep hill or slope goes up or down sharply.
2 (adj) If there is a steep increase in prices, etc they rise quickly.

steeple steeples (n) A steeple is the tall, pointed top of a church tower.

steeplechase steeplechases (n) A steeplechase is a long race with hurdles and water jumps for people or horses.

steer steers steering steered (vb) If you steer a car, boat, etc you control it so that it goes where you want it to go.

stem stems stemming stemmed
flower p112
1 (n) The stem of a plant is the long vertical part supporting the leaves and flowers.
2 (vb) If an idea stems from a certain place, this is where it comes from.

stencil stencils (n) A stencil is a piece of thick card or plastic in which letters, patterns, etc have been cut. They can be copied by pressing paint or ink through the holes onto a flat surface.

stepfather stepfathers (n) Your stepfather is the man married to your mother after your real father's death or a divorce. **stepmother** (fem.n)

stereo (adj) describes music or apparatus used to play music through two different speakers.

stereotype stereotypes (n) A stereotype is a simplified idea of a person or thing.

sterilise sterilises sterilising sterilised (vb) If you sterilise something, you clean it thoroughly to get rid of germs.

sterling (n) describes the British money system.

stern sterns; sterner sternest
1 (adj) A stern person is rather strict and serious.
2 (n) The stern is the back part of a boat.

stethoscope stethoscopes (n) A stethoscope is an instrument that doctors use to listen to a patient's heart, lungs, etc.

stew stews stewing stewed (n) A stew is a meal of meat, vegetables, etc cooked slowly in a liquid at a low temperature.

steward stewards (n) A steward is a man who works on a boat, plane or train looking after the passengers. **stewardess** (fem.n)

stick sticks sticking stuck
1 (n) A stick is a small piece of wood.
2 (n) A stick is a long, thin piece of material such as a licorice stick.
3 (vb) If you stick something to a surface, you fix it there with glue, tape, etc.
4 (vb) If something sticks in your mind, you remember it for a long while.

stiff stiffer stiffest
1 (adj) If something is stiff, it is difficult to bend or to move easily.
2 (adj) If you feel stiff after exercise it is difficult to move your muscles.
3 If you have stiff competition in an activity, you find it difficult to win.

stifle stifles stifling stifled
1 (vb) If you stifle a noise, you stop it.
2 (vb) If you stifle something, you stop it from continuing. *Her father stifled her plan to go abroad.*
3 (adj) In stifling weather it is very hot and difficult to breathe.

still stiller stillest
1 (adj) A still person makes no movement.
2 (adj) When the air is still, there is no wind.
3 (adj) A still drink is not fizzy.
4 (adv) If something still happens, it is going on now, even though it started long ago.
5 (adv) Still means even more. *I've worked all day and there's still more to do.*

stimulate stimulates stimulating stimulated (vb) If someone or something stimulates you, they excite you with new ideas and interests. **stimulation** (n)

sting stings stinging stung (n) The sting of an animal, insect or plant is the part that pricks through a person's or animal's skin leaving a soreness, swelling or poison there.

S

288

stink stinks stinking stank stunk (vb) If something stinks, it smells very bad.

stir stirs stirring stirred
1 (vb) When you stir a mixture, you move it round and round with a spoon or fork.
2 (vb) If you stir when you are asleep, you move a little but do not wake up.
3 (adj) Stirring music is exciting.

stirrup stirrups (n) Stirrups are the metal foot rests hanging on either side of a saddle.

stitch stitches stitching stitched
1 (vb) If you stitch clothes, you use a needle and thread to sew them together.
2 (n) A stitch is a sharp pain you feel in the side after running.

stoat stoats (n) A stoat is a small, brown carnivorous animal. In winter, its fur turns white and is called ermine.

stock stocks stocking stocked
1 (vb) If a shop stocks something, they have it ready to sell.
2 (n) The stock on a farm is all the animals kept there.
3 (n) The stocks were a wooden frame used to hold people's feet and hands as a punishment during medieval times.
4 (n) Stocks are shares which are large parts of the ownership of a company or industry and which can be bought as an investment.
5 If you take stock of a situation, you think about different aspects of it.

stockbroker stockbrokers (n) A stockbroker is a person whose job is to buy and sell shares in a company for people.

stomach stomachs (n) The stomach is the part of the body where food is digested before moving on to the intestines.

stone stones
1 (n) A stone is a piece of rock found on the surface of the ground.
2 (n) A stone is a hard seed found in the middle of fruits like peaches, plums, etc.
3 (n) A stone is a measurement of weight. 1 stone equals 14lbs.
4 (n) A precious stone is a jewel, a diamond or ruby, for example.

Stone Age (n) The Stone Age is the earliest known time of human history, when tools and weapons were made of stone.

stool stools (n) A stool is a seat of varying height without a back rest.

stoop stoops stooping stooped (vb) If someone stoops, they walk with their shoulders bent forwards.

stop stops stopping stopped
1 (vb) If you stop what you are doing, you do not do it anymore.
2 (vb) If you stop someone from doing something, you do not allow them to do it.
3 (n) A stop is a place at a roadside, etc. where coaches and other vehicles halt for people to get on and off.

stopwatch stopwatches (n) A stopwatch is a watch which can be stopped and started easily so that exact time measurements can be made.

storage
1 If something is in storage, it is kept in a safe place until it is needed.
2 (n) Storage is the method of keeping data in a computer.

store stores storing stored
1 (n) A store is a large shop, selling a wide range of goods.
2 (vb) If you store things somewhere, you put them away until needed.

storey storeys (n) A storey in a building is one of its floors or levels.

stork storks (n) A stork is a large white bird with a long, pointed beak and long legs.

storm storms storming stormed
1 (n) A storm is very bad weather with thunder, lightning and strong winds.
2 (vb) If soldiers storm a defended place, they make a surprise attack on it.
3 If there is a storm of protest, many people complain loudly.

story stories
1 (n) A story is a telling of events, either true or imagined, spoken or written.
2 (n) If you want to know the story of a play or film, you want to know what it's about.

stout stouter stoutest (adj) A stout person is quite fat.

straight

straight straighter straightest
1 (adj) A straight line or road has no bends in it.
2 (adv) If you stand up straight, you stand upright.
3 (adv) If you go straight home, you go there as quickly as possible.
4 (adj) Straight hair has no waves or curls in it.
5 If you keep a straight face, you try hard not to laugh.

straightforward (adj) If someone or something is straightforward, they are easy to understand.

strain strains straining strained
1 (vb) If you strain a muscle, etc you injure it so that it is painful.
2 (n) If you feel under a strain, you feel tense and anxious.
3 (vb) If you strain to hear something, you try very hard to hear it.

strait straits
1 (n) A strait is a narrow piece of water between two pieces of land or two seas.
2 If you are in dire straits, life is very difficult for you.

strange stranger strangest (adj) If something is strange, it is unusual, confusing or frightening.

stranger strangers (n) A stranger is someone you have never met before, or someone new to a place or situation.

strangle strangles strangling strangled (vb) If someone strangles another person, they kill them by pressing on their throat so that they cannot breathe.

strap straps (n) A strap is a narrow length of material, leather, webbing, etc used to hold something together.

strategy strategies (n) A strategy is a plan so that things get done successfully.

stratosphere (n) The stratosphere is the layer of atmosphere lying between 10 and 50 km above the earth's surface.

stratum strata (n) A stratum is a layer of something especially rock.

straw straws
1 (n) Straw is the dried stems of wheat, oats, etc used for animals' bedding and for making such things as mats.

2 (n) A straw is a thin tube of plastic or paper used to suck up a drink from a glass.
3 If something is the last straw, it is the last disheartening event in a series of disasters.

strawberry strawberries (n) A strawberry is a small, soft red fruit.

stray strays straying strayed (vb) If a person or animal strays from a group they wander off on their own.

streak streaks streaking streaked
1 (n) A streak is a long, thin mark on the surface of something.
2 If someone has a nasty streak in their character, part of their personality is unpleasant.
3 If you have a lucky streak, a number of good things happen for you.

stream streams
1 (n) A stream is a small river.
2 (n) A stream of traffic is a line of vehicles one behind the other.
3 (n) If two people are in the same stream for maths, for example, they have similar ability in the subject.

streamer streamers (n) A streamer is a long, thin roll of paper which unrolls when thrown at parties, carnivals, etc.

street streets
1 (n) A street is a road with buildings on both sides.
2 If something is right up your street, you are really interested in it.

streetwise (adj) If you are streetwise, you can look after yourself well, despite threatening situations in day-to-day life.

strength strengths
1 (n) Strength is how strong someone or something is.
2 If you show particular strength of feeling about something, you show how much this matters to you.
3 If you go from strength to strength, you get better and better at something.

strenuous (adj) A strenuous activity needs a lot of effort and energy.

S

stress stresses stressing stressed
1 (n) If you feel stress, you feel tense because you cannot cope with your problems.
2 (vb) If you stress certain points when you are speaking, you make them stand out clearly.

stretch stretches stretching stretched
1 (vb) When you stretch, you move your arms and legs away from your body as far as possible.
2 (vb) If woodland, for example, stretches over a wide area, it covers the area.
3 (vb) If an activity stretches you, it makes you use all your energies and abilities.

stretcher stretchers (n) A stretcher is a long piece of canvas on poles for carrying injured people.

strict stricter strictest
1 (adj) A strict person does not allow others to behave badly.
2 (adj) Strict instructions have to be carried out in a very particular way.

stride strides
1 (n) A stride is a long step taken when walking or running.
2 If you take something in your stride, you do it easily.

strike strikes striking struck
1 (vb) If you strike someone or something, you hit them.
2 (vb) If people strike, they refuse to work because they want more money or better working conditions.
3 (vb) If an idea strikes you, it comes to you suddenly.

string strings
1 (n) String is the thin cord used to tie up things.
2 (n) A string on a guitar, violin, etc is a very thin piece of wire, etc which gives a musical sound when touched.

strip strips stripping stripped
1 (n) A strip of land or water is a narrow piece of it.
2 (vb) If you strip, you remove all your clothes.
3 (vb) If you strip a surface, you remove everything covering it.
4 (n) A comic strip is a series of cartoon-type drawings which tell a story.

stripe stripes
1 (n) A stripe is a band of colour usually next to other different-coloured bands.
2 (n) A stripe on a person's uniform shows their rank.

stroke strokes stroking stroked
1 (vb) If you stroke someone or something, you touch them gently moving your hand backwards and forwards to show that you care for them.
2 (n) A stroke in swimming is a particular way of swimming. *Back stroke... butterfly stroke.*
3 (n) A stroke is a sudden illness which may cause paralysis and brain damage.
4 If you have a stroke of luck, something good unexpectedly happens.
5 If you do not do a stroke of work you are very lazy.

stroll strolls strolling strolled (vb) If you stroll, you walk along in a slow and easy way.

strong stronger strongest
1 (adj) A strong person or animal shows physical power.
2 (adj) If you have strong feelings about something, your ideas are not easily changed.
3 (adj) A strong cup of coffee or tea, etc is highly flavoured.

structure structures (n) The structure of something is the way it is organised.

struggle struggles struggling struggled
1 (vb) If someone holds on to you and you struggle, you try to free yourself.
2 (n) If you struggle to do something difficult, you have to make a great effort.

stubble
1 (n) Stubble is the very short stems left after corn, wheat, etc has been cut.
2 (n) Stubble is the short hair on a man's face just before he needs to shave.

stubborn
1 (adj) Stubborn people cannot be easily persuaded to change their minds.
2 (adj) A stubborn stain, for example, is very difficult to remove.

S

stud

stud studs
1 (n) A stud is a small metal fastener on clothing.
2 (n) A stud is a small piece of metal used for decoration, for example, an earring.
3 (n) A stud is one of the small, round pieces on the bottom of sports shoes.
4 (n) A stud is a place where horses are kept for breeding.

student students (n) A student is someone who studies at college, university or school.

studio studios
1 (n) A studio is a place or room where artists such as actors, painters or musicians work.
2 (n) Television studios are the buildings where programmes are put together and televised.

studious (adj) A studious person spends a lot of time studying.

study studies studying studied
1 (vb) If you study a subject, you spend a long time reading and learning about it.
2 (vb) If you study someone or something, you look at them closely.
3 (n) If someone makes a study of something, they explore it in great detail.
4 (n) A study is a room in a house used for writing, reading and other quiet activities.

stuff stuffs stuffing stuffed
1 (n) Stuff is a word you use when you cannot think of a more precise word. *Tar is sticky, black stuff.*
2 (vb) If you stuff something, you fill it without much care.

stumble stumbles stumbling stumbled
1 (vb) If you stumble, you trip over something and nearly fall to the ground.
2 (vb) If you stumble while reading aloud, you have difficulty in saying the words clearly.

stump stumps stumping stumped
1 (n) A stump of a tree or tooth is the small part left after the larger part has been removed.
2 (n) A stump is one of the three vertical wooden pieces in a cricket wicket.
3 (vb) If a problem stumps you, you cannot work out the answer.
4 (vb) If you stump along, you move along heavily.

stun stuns stunning stunned
1 (vb) If you stun someone, you knock them on the head and make them unconscious.
2 (vb) If you stun someone, you amaze them.
3 (adj) A stunning person or event is very attractive or amazing.

stunt stunts stunting stunted
1 (n) A stunt is an event or act involving daring or dangerous actions to attract people's attention.
2 (adj) A stunted plant, for example, has not grown fully.

stupid stupider stupidest (adj) Someone or something stupid is lacking in common sense.

sturdy sturdier sturdiest (adj) A sturdy person or thing is strong and unlikely to be knocked over easily.

stutter stutters stuttering stuttered (vb) If you stutter, you find it difficult to say the first letter of a word.

sty sties (n) A sty is a pig's home.

stye styes (n) A stye is an infected place on the eyelid which gets red and swollen.

style styles
1 (n) Your style of doing something is the way you do it.
2 If someone has style, they have a clever and attractive way of dressing and behaving.

stylus styluses (n) A stylus is a small, pointed device with a tiny diamond or sapphire set in it, which picks up sound signals on a record as it goes round.

subject subjects subjecting subjected
1 (n) The subject of a book, programme, discussion, etc is the main thing or person in it.
2 (n) A subject is something you study in a place of education. *My favourite subject is history.*
3 (n) The subjects of a country are the people who live there and have the right to live there.
4 (vb) If you subject someone to something, you make them undergo it. *He was subjected to punishment.*

submarine submarines (n) A submarine is a type of ship that can move under the water. **submariner** (n)

submerge submerges submerging submerged
1 (vb) If you submerge something or someone, you push them under the water.
2 (vb) If you submerge yourself in your work, you give all your time and attention to it.

submit submits submitting submitted
1 (vb) If you submit to someone or something, you give in to them.
2 (vb) If you submit an application for something, you hand it in or send it off.

subscribe subscribes subscribing subscribed (vb) If you subscribe to a magazine or newspaper, you pay for it and receive it regularly. **subscription** (n)

subside subsides subsiding subsided
1 (vb) If water subsides, after a flood for example, it goes back down to a lower level.
2 (vb) If noise subsides, etc it gets quieter.

substance substances
1 (n) A substance is a solid, a liquid or a powder.
2 (n) If an argument or a book has substance to it, it has something important to say.

substantial (adj) Something substantial is large and easily noticed. *A substantial fortune . . . a substantial meal.*

substitute substitutes (n) If a person or thing is a substitute for someone or something else, they replace them.

subtle subtler subtlest (adj) If something is subtle it is not very obvious and hard to describe. *Subtle smells . . . Subtle tastes.*

subtract subtracts subtracting subtracted (vb) If you subtract one number from another larger number, you take it away to leave a smaller number. $15 - 4 = 11$

suburb suburbs (n) A suburb is the outer area of a town or city where many people live. **suburban** (n)

subway subways (n) A subway is a pathway under a road.

succeed succeeds succeeding succeeded
1 (vb) If you succeed in doing something, you are able to do it. **success** (n)
2 (vb) If you succeed someone else, you take over their job or position.

succulent succulents
1 (adj) If meat is succulent it is tender and juicy.
2 (n) A succulent is a type of plant that has a thick stem or thick leaves which are full of moisture.

suck sucks sucking sucked
1 (vb) If you suck liquid through a straw, you take it in through your mouth by pulling in your face muscles.
2 (vb) If you suck a sweet, for example, you put it in your mouth and dissolve it slowly.

sudden (adj) A sudden event is something you had not expected to happen.

sue sues suing sued (vb) If you sue someone, you make a claim against them through the law courts, usually to get money.

suede (n) is soft leather with a rough surface, used for shoes, jackets, etc.

suet (n) is hard animal fat used in steamed puddings.

suffer suffers suffering suffered
1 (vb) If you suffer, you are upset because of a sad or unpleasant incident.
2 (vb) If you suffer from a disease or illness, you have it.

sufficient (adj) If you have sufficient food or do sufficient work, this is enough for what is needed.

suffocate suffocates suffocating suffocated (vb) If someone suffocates, they die because they have no air to breathe.

S

suffragette suffragettes (n) In the early 20th century a suffragette was a woman who campaigned to get the vote for women.

sugar sugars (n) Sugar is a white or brown sweet substance used in cooking and in drinks.

sugar beet (n) is a plant, the root of which produces sugar.

suggest suggests suggesting suggested
1 (vb) If you suggest an idea or suggest a person for something, you offer them for others to think about. **suggestion** (n)
2 (vb) If one thing suggests another to you, you feel there is a definite connection between them.

suicide suicides (n) If someone commits suicide, they kill themselves.

suit suits suiting suited
1 (vb) If certain clothes suit you, they make you look attractive.
2 (vb) If an arrangement suits you, it is convenient for you.
3 (n) A suit is a jacket and matching trousers or skirt.
4 (n) A suit in a pack of cards is one of the sets of diamonds, spades, hearts or clubs.

suitable (adj) If something is suitable, it is what you need at the time you are looking for it.

suitcase suitcases (n) A suitcase is a firm bag with handles used to carry clothes.

suite suites
1 (n) A suite is a set of rooms in a hotel or office for a special purpose. *Honeymoon suite... director's suite.*
2 (n) A suite is a set of matching furniture such as a three-piece suite.

sulk sulks sulking sulked (vb) When you sulk, you show you are annoyed or upset by refusing to talk to others and by acting in a bad-mannered way.

sullen (adj) A sullen person has little to say and is moody and unpleasant to people.

sulphur (n) is a yellow substance with a powerful smell. It can burn fiercely.

sultana sultanas (n) A sultana is a small, dried, seedless grape used in cooking.

sultry (adj) When the weather is sultry it is hot and humid.

summary summaries (n) A summary is a short version of something written or spoken.

summer summers (n) Summer is the season between spring and autumn when the weather is usually fine and sunny.

summit summits
1 (n) A summit of a mountain is its highest point.
2 (n) If you reach the summit of your ambitions, you are able to do everything you wanted to do.

summon summons summoning summoned
1 (vb) If the headteacher summons you to his or her office, for example, you are ordered to go there.
2 (vb) If you summon your energy for a difficult task, you make great effort.
3 (n) If you commit an offence, you may receive a summons to appear in court.

sun suns
1 (n) The sun is a very hot, bright ball of fire in the sky which gives Earth its light and heat.
2 If you catch the sun, you get sunburnt.

solar syste
p278

sunrise sunrises (n) Sunrise is the time in the early morning when the sun first appears in the sky.

sunset sunsets (n) Sunset is the evening time when the sun disappears.

sunstroke (n) is an illness with sickness, high temperature, etc. caused by too much strong sun.

superb (adj) Something superb is of a very high standard.

superficial (adj) If you have a superficial interest in someone or something, you are not very interested in them.

superfluous (adj) Something superfluous is unnecessary.

superintendent superintendents (n) A superintendent is someone who holds a position of authority in the police force.

superior
1 (adj) If something is superior to something else, it is of better quality.
2 (adj) If you are superior to someone else, you hold a higher position.
3 (adj) If you feel superior to other people, you believe you are better than they are.

supermarket supermarkets (n) A supermarket is a large shop selling a wide variety of foods and other goods, which you select yourself and pay for at the check-out.

supernatural (adj) things and events cannot be explained in the usual way.

superpower superpowers (n) A superpower is a country with a strong economy and army. The USSR and the USA are superpowers.

supersonic (adj) A supersonic aircraft can travel faster than the speed of sound.

superstitious (adj) If you are superstitious, you believe that certain things bring good or bad luck and you may also believe in ghosts, magic, etc.

supervise supervises supervising supervised (vb) If you supervise someone or something, you watch them to make sure everything runs smoothly. **supervision** (n)

supper suppers (n) Supper is a meal eaten in the evening.

supple (adj) If you are supple, you are able to move easily and gracefully.

supplement supplements supplementing supplemented
1 (n) A supplement to a newspaper or magazine is an extra part, sometimes dealing with a topic in detail.
2 (vb) If someone supplements their income, they add to their money by doing an extra job.

supply supplies supplying supplied
1 (vb) If you supply something for someone, you provide it.
2 (n) If you have a supply of something, you have a certain amount of it.

support supports supporting supported
1 (vb) If you support someone's ideas, you agree with them and help them.

2 (vb) If you support a team, you follow them by going to their matches and wearing their colours.
3 (vb) If a person works to support their family, they earn money to buy them clothes, food, etc.
4 (vb) If a shelf supports a number of books, it holds them up.
5 (n) If you are a support to a sad or ill person, you help them and comfort them.

suppose supposes supposing supposed
1 (vb) If you suppose that something will happen, you think that it will.
2 (vb) If you are supposed to do something, you are expected to do it.
3 (vb) If you add 'I suppose' when commenting on something or someone, you show you are not certain about it.

suppress suppresses suppressing suppressed (vb) If you suppress information or your feelings, you do not let these be known to others. **suppression** (n)

supreme (adj) If you make a supreme effort to do something, you make the greatest possible effort.

sure surer surest
1 (adj) If you are sure about something or someone, you can trust them.
2 If you are sure of yourself, you have self-confidence.
3 (adj) If you are sure that something will happen, you are certain that it will.

surf surfs surfing surfed
1 (n) Surf is the white foam of water as the waves break on a beach or rocks.
2 (vb) If you surf, you ride towards the shore on top of a big wave while standing or lying on a surfboard.

surface surfaces (n) The surface of something is the outer part or the top part of it.

surfboard surfboards (n) A surfboard is a long narrow plastic or wooden board used for surfing.

surge surges surging surged (vb) If a group of people surge forward, they move together in a forceful way.

surgeon surgeons (n) A surgeon is a doctor specially trained to operate on people.

S

surgery surgeries
1 (n) A surgery is a place where you can visit a doctor or dentist for advice or treatment.
2 (n) Surgery is the treatment of a sick person which involves cutting open their body to repair damage or injury.
surgical (adj)

surly (adj) A surly person is rude and bad-tempered.

surname surnames (n) Your surname is your last name, often shared with others in your family.

surplus surpluses (n) If you have a surplus of something, you have more than you need.

surprise surprises surprising surprised
1 (vb) If you surprise someone, you appear or do something when they are not expecting it.
2 (n) If you receive a surprise, you get something you did not expect.
3 If someone or something takes you by surprise, they turn up unexpectedly.

surrender surrenders surrendering surrendered (vb) If an army surrenders, it admits defeat.

surround surrounds surrounding surrounded
1 (vb) If something surrounds something else, it is positioned all around it.
2 (n) Your surroundings consist of the place where you live and the conditions in which you live.

survey surveys surveying surveyed
1 (vb) If you survey land, you measure it and make a map of it.
2 (vb) If you survey a scene, you spend time looking at it closely.
3 (n) A survey is an investigation of something, such as people's habits, or shops in an area or local bird life, for example.

survive survives surviving survived
1 (vb) If you survive, you carry on living despite difficulties. **survival** (n)
2 (vb) If you survive someone, you live on after their death.

suspect suspects suspecting suspected
1 (vb) If you suspect someone of a crime, you think they are guilty.
2 (vb) If you suspect that something is happening, you feel it is likely to be taking place.
3 (adj) If someone or something is suspect, they cannot be trusted.
4 (n) A suspect is someone who may be guilty of a crime.

suspend suspends suspending suspended
1 (vb) If you suspend something from a high place, you let it hang down.
2 (vb) If a headteacher suspends a badly behaved pupil, they punish them by not allowing them to attend school for a set time.

suspense (n) Suspense is a feeling of excitement or fear when you have to wait for something special to happen.

suspicious
1 (adj) If you are suspicious about someone you think they may be doing something wrong. **suspicion** (n)
2 (adj) If there are suspicious circumstances surrounding a person's death, there is doubt about how they died.

swallow swallows swallowing swallowed
1 (vb) When you swallow food or drink, you take it into your mouth and make it go down your throat.
2 (n) A swallow is a bird with long wings and a tail with two points.

swamp swamps swamping swamped
1 (n) A swamp is a very wet area of land.
2 (vb) If you swamp someone with work, you give them too much to do.
3 (vb) If heavy rain swamps a boat, it fills it with water.

swan swans (n) A swan is a large water bird, usually white and with a long neck.

swap swaps swapping swapped (vb) If you swap one thing for another, you exchange it for something else.

swarm swarms (n) A swarm is a large group of bees or other insects.

sway sways swaying swayed (vb) If someone or something sways, they move gently from side to side.

S

swear swears swearing swore sworn
1 (vb) If you swear, you use bad language.
2 (vb) If you swear you did something, you state it very strongly.
3 (vb) If you swear in a court of law, you promise that what you say is true.

sweat sweats sweating sweated
1 (n) Sweat is the liquid that comes from your skin when you get hot or anxious.
2 (vb) If you sweat, small beads of liquid come out of your skin.

sweater sweaters (n) A sweater is a warm knitted piece of clothing worn on the top part of the body.

sweatshirt sweatshirts (n) A sweatshirt is an item of clothing usually worn for sports or relaxation.

swede swedes (n) A swede is a round, orange root vegetable.

sweep sweeps sweeping swept
1 (vb) If you sweep a floor, path, etc, you clean it with a brush or broom.
2 (vb) If a craze sweeps through a group of people, it spreads very quickly.
3 (n) A sweep is someone whose job it is to clean chimneys.

sweet sweeter sweetest
1 (adj) Sweet foods contain a lot of sugar.
2 (n) A sweet is a pudding.
3 (n) Sweets are chocolates and other small, sweet things eaten for pleasure.
4 If you have a sweet tooth, you enjoy sweet foods.

sweetcorn (n) is another name for maize.

sweet potato sweet potatoes (n) A sweet potato is a vegetable with pinky-brown skin and yellow flesh.

swell swells swelling swelled swollen
1 (vb) If a part of your body swells, it grows larger because you are injured or ill.
2 If you join a group to swell the numbers, you join it to make it larger.

sweltering (adj) When the weather is sweltering, it is very hot.

swerve swerves swerving swerved (vb) If you swerve, you change direction suddenly to avoid a collision.

swift swifts; swifter swiftest
1 (n) A swift is a small bird with crescent shaped wings which moves very fast.
2 (adj) A swift movement is a quick one.

swim swims swimming swam swum
1 (vb) When you swim, you move through the water by moving your arms and legs.
2 (vb) If your head swims, you feel dizzy.

swimsuit swimsuits (n) A swimsuit is a piece of clothing for swimming in.

swindle swindles swindling swindled
(vb) If you swindle someone, you cheat them out of money or goods.

swing swings swinging swung
1 (vb) If you swing something, you move it backwards and forwards.
2 (n) A swing is a seat which hangs from two upright posts and on which a person can move backwards and forwards.

switch switches switching switched
1 (n) A switch is a control on a machine, for example, which you move to turn it on and off.
2 (vb) If you switch to something different, you change.
3 (vb) If you switch a machine on, you start it.

switchboard switchboards (n) A switchboard is a place in a building, office, etc. where the telephone lines connect and can be answered.

swivel swivels swivelling swivelled (vb) If something swivels it twists around.

sword swords (n) A sword is a weapon with a long, sharp blade.

sycamore sycamores (n) A sycamore is a tree with five-pointed leaves and winged seed cases.

syllabus syllabuses (n) A syllabus for a subject gives all the details of that particular course.

symbol symbols
1 (n) A symbol is a shape or design used to express an idea, a person, etc.
symbolic (adj)
2 (n) A symbol is a letter or number which stands for a chemical, sound, etc. *H_2O is the chemical symbol for water.*

S

sympathy

sympathy sympathies
1 (n) If you show sympathy for someone after something sad happens, you show that you are sorry and want to help. **sympathetic** (adj)
2 If you are in sympathy with someone's point of view, you agree with them.

symphony symphonies (n) A symphony is a detailed piece of music written for an orchestra.

symptom symptoms (n) A symptom is a sign of illness. **symptomatic** (adj)

synagogue synagogues (n) A synagogue is a building where Jewish people meet to worship.

synchronise synchronises
synchronising synchronised (vb) If you synchronise your watch with someone else's, the two watches show exactly the same time.

synonym synonyms (n) A synonym is a word with nearly the same meaning as another one.

synthesiser synthesisers (n) A synthesiser is an electronic machine which uses a computer to mix different sounds and words often used in popular music.

synthetic (adj) Something which is synthetic is made from artificial, rather than natural, substances.

syringe syringes (n) A syringe is a small instrument used to draw up liquids and push them out. Doctors and vets use them to give injections to patients.

syrup syrups (n) A syrup is a very sweet liquid made from sugar and water.

system systems
1 (n) A system is a way of working or organising something. *He had a very efficient system for planning his homework.* **systematic** (adj)
2 (n) A system is the way that a particular aspect of society is arranged. *The English legal system is different to many European systems.*
3 (n) The system of something is the way in which the parts are linked together so that they work successfully. *His new computer system operated faster than the old one.*

Tt

tabernacle tabernacles
1 (n) The tabernacle was the tent containing the most sacred writings of the ancient Jews.
2 (n) The tabernacle is the Jewish Temple.
3 (n) The tabernacle is a temporary structure used by Jews on feast days as an eating area.

table tables
1 (n) A table is a piece of furniture with a flat top used for working on or eating from.
2 (n) A table is a chart showing information arranged in columns and rows. *A timetable.*
3 (n) Tables are lists of multiplication facts that you learn at school. *1 × 2 = 2, 2 × 2 = 4.*

tablespoon tablespoons (n) A tablespoon is a large spoon used for serving or measuring food.

tablet tablets
1 (n) A tablet is medicine in the form of a small, hard, round shape.
2 (n) A tablet is a flat piece of stone on which people carved writing before paper was invented.
3 (n) A tablet of soap is a small block of soap.

table tennis (n) is a game played indoors by two or four people. They stand at each end of a long table with a low net in the middle and hit a small, light ball across it using small bats.

tabloid tabloids (n) A tabloid is a small format newspaper containing articles and many photographs.

taboo taboos
1 (n) A taboo is a religious or tribal rule forbidding people to do certain things.
2 (adj) Things that are taboo are avoided because they cause embarrassment or are unpleasant. *Talk of death is taboo.*

tackle tackles tackling tackled
1 (n) Tackle is the equipment you need for a certain activity, such as fishing tackle.

tape

2 (n) Ropes and pulleys used to lift things are called tackle.
3 (vb) If you tackle a job or problem, you deal with it.
4 (vb) If you tackle someone in a sport, you try to get the ball from another player.

tact (n) is the ability to deal with difficult situations without upsetting people or hurting their feelings. **tactful** (adj)

tactic tactics (n) Tactics are the methods that you use in order to achieve what you want. *His usual tactic was to pretend to be ill.*

tail tails tailing tailed
1 (n) A tail is a part of an animal that grows out of the back end.
2 (vb) If you tail someone or something, you follow them closely.

tailor tailors (n) A tailor is a person who makes clothes for people who have ordered garments to fit their requirements.

takeaway takeaways (n) A takeaway is a cooked meal you buy in a shop and take somewhere else to eat.

tale tale (n) A tale is a story.

talent talents (n) A talent is a special ability or skill. **talented** (adj)

talk talks talking talked
1 (vb) If you talk, you speak and say things to communicate with other people.
2 (n) A talk is a conversation, discussion or lecture.

talkative (adj) people talk a lot.

tall taller tallest (adj) Someone or something tall is above average in height.

Talmud (n) The Talmud is the collection of laws and traditions which govern the lives of Orthodox Jews.

talon talons (n) Talons are the sharp, hooked claws of birds of prey.

tambourine tambourines (n) A tambourine is a musical instrument which you shake or hit with your hand.

tame tames taming tamed; tamer tamest
1 (vb) If you tame an animal, you train it to obey or to be at ease with humans.
2 (adj) A tame animal is at ease with humans and will not attack them.

tamper tampers tampering tampered
(vb) If you tamper with something, you touch or interfere with it or alter it when you shouldn't.

tandoori (n) is an Indian way of cooking meat, vegetables, etc in a clay oven.

tangerine tangerines
1 (n) A tangerine is a small fruit similar to an orange but easier to peel.
2 (n) Tangerine is a pale, orange colour.

tangle tangles tangling tangled
1 (n) A tangle is a jumbled mass of something like string, wool, etc.
2 (vb) If something tangles or you tangle something, it gets twisted into knots.
3 (n) A tangle is a muddle or a mess. *I'm in a tangle with my homework.*

tank tanks
1 (n) A tank is a large, metal or glass container for liquids.
2 (n) A tank is an armoured military vehicle that runs on tracks rather than wheels.

tankard tankards (n) A tankard is a metal drinking mug.

tanker tankers
1 (n) A tanker is a very large ship designed to carry oil.
2 (n) A road or railway vehicle that carries large amounts of gas, oil, etc is called a tanker.

tantalise tantalises tantalising tantalised (vb) If you tantalise someone, you torment them by pretending they can have something which you constantly keep out of reach.

tantrum tantrums (n) A tantrum is a sudden, childish fit of bad temper.

tape tapes taping taped
1 (n) Tape is a long, thin, plastic strip treated so that it can record sounds or images for cassette recorders, video recorders or computers.
2 (n) A tape is a cassette or spool containing magnetic tape for video or sound recorders.
3 (vb) If you tape something, you record sounds or images on a recorder.
4 (n) Tape is sticky-backed plastic used to stick things together.

taper

taper tapers tapering tapered (vb) If something tapers, it gradually becomes narrower.

tape recorder tape recorders (n) A tape recorder is a device which will record and play back sounds on tape.

tapestry tapestries (n) A tapestry is a cloth with pictures or patterns stitched or woven into it in coloured threads.

tapioca (n) is a food with small round grains, like rice, which comes from the cassava plant.

tar tars tarring tarred
1 (n) Tar is a thick, black substance made from oil and used for making roads. It is also produced when tobacco burns.
2 (vb) If you tar a road, you cover it with tar.

tarantula tarantulas (n) A tarantula is a large, furry spider with a poisonous bite.

target targets
1 (n) A target is a place such as a town or building at which a weapon, a bomb or a missile, for example, is fired.
2 (n) A target is an object at which you fire bullets or arrows for sport.

tarn tarns (n) A tarn is a small mountain lake.

tarnish tarnishes tarnishing tarnished
1 (vb) If a metal tarnishes, it becomes stained or discoloured.
2 (adj) If someone's reputation is tarnished, they have done something which makes them less popular or respected.

tarpaulin tarpaulins (n) A tarpaulin is a heavy, waterproof sheet, used to protect things from the rain.

tart tarts; tarter tartest
1 (n) A tart is a piece of baked pastry filled with jam or fruit.
2 (adj) Something tart has a sharp taste.

tartan tartans (n) Tartan is woollen cloth with colourful check patterns. There are many designs of tartan, which is traditionally associated with Scotland.
plaid p21

task tasks (n) A task is a job that has to be done.

tassel tassels (n) A tassel is a bunch of threads tied together at one end and used as decoration.

taste tastes tasting tasted
1 (n) Taste is one of the five senses that makes you aware of the flavour of things.
2 (n) The taste of something is its particular flavour: sweet, sour, etc.
3 (vb) If you taste something, you put it into your mouth to find out its flavour.
4 (n) Your taste is also your own particular choices of things such as clothes, food, furniture, music, etc.
mouth p186

tasty tastier tastiest (adj) Food which is tasty has a good flavour.

tattered (adj) things are torn and ragged.

tattoo tattoos
1 (n) A tattoo is a permanent design or picture made on a person's skin.
tattooist (n)
2 (n) A tattoo is a signal played on a drum or bugle.
3 (n) A tattoo is a public, military display of marching and music.

taught see **teach**

taunt taunts taunting taunted (vb) If you taunt someone, you say or do cruel things to hurt or anger them.

taut tauter tautest (adj) If something is taut, it is stretched tight. *The guitar string was taut.*

tawny tawnier tawniest (adj) Something which is tawny is a yellowish-brown colour.

tax taxes taxing taxed
1 (n) A tax is a sum of money people pay to the government so that it can pay for public services. *The community charge is a tax.*
2 (vb) If something taxes you, it exhausts you and drains your energy. *The marathon taxed my strength.*

taxi taxis; taxies taxiing taxied
1 (n) A taxi is a car with a driver which you can hire to take you on journeys.
2 (vb) If a plane taxies, it moves slowly along a runway before take off or after landing.

taxidermist taxidermists (n) A taxidermist is someone who stuffs dead animals so that they can be displayed.

tea teas
1 (n) Tea is the dried and chopped leaves of the tea bush.
2 (n) Tea is a drink made by pouring boiling water over the tea leaves.
3 (n) Tea is a light meal taken in the afternoon around 4.00 p.m.
4 (n) Tea is also a more substantial meal eaten in the early evening.

teach teaches teaching taught (vb) If you teach someone a subject or a skill, you explain it to them or show them how to do it. **teacher** (n)

teak (n) is a hard wood used for making furniture.

team teams
1 (n) A team is a group of people who play a particular sport together, against other teams.
2 (n) A team is a group of people who work together on a job or project.
3 (n) A team is a group of animals such as horses, that work together.

tear tears; tearing tore torn
1 (n) A tear is a small drop of water that comes from your eyes when you cry. **tearful** (adj)
2 (vb) If you tear something, you damage it by pulling it apart, or catching it on something.
3 (n) A tear is a rip in clothes or cloth.
4 (vb) If you tear someone away, you snatch them away violently.

tease teases teasing teased
1 (vb) If you tease someone, you make fun of them or joke about them. *My sister will tease me about my new haircut.*
2 (vb) If you tease an animal, you annoy it in a cruel way.
3 (n) A tease is someone who enjoys teasing people.

teaspoon teaspoons (n) A teaspoon is a small spoon often used to measure sugar into drinks. It is also the amount a teaspoon holds. *A teaspoon of spice.*

teat teats
1 (n) A teat is the soft pointed part on the body of a female mammal which babies suck to get milk.
2 (n) A teat is made from rubber or plastic that is shaped like a teat, and is fitted to a bottle so that a baby can suck from it.

technical
1 (adj) Technical things are concerned with machines, technology, etc and the way things work.
2 (adj) Technical describes the skills and the methods needed to carry out a practical activity or process. **technician** (n)

technical college technical colleges (n) A technical college is mainly concerned with teaching technical subjects.

technology technologies (n) Technology is the study of science and how to apply it to improve industry, medicine, etc.

tedious (adj) Something that is a tedious activity makes you feel bored and tired because it is long and monotonous.

tee tees (n) A tee is a small stand used to support a golf ball before it is hit.

teenager teenagers (n) A teenager is a person aged between thirteen and nineteen.

telecommunications (n) is the technology which sends messages and signals across long distances by radio, television, telephone, etc.

telegram telegrams (n) A telegram is a message sent by telegraph to an office and delivered by hand to a person's home.

telegraph telegraphs telegraphing telegraphed (n) The telegraph is a system of sending messages over a distance by means of electricity or by radio signals.

t

telepathic (adj) A telepathic person has extraordinary mental powers, for example, the ability to communicate or read thoughts without using speech, writing or touch. **telepathy** (n)

telephone telephones (n) A telephone is an electrical device which allows people to speak to one another over long distances.

teleprinter teleprinters (n) A teleprinter is an electrical device which prints out messages sent from machines in other places.

telescope telescopes (n) A telescope is a tube-shaped instrument with lenses. You look through it with one eye and it makes distant things appear closer.

television televisions
1 (n) Television is the system which allows you to receive sounds and pictures sent over a long distance on a television set.
2 (n) A television is the piece of electrical equipment that receives pictures and sounds transmitted by the television system.
3 (n) Television is all the programmes you can watch on your television set.

telex telexes telexing telexed (n) Telex is a world-wide system of sending written messages from one place to another. A message typed at one machine is received and is immediately printed by another.

tell tells telling told
1 (vb) If you tell someone something, you give them information by speaking or writing to them.
2 (vb) If you tell someone off, you make clear to them that they have done something wrong.

temp temps (n) A temp is a person, usually a secretary, who works in an office for a short time while a permanent employee is on leave.

temper tempers (n) Your temper is your state of mind and feelings, whether you are irritable and angry or calm and peaceful.

temperament temperaments (n) A person's temperament is their basic nature or character.

temperamental (adj) A temperamental person is moody and unpredictable.

temperate
1 (adj) A temperate climate is not too cold or too hot.

temperature temperatures
1 (n) Temperature is the amount of heat that can be measured or felt.
2 (n) If you have a temperature, your blood is hotter than it should be, usually because you are ill. The normal body temperature is about 37°C.

fahrenh
p105

temple temples (n) A temple is a building where people worship a god or gods.

tempo tempos (n) Tempo is the speed at which music is played.

temporary (adj) Something temporary lasts only for a short time.

tempt tempts tempting tempted
1 (vb) If you tempt someone, you offer them something in order to persuade them to do what you wish.
2 (adj) Something that is tempting is attractive and difficult to resist. **temptation** (n)

tenant tenants (n) A tenant is a person who lives in a building belonging to another person to whom they pay rent.

tend tends tending tended
1 (vb) If you tend something, you care for and look after it.
2 (vb) If something tends to happen, it is likely to happen. *We tend to get angry if people annoy us.* **tendency** (n)

tender tenders; tenderest
1 (adj) Something tender is delicate and easily damaged.
2 (adj) Tender meat is soft and easy to cut or chew.
3 (adj) A tender person is loving and caring.
4 (adj) If part of your body is tender, it is sore and painful to the touch.
5 (n) A tender is a coal or water truck towed behind a steam engine.

tendon tendons (n) A tendon is a strong cord inside the body attaching muscles to bones.

t

tendril tendrils
1 (n) A tendril is a thin shoot, by which plants attach themselves to brickwork, etc.
2 (n) A tendril is a thin wisp of something, hair, for example.

tennis (n) is a game for two or four players, played on a court using racquets and a ball. The players hit the ball to one another across the net.

tense tenses tensing tensed; tenser tensest
1 (vb) If you tense your muscles, you tighten them up.
2 (adj) If you are tense, you feel worried and unable to relax.
3 (n) The tense of a verb shows whether it is the past, present or future.

tension tensions
1 (n) Tension is the degree of tightness when something is stretched tight.
2 (n) Tension is the atmosphere of anxiety and fear which arises when there is likely to be trouble, violence or danger.

tent tents (n) A tent is a shelter made from canvas or nylon and held up by ropes and poles.

tentacles tentacles (n) Tentacles are the long, thin limbs of an octopus and other creatures.

tepee tepees (n) A tepee is a North American Indian tent.

tepid (adj) Tepid water is only slightly warm.

term terms
1 (n) A term is a period of time at a school or college. There are usually three terms in a year.
2 (n) Terms are words which relate to a special subject. *Medical terms, scientific terms, legal terms.*
3 (n) Terms are a condition or agreement. *He made a list of his terms for doing the job.*
4 If you are on good terms with someone you get on well with them.

terminal terminals
1 (n) A terminal is a place where journeys by plane, bus, etc end.
2 (n) A terminal is a keyboard and screen connected to a main computer.
3 (adj) A terminal disease or illness causes death, often slowly, and cannot be cured.

terrace terraces
1 (n) The terraces at a football ground are the steps where people stand to watch the game.
2 (n) A terrace is a row of houses joined together. **terraced** (adj)
3 (n) A terrace is a flat area, usually paved and outside a house, where people can sit.

terrapin terrapins (n) A terrapin is a small North American turtle.

terrible
1 (adj) Something terrible is frightening, unpleasant, tragic, etc.
2 (adj) If you feel terrible, you feel ill or upset.
3 (adj) If something is terrible, it is of very poor quality. *This is a terrible piece of work.*

terrier terriers (n) A terrier is a small dog. There are several kinds of terrier.

terrific
1 (adj) Something terrific is very great in extent or amount. *A terrific crash... A terrific volume of water.*
2 (adj) Someone or something terrific is excellent.

terrify terrifies terrifying terrified. (vb) If someone or something terrifies you, it frightens you badly. **terror** (n)

territory territories
1 (n) An animal's territory is the area it defends and feels safe in.
2 (n) Territory is land belonging to a particular country.

terrorist terrorists (n) A terrorist is a person who uses violence to force others to do what they want.

tessellate tessellates tessellating tessellated (vb) If shapes tessellate, they fit together leaving no spaces. **tessellation** (n)

test tests testing tested
1 (n) A test is a series of questions, tasks, etc that you do to show how much you have learned, or how well you can do certain things.
2 (vb) If you test someone, you question them to see how much they know.
3 (vb) If you test a piece of equipment, you make sure that it works.
3 (adj) A testing time or situation is difficult and demands a lot from you.

t

Test match

Test match Test matches (n) A Test match is an international rugby or cricket match.

test tube test tubes (n) A test tube is a thin, glass container used in scientific experiments.

test-tube baby test-tube babies (n) A test-tube baby is a baby that develops from an egg which has been removed from the mother's body, fertilised and then replaced in her womb so that it can continue developing.

tetanus (n) is a very painful disease caused by infected wounds.

tether tethers tethering tethered (vb) If you tether an animal, you tie it so that it cannot escape.

textbook textbooks (n) A textbook is an information book used by people studying a particular subject. *A French textbook.*

texture textures (n) The texture of something is the way it feels to the touch.

thank thanks thanking thanked (vb) If you thank someone, you show you are grateful to them for something .

thatch thatches thatching thatched
1 (vb) If you thatch a house, you make a roof from straw and reeds.
2 (n) Thatch is straw or reeds used to make a roof.

Thatcher, Margaret (1925–) Mrs Thatcher was the first woman Prime Minister of the United Kingdom; the longest serving Prime Minister of this century. (1979–1990) and leader of the Conservative Party from 1975.

thaw thaws thawing thawed
1 (vb) If something frozen thaws, it melts.
2 (n) A thaw is a time when ice and snow melt.

theatre theatres (n) A theatre is a building where plays, shows, etc are performed.

theft thefts
1 (n) If someone is convicted of theft, they have been caught stealing.
2 (n) If there is a theft, something is stolen.

theme themes (n) The theme of a play, film, book, lecture, etc is the main idea that is developed.

theology theologies (n) Theology is the study of religions and religious ideas.

theory theories (n) A theory is an idea which has been carefully thought out, but is not yet proven.

therapy therapies (n) Therapy is the treatment of illnesses or conditions without drugs or surgery. **therapeutic** (adj)

Theresa of Calcutta or **Mother Theresa** (1910–) She is the missionary who has devoted her life to helping the poor, the homeless and the dying. She won the Nobel Peace Prize in 1979.

therm therms (n) A therm is a measurement of heat.

thermal thermals
1 (n) A thermal is the rising movement of warm air.
2 (adj) Thermal clothes keep you particularly warm in cold weather.

thermometer thermometers (n) A thermometer is a device used to measure temperatures.

Thermos Thermoses (n) A Thermos or a Thermos flask is a container which will keep its contents hot or cold.

thermostat thermostats (n) A thermostat is an automatic device to control the temperature in a room, engine, etc and to keep it constant.

thesaurus thesauruses (n) A thesaurus is a reference book in which words with similar meanings are grouped together.

thick thicker thickest
1 (adj) Anything which is thick has a greater distance between its surfaces than is normal. *A thick rope.*
2 (adj) Thick snow or fog is deep or dense.

thick-skinned (adj) A thick-skinned person is not easily hurt by criticism.

thief thieves (n) A thief is a person who steals things from others.

thigh thighs (n) Your thighs are the top parts of your legs.

thimble thimbles (n) A thimble is a small cup that you wear on a finger to protect it while you are sewing.

thin thinner thinnest
1 (adj) A thin person or animal has little fat on their bodies.
2 (adj) Anything that is thin has only a small distance between its sides. *A thin rope.*

think thinks thinking thought
1 (vb) If you think about something, you consider it carefully.
2 (vb) If you think something is true, you believe it is, but cannot prove it.
3 If you think a lot of someone, you admire or like them.
4 If you think twice before doing something, you consider whether to go ahead or not.

third thirds
1 (n) A third is one of three equal parts of anything.
2 (adj) Anything that is third, comes after the first and second.

Third World (n) The Third World refers to poor, underdeveloped countries, often in Africa, Asia or South America.

thirst thirsts
1 (n) A thirst is a feeling that you need a drink. **thirsty** (adj)
2 (n) If you have a thirst for something, you want it very much. *A thirst for adventure.*

thistle thistles (n) A thistle is a wild plant with prickly leaves and coloured flowers.

thorn thorns (n) A thorn is a short, sharp, point on a stem of a plant or bush. **thorny** (adj)

thorough (adj) If you do something in a thorough way, you do it very carefully and in detail. **thoroughly** (adv)

thought thoughts (n) A thought is an idea or opinion in your mind. **thoughtful** (adj) **thoughtless** (adj)

thrash thrashes thrashing thrashed
1 (vb) If you thrash someone, you hit them very hard.
2 (vb) If you thrash someone at a sport, you defeat them easily.
3 (vb) If you thrash out a problem, you discuss it thoroughly with someone.

thread threads threading threaded
1 (vb) If you thread a needle, you push cotton through the eye.
2 (n) Thread is a fine cotton, silk, etc used in sewing, embroidery, etc.
3 If someone's life hangs by a thread, they are unlikely to survive.

threaten threatens threatening threatened
1 (vb) If you threaten someone, you say that you intend to harm them in some way. **threat** (n)
2 (vb) If danger threatens, it seems very likely to happen.
3 (adj) If you feel threatened by someone you feel that they will harm you.

three-dimensional (adj) Anything three-dimensional has height, length and depth. It looks solid rather than flat.

three-quarters (n) is a measurement which is three out of four equal parts of anything.

thrill thrills thrilling thrilled
1 (vb) If something thrills you, you feel very excited about it.
2 (n) A thrill is a sudden feeling of excitement.
3 (adj) If something is thrilling, it is exciting and enjoyable.

thriller thrillers (n) A thriller is a book, play or film that tells an exciting story usually about a crime.

throat throats (n) Your throat is the passages in your neck which lead to your stomach and lungs.

t

throb

throb throbs throbbing throbbed
1 (vb) If a part of your body throbs, it beats with pain.
2 (vb) If a place throbs, it is full of people and noise. *The disco throbs on Saturday nights.*

throne thrones (n) A throne is a special seat for a king, queen or other important leader.

throng throngs thronging thronged
1 (vb) If people throng to a place they go in large numbers.
2 (n) A throng is a crowd of people.

throw throws throwing thrown
1 (vb) If you throw something you are holding, you send it flying through the air with a quick movement of your arm.
2 (vb) If you throw yourself into an activity, you give all your energy to it.
3 (vb) If you throw a party, you organise and hold one.
4 (vb) If a potter throws a pot, he or she shapes clay on a potter's wheel.

thrush thrushes (n) A thrush is a brown bird with a speckled breast and a sweet song.

thrust thrusts thrusting thrusted
1 (vb) If you thrust your way into a place, you push past people to get there.
2 (vb) If you thrust something into a bag, pocket, etc you push it there forcibly.

thug thugs (n) A thug is a violent, often criminal person.

thumb thumbs (n) Your thumbs are the jointed parts of your hands slightly lower than the four fingers.

thump thumps thumping thumped
1 (n) A thump is a hard blow that you give to someone or something, usually with your fist.
2 (vb) If you thump someone, you hit them hard.
3 (vb) When your heart thumps, it beats strongly.

thunder thunders thundering thundered
1 (n) Thunder is the loud noise heard in a storm, and often associated with lightning.
2 (vb) If someone or something thunders, they make a loud angry noise.

thunderstorm thunderstorms (n) A thunderstorm is a storm of thunder, lightning and heavy rain.

thyme (n) is a small plant whose leaves are used in cooking.

tick ticks ticking ticked
1 (n) A tick is a mark used to show that something written is correct or satisfactory.
2 (vb) When a clock, watch, etc ticks, it makes a clicking noise.

ticket tickets (n) A ticket is a paper which shows that you are entitled to enter a place, or travel on something. *A train ticket, a theatre ticket.*

tickle tickles tickling tickled
1 (vb) If you tickle someone, you touch them in such a way that they laugh.
ticklish (adj)
2 (vb) If something tickles you, it amuses you.
3 (n) A tickle in your throat is an irritation.

tide tides (n) The tide is the regular change in the level of the sea on the shore.

tidy tidier tidiest (adj) A tidy person or thing is neat and well presented.

tie ties tying tied
1 (n) A tie is a piece of material worn around the neck and knotted in a special way.
2 (vb) If you tie something you fasten it with string, wool, etc.
4 (vb) If you tie with someone in a competition, you finish in the same position as they do.

tier tiers (n) A tier is one of several layers or levels that are placed on top of one another. *The cake had four tiers.*

tiger tigers (n) A tiger is a very large wild cat with black and orange stripes. Tigers live in Asia.

tight tighter tightest
1 (adj) If clothes are tight, they fit you very closely.
2 (adv) If you hold something tightly, you hold it firmly.

tights (n) are an item of clothing worn to cover the hips, legs and feet.

tighten tightens tightening tightened (vb) If you tighten something, you make it more secure.

tightrope tightropes (n) A tightrope is a rope or wire at a high level on which acrobats walk and perform.

tile tiles
1 (n) A tile is a flat piece of baked and glazed clay, carpet, etc that is used with others to cover floors, walls, etc.
2 (vb) If you tile an area, you cover it with tiles.

tiller tillers (n) A tiller is the long handle which moves the rudder and steers a boat.

tilt tilts tilting tilted (vb) If you tilt something, you move it so that it slopes.

timber timbers (n) Timber is wood used for building, ships, etc.

time times
1 (n) A time is what we measure in minutes, hours, days, etc.
2 (n) A time in history is a particular period. *Roman times… Norman times… Modern times.*
3 (vb) If you time a race, you measure how long it takes.
4 If something happens from time to time, it happens occasionally.
5 If something happens in no time, it happens very quickly.
6 If you make time for someone, you make sure that you have enough time to see them.

time share (n) is an arrangement where people buy shares in a holiday home and each of them spends a certain amount of time in it every year.

timetable timetables
1 (n) A timetable is a plan showing lessons and breaks and at what time they happen.
2 (n) A timetable can show the arrival and departure of buses, trains, etc.

timid (adj) A timid person is shy and lacks confidence.

timpani (n) are kettledrums played in an orchestra.

tin tins
1 (n) Tin is a soft, silvery-white metal.
2 (n) A tin is a metal container for food, paints, drinks, etc.

tingle tingles tingling tingled (vb) If part of your body tingles, it produces a prickly sensation.

tinsel (n) is made up of pieces of shiny glittering material and is used to decorate Christmas trees, etc.

tint tints tinting tinted
1 (n) A tint is a light shade of a colour.
2 (vb) If you tint something, you change the colour of it slightly.

tiny tinier tiniest (adj) Something tiny is very small.

tiptoe tiptoes tiptoeing tiptoed
1 (vb) If you walk on tiptoe, you walk as quietly as you can.
3 If you stand on tiptoe, you stand on your toes.

tire tires tiring tired
1 (vb) If you tire, you become sleepy or exhausted.
2 (adj) If you are tired you need a rest or sleep.
3 (adj) A tiring job is one that exhausts you.
4 (vb) If you tire of someone or something, you become bored or fed up with them.

tissue tissues
1 (n) Tissue is thin paper used to wrap fragile things.
2 (n) A tissue is a thin paper handkerchief.
3 (n) Tissue in plants or animals is made up of similar cells.

tit tits (n) A tit is a small kind of bird.

title titles
1 (n) The title of a book or play is its name.
2 (n) A person's title is the name such as Mr, Mrs, Lord, Doctor, etc used in front of their own name.

toad toads (n) A toad is an animal rather like a frog, but which lives more on the land and has a drier skin.

toast toasts toasting toasted
1 (n) Toast is bread that has been heated in a grill until it is brown and crisp.
2 (vb) If you toast bread, you heat it until it is brown and crisp under a grill.
3 (vb) If you toast someone, you show your respect by drinking to their health.

t

tobacco

tobacco tobaccos Tobacco is a plant whose leaves are dried, shredded and smoked in pipes, cigars or cigarettes.

toboggan toboggans tobogganing tobogganed
1 (n) A toboggan is a sledge.
2 (vb) If you toboggan, you travel over the snow on a toboggan.

today (n) is the present day.

toddler toddlers (n) A toddler is a young child who has recently started to walk.

toe toes (n) A toe is one of the five parts at
skeleton p273 the end of your feet.

toffee toffees (n) Toffee is a sticky chewy sweet made from boiled sugar and butter.

toga togas (n) A toga was a garment worn by the male citizens of ancient Rome.

together
1 (adv) If people do things together, they do them with one another.
2 (adv) If you join things together, you attach two or more things to each other.

toggle toggles (n) A toggle is a small wood, plastic or metal rod which is used on some coats in place of buttons.

toilet toilets (n) A toilet is the large bowl connected to the plumbing of a building that people use to get rid of waste matter from their bodies.

token tokens (n) A token is a flat disc that can be used in machines instead of money, or a card worth a certain amount of money which you can exchange for goods.

tomato tomatoes (n) A tomato is a small, red fruit which can be eaten raw or cooked.

tomb tombs (n) A tomb is a place above ground where dead people are buried.

tomorrow tomorrows (n) Tomorrow is the day after this one.

tom-tom tom-toms (n) A tom-tom is a small drum from Africa or Asia, which is played with the hands.

ton tons (n) A ton is a unit of weight equal to 2240 pounds. It is the same as a metric tonne.

tone tones toning toned
1 (n) Tone is a particular quality in a sound. *He sang in clear tones.*
2 (n) A tone is a particular quality in a colour which makes it lighter or darker.
3 (vb) If you tone up your muscles, you make yourself fitter.

tongs (n) are tools which look like scissors, but are used to hold things.

tongue tongues (n) Your tongue is the muscle in your mouth which tastes things, and with which you talk.
 mouth p18

tongue-twister tongue-twisters (n) A tongue-twister is a sentence or rhyme in which many of the words begin with the same letters or sounds so that it is very difficult to say. *She sells sea shells on the sea shore.*

tonight (adv) is the evening and night which follows today.

tonne tonnes (n) A tonne is a metric unit of weight. One tonne is the same as 1000 kilos.

tonsillitis (n) is an infection of the tonsils.

tonsil tonsils (n) Your tonsils are the small, soft lumps at the back of your throat.

too
1 (adv) We use the word too at the end of a sentence to mean as well. *Peter came too.*
2 Too is used to mean an excess of something or some quality. *Too little, too much, too hot, too cold, etc.*

tool tools (n) A tool is a piece of equipment used to help with work of any kind. *Hammers, chisels and computers are all useful tools.*

tooth teeth
1 (n) Teeth are the hard, white objects in your mouth which grow in rows and which you use to chew or bite food.
2 (n) A tooth is the part of a cog wheel, comb, etc which sticks out along the edge.
mouth p18

toothache (n) is a pain in your tooth.

toothpaste toothpastes (n) Toothpaste is a cream for cleaning the teeth.

topiary (n) is the art of trimming bushes into the shape of animals, patterns, etc.

topic topics (n) A topic is a specific subject being discussed, or written about.

topical (adj) things are in the news at the moment.

torch torches
1 (n) A torch is a light that can be carried in your hand and is powered by batteries.
2 (n) A torch is a flaming wad of material on the end of a stick.

torment torments tormenting tormented
1 (vb) If you torment a person or an animal, you hurt or distress them, often over a long period of time.
2 (n) Torments are the things which cause you physical pain or mental suffering.

tornado tornadoes (n) A tornado is a very violent storm. It is often accompanied by a very strong funnel-shaped wind.

torpedo torpedoes (n) A torpedo is a long, cylindrical, under-water missile, fired from ships or submarines.

torrent torrents (n) A torrent is a lot of water falling or flowing very quickly.
torrential (adj)

tortilla tortillas (n) A tortilla is a hard, Mexican pancake made of corn and eggs.

tortoise tortoises (n) A tortoise is a slow-moving reptile with a shell on its back for protection.

torture tortures torturing tortured
1 (vb) If a person tortures another person, they deliberately cause them great pain in order to punish them or to get information.
2 (n) Torture is the act of hurting people in order to get information or confessions.

toss tosses tossing tossed (vb) If you toss something, you throw it in the air.

total totals totalling totalled
1 (n) A total is a number that you get when you have added or counted all the things you are supposed to be counting.
2 (vb) If you total up things, you add them together.
3 (adj) You can use total to emphasise the completeness of something. *It was a total failure.*

toucan toucans (n) A toucan is a South American bird with a large, brightly coloured beak.

touch touches touching touched
1 (vb) If you touch something, you come into contact with it, or feel it with your hands.
2 (n) Your sense of touch is the sense that lets you know how things feel.
3 (vb) If something touches you, it affects your emotions.

touchdown touchdowns (n) A touchdown is a scoring move in American football.

tough tougher toughest
1 (adj) Something tough is very strong and difficult to tear or break.
2 (adj) A tough person is physically strong and aggressive.
3 (adj) A tough problem is very difficult to solve.

toupee toupees (n) A toupee is a small wig.

tour tours touring toured
1 (vb) If you tour, you travel around visiting many places.
2 (n) A tour is a trip around many places lasting several days.

tourism (n) is the business of providing hotels and entertainment for visitors to a place or country. **tourist** (n)

tournament tournaments (n) A tournament is a competition where competitors are eliminated at each stage until one winner is left.

tourniquet tourniquets (n) A tourniquet is a piece of cloth wound tightly around an injured limb to stop bleeding.

t

tow

tow tows towing towed (vb) If one vehicle tows another vehicle, one of them pulls the other.

towards (prep) If you move towards something, you move in its direction.

towel towels (n) A towel is a piece of soft cloth that you use to dry yourself.

tower towers towering towered
1 (n) A tower is a tall building or structure.
2 (vb) If one thing towers over another, it is very much higher. *The pylons towered over the cottage.*

town towns (n) A town is a large collection of houses, offices, and factories where people live and work.

toxic (adj) substances are poisonous.

trace traces tracing traced
1 (vb) If you trace a drawing, etc you copy it by drawing on thin paper put over the top.
2 (vb) If you trace the origins of something, you find out how it began.
3 (n) A trace is a tiny amount of something or a sign that something has been in a particular place. *A trace of dust proved that he had been at the scene of the crime.*

track tracks tracking tracked
1 (n) A track is a narrow path.
2 (n) A track is a metal rail that trains or trams travel on.
3 (n) A track is a piece of ground, usually in the shape of a ring, where athletics or motor races are held.
3 (n) A track is a song on a record or tape.
4 (n) The track of a satellite, planet, etc is the path it takes through space.
5 (n) Tracks are the footprints of animals or people left in the ground behind them.
6 (vb) If you track someone or something, you follow them by following the marks they leave as they pass.

tracksuit tracksuits (n) A tracksuit is a warm set of clothes, consisting of a top and trousers, worn by athletes when they are waiting to perform or for training.

traction engine traction engines (n) A traction engine is a steam-driven vehicle used in the past to pull heavy loads.

tractor tractors (n) A tractor is a farm vehicle used to pull trailers, ploughs, etc.

trade trades trading traded
1 (vb) If you trade, you buy and sell goods.
2 (n) A trade is a skill that you use to earn your living. *Her trade is plumbing.*
4 (n) Trade is the act of buying and selling goods between people or countries.

trademark trademarks (n) A trademark is a name or symbol used by a company on their goods, vehicles, etc. It is protected by law so that it cannot be copied.

trade union trade unions (n) A trade union is an organisation formed to look after the interests of workers in particular industries or jobs.

tradition traditions (n) A tradition is a belief or activity that a particular group of people hold or have carried on for a long time. **traditionally** (adj)

traffic traffics trafficking trafficked
1 (n) Traffic is the name for all the vehicles that pass along roads.
2 (vb) If you traffic in something, you sell it, often illegally. *He was caught by the police trafficking drugs.*

traffic warden traffic wardens (n) A traffic warden makes sure that car drivers park their cars properly in towns.

tragedy tragedies
1 (n) A tragedy is a very sad or disastrous happening especially one in which people are killed.
2 (n) A tragedy is a type of play, with a sad ending.

trail trails trailing trailed
1 (n) A trail is a small, narrow path.
2 (n) A trail is the scent, footprints, etc that an animal or person leaves behind them.
3 (vb) If you trail someone or something, you follow them by looking for the marks that they leave as they pass.

trailer trailers (n) A trailer is a cart or a large container towed behind vehicles.

train trains training trained
1 (vb) If you train a person or an animal to do something, you teach them how to do it.
2 (n) A train is a vehicle which travels on rails and carries goods or passengers.
3 (n) A train is the long part of some formal dresses which trails behind the wearer.

t

trainer trainers
1 (n) A trainer is a person who trains other people or animals.
2 (n) Trainers are a type of shoe worn for sporting events or casual wear.

traitor traitors (n) A traitor is a person who betrays their country or friends, etc.

tram trams (n) A tram is an electric, passenger vehicle that runs on rails through towns.

tramp tramps tramping tramped
1 (vb) If you tramp somewhere, you walk in a heavy way.
2 (n) A tramp is a person with no home or permanent job and very little money. Tramps go from place to place getting food and money by taking occasional jobs or begging.

trample tramples trampling trampled
(vb) If you trample on something, you walk over it and crush it.

trampoline trampolines (n) A trampoline is a strong cloth held to a frame with springs, that is used by gymnasts to jump or bounce very high.

trance trances (n) A trance is a state in which a person seems to be asleep, but can see and hear and respond to orders.

tranquillity (n) is a state of calm and peace. **tranquil** (adj)

tranquilliser tranquillisers (n) A tranquilliser is a drug used to calm or relax people or animals.

transaction transactions (n) A transaction is a business deal between two or more people.

transatlantic (adj) is used to describe anything that crosses the Atlantic ocean, especially between the USA and Europe.

transcript transcripts (n) A transcript is a written account of a conversation. **transcription** (n)

transfer transfers transferring transferred
1 (vb) If you transfer someone or something, you move them officially from one place to another. **transferable** (adj)
2 (n) A transfer is a design on a piece of paper which can be put on to pottery, material, etc.

transfix transfixes transfixing transfixed (vb) If something or someone transfixes you, you are so impressed or frightened by them that you cannot move.

transform transforms transforming transformed (vb) If something transforms you, it changes you. **transformation** (n)

transformer transformers (n) A transformer is a device which changes the voltage of an electric current.

transfusion transfusions (n) A transfusion is a process where blood is given to a person who is injured or ill.

transistor transistors (n) A transistor is a very small device in something such as a television or a radio.

transit
1 (n) Transit is the process of moving goods or people from one place to another.
2 If things or people are in transit, they are being moved from one place to another.

translate translates translating translated (vb) If you translate speech or writing, you change it from one language to another. **translation** (n)

translucent (adj) Something that is translucent allows light to pass through it, and appears to glow.

transmit transmits transmitting transmitted
1 (vb) If you transmit a message or programme, you broadcast it through television or radio. **transmitter** (n)
2 (vb) If you transmit something, you send it to a different place.
3 (vb) If you transmit a disease, you pass it on to other people. **transmission** (n)

transparent (adj) If something is transparent, it is completely clear and you can see through it.

t

transplant

transplant transplants transplanting transplanted
1 (vb) If you transplant a flower or plant, you move it from one place to another.
2 (n) A transplant is an operation where an organ, such as a heart or a kidney, is taken from one person and put into another.

transport transports transporting transported
1 (n) Transport is the moving of goods or people from one place to another.
2 (vb) If you transport someone or something, you take it from one place to another.

trapeze trapezes (n) A trapeze is a high swing that circus acrobats use.

trauma traumas (n) A trauma is a very unpleasant occurrence or emotional shock which affects you badly. **traumatic** (adj)

travel travels travelling travelled
1 (vb) If you travel, you move from one place to another. **traveller** (n)
2 (n) Travels are the journeys that people make.
3 (vb) If you travel a certain distance or at a certain speed, you move that distance or at that speed.

travel agent (n) A travel agent is a person whose job it is to arrange holidays or journeys for people.

trawl trawls trawling trawled
1 (vb) If you trawl for fish, you try to catch them in a huge net towed behind a fishing boat called a trawler.
2 (n) A trawl is the name of the net used in trawl fishing.

tray trays (n) A tray is a flat piece of wood, metal or plastic used for carrying things.

treachery treacheries (n) Treachery is the act of betraying friends or your country.

treacle (n) is a thick, sticky, sweet liquid made from sugar and used in cooking.

tread treads treading trod
1 (vb) If you tread on something, you place your foot on it.
2 (n) The tread is the pattern on tyres.
3 (n) A tread is the upper surface of steps.
4 (vb) If you tread water, you move your arms and legs enough to stay afloat.

treason (n) is the crime of betraying your country to another country.

treasure treasures treasuring treasured
1 (n) Treasure is a collection of valuable jewellery, money, etc. especially one that is hidden or buried.
2 (n) A treasure is a valuable painting, jewel, etc. which is kept in a museum or art gallery.
3 (vb) If you treasure something, you look after it carefully, because it is important to you.

treasury treasuries
1 (n) A treasury is a place in a castle or cathedral where valuable treasure is kept.
2 (n) In Britain and some other countries, The Treasury is the department of the government that deals with money, taxes, etc.

treat treats treating treated
1 (vb) If you treat something, you put a special substance on it to alter it in some way. *The wood was treated to make it fire resistant.*
2 (vb) If you treat someone or something in a particular way, you deal with them in that way.
3 (vb) If a doctor treats a person, they try to cure their illness.
5 (vb) If you treat a person, you buy them a special gift, or do something that they like.
treatment (n)

treaty treaties (n) A treaty is an agreement between two countries.

treble trebles trebling trebled
1 (vb) If you treble something, you make it three times bigger than it was.
2 (n) A treble is a singer or instrument that has a very high voice or sound.

tree trees (n) A tree is a tall plant with a long trunk made of wood, which usually has leaves and branches, and can live for many years.

trek treks trekking trekked
1 (n) A trek is a long, hard walk.
2 (vb) If you trek somewhere, you go on a long, hard journey, often by foot.

trellis trellises (n) A trellis is a framework of wood for plants to climb up.

tree

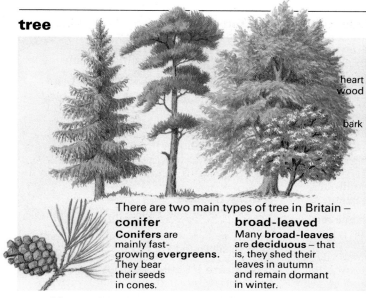

heart wood

bark

new wood

old wood (annual rings)

There are two main types of tree in Britain –

conifer
Conifers are mainly fast-growing **evergreens**. They bear their seeds in cones.

broad-leaved
Many **broad-leaves** are **deciduous** – that is, they shed their leaves in autumn and remain dormant in winter.

How trees grow
Each year the whole stem puts on a new outer layer, so that the trunk becomes gradually thicker towards the base. This outward growth means that the newer tissues which carry water to the leaves are always on the edge of the trunk and the older wood in the centre serves as tough supporting tissues. When the tree stops growing in the winter this produces annual rings which can be used to date a felled tree.

tremble trembles trembling trembled
1 (vb) If you tremble, you shiver with cold or fright.
2 (vb) If your voice trembles, it is shaky.

tremendous
1 (adj) Something that is tremendous, is very large, impressive or important.
2 (adj) Tremendous is also used to mean very good. *That's tremendous news!*

tremor tremors
1 (n) A tremor is a shaking movement that you are unable to control.
2 (n) A tremor is a small earthquake.

trench trenches (n) A trench is a long, narrow ditch or channel in the ground, dug either to put plants, pipes etc in, or for soldiers to shelter in.

trend trends (n) A trend is a general movement of events, styles, tastes, etc.

trespass trespasses trespassing trespassed (vb) If you trespass you go onto someone's land without their permission.

trial trials
1 (n) A trial is a legal process in which a court listens to evidence to decide whether a person is guilty or innocent of a crime.
2 (n) A trial is a type of experiment in which someone or something is tested to see how well they perform.
3 (n) Trials are difficulties and hardships.

triangle triangles
1 (n) A triangle is a flat shape with three straight sides and three angles.
triangular (adj)
2 (n) A triangle is a musical instrument which produces a note when hit with a metal bar.

tribe tribes (n) A tribe is a group of people belonging to the same race, and usually living together, sharing the same customs, beliefs, language, etc. **tribal** (adj)

tributary tributaries (n) A tributary is a stream or river that flows into a larger river.

tribute tributes (n) A tribute is something done or said to show respect for someone. *Hundreds of people came to pay tribute to the Queen on her birthday.*

trick tricks tricking tricked
1 (n) A trick is something you do in order to deceive someone or to make them look foolish.
2 (vb) If someone tricks you, they deceive you, cheat you or make you look foolish.
3 (n) A trick is something clever and skilfully done to entertain people.
4 (n) A trick can also be a joke. *We played a trick on the teacher.*

t

trickle

trickle trickles trickling trickled (vb) If a liquid trickles, it flows slowly and in very small quantities. *Water trickled down the walls.* trickle (n)

tricky trickier trickiest (adj) Something tricky is difficult to deal with or manage.

tricycle tricycles (n) A tricycle is a three-wheeled pedal cycle.

trifle trifles
1 (n) A trifle is a pudding made from cake, jam or fruit, custard and cream.
2 (n) A trifle is a very small amount of something or something unimportant.

trigger triggers triggering triggered
1 (n) A trigger is a small lever on a gun or machine. You press it to make the gun or machine work.
2 (vb) If you trigger an event or situation, you cause it. *His jealousy triggered off the quarrel.*

trim trims trimming trimmed (vb) If you trim something, a lawn for example, you cut it so that it looks neat.

trinity
1 (n) A trinity is a group of three things or people.
2 (n) In the Christian religion, the Trinity is the union of the Father, Son and Holy Spirit in one God.

trio trios (n) A trio is a group of three people or things that have something in common. *A trio of musicians.*

trip trips tripping tripped
1 (vb) If you trip, you catch your foot against something and stumble.
2 (n) A trip is a return journey or an excursion, which can last for a day or longer.

tripe (n) is the stomach of an ox, cow or pig which is cooked and eaten as food.

triple (adj) Something described as triple consists of three things or three parts. *The triple jump is a three-part jump.*

triplet triplets (n) Triplets are three children born to the same mother at the same time.

tripod tripods (n) A tripod is a stand with three legs often used with a camera.

triumph triumphs triumphing triumphed
1 (n) A triumph is a great success.
2 (n) Triumph is the feeling you have when you have achieved a great success or victory.
3 (vb) If someone triumphs, they gain a complete victory, often after a long struggle. **triumphant** (adj)

trivial (adj) things are unimportant.

troll trolls (n) A troll is an ugly imaginary creature from Scandinavian mythology.

trolley trolleys
1 (n) A trolley is a wheeled cart which you pull or push and use to carry things.
2 (n) A trolley is a small table on wheels, used to serve food or drink.

trombone trombones (n) A trombone is a large, brass musical instrument with a slide that you move to vary the note.

troop troops trooping trooped
1 (vb) If you troop somewhere, you go in a large group. **troop** (n)
2 (n) Troops are soldiers.

trophy trophies
1 (n) A trophy is a prize awarded to the winners of games or races.
2 (n) A trophy is something you keep to remind you of a victory of some kind.

tropics (n) The tropics are the hottest regions of the world. The tropics lie north and south of the equator. **tropical** (adj)

trouble troubles troubling troubled
1 (n) Troubles are problems or difficulties.
2 (vb) If something troubles you, it worries you.
3 (adj) Troubling things cause worry and distress.

trough troughs (n) A trough is a long, narrow container from which animals drink or eat.

troupe troupes (n) A troupe is a group of entertainers.

trousers (n) are a piece of clothing. Trousers cover your bottom and have two tubes of fabric which cover your legs.

trout trout (n) A trout is a freshwater fish that can be eaten.

trowel trowels (n) A trowel is a small, hand tool used in gardening or in building.

truant truants (n) A truant is a child who stays away from school without good reason. **truancy** (n)

truce truces (n) A truce is an agreement between two people or groups of people to stop fighting for a time.

truck trucks
1 (n) A truck is a lorry or large open-backed vehicle used to carry goods.
2 (n) A truck is an open goods wagon on the railway.

trudge trudges trudging trudged (vb) If you trudge somewhere, you go there with heavy, tired steps.

true truer truest
1 (adj) If something is true, it is based on fact and really happened.
2 (adj) Something that is true is genuine.
3 (adj) Your true feelings are what you actually feel although you may not show them.

truffle truffles
1 (n) A truffle is a soft, sweet chocolate often flavoured with rum, cherries, etc.
2 (n) Truffles are mushroom-like fungi, which grow underground and can be eaten.

trumpet trumpets trumpeting trumpeted
1 (n) A trumpet is a brass musical instrument that you play by blowing into it.
2 (vb) If an elephant trumpets, it makes a loud noise.
3 If you blow your own trumpet, you boast about your own achievements.

truncheon truncheons (n) are short wooden sticks carried by British police.

trunk trunks
1 (n) A trunk is the thick main stem of a tree.
2 (n) Your trunk is your body, excluding your arms, legs and head.
3 (n) An elephant's trunk is its long nose.
4 (n) A trunk is a large, strong box or piece of luggage.
5 (n) Trunks or swimming trunks are the briefs worn by men and boys when swimming.

trust trusts trusting trusted
1 (vb) If you trust someone, you believe they will treat you fairly and will do as they have promised.
2 (n) Trust is the responsibility you have to the people who rely on you. *She was determined to repay the trust shown in her.*

truth truths
1 (n) A truth is a fact or an idea which people believe to be correct.
2 (n) The truth about something is what actually happened, rather than imaginary versions of it.
3 If you tell the truth you are honest and do not tell lies. **truthful** (adj)

try tries trying tried
1 (vb) If you try to do something, you make an effort to do it.
2 (vb) If you try something, you use it, taste it or experiment with it to see how good or suitable it is. *Try this cake it's delicious.*
3 (vb) When a court tries a person, they question them to see if they have committed a crime or not.
4 (vb) A person who tries your patience is extremely irritating and difficult.
5 (n) A try is an attempt to do something.
6 (n) A try in rugby is when a player scores by carrying the ball over the opponents' goal line and putting it on the ground.

tsar or **czar** tsars or czars (n) The tsar was a king of Russia in former times. His wife was known as the tsarina.

T-shirt T-shirts (n) A T-shirt is a round-necked, short-sleeved casual shirt, usually made from a knitted cotton fabric.

tuba tubas (n) A tuba is a large brass instrument. It has a curved tube of brass with a very large funnel at the end.

tube tubes
1 (n) A tube is a long, hollow length of metal or glass, etc.
2 (n) The Tube is another name for the London underground train system.

tuber tubers (n) A tuber is a part of the roots of some plants which swell up into round lumps. *Potatoes are tubers.*

tuberculosis (n) is an infectious disease which damages lungs and other parts of the body. It is also known as T.B.

t

tuck

tuck tucks tucking tucked
1 (vb) When you tuck a loose end of cloth or thread in, you push it where it is secure and tidy.
2 (n) A tuck is a fold sewn into a garment to make it fit well.
3 (vb) If you tuck in to a meal, you eat eagerly and with pleasure.
4 (n) Tuck is the food that schoolchildren buy to eat between meals.

tuft tufts (n) A tuft is a bunch of grass, hair, etc which grows closely together, and stands above the surrounding grass or hair. **tufted** (adj)

tuition (n) If you receive tuition in a subject, you are taught, often on your own or in a small group.

tulip tulips (n) A tulip is a flower that grows from a bulb in spring.

tumble tumbles tumbling tumbled
1 (vb) If you tumble, you fall and roll over.
2 (vb) If the price of something tumbles, it falls very suddenly.

tumble drier tumble driers (n) A tumble drier is a machine that dries clothes, by turning them over and over in warm air.

tuna tuna (n) A tuna is a large, edible sea fish.

tune tunes tuning tuned
1 (n) A tune is a pleasing pattern of musical notes.
2 (vb) If you tune an instrument, you make sure that it will play the correct notes.
3 (vb) If you tune a vehicle, you make sure that the engine is running properly.

tunnel tunnels tunnelling tunnelled
1 (n) A tunnel is a passage underground.
2 (vb) If you tunnel, you dig a passageway under the ground.

turban turbans (n) A turban is a long piece of cloth worn around the head, especially by Sikh men.

hydro
electricity
p142

turbine turbines (n) A turbine is an engine powered by water, steam, gas, etc which turns the blades of a wheel and makes it turn round.

turbo turbos (n) A turbo is a fan in an engine, which is driven by exhaust gases and which improves the engine's performance.

turf turfs or **turves**
1 (n) Turf is short, thick, even grass.
2 (n) A turf is a piece of good grass with roots and soil used to make a lawn.

turn turns turning turned
1 (vb) When you turn, you move your body, for example, to face a different direction.
2 (vb) If you turn a key, switch, etc you move it so that it starts to work or goes on.
3 (vb) If you turn to a page in a book, you find that page.
4 (vb) If something turns into something else, it becomes something different.

turnip turnips (n) A turnip is a round, white root vegetable.

turret turrets (n) A turret is a small tower on top of a castle, for example. **turreted** (n)

turtle turtles (n) A turtle is a large reptile with a shell, that lives mainly in the sea.

tusk tusks (n) A tusk is a long pointed tooth of the elephant, walrus, wild boar, etc.

tweed tweeds (n) Tweed is a thick, woollen cloth, woven in many colours.

tweezers (n) are a small tool of two metal arms, joined at one end and used for holding or picking up small objects.

twice
1 (adv) If something happens twice, it occurs two times.
2 (adv) If one thing is twice as big as another thing, it is double the size.

twilight (n) is the dim light just after the sun sets at night.

t

twin twins twinning twinned
1 (n) Twins are two people born to the same mother at the same time.
2 (vb) If one town twins with another in a different country, they have close links.

twist twists twisting twisted
1 (n) A twist is a bend in a road.
2 (vb) If you twist something, you move one part of it to face a different direction.
3 (n) A twist in a story, play, film, etc is an unexpected change in the plot.
4 If you twist someone around your little finger, you are able to make them do whatever you want.

tycoon tycoons (n) A tycoon is a businessman with a lot of money and power.

type types typing typed
1 (n) A type of something is a particular kind of it. *They used many types of ink.*
2 (vb) If you type something, you write it on a typewriter or wordprocessor.
3 (n) Type is the printed words produced by a typewriter, wordprocessor or type-setting machine.

typhoid (n) is a serious, infectious disease that causes a fever and diarrhoea.

typhoon typhoons (n) A typhoon is a violent storm in the Western Pacific area.

typical (adj) If something is typical, it has the usual features of the group to which it belongs.

tyre tyres (n) A tyre is a thick band of rubber, either solid or filled with air, which fits on the wheels of cars, prams, bicycles, etc.

Uu

udder udders (n) The udder of a female animal, a cow for example, is the large, bag-like organ hanging between the legs which produces milk.

ugly uglier ugliest
1 (adj) If someone or something is ugly, they are not pleasant to look at.
2 (adj) An ugly situation is unpleasant because it is dangerous or threatening.

ulcer ulcers (n) An ulcer is a sore inside or outside the body which can become septic. **ulcerated** (adj)

ultimate
1(adj) Ultimate describes the final outcome of a long series of events. *The ultimate goal of their months of training was to sail round the world.*
2 (adj) Ultimate power is the greatest or supreme power.
3 (adj) The ultimate describes the most extreme example of something. *The ultimate joy . . . the ultimate evil.*

ultrasonic (adj) sounds are those that are too high pitched for human beings to hear.

ultraviolet light (n) is the radiation from the sun which causes the skin to darken. Too much can be harmful.

umbilical cord (n) The umbilical cord is the tube connecting an unborn baby to its mother through which it receives food and oxygen.

umbrella umbrellas (n) An umbrella is a folding frame covered with fabric which you open over you to protect yourself from rain.

umpire umpires (n) An umpire's job is to supervise sporting contests or matches, to keep the score and to make sure that the rules are kept.

unacceptable (adj) If something is unacceptable, it is not satisfactory and should be changed.

u

unanimous

unanimous (adj) A unanimous vote or decision has the support or agreement of everybody concerned.

unbearable (adj) things are those that we find so painful or upsetting that we cannot endure them.

unbelievable
1 (adj) Something that is unbelievable is so unlikely that we cannot think that it can be true.
2 (adj) If something is unbelievable it is very surprising or wonderful. *Her piano playing is unbelievable.*

unbiased (adj) Someone who is unbiased shows no favouritism in making judgements or decisions.

uncanny uncannier uncanniest (adj) Uncanny things are unusual, strange or have no easy explanations. *She bore an uncanny resemblance to my sister.*

uncertain
1 (adj) If you are uncertain about something, you are not sure about it. *I am uncertain about which road to take.*
2 (adj) If something is uncertain, it may or may not take place. *Rain made play in the Test match uncertain.* **uncertainty** (n)

uncivilised (adj) Uncivilised people or tribes are thought to lead primitive or simple lives because they have no written culture, science, technology, etc.

uncle uncles (n) Your uncle is the brother of your father or your mother.

unclean (adj) Things that are unclean are dirty and liable to cause disease.

uncomfortable
1 (adj) If you are uncomfortable your body does not feel relaxed and at ease. *We were uncomfortable because three of us had to share one seat.*
2 (adj) An uncomfortable chair, room etc is one in which you cannot relax or feel at ease.
3 (adj) An uncomfortable situation makes you worried or nervous.

unconscious
1 (adj) If someone is unconscious, they are not aware of anything around them because they are in a coma caused by an accident or illness.
2 (n) The unconscious is the part of your mind that you do not know about and cannot control but which influences conscious activities.

uncontrollable (adj) If someone or something is uncontrollable, they are difficult and you have no control over them.

uncooperative (adj) people refuse to help or work with anyone.

undaunted (adj) If you are undaunted, you are not put off or discouraged by disappointments or set-backs or by unkind things that people say.

undecided (adj) If you are undecided, you can't make up your mind about something.

undeniable (adj) If something is undeniable, it is so obviously true that you cannot argue against it or disagree with it.

under
1 (prep) Under means beneath. *The cat was under the table.*
2 (prep) Under means below the surface *The rocks under the water are dangerous.*
3 (prep) If you are under the influence of something or of someone, they affect the way you behave or think.
4 (prep) If something is under construction, a road or a house for example, then it is the process of being built.
5 (prep) If a person is under someone's command, then they must obey that person's orders.
6 (prep) If you are under observation, attack, guard, etc you are being observed, attacked, guarded, etc.
7 (prep) If you say that something is under a particular number or amount, you mean that it is less than that figure. *She was under seven stone . . . Are you under sixteen?*

undercarriage undercarriages (n) The undercarriage of an aeroplane is the part including the wheels which supports it on taking off and landing.

aircraft p5

underdeveloped (adj) Underdeveloped means not fully grown or not at full strength. *Underdeveloped countries have few industries at the moment.*

underdog underdogs (n) An underdog is an unfortunate person who tends to be a loser.

underestimate underestimates underestimating underestimated (vb) If you underestimate something you do not realise how big it is or how long it will take. *We underestimated how thirsty you'd be and we've run out of coke.*

undergraduate undergraduates (n) An undergraduate is a student at university who is studying for a degree.

underground
1 (adj) An underground car park or store room, for example, is below the surface of the earth.
2 (adj) Underground activities are secret or illegal.
3 (n) The Underground in Britain is a railway system with electric trains which travel mainly in tunnels under a city.

undergrowth (n) refers to all the plants and bushes growing close together under the trees in a wood or jungle.

underhand (adj) activity or behaviour is done secretly and is usually dishonest or deceitful.

underline underlines underlining underlined
1 (vb) If you underline a word or sentence you draw a line under it.
2 (vb) If something underlines a fact, a problem or a feeling, it emphasises it. *The recent article in the paper underlines the dangers of smoking.*

undermine undermines undermining undermined
1 (vb) When the sea undermines a cliff, for example, its base is gradually worn away or weakened so that it is in danger of collapsing.
2 (vb) If you undermine a person, system or an idea, etc you weaken it to make it less powerful or convincing.

undernourished (adj) Undernourished people are unhealthy because of lack of food or because they eat the wrong kinds of food.

underprivileged (adj) people do not have the advantages that others have, such as possessions, good food and comfort.

understand understands understanding understood
1 (vb) If you understand what someone is saying or what you read, then you know what it means.
2 (vb) If you understand how something works, you know how it works.
3 (vb) If you understand someone, you think you know why they behave in the way they do.
4 (vb) If you say that you understand that something is so, then you have been told about it. *I understand you are going to Spain in May.*

understudy understudies (n) An understudy is an actor who learns the lines and moves of another actor, and so is able to stand in for him in an emergency.

undertake undertakes undertaking undertaken
1 (vb) If you undertake a job or undertake to do something, you promise to be responsible for it.
2 (n) An undertaking is a task or job that you have promised to do.

undertaker undertakers (n) An undertaker's job is to prepare dead bodies for burial or cremation and to arrange for the funerals.

underworld
1 (n) The underworld is all the people involved in crime in a city or society.
2 (n) In many old myths and religions the underworld is the place beneath the earth where the spirits of the dead go.

undesirable (adj) things or people are those which are disliked because they are a bad influence.

undignified
1 (adj) Undignified behaviour is rather silly or foolish.
2 (adj) If you feel undignified, you feel foolish and uncomfortable.

u

undisciplined

undisciplined (adj) Undisciplined people have no self-control and behave badly.

undue (adj) is used to describe something that is more extreme than was expected. *There was an undue amount of noise from the party.*

undulate undulates undulating undulated (vb) Something that undulates, a road for example, has slight slopes that rise and fall gently.

unearth unearths unearthing unearthed
1 (vb) If you unearth something, you dig it up from where it has been buried.
2 (vb) If you unearth a secret or an unknown fact, you discover it.

uneasy uneasier uneasiest (adj) If you are uneasy, you feel anxious, afraid and threatened. *The constant howling wind made the dogs uneasy.* **uneasily** (adv)

uneducated (adj) An uneducated person has not received any teaching.

unemployed (adj) An unemployed person does not have a job.

unequal (adj) If two things are unequal, they do not match or balance or are unfair because one is larger, heavier, etc than the other.

uneven
1 (adj) An uneven surface is not flat or smooth.
2 (adj) An uneven edge is not straight.

uneventful (adj) In an uneventful day or journey, etc nothing very interesting or exciting happens.

unexpected (adj) events take you by surprise because you did not think that they would happen.

unfair (adj) Something that is unfair is, or seems wrong or unjust. *The referee gave an unfair penalty.* **unfairly** (adv)

unfaithful (adj) People who are unfaithful are not loyal in their relationships.

unforgivable (adj) If someone does something that is unforgivable, it is so bad that you cannot excuse them.

unfortunate
1 (adj) Someone who is unfortunate is unlucky or has something unpleasant happen to them.
2 (adj) An unfortunate situation or happening is one that could make you feel embarrassed or sorry. **unfortunately** (adv)

unfriendly unfriendlier unfriendliest
1 (adj) An unfriendly person makes no effort to make friends and doesn't seem to want them.
2 (adj) Something that is unfriendly is not warm or welcoming. *The land was bleak and unfriendly.*

unfurl unfurls unfurling unfurled (vb) If you unfurl something that is rolled up, a flag or sail for example, you unroll it or spread it out.

unhappy unhappier unhappiest
1 (adj) If you are unhappy, you are sad or upset.
2 (adj) An unhappy choice or situation is a bad one that might cause problems or sadness. *It was an unhappy choice of hotel; the food was disgusting and the beds were too hard.*

unhealthy unhealthier unhealthiest
1 (adj) Something that is unhealthy is likely to cause illness or poor health.
2 (adj) If you are unhealthy you are in poor health.
3 (adj) If you have an unhealthy interest in something, you are more interested in it than is considered good for you.

unhygienic (adj) Something that is unhygienic is dirty and likely to be a health hazard.

unicorn unicorns (n) A unicorn is a mythical creature. It looks like a horse with a single horn growing on its forehead.

unidentified (adj) If someone or something is unidentified, nobody is able to say who or what it is.

uniform uniforms
1 (n) A uniform is clothing worn by members of the same group such as the army, the police, schoolchildren. Uniforms are always the same.
2 (adj) Things that are uniform are the same in size, weight and colour. *The children are of uniform height.*

u

unify unifies unifying unified (vb) If a number of things or people unify, they come together and share a common aim or function. *They were unified by their efforts to help the victims of the earthquake.*

uninhabited (adj) houses or places have no people living there.

unintelligible (adj) speech or writing is impossible to understand.

union unions
1 (n) A union (or trades union) is an organisation formed by workers to represent their rights and try to improve pay and working conditions.
2 (n) Union is the joining of two or more things together. *The Soviet Union is made up of a number of different states... The vicar blessed the union of the young couple after their wedding.*

unique (adj) If something is unique, it is the only one of its kind.

unison (adv) If two or more people do something in unison, they do it together at exactly the same time.

units units
1 (n) A unit is a single complete thing.
2 (n) A unit is one part of the furniture or equipment designed to fit into a given space. *Kitchen units... hi-fi units.*
3 (n) A unit is an organised group of people who work together at a particular job. *The intensive care unit... army units.*
4 (n) A unit is a term used to describe a fixed quantity of measurement. *A centimetre is a unit of length... a litre is a unit of liquid measurement... a penny is a unit of currency... a minute is a unit of time.*
5 (n) In arithmetic one unit is a whole number less than 10.

unite unites uniting united (vb) If a group of people or countries unite, they join together to form a single larger group or country.

universe (n) The universe is the whole of space and everything it contains; galaxies, stars, planets and all matter and energy.
universal (adj)

university universities (n) A university is a place of higher education where students go to study for degrees and to do research.

unknown
1 (adj) If someone or something is unknown to you, you know nothing about them.
2 (n) The unknown refers to all the things that people do not know about or understand.

unless (conj) is used to introduce a condition that may or may not happen according to your choice. *Unless you turn down the music, I shall take away your radio... You will not be able to buy a bicycle unless you save some money.*

unlimited (adj) If there is an unlimited amount of something, there is plenty of it.

unmanageable (adj) Something unmanageable is difficult or impossible to control.

unnecessary Something unnecessary is not needed.

unpleasant (adj) If something is unpleasant, it is not enjoyable.

unpredictable (adj) If someone or something is unpredictable, you cannot say what will happen or how they will behave.

unqualified (adj) An unqualified person has no formal training or licence to do a job. *I would not fly in an aeroplane with an unqualified pilot.*

unrecognisable (adj) If someone or something is unrecognisable, you cannot be sure who or what they are because they have changed for some reason.

unreliable (adj) Someone or something that is unreliable cannot be trusted.

unskilled (adj) Unskilled work requires no special training to do it.

unsociable (adj) An unsociable person does not like the company of others.

unsuccessful (adj) If you are unsuccessful in something, you do not manage to do it.

unsuitable (adj) An unsuitable person or thing is not fitting to the particular circumstances. *The dirty boy was unsuitable for work in the kitchen.*

unsure (adj) If you are unsure about something, you are not confident about dealing with it.

u

unsuspected (adj) Something that is unsuspected has not been forseen. *She had unsuspected talents in music.*

until (prep or conj) Until means up to that time. *I will wait until he comes... until you help me, I cannot do the work.*

unusual (adj) Someone or something that is unusual is surprisingly different or rare.

upbringing (n) Your upbringing is the way you have been brought up, and the ideas and opinions you have formed as a result.

upheaval upheavals (n) An upheaval is a major change or disturbance. *Losing all our money caused an upheaval in our lives.*

upholstery (n) is the padding and fabric used in furniture to make it comfortable.

upmarket (adj) Upmarket things are expensive.

upper uppers
1 (adj) The upper part of something is the higher or highest part of it. *We skied on the upper slopes of the mountain.*
2 (n) The upper of a shoe is the part above the sole that covers the top of the foot.
3 (adj) If you have the upper hand in a contest, you are winning.

upright
1 (adj) Someone or something that is upright is in a vertical position.
2 (adj) Someone who is upright has very high moral standards.

uproar (n) An uproar is a lot of angry noise or loud protests made by a group of people.

upset upsets upsetting upset
1 (vb) If you upset a drink, you spill it.
2 (vb) If you upset someone's plans, you spoil them.
3 (vb) If you upset yourself about something, you become unhappy and angry about it.
4 (n) If you have a stomach upset, you feel sick.

upstairs
1 (adv) if you go upstairs, you move to a higher floor in a building.
2 (adj) An upstairs room is on a higher floor.

upstream (adv) If a fish swims upstream, it swims against the current towards the source of the river.

uranium (n) is a radioactive metal used to produce nuclear energy.

urban (adj) describes things to do with towns and cities. *Urban development... urban roads... urban living.*

urge urges urging urged
1 (vb) If you urge someone to do something, you tell them very forcefully to do it.
2 (n) If you have an urge to do something, you have a very strong wish to do it.

urgent (adj) If something is urgent it needs to be dealt with immediately.

urine (n) is the liquid you pass from your body when you go to the lavatory.

use uses using used
1 (vb) If you use something, you do something with it to perform a job, sort out a problem, etc. *I use my calculator for arithmetic.*
2 (vb) If you use people, you selfishly get them to do things for your benefit.
3 (n) If something is of no use, it has no value or is pointless. **useless** (adj)
4 (adj) A used item has already been used, owned or is second-hand. *A used car... a used plate... a used handkerchief.*

useful
1 (adj) If something or someone is useful, they are of some help.
2 (adj) If something you have comes in useful, it helps you in some way.

usher ushers (n) An usher is someone who shows you to your seat in a theatre, at a wedding, etc.

usual
1 (adj) The usual things or the usual people are those that we know well.
2 (adj) If something happens as usual, it happens as you would expect.
usually (adv)

utensil utensils (n) A utensil is a tool used for certain jobs.

utter utters uttering uttered (vb) If you utter words, you speak them.

u

Vv

vacant
1 (adj) A vacant room or building is not occupied.
2 (adj) If a job is vacant, no-one is doing it and it can be applied for. **vacancy** (n)

vaccinate vaccinates vaccinating vaccinated (vb) If a doctor vaccinates you, he or she injects you with a medicine to protect you from disease. **vaccine** (n) **vaccination** (n)

vacuum vacuums (n) A vacuum is a complete absence of air or atmosphere. *Space is a complete vacuum.*

vacuum-cleaner (n) A vacuum-cleaner is a machine that sucks up dust and air.

vacuum flask vacuum flasks (n) A vacuum flask keeps food hot or cold.

vacuum-packed (adj) Something that is vacuum-packed is wrapped in a packet from which all the air has been removed.

vagina vagina (n) The vagina is the part of the female body which leads to the womb.

vagrant vagrants (n) A vagrant is a person who sleeps outdoors and has no home. **vagrancy** (n)

vague vaguer vaguest (adj) Something vague is unclear and uncertain.

vain vainer vainest
1 (adj) A vain person is proud and conceited.
2 If you do something in vain, you do it without success.

valentine valentines (n) A valentine is a card or message sent to someone you love on St. Valentine's Day which is February 14th.

valiant (adj) A valiant person is brave.

valid
1 (adj) Something which is valid is correct or legally acceptable.
2 (adj) A valid opinion or comment is one that can be confirmed by evidence.
validity (n)

valley valleys (n) A valley is low land between hills or mountains.

value values valuing valued
1 (n) The value of something is its worth.
2 (vb) If you value something, you regard it as important.
valuable (adj)

valve valves
1 (n) A valve is a device which controls the flow of liquids or gases.
2 (n) A valve is an electronic device used in radios, etc.

vandal vandals (n) A vandal is a person who destroys or spoils property for no obvious reason. **vandalism** (n)

vanilla (n) is a flavouring used in sweets.

vanish vanishes vanishing vanished (vb) If someone or something vanishes, it disappears.

vain (adj) If you are vain, you are too interested in the way you look. **vanity** (n)

vapour vapours (n) Vapour is a mass of tiny droplets in the air which look like a gas, smoke, etc. *Water vapour pours out when the kettle boils.*

variety varieties (n) A variety is a wide range of choices or things.

various (adj) means different or several. *There were various cheeses on display.*

varnish varnishes varnishing varnished (n) Varnish is a clear, sticky liquid which is painted on objects to give a hard, protective coat.

vary varies varying varied (vb) When things vary, they alter and change.

vase vases (n) A vase is a container for flowers, etc.

vast (adj) Something vast is very large.

vat vats (n) A vat is a very large container used for storing liquids.

V

Vatican

Vatican (n) The Vatican is a city-state within the city of Rome which is the home of the Pope.

vault vaults vaulting vaulted
1 (n) A vault is a large cellar.
2 (vb) If you vault in gymnastics you jump over or onto something, often using your hands to steady yourself.
3 (adj) A vaulted roof is arched.

veal (n) is meat from calves.

vegan vegans (n) A vegan is a person who does not eat or use any animal products.

vegetable vegetables (n) Vegetables are plants, especially those we eat.

vegetarian vegetarians (n) A vegetarian is a person who does not eat meat or fish.

vegetation (n) refers to all the plants which fill an area. *We walked through dense vegetation.*

vehicle vehicles (n) A vehicle is a machine, such as a car, bus or truck, which carries people or goods from one place to another.

veil veils (n) A veil is a thin piece of cloth used by women to cover the face and head.

vein veins
1 (n) A vein is a tube in the body which carries blood back to the heart.
2 (n) A vein is a tube for liquids in a leaf or insect or a layer of metal or mineral in rock.

velocity velocities (n) Velocity is the speed at which something travels.

velvet velvets (n) Velvet is a thick, soft material used in curtains and clothing.

veneer veneers (n) A veneer is a thin layer of wood, plastic, etc glued on to a cheaper material to give an attractive appearance.

vengeance (n) is the act of harming someone, in return for something they have done to harm you.

venison (n) is the meat from deer.

venom (n) is the poison which some insects and snakes are able to inject into their prey. **venomous** (adj)

vent vents venting vented
(n) A vent is a hole in a roof or wall allowing smoke or air in or out of a room, building, etc.

venture ventures venturing ventured
1 (n) A venture is something new that you do that involves risk of some kind.
2 (vb) If you venture an opinion, you let your opinion be known.

verb verbs (n) A verb is a word which shows what people or things do. Words such as *walk, talk* and *run* are verbs.

verdict verdicts
1 (n) A verdict is the decision of guilt or innocence given at the end of a trial.
2 (n) A verdict can be an opinion on something.

verge verges
1 (n) The verge is the grass at the side of a motorway or road.
2 (prep) If you are on the verge of something, you are very close to doing it.

verger vergers (n) A verger is a person whose job is to look after the contents of a church and the building itself.

verify verifies verified (vb) If you verify something, you check it to make sure that it is true. **verification** (n)

vermin (n) are animals such as rats, mice, etc which damage crops, and are seen as pests.

versatile (adj) people can do many things or jobs. **versatility** (n)

verse verses
1 (n) A verse is a section of a poem.
2 (n) A verse is one of the numbered sections into which chapters of the Bible are divided.
3 (n) Verse is writing which has rhythmic patterns, and which sometimes rhyme.

version versions (n) A version is a form of something, which is different in some ways to other forms of the same thing. *Her version of events was different.*

versus (prep) Versus means against. *The final will be Hull versus Widnes.*

vertebra vertebrae (n) Vertebrae are the pieces of bone which make up your spine.

vertical (adj) If something is vertical, it is in an upright position, or points upwards.

very (adj) Very is used to emphasise what you are saying. *It was a very tall building.*

vessel vessels
1 (n) A vessel is a ship of some sort.
2 (n) A vessel is a container for liquids.
3 (n) A vessel is one of the tubes in an animal or plant which carries the blood or liquid around the body.

vest vests (n) A vest is a garment worn underneath a shirt or blouse.

vet see **veterinary surgeon**

veteran veterans

a veteran car

1 (n) A veteran is a retired serviceman, especially one who has served in a war.
2 (n) A veteran is a person who has been involved in some activity for a long time. *He was a veteran of many meetings.*
3 (adj) Veteran cars and motorcycles are those made before 1905.

veterinary surgeon (n) A veterinary surgeon treats sick or injured animals.

via (prep) is used to mean 'by way of'. *We went via Cotteridge to get to Bourneville.*

viaduct viaducts (n) A viaduct is a bridge which carries a road or railway across a valley.

vibrate vibrates vibrating vibrated (vb) If something vibrates, it moves with very quick, small movements, to and fro.
vibration (n)

vicar vicars (n) A vicar is a priest in the Church of England.

vice vices
1 (n) A vice is a fault in your character or a particularly bad habit.
2 (n) A vice is a tool used to grip things and hold them steady.
3 Vice is used in people's titles to show that they are a deputy or second in rank. *He was vice-captain for two games.*

vice-versa (adv) You use vice-versa to show that something can be true either way around. *He was a bad influence on her and vice-versa.*

vicinity vicinities (n) A vicinity is an area around something. *She was seen in the vicinity of the school.*

vicious (adj) people or things are cruel, aggressive and hurtful.

victim victims (n) A victim is a person who has suffered in some way. *Victims of war, disease, poverty, crime, etc.*

victor victors (n) A victor is a person who defeats another in a competition or war.

Victorian (adj) Something or someone Victorian existed in the reign of Queen Victoria which lasted for sixty-four years. (1837–1901)

victory victories (n) A victory is a success against an opponent in sport, battle, etc.
victorious (adj)

video videos videoing videoed
1 (n) A video is a tape cassette used to record television programmes, or used with a camera.
2 (n) A video is a machine which plays and records on video cassettes.
3 (vb) If you video something, you film or record it onto video tape.

view views viewing viewed
1 (n) A view is everything which can be seen from a place.
2 (n) Your views are your beliefs and opinions.
3 (vb) If you view someone or something you look at them carefully.

vigilant (adj) If you are vigilant, you pay careful attention in certain situations so that you do not miss anything.

vigorous (n) people are energetic.
vigour (n)

Viking Vikings (n) The Vikings were peoples from Scandinavia who in past times raided and settled in countries all over north-west Europe.

villa villas (n) A villa is a house, often with large gardens and terrace.

V

village

village villages (n) A village is a small group of houses, usually with a church, shop and school.

villain villains (n) A villain is someone who deliberately harms others or breaks the law.

vindictive (adj) A vindictive person is spiteful and determined to hurt someone they think has hurt them.

vine vines
1 (n) A vine is a plant which produces grapes.
2 (n) Some long, trailing plants are called vines.

vinegar vinegars (n) Vinegar is a sharp-tasting liquid, made from wine or malt, which is used to flavour food.

vineyard vineyards (n) A vineyard is a place where grapes are grown to make wine.

vintage
1 (adj) A vintage car is a car made between 1919 and 1930.
2 (adj) A vintage wine is a good quality wine produced in a particular year.
3 (adj) Something described as vintage, is a particularly good example of its type.

vinyl vinyls (n) Vinyl is a plastic material used for seat coverings, etc.

viola violas (n) A viola is a stringed musical instrument like a large violin and with a deeper tone.

violate violates violating violated
1 (vb) If you violate a law or promise, you break it.
2 (vb) If you violate a place or person, you treat it badly, or damage it.

violent
1 (adj) A violent person behaves in a way that is meant to hurt or frighten others.
2 (adj) A violent event is sudden and frightening. **violence** (n)

violet violets
1 (n) A violet is a small, sweet-smelling, purple or white flower.
2 (adj) Something that is violet is bluish-purple in colour.

violin violins (n) A violin is a wooden stringed instrument played with a bow and held under the chin.

viper vipers (n) Viper is another name for an adder.

virgin (adj) means unused or untouched.

virtue virtues (n) Virtue is a good quality such as kindness, generosity, honesty, etc. **virtuous** (adj)

virus viruses (n) A virus is a kind of small germ which can cause disease in living things.

visa visas (n) A visa is a stamp on your passport which allows you to enter certain countries.

visible (adj) Something that is visible can be seen.

vision visions
1 (n) Vision is the ability to see with your eyes.
2 (n) A vision is a picture in your mind in which you imagine how things might be different from the way they are now.
3 (n) A vision is a religious experience in which a person believes that they see something miraculous.

visit visits visiting visited (vb) If you visit a person or a place, you go there. **visitor** (n)

visor visors
1 (n) A visor is a transparent screen on a helmet which protects the wearer's eyes.
2 (n) A visor is a small sun screen above the windscreen inside a car.

visual (adj) Anything visual is to do with your sight.

vital
1 (adj) Something vital is neccessary to keep an animal or person alive.
2 (adj) Something that is vital is very important.
3 (adj) A vital person is full of life and energy. **vitality** (n)

vitamin vitamins (n) Vitamins are substances which are essential in small quantities for good health. Normally found in foods, they can also be taken as tablets.

vivacious (adj) people are lively and exciting. **vivacity** (n)

vivid (adj) things are very bright or clear.

vivisection (n) is the practice of experimenting on live animals.

vixen vixens (n) A vixen is a female fox.

vocabulary vocabularies
1 (n) Your vocabulary is the total number of words you know in a particular language.
2 (n) A vocabulary is a list of words, espcially for a particular subject.

vocal (adj) Anything vocal is to do with the human voice.

vocation vocations (n) If you have a vocation, you have very strong feelings about a job you want to do. *He had a strong vocation for nursing.*

voice voices voicing voiced
1 (n) Your voice is the sound you make when you speak or sing.
2 (vb) If you voice an opinion, you tell people what you think about something.

void voids
1 (n) A void is a very large space or a deep hole. *He tumbled headlong into the void.*
2 (n) A void can also be an empty feeling in your life caused by the loss of someone or something. *There was a void in her life when her dog died.*

volcano volcanoes (n) A volcano is a mountain with a crater at the top. Sometimes gases, lava and ash erupt from them. **volcanic** (adj)

vole voles (n) A vole is a small, mouse-like rodent with short ears and tail.

volley volleys
1 (n) A volley is a shower of bullets or missiles.
2 (n) In ball games, a volley is a shot where the ball is hit before it bounces.

volleyball (n) is a game in which two teams hit a large ball with their hands, backwards and forwards over a high net.

volt volts (n) A volt is a unit for measuring the force of electricity.

volume volumes
1 (n) The volume of an object is the amount of space it occupies or contains.
2 (n) Volume is an amount of something, especially when it is a large amount. *There is a large volume of mail at Christmas.*
3 (n) A volume is a book, especially when it is one of a series, encyclopaedias, etc.
4 (n) The volume of a television, radio etc, is the loudness of the sound it produces.

voluntary (adj) If an action or job is voluntary, it is done willingly without payment. **volunteer** (n)

vomit vomits vomiting vomited
1 (n) Vomit is partially digested food, bought up from the stomach and expelled through the mouth.
2 (vb) If you vomit, you are sick.

vote votes voting voted
1 (vb) If you vote for someone or something you choose them, and show your choice by marking a piece of paper, or putting up your hand.
2 (n) A vote is a choice made by one person or a group of people.
3 (n) If you have the vote you are legally allowed to vote in a political election.

voucher vouchers
1 (n) A voucher is a piece of paper which can be used instead of money. *My aunt gave me a £5 gift voucher.*

vow vows vowing vowed
1 (vb) If you vow to do something, you make a solemn promise to do it.
2 (n) A vow is a solemn promise.

vowel vowels (n) In the English language the vowels are the letters a, e, i, o, u, and the sounds that they represent.

voyage voyages (n) A voyage is a long journey by sea or through space. **voyager** (n)

V

vulgar
1 (adj) Something that is vulgar is not very artistic or elegant and is thought to show bad taste.
2 (adj) Vulgar people are crude, bad-mannered and unpleasant.

vulnerable (adj) things or people are easily hurt or damaged because they are not protected. *Old people living alone are vulnerable.*

vulture vultures (n) A vulture is a large bird which feed on carrion (the flesh of dead animals).

Ww

wade wades wading waded (vb) If you wade through water, you walk slowly through it, often with most of your body in the water.

wafer wafers
1 (n) A wafer is a very thin biscuit.
2 (n) A wafer is a thin piece of bread given at the Communion service in some Christian churches.

waffle waffles waffling waffled
1 (n) A waffle is a thick, crisp pancake often eaten with syrup.
2 (vb) If you waffle, you talk or write at length about irrelevant ideas.

wage wages (n) A person's wage is the money paid to them for their work.

waist waists (n) Your waist is the narrower middle part of your body, just above your hips.

wait waits waiting waited
1 (vb) If you wait, you remain in a place until someone arrives or something happens.
2 (n) A wait is time spent before something happens.
3 (vb) If you wait on people, you serve food in a restaurant or house. **waiter** (n) **waitress** (fem. n)

wake wakes waking woke woken
1 (vb) When you wake, you become fully conscious after a period of sleep.
2 (n) The wake of a ship is the trail of disturbed water it leaves behind.

walk walks walking walked
1 (vb) If you walk, you move along putting one foot in front of the other.
2 (n) A walk is a journey you make on foot.

walkabout walkabouts (n) If a famous person has a walkabout, they walk through the crowds to talk and meet them.

wallaby wallabies (n) A wallaby is an animal like a small kangaroo, found mainly in Australia.

wallet wallets (n) A wallet is a small case used for carrying money, credit cards, etc.

walnut walnuts (n) A walnut is an edible nut.

walrus walruses (n) A walrus is a big sea animal like a seal, with two large tusks growing downwards.

waltz waltzes (n) A waltz is a graceful dance for two people together.

wander wanders wandering wandered
1 (vb) If you wander, you walk with no clear direction or purpose.
2 (vb) If your mind wanders, you do not concentrate.

want wants wanting wanted
1 (vb) If you want something, you have a desire for it.
2 (adj) A wanted person is someone whom the police are trying to find.
3 (n) Want is a general lack of something. *She suffered from a want of care.*

war wars
1 (n) War is fighting between countries or groups of people which goes on for a long time.
2 If you have been in the wars, you have been hurt in a fight or accident.

ward wards
1 (n) A ward is a room section of a hospital where patients stay until they are better.
2 (n) A ward is a young person who is officially put in the care of a court or a guardian.

warden wardens (n) A warden is a person who is in charge of a place and who sees that certain laws are obeyed. *Traffic warden... hostel warden.*

wardrobe wardrobes (n) A wardrobe is a large cupboard for storing clothes.

warehouse warehouses (n) A warehouse is a large building used to store goods.

warhead warheads (n) A warhead is the exploding part of a missile or bomb.

warm warms warming warmed;
warmer warmest
1 (vb) If you warm something, you heat it slightly.
2 (adj) Someone or something that is warm has some heat in it.
3 (adj) A warm person is friendly and easy to get along with.

warm-blooded (adj) A warm-blooded animal is able to keep its body temperature quite high even when the weather is cold.

warn warns warning warned
1 (vb) If you warn someone about something, you make them aware of the problems they may face.
2 (n) If you give someone a warning about something, you tell them not to do it.

warp warps warping warped (vb) If something warps, it bends and twists.

warrant warrants (n) A warrant is an official form which allows the police to search a house, or arrest someone, for example.

warren warrens (n) A warren is a collection of tunnels underground where rabbits live.

warrior warriors (n) A warrior is someone especially skilled in fighting.

wart warts (n) A wart is a small, hard growth on the skin.

wary warier wariest (adj) If you are wary about something or someone, you are unsure of them and therefore suspicious.

wash washes washing washed
1 (vb) If you wash someone or something, you clean them with water, soap, etc.
washable (adj)
2 If clothing is in the wash, it is dirty and is being washed.

wasp wasps (n) A wasp is a striped yellow and black insect that can sting.

waste wastes wasting wasted
1 (vb) If you waste something, you use too much, or use it to no purpose.
2 (n) Waste is rubbish or unwanted things.
3 (n) If something is a waste of time, there is no point in doing it.
4 (vb) If you waste no time in doing something, you do it quickly.

watch watches watching watched
1 (vb) If you watch something or someone, you look at them for some time.
2 (n) A watch is a small clock on your wrist.
3 If you watch out for someone or something, you are on the lookout for them.

water waters watering watered
1 (n) Water is a clear liquid with no taste or smell which people and animals drink, and which falls as rain.
2 (vb) If you water something, you pour water on it to help it grow.
3 (vb) If your mouth waters, saliva enters your mouth because you think of food.
4 If you are in hot water, you are in trouble.
5 If you keep your head above water, you manage to survive your troubles.

watercolour watercolours (n) Watercolours are paints which are mixed with water, and also the paintings produced by using them.

waterfall waterfalls (n) A waterfall is a natural fall of water from a river or stream on one level to a lower level.

W

waterlogged

waterlogged (adj) Something that is waterlogged is completely soaked with water and cannot soak up any more.

watermark watermarks (n) A watermark is a mark in a piece of paper, especially banknotes and writing paper, which can be seen if you hold it to the light.

water polo (n) is a ball sport played in a swimming pool between two teams.

waterproof (adj) Something that is waterproof does not let in water.

watertight
1 (adj) Something that is watertight does not let water out.
2 (adj) If you have a watertight argument it is difficult to find points against it.

waterworks (n) are places where water is cleaned and treated so that it can be used.

watt watts (n) A watt is a unit of electricity. *A 100 watt bulb.*

wattle wattles (n) Wattle is made up of thin sticks, woven to make a wall or fence.

wattle and daub (n) is a method of making walls by covering woven sticks with clay.

wave waves waving waved
1 (vb) If you wave, you move your hand back and forward to attract someone's attention.
2 (vb) If you wave something, you move it back and forward to attract attention.
3 (n) A wave is a raised line of water in the sea, river, etc.
4 (n) A wave is the form in which some energies travel. *Light waves ... sound waves.*

waveband wavebands (n) A waveband is a set of radio waves of the same length.

wax waxes (n) Wax is a solid, fatty substance which becomes liquid when heated. It is produced naturally by some insects, and is used for polishing, making candles, etc.

weak weaker weakest (adj) If someone or something is weak, they are not very strong.

wealth (n) is the amount of money and possessions that you have, especially if you have a lot. **wealthy** (adj)

weapon weapons (n) A weapon is something that is designed to kill or hurt people.

wear wears wearing wore worn
1 (vb) When you wear clothes, you cover parts of your body with them.
2 (vb) If something wears well, it lasts a long time with plenty of use.
3 If something is the worse for wear, it looks shabby through heavy use.

weary wearier weariest (adj) A weary person is tired.

weasel weasels (n) A weasel is a small wild animal with red-brown fur that lives by killing mice, etc.

weather weathers weathering weathered
1 (n) The weather refers to the conditions of rain, wind, sunshine, etc present at any one time.
2 (vb) If something weathers, it is affected by the time spent in the wind, rain, sun, etc.

weather forecast weather forecasts (n) A weather forecast is a statement about what the weather will be like in the next few days, weeks, etc.

weave weaves weaving wove woven. (vb) If you weave, you make threads go over and under one another to make a piece of cloth.

web webs (n) A web is a fine net of threads spun by a spider to trap insects.

wedding weddings (n) A wedding is a union of two people in marriage.

wedge wedges wedging wedged
1 (n) A wedge is a triangular piece of something, that is wider at one end than at the other.
2 (vb) If you wedge something, you fix its position with shaped pieces of wood or other material.

weed weeds weeding weeded
1 (n) A weed is a wild plant, that grows where it is not wanted.
2 (vb) If you weed, you pull up unwanted plants from a piece of land.

week weeks
1 (n) A week is a period of seven days.
2 (n) A week sometimes refers to the days from Monday to Friday.

weekday weekdays (n) A weekday is any day between Monday to Friday.

weekend weekends (n) The weekend is the days Saturday and Sunday.

weekly weeklies
1 (adj) A weekly event happens once a week.
2 (n) A weekly is a magazine or newspaper that is published once a week.

weep weeps weeping wept (vb) If you weep, you cry because you are unhappy, or sometimes because you are very happy.

weevil weevils (n) A weevil is a small insect that destroys crops.

weigh weighs weighing weighed (vb) If you weigh something, you find out how heavy it is by using scales. **weight** (n)

weightlifting (n) is a sport in which people try to lift increasingly heavy weights. **weightlifter** (n)

weir weirs (n) A weir is a structure across a river which controls the flow of the water.

weird weirder weirdest (adj) Someone or something that is weird, is strange and unusual.

welcome welcomes welcoming welcomed
1 (vb) If you welcome someone, you greet them in a friendly way when they arrive.
2 (vb) If you welcome someone's ideas, you are glad to hear them.
3 If you make someone welcome, you make them feel at home and cared for.

weld welds welding welded (vb) If you weld two pieces of metal, you join them using heat to melt the edges so they can be pressed and sealed together. **welder** (n)

welfare (n) Someone's welfare is their state of health, comfort, etc.

welfare state (n) The welfare state is a country's system through which education, healthcare, etc are provided by the state.

wellington wellingtons (n) Wellingtons are long rubber boots worn to keep your feet and legs dry.

west (n) West is one of the four main points of the compass. You look in the direction of west to see the sun set.

western westerns
1 (adj) Western describes anything from the west part of a country, continent, or even the world.
2 (n) A western is a story or film about the West of the U.S.A. in the 19th Century, involving cowboys, gunfights, etc.

whale whales (n) A whale is the largest mammal on earth but which lives in the sea.

wharf wharves (n) A wharf is a platform built out into the sea or a river where ships can load and unload.

wheat wheats (n) Wheat is a cereal crop which produces wheat grains which are ground into flour for bread, etc.

wheatgerm (n) is at the centre of the wheat grain and contains many vitamins.

wheel wheels wheeling wheeled
1 (n) A wheel is a circular object that moves on an axle. Cars, trains, bicycles, etc all run on wheels.
2 (vb) If you wheel something, you push it along on its wheels.

wheelbarrow wheelbarrows (n) A wheelbarrow is a cart with one wheel at the front and two legs at the back. It is used by builders and gardeners to carry things.

wheelchair wheelchairs (n) A wheelchair is a seat on wheels used by disabled, elderly or sick people to allow them to move themselves or to be pushed by others.

wheeze wheezes wheezing wheezed (vb) If you wheeze, you find it difficult to breathe, and may make hissing sounds.

whelk whelks (n) A whelk is an edible shell-fish.

whenever (conj) means any time. *Come whenever you can.*

wherever

wherever (conj) means in or to any place. *Go wherever you like ... Wherever you go in Wales there are hills.*

whether (conj) When whether is used, it shows that there is a choice between two or more possibilities. *I'm not sure whether to give up history or geography next year.*

which
1 Which is used when you are asking a question and there is a choice of answers. *Which bus did you come on? .. Which car is yours?*
2 Which is used when you are specifying or explaining the thing you are talking about. *He used a special bike, which was made of plastic.*
3 Which can also be used to give opinions. *He gave me a price of £25, which was not bad.*

whiff whiffs (n) A whiff is a faint smell of anything.

while
1 (n) A while is a short or long period of time. *He waited for a while.*
2 While means during a period of time. *Can you do this while I check the cooker?*
3 While can also be used to show a contrast. *She was very quick and untidy, while her brother was slower but neater.*

whim whims (n) A whim is a sudden wish to do something or have something.

whimper whimpers whimpering whimpered (vb) If an animal or person whimpers, they make a quiet moaning noise caused by fear or pain.

whine whines whining whined
1 (vb) If something whines, it makes a long, high-pitched noise.
2 (vb) If someone whines, they complain in an irritating way about something.

whip whips whipping whipped
1 (vb) If you whip someone or something, you hit them with a whip.
2 (n) A whip is a thin cane or leather strip used to hit people or animals.
3 (vb) If the wind whips something, it blows it sharply.
4 (vb) If you whip cream, eggs, etc. you beat them.

whippet whippets (n) A whippet is a small, thin dog often used in racing.

whirl whirls whirling whirled
1 (vb) If something or someone whirls, they turn round and round very quickly.
2 Someone in a whirl is very excited but confused and disorganised.

whirlpool whirlpools (n) A whirlpool is an area of water moving round and round and drawing things into its centre.

whirlwind whirlwinds (n) A whirlwind is a column of air which turns quickly and can pull things into its centre.

whisk whisks whisking whisked
1 (vb) If you whisk food, you stir air into it very quickly. *Whisk the egg whites until they stand in peaks.*
2 (n) A whisk is a kitchen tool used to beat food into a froth.
3 (vb) If someone whisks another person away they take them away quickly.

whisker whiskers
1 (n) Whiskers are the hairs which stand out from the side of animal's faces.
2 (n) A mans whiskers are the hairs on his face which grow if he does not shave.
3 (n) A whisker can mean a very small distance or amount. *We missed the other car by a whisker.*

whisky whiskies (n) Whisky is a strong alcoholic drink made from barley or other grain.

whisper whispers whispering whispered (vb) If you whisper, you speak very quietly. **whisper** (n)

whistle whistles whistling whistled
1 (vb) If you whistle, you make a noise by blowing out through your lips.
2 (n) A whistle is a device which makes a whistling noise.
3 (vb) If something such as an arrow whistles, it makes a high pitched noise as it travels through the air.

white
1 (adj) Something that is white is the lightest colour there is; the colour of new-fallen snow.
2 (n) The white of an egg is the part that surrounds the yolk.

Whitehall (n) is the name of the street in London where many government offices are.

Whitsun (n) is the seventh Sunday after Easter in the Christian calendar.

whole (n) A whole thing is complete.

wholefood **wholefoods** (n) Wholefoods are those foods which are considered good for you, and contain no additives.

wholemeal (adj) flour is made from the grain and husks of wheat.

wholesome (adj) Something wholesome is considered good for you. *Wholesome food... wholesome entertainment.*

whose You use whose when asking a question about who owns or is associated with something. *Whose car is this? Whose little girl is this?*

wick **wicks** (n) A wick is a thin cord in the middle of a candle or oil lamp which burns and carries the fuel to the flame.

wicked (adj) Someone or something that is wicked is evil or bad. **wickedness** (n)

wickerwork (n) Something made from wickerwork is made from woven cane or reeds.

wide **wider** **widest**
1 (adj) If something is wide, it has a greater distance from one side than other things of the same type. **width** (n)
2 (adj) A wide variety is a selection that contains many items of the same type. *There was a wide variety of cheeses on display.*
3 (adj) Something that has wide support or appeal is supported by a great many people.

widow **widows** (n) A widow is a woman whose husband has died.
widower (masc.n)

wield **wields** **wielding** **wielded**
1 (vb) If you wield something, you hold and use it. *She wielded the sword with great skill.*
2 (vb) If you wield power, you have it and use it.

wife **wives** (n) If you are a man, your wife is the woman to whom you are married.

wig **wigs** (n) A wig is artificial hair worn to cover baldness, or to change someone's appearance.

wiggle **wiggles** **wiggling** **wiggled** (vb) If you wiggle something, you move it in small movements from side to side or up and down.

wigwam **wigwams** (n) A wigwam is a tent made from animal skins by North American Indians.

wild
1 (adj) Animals or plants which are wild live naturally.
2 (adj) Wild land is not cultivated or developed but is in its natural state.
3 (adj) Wild weather is stormy and windy.

wilderness **wildernesses** (n) A wilderness is an area of wild or desert land.

wilful
1 (adj) Wilful people want their own way.
2 (adj) A wilful act is one done with the intention of hurting others.

will **wills**
1 (n) Will is the determination to do a particular thing. *He can walk the distance if he has the will.*
2 (n) A will is a document in which you tell people what you want to happen to your belongings after you are dead.
3 If you do something against your will you don't really want to do it.

willow **willows** (n) A willow is a type of tree often found near water.

wilt **wilts** **wilting** **wilted** (vb) If a plant or a person wilts, they become weak or tired.

wily (adj) Someone or something that is wily, is cunning and crafty.

win **wins** **winning** **won** (vb) If you win a competition, etc, you come in first place or have the best score. **winner** (n)

wince **winces** **wincing** **winced** (vb) If you wince, you tighten the muscles in your face, because of a pain or because you have seen or remembered something unpleasant.

winch **winches** **winching** **winched**
1 (vb) If you winch someone or something up or down, you raise or lower them using a winch.
2 (n) A winch is a device for lifting heavy objects.

wind

wind winds winding wound
1 (n) The wind is the movement of air that we can feel around us. **windy** (adj)
2 (adj) If you are winded, you have difficulty breathing for a short while because the air is knocked out of your lungs.
3 (n) Wind is the name for the gases produced in the stomach or intestines.
4 (adj) The wind section of an orchestra is the group of musicians who blow through their instruments.
5 (vb) If you wind something up, you use a key to tighten a spring to make a clockwork machine work.
6 (vb) If you wind something around something else, you wrap something around it.
7 (vb) If something winds, a path, for example, it does not go in a straight line, but has bends and curves in it.

windmill windmills (n) A windmill is a building where corn is ground into flour or water is pumped. The power is provided by the wind.

window windows (n) A window is a large space in a wall or vehicle which lets in air and light and is usually covered with glass.

windscreen windscreens (n) A windscreen is the glass window in the front of a vehicle.

windsurf
windsurfs
windsurfing
windsurfed (vb) If you windsurf, you ride over water on a board which has a sail to power it.
windsurfer (n)

wine wines (n) is an alcoholic drink usually made from grapes.

wing wings
1 (n) A wing is one of the feathered limbs on a bird or insect which enable it to fly.
2 (n) The wings of an aeroplane are the large, flat surfaces which allow it to fly.
3 (n) In games such as hockey or football, the wing is the extreme left or right position of the playing area.

aircraft p

wink winks winking winked
1 (vb) If you wink, you open and shut one eye as a sign to others that you are joking or as a greeting.
2 (vb) If a light winks, it flashes on and off.
3 Wink is also used to describe sleep. *I didn't sleep a wink... I'll just have forty winks.*

winkle winkles (n) A winkle is a small, edible sea snail.

winter winters (n) Winter is the coldest season of the year between Autumn and Spring.

wipe wipes wiping wiped
1 (vb) If you wipe something, you clean it with a cloth.
2 (vb) You wipe a videotape, audio tape or computer tape, when you remove the music, pictures or information from it.

wire wires wiring wired
1 (vb) If you wire a building, you put the electrical cables into place.
2 (vb) If you wire a machine, you connect it so that electricity or electrical signals can go through it.
3 (n) Wire is a thin strip of metal used to carry electricity or electrical signals.
4 (n) Wire is a long, thin strip of metal used to make fences, or to tie things up.

W

wisdom (n) is a person's ability to use their knowledge and experience to give good advice or make good judgements.

wise (adj) A wise person is clever, experienced and make good decisions.

wish wishes wishing wished
1 (vb) If you wish for something, you hope that it will happen. **wish** (n)
2 (vb) If you wish someone happy birthday, best of luck, etc you hope for those things for them.

wishbone wishbones (n) A wishbone is the v-shaped bone in the breast of birds.

wisp wisps (n) A wisp is a slight or small trace of something. *A wisp of hair, a wisp of smoke.*

wit wits
1 (n) Your wits are the intelligence or cunning which help you in difficult situations.
2 (n) Wit is the quality of humour or skill with words which amuses other people.
3 If you are at your wits' end you cannot solve a problem that is seriously worrying you.

witch witches (n) A witch, in the past, was a woman believed to have magical powers, usually evil. **witchcraft** (n)

withdraw withdraws withdrawing withdrew withdrawn
1 (vb) If you withdraw from something, you take no further part in it. *He withdrew from the interviews.*
2 (vb) If you withdraw money from a bank account, you take it out to spend.
3 (adj) Withdrawn people are very quiet and keep their thoughts and feelings to themselves.

wither withers withering withered (vb) If something withers, it shrivels up or becomes weaker.

without
1 (prep) Without shows that someone does not have something. *He was without money.*
2 (prep) If you go without someone, you leave them behind. *He went without me.*
3 (prep) You use without to show that something would happen if it were not for someone or something else. *We would have starved without the help of the Red Cross.*

witness witnesses witnessing witnessed
1 (n) A witness is a person who sees an event and can describe what happened, particularly in court.
2 (vb) If you witness something, you see it happen.
3 (vb) If you witness a legal document for someone, you sign it to confirm that they are the person who has signed it.

witty (adj) A witty person or story, etc is clever and amusing.

wizard wizards (n) A wizard is a man who is supposed to have magic powers.

wizened (adj) Someone or something that is wizened is shrivelled and wrinkled.

wobble wobbles wobbling wobbled (vb) If someone or something wobbles, it moves in a shaky and unsteady way from side to side.

woe woes (n) Woe describes unhappiness or distress.

wolf wolves (n) A wolf is a large, dog-like, carnivorous animal which hunts in packs.

woman women
1 (n) A woman is an adult female human.
2 (n) Women is used to mean the female sex in general.

womb wombs (n) The womb is the part of a woman where the unborn baby grows and develops.

wonder wonders wondering wondered
1 (n) Wonder is the feeling you have when you see something surprising, or startling.
2 (vb) If you wonder about something, you want to know more about it.
3 (vb) If you wonder at something, you are surprised by it. *I stood and wondered at the sight.*

wonderful (adj) Someone or something wonderful is of very high quality or is very good in its own way. *That's wonderful news!*

wood woods
1 (n) A wood is a group of trees growing close together.
2 (n) Wood is the material which makes the trunk and branches of trees and is used for furniture, building, etc.

woodland

woodland woodlands (n) Woodland is land covered with trees.

woodlouse woodlice (n) These are small grey creatures that live in damp places.

woodpecker woodpeckers (n) A woodpecker is a bird that makes holes in trees to feed on the insects which live there.

woodwind (n) Woodwind is the family of musical instruments that you play by blowing though a mouthpiece and into a hollow tube. Different notes are made by opening and closing holes in the instrument.

woodwork
1 (n) Woodwork is the craft of making things from wood.
2 (n) The woodwork of a building describes those parts made from wood.

woodworm (n) are beetle larvae which eat wooden things, causing great damage. Woodworm is also the word used to describe damage done by the larvae.

wool wools
1 (n) Wool is the hair growing on sheep and other animals which is often used for making clothes. **woollen** (adj)
2 (n) Wool is used to mean the threads from which woollen clothes are made.

word words wording worded
3 (n) A word is a unit of language which has one or several meanings.
4 If you repeat something word for word, you repeat it exactly as you heard it.
5 If someone gives their word, they promise to do something.

word processor word processors (n) A word processor is a machine similar to a computer but which is used to print documents, letters, dictionaries, etc.

work works working worked
1 (n) Work is the activity that people do to earn a living.
2 (n) Work is a task or duty you have to do.
3 (vb) If you work metal or leather, for example, you use it to make things. *He worked metal for a living.*
4 (vb) If you work the land, you grow things to eat.
7 (vb) If a machine, for example, works, it performs properly and does what is expected from it.
8 (vb) If you work with people, you co-operate to achieve something.
10 (n) A work is a painting, play, etc that has been created by someone. *The painter's greatest works were on show.*
11 (n) A works is a place where something is manufactured or treated, such as a sewage works.
12 (vb) If you work out the answer to a problem, you solve it.

workman workmen (n) A workman is a man whose job involves working with his hands, such as a plumber or a builder.

workshop workshops (n) A workshop is a place where things are made, repaired or mended.

world worlds
1 (n) The world is the planet Earth.
2 (n) The world also refers to all the people in the world.
3 (n) A person's world is the life they live and the people they know. *He moved in a small world of writers.*

worldly
1 (adj) Someone who is worldly is experienced in the ways of the world and other people.
2 (adj) Your worldly goods are all the things you own.

worm worms worming wormed
1 (n) A worm is a small animal that lives in the soil and has no limbs or bones.
2 (n) Some worms are parasites which live in some people and animals.
3 (vb) If you worm information out of someone, you gradually persuade them to tell you although they are trying to keep it a secret.

W·

worn
1 (adj) If something is worn, it has had a great deal of use and is old or damaged.
2 (adj) If someone looks worn, they look old and tired. *People who write dictionaries look worn when they get to W!*

worry worries worrying worried
1 (n) A worry is a problem. **worrying** (adj)
2 (vb) If you worry, you feel concerned about something.

worship worships worshipping worshipped
1 (vb) If you worship, you pray to and praise God or gods.
2 (vb) If you worship a person, you love or admire them so much you think they can do no wrong.

worth
1 (n) The worth of something or someone is their value. **worthless** (adj)
2 (prep) If something is worth a certain amount it can be sold for that amount of money.
3 (n) If you have a week or a day's worth of something, you have enough to last that long. *We have a day's worth of water.*
4 If you say that something is worth doing, you feel that it will be useful or fun.

would
1 You use would to talk about a situation that was in the future at the last time you were talking about it. *I thought we would win.*
2 You use would when you are referring to someone's willingness to do something. *He would do it if he could.*
3 You use would when you ask a polite question. *Would you like a sweet?*

wound wounds wounding wounded
1 (n) A wound is an injury to a person's or animal's body.
2 (vb) If you wound someone, you injure them in some way.
3 (vb) If you wound someone, you hurt their feelings.

wrangle wrangles wrangling wrangled
1 (n) A wrangle is a noisy argument.
2 (vb) If you wrangle you argue noisily.

wreak wreaks wreaking wreaked (vb) If someone or something wreaks damage or havoc, they cause it.

wreath wreaths
1 (n) A wreath is a ring of flowers or leaves usually placed on graves, war memorials, etc.
2 (n) A wreath can also be a ring of flowers and leaves worn around your head or neck. *The children hung wreaths around our necks to welcome us.*

wreck wrecks wrecking wrecked
1 (vb) If you wreck something, you destroy it or ruin it. *He wrecked the car. She wrecked her chances in the exam.*
2 (n) A wreck is a ship that has been destroyed or sunk at sea or any vehicle which has been badly damaged. **wreckage** (n)
3 (n) If someone or something is a wreck they are unhealthy or in poor physical condition.

wren wrens (n) A wren is a tiny brown bird, with a turned up tail.

wrench wrenches wrenching wrenched
1 (vb) If you wrench something, you pull or twist it sharply.
2 (vb) If you wrench your arm or leg, you twist and injure it.
3 (n) A wrench is a tool for turning nuts on a bolt.

wrestle wrestles wrestling wrestled
1 (vb) If two people wrestle, they fight by holding and trying to force each other to the ground.
2 (vb) If you wrestle with a problem you try hard to find a way of solving it.

wretch wretches (n) A wretch can be a wicked person or someone for whom you feel very sorry.

wretched
1 (adj) Someone who is wretched is very unhappy or ill.
2 (adj) Something wretched is uncomfortable or of very poor quality. *He lived in a wretched room, cold and damp.*

wriggle wriggles wriggling wriggled
1 (vb) If a person or animal wriggles, they twist about in a lively or excited way.
2 (vb) If you wriggle through a narrow space, you squeeze through by twisting and turning.
3 (vb) If you try to wriggle out of something, you try to get out of doing it.

wring

wring wrings wringing wrung
1 (vb) If you wring something, you twist it, often to get the water out.
2 (vb) If you wring an animal's neck, you break it by twisting it.
3 (vb) If you wring your hands, you twist them together because you are worried.

wrinkle wrinkles wrinkling wrinkled
1 (n) A wrinkle is a small crease.
2 (vb) If something wrinkles, it becomes creased.

wrist wrists (n) Your wrist is the joint between your arm and your hand.

write writes writing wrote written
1 (vb) When you write, you put words, letters, numbers, etc onto paper or another surface. **writing** (n)
2 (vb) If someone writes a book, story, etc they create it. **writer** (n)
3 (vb) When you write to someone, you send them a letter.

writhe writhes writhing writhed (vb) If a person or animal writhes, they twist and turn their bodies violently.

wrong wrongs wronging wronged
1 (vb) If you wrong someone, you treat them badly or unfairly.
2 (adj) Something that is wrong is bad or unfair. *Many people believe it is wrong to kill animals for sport.*
3 (adj) Something that is wrong is incorrect. *Two of my sums were wrong.*
4 (n) Wrong behaviour is not acceptable behaviour.

xerox xeroxes xeroxing xeroxed
1 (n) A xerox is a machine that makes copies of writing or drawings.
2 (vb) If you xerox a piece of writing, you make a copy of it on a xerox machine.

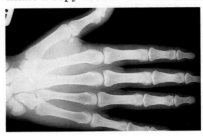

X-ray X-rays X-raying X-rayed
1 (n) An X-ray is a ray of radiation that can pass through some solids. Doctors use the X-ray photograph to examine the interior parts of the body.
2 (vb) If a doctor X-rays you, they photograph the inside of you using an X-ray machine.

skeleton p273

xylophone xylophones (n) A xylophone is a musical instrument made of wooden bars of different lengths which produce notes when hit with special hammers.

X

Yy

yacht yachts (n) A yacht is a large boat used for racing, sailing or cruising. **yachting** (n)

yak yaks (n) A yak is a long-haired ox from Tibet and the Himalayas.

yam yams (n) A yam is a potato-like vegetable that grows in hot countries.

yard yards
1 (n) A yard is a unit of measurement of length equal to 36 inches or about 91 centimetres.
2 (n) A yard is a paved space with walls around it, next to a building.
3 (n) A yard is a place where certain types of work are carried out. *A shipyard . . . builders yard.*

yarn yarns
1 (n) Yarn is thread made from wool or cotton and used for weaving or knitting.
2 (n) A yarn is a story that is spoken.

yashmak yashmaks (n) A yashmak is a thin veil worn by some Muslim women to cover their faces in public.

yawn yawns yawning yawned
1 (vb) When you yawn, your mouth stretches and you take in a lot of air, often because you are tired or bored.
2 (adj) A yawning gap is a wide gap. *There was a yawning gap in the earth.*

year years (n) A year is a unit of time. There are 52 weeks, or twelve months in a year. Most years have 365 days except for leap years which have 366. It takes one year for the Earth to orbit the sun. **yearly** (adj)

yeast yeasts (n) Yeast is a type of fungus used to make bread rise, and to ferment alcoholic drinks.

yell yells yelling yelled
1 (n) A yell is a loud shout.
2 (vb) If you yell, you shout loudly.

yellow yellows yellower yellowest
1 (n) Something that is yellow is the colour of butter or of daffodils.
2 (adj) If something is yellow, it is coloured yellow.

yesterday yesterdays (n) Yesterday is the day before today.

yet
1 (adv) If something has not happened yet, you expect it to happen in the future.
2 (adv) Yet can mean even more. *There were yet more people arriving.*
3 (conj) Yet can also mean but, or even so. *She was very unhappy, yet she kept on working.*

yeti yetis (n) A yeti is said to be a large, hairy, ape-like creature living in the mountains of Northern India, but nobody is really sure that it exists.

yew yews (n) A yew is an evergreen tree with small, dark, needle-like leaves.

yield yields yielding yielded
1 (vb) If someone or something yields, they collapse or gives way.
2 (n) The yield of a farm, field, etc is the amount of the crop it produces.

yodel yodels yodelling yodelled (vb) If someone yodels, they make a high trilling noise as part of a song.

yoga (n) is an exercise which develops the body and the mind, making you both mentally and physically relaxed and fit.

yoghurt yoghurts (n) Yoghurt is a creamy food made from milk.

yogi yogis (n) A yogi is a person who has spent many years practising yoga.

yoke yokes yoking yoked
1 (vb) If you yoke two animals together, you put a bar across their shoulders, so that they can pull a cart.
2 (n) A yoke on a dress or coat is the part that covers the shoulders.

y

yolk yolks (n) A yolk is the yellow part of an egg.

Yom Kippur is the time of fasting when Jews ask for God's forgiveness for their sins.

young younger youngest
1 (adj) Young people or animals are not yet adult.
2 (adj) A young child is a baby or toddler.

youth youths
1 (n) A youth is a young man between the ages of thirteen and twenty.
2 (n) Youth is the time when you are between thirteen and twenty.
3 (n) The youth of a country are the young people who live there. **youthful** (adj)

Yule (n) is an old-fashioned word for Christmas.

Zz

zany zanier zaniest (adj) Someone or something zany is odd in an amusing way.

zeal (n) If you do something with zeal, you do it eagerly and with great enthusiasm. **zealous** (adj)

zebra zebras (n) A zebra is a striped, African animal like a horse.

Zen (n) is a form of Buddhism which emphasises learning through meditation.

zest
1 (n) Zest is a feeling of pleasure and excitement.
2 (n) Zest is the skin of oranges, lemons, etc. when used for flavouring in cookery.

zigzag zigzags zigzagging zigzagged
1 (n) A zigzag is a line which looks like a series of v's: VVVVVVVVV
2 (vb) If you zigzag, you move in a series of sharp turns to left and right.

zinc (n) is a bluish-white metal often used to cover other metals to protect them from rust.

zip zips (n) A zip is a device with small, interlocking teeth used to fasten clothes, suitcases, etc.

zodiac (n) The zodiac is a chart used by astrologers to represent the paths of the planets and stars.

zone zones (n) A zone is a particular area of land.

zoo zoos (n) A zoo is a place where animals are kept so that people can see or study them.

zoology (n) is the scientific study of animals.

zoom zooms zooming zoomed (vb) If something zooms, a rocket for example, it shoots up into the sky at high speed.

Abbreviations

AAA	Amateur Athletic Association		HGV	heavy goods vehicle
abbr	abbreviation		HM	His or Her Majesty
ac	alternating current		HMS	His or Her Majesty's Ship
AD	Anno Domini (In the year of our Lord)		hp	horse power
			HQ	headquarters
am	*ante meridiem* (before noon)		HRH	His or Her Royal Highness
anon	anonymous			
approx	approximately		ID	identification
			ie	*id est* (that is)
b	born		IQ	intelligence quotient
BA	Bachelor of Arts			
BBC	British Broadcasting Corporation		JC	Jesus Christ
BC	Before Christ		JP	Justice of the Peace
BEd	Bachelor of Education			
bhp	brake horse power		kb	kilobyte
BMA	British Medical Association		km	kilometre(s)
BR	British Rail		kph	kilometres per hour
BSc	Bachelor of Science		kW	kilowatt
CAD	Computer Assisted Design		lat	latitude
CAL	Computer Assisted Learning		lbw	leg before wicket (cricket)
CC	County Council, cricket club		LCD	liquid crystal display
cc	cubic centimetre		LEA	Local Education Authority
CD	compact disc		LED	light emitting diode
CID	Criminal Investigation Department		long	longitude
cm	centimetre			
CND	Campaign for Nuclear Disarmament		MA	Master of Arts
CV	curriculum vitae (progress of life)		MCC	Marylebone Cricket Club
			MD	managing director
dc	direct current		MI	military intelligence
DES	Department of Education and Science		mg	milligram(me)
			ml	millilitre(s)
DHSS	Department of Health and Social Security		mm	millimetre(s)
			MOD	Ministry of Defence
DIY	do it yourself		MOT	Ministry of Transport
DJ	Disc Jockey, dinner jacket		MP	Member of Parliament, military police
DOE	Department of the Environment		mpg	miles per gallon
			mph	miles per hour
EEC	European Economic Community		MS	multiple sclerosis
eg	*exempli gratia* (for example)		ms	manuscript
etc	*et cetera* (and so forth)		MSc	Master of Science
			Mw	medium wave
FA	Football Association			
			NATO	North Atlantic Treaty Organisation
g	gram(me)		NCO	non-commissioned officer
GB	Great Britain		NLQ	near letter quality
GCSE	General Certificate of Secondary Education			
			OAP	old age pensioner

P	parking	UFO	unidentified flying object
p	new penny	UHF	ultra high frequency
PC	Police Constable, personal computer	UN	United Nations
PO	Post Office	USA	United States Of America
pm	*post meridiem* (afternoon)	USSR	Union of Soviet Socialist Republics
PM	Prime Minister		
PS	*post scriptum* (written after)	VAT	value added tax
		VCR	video cassette recorder
RAM	random access memory	VDU	visual display unit
RIP	Rest In Peace	VHF	very high frequency
ROM	read only memory	VIP	very important person
SEN	State Enrolled Nurse	WC	water closet
SRN	State Registered Nurse		
St	saint, street	YHA	Youth Hostel Association
		YMCA	Young Men's Christian Association
TNT	Trinitrotoluene	YWCA	Young Women's Christian Association
TT	teetotal, Tourist Trophy		
TU	Trade Union		
TUC	Trades Union Congress		
TV	television		

Some people put full stops in abbreviations, but not everybody does and both ways are right.

Endangered species

As we were compiling this dictionary, we noticed that some of the animals and plants we included were **endangered species**. So we have grouped some important endangered species together on these pages for easy reference.

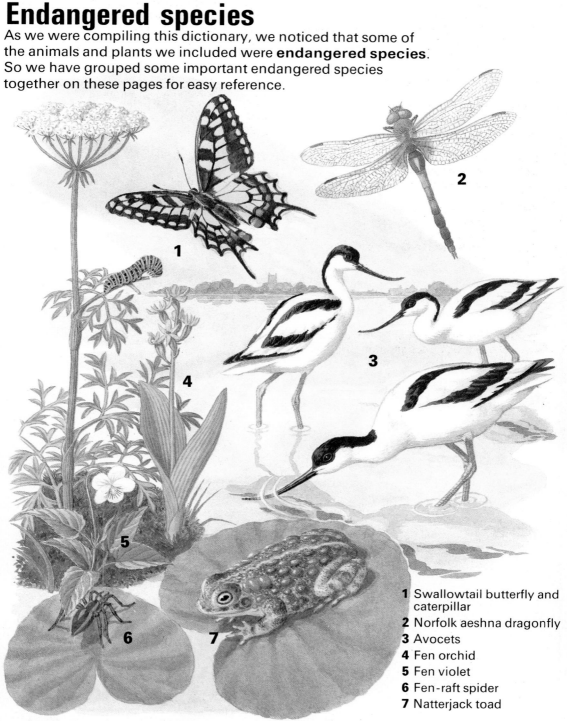

1 Swallowtail butterfly and caterpillar
2 Norfolk aeshna dragonfly
3 Avocets
4 Fen orchid
5 Fen violet
6 Fen-raft spider
7 Natterjack toad

Endangered species of the East Coast

344

1 Common crossbill   7 Greenland white-
2 Red squirrel   fronted geese
3 Golden eagle   8 Otter
4 Whooper swans   9 Pine marten
5 Snowy owl   10 Mountain hare
6 Polecat   11 Scottish wildcat

Endangered species of open grassland and heath

1 Wryneck
2 Red-backed shrike
3 Dormouse
4 Great-crested newt
5 Sand lizard
6 Smooth snake
7 Large blue butterfly